THE OUTLINE OF KNOWLEDGE
EDITED BY
JAMES A. RICHARDS

THE HISTORY OF THE WORLD
By Arthur Donald Innes

THE ROMANCE OF MONEY
By Russel M. Knerr

THE READER'S GUIDE

VOLUME XX

J. A. RICHARDS, INC.
NEW YORK

Copyright 1924
J. A. RICHARDS, INC.
MANUFACTURED IN U. S. A.

Typesetting, Paper, Printing, Binding and Cloth
By THE KINGSPORT PRESS
Kingsport, Tenn.

CONTENTS

PART ONE
THE HISTORY OF THE WORLD

CHAPTER		PAGE
XLIII	The Consolidation of Germany	1
XLIV	Asia	24
XLV	American Nationalism	44
XLVI	Great Britain and Greater Britain	63
XLVII	International Relations and the Eastern Question	75
XLVIII	The European States	99
XLIX	Outside Europe	119
L	Features of the Nineteenth Century	147
LI	Will to Power	163
LII	Crisis	202
LIII	Catastrophe	216

PART TWO
THE ROMANCE OF MONEY

I	When Every Man Was His Own "Mint"	231
II	The Gold of Egypt and the Lands of the East	237
III	The Money-Bags of Crœsus and the Treasuries of Greece	244
IV	When Rome Was the Nerve-Center of the Money-World	254
V	The Money Shortage of the Gothic Age	265
VI	Merchant Princes Who Reigned In Baroque Days	279
VII	England, Monied Mistress of the Seven Seas	294

THE ROMANCE OF MONEY TO-DAY: AMERICA

I	The Romance of Making and Growing (Production)	315
II	The Romance of Rail and Rudder (Transportation)	328
III	The Romance of Buying and Selling (Store and Stock Exchange)	342
IV	The Romance of Lending and Borrowing (Banking and Foreign Exchange)	361
V	The Romance of National Housekeeping (U. S. Treasury and Mint)	381

PART THREE

I	THE READER'S GUIDE	401

THE
HISTORY OF THE WORLD

Continued from Volume V

CHAPTER XLIII

THE CONSOLIDATION OF GERMANY, 1851-1871

I.—First Phase: Enter Bismarck, 1851-1862

In the years which followed the breakdown of the nationalist and popular movements in Central Europe, the reaction ruled both in the Austrian Empire and in Prussia. In the former, centralization and uniformity provided the keynote: nationalist ideas were suppressed as rigorously among the Slavs who had stood by Imperial unity as among the Magyars who had defied the government in arms. In Prussia the dominating influence was that of the landowning class, the Junkers; whose extreme narrowness of outlook, however, soon became distasteful even to such convinced monarchists as the Prince of Prussia—the king's brother William, the heir presumptive to the throne, a special object of popular hostility in 1848—and the rising statesman Otto von Bismarck, who had not yet become a controlling factor in Prussian policy.

Bismarck's primary interest was in foreign policy. Starting from the point of view of Frederick the Great, the grand aim was to make Prussia indubitably on an equality with the mightiest of the Powers, but practically something more; she was to be *prima inter pares*. The point of departure from Frederick's position was that involved by the altered conditions of Europe. Prussia could only reach the goal as the acknowledged head of a consolidated German nation; only with united Germany at her back, and under her direction, could she become dominant. That is, consolidation as distinct from merely a front rank position in a loose confederation was added by Bismarck to Frederick's program. To both, Austria was the rival whose ascendency in Germany must be broken; but to Bismarck this meant farther her positive extrusion from Germany. To both, the cultivation of Russian friendship was essential, while goodwill between Russia and either France or Austria was to be discouraged. It followed, for both, that Prussia must wield such a military engine as could not only defy foreign attack, but could assume the aggressive swiftly and suddenly when and where she willed. This again involved that the government must have complete control of the military engine, unhampered by popular interference. Apart from this specific purpose, Bismarck was entirely opposed to anything in the nature of popular control, which, as the representative of Prussia, he resisted in the Frankfort Diet—popular control meant in his eyes merely wordy debates which generate nothing but what is still-born—though he was quite ready on occasion to placate public opinion by such formal concessions to constitutional doctrine as pleased the theorists but were in practice ineffective.

It cannot be said that Frederick William adopted Bismarck's counsels, but the actual effect of his policy in relation to the Crimean War was very much the same as if he had done so. He did not want to quarrel with Nicholas, and would not back Austria with armed intervention, though his chief reason was probably a scruple, at which Bismarck would have scoffed, to smirch himself by an alliance with Napoleon, or with a Moslem against a Christian Power. Lacking Prussian support, Austria vacillated, earned the resentment of Russia on one side and France on the other, and ended by finding herself in isolation. A year after the Peace of Paris the sensitive and ill-balanced brain of Frederick William gave way, and it became necessary to appoint his brother, the Prince of Prussia, regent. Thus, at the age of sixty, William practically began a reign of thirty years which saw the creation and consolidation of a new German Empire. The crown did not actually pass to him till 1861; in the next year he gave the helm of the State into the hands of Bismarck, who steered the ship till William's grandson "dropped the pilot" in 1890.

During the regency William appointed a ministry somewhat more liberal than that of the last years. He was a man of a very different calibre from his brother; lacking in imagination, and not very far sighted, but with certain definite practical ideas on which he was unyielding. A soldier from his boyhood, he was convinced that Prussia needed a supreme army. He had no doubts about the Right Divine of the monarchy, or the necessity for a Prussian—not an Austrian—hegemony of Germany. He would have supported his brother in accepting the Imperial crown, even at the risk of war with Austria; but he retained the old Hohenzollern sentiment of loyalty to the Hapsburgs, which had been lacking in Frederick II. alone of the whole Prussian dynasty. In 1859 he was ready to support Austria in arms in her struggle against the alliance of Napoleon and Victor Emmanuel, with the French threat to the Rhine Province as an excuse;

but the condition of his aid was that he should be in supreme command of the German contingents. His attitude was responsible, more than any other thing, for the peace of Villafranca; for it had the effect of frightening Napoleon on one side, and alarming the pride of Austria on the other. Francis Joseph preferred the loss of Lombardy to its retention on terms which implied the military primacy of Prussia. He rejected the offer and ceded Lombardy, lest he should have to cede more; Napoleon dropped the demand for Venetia, lest Prussian armies should attack him on the Rhine; and the coolness between Prussia and Austria was accentuated.

The progress of Italian unification farther gave a new impulse to the idea of German unification, both in the "little Germans," who wished to exclude Austria, and in the "Pan-Germans," who demanded her inclusion, and the question again became acute before Bismarck had been minister of King William I. for a twelvemonth.

During this decade (1851-61) there were other developments in Central Europe which were to become important in the approaching conflict between Austria and Prussia. The former had at last awakened to the effect of the Zollverein in identifying the economic interests of the German states with those of Prussia and providing a bond of union between them and her rival. She therefore sought first admission to it for herself. Prussia countered the move by external tariff proposals that verged on free trade, which Great Britain had adopted in the last decade under Peel's leadership. Austria's protectionism was too strong for her to join the Zollverein under such conditions, whereas Hanover was drawn into the ring. An attempt on Austria's part to detach the south Germans failed, since they were too much alive to the advantages they derived from the union; with the practical effect that all Germany was included in it with the exception of Austria, which remained outside. Thus the economic union supplied a very strong groundwork for a political unification which should exclude Austria. Perhaps the main counteracting force was the jealousy of Prussia in the bigger states, coupled with the Catholicism of the south attracting it to Catholic Austria.

The second development was in Prussia, where William was hardly regent before he set about the preparations for army reorganization which were heralded by the appointment of Moltke as Chief of the General Staff and Albrecht von Roon as war minister. William was no great genius himself, but he had the faculty, invaluable to a monarch, of choosing the best brains to advise him, and the farther quality, which some princes similarly gifted have accounted superfluous, of an absolute and unswerving loyalty to the men whom he had chosen. When he had given his confidence to these two, and finally to Bismarck, all the three were equally loyal to him and to each other. And the quartet made the German Empire.

The army policy of the regent was formulated at the moment when he became king (1861), and at once produced the constitutional crisis which caused him to summon Bismarck to his side from his post as ambassador at St. Petersburg. The king demanded a revised application of the principle of universal military service, coupled with an increased term of service, which added thirty-nine regiments to the army. The Prussian Parliament fought the Bill; the king would not give way. A general election in January 1862 strengthened the opposition. On the dissolution of the Chambers, an entirely conservative ministry was formed; but in the new Assembly the opposition was raised to overwhelming strength, and refused supplies; and the new ministry lacked the strength and courage, if not the will, to override the law—which was the only way of saving army reform. William was ready to abdicate rather than give way; but Bismarck was ready to break Parliament and take the risk of a revolution, which might well have cost king and minister their lives. He carried the king with him. There was a conflict between the two Chambers, the upper supporting the government; the assent of both was necessary to the passing of any budget; and meanwhile the government was spending the money which had not been voted. While the struggle was still going on the Polish question supervened (1863), and in effect Bismarck promised the Tsar Prussia's support, since, in his view, Prussian Poland was threatened by the insurrection. But liberal opinion supported the Poles. The king supported Bismarck; the government established a vigorous press-censorship, went resolutely on its course, levied the unauthorized taxes—and there was no revolution. Bismarck had saved the new army organization, and won the supremacy of the Crown. Incidentally he had incurred the displeasure of England and France, which was of minor consequence, but had established the understanding with Russia which was vital to his plans.

In the Austrian Empire the policy of extreme centralization and of subordinating all other national elements to the German prevailed—unchecked but detested—under what was known as the Bach system, from the suppression of Hungary in 1849 till the loss of Lombardy ten years later. The Italian campaign revealed the failure of the system, and the government itself at last recognized the necessity for reforms. Two alternative lines of reforms were available: to preserve the principle of centralization and unity, but through the machinery of a general Imperial Parliament, or to develop autonomy through provincial Parliaments with a central authority whose powers were strictly limited; the German elements generally desiring the former and the nationalities the latter. But, as in the past, the aim of the one group was primarily democratic, that of the other primarily nationalist; with the result that the crown and the aristocracy favored the second. Hence came the promulgation of the October Charter of 1860 which, broadly speaking, restored the provincial Constitutions of 1847. But the immediate effect was to revive the Hungarian aspirations of 1848, and this demand was backed by the refusal of the Magyar officials to levy the taxes and the recruits required by the central government. The Bach system had not been wiped out in order that anarchy might take its place. The alternatives now were either the full concession of the Hungarian demands or the substitution of an Imperial Parliament, and the latter course was adopted by the Imperial Constitution of February 1861. But this too was rejected by Hungary, in spite of the concessions to her of a separate administration. The exiled Kossuth urged the separatist demands of 1849; the leaders in Hungary were not prepared to go so far, and were willing to compromise on the lines of Hungarian autonomy, subject to Imperial control of foreign and military affairs. But the Emperor had reached the limit of the concessions he was as yet prepared to make, and the unrest continued.

II.—Second Phase: Exit Austria, 1862-1866

In the summer of 1863, Austria had formulated her own scheme of a revised Constitution for the German Confederation. Prussia, in the first year of William's actual kingship, had reasserted her doctrine, that German unity required the closer union of the secondary and minor states under her own headship. The secondary states had as little liking for subordination to Prussia in 1861 as in 1850, and favored a triple control divided between Austria, Prussia, and the Rest—which would have enabled them to hold the balance between Austria and Prussia. Liberalism everywhere demanded a common Parliament democratically elected; a reform which found no favor with the governments, since they alone, not their subjects, to whom they had no disposition to surrender their authority, were represented in the ruling Diet. In 1863 Austria had promulgated her Imperial Constitution, and believed herself to have solved her own internal problem; Prussia was in the throes of the constitutional struggle, in which the world at large believed that William and Bismarck would be defeated; and the moment seemed opportune for Austria.

She proposed, then, a Conference of the Princes to settle on a new Federal Constitution—that is, to adopt her scheme, which was devised to make her own hegemony permanent and decisive, without conceding anything to democracy. Bismarck wrecked the plan by persuading the king, much against his will, to refuse attendance at the Conference. Nor did it attract the secondary states, since it would have left them no hope of holding the balance. Bismarck also surprised the public—since he was reputed to be the incarnation of reaction—by declaring for a directly elected Federal Parliament. Austria, being unsupported, had no choice but to revert to the joint hegemony of the past, involving, in effect, agreed co-operation with Prussia. On the other hand, of the two foreign Powers which at present mattered to him, Bismarck had already secured Russia; and he now found France making overtures which he was quite ready to encourage without committing himself, because Napoleon was now seeking to bring about another Congress for the settlement of outstanding European questions, on which French and Austrian views were in conflict. Bismarck secured Napoleon by intimating Prussia's willingness to take part in the Congress. Thus at the end of 1863 Prussia was in a far stronger position in relation to Austria than she had been at any time since Frederick William had let his opportunities slip. Time would show how much more her position was still to be strengthened when the new army organization should be in full working order.

The result was that Bismarck found ready co-operation from Austria on the question of Schleswig-Holstein, which had again become acute on the death of Frederick VII. of Denmark and the accession of Christian IX., which revived the whole business of the Augustenburg right to the succession in the duchies. That claim had been set aside by the Powers in the London Treaty of 1852, to which Austria and Prussia were both parties, while the German Confederation had been unrepresented; and Germany as well as the duchies themselves desired their severance from Denmark and incorporation with Germany through the Augustenburg succession. Meanwhile Denmark herself, in her treatment of both the duchies, had been defying the terms of the treaty, which Frederick VII. in effect had repudiated in March, seven months before his death. Holstein appealed to the Confederation, which threatened Denmark with federal action (as in Frederick William's time), only to be defied in turn by the promulgation of a fresh Constitution for Holstein. When Christian, who only succeeded in right of the London Protocol, confirmed the Constitution, which treated the Protocol as waste paper, the Confederation Diet could not be restrained from taking action. Refusing to recognize Christian as Duke of Holstein, it ordered the occupation of the duchies in the name of the Confederation; which was begun by Saxon and Hanoverian troops.

Neither Austria nor Prussia was a party to the action of the Diet which was an invitation for the signatories of the Protocol to intervene. Neither of them wanted the Augustenburg succession; Bismarck wanted to create an occasion for annexing the duchies to Prussia. Austria was readily persuaded to joint intervention as champions of the Treaty of London; rejecting the Augustenburg claim in spite of the Diet, but at the same time requiring Christian to carry out his treaty obligations in the duchies on pain of forfeiture. Thus the Western Powers had the ground for adverse intervention cut from under their feet, however ill pleased they might be, while Christian would have to withdraw the Constitution or take the consequences of his refusal. On the other hand, if he did not refuse, he would risk his Danish crown, since the whole Danish people were hot for the Constitution. To make the refusal more secure, Bismarck tricked the Danish Government into a belief that the British Government was threatening Prussia with intervention on their behalf; which produced the effect desired. In February 1864 Prussian and Austrian troops crossed the Eider, and in three weeks were on Danish soil. However valiantly the Danes might fight, they were overwhelmed.

The campaign continued while Great Britain was arranging a Conference which the belligerent Powers could not decline. It met in April. Three months later it was dissolved without having accomplished anything, since no agreement could be reached. Count Beust, for the Confederation, wanted Augustenburg. Austria was now inclining in the same direction lest the duchies should go to Prussia, a solution encouraged by Napoleon. England objected to the severance of the duchies from Denmark. Napoleon proposed his favorite method, a *plébiscite;* to which Austria, with Venice in her purview, objected. Bismarck felt sufficiently secure to submit the Augustenburg claims to the Congress, confident that they would be rejected by the Powers which had committed themselves to the London Protocol; but he also made Prussia's support of the candidature conditional on the naval and military subordination of the duchies to Prussia, which scotched the whole plan for Austria.

When the ineffective Conference broke up, it only remained for Prussia and Austria to settle things between them. Bismarck had preserved a technically unassailable position by basing it on the old treaty, and he had kept Augustenburg out. Christian could only submit to the terms dictated by the two Powers to whom he had to hand over his rights in the duchies. But another year passed before Bismarck established an agreement with Austria at Gastein (August), under which Prussia undertook the administration of Schleswig and Austria that of Holstein, reference of the question to the Diet being expressly barred. Bismarck had found it difficult to carry the king with him, and had earned the hostility of the Diet by his attitude to Augustenburg; but Austria's surrender on that point left her in hardly better plight, and now he had, in the duchies, a level by which he could force on a quarrel with Austria at the moment of his own choice.

The accession of military and maritime strength to Prussia through the acquisition of the duchies was Bismarck's immediate, but not his ultimate, objective throughout. His whole policy was directed to an unqualified Prussian hegemony of Germany, attainable only through the total exclusion of Austria, and that was an end which could never be achieved without an armed conflict and a decisive victory. The conflict must be postponed till the victory was assured. The Schleswig-Holstein war had proved the efficiency of the military instrument forged in the newly organized army. The government had weathered the constitutional struggle. Prussia was all but ready for a duel; but Austria must be inveigled into technical aggression, and an ally was wanted who would make no claim to spoils which would inconvenience Prussia. Russian goodwill and British neutrality might be taken for granted. Italy, with her eyes on Venetia, was the obvious ally; France must be hoodwinked into benevolent acquiescence until it should be too late to take action. And there was always in the background the difficulty of convincing King William that the war was necessary and just, and of counteracting his dislike to fighting against Germans.

To hoodwink Napoleon was not so difficult as the world imagined. His reputation for astuteness and impenetrability were largely due to the fact that when he did speak and act the words and actions were apt to be unexpected because they had only been decided upon at the last moment. Bismarck had taken the measure of his man, but outside Prussia no one had yet taken Bismarck's measure. Napoleon did not want a united Germany; it would not suit him that Germany should be an instrument in the hands of Austria; he would like to see Austria and Prussia at odds, and out of the conflict he would hope to snatch "compensation" on the Rhine. Bismarck engineered an informal meeting at Biarritz (October), with the result of which both were well contented, because Napoleon thought he had secured what he wanted, whereas Bismarck knew that he himself had won the trick. His assumption of blunt candor and simplicity was the most effective mask possible. He left the Emperor under the impression that a prolonged war was coming, in which Prussia would find herself compelled to appeal for his aid; he in due time would step in, dictate terms to the belligerents, and take the Rhine Provinces or Belgium as the reward or compensation for his benevolent and disinterested intervention.

Bismarck's business was to bring the war to a swift and decisive issue while Napoleon was still only preparing to intervene at leisure. An Italian flank attack on Austria at the right moment would be an extremely useful diversion. But Italy received his first overtures with coolness, suspecting his sincerity. She had no mind to be used as a cat's-paw and then to be left in the lurch after the fashion of Villafranca. She invited Austria to cede Venetia for cash. Austria declined to sell an inch of territory. Bismarck succeeded in removing the suspicions of the Italian Government, partly by effecting a commercial treaty between Italy and the Zollverein; and on 8th April

THE CONSOLIDATION OF GERMANY

(1866) the bargain between Prussia and Italy was struck and ratified. If war was declared within three months, Italy would strike simultaneously; neither Power would make a separate peace, or any peace which did not give Venetia to Italy and a corresponding accession of territory in North Germany to Prussia. But Bismarck would have to force the crisis before the three months were passed.

Meanwhile, friction had developed in the duchies. Gablenz, the Austrian governor in Holstein, appeared to Manteuffel, the Prussian governor in Schleswig, to be fomenting the popular agitation in favor of Augustenburg, thereby adding to his own difficulties. Gablenz was deaf to his remonstrances; and in January Austria declared that she still adhered to the views of the Diet in regard to Augustenburg; whereby she helped Bismarck over his difficulties with King William, whose sentiment of loyalty to Austria was not proof against such a breach of faith. The acrimonious notes which followed were significant of the real relations between the two Powers. There was very little left of the Gastein veneer. By the end of March both were dispatching circular notes to the German princes which indicated a critical session of the Diet; Bismarck at the same time proposing a Prussian scheme of federal reform which included a Parliament elected by universal suffrage; which may have been a bid for popular support, carrying with it no serious risk since the Diet was quite certain to reject it. Ominous military preparations were going on, conspicuously in Austria and Italy during April.

A month's postponement of the crisis was due to Napoleon. French statesmen were awakening to Bismarck's project of unifying Germany under Prussian hegemony by means of a war for the exclusion of Austria, and were demanding that the war should be prevented. The Emperor again proposed a Congress, and urged upon Austria the cession of Venetia—which would have settled the Italian question and deprived Prussia of her ally. But though Austria made the offer, Italy refused it on the point of honor; and the Congress fell through because Austria laid down conditions for her participation in it which would have made it meaningless. Napoleon, however, still believed that the pose of neutrality would enable him to intervene at his own time as the arbiter.

At the beginning of June Austria played straight into Bismarck's hands by referring the duchies question to the Diet, breaking the Gastein Convention; whereby Bismarck was warranted in declaring that her action had restored the pre-Gastein conditions of joint occupation; that Prussia and Austria had both been acting, not as members of the Confederation, but as independent European Powers; and that Prussia could not recognize the right of the Confederation to settle affairs in the duchies till its own Constitution was reformed. And he handed in to the Diet, along with his protest against Austria's action, the Prussian scheme of federal reform. It included the demand for a German Parliament elected by manhood suffrage. It excluded Austria. And in the meanwhile Prussian troops entered Holstein, of which Manteuffel took the administration into his own hands, while the Holstein Government betook itself to Altona.

In the eyes of most of Germany this was an act of brigandage. Austria responded with a demand for "federal execution" in Holstein upon Prussia (as previously upon Christian); which was laid before the Diet for consideration, simultaneously with the Prussian proposal for federal reform, on 14th June. The Diet carried the Austrian motion, and Prussia withdrew from the Diet and the Confederation.

The reorganization of the Prussian army bore instant fruit. Its units were disposed ready for this precise juncture. In fourteen days Prussian troops were in occupation of Hesse-Cassel, of Hanover, and of Saxony; in a fortnight resistance in North Germany ended with the surrender of the Hanoverian army (28th June). Italy declared war simultaneously, but met with disaster at Custozza. The decisive issue, however, lay with the main Prussian armies and Austria. On 2nd July, a week after Custozza, it was reached at Sadowa or Königgrätz, where the Austrians and Bavarians were completely shattered by the arrival on the field, at the critical moment, of the Prussian Crown Prince's converging army, the advance of which had been delayed. The victory was won largely by the infinite superiority of the Prussian armament; its breech-loading needle-gun had already been tested in the Danish war, while the Austrians were still armed with the muzzle-loading musket. At the end of the day the "Seven Weeks' War" was practically over, though the extent of Austria's power of continued resistance was still uncertain.

A check or even an inconclusive victory at Königgrätz would have placed Prussia in a critical position; even as matters stood, prompt and vigorous intervention by France was a menacing possibility. But Napoleon knew that he was not ready to march against Prussian troops flushed with victory. He did indeed—in response to public feeling—half threaten intervention. But while he talked and Prussia replied, Bismarck continued to act. South Germany was occupied so that, if Napoleon sought to move, he would find no co-operation there. Italy stood by her word, and the Austrian troops there could not be released.

Bismarck, however, knew when and how to hold his hand as well as when and how to strike. The fundamental necessity was the separation of Austria from Germany. The unification of Germany was to follow, but the time had not arrived for it; the south must come in willingly, and it was not yet willing. Napoleon must be placated as yet. To use the defeat of Austria for her humiliation would be folly

THE CONSOLIDATION OF GERMANY

—her rivalry in Germany once for all ended, the way should be paved for renewed friendship and alliance. Moderation must be the note. Italy, of course, must have Venetia, according to promise; but the Prussian king and the soldiers must restrain their desire for a triumphal entry into Vienna and for penalizing Austria by demanding a cession of territory to Prussia. There must be no forcible absorbing of South Germany—which, however, must be secured against attaching itself either to Austria or to France; whereas North Germany must become dependent on Prussia, ostensibly in the form of a North German Confederation already in process of formation, but partly by direct annexation—and to this Napoleon could hardly raise objection, though he might demur on details. In procuring King William's assent to his policy, he had an unaccustomed ally in the Crown Prince, whose liberal views were usually antagonistic to the chancellor's.

Bismarck still triumphed over his difficulties. An armistice was concluded on 22nd July, and peace preliminaries were signed at Nikolsburg on 26th July. Suggestions from Russia, now perturbed by the immensity of Prussia's success, for a Congress, were met by what was tantamount to a threat that Prussia, if driven to it, would encourage insurrection in Poland and in Hungary—but the threat was accompanied by a private hint to the Tsar that Prussia's friendship would be useful to him in the East. On 24th August the definitive peace was concluded at Prague. Italy acquired Venetia, but not the Trentino which she demanded—that was not in the bond. Prussia took no territory from Austria. A belated claim by Napoleon to "compensation" on the left bank of the Rhine could be curtly rejected, and served mainly to throw the alarmed South German states into the arms of Prussia, on which they must now rely for defense against French aggression, and to confirm them in forming with her an alliance offensive and defensive. In North Germany, Saxony was left intact in deference to Austria; but Nassau, the electorate of Hesse, and the kingdom of Hanover, as well as Schleswig-Holstein, were annexed to Prussia; whose eastern and western portions were now united by continuous territory instead of being separated as hitherto.

III.—Third Phase: Reorganization, 1866-1869

In 1859 Napoleon III. was at the zenith of his reputation; under his rule France was enjoying material prosperity on the one hand, while on the other she could believe that the Emperor had raised himself to the position of the arbiter of Europe. The French arms had been victorious over Russia in the Crimea and over the Austrians in Italy. In both cases the peace which was made could be claimed as a French peace. Only the shrewder observers could detect the pinchback quality of the attendant glories which could be claimed as the outcome of the personal rule of the great Napoleon's nephew. But the Emperor himself was aware of the insecurity of the foundations on which his power rested. The warrant for the arbitrary system he had created had been found in the necessity for crushing the Red Terror; as the savior of Society, popular sentiment could condone the unscrupulous methods by which his power was achieved and inaugurated, but something more was needed to retain for the government the popularity necessary to its stable continuance. The pose of the Liberator and the application of the plébiscite had been the strong cards in playing for Liberal support; but Liberals were not satisfied to have their principles reserved for foreign consumption, nor could they view with equanimity the necessity under which Napoleon constantly found himself of placating the ultramontane Catholics. The Malakoff and Solferino were pallid reflections of Austerlitz and Wagram; and the Emperor, after 1859, strove in vain to save the fading luster of his rule. He failed conspicuously to save Poland, and then Denmark; his intervention in Mexico, to be recounted later, brought not glory but humiliation; and now Bismarck in the most friendly manner had baffled him at every turn, and France saw with intense and growing alarm the consolidation of a new and tremendous power in Prussia following upon the organization of a united kingdom of Italy, which was more likely to be friendly to Prussia than to France. What France did not know was that her own organization for war was rotten, and under the existing régime incurable. It was all but inevitable that sooner or later Napoleon would find himself driven to stake the Second Empire on the desperate throw of a life and death struggle with Prussia. For never in her whole history had France been face to face with a great consolidated Power on the Rhine.

Prussia, by the war of 1866, severed Austria both from Germany and from Italy; perhaps the best service that could have been rendered to the composite Empire. Of old the Netherlands, and latterly North Italy, had been appendages impossible to co-ordinate with the rest of the Austrian dominions, distractions to her government, hotbeds of disaffection, openings for flank attack. The loss of North Italy benefited her in much the same way as, centuries before, England had gained by the loss of her French possessions; while the *Italia Irredenta* which she still retained was both strategically and commercially of real advantage to her. Hardly less to her benefit was the severance from Germany, since with it Prussia ceased to be her rival, the conflict of interests between the two Powers disappeared, and both would derive advantage from a permanent understanding; and while neither could afford to encourage the aggrandizement of Russia at the expense of the other, it was to the interest of both to conciliate their powerful neighbor, and to discourage on her part any tendency to a friendly understanding with France. It was true that Bismarck could not hope to win immediately the cordial friendship of the Power which he had just so signally defeated, but by his skillful avoidance of humiliating terms he had made the desirable *rapprochement* a possibility of the near future. Finally, when there was no longer any question of the position of the Austrian Empire in the German Confederation, a grave complication in the settlement of her internal arrangements was removed. Pan-Germanism, and the simple subordination of the other racial elements to the German, ceased to be a possible ideal. Magyar and German found a prompt compromise in a dualism which shared between them severally the supremacy over the divided Slavonic elements which together outnumbered either of them.

The Constitution of 1861 had given but brief promise of working well. The Magyars were solidly determined to resist the centralized control under the single Parliament of the Empire; the hotter headed among them clung to Kossuth's demand for complete separation, saving only the union of crowns; and their general insistence on autonomy gave the cue to other sections. In 1865 the Constitution was suspended, but the Hungarian patriot, Deàk, who had opposed Kossuth and the extremists in 1848, acquired the controlling influence. In his view there was to be no separation, but complete autonomy—the essential unity being maintained by central control of the army, foreign affairs, and finance. This was the basis of the scheme propounded by Hungary in the Diet, summoned some three months after the Treaty of Prague. It was acceptable neither to the German party, which saw in it the loss of their ascendency and the break up of the Empire, nor to the Slavs, who wanted a federal union with provincial autonomy. Agreement seemed out of reach till, in February 1867, Baron Beust— the former minister of Saxony and representative of the German Confederation at the Schleswig-Holstein Conference—became minister. Under his management the Magyar scheme was practically adopted. The Empire was divided into two halves, the Austrian and the Hungarian, with the Leitha as the boundary, forming the Dual Monarchy of Austria and Hungary. The common Imperial Government, presided over by the Imperial Chancellor was to control foreign affairs, the army, and Imperial finance; in everything else each kingdom was to manage its own affairs. A delegation of sixty members from either Diet assembled annually to discuss Imperial questions—separately. Failing agreement between the two groups, they met, not to discuss but to vote. The respective contributions of the two monarchies to the Imperial treasury were settled by the *Ausgleich* or Compromise, in proportions highly advantageous to Hungary. Finally, the practical effect was to give the Magyars complete domination over the south Slavs, the Germans a domination less complete over those of the north, while as concerned Imperial policy Magyars and Germans were on an equal footing; an arrangement highly satisfactory to the former, sufficiently so to the latter, but much the reverse to all the Slav and Rumanian populations of the Empire. The Magyars had steadily refused to recognize the authority of the Emperor as King of Hungary until his formal coronation with the "crown of Stephen." After nearly thirty years, Francis Joseph now acceded to the demand, and was duly crowned at Pesth in June 1867. So the curtain rang up on the last act in the drama of the Hapsburg dynasty.

Meanwhile Bismarck was organizing that consolidation of Germany which was to attain completion at Versailles when France lay prostrate before the victorious German armies. That struggle, he knew, must precede the consummation, and before it Germany must be practically united. Because he chose that the issue should not be precipitated but made certain, he abstained from immediate formal unification. The North German Confederation which he had planned was geographically separated from the south—which might form a Confederation of its own if it chose—by the Main. For the time being, alliance with the south, not unification, was the object in view.

First, however, he had to put on a secure basis in Prussia itself the sudden and startling access of popularity which attended the triumph over Austria. Hitherto in Prussian eyes he had been the arch-enemy of liberalism, riding rough-shod over the Constitution, the ally of the Tsar in trampling on the liberties of Poland. But the victory over Austria was his justification. Every one could see that it was the outcome of the iron rule, without which it could never have been achieved. At such a moment, magnanimity could not be taken for weakness. Bismarck was not magnanimous, but he could assume the virtue though he had it not when he saw political advantage to be reaped from it—as in his dealings with defeated Austria. He came to the Prussian Diet with a Bill indemnifying his government for the unconstitutional procedure whch, as the event had proved, had been forced upon it, but only by dire necessities of state. That shrewd move was entirely successful. A substantial section of the Liberals had already been won to an enthusiastic support of his foreign policy; now as the National Liberal party they were converted into a mainstay of the government, which had chosen the hour of decisive victory to free itself from the reproach of unconstitutionalism. And Bismarck lost nothing; he was sure now of getting his own way under constitutional forms, whereas by following unconstitutional methods he would only create difficulties for himself by arousing opposition. He was not a convert to constitutional principles, but he had no sort of objection to constitutional practice when opposition was silenced thereby.

The same principle characterized the Constitution he propounded for the North German Confederation. It secured the substance of power for Prussia while mollifying the susceptibilities of the minor states, his own supremacy while conciliating democratic and constitutional sentiment, federal authority while apparently studious of particularist interests. Each state would continue to govern itself, but the federal authority would control matters of common interest—all that affected the army and foreign affairs. The army command and organization must be single, and must therefore inevitably be vested in Prussia—a practical guarantee that she would direct foreign policy. The federal legislature was twofold, a representative Assembly *(Reichsrath)* elected directly by universal suffrage, and a Federal Council *(Bundesrath)* of delegates from the governments, with powers carefully undefined and consequently elastic. Its president would, of course, be the King of Prussia, represented by the chancellor. Of the forty-three members of the Bundesrath, Prussia had no more than seventeen, giving the minor states a clear majority; but if five of their twenty-six votes were given to Prussia her predominance was secured, so that the chance of her ever being outvoted was infinitesimal. As to the Reichsrath, it was Bismarck's personal view that the sentiment of liberalism was a disease of the middle classes, and that universal suffrage would in practice strengthen the actual government from above. The Zollverein, of which the South German states were members, could not at once be pleased under federal control; but that was soon to follow. Finally, when it suited the Federal Government to encroach upon the domain of the particular governments, it would always be with the two pleas that the specific action was in the common interest and that it was not barred by the Constitution. Bismarck relied not upon challenging and crushing opposition, but on reducing the sources of friction to a minimum. To the minor states it could be pointed out that their interests were safeguarded by their power of outvoting Prussia, to the Liberals that the Reichsrath was constituted on the most approved lines of democracy, to dissatisfied Prussians that, as a matter of fact, Prussia held the whole Confederation in her own hands—the apparent limitations on her powers having no corresponding reality behind them. The Constitution of the North German Confederation was accepted by the governments in February 1867, was passed after much discussion by a constituent *Reichstag* in April, was then adopted by the several Diets of the states, and came into force in July.

Of the southern states, which had not formed a similar Confederation of their own but had individually, in fear of France, made military alliances with Prussia, Baden alone was anxious for immediate admission to the northern Confederation. To this the rest were opposed; not wishing as yet themselves to do so, they claimed that no single one of them was free to join without the rest. Bismarck, content to wait, and aware that a premature union might bring on an alliance between France and Austria, agreed to the adverse contention, and Baden remained outside. But if the form of union was still to be avoided, its substance was within reach. Besides the alliances for military purposes, there was the Zollverein, the economic union, which could be drawn closer, though already the community of economic interests had served to keep the south within it despite the political leaning towards Austria. Now on Prussia's initiative it was reorganzied, and its affairs were placed under control of a Tariff-parliament and council—the tariff committees of the Reichsrath and Bundesrath joined by delegates from the south.

On the other hand, Napoleon's position was in the meanwhile growing more critical. The Mexican fiasco culminated with the capture and execution of his protégé, the "Emperor" Maximilian, by the republicans. Foiled on the Rhine, Napoleon sought compensation in the acquisition of Luxemburg, which the Dutch Government was willing to sell to him; but Prussia refused to withdraw the garrison maintained there under the 1815 treaties, and a Conference tided over the difficulty by procuring the withdrawal, but coupling it with the neutralization of Luxemburg. Napoleon had really succeeded only in reviving the general suspicion of his acquisitive proclivities; while within France republicanism and anti-clericalism were finding a new and dangerous leader in Léon Gambetta, whose hands were strengthened by affairs in Italy. For, at the close of 1866, the French troops were withdrawn from Rome, in accordance with an agreement entered upon fifteen months before. Within a few months Garibaldi had collected his volunteers to seize the Eternal City. Napoleon yielded to the pressure of the clericals and sent French troops to its defense; and Garibaldi was hopelessly defeated at Mentana (November). The ascendency in France of the clericals was established, but at the cost of the irreconcilable hostility of the new republican party, while Italy was completely alienated. Nor were the tottering foundations of the Empire secured by the series of ostensibly democratic reforms which preceded the catastrophe of 1870, and in May of that year culminated with the confirmation of the "Liberal Empire" by plébiscite.

IV.—Fourth Phase: The Struggle with France, 1869-1871

When Bismarck took office in 1862 it had been perfectly clear to him that Prussia could never attain the position to which he aspired until Austria had been ejected from Germany by force of arms. The primary need, therefore, was to prepare for war with Austria; which meant not only to get ready for the fight when it should come, but first to avoid an open rupture till Prussia was ready, and secondly, to force on the conflict when that moment had arrived. But he had also held it essential that Prussia should be able to lay a technically incontrovertible case before the world when the signal was given for the conflict, that Austria should be seduced into assuming ostensibly the rôle of aggressor. After 1866 France stood to the second stage of his program, the consolidation of Germany, as Austria had stood to its first stage, the establishment in Germany of a Prussian hegemony. She was all but certain to fight rather than permit that consummation. And there was a still greater risk that a false step on Prussia's part would bring allies to the aid of her enemy. It was all the more necessary that the conflict should be forced when Prussia was sure of victory in a duel, but not before, and in circumstances which should provide no other Power with an excuse for going to the help of France. The necessary conditions were brought about in 1870 by events with which, in the first instance, Prussia had no concern.

For twenty years after the sordid business of the Spanish marriages, the affairs of Spain, like those of Portugal, were without influence on the rest of Europe, except so far as monarchism was besmirched by the gross scandals of the Spanish court. The sexual vagaries of kings and princes may be regarded as matter of course, but those of queens and princesses are not so lightly condoned, and Queen Isabella stood in painful contrast to the sovereigns of England, Russia, and Prussia. Carlists continued to give the title of Carlos VI. to the son of the late pretender to the Spanish throne, but Isabella was upheld by the "brigand of considerable intelligence," General Narvaez, who was at the head of the government in the year of revolutions, ruled despotically, and crushed mercilessly what there was of revolutionary movement when most of Europe was in a state of upheaval. Between crises, it was the habit of his temporary supporters to turn against him and drive him from office till a fresh crisis necessitated his return. Occasionally his place was taken by the military adventurer O'Donnell, who had played a variegated part in the earlier revolutions.

In 1860-1, when O'Donnell was in power, campaigning in Morocco brought to the front General Prim, a soldier of liberal ideas; who, that he might be kept out of the way, was dispatched to Mexico in 1862. There Prim found himself in direct disagreement with Napoleon, whose aim was to overthrow the Mexican Republic, and in its place to set up the Austrian Archduke Maximilian as Emperor. Spain, France, and England had combined to compel Mexico to pay her debts, but when Napoleon's real purpose manifested itself, Prim, supported by the British, withdrew his troops. On his return to Spain he became the third of the trio, one of whom must inevitably control the Spanish Government, the other two being Narvaez and O'Donnell. They were incompatibles. Prim had to pursue his own designs—which included the deposition of the impossible queen—in exile. O'Donnell and Narvaez alternated; but the former died in 1867, the latter in 1868, and Prim reappeared on Spanish soil on 17th September of that year. On 30th September the queen fled, and a week later Prim had formed a Provisional Government.

A new Constitution was prepared. The Constituent Cortes declared by a three to one majority for a limited Monarchy, and in the summer of 1869 Prim had to find an occupant for the Spanish throne. Isabella's son, Alfonso, would hardly have been possible in any case; being only eleven, he was doubly impossible. Montpensier, the Orleans brother-in-law of the ex-queen, was willing, but unacceptable either to Prim or to Napoleon, whose hostility was to be avoided. The Duke of Aosta, younger son of Victor Emmanuel was unwilling; so were Ferdinand of Saxe-Coburg, the father of Luiz, King of Portugal, and Luiz himself, whose candidature would have been acceptable to those who desired to see the crowns of Spain and Portugal once more united. The Duke of Genoa, Victor Emmanuel's nephew, was approached in January 1870 with like unsuccess. The republican party was gaining ground in Spain and Prim was becoming unpopular. He turned his eyes to Prince Leopold of Hohenzollern-Sigmaringen, of the actually senior and Roman Catholic branch of the reigning house of Prussia, whose younger brother Charles had recently been chosen Prince of Rumania. In Spain the candidature of Leopold, finally declined by the prince himself, led only to a fresh invitation to the Duke of Aosta, who this time accepted the crown which he was to abdicate after two dreary years. Prim himself was assassinated in December, when the Franco-Prussian War was in full progress, three days before the new king landed on Spanish soil.

But in the meanwhile the Spanish negotiations, by good or evil luck more than by the Chancellor's skilful management, had brought about the open rupture between Prussia and France at the moment and under the conditions which he desired.

Tentative approaches had been first made to Prince Leopold early in 1869. The House of Sigmaringen was connected with the Bonapartes, and Napoleon had viewed without disfavor the election of one of its scions to the Rumanian princedom. But Spain was another affair. Leopold's father was fervently, even quixotically loyal to the Prussian branch of the Hohenzollerns, to which he had voluntarily surrendered his own principality, and had found his reward in being admitted a member of the Royal Family. A devoted adherent of Prussia might be harmless on the Rumanian throne, but not in Spain on France's flank. It was not possible for France to view with equanimity the attachment of Spain to Prussia. Bismarck from the outset apparently wished the candidature to be carried—perhaps with the intention that Spain in the

French war should play a part corresponding to that of Italy in the Austrian war; but it is difficult to see how he hoped to escape the consequences of what would have been the universal conviction of South Germans as well as of the rest of Europe—that the selection had been engineered by Prussia in the dynastic interest of the Hohenzollerns. The one chance was to obliterate every shadow of evidence that Prussia had had a voice or a finger in the matter. In actual fact he seems to have stood alone. King William was against him; the prince and his father were against him. Leopold had given his last definite refusal, and Bismarck believed that his own public career was at an end, when the French Government played straight into his hands as Austria had done in 1866, enabling him to portray her to Europe as the wanton aggressor, and Prussia as the insulted party.

The negotiations which were passing at intervals during 1869 and the first months of 1870 were studiously kept secret. The Prussian Government, as a government, had no knowledge of them. It would appear to have been Bismarck's object to bring about the election of Leopold by Spain without any appearance of Prussia in the matter, and to leave to Napoleon the risk of the odium attaching to an intervention, after the thing was done, in order to demand from Spain the reversal of the nation's choice. That object was almost achieved, for he did at last reach a point when King William gave Leopold a reluctant permission to accept if he chose, and Leopold was over-persuaded by Bismarck into yielding the assent; though his father's doubtful approval would only be given conditionally on a positive order from the Prussian head of the House of Hohenzollern, which was never forth-coming. The king himself had only given way so far under the unanimous pressure of a confidential council. In June it remained only for the Spanish Government to carry the election through the Cortes; nothing was as yet known outside, though France was angrily suspicious. Once the thing was through, France would probably turn on Spain, put herself in the wrong, and either cripple herself thereby for an immediate struggle with Prussia, which could complete the consolidation of Germany without French interference, or drag Prussia into a war apparently forced on her.

Then the plan broke down, because the Cortes—owing to a misapprehension—was adjourned till the autumn instead of being kept sitting to carry the election through. Something of the facts leaked out; France exploded into a demand that the King of Prussia should squash the candidature before it could be submitted to the Cortes. William, at Ems, could only tell the French ambassador, Benedetti, what he believed to be the honest truth, that his government had nothing to do with the matter, and that he personally had only sanctioned his kinsman acting as he himself judged best—an attitude from which he was not prepared to depart. Europe heaved a sigh of relief and imagined that the menace of war had passed when it became known on 12th July that Leopold, of his own motion, had withdrawn his candidature.

On the issue France had won a complete victory; Bismarck was routed. There was nothing approaching a *casus belli* for either party to the diplomatic contest. Unhappily she was not content. For the sake of adding humiliation to defeat, she threw away the victory she had won. The French minister, Grammont, demanded, in effect, an apology from the King of Prussia, and a pledge that he would prohibit any revival of the candidature. Bismarck was now in Berlin. On the 13th, the ambassador, Benedetti, in a conversation with the king at Ems, presented Grammant's demand. William refused to give pledges for all time, and later sent an aide-de-camp to say that he had a private letter confirming Leopold's withdrawal, and that the incident must now be regarded as closed. In fact, he imagined that it was ended, and telegraphed to the chancellor an account of what had happened. The telegram, condensed by Bismarck, was published late that night in the *Nord Deutsche Zeitung*. Twenty-four hours later Napoleon, overborne by the public excitement and the pressure of the war party, which foresaw a triumphal march to Berlin, signed the French declaration of war.

Bismarck in his condensation had not altered the words, phrases, or statements; he had merely penciled out what was superfluous; but the "superfluities" were essential to a true understanding of what had actually taken place. Benedetti had carried out a distasteful task with courtesy, the king had given the inevitable reply with equal courtesy; but from the Ems telegram, as published, it appeared to all Germans that William had met an insolently expressed demand with becoming firmness, to all France that his answer was a direct defiance. All France and all Germany, north and south, rose to the call as one man. But it was Germany's hour, for she was ready, and France was not. And the circumstances virtually ensured that the conflict would be fought out as a duel. Bismarck's object was achieved.

Each side was confident of victory; probably there was no man in France who feared the outcome so much as Napoleon himself; but he dared not refuse the ordeal—to him its acceptance was the last desperate chance of the gambler who sees ruin staring him in the face. Grammont's blunder, turned to account by the Ems telegram, left him no alternative. William did not wish for war, but for him too there was no alternative. What Grammont had done was to fuse all Germany into unity, and to give to Bismarck what

THE CONSOLIDATION OF GERMANY

he had hitherto lacked, an incontrovertible case to present to the Powers. British neutrality—with Gladstone at the head of the government and Granville at the foreign office—could be taken for granted. Bismarck's publication of Napoleon's earlier proposals for a French annexation of Luxemburg provided the finishing touch. Russian friendliness was assured, since the moment had passed when a Franco-Russian *rapprochement* had seemed more than possible. A delay of a few months might have completed an Austro-French understanding which had not yet been reached, but as matters actually stood, Russia could be counted on to keep the ring so far as Austria was concerned—her attitude was confirmed by a hint from Bismarck that the moment was at hand for denouncing the Black Sea clauses of the post-Crimean treaty. No danger was to be apprehended from Italy; clerical pressure still forbade Napoleon to withdraw the French garrison from Rome, which was the price of Italian support for France. As to Germany's readiness, Roon and Moltke had no qualms; they had had time to bring the whole organization of the armies up to the Prussian standard. Their confidence was the confidence of knowledge; that of France was the confidence of temperament—and of ignorance.

There was no question of violating neutral territory in 1870; Bismarck knew his business too well. The first serious collision took place on 2nd August at Saarbrucken, an advanced post of the Prussians, which they were forced to evacuate. This was the first French victory—and the last. On 4th August the Third Army—South German troops led by the Prussian Crown Prince—was victorious at Weissenburg; two days later the First and Second Armies carried the heights of Spicheran, and the Crown Prince defeated MacMahon's smaller forces in a fiercely contested battle at Wörth. Bazaine attempted to withdraw the main army from Metz for a concentration at Verdun of Châlons; the retreat was held up by an attack at Colombières on 14th August; and the bloody battles of Vionville, Mars-la-Tour, and Gravelotte on 16th and 17th August, cooped up Bazaine in Metz with 170,000 men. MacMahon was driven north by the Crown Prince on Sedan, where he joined the Emperor; but after a fierce struggle Napoleon was obliged to surrender himself with his whole force of 70,000 men to the King of Prussia (1st September).

Sedan shattered the Second Empire. The first defeats drove Napoleon's ministry from office; on the news of the surrender the new ministry vanished; the Empress, deserted, took flight to England; the third republic was proclaimed, and a provisional government of national defense was formed in Paris, headed by General Trochu, Jules Favre, and Léon Gambetta. To the Empire William could have dictated terms; the republic, while announcing that there was now no reason for continuing a war of Napoleon's making asserted its determination not to yield a foot of French soil. Bismarck reckoned that it was France which had driven Napoleon into the war, and France which must be deprived of the power of renewing the war at a more promising opportunity. To that end, Alsace and Lorraine with Metz and Strassburg must cease to be French and must become German. The answer to the republic's declaration was the Crown Prince's march on Paris, of which the siege began on 19th September. On 27th September Strassburg fell.

A government shut up in Paris could not direct the affairs of France; to which it was represented by some members who escaped to Tours before the investment was completed. In the provinces, sectional leagues began to be formed. On 7th October Gambetta escaped in a balloon from the beleagued capital to Tours, and at once became incarnate France, indomitably defiant of her foes. He flung all his energies into raising and organizing four new armies in the provinces while Metz and Paris held vast German forces wrecked by the surrender of Bazaine at Metz (27th October) with 170,000 men and vast military stores. The main German armies were released; but Gambetta responded by proclaiming a *levée en masse*. The raw troops could and did fight heroically, but they were hopelessly over matched. Desperately won successes were followed by fatal defeats. Every attempt to relieve Paris failed. On the southward, through the winter, Bourbaki strove to create a diversion by thrusting past Belfort on to German soil; but he could not break through the German lines and was driven over the Swiss frontier on to neutral soil, where his shattered but still numerous forces had to disarm on 1st February. By that time the fate of Paris was sealed. The last sortie from the already starving city was made and failed on 21st January, and on 28th January the government in Paris signed the capitulation and an armistice; all her forts were surrendered and all war material, and all the troops save the National Guard laid down their arms. For the creation of an authoritative government with whom the victors could treat, a National Assembly was summoned to meet at Bordeaux; the veteran Thiers was called to the head of affairs and conducted the negotiations which concluded in the peace, of which the preliminaries were signed on 26th February (1871), the definite Treaty of Frankfort following on 10th May.

The terms for France were crushing—dictated primarily by the strategical demands of the Prussian military chiefs. With Metz and Strassburg she had to cede Alsace and the best part of Lorraine, to pay an enormous indemnity, and to submit to a partial military occupation, which was to be reduced as the indemnity was paid off—an end which, to the world's amazement, she attained in three years. Bismarck, acting not from generosity but from policy, saved her only from the most extreme claims of the soldiers which, if pressed, would have forced her to yet one more desperate struggle which might have brought outraged Europe to her aid. Some concessions were also made, not without secret resentment, to British pressure. But deep in the heart of every Frenchman was planted a hostility to Germany, which before fifty years were over was to bear terrible fruit.

Incidentally, the war had compelled at an early stage the withdrawal of the French garrison from Rome, enabling Victor Emmanuel to occupy the city, make it the long-desired capital of his kingdom, and finally put an end to the Pope's temporal sovereignty. Also it gave Russia an opportunity, extremely convenient for Bismarck, of deserting her old attitude as champion of the irrevocable character of treaties, denouncing the Black Sea clauses of the Treaty of London, and procuring a revision of that treaty in her own interests, for which she was assured of Prussian support. By doing so she was effectively debarred from backing Austria's suggestion that the German annexation of Alsace-Lorraine was a matter which could only be settled by agreement of the Powers, as contravening the Vienna Treaties.

The most tremendous outcome of the duel, however, was the birth of the new German Empire. It had set free the flood of national sentiment, overwhelming the barriers that still stood in the way of unification. During its progress one after another of the southern states had been admitted to the northern Confederation; Bismarck had overcome, on the one hand, the reluctance of the Kings of Bavaria and Würtemburg, on the other, the prejudices of King William; and the coping stone was set on the fabric he had created when, on January 18, 1871, a few days before the capitulation of Paris, the King of Prussia was acclaimed German Emperor in the Hall of Versailles by the assembled princes, ministers, and generals of the German states.

CHAPTER XLIV

ASIA, 1848-1871

I.—*China and the Japanese Revolution*

THE treaty of Nanking between British and Chinese in 1842 led the way to corresponding arrangements with the United States and with France. Canton, however, was not made an open port as promised, and the local governors continued—with the Imperial sanction—to encourage hostile demonstrations against foreigners. In 1856 matters were again brought to a head by what is known as the *Arrow* incident. A Chinese *lorcha*, which during the previous twelvemonth had been registered as a British vessel, and was still flying the British flag, though not technically entitled to do so, was boarded by the orders of Yeh, the viceroy at Canton, and her crew were taken prisoners as pirates. Sir John Bowring, the British Governor—officially "Superintendent of Trade"—demanded the release of the men. Yeh would at first neither give them up nor apologize. Bowring and Parkes, the Consul at Canton, called upon the British admiral on the China station to intervene, and Canton was seized, though not held for the time, the forces being insufficient for occupation; Yeh having meanwhile set a price upon the head of every Englishman.

In view of the serious position which had arisen through the action of the local officials, British and Chinese, Lord Elgin was sent out as Commissioner in 1857. Yeh continued obdurate, and after various minor operations Canton was again seized, and Yeh himself was captured and deported. France having, in the murder of a missionary, a grievance of her own, joined Britain as an ally; the United States and Russia associated themselves with the demands of the allies, but only diplomatically. The Imperial Government professing to hold no direct communication with the foreigners, the allies proceeded against Peking itself, capturing the Taku forts. The approach of their forces to the capital brought the Government to reason, and fresh treaties were signed in 1858.

The trouble however, did not end here. A fundamental point in the treaties was the permanent appointment of diplomatic agents by the Powers, to reside in Peking, or at least to visit it on occasion. This the Chinese sought to evade; and matters reached such a point that hostilities were renewed in 1860. The Taku forts were again captured; British and French marched on Peking. In the course of the advance and the opening of negotiations British officials were treacherously seized, carried off, and subjected to gross indignity and violence; and when the allied troops entered Peking a sharp penalty was inflicted by the destruction of the summer palace.

The main object was now achieved. The primary purpose of the allies was to enforce responsibility upon the Central Government, which had hitherto held itself celestially aloof, leaving provincial demonstration to the governors, each of whom acted on his own responsibility without direct support from his neighbors, and all with a comfortable assurance that Peking held the outer barbarians in utter contempt, and would approve the most ignominious treatment of them. A new situation was created when it was impressed upon the court of Peking that the Europeans regarded it as responsible for the doings of its subordinates, and would not content themselves with calling the latter to account if they transgressed international practice as understood in Europe. Peking had never looked upon foreign Powers as anything more than troublesome visitors of inferior grade, who should be kept at arm's length, but otherwise as far as possible ignored. With permanent Residents at Peking they could not be ignored. And besides this, Peking had never felt called upon to interfere with the mandarins. In short, its own conception and the Chinese conception of its duties and responsibilities were entirely different from that which the Europeans expected and required it to adopt.

For the time being, however, the treaties of 1860 ended the active hostility of the Government to the foreigners. For it was mainly to the vigor and skill of the foreigners who now came to its aid that it owed the suppression of the Taeping rebellion. This movement had started about 1850 in South China under the leadership of Hung Siu-tsuen, who claimed to be a Prophet or Messiah, and assumed the title of Tienwang, united himself with the great secret, "Triad" Society, which aimed at the overthrow of the Manchu dynasty and dominion, overran much of the south, and established a kind or rule over a considerable area, with Nanking as its center. The Taepings, as the rebels were now called, relapsed into comparative inactivity, but their energies were revived by the collapse of the Imperial Government before the European forces. Their renewed expansion threatened Shanghai, a position of such importance to the Europeans that they became actively concerned in its defense. A Chinese force was raised in the service of the Government under an American named Ward. After he had been killed in action these troops were placed under the command of "Chinese Gordon," to whose unique character and abilities was mainly due the final break-up of the rebels in 1864.

Intercourse between Japan and the rest of the world had always been of the slightest, though in early ages there had been sufficient connection with China to implant both Confucianism and Buddhism in the midst of the native Shintoism. Of the Europeans, none save the Dutch had succeeded in obtaining any sort of footing in Japan, and since the early seventeenth century the only intercourse with foreigners permitted had been with Dutch and Chinese. During this whole period the rulers of Japan had been the Tokugawa Shoguns or Tycoons, although no one questioned that the supreme head and incarnation of the State was the divinely descended Mikado, whose line dated from an immemorial and mainly mythical antiquity. The Mikado was sacrosanct, almost if not quite a divine being; but for centuries he had taken no part in the government which professedly acted by his authority. The Shogun, theoretically his minister, was in effect the sovereign; his council of state and ministers were taken from his own feudal vassals, not from the daimyios, the great feudatories of the Crown; but there was no pretense of any divine character pertaining to his office, as to that of the Mikado.

The Tokugawa rule was no tyranny. The country was self-sufficing so far as concerned the immediate needs of the population; it appeared to be immune from foreign attack; the people were contented; the era of raging civil strife had passed; there were no foreign influences to disturb its equilibrium; it had no craving for the products of other lands nor any fervent desire to find markets for its own products; while the arts of peace flourished. But when the second half of the nineteenth century opened, it was on the verge of one of the most startling revolutions in history—a revolution which entirely changed the system of government, and at the same time leveled the barriers which had sheltered or cut off Japan from the rest of the world.

Deliberately aiming at isolating themselves, the Japanese *literati* concentrated upon national history and traditions with a bias against whatever was of foreign origin, and the first half of the century saw a revival of the indigenous Shintoism as against the Buddhism and Confucianism imported from China. The divinity of the Mikado was an integral part of Shintoism, and thus the way was prepared for a Mikado to assert the authority which had been so long in suspense; not as a political expedient, but as bringing again into practical operation the theocratic conception of the State. In the ordinary course there would have been no particularly strong incentive for him to emerge from the seclusion of his somewhat confined Elysium; but circumstances were to bring about a divergence between Shogun and Mikado, capped by the accession of a Mikado who had at once the will to play the long-forgotten part, and the character and ability to do it with supreme success.

The first serious stirrings of perturbation were, perhaps, caused by the unexpected developments in the relations of China and Europe. Through Dutch and Chinese, some report of what was going on in the outside world penetrated into Japan. If China was being attacked, Japan's turn might come. Warnings were forthcoming that Japan was in no condition to resist European armament. She might have no doubts about her own martial spirit and capacity, but something more was needed to cope successfully with this new military science. If Japan was to keep her gates closed to the foreigner she must make them impregnable, for the foreigner was more than likely to attempt to force them, and if he succeeded a vista of farther dangers would be opened. The appearance of an American warship in 1846 gave ocular demonstration of the peril, though her mission was merely to request leave to trade. The request was declined; but the Shogun, Iyeyoshi, was alarmed.

There was reason enough, for adequate defense would need an immense immediate outlay, which Japan's finances were quite incapable of meeting. There was a grave deficiency of treasure in the country since the foreign trade, conducted exclusively through the Dutch channel, had meant for Japan the export of treasure in exchange; and the lack of specie had led to the development of the fatal expedient of debasing the coinage so that its purchasing power was far below its face value. The natural conclusion of Japanese conservatism was that trade with the foreigner was in itself an evil thing which should be reduced to the lowest limits—that the barriers which excluded him ought to be stiffened. And precisely at this juncture a Mikado, Komei, strongly imbued with these ideas, succeeded to the throne, and departing from the aloofness of the past, proceeded to impress his views upon the Shogun.

Thus, on the one hand, there was the enormous body of opinion, wherewith the Mikado identified himself, which demanded an increased stringency in the exclusion of the foreigner; on the other, the menace that the foreigner was on the point of demanding its relaxation, with European armament to emphasize his arguments. That form of logic could only be answered in kind—by corresponding armament; while the fact was being brought home to the Shogun's mind that such armament was—immediately at least—unattainable. The difficulty was increased by the consciousness that most of Japan had not realized the inadequacy of his defensive system, still less the enormous burden which would be involved in any attempt to raise it to the necessary standard. And finally, there was the small, unpopular section which believed that the whole conservative policy was wrong, and that the admission of foreigners, foreign traders, and foreign ideas, all that the breaking down of the barriers would entail, was in itself desirable and necessary to the future welfare and prosperity of Japan.

Anxiety was increased by the activities of France and still more of Russia in the China seas; and the Western menace definitely materialized when, in 1853, Commodore Perry of the United States Navy, with four ships and a letter to the "Emperor" from President Fillmore, arrived in the Bay of Yedo (the headquarters of the Shogun Government) with suggestions which, if conceded, would obviously introduce the thin end of the dreaded wedge. Iyesada, the new Shogun who succeeded Iyeyoshi during the negotiations, took the only course open to him, which was to temporize. To fight as matters stood was out of the question, while unqualified submission to a scarcely veiled threat would be a humiliation which the Shogun Government could not afford to face. Perry was, in effect, informed that proposals so revolutionary could not be dealt with until the nobles had been consulted and the whole matter referred to the Mikado. Perry withdrew, but intimated that he would return in the spring, when he anticipated a satisfactory reply.

At this time the Europeans assumed that the Shogun, whom they called the Emperor, was in fact the head of the State, and that the Mikado was not a secular but a spiritual authority. In fact, according to the practice of centuries, there was no need for referring any political question to the Mikado, whose intervention from an English point of view would have been flagrantly unconstitutional; but in the Japanese view there was nothing to prevent him from resuming political control if he chose to do so. The Shogun and his ministers knew that they could not fight; whereas public opinion, unconscious of the financial difficulties, and only half alive to the military necessities, would force them on to a disastrous conflict, while some of them already held the unpopular view that even if exclusion could be maintained it would be wrong policy. It was a sheer necessity, then, to placate the foreigner, but to do so under the pretext, for home consumption, that concessions were being made only to gain time for placing the country in an adequate state of defense. If the Conservatives appealed to the Crown against the Shogunate, the Shogunate would fall, the foreigners would invade the country, and red ruin would follow. It was therefore imperative that the Shogun should be able to claim that his policy had the ostensible approval of the Mikado. The question was, in short, one in regard to which the Shogunate felt that it was unable openly to impose its own will on the community, and could only get its own way by dexterous management of the factors in the situation. It could not face a conflict in which the Mikado would be the figurehead of a popular opposition; but it followed inevitably from the course taken that an actively disposed Mikado would once more recover political control in fact as well as in name.

In actual fact the contest in Japan became one between the section who wished the barriers to be broken down and the section who saw that an immediate collision with the foreigners must be averted, but only desired the delay to be employed in preparation for a struggle for which all the energies and resources of Japan must be vigorously organized. The sympathies of the Shogun and his principal minister, Kamon no Kami, were with the former, while it was still necessary to act as though the real aim was to carry out the policy of the latter, who included the majority of the nobles as well as the Mikado and his entourage.

So when Commander Perry returned in 1854 the thin end of the wedge was reluctantly admitted. An agreement was made under which American ships were to be admitted to the two ports of Shimoda and Hakodaté for certain specified purposes, which included only very limited rights of trading; and there was to be an American Consul at Shimoda. The general ignorance of the financial situation, however, caused even these concessions to be regarded as signs of lamentable feebleness in the Government. In the same year somewhat similar agreements were made by the embarrassed rulers with the British and Russians, who were now engaged in the Crimean War.

When the American Consul, Townsend Harris, arrived in 1856, arguments in favor of further concessions were greatly strengthened, in the view of the Shogun, by the course of the European quarrel with China. While he and his ministers were convinced of the necessity of yielding lest worst should befall, the Conservatives were no less convinced that a more vigorous policy of defense and a more skilful diplomacy would succeed in postponing farther concession till the mask could be dropped and the foreigner sent about his business elsewhere. Delay was carried to the utmost limits of safety; but in July 1858 the Shogun was obliged on his own responsibility, without having secured the Mikado's formal assent, to sign the treaty for which Harris was pressing, which was followed next month by corresponding treaties with Holland, Russia, and Great Britain, and a little later with France. Four more ports were to be opened, and freedom of religious worship, with other rights, was conceded, including the establishment of legations of the several Powers at Yedo.

At this juncture Iyosada died; his adopted heir was a boy, and the government was carried on by the ministers, with Kamon no Kami at their head. The anti-foreign temper was rising. The foreign legations took up their residence in Yedo, but every possible difficulty was put in the way of trading. One of the accepted theories was that the Europeans wanted to come to Japan only for the sake of trade, and would retire of their own accord, leaving Japan in peace if trade proved unprofitable. Outrages were committed; half a dozen foreigners at intervals were assaulted and murdered. Then (March 1860) Kamon no Kami was attacked and slain by a band of retainers—*Samurai*—of the "patriotic" faction. The irritation increased when another Power, Prussia, demanded and obtained concessions similar to those already granted. The murder of a member of the United States legation induced the other legations to remove from Yedo to safer quarters, and they had hardly been persuaded to return when an attack was made on the British legation.

Meanwhile relations were growing more and more strained between the Mikado and the Government, which had conciliated him by professions that the moment for open defiance of the foreigners was at hand—while it actually knew itself to be helpless. It now found itself practically compelled to accept one of the Opposition leaders as guardian of the young Shogun, and another as President of the Council—the post formerly held by Kamon no Kami. A few weeks later a British party, heedless of etiquette, came in the way of march of Satsuma, one of the great nobles, and his retainers; whereupon they were attacked and one of them named Richardson, was killed. Demands for reparation and punishment of the guilty parties made by the British Government, and backed by a naval squadron, were only partially met. The British admiral seized some steamers belonging to Satsuma under the guns of his forts at Kagoshima—on their own estates the daimiyos were practically beyond the Government's authority; the forts opened fire, and were bombarded in return. Satsuma made terms with the British, while his action was represented to the Mikado at Kioto as a spirited resistance to the barbarians.

Meanwhile the Shogun had been summoned to Kioto, where he had undertaken to ignore the treaties and open a campaign against the foreigners, which the whole council knew to be wholly impracticable. Nevertheless the order was issued to the daimiyos to take measures for driving the barbarians from their coasts. The lord of Choshiu, whose estate lay on the Strait of Shimonoseki, straightway turned his guns upon the foreign shipping passing through the strait—ignoring the remonstrances of a young Samurai the future Marquis Ito, who had just returned from a visit to Europe with enlightened eyes. The result was inevitable. The forts were dismantled and a substantial indemnity was demanded from Choshiu, which was ultimately paid by the Shogun's Government. It is to be observed that after the fighting relations entirely friendly were established with both Satsuma and Choshiu.

These events, which took place in 1863, opened eyes which had been closed to the realities of the situation. The Mikado and his conservative advisers informed the Shogun that the time was not yet ripe for the expulsion of the foreigners—as though they had not themselves incited or enforced premature action—reprimanding him for not having kept the Mikado properly informed. Choshiu was also reprimanded. A change had come over the spirit of court and the daimiyos; though far from favorable to the Shogun Government, it was even more condemnatory of the ultra-reactionaries, while still anxious, at least as concerned the Mikado, to work towards the exclusion policy.

Now there appear to be these three divisions: the Mikado and the anti-Shogun faction, who meant to increase the direct control exercised by the Mikado; the Shogunate, which had the difficult task of justifying without explaining its ambiguous policy; the Choshiu faction, which in its vew had been penalized for acting upon the Government's instructions, and was smarting under a sense of injustice. A compromise was reached between Mikado and Shogun in 1864; but the Choshiu clansmen or retainers assembled in arms in the familiar mediæval fashion of England, to protest their own loyalty but to demand the removal of evil counselors.

This demonstration was the opening of civil war. The Choshiu nobles were in effect denounced as rebels by the Mikado; the forces at the disposal of the Government moved against them; the nobles submitted, and executed the samurai who had urged them on. This was not enough for the Shogun, who ordered their arrest, and issued farther decrees displeasing both to the Mikado and to leading daimiyos. The Shogun was again summoned to Kioto, and the Choshiu clansmen again rose in arms and inflicted defeats on the Government troops, which now represented only the Shogun's party.

Meanwhile, the Europeans had grasped the fact that there was now in Japan a dual authority, that the Shogun was not in effective control, and that they must require positive ratifications of the treaties from the Mikado himself, which had hitherto not been forthcoming. It was at this juncture that, in 1865, they presented their demands for the ratification of the treaties by the Mikado for their still deferred fulfilment. A combined squadron of warships in the bay of Osaka emphasized the pressure. The Government succeeded in procuring the Mikado's ratification, but only with a reservation as to opening the port of Hiogo which was withheld from the diplomatists. On the other hand, in view of the manifest signs that the Choshiu nobles would be acquitted, the Shogun's council sought to pass upon them sentences of seclusion and confiscation which roused the ire of the dissatisfied daimiyos. Again the Council found themselves unable to give effect to their decrees (1866). Then in quick succession died, first the Shogun, who was succeeded by his cousin and principal adviser, best known as Kokei, and then the Mikado, who was succeeded by the boy of fifteen, Mutsuhito, who ruled over Japan until 1912.

There were now two primary questions—the demand of the foreigners for the prompt opening of Hiogo under the treaties, as to the reservation of which by the late Mikado they had not been informed, and the domestic question as to the treatment of Choshiu. After some delay the argument that the honor of Japan required the carrying out of what had been represented to the foreigners as a positive pledge to open Hiogo was accepted as convincing by the Mikado's court; but while there the reinstatement of the nobles was strongly favored, it was incompatible with the line the Shogun had taken both before and after his accession to that office. The dual control had become impossible; the Shogun could not override the Mikado or attempt to do so with any prospect of success; there must be a single universally accepted head of the State. Kokei recognized the facts, and tendered his resignation in October (1867). It was accepted, and so ended the Shogunate which had ruled unchallenged in Japan since establishment of the Tokugawa dynasty of Shoguns.

Kokei was, however, instructed to carry on the government, pending an assembly of the daimiyos to arrange reconstruction. But, in fact, what was now taking place in Japan was a revolution. In January (1868) the young Mikado proclaimed that he had resumed the direction of the Government; old offices were abolished, new officials were created, none of the Shogun's adherents were among their number; the Choshiu nobles were reinstated, and others who had suffered in the earlier stages of the conflict with the Shogunate were restored. Against his own judgment, but urged on by his more hot-headed kinsmen and clansmen, the ex-Shogun attempted resistance, but was completely overborne. The foreigners received satisfactory assurances from the Mikado that the creation of the new Government was not a party move but his own act, and that they might rely upon his protection and the full observance of the treaties; and when popular demonstrations were made against them, the prompt and effective action of the Government was convincing evidence of its good faith. In less than three months Kokei submitted, and though hostilities were prolonged by other members of what had now become only a faction, all resistance had disappeared before the end of the year. Yedo, as the administrative center, became also the Imperial capital in place of Kioto, under the name of Tokio.

The new Government deliberately based itself on the counsels of the men who had enjoyed and made full use of the best opportunities for studying and appreciating the political methods and the manners of the most prosperous foreign countries. It accepted the international etiquette of the great nations; it modeled its own structure upon theirs. By their own act the daimiyos surrendered their feudal independence, and transferred the allegiance of the samurais to the Emperor. As early as 1869 began tentative experiments in the creation of parliamentary institutions. Free speech was among the first principles proclaimed by the new Government; religious toleration was almost immediately granted, as fully as was possible to a monarchy which based its claim to authority not on the divine right of kings but on the divine descent of the monarch. Japan had not yet asserted herself as a fighting force, but she had definitely claimed a place among the progressive nations of the world at the moment when William of Prussia was hailed German Emperor.

One of the most surprising features of the Japanese revolution was the paradox that it derived its original momentum from popular hostility to the foreigner, whereas the goal it attained, ultimately with deliberate intention, was precisely what its first promoters were most zealous to prevent. The imperialist movement arose from the suspicion that the Shogun had foreign sympathies while the Mikado was a fervent exclusionist. It ended by placing the reins of power unreservedly in the hands of a young emperor who represented all that was most tolerant, most enlightened, most receptive of new ideas in Japan. In the name of a spiritual autocracy it abolished the feudalist Shogun monarchy and the whole national system of feudalism, and substituted for the former the machinery of European constitutionalism. It did, indeed, involve a civil war, but one which was singularly free from terrorism or vindictiveness. It is unique in this that the very class which in 1850 was most hostile to change was in 1870 the stronghold of the new ideas; and the most far-reaching of revolutions was carried to its definite completion peacefully and by consent, so that after fifty years there is still no sign that its stablility is in doubt.

II.—*Russia in Asia; and India*

From the Far East we turn to the main area of Russian and British activities in Asia, commonly known as the Middle East, but in effect comprising the whole Asiatic Continent outside the Chinese and Ottoman Empires.

The progress of Russia in Siberia, the territories on the north of the Chinese Empire, did not as yet affect the European Powers. In effect she was dealing so far with barbarian tribes, not with organized states. While Nicholas I. was still reigning Russia had recently established herself on the shores of the Pacific, though she lacked an ice-free port, with posts at Petropavlovsk in Kamschatka and Nikolaievsk at the mouth of the Amur. Her expansion in this region was soon to become a source of anxiety both to China and to Japan, but did not as yet bring on any collision with either.

Between the Black and the Caspian Seas, her pressure into Asia was held up by the Caucasus and its independent tribes. Here a long struggle was maintained for more than twenty years by the great leader known as Schamyl (that is, Ishmael). Perhaps the most serious error of the British in the Crimean War was their neglect to give energetic support to that indomitable chief; of which the result was his final submission in 1859. The last resistance of the mountaineers was crushed in 1864; and with complete command of the Caucasus, Russia was enabled to bring to bear a constant pressure upon Turkish Armenia on one side, and Persian Ajerbizan on the other.

British interests, however, were more directly challenged by the advance of Russia in Central Asia—by her pressure, that is, over her southern boundary, from the Caspian to the Sea of Aral, and from the Sea of Aral to Lake Baikal, and so to the Chinese Marches and Lake Balkash. In this region of Turkestan lay the three great Khanates of Khiva, Bokhara, and Kokand, with Afghanistan on their south, and beyond Afghanistan, India. Every Russian movement into the Khanates on the Amu Darya and east of it, or among the miscellaneous Tartars on the west of it, was an advance towards the Persian or the Afghan frontier, bringing Russia a step nearer to India. For Russians in Central Asia, as for British in India, incontrovertible reasons which made every fresh advance imperative were always forthcoming, and in 1848 the British were on the point of annexing the Punjab and carrying their own frontier up to Peshawar; nevertheless they never for a moment doubted that the Russian advances were dictated by a deliberate policy which had India herself for its goal. Just so, Persian attacks on Afghanistan were imputed by the British to Russian influences making use of Persia as a cat's-paw with the same object in view.

In 1842 the Khan of Khiva had been forced to make a treaty with Russia which gave her entry to the basin of the Amu Darya; in 1846 she had established herself at the mouth of the Sir Darya. To protect herself against Tartar raids more or less sanctioned by the Khan of Kokand, she advanced up the latter river and fortified Perovski in 1853. Next year, penetrating eastwards, she established a fort at Vernoye, between Lakes Baikal and Issik Kul. But the raiding of caravans continued. A Russian expedition into Kokand in 1863 which captured Clemkent led to an unauthorized attack on Tashkend next year, and to the avowedly reluctant annexation of the "Province of Turkestan," between the Sea of Aral and Lake Issik Kul, in 1865.

This alarmed the Khan or Amir of Bokhara, who proclaimed a *jehad*, a religious war, against the Russians. The Russian commander, Romanovski, ignored, as hopelessly impossible of execution, his official instructions to make a peaceful arrangement, and in May 1866 inflicted on the Khan's forces at Irjai a defeat which had its Indian precedents at Plassey and Buxar. Continued resistance led to the capture of Khojend and other fortresses, the annexation of which drove a great Russian wedge between Kokand and Bokhara; and the whole of this enlarged Turkestan was in 1867 placed under General Kaufmann as Governor-General. Still the Khan of Bokhara remained obstinately hostile, and Kaufmann's consequent operations in 1868 resulted in the capture of Samarkand. The fall of Samarkand was decisive; the Khan Muzaffar-ed-Din made complete submission, but was permitted to remain Amir of Bokhara, as a dependent ally. The shadow of approaching Russia was not far from the border of Afghanistan. However anxious British statesmen might feel, protest was rendered ineffective by the rejoinder that Russia had only been driven to act by the same impelling necessities as successive Governors-General in India from Wellesley to Dalhousie. With the most peaceable intentions, a civilized government, having aggressively hostile unorganized tribes or semi-organized states on its borders, is forced to a perpetual extension of the area both of its direct dominion and of its responsibility and authority for the general maintenance of order.

Moreover, during the first half of this same period the British Government in India had been both developing its control and extending its direct dominion by annexation, and had then been forced to throw all its energies into a fierce struggle for the maintenance of its authority, even the preservation of its existence; in which it had won a decisive victory. That victory opened a new chapter in the story of the Great Experiment.

Dalhousie had hardly reached India in 1848 when a revolt broke out in the Punjab against the government which had been established there for two years under the ægis of the British. The Sikhs believed, not without some warrant, that they had been betrayed by their leaders, not beaten in fair fight. But for the British officers in the Punjab and the Pathan tribesmen, who very much preferred British to Sikh administrators, the Lahore Government would have been overturned and Sikh armies would probably have again invaded British territory. That result was averted by the small forces which were immediately brought into the field. In November the main British army entered the Punjab to crush the revolt; in a fiercely fought battle at Chillianwalla, a very dubious victory was won in which the British after barely escaping grave disaster were left actual masters of the field, while the Sikhs only fell back to an impregnably entrenched position. The final engagement, however, at Gujerat in February (1849) was absolutely decisive. The Sikh army was shattered, and this time there was no doubt left in the Sikh mind that it had been soundly beaten in a straight stand-up fight. It was equally clear that there was only one man—if any—in India capable of reorganizing a strong native government in the

Punjab, Henry Lawrence. Dalhousie and his advisors were not prepared to take that risk, and the only possible alternative was annexation. The Punjab was annexed and placed under direct British administration; eight years later it was to prove itself the staunchest adherent and supporter of the British Raj in India.

Wellesley and Dalhousie stand alone among the British Governors-General as men who were definitely convinced that the extension of British rule was desirable from the British point of view as well as being wholly to the advantage of the natives of India. The rest had all worked on the theory that annexation was to be resorted to only with reluctance and in circumstances which made any other course a danger to the maintenance of public order. These two held that wherever there was legitimate warrant for it it was the preferable course to take—a view never at any time endorsed by the authorities at home.

The annexation of the Punjab was almost universally recognized as a necessity. Every other autonomous state in India was already so far a dependency as to accept the British sovereignty, as of the lawful lord-paramount who had taken the place of the Moguls, and the sovereign's prerogative of controlling foreign relations and imposing peace; while the hereditary prince conducted the actual government as he pleased, provided that he maintained a passable standard of respectability. In such states the supreme Government only placed the administration in the hand of its own officials during minorities and then only when it appeared to be an imperative necessity. With the passing of the Punjab autonomy, the whole of India proper came under the British sovereignity, and there was no state left which was ready to measure swords with the sovereign.

Nevertheless, sundry of the dependent states lost their autonomy under Dalhousie's rule, and were absorbed into the British dominion—by a process strictly and admittedly legal but novel at least in its extended application. By immemorial custom, a childless ruler might adopt an heir who, with the sovereign's sanction, would succeed to his throne as well as to his personal estates. The sanction might be, but rarely was, refused, in which case the crown passed to the paramount authority by lapse or escheat. By the simple process of refusing to authorize adoption or to sanction adoptions made without authority, Dalhousie was enabled to bring several autonomous states, notably Nagpur, Jhansi, and Sattara, under direct British rule on the death of the childless Rajahs. At the moment when Dalhousie left India, the question of the annexation of Oudh, the greatest of the Mohammedan states with the exception of Haidarabad, was under consideration, though here the reason was the persistently intolerable misrule of its princes. The actual decision to depose the ruler and annex Oudh was carried out by Dalhousie's successor, Lord Canning.

Besides these absorptions, there was an expansion. Burmah once more challenged the Government of India in a fashion to which a military expedition was the only possible answer, and the annexation of Pegu was the only possible sequel.

Now the annexations of the Punjab and of Pegu, each the result of victory in an armed conflict which had not been provoked by the British, both presented themselves as perfectly legitimate conquests in complete accord with Oriental and British precedent. Systematic refusal to recognize adoption was a new thing. There were few Hindu dynasties which had not, more than once or twice in their history, been saved from extinction by this practice, and in one case, that of Sindhia, every one of the entire line since its founder had succeeded by adoption. As a matter of fact Dalhousie's intention was still to recognize it as the rule in the greater states, and generally to depart from the established rule only in minor states whose government was unsatisfactory; but Rajput princes and clansmen were alarmed and uneasy (though their anxiety was considerably allayed by the tact of Henry Lawrence, who was transferred from the Punjab to Rajputant); and an impulse was given to the sense of unrest which was developing beneath the surface, unsuspected for the most part by the British authorities. For British administration, however excellent, closed advancement to the ambitious native. Suspicion and hostility were stirred, akin to the sentiment in the Scottish Highlands in the seventeenth and eighteenth centuries, which clung to accustomed institutions and resented all interference with them in the name of an unfamiliar law, whatever increase of prosperity the law might bring with it.

Farther, the enlightenment and energy of Dalhousie's rule were neither understood nor appreciated by the populations, though they were of infinite value. The beginnings of railways and laying of telegraph lines savored of deviltry; railway traveling was incompatible with castes-segregation. Public works appeared to be undertaken only for the sinister purpose of tightening the grip and increasing the power of the British Raj; time was needed before their beneficial effects could be felt. The feebler folk who were shielded by the strong hand of the law hardly realized that they were being protected; the more vigorous found themselves restrained from the license they had enjoyed under lax rulers; in other words, the active predatory classes had the strongest of reasons for objecting to British rule, while the passive and peaceable classes were scarcely conscious of the benefits they derived from it, and were to derive from it in still greater measure in the future.

It was, in fact, an era of extremely benevolent, far-sighted, and just despotism; but its benevolence was not understood, its foresight was unrecognized, and its justice was rather resented than approved; while it emphasized the supremacy of a ruling race whose religion and social customs were wholly alien alike to the Hindu and the Mussulman. Its obvious sanction was the control of an army which, under British leaders, had repeatedly and decisively proved its overwhelming superiority to any other force in India or within reach of India which might be brought against it; the time had passed when its power of compelling obedience, with that army, could be doubted. It was not so clear what would happen if that army failed it. Only in the event of the army turning against it was there any possibility of dislodging the British Raj.

This, however, was precisely the danger that was about to take a manifest form. The great bulk of the army was composed of native regiments. During Dalhousie's governorship the proportion of white to native troops was greatly reduced. White troops were called away by the Crimean War, and were not replaced; the strength of the native regiments was raised, and their number increased on account of the Punjab and Burmese Wars and the annexations; and the native troops began to believe themselves capable of overwhelming their white associates. Their loyalty was subjected to a severe strain by government orders which, as they were taught to believe, were directed against their religion as Mohammedans, and still more as Hindus. Their disaffection was deliberately fomented by malcontents who were thirsting for the overthrow of the British dominion, though their views of the dominion which was to take its place were irreconcilably diverse.

Thus the great revolt, when it came, was primarily a revolt of the Sepoys, brought about for their own ends by political intrigues. It failed because while there was plenty of disaffection outside as well as inside the army, the movement was not a national one with a national goal or any common constructive aim, and because the disaffection outside and inside was far from being universal. The princes knew that without some paramount controlling authority, India would fall into a welter of aimless bloodshed; and no ruling prince from first to last gave his countenance to the revolt, because there was no conceivable prospect of any power imposing itself or being generally accepted as paramount other than that of the British; certainly of any which would be preferable. If some of them felt ill-will to the British for the restraints imposed on them, none of them wanted the restraints on more powerful neighbors withdrawn; none but Mahrattas wanted a Mahratta domination, while no Hindu could desire an effective Mogul or Mussulman restoration, which was the aim of the Mohammedans who fostered the revolt.

But the trouble, though so little suspected, was brewing before

Dalhousie, in shattered health, left India in 1856. His successor, Lord Canning, was practically in the hands of the officials who had been admirable subordinates to a masterful chief—men who were for the most capable of carrying out but not of originating a policy. His first task was the annexation of Oudh, which was hotly resented not only by every one connected with the old government and the Oudh army, but by half the Mussulmans in India. Promises made with regard to the settlement there to the Talukdars, the great landholders, many of whom were in effect Rajput clan chiefs, were not properly carried out by the British officials, and this was resented both by the Talukdars and by their clansmen, whose interests the officials conceived themselves to be safeguarding. The Bengal army was gravely perturbed by the General Service Enlistment Act, which made the troops liable for service overseas—that is, in Burmah—though crossing the sea was a violation of the caste obligations of the high-caste troops of which the Bengal regiments, unlike those of Madras, Bombay, and the Punjab, were mainly composed. Also a quarrel with Persia compelled Canning to send thither white troops and some of the most efficient officers.

On the top of all this came the "cartridge incident"—a godsend to the agitators. The Government ordered the adoption of the Enfield breech-loading rifle instead of the muzzle-loading musket, and in the ingredients of the new cartridges the makers—against orders—introduced animal fat, contaminating both to Hindus and Mussulmans. None of them were issued, but some were made; the fact became known, and the sepoys almost to a man were made to believe that they would suffer contamination if they used the new weapons which were served out to them. The panic among them grew; one regiment, then another and another mutinied; and then at the great Mirat-cantonment, on May 10, 1857, the sepoys rose in a body, slew their officers, and marched on Delhi, where the Mussulman conspirators promptly proclaimed the Mogul restoration.

From Delhi to Benares the white troops numbered hundreds, the sepoys thousands. In this area, during the next seven weeks, all but some hundreds of the sepoys had mutinied and joined the revolt, reinforced by the disbanded troops of the Oudh army and by the followers of Nana Sahib, the adopted son of the last of the Mahratta Peshwas, who had been deposed in 1819. South of the Ganges, the ex-Rani of Jhansi raised a revolt and while Sindhia and his minister, Dinkar Rao, remained loyal, the Gwalior contingent broke away. The British and the loyal sepoys were shut up, surrounded by hostile swarms, in Lucknow and Cawnpore, in greater security at Agra, or gathering on the ridge facing Delhi. Benares and Allahabad, however, points of strategic importance, had been secured. Outside this area the mutinies were sporadic and local. South of the Nerbudda none actually occurred, though many of the troops were restrained with difficulty. In Bengal, from Patna to Calcutta, such mutinies as took place were promptly crushed, and the same occured in the Punjab, where it presently became possible to raise new loyal regiments of Sikhs and Pathans, which rendered invaluable service in the main theater of war.

The critical struggle, then, was confined to the Ganges basin between Delhi and Allahabad, and its most critical period, its second stage, was from the end of June, when the siege of the Lucknow Residency began, till the reinforcement of the garrison by Havelock and Outram at the end of September, following immediately upon the capture of Delhi. From that time it was certain that the British would be able to hold their own until new forces pouring in should thoroughly break the back of the rebellion. This end was accomplished in the third stage by the campaigns of Sir Colin Campbell in Oudh and the Doab (between the Jumna and the Ganges), and of Sir Hugh Rose in the next six months. The fourth stage, from April 1858, was the crushing of the still stubborn resistance of the forces which kept the field through the summer, and the quenching of the last embers of the conflagration, which was not actually completed till 1859.

In the critical stage the main interest centered in the siege of Delhi, the defense of the Lucknow Residency, the campaign in which Havelock fought his way through from Allahabad to Lucknow, and the brief but terrible episode of the hopeless defense of Cawnpore and the treacherous massacre of its garrison. Most vital of all was the siege of Delhi, where some 60,000 British loyal sepoys occupied the famous ridge, held it against overwhelming odds, and finally stormed the great city, which was occupied by at least 30,000 mutineer troops. The capture of Delhi was made possible only when troops and a siege train could be sent down from the Punjab, and at the outset no loyal soldiery could be spared from that province. Yet the risk was taken of raising to fight British battles regiments of Sikhs who only eight years before had been fighting their hardest against the British; and if the step was bold to rashness, it was fully justified by the event. The admirable work of the engineers prepared the way for the assault on 14th September, which gave the British a footing within the ramparts, though it took a week of desperate street-fighting before the mutineers were cleared out and in full flight towards Lucknow.

Cawnpore belongs rather to the first than the second phase; for the position was indefensible, in spite of its importance as commanding the passage of the Ganges into Oudh; and though the little garrison held out for nearly three weeks against Nana Sahib's followers, it had been forced to surrender, on terms, as early as 26th June. The terms were deliberately broken, the men of the garrison were shot down on embarkation for Allahabad under a "safe-conduct"; the women and children were kept as hostages, to be butchered in cold blood not three weeks afterwards.

From 30th June to 25th September the British and the loyal sepoys in Lucknow held the Residency, begirt by thousands of mutineers and the hostile town population. The heaviest work fell on the engineers, since the mining works of the enemy could be carried on completely under cover at short distance from a score of different points. Of thirty-seven several mines, some were short, twenty-five were detected by the counter-mining vigilance of the engineers, and only one effected a breach, which was repaired before the besiegers tried to storm it. But the engineers were few and the lines long; the garrison was almost exhausted, and some of the sepoys had already declared that unless relief came in a week they would march out; when the little force of Havelock and Outram stormed its way through Oudh, and the Residency was saved.

Havelock with less than 2,000 men, Highlanders, Sikhs, and others, was at Allahabad on 30th June. He fought his way up to Cawnpore, which he entered on 17th July, to find it still reeking with the blood of the helpless victims whom the Nana had slaughtered when he found that Havelock's advance was not to be resisted. He crossed the Ganges and routed the mutineers. The depletion of his forces by cholera forced him to fall back, yet again he made a desperate thrust forward, again routed the mutineers, but again had to fall back, and this time across the Ganges—out of Oudh—to Cawnpore. The retreat convinced the Oudh population that the British were beaten, and numbers of them who had hitherto been with difficulty restrained by the Talukdars, now swelled the mutineer army in Lucknow (August). It was not till 15th September that Outram with a couple of fresh regiments joined Havelock. Ten days later the two had driven their way into the Residency, and the garrison thus strengthened was well able to maintain the defense.

Now the second phase opened. Reinforcements were arriving in Calcutta, including troops diverted from the China War, which was also in its first stages. Sir Colin Campbell, now in supreme command, relieved the Lucknow Residency with 5,000 men on 17th November; left the Alam Bagh fortress—in place of the Residency—securely garrisoned; routed on 17th December the Gwalio contingent which, inactive at first, had lately advanced on Cawnpore; in March returned to Lucknow, where the city was still occupied by the mass of the mutineer armies; and after hard fighting drove them completely out of it, though he failed to annihilate them, on 17th March. On 21st March Sir Hugh Rose's column, advancing from Bombay, was before Jhansi, which fell on 3rd April.

From this time the resistance came from the Jhansi Rani and the Gwalior contingent south of the Ganges, and from the Oudh Talukdars, who previously had held aloof from the revolt, in Oudh itself. The cause of this was a proclamation issued by the Governor-General, under the mistaken impression that they had been active participants, which led them to expect a general confiscation of their estates. Conceiving that their loyalty was to be repaid by robbery, they rose, and months of protracted jungle warfare resulted. The Rani was killed in action—fighting like a Joan of Arc—in June; but the last leader of rebellion, Tantia Topi, was not finally hunted down till next year, when he suffered death as an active accomplice in the crime of Cawnpore.

The stories of treachery, murder, and massacre had roused in the British public both at home and in Bengal an indiscriminating wrath which might have taken the shape of a wholesale vengeance but for the unswerving front with which Canning faced the storm of obloquy, and insisted that punishment should fall only on the instigators of crime, not upon those whom they had misled. The mutiny had served to demonstrate finally and conclusively the irresistible power of the British Raj. It had emphasized the necessity for a more sympathetic appreciation, on the part of the ruling race, of ingrained points of view and habits of mind which they were apt to dismiss as mere superstitions and prejudices; the need also for a more complete recognition by the people of Great Britain of their responsibility for the Indian Empire which, in the course of a century, had passed under British sway.

By general consent the dual control by the Company which, without in the least intending it, had created the territorial dominion, and by a separate ministerial body responsible to Parliament, was abolished, and the government of India was assumed solely and directly by the Crown. India became, by the Act of 1858, definitely one of the great departments of the British Government, with its governor-general in India responsible to the Secretary of State at home. The Queen's proclamation which accompanied the inauguration of the new order announced her lively interest in the welfare of her Indian subjects, her desire for harmony and sympathetic understanding, her sense of loyalty displayed as outweighing the disaffection which could be understood and pardoned. But probably its most convincing and effective clause was that which repudiated for ever the Dalhousie doctrine of "Lapse," whereby the continuity of the dependent or feudatory dynasties was permanently assured. The Oudh Talukdars found that they had no such confiscations to fear as had seemed to threaten them; and the appointment of "Clemency Canning" as the first governor-general under the new régime was an unmistakable earnest of goodwill.

The years following were marked not by dramatic events but by a strikingly rapid recovery from the violent upheaval, and by the development of material and, especially, commercial progress. Canning, his successor Lord Elgin, Sir John Lawrence, who was governor-general from 1864 to 1869, and Lord Mayo were all imbued with the spirit of reconciliation, and Lawrence may be called the incarnation of the Liberal conceptions of Indian government. The moment had not yet come when apprehension was once more to be keenly aroused by the approach of Russia to the borders of Afghanistan, and though after the death of Dost Mohammed—who had kept his Afghans firmly in check during the Mutiny—the succession to the throne of Kabul was long disputed before his son, Sher Ali, finally established himself there, the Indian Government refused all invitations to intervene, preserving merely a friendly attitude to the *de facto* ruler, whoever he might be. And within the bounds of India peace reigned unbroken.

CHAPTER XLV

AMERICAN NATIONALISM, 1848-1871

I.—*South America and Mexico, 1848-1871*

By the middle of the nineteenth century the South American Continent was divided between the Empire of Brazil—formerly Portuguese—and the nine Spanish-American republics, with approximately the same boundaries as at the present day; though on the northern shoulder, wedged between Brazil and Venezuela, there remained the three European Guiana colonies, French, Dutch, and British. In Chile a constitutional republic acquired a greater stability than any of the other Spanish-American governments. Columbia in 1861 and Venezuela in 1864, adopted Constitutions modeled on that of the United States, which brought peace to the former, but by no means ended the civil strifes in the latter. The general picture is one of successive dictatorships everywhere, for the most part violent tyrannies violently subverted.

The same description applies to the Central American republics and to Mexico—in other words, to all of the mainland that had been Spanish America. Throughout it there was at most only a reflection of the European revolutionary movements. In Europe the Democratic movement was one for equality before the law, political and social, for all classes of the community, accompanied by an extremist tendency to capture for the manual workers the political predominance enjoyed in the past by the landowners which was now in some countries passing to the manufacturers and traders. In Spanish America there was neither a peasantry in serfdom to a landowning aristocracy, nor a proletariat dependent on capitalist employers; nor were there established monarchies with an arbitrary control of the whole political machine.

Theoretically, the alternative to the rejected Spanish monarchy, with its immemorial lack of governance, was democratic republicanism; but there was neither machinery ready to hand for carrying on the business of government, political genius capable of creating such machinery, nor the political experience and political habits of mind necessary to work such machinery as could be created. Hence when what there was of system in the old order collapsed, there was merely a constant strife not of principles but of factions and persons to capture a purely dictatorial mastery dependent on the temporary control of the strongest available military force; and the era of successive dictatorships, insurrections, *coups d'état,* and pronunciamentos was still in full operation half a century after the last vestige of the authority of the Spanish Crown had disappeared from the American continent.

In Europe the Nationalist movement had its two aspects—one seeking the liberation of peoples of common nationality from the control of alien authority, the other seeking the consolidation into a single nation of peoples conscious of common nationality. The liberation achieved in America was liberation only from the control of a government with its headquarters on the other side of the Atlantic, and of its imported functionaries, who were of the same blood, religion, and traditions as a large proportion of the natives. The successful movement for independence in the first quarter of the century could be called nationalist only to the precise extent to which this imported government could be called alien. As for national consolidation, the disruptive forces were far stronger than those which made for unity. Bolivar's attempt to construct a United States of the North ended in the emerging of five separate republics which were not united at all, and two of them, Columbia and Venezuela, only just escaped farther disintegration.

Brazil meanwhile, under its constitutional Emperor Pedro II., enjoyed a Liberal Government, free from the frequent and violent perturbations of her neighbors, though not unaffected by republican propaganda. Neither South nor Central America materially influenced or was influenced by Europe in the political sense after their separation from the Spanish and Portuguese crowns.

Mexico, however, occupied a somewhat different position. Bordering on the United States, she was from time to time involved in differences with that great Power, and in the period now under review she provided also a disastrous field of adventure for the restless ambitions of the Emperor of the French.

Though Santa Ana was driven from power by the ill success of the resistance offered to the United States in the Texan quarrel, he recovered the dictatorship, but only to lose it again in 1855. From the strife of factions which followed his final fall, Benito Juarez emerged in 1860 as President and head of an anti-clerical party. The Clericals were already seeking financial and other assistance in Europe, and had gained the ear both of the Spanish Government and of Napoleon's Empress, Eugénie, when Juarez, being in financial straits, simultaneously secularized ecclesiastical property in Mexico, and stopped the payment of the Mexican debt, in 1861, just at the moment when the United States had plunged into the great Civil War. At any other time, European intervention in Mexico would have been barred by an emphatic reminder of the Monroe doctrine; but President Lincoln had too much on his hands, for some time to come to permit of any serious protest.

Napoleon, then, saw an opportunity for glory, and at the same time for restoring the confidence of the French Clericals, perturbed by the course of events in Italy. The establishment of a Latin monarchy in Mexico resting on Clericalism under the ægis of the French Empire seemed to offer a promising program. It was encouraged by Saligny, the French envoy in Mexico; Spain was favorably disposed; England was willing to demonstrate against the suspension of payments in which she had a strong interest. The co-operation of those Powers might be useful and their antagonism dangerous at the outset, though they were not likely to fall in with later developments of the plan. Austria also might be rendered more amenable in Italy if the Archduke Maximilian accepted the invitation of the Mexican Monarchist-Clericals to a Mexican throne for which he would in fact be indebted to France.

So at the end of 1861 a joint demonstration was arranged with the Spanish and British Government, ostensibly to impress the Mexican Government with the necessity for establishing order, security for foreign residents and their property, and the due payment of Mexico's debts. Farther than that Britain never dreamed of going; Prim, who was given the Spanish command, had no disposition to commit himself to costly and difficult operations of which Napoleon would reap the advantage—which he soon perceived to be the purpose of the Emperor, whose expedition was on a more ambitious scale than were those of his allies. In February 1862 both British and Spanish had already recognized Juarez and come to terms with him. If Napoleon was bent on more, he would have to go on alone.

He went on alone, and an initial reverse involved the dispatch of larger armies, of which the chief command was intrusted to Bazaine, who was raised to the rank of Marshal. In the summer the city of Mexico was occupied, and Maximilian, who had given his assent, was proclaimed Emperor; but Juarez and Porfirio Diaz kept the flame of resistance burning. The business was not bringing the *éclat* for which Napoleon had vainly hoped, and it fettered him in his European policy, but France felt herself too deeply committed to retire. In 1864 Maximilian arrived in person with his wife, and had a triumphant reception in the capital; but his amiable qualities did not make him equal to the intricate situation in which half the country was in arms against him, his Clerical supporters were making demands which he was neither willing nor able to satisfy, and Bazaine, the strongest military factor, was playing in the interests of France or of himself a game which was not Maximilian's. The resistance remained irrepressible. In 1865 the war in the United States was ended, and the government was soon demanding, in the name of the Monroe doctrine, that the French troops should be withdrawn and Mexico left to settle her own form of government. War with the United States was more than Napoleon could risk as matters then stood in Europe, where the relations between Prussia and Austria were strained; and in the beginning of 1866 the order was given for Bazaine's withdrawal, though the embarkation did not begin till a year later.

Maximilian, who had been seduced into his venture mainly by Napoleon's persuasions, was left in the lurch. His chance was gone, but he would not desert the lost cause. Treason delivered him into the hands of his enemies—who claimed to be the legitimate Government of Mexico and had in fact been so recognized by the United States—and he was shot after a form of trial. So tragically ended the Mexican adventure. Juarez was re-established as President of the Mexican Republic, and his dictatorship during the next five years laid the foundations of a rule which had at least the merit of comparative stability, though neither he nor Diaz after him succeeded in giving it permanency.

II.—*The United States: The Breach*, 1848-1861

While the Mexican War of 1847 secured the next Presidential election to one of its Generals, Zachary Taylor, the acquisition of California by the treaty of 1848 had unexpected results. The simultaneous discovery of gold there led at once to a huge immigration of gold-diggers. By the end of 1849 the immigrants, since the new territory still awaited organization by the United States Government, resolved to claim admission to the Union as a State. The majority of them were Northerners, and in the Constitution which they formulated slavery, though a great part of the territory was south of the Missouri line, was prohibited; to the great indignation of the men from the south. President Taylor proposed that in the whole of the newly acquired area, New Mexico as well as California, the territorial organization should permit the populations to form slave or free States as they might choose. Henry Clay, a lover of compromise, had a different solution. Taylor's unexpected death left the settlement of the question to his Vice-President, Fillmore, who succeeded to the Presidential office, and Fillmore accepted Clay's plan, the "compromise of 1850," to which Daniel Webster had already committed himself in the "Seventh of March Speech."

Now the southern extremists objected entirely to the principle of local option, believing that the southern voters would be swamped by the northern, as in California; the South in the new territories must be on an equal footing of power with the North. Otherwise, the preponderance of the North in the Central Government would be increased; the North would be able to impose its will on the South, whose interests would be fatally overridden; and the South, to save itself, would sever the Union. The anti-slavery extremists were bent on preventing slavery in the new territory altogether, claiming that there was a "higher law" than the Constitution, and the accursed thing must go, whether or not the Constitution permitted. They demanded the "Wilmot proviso" which in 1846 had proposed—though it had not become law—the exclusion of slavery from any territories acquired from Mexico, the Missouri Compromise having applied expressly only to the Louisiana Purchase. Clay, the southern moderate, backed by Webster, the northern moderate, desired the Compromise; under which the decision of California would be ratified, slavery would not be abolished in Columbia, and in the rest of the territories the question would be settled by local option. But to mollify the South, a "fugitive slave law" was to enable slave-owners, in fact as well as in theory, to recover slaves who had escaped into free territory.

The Compromise was passed; but the stringency of the new Fugitive Slave Law defeated its own objects. When the slave-owner's agents came into the free States to seize and carry off the fugitives, the abolitionists rescued them, and convictions for so doing were hardly obtainable—as constantly befalls where trial by jury is in force, and the law violates, or is not supported by, popular opinion and the public conscience. Moreover, the public conscience was violently inflamed by the publication in 1852 of "Uncle Tom's Cabin," the one work of fiction which has had an immediate and powerful influence on the making of history. Regarded as a picture of the institution as normally practised in the south, it was unquestionably a flagrant misrepresentation; but it painted with a fervid appeal to humanitarian sentiment conditions actually prevalent in some cases under the ægis of the law, and the revolting possibilities logically involved in the whole theory of slavery, the immorality of the root-principle of a system which treated a human being as a chattel at the absolute disposal of his owner.

For the moment, however, the Compromise offered hopes of peace, and the next Presidential election returned a northern Democrat, Franklin Pierce, from Vermont, the general supposition being that the Democrats were less likely than the Whigs to trouble the comparatively quiet waters. Yet it was a northern Democrat, Stephen Douglas, who stirred them afresh in 1854. West of the Missouri River and of the State of Missouri and north of Texas lay the greater part of the "Louisiana Purchase" territory still unorganized, the whole area being subject to the Missouri Compromise—and on the north or free side of the Missouri line of demarcation. In a broad spirit of conciliation as his friends maintained, or to secure the southern vote at the next Presidential election as his opponents affirmed, Douglas introduced the Kansas-Nebraska Bill for the organization of this region. Assuming that the Missouri Compromise had been abrogated when its principle was set aside in the 1850 Compromise, he proposed that the 1850 principle of local option, popularly known as "squatter sovereignty," should be applied here as well as in the once Mexican area.

If any other question than that of slavery had been the point of issue, territorial option would have been difficult to challenge after the classic case of California. But slavery was a moral no less than a political problem. Its opponents for the most part recognized that where it had been established before the union its disappearance must be left to time. They could reconcile themselves to its admission elsewhere only where an obligation had been imposed by past pledges, as under the Missouri Compromise; no equivalent obligation had been imposed by the acceptance of local option in the 1850 Compromise; yet they were invited to open to it gratuitously the door which the Missouri Compromise itself had closed. No such concession ought to be made to the Powers of Darkness, however sincerely Douglas and his supporters might affirm that it was a concession in name only, since—as Webster had said of California—"slavery was excluded by nature" from Nebraska (as the region was then called), and that Nebraska or any part of it should voluntarily become a slave State was almost unthinkable. The Bill was passed, incidentally providing for division into the two territories of Nebraska and Kansas. But it was taken as a direct challenge on the principle of slavery, ignoring the essence of the past compromises and making all compromise in the future impossible.

The Act broke the Democratic Party and practically created and developed the new party which took the old name of Republican. The elections to Congress placed the Democrats in a minority about as great as their previous very substantial majority had been. The cleavage which had shaped the parties of Democrats and Whigs had been one of forms and factions much more than of principles; now, issues of principle had forced themselves to the front, and the cleavage was unmistakably on the two questions indissolubly bound up with each other, of slavery, and State versus Federal Rights.

It was at once manifest that Kansas, the southern territory marching with Missouri, would be the field of an acute struggle. North and South were each zealous to carry out an immigration which would give it the predominance. The advantage lay with the North, for a planter's establishment was not easily transferred to distant virgin territory. The northern settlers were more numerous, being helped by societies organized with that end in view, but were swamped by a rush of temporary immigrants from Missouri, who captured the territorial legislature; though not without so much intimidation and corruption that the "free state" men refused to recognize its authority, set up a separate Convention, and demanded admission to the Union as a Free State. The legislature, on the other hand, held a convention to formulate a Constitution, under promise that its decision should be submitted to a popular vote for ratification; but when the question to be submitted turned out to be only whether slavery in the new State should be limited or unlimited, they thereby enlisted against themselves the very men, including Douglas, who had advocated the principle of squatter sovereignty. Free fighting and acts of personal violence on both sides exasperated the situation. A fresh election resulted in an enormously preponderant vote against slavery.

Meanwhile the Supreme Court of the United States had given, in 1857, a remarkable judgment in regard to the case of an escaped slave named Dred Scott, in which it was laid down that the restriction of slave-owners' rights in "National" territory by the Missouri Compromise was unconstitutional and therefore invalid, and that slave-owners might take their slaves into free territory. On those principles there would be practically no check on the expansion of slavery, if the law was strong enough to protect the "property" of slave-owners in the free States, where it was in actual practice already unable to enforce the fugitive slave law; a fact emphatically illustrated at the end of 1859 when John Brown of Kansas raided the National arsenal at Harper's Ferry in Virginia in order to arm the slaves, and won immortality by his own capture and execution—an event celebrated in one of the most popular spirited and famous of war-songs.

Thus during the Presidency of Buchanan, the successor of Franklin Pierce, a crisis was rapidly approaching. At the close of 1860 came the Presidential election which brought the issues to a head. The Democrats of the North and of the South were definitely split. The solid South held that the time had come for asserting without qualification that the institution of slavery was merely an economic necessity for them, but was a positive benefit to society, right in itself, a moral civilizer. The northern Democrats admitted the economic necessity, and while they condemned slavery morally recognized the right of the southerners to take a different view and to act upon it. They were willing to leave the question an open one for the new States, which should be free to settle it for themselves. The Republicans generally, as distinguished from the Abolitionist group, declined to regard the moral question as an open one, while acknowledging the constitutional right of the southern States to retain the institution, but only within their own borders. Of the two sections of the Democrats the northern was in fact nearer to agreement with the Republicans than with the South. The northern Democrats nominated Douglas, the South chose the Vice-President Breckinridge; and the Republicans concentrated upon Abraham Lincoln, latterly the most powerful champion of their views; while a "Constitutional Union" party of ultra-conservatives nominated a fourth candidate of their own. The result was that Lincoln carried the election, though the Republican Party was actually in a minority. With his election, the primary issue became not slavery but secession.

In actual fact, Lincoln, even with a majority behind him, would not have entered upon an abolitionist program; as matters stood, such an attempt would have been doomed to complete failure. But the South recognized in the event a victory of the principles which they repudiated with entire conviction, whether from the point of view of morals or of expediency; a victory which would be pressed—and if pressed would mean more and more the subordination of the South to the North, the gradual disappearance of their rights and depression of their interests, the constant increase of the northern predominance in a Central Government, which would encroach more and more upon State rights as understood in the South.

The time, then, had come when severance of the union was the only way of escape. South Carolina took the lead and summoned a State Convention which, on December 20, 1860, unanimously passed an Ordinance to dissolve "the compact of union between South Carolina and other States, known as the Constitution of the United States of America." In the course of the next month Georgia and the five Southern states which touch the Gulf of Mexico followed suit. In February they drew up for themselves, under the name of the Confederate States of America, a Constitution modeled on that of the United States. Later, the rest of the slave-owning States, with the exception of the most northern—Missouri, Kentucky, part of Virginia, Maryland, and Delaware—joined the secession; and Jefferson Davis of Mississippi was elected Confederate President. Meanwhile, on March 4, Lincoln was inaugurated President of the United States; and his inaugural address declared that the Union was unbroken, and that he would fulfill his duty in taking care that the laws of the Union were duly executed in all the States—a clear pronouncement that secession was a defiance of the law.

The seceding States for their part had already taken possession of most of such National (not State) property, arsenals and military posts, as lay within their borders. Fort Sumter being garrisoned by United States troops, the President informed the Governor of South Carolina that it would be provisioned, which it was not at the time. Thereupon the Southerners closed on it, and it was forced to surrender on April 14. Next day the President's proclamation appeared calling for 75,000 volunteers. The great Civil War had begun.

III.—*The United States: The War for the Union,* 1861-1865

The southern States seceded on the ground that if they so desired it was within their right, that they did so desire, and that they had that desire a justification potent enough to outweigh the claims of the sentiment in favor of unity. On these points the South was virtually unanimous. The North held that they had no such right technically; and that in any case the future welfare of the continent depended on the preservation of unity, the maintenance of which had therefore a justification which outweighed any local sentiment in favor of separation.

On the technical point, it was extremely difficult to controvert the Southern or Confederate contention as a matter of history. A number of States which had successfully repudiated the only authority which was common to them—that of the British Crown—had then entered on a compact again instating a common authority. The South claimed that this was a compact between a group of sovereign States, from which each one was at liberty to withdraw at will. The North, the Federals, could only reply that the compact was an act not of the several States but of a whole people—which at the time had no legal National existence—though it was beyond question accepted by the several States acting individually; that the Union was therefore not a dissoluble Confederation, but a Federation indissoluble except by common consent, as much as if a clause to that effect had been included in the Constitution itself. On the modern hypothesis of the unqualified right of self-determination, it is not easy to see how the Southern claims could be denied—or upon the principle which the whole of the sometime colonies had asserted when they severed themselves from the British Crown.

On the other hand, no less incontrovertible was the Northern contention that, unless there was an indissoluble Union, a complete break up into a number of antagonistic States, with all the evils of the European State system, would follow. Even at the best there would be two rival Confederations with antagonistic interests. Stated in the simplest terms, the public security and welfare imperatively demanded a unity admittedly indissoluble by the action of a section. A National patriotism could not be challenged on the plea of an academic technicality. This was a question not of forcibly and artificially combining the disunited but of maintaining a natural union voluntarily achieved three-quarters of a century ago.

Secession was the issue. The North would not have fought the South in order to put down slavery; it fought the South because the

South rejected the principle of Federal Union not only in word but in act. The struggle had only been postponed hitherto by concessions to the southern interests. But it was the particular southern interest in slavery, the fear that the institution could be saved only by secession, that made the South act at last upon its theory of the right of secession. It was northern hostility to slavery which excited to fighting point the apprehensions of the South. In the course of the war, emancipation became an instrument of victory in the hands of the North; and as a war for emancipation, the conscience of the civilized world sympathized with the northern cause, though on the secession issue the South had won the same sort of sympathy across the Atlantic as the Thirteen Colonies when they challenged British domination.

To the South it was always incredible that the right of secession could be honestly questioned by a disinterested spectator. To the North it was equally incredible that it could be honestly defended. The world at large assumes that with its neighbors economic interests count for more than principles of abstract justice, and it saw that the economic interests of the South would gain, apparently, at least, by secession, those of the North by maintenance of the Union. On the other hand, such advocates of political freedom as Gladstone favored the South, whereas the fact that negro slavery was at stake made all those to whom slavery was an abomination supporters of the North. Governments, however, acted on the view that if the North and the South chose to fight each other for whatever reason, it was their business not to pronounce on the rights or wrongs of the quarrel, but to observe strictly an official neutrality; an attitude which was at once questioned and resented by both. The Federals, in fact, had some justification for complaining that the official neutrality of the British Government was belied by the negligence which, whether intentional or not, permitted the departure from British ports of the *Alabama* and other vessels destined to serve the Confederate cause, and omitted to lock the stable doors till the horse had been stolen. On the other hand, the contention of the South that its independence ought to have been recognized but was not, and of the North that the South ought not to have been but was recognized as belligerent instead of rebel, were equally untenable on the principles of non-intervention consistently maintained by every British minister since the meeting of the Vienna Congress.

Most of Virginia, North Carolina, Tennessee, and Arkansas joined the Confederates; Kentucky and Missouri, not without conflict, were retained for the Union. The primary object of the Confederates was to capture the capital, Washington, on the northern or Maryland side of the Potomac; to cover Washington was the object of the Federals as soon as they had secured Maryland itself.

The first big battle of the war at Bull's Run (July 21, 1861) was also the first example in modern warfare of a fight for a railway junction as a point of first-class strategic importance. The victory of the South gave the Confederates possession of Manassas Junction, where the west-to-east rail crossing the Blue Ridge from the Shenandoah Valley on the west joins the north-to-south rail from the Potomac, opposite Washington, on the east. It was won because the Federal commander in the Shenandoah Valley failed to prevent the Confederate chief, Johnston, from entraining his troops which took a decisive part in the struggle. The battle gave the Confederates an unwarranted assurance of an early triumph, and many of them went home; but it also roused the North to consciousness of the immensity of the effort which would be demanded from it; recruits came in to Washington in large numbers, and the increased force was effectively organized by M'Clellan.

In November occured the *Trent* incident, which nearly forced Great Britain into war with the Federal Government. The Confederates dispatched two commissionaries for England and France, who took passage on a British ship, the *Trent*. On a strained interpretation of the "right of search" as maintained by the British, but denounced hitherto by the United States, the Trent was boarded and the commissioners were carried off by a Federal warship. The Federal Government yielded to the very emphatic demand of the British Government that the commissioners should be released, while claiming that in doing so they were acting upon their own doctrine of the right of search, not that of the British, which had, in their view, fully warranted the seizure—a view repudiated by the British Government. War was averted, but the North persisted in the opinion that the British had been guilty of an unfriendly act, intended to embarrass the Federals; the British claimed that the only course open to them as neutrals was the course which they had taken; and the whole incident intensified the mutual suspicions of the two nations, each of which was perfectly satisfied that it had been itself entirely in the right and the other inexcusably in the wrong.

Though Bull's Run had secured the railway to the Confederates, it did not give immediate access to Washington, where M'Clellan was organizing the army of the Potomac. The area of conflict extended; in the year following Tennessee became a third theater, in addition to the Potomac and the Shenandoah, and the naval superiority of the North enabled it to declare a blockade of the southern ports, and to establish control of the lower Mississippi by the capture of New Orleans in April. The victory of Thomas at Mill Spring, and the capture of Forts Donelson and Henry by Ulysses Grant and of New Madrid by Pope gave the Federals the entry of Tennessee; and Grant's conversion of defeat into victory at Shiloh gave them control of the upper Mississippi down to Memphis (where it enters the State of Arkansas), which was captured in June. The Confederate command of the river at Vicksburg, however, severed the communication between its upper and lower portions.

The main campaign should have been conducted in Eastern Virginia by M'Clellan, whose talents as an organizer were not equaled by his abilities as a commander, which were, moreover, hampered by the control from Washington. His aim was to attack Richmond from the "Peninsula" between the rivers York and James; but a large force was placed in the Shenandoah Valley, where it was faced with a smaller army under "Stonewall" Jackson, whose activities so alarmed the Federal headquarters that another still larger fence was detained to cover Washington. M'Clellan's advance on Richmond was checked first at the end of May by Johnston. The Confederate general was severly wounded, and his place was taken by Lee, who now, with the aid of Jackson, inflicted a series of blows on M'Clellan in the "Seven Days" (26th June—2nd July), driving him away from Richmond; though a final attack at Malvern Hill was repulsed decisively and with heavy loss to the Southerners. Lee, with Jackson, turned to fling himself upon Pope, who commanded the covering army before Washington, and Pope was driven back to the covering lines by the second Battle of Bull's Run.

Lee next proposed to invade and recover Maryland; but the great numerical superiority of the Federals forced him to retire, after the fierce but indecisive Battle of Antietam, to Fredericksburg, and the year's campaigning in the east closed with an unsuccessful and very sanguinary attack upon his lines there (December 13, 1862).

In the west, since midsummer, a fierce conflict had developed in eastern Tennessee between the Federals Buell and Rosecrans and the Confederate Braxton Bragg, culminating in the desperate Battle of Murfreesboro', or Stone River (31st December), where the casualties numbered a quarter of the forces engaged, and the Confederates were finally obliged to retire. Grant, left in command of the Mississippi army, but hampered by orders from Washington, endeavored to capture Vicksburg; but the plan of attack imposed on him was foiled by a successful attack on his communications which checked his own advance on the eastern side, and enabled the Confederate commander, Pemberton, to meet in force and repulse at Haines' Bluff (29th December) the second column under Sherman which was advancing down the Mississippi directly upon Vicksburg. It was not till May 1863 that Grant was able to shut Pemberton up in Vicksburg.

But meanwhile an event of supreme importance had occurred. In September 1862 President Lincoln issued the Proclamation announcing that all slaves in any State which should be in rebellion at the New Year would then be declared free; and on January 1, 1863, the

Emancipation Proclamation was duly sent forth. It did not apply to the border slave States which had held by the Union, nor effectively elsewhere except in areas dominated by Federal forces. But it meant to the world outside that the conflict had definitely taken the shape of a war of emancipation; the North was irretrievably committed to that particular issue, which no less definitely had not been the case heretofore. To Lincoln, intensely as he hated slavery, the Union, not slavery, was the issue, and he committed himself and the North to emancipation only when it presented itself as a means to victory in the struggle against disintegration. It served that purpose because it consolidated foreign sentiment in favor of the North, and because it created for the South an enemy within its own gates, complicating for it the problem of defense by the distraction of an internal danger which must be guarded against.

Between January and May there were no decisive engagements, east or west. At the beginning of May, Hooker, who had taken M'Clellan's place as commander of the Potomac army, crossed the Rappahannock in force to renew the attack on Lee's much smaller army. The Confederates accepted the challenge; Hooker found his right suddenly assaulted by Jackson, and was all but routed at Chancellorsville. Jackson was killed by an accidental shot, but Lee next day drove Hooker over the river, though the numbers of the Federals were double his own. Continuing his offensive, he advanced to invade Pennsylvania, the Potomac army following under a new commander, George Meade. The two forces came to grips in a three days' battle at Gettysburg, where Meade occupied a very strong position, whence Lee's desperate attacks failed to dislodge him; both the forces again lost more than a quarter of the combatants, but Lee had to fall back over the Potomac. Next day (4th July) the Confederates beleaguered at Vicksburg by Grant were compelled to surrender.

Meanwhile the operations were renewed in Tennessee where two northern armies were shut up in September by Bragg at Chattanooga and at Knoxville. Then Hooker, with reinforcements from the Potomac, joined Thomas at Chattanooga, and Grant arrived with Sherman from Vicksburg to take the supreme command. Another complicated three days' "Battle of Chattanooga" drove Bragg in hasty retreat to Atlanta, in Georgia (November 1863).

The decisive struggle opened in May 1864 when the supreme command of all the Federal forces had at last been intrusted to one chief, the victor of Vicksburg and Chattanooga. The Confederates had been fighting for three years with no reserve power, the Federals with an immense reserve power only brought into the field by slow degrees. The victories of the South had been won by armies always smaller and often very much smaller than those of their opponents. The northern armies were constantly increasing, and all their losses were much more than made good; the southern armies were constantly diminishing, and their losses could not be made good. The South had perforce left its business of production entirely to the slaves; the north had never depleted its industrial population for the armies, and its production and its wealth advanced; while its blockade of the ports had deprived the South of the imports on which— cut off from trade with the North—it was almost wholly dependent. In the fourth year of the war the results manifested themselves. The South was overwhelmed by depletion, exhaustion, and the blockade.

The struggle resolved itself into two main divisions, though they were co-ordinated—Grant's duel with Lee, who after Gettysburg had fallen back into Virginia, and Sherman's campaign in the south. Grant, having deputed the command of the Tennessee armies, numbering 100,000, to Sherman, advanced with Meade into Virginia, where his own 120,000 were faced by Lee with about half the number. Continuous heavy fighting from 5th-12th May about Chancellorsville and Spotsylvania Court House, failed to eject Lee from his positions. Every effort to outflank him and threaten Richmond failed; every movement still found Lee's army impregnably stationed to repel the approach to Richmond; and again Grant's attacks were beaten off after continuous heavy fighting from 31st May to 12th June in the region of Cold Harbor. Then Grant moved on Petersburg (on the south of Richmond), and began a siege which lasted into the following spring. In all the fighting, Grant's losses were very much the heavier, but the gaps were promptly filled up, while those in Lee's forces were not, so that Grant gained heavily by the policy of refusing to exchange prisoners. The re-election of Lincoln to the Presidency increased the vigor of the prosecution of the war by the North, and the energy with which the losses were more than made good. At last, in April 1865, Grant, whose forces were now in the proportion of five to two, was able to carry out an enveloping movement, and Lee was forced to attempt an escape westward by the valley of the Appomattox. A delay in the arrival of Lee's supplies enabled a column under Sheridan to block the line of his retreat, while Grant's main force was close on Lee's heels. The Confederate army had no other alternative than annihilation or surrender, and the terms of surrender were generous enough. The troops were required only to lay down their arms and cease from farther hostilities. The surrender at Appomattox Court House (April 9, 1865) ended the fighting.

While Lee was making his long, indomitable stand for the South against Grant in Virginia, Sherman began his southward movement on Atlanta. Facing him was Johnston, who, restored to command after recovering from the wound which had compelled his retirement, had vainly endeavored to break up the seige of Vicksburg. Repeatedly outflanked by Sherman's superior numbers, Johnston fell back and back, always upon fresh entrenchments, always fighting but never joining in a pitched battle, until he was superseded by a less cautious commander, Hood, who thrice in July and again a month later assumed the offensive, but was repulsed each time. Then by a turning movement Hood fell on Sherman's communications; but Sherman, detaching Thomas to attend to Hood, himself pushed forward, captured Atlanta, and then started westward on his famous "march to the sea." Unless Hood could eliminate Thomas or Lee should elude Grant, he was not likely to meet any very serious resistance, his troops would live on the enemy's country, and the political effect of a march through Georgia would be immense—equaled by the strategic value of the next stage, a northward march in rear of the southern ports.

Thomas was not eliminated. He retired north to Nashville, keeping Hood occupied, held him there while he bided his own time, and in mid-December shattered the western Confederate army in a two days' battle. Three days later Sherman was in Savannah; in January he started on the northward march. Johnston with what troops it was still possible to collect could only check, without stopping, his advance through the Carolinas. Reinforced from Tennessee and elsewhere, Sherman before the end of March had Johnston in his grip, so that no relief or diversion in aid of Lee was possible to him, and the victory of the North was sealed by the surrender at Appomattox on April 9, 1865.

IV.—*The United States: Reconstruction,* 1865-1871

The victory of the North over the South, of union over disintegration, of personal freedom over slavery, was sealed by the blood of the great man to whom more than to any other single person it was due. On 14th April Abraham Lincoln was murdered by a crazed devotee of the lost cause—the victim of an insane plot to which less than a dozen irresponsible persons were privy. No crime was ever so unspeakably stupid. The lank, uncouth form of this man of the people enframed the grandest figure the century produced. Clear-eyed, single-hearted, indomitable, the pilot had remained at the helm from the beginning to the end of the storm; infinitely patient, utterly selfless, wholly confident in the righteousness of his cause; yielding not an inch to excited clamor, to vindictive passions, to sentimentalism, to intrigue; seeking always to be just, willing always to be generous, to those against whom he was fighting, but with no wavering, no compromising on the principles for which a complete victory must be won. He was the one man capable of assuaging the bitter vindictive spirit which had been aroused on both sides, and carrying through a successful policy of reconciliation. He fell; his task passed to less able hands; and there was little enough of idealism in the reconstruction which followed.

During the struggle parties in the North had been merged in the single aim of preserving the Union; even actual emancipation within the slave States had become a positive issue only in the course of the struggle when the President had recognized it as an inevitable condition of decisive victory, for which to the last he would have urged generous compensation. When he was gone there were many, including his successor, Andrew Johnson, who wished to give effect to his policy, but none who could control the revival of the old party rancour.

With the submission of the South the complete abolition of slavery was a certainty. There was no civilized Power left in the world under whose ægis the institution could shelter, though the "Thirteenth Amendment" to the Constitution, which abolished it, awaited ratification. Emancipation, however, involved other problems besides the moral issue. The personal freedom of the negro created a new economic position in the South, while his political freedom altered in favor of the South the basis of representation in the Federal Government. The South with increased representation would in the natural course again unite with the northern Democrats, who during the war had combined with the Republicans—actually a minority—in support of the Union; and the Republicans might lose the fruits of victory.

Now it was common ground that those persons who had participated in secession had forfeited their political rights. In Lincoln's view it was right and wise that they should be reinstated, with as little exception as possible, by an act of grace. Then the States would resume the normal discharge of their normal functions. But the Republicans desired the minimum of reinstatement and the resumption by the South of State functions under severe limitations; while they claimed that the South by rebellion had forfeited State rights which the Federal Government could restore on its own terms. Johnson, free, as he judged, to act on his own initiative without waiting for the meeting of the recently-elected Congress, which custom deferred till the end of the year, issued a much more limited amnesty than Lincoln had proposed, virtually excluding all owners of substantial estates, while requiring, as a condition of restoring the State governments, the abolition of slavery, acceptance of the Thirteenth Amendment, and repudiation of debts incurred in aid of the war. The South in effect accepted the situation. The reinstated governments, however, took in hand the problem of the emancipated negroes on the hypothesis that while they enjoyed personal freedom they were not fit for or entitled to full citizen rights—they were a class apart, for whom it was necessary to legislate in a restrictive sense.

But when Congress met, it had taken alarm very thoroughly. It resented the autocratic action of the President when war was over. It saw the South under control of the class which had been in rebellion. It saw, or thought it saw, the negro being legislated back into a virtually service condition. And it anticipated a Democratic combination not only revived but strengthened, with a Southern element larger than before the war. It refused to recognize as valid or to ratify Johnson's reconstruction, or to admit the representatives of the "rebel" States; and without the South the Republicans were approximately in a majority of two to one.

A prolonged conflict followed between President and Congress, which formulated the Fourteenth Amendment, disfranchising every one who had held office under the Confederate Government, affirming equality of civil rights for negroes and whites, and restricting the representation in Congress of States which denied the franchise to negroes. Acceptance of the Amendment by any State would carry with it recognition of its reconstruction. A new Congressional election at the end of 1866 made the Republicans still stronger in the North, where Johnson damaged his own case by injudicious and violent oratory; the South with practical unanimity rejected the Fourteenth Amendment; and the Republican two-thirds majority was secured—a matter of first-rate importance with them, since it enabled them to override the President's veto.

In these circumstances, they forced through their own reconstruction over the President's head, in 1867. Each State was to hold a constituent Convention—elected on a franchise which included negroes and excluded Confederates—which was to draft a Constitution establishing a similar franchise; on the ratification of the Constitution by the electors and acceptance of the Fourteenth Amendment, it was to be admitted to full place as a State in the Union. Meanwhile the South was placed under military government. And, farther, the Congress passed a series of Acts restricting the President's powers of independent action; party hostility was carried so far that the President was impeached and only escaped condemnation by a single vote in the Senate.

The Republican victory was completed by the Presidential election of 1868 which placed General Grant in the Presidential chair. The new franchise had given to almost all the southern States Republican governments and a dominant Republican party, by in effect substituting black electors for white. (Incidentally, the conditions laid down for the readmission of southern States could not be imposed upon those which were already in the Union, and several northern States refused to admit the negroes within their own borders to their own franchise, the Republicans being too strong to need their votes.) The Republican general was elected President by an overwhelming majority. As an immediate consequence a Fifteenth Amendment, expressly prohibiting disfranchisement on the ground of race or color, was carried through, nor without difficulty, and at length in 1870 the last of the southern States which had not hitherto conformed to all the conditions was once more admitted as a member of the Union. Farther, although the attitude of the Supreme Court was long doubtful, a series of decisions on the constitutional validity of certain points in the reconstruction laws served practically to confirm them.

Nevertheless, the Republican method of dealing with the South had established there anarchy instead of orderly and loyal government. The rule of the negro, tempered by "carpet-baggers" and "scalawags," professional politicians from the north and outcaste southerners, was in itself incompetent and intolerable; at the best inefficient, because every man fitted by training or experience for administration was excluded from it, and at the worst hopelessly corrupt as well. The spectacle of white men with an age-long tradition of freedom, responsibility, and authority under the political domination of men born and bred in slavery, and with no traditional standards at all, was one without parallel, fatal to the maintenance of law. The law was in fact powerless to conquer its social resistance to it, and it was for the most part by concerted lawlessness, overt or covert, that the whites were able—though still not for some years—to recover an ascendency where they had once been undisputed masters, and where, admittedly and obviously, it was a necessary condition of anything which could reasonably claim the title of government at all.

The old system of production in the South vanished with emancipation. The negro, if he chose to work, was a free laborer, and the South, hitherto content to purchase with its own produce the goods which it needed for its own consumption, began to turn to those industrial occupations which it had deemed superfluous in the past. The industrial Protection which heretofore had been a source of contention between North and South, and had during the war been developed as an immediate source of revenue, became firmly established, since no protected industry is willing to relinquish its own safeguards against external competition till it feels its own interests hampered by the safeguards extended to its neighbors.

Finally, the Republican administration could claim a successful record in respect of its foreign policy, in the form of commercial treaties—notably with China and Germany—the purchase of Alaska from Russia (though this was opposed by the Senate), and the settlement of outstanding questions with France and Great Britain. Napoleon's Mexican adventure had been undertaken at the moment when the war was beginning and intervention on the part of the

United States was out of the question; but the war once over, diplomatic pressure could be brought to bear, and secured the withdrawal of French troops from American soil. The Treaty of Washington (May 1871) provided for arbitration on the fisheries question and the Vancouver boundary question with Canada, the former being referred to the new German Emperor; and on the *Alabama* claims, which were referred to an international tribunal to be held at Geneva. The subsequent awards in these cases were very much more satisfactory to the United States than to Canada and Great Britain; but they presented the first examples of the volunary reference of international disputes to arbitration which, in some form or other, was beginning to offer the one possible alternative to war as the sole arbiter.

CHAPTER XLVI

GREAT BRITAIN AND GREATER BRITAIN, 1848-1871

I.—*The British Isles*

THE collapse of Chartism in England rather than the movement itself advanced the cause of democratic development, which had been impeded primarily by fears of violent revolution, of attacks on property, and generally of the unfitness of the unenfranchised to exercise political power. The Chartist episode of 1848 proved that the working classes were not bloodthirsty revolutionaries; the development of the great trade unions, notably among miners and engineers and in the building trade, proved that they possessed powers of organization and discipline; the conduct of the cotton operatives in particular during the American War manifested in them a capacity for self-restraint and self-denial of which the whole nation was justly proud. The attitude of the governing classes changed. If they were still nervous about admitting the proletariat to political power, sympathy at least for the demand could no longer be denied; and though hesitation to make a vast experiment delayed franchise extension for nineteen years, the Reform Act of 1867, passed under the auspices of a Conservative Ministry, enormously increased the electoral body by including in it practically the whole of the urban artisan class; giving to the hitherto unenfranchised a numerically dominant control. The extension fell very far short of conceding the manhood suffrage which was always the goal of ultra-democrats; but it at once made Great Britain the most democratically governed of the European nations, because its governments were definitely responsible to a Parliament which was itself definitely responsible to the electorate; which was not the case elsewhere, even though the electorates themselves might enjoy a wider franchise.

From 1846 to 1874 the Liberals dominated every Parliament, whether Liberal or Conservative ministers were actually in office. The Aberdeen ministry, which was responsible for the Crimean War, was in form a coalition of Liberals and Peelites, while in fact it led to the absorption of the latter by the former. The Conservatives, led by Derby and Disraeli, were in office for most of 1852, again in 1858 and a part of 1859, and for a third time from the end of 1866 to the end of 1868; but in each case the Conservatives, in actual minority, were dependent on the support of at least a substantial section of the formal Opposition.

Franchise extension, whether granted through fear or sympathy or dictated by the abstract sense of justice, is always a concession from the governing classes to those who are outside it—in form at least a voluntary surrender of a part of the power they wield to those who may or may not prove themselves fit to shart it. When threats to extort it by violence ceased to cause alarm and to stiffen resistance, sympathy and the sense of justice came gradually into full play; and the dominant middle class, though not without some perturbation of spirit, recognized the claims of the "intelligent artisan" to the suffrage, though not yet that of the bucolic or the casual laborer. The boldest of franchise reformers was Benjamin Disraeli, who, like Bismarck, believed that a popular vote would strengthen his own party rather than the Liberals. When in office in 1858-9 he carried one of the points in the democratic Charter—abolition of property qualification for Members—but failed to pass an ingeniously complicated Franchise Reform Bill. Till Palmerston's death in 1865 the question was shelved; but in 1866 the Liberals brought in a Bill which was defeated by the action of a section of their own party. The Conservatives returned to office, and in 1867 Derby and Disraeli took their "leap in the dark," and Disraeli's Bill in the end went farther in some respects than what the most advanced Liberals would have suggested, though, on the other hand, most of the checks and balances he had desired disappeared under the stress of criticism from the Opposition, which when combined was stronger than the Government.

With the artisan vote actually preponderant in the urban electorate, what may be called a limited Democracy was definitely established; limited, first because the suffrage was still a long way from being universal, secondly because the business of administration still remained in the hands of the same governing classes as before, and there was still a hereditary chamber representing only one section of the community but enjoying theoretically equal powers with the elective Chamber except in finance; but Democracy, because the administrators were responsible to a wide popular electorate.

During the same period the last vestiges of Protectionism disappeared. For fifty years hardly a voice was again raised in its favor, wailing to deaf ears. The Navigation Acts, already modified by Huskisson when George IV. was king, disappeared in 1849, and with them the preferences which colonial trade had hitherto enjoyed, though this to the colonies was far more than compensated by the accompanying freedom of export, the restrictions on which under the Acts were a serious grievance, especially in Canada. All taxation of trade, except what applied equally to home-produced and imported goods and was imposed for revenue purposes alone, vanished with the Gladstone budgets of 1859 and 1860. Prices sank; the laborer was able to resist a corresponding reduction in his money-wage, so that his purchasing power increased; competition stimulated every kind of production except that of the farmer, so that the manufacturer as well as the trader flourished exceedingly.

It was found, moreover, that the restrictions, imposed for the most part by benevolence in opposition to the prevalent economic theory, upon the employment of women, young persons, and children increased productively instead of diminishing it; while the organization of trade unions, directed to enabling the operative to bargain with the employer on equal terms, was slowly becoming effective. An inquiry into the methods of the unions in 1867 exonerated the greater organizations from the charges of gross intimidation which had been freely leveled against them, and their establishment with a secure legal status became one of the first demands of the new electorate, which decisively returned the Liberals to power under the leadership of W. E. Gladstone at the end of 1868. Accordingly in 1871 they became legalized associations, though the prohibition of "picketing" made strikes for a time practically futile. Protection of the workman from the terrorism which had actually been exerted in several of the minor unions was the object of this latter enactment.

In 1870 a great step was made towards the education of the rising generation of the new electorate by an Act organizing compulsory education under the management of elected local schoolboards, where the National Church schools—the only existing institutions for the purpose—were insufficient for the needs of the locality. It was only the need for "educating our masters," in Robert Lowe's phrase, that at last aroused the State in England to take an active hand in education, though France had awakened to the national necessity of education even in the days of the Terror. In theory at least the purpose of State education must be to fit the youth of the country for the full and intelligent exercise of citizenship.

Anti-nationalist governments in other European states have always had a retort to British expressions of sympathy with Nationalist movements and aspirations; they have always pointed to Ireland as a field where an alien government is constantly met with defiance of its authority by a population which demands full autonomy; while it has not been equally obvious to the foreign observer that a substantial and vital section is no less vehement in its abhorrence of autonomy and its preference for the system which gives it representation in the central government on an equal footing with the rest of the United Kingdom. Eighteen years of experimental and partial autonomy at the end of the eighteenth century had in fact proved a melancholy failure; and ever since then the central government had striven laboriously and ineffectively to remedy grievances in accordance with English ideas of justice, without producing any appreciable effect on the popular hostility to and defiance of the law and all its agents, which could be met only by the periodical suspension of normal liberties known as Coercion.

After the futile "Young Ireland" insurrection of 1848 there was a lull in the Irish troubles. But the famines of the "forties" joined with other causes brought about a great emigration to America, where the emigrants still cherished a hostility to England which flourished in the congenial atmosphere of the United States; and the ill-feeling was intensified by the American Civil War. Not autonomy but complete independence for Ireland was the aim of the Fenian Brotherhood which planned in America the campaigns to be conducted in Ireland and England for the subversion of the government; not by war in the field, which would obviously be futile, but by what any and every government responsible for the maintenance of order and personal security could only call organized crime. The government was able to detect and suppress the agencies in Ireland in 1865 and again in 1867, but the headquarters of the movement were out of reach on foreign soil; and the movement itself emphasized the existence of a bitterness spirit, to remedy which became one of the leading aims of the Liberal party under Gladstone's leadership.

Catholic emancipation had still preserved as the Established Church of the country the Church of a small minority. Gladstone disestablished it, but failed thereby to conciliate the Roman Catholic clergy, whose influence with their flocks continued to encourage hostility to the government. The second conspicuous grievance was that of the land and the legal relations between landlord and peasant; and the long series of Irish Land Bills was opened with that of 1870, which sought to give fixity of tenure with compensation for tenants' improvements. But the continuance of agrarian outrages caused the Bill to be accompanied by a Coercion Act, so that it served as little as disestablishment to conciliate the Catholic peasant population.

The third grievance, expressed whether with moderation or violence in the demands for autonomy, did not, so fàr, impress the statesmen of Great Britain as a genuine grievance at all; for the simple reason that half the Irish representatives at Westminster were opposed to what was now beginning to be known as Home Rule. The Irish peasant, like the English agricultural laborer, did not come within the extended electorate, and it was still the general conviction not only that Home Rule could not be granted without injury both to the State in general and to Ireland in particular, but also that it was not seriously desired by the majority of the population. Anything, in short, in the nature of a repeal of the incorporating Union was looked upon as outside the sphere of practical politics, a thing on which no statesman would waste serious consideration.

II.—Colonial Self-Government

While England was hesitating, and finally deciding, to take the second great step towards Democracy, the British colonies proper were advancing along the path of development which was to transform them into semi-sovereign states, united with each other and with the mother country as a commonwealth of democracies, in groups having distinctive national characteristics as well as a preponderant element of common nationality; the oldest group, the American, leading the way.

In Canada the establishment of a Representative Legislature by the Act of Reunion developed into definite responsible government with the arrival of Lord Elgin as Governor in 1848. He acted, that is, explicitly on the principle of placing the selection of ministers in the hands of the leader of the party dominant in the Legislature, and of himself acting, as representative of the Crown, through the ministers and on their advice. Contests between Governors and popular leaders had been proceeding simultaneously in New Brunswick and Novia Scotia, both of which acquired responsible government practically at the same moment as Canada, and in 1851 it was extended to Prince Edward Island.

The British Government ceased after 1846 to exercise control over tariffs, and the abolition of the Navigation Acts in 1849 freed the colony from the last hampering regulations of commerce imposed by the mother country, though in other respects the adoption of Free Trade for the British Isles deprived the colonies of the preference which their products had hitherto enjoyed.

Self-government proceeded apace. Vexed questions concerning compensation for losses suffered through Papineau's rebellion were dealt with in the first two years of Lord Elgin's rule; and in 1854 two outstanding problems, the "Clergy reserves" and the seignorial rights, which were a legacy of the old French system, at last found a satisfactory settlement. A French-Canadian grievance was removed by the repeal of the clause in the Act of Reunion which had restricted the use of the French language in the Legislature, in the vain hope that the fusion of the French and British elements would thereby be hastened. Non-recognition of a popular language in general use becomes, wherever applied, a racial grievance implying subordination, and preserves instead of modifying racial divisions. Material progress also was rapid, especially in Upper Canada, which in population and wealth soon overtook and surpassed the Lower Province; a development largely due to railway extension.

The growth of Upper Canada had political consequences of the first importance. The provinces had equal representation in the Legislature, and the equality, at first unduly favorable to the Upper Province, was now becoming more unfair to it year by year. The idea of a general federation of the British North American provinces gained ground, especially after the moving of a formal resolution on the subject in the Nova Scotia Legislature in 1854. In Canada, while reunion had brought about responsible government, it had failed to produce unity, and in any federation of provinces Upper and Lower Canada would take their places severally; and in 1860 the delegation of local affairs to the control of separate parliaments was mooted—unsuccessfully, owing to the opposition in French Canada which was unwilling to surrender the advantages it now enjoyed under the settlement of 1842.

The next important steps were taken in 1864. In that year a Coalition Government was formed in Canada with the avowed purpose of substituting for the existing unitary system in Canada a federal system with autonomy for the separate provinces. At the same time, on the initiative of Nova Scotia, a conference was summoned with a view to a federation of the three maritime provinces, to which Canada also resolved to send delegates, with the result that it was decided to hold the Quebec Convention to prepare a scheme for a general federation, Newfoundland also being represented.

Now is was the general intention to approximate parliamentary institutions as closely as was practicable to the system of Great Britain as the grand exemplar. The United States, on the other hand, offered the one obvious model for federation, and experience had proved that the great difficulty was an indisputable adjustment of State rights and federal rights. For the Canadas alone, federation would have meant the retention of a central government with devolution of State control to State governments; the obvious course being that the State governments should have such powers only as were expressly delegated to them. On the other hand, a general federation would mean that a number of independent States were preparing to delegate to a common central authority the control over common interests; and the obvious course would be for the central authority to have such powers only as were expressly conferred upon it. The former plan, however, prevailed with the Convention, and it was decided that the Federal Government should have vested in it all powers which were not explicitly appropriated to the provincial parliaments. Canadian experience also proved the necessity for a certain elasticity in the proportion of representation in the central government to be enjoyed by the several states. When the Convention had prepared its scheme it found ready acceptance in Canada; but objections were raised to it in the maritime provinces on three issues—that the Conference had no mandate to deal with a general federation, that the financial adjustments were unfair, and that the smallest provinces, unless disproportionately represented, would find their interests over-ridden. Consequently Newfoundland withdrew from the scheme altogether, and Prince Edward Island for some years. Fenian raids into New Brunswick and Upper Canada in 1865 emphasized there and in Nova Scotia the need for union and roused the loyalist spirit—an invariable result of external attack—and the two maritime provinces accepted the scheme during that year. In 1867 it received the sanction of the Imperial Parliament in the British North America Act, which united the provinces of Upper Canada, Lower Canada, New Brunswick, and Nova Scotia in the Dominion of Canada; with provision for admitting to the Dominion such other British North American territories as might so desire.

In 1869 the Dominion purchased the rights of the Hudson Bay Company in the Hudson Bay or Rupert's Land territory on the north-west, and began to organize a government. A rising on the part of the half-breeds led by Louis Riel was suppressed by the Red River expedition in 1870, and next year the Province of Manitoba was incorporated in the Dominion, and also the western Pacific province of British Columbia, including Vancouver Island. Vancouver had been organized as a Crown colony in 1849, and British Columbia in 1858, owing to the influx of immigrants consequent upon the discovery of gold, and the two had been united in 1866.

Anticipating matters slightly we may here remark that the completion of the Dominion was practically effected in 1873 by the accession of Prince Edward Island, though Newfoundland has resolutely refused inclusion. The preservation of the aboriginal races was provided for by the establishment of Indian Reserves.

In Australasia the premier colony, New South Wales, had received a measure of representative government in 1842, following on the Canadian Act of Reunion; that is, it had been granted a Legislative Council on which two-thirds of the members were elected, the Governor's Council having hitherto been an exclusively nominated body. This new legislature could initiate and pass laws, subject to the Governor's veto, and to the proviso that they must not be repugnant to the laws of England; but it did not control administration or customs. The next step was an Act of the Imperial Parliament conferring a like privilege upon Tasmania, South Australia, and the Port Phillip district, which was now constituted a separate colony under the name of Victoria. (The names of the capitals, Adelaide and Melbourne, are reminders of the dates at which South Australia and the Port Phillip District were first organized, the former being named after Queen Adelaide, the consort of William IV., and the latter after Queen Victoria's first prime Minister). All these colonies were at the same time authorized to submit Constitutions for themselves to the consideration of the Home Government when they should so desire, though none of them at the time took immediate advantage of the right. But between 1842 and 1850 Great Brtiain had adopted Free Trade for herself, and it was a practical corollary that with the nucleus of self-government a practically complete financial control was conceded, with only the reservations that no customs must be imposed which were contrary to treaty rights or differentiated adversely against British goods. Only the land sales remained outside the colonial control as being concerned with Imperial property and revenues, though the latter were allocated by the Crown for the benefit of the colony.

Now for the second time the discovery of gold produced big political results, California having provided the first example, as the Transvaal was to supply another at a later date. In 1851 Edward Hargraves, an unsuccessful prospector in the Californian gold fields, found better fortune—and alluvial gold deposits—at Summer Hill Creek, in New South Wales. The first discovery was followed by others. There ensued a rush for the gold fields which surpassed that in California. All other occupations were deserted; the population crowded into the diggings; more hosts poured in from every ship that reached an Australian port, and ocean traffic was developing rapidly, for it was just at the moment when fleets of ocean steamers were beginning to be launched. And the newcomers were not bred agriculturists like the previous free settlers; they came from every class, imbued with the political ideas to which they were accustomed at home. If many of them returned to their native soil with their fortunes made, an infinitely larger number who had not made their fortunes stayed where they were, material for an industrial population which had not hitherto existed.

The Home Government, alive to the new position, pressed the four colonies which had a representative system established to act on the authorization and formulate constitutions. Demands for completer self-government and extension of the franchise to the new settlers were already arising, and in 1854 each of them submitted its own scheme. All proposed a bicameral system with one chamber entirely elected on a broad franchise, though on the composition of the several second chambers they varied. All assumed the principle of ministerial responsibility to the legislature which was now in full operation in Canada. In 1855 the schemes received the royal assent, two of them, which on technical grounds had to be submitted to the Imperial Parliament, being slightly modified. Western Australia alone, created under different conditions, remote from the gold-fields, isolated from the rest by intervening deserts, and still adhering to convict labor after transportation to all the other colonies had ceased, remained under the old system, rejecting even a Representative Council until 1870, and waiting still another twenty years for responsible government. But in 1859 a fifth autonomous colony was added by the separation of Queensland from New South Wales, and its erection into a distinct self-governing colony with a Constitution of its own similar to those of the other four. The federation of British North America in the next decade, as the Dominion of Canada, did not for many years excite a corresponding movement in the Australian group.

New Zealand stood apart from Australia, and differed from it in having a pressing native question of its own. The Australian blackfellows were not only few in numbers, but were too primitive, physically, intellectually, and politically, to present the same problems of treatment as the more vigorous and comparatively organized "barbaric" peoples with whom the white man has for the most part come in contact in his expansion over the globe. The New Zealand Maoris, however, were on an altogether different and very much higher type. In New Zealand the British had not, as in Australia, established themselves by the occupation of unsettled territories, or by conquest; they had entered in 1839 by treaty with organized tribes already in occupation, tribes which by treaty had accepted the British sovereignty on terms; and the main causes of friction had lain in unwarrantable breaches of those terms not by the Maoris, nor by British officials, but by British settlers.

The happy combination of justice, vigor, and tact in the Governor, George Grey, saved the colony from disaster, and did much to restore the confidence of the Maoris; fortunately also he was strong enough to override the inept intervention of the House Government, which was misled by interested advisers, and to ignore a quite unworkable Constitution with which it provided him. In 1851 the Home Government was becoming eager to press responsible government on every colony which would adopt it; but, this time, in framing a Constitution for New Zealand, it was guided by the Governor himself, and the new Constitution, with responsible government, was set up in 1852, three years earlier than in Australia.

At that time the Maori population—between 50,000 and 60,000—was about twice as large as the British. The latter were few and the former were especially numerous in the north island. After Grey's departure in 1853 the settlers again sought to acquire land in the north island by methods of doubtful legality, much resented by the Maoris; ill-feeling revived, and in 1860 there began a struggle on the part of the Maoris for the ejection of the British. Though Grey returned, the Maoris war was not finally brought to an end till 1871. The Governor was in disagreement with his ministry, and—as always happens —the Government on the spot, very much alive to the dangers to white folk among a hostile colored population, was very much at odds with a Home Government, always more anxious to avoid and more ready to condemn excessive harshness than a dangerous leniency in the treatment of natives. In 1871, however, the Maoris recognized the futility of continuing a hopeless contest, maintained though it had been with remarkable skill and tenacity. They accepted the situation with a sober acquiescence which gave no guarantee for continuous peace. But it may here be remarked that since that time there has been no renewed outbreak; their numbers have fallen away greatly while the white population has increased; and with consistent prosperity and sound administration in the Dominion, the Maori, if we may judge by recent developments, has become more than reconciled to his position as a subject in the British Empire.

In South Africa, the third great colonizing area, the Home Government was in advance of the colonists in its desire to extend autonomy. At its instance, and with considerable reluctance on the part of the colonists, an elective Legislature was created for the Cape Colony, having, however, no control over the executive. The electorate was formed without discrimination of race or color on a low property qualification, which sufficed in practice to exclude negroes and Hottentots, though there were no barriers to their acquisition of the necessary qualification. Responsible government did not follow till 1872. Natal, annexed in 1843, was not separated from Cape Colony till 1856, after which it was satisfied with the status of a Crown colony for over thirty years.

In this area, however, the more pressing questions were those which concerned the native tribes and the Dutch who had migrated across the Orange and Vaal Rivers. Those who had settled down between the Orange and the Vaal were less fervently hostile to the British supremacy than the stalwarts who penetrated farther north (or retired thither again over the Drakensberg when the Cape Government asserted its authority over Natal. In 1848, in consequence of renewed troubles with the Kaffir tribes, a considerable Kaffir area was brought into direct dependence, under the supervision of a Commissioner, as Kaffraria; and the districts between the Orange and Vaal was formally included in the British Dominion as the Orange River Sovereignty, the more hostile element among the Boers removing themselves out of reach across the Vaal.

Kaffraria covered the district between the hills and the coast, from the Kei River (the old boundary between the colony proper and the Kaffir territory) up to the newly-annexed Natal, beyond which again lay the Zulu kingdom. Basutoland, in the angle formed by the river Caledon (a tributary of the Orange) and the Drakensberg, was still nominally independent. Kaffraria was encouraged to revolt by the Basuto chief Moshesh, who, having secured the neutrality of the Orange River Sovereignty farmers, sought active help from the Boers beyond the Vaal, fearing that he would have to pay the penalty for his intrigues when the British brought the Kaffir War to its inevitable conclusion. The Boer leader, Pretorius, offered the Cape Government neutrality on condition that the independence of the Transvaal should be recognized. The result was the Sand River Convention (January 1852), which guaranteed autonomy to the Transvaal; and Moshesh promptly came to terms.

The Home Government not only acquiesced in the establishment of the "South African Republic" beyond the Vaal, but in its newly-born enthusiasm for colonial autonomy—in other words, its desires to escape responsibility—pressed the Orange River Sovereignty to follow the example of the Transvaal. The farmers there were in no haste to purchase a formal independence at the price of losing British protection; still they acceded, since there was no doubt that in the long run at least the Cape Government would be obliged to protect any white settlers against an organized attack by negro tribes; and so by the Bloemfontein Convention (1854) the Orange Free State was established in place of the Orange River Sovereignty. As a matter of fact the Orange Free State found itself repeatedly involved in difficulties with the Basuto Moshesh, which were only settled by the intervention of the Governor of the Cape as arbitrator at the request of President Brand; after which, at the request of Moshesh himself, Basutoland was formally taken under British sovereignty and made a Protectorate (1869).

Before leaving South Africa we may note the extraordinary affair of the Kosa Kaffirs in 1857 as an instance of the problems of the "White Man's Burden." At the time, Sir George Grey was Governor of the Cape, whither he had been transferred from New Zealand. The tribes in Kaffraria belonged chiefly to the Kosa group. They had at last learnt if they persisted in forcing war on the British they were bound to be beaten unless an actual miracle should save them. But a native prophet inspired them with a firm conviction that a miracle was to save them. The benevolence of the British administration had not removed their objections to the predominance of the white man, and a great rising was planned. The spirits of the dead were going to return to earth on a certain day and lead them to overwhelming victory. Not only would the white men be wiped out, but the earth would straightway bring forth her fruits in abundance, and the pastures would be filled with cattle. Only, as a demonstration of faith, they were to leave the soil untilled, and when the great day came they must have completed the destruction of their grain and their cattle. To fight the madness was hopeless; all the Cape Government could do was to make ready for the rising, and provide for the impending famine. The day came. The promised leaders did not return to earth, and all the food in the country had been religiously destroyed. There was no rising; the Kaffirs poured over the border not to fight but to cry for food. All the efforts of the Government to provide for the emergency had left them still far short of the necessary supplies, and thousands of Kaffirs perished of sheer starvation. Kaffiraria was half depopulated, was largely resettled by white settlers, and the whole district ceased to be, as since 1848, a purely native Protectorate, and was incorporated in Cape Colony in 1865.

CHAPTER XLVII

INTERNATIONAL RELATIONS AND THE EASTERN QUESTION, 1871-1889

I.—*The European Powers,* 1871-1875

ON May 27, 1859, the Austrian crossed the Ticino; on May 10, 1871, the Peace of Frankfort was signed. In those twelve years momentous changes had taken place in the European system. At the beginning, Italy was still a "geographical expression"; at the end she was a united monarchy. At the beginning the Pope was a temporal prince, besides being the supreme pontiff of half Christendom: at the end, the Church had affirmed his Infallability; but he was a "prisoner in the Vatican." At the beginning Austria was the premier state in Germany, dominated Italy, and held Magyars and Slavs in subjection within her own borders; at the end, she was extruded from Italy and from Germany, and her unitary empire had become the Dual Monarchy of Austria-Hungary. The congeries of disunited states which had formed the German Confederation when William became Regent of Prussia was now—with the omission of Austria—consolidated under Prussian supremacy in what was in name the German and in effect the Prussian Empire, holding Schleswig-Holstein, which had been wrung from Denmark, and Alsace-Lorraine, which had been torn from France. And no one any longer regarded "the treaties" by which Metternich, Nicholas, and others when it suited them, had set such store, as anything but waste paper. The system set up by the Vienna Congress had gone completely to pieces, leaving nothing but a remnant of the Concert of Europe which only made itself heard—and then somewhat discordantly—when the Eastern question became dangerously insistent.

The Vienna Congress had served a purpose. Almost forty years passed after Waterloo before any of the greater States were again at war with each other. Then in rapid succession came the Crimean War, the War of Italian Liberation, the Seven Weeks' War, the Franco-Prussian War, followed again by forty-three years of European peace, unbroken save in the Balkan Peninsula. But in strict truth these were years of armed truce rather than of peace, during which Europe lay under the incubus of ever-swelling armaments, though no Power was willing to fling down a direct challenge to a foe ready to take it up.

For twenty years the master-statesman of Europe made it his business to foster dissensions between Powers whose *rapprochement* might threaten Germany with a dangerous isolation, to bind to her indissolubly Austria, which had ceased irrevocably to rival the Prussian supremacy in the new Empire, to keep Russia conveniently detached from Western allies and amicably disposed towards that new empire which needed time to solidify. From France in isolation there could be no serious menace, at least for years after her overwhelming defeat, and nowhere was there any direct collision to be anticipated between German and British interests.

And yet no one knew better than Bismarck that while France was prostrated by the war, the peace had implanted in her an implacable hostility, and that, however friendly the relations of Germany and Russia might be, the day might come when Teutonism and Slavism headed by Russia would find themselves in perilous antagonism. Then Russia would look to France and France would look to Russia. Hence it was the third article of Bismarck's political creed that France and Russia must be kept apart, as the second was that Germany and Austria must hold together—and the first that the military strength of Germany must be maintained at a level which would render her equal to any conceivable emergency or possible combination of enemies. To seek friendship with France would be a useless waste of energy. As for Great Britain and Italy, the main thing was to check any disposition on the part of either to gravitate towards either Russia or France, no very difficult problem for a diplomatist so astute as the Chancellor.

If Italy had not yet achieved her full desire, her unsatisfied craving for the Trentino, Trieste, and Dalmatia was not likely to produce any present disturbance, though it did not facilitate a genuine reconciliation with Austria; and though her unity was assured, she contained within herself so many antagonistic elements as to make the task of organizing the newly-born kingdom by no means an easy one. She had too many domestic problems to face with too much diversity of opinion as to the method of dealing with them, for any settlement of them to be rapidly reached unless by an accepted dictator; while there was no man in Italy capable of exercising such an authority as Bismarck now wielded in Germany. Hence in any international combinations, she could be no more than a make-weight.

What was true of Italy was for the time still more true of France. Heavy as her sufferings and her losses had been during the war, the peace left her not only bereft of territory which had been hers for much more than a century, but burdened also with an indemnity which seemed, and was intended by the victors, to be altogether crushing. More than this, she was without a settled government. Provisionally she was a Republic, but how long she would be so remained to be seen. Her chosen "Chief of the Executive," Thiers, was a convinced monarchist, who forty years before had played no small part in raising the "citizen king" to the throne; there was a large party which would have welcomed an Orleans restoration, another great body of Legitimists who would have recalled the Bourbons, a third group of Bonapartists. It was possible that any one of the three might carry the day, certain that none of the three would rest satisfied with the success of either of the others; while if the Republic survived, it would be owing not to enthusiastic Republicanism but to the irreconcilable ideals—and candidates—of the several monarchist groups, each of which preferred its own type of monarchy—Napoleonic, Legitimist, or Constitutionalist—to a Republic, but failing its own type, would acquiesce in the Republic with various degrees of reluctance rather than accept a rival type. The recuperation of France was indeed so extraordinarily rapid as to inspire no little anxiety at Berlin; but it was many years before her government was sufficiently stabilized for her to recover her full front rank position among the European States. Nor could she again become a prospective storm-center till her recovery had reached such a point that she could again challenge Germany to a duel with the lost provinces as the stake, or at least could secure a powerful ally with an equally strong desire to overthrow the great Central Power. Such an ally she would find neither in Italy nor in Great Britain, which was conscious of no interests incompatible with those of Germany or of Austria.

In the East, however, still lay the materials for international conflagration; more than ever, for two reasons. The Treaty of London in 1871 wiped out the Black Sea clauses in the treaty of 1856, reviving the old acuteness of the British suspicious of Russian designs on the Dardanelles. The extrusion of Austria from Germany as well as from Italy forced her to concentrate upon the East the attention which had hitherto fluctuated between East and West, accentuating the antagonistic interests of Austria with her South Slav population and the great Slavonic power of Russia in the mainly Slavonic Balkans. Neither England nor Austria could afford to see a Russian protectorate of the Balkan Slavs and semi-Slavs, which was just what Russian sentiment, national and religious, demanded; neither Austria nor Russia was willing to see an independent Balkan confederation strong enough to protect itself; while Great Britain was possessed with the conviction that the integrity of the Turkish Empire was vital to her own interests. Germany as yet had no interests of her own in the Balkans, but if Russian and Austrian interests should clash too seriously she was bound to be Austria's shield-bearer; though Bismarck would by no means quarrel with Russia if he could possibly help it, seeing that while East Germany marched with Russia West

Germany marched with France. The most useful wile for Bismarck was to avert disagreement between Russia and Austria by encouraging Russian expansion in East and Central Asia; neither Germany nor Austria would suffer, if by so doing she should be involved in purely Asiatic complications with Great Britain.

Bismarck had made the German Empire by a series of carefully prepared wars of aggression in which he had always succeeded in making his antagonist the technical aggressor. Having made it, he wanted not war any more but peace—in particular, peace between Austria and Russia, since there was no sort of risk of their forming a combination hostile to Germany, whereas a quarrel between them would compel Germany to take a side, which would mean quarreling with Russia. Germany was now indisputably the first military Power in Europe. Bismarck did not want another mile of territory; he did not want alien populations subjected to her rule; but for Moltke and the soldiers, he would have taken less territory from France and would not have embarrassed Prussia with so many Lorrainers who remained French in sympathy and sentiment even if they bore German names. He had no oceanic ambitions for Germany, no illusion that her future was on the sea. He had so dealt with Austria in her hour of defeat that a recognition of common interests was enough to secure her friendship; he had so dealt with France that her enmity might be troublesome but at least for a long time to come hardly dangerous. Having no positive motive for aggression, nothing substantial to gain by it, he had no desire to rouse hostility by indulging dreams of conquest and glory, preferring the rôle of the judicious moderator whose positive opposition on one would invite without thinking twice —a moderator with no interests at stake and inspired by goodwill towards every one.

In the year of Bismarck's birth Alexander I., in a fit of idealism, had designed the Holy Alliance which Metternich had transmuted into a league between Austria, Russia, and Prussia for the preservation of the peace of Europe by the suppression of "the Revolution" wherever it might raise its head. In the year of Bismarck's triumph the Revolution was entering upon new paths, but he was not in the least afraid of it. Experience had proved sufficiently that in Germany Otto von Bismarck was stronger than the Revolution, to the good or ill success of which among the western nations he was indifferent. Bismarck set about reviving not the Holy Alliance but Metternich's league; but with the entirely different object of so adjusting the interests of the three Empires that they should not fall out among themselves to the detriment of Germany. The league of the Three Emperors, inaugurated in 1872, was a guarantee of European peace so long as it remained effective; and this was Bismarck's object, though it was convenient to base it ostensibly on the old foundation of maintaining treaties and suppressing anarchism. It ceased in the long run to be effective when the incompatibility of Russian with Teutonic interests became too marked for glozing over. Meanwhile if the three Central and Eastern Powers were in harmony, disagreements among the rest would not disturb them—would indeed be rather agreeable; Italian troubles to Austria, French troubles to Germany, British troubles to Russia.

So dissensions between those three Powers were to be judiciously fostered. On the European continent they had nothing to quarrel about, but in Africa there were on the horizon clouds big with conflict, in Egypt, in Tunis, and in Morocco, between France and England; between France and Italy, and incidentally between France and Spain; and finally Asiatic quarrels between England and Russia were eminently desirable from Bismarck's point of view as drawing Russia's aggressive energies away from the danger-point in the Balkans. For Bismarck's friendliness to Russia meant not that he loved her but that he feared her enmity. France would not profit and Germany would not suffer from any awkward consequences of an Anglo-Russian conflict, whether for Russia or for Great Britain.

By the end of 1872 Bismarck's immediate object was achieved. France was still isolated, still laboring under the burden of the war indemnity, still in the throes of the struggles between the monarchist factions, each of which was anticipating the success of its own candidate for a Royal or Imperial crown; England, under the Gladstone ministry, with a foreign policy deriving not from Palmerston but from Aberdeen, was unlikely to give trouble; and the German Chancellor had succeeded in producing at least the appearance of a cordial spirit of co-operation between St. Petersburg, Vienna, and Berlin. Nihilism in Russia and the Commune in Paris enabled him to play upon the fears of Alexander and Francis Joseph, and to convince them of the need for mutual support against the revolutionary menace. For the moment the Eastern question was in the background. Russia had every reason for believing in the goodwill of Germany, which she had more than earned by effectively restraining Austria from intervention in the war with France, and which had been comfortably displayed by Bismarck's attitude in regard to the annulling of the Black Sea clauses. The calculated magnanimity of his treatment of Austria after Königgrätz bore fruit the more readily when she saw herself— after Sedan—without hope of any continental ally unless she accepted Germany's proffered friendship. The earnest of her conversion was given when the Hungarian Count Andrassy took the place of the anti-Prussian Beust as Francis Joseph's minister; for whereas the German interests of Vienna and Berlin had clashed, those of Hungary and Prussia did not. For the present reconciliation of Austria and Russia, fear of the Revolution was a sufficiently pressing motive—

little as it weighed with Bismarck himself, who for his own reasons preferred a republican to a monarchist France. And so in September 1872 the three Emperors met and set up that simulacrum of the Holy Alliance which was known as the *Dreikaiserbund,* though unratified by any formal written treaty.

The amazing energy which enabled France to pay off the war debt and free her soil from the last German troops in May 1873, and to build up in two years more an army of two and a half millions, perturbed the German militarists, who in 1875 were urging active measures against France; but Bismarck did not fear his neighbor so long as she was without the allies, who were certainly not forthcoming, and the war scare passed. But even at that moment the storm clouds were gathering in the East.

II.—*The Balkan Ferment, 1875-1877*

The clouds rose in Herzegovina. Serbia and Montenegro were virtually independent States since the former had procured the evacuation of the Turkish garrisons in 1867; but on the west of them Bosnia and Herzegovina remained under Moslem rule, for the Christian peasantry, whether Orthodox or Roman Catholic, were the serfs of Moslem landowners who were followers of Islam, the more zealous because their forefathers had been renegades from Christianity, and whose zeal expressed itself in tyrannizing over the peasants, who suffered hardly less from the exactions of the tax-farmers and the monstrous corruption of what passed in the courts of justice. A population of agricultural serfs is for obvious reasons not easily roused to the point of armed defiance, but when it has been so roused it fights desperately. In the summer of 1875 Herzegovina resolved to fight; the peasants solidly refused to pay the taxes demanded and defied their overlords. The Ottoman Government sent troops to bring them to heel, and the troops were disastrously defeated.

The success of the insurgents promptly brought to their support flocks of volunteers from the neighboring Slavonic districts, not only Bosnia, where conditions similar to those in Herzegovina prevailed, but also from Serbia and Montenegro, and it stirred the sympathies of the South Slavs within the Austrian Empire. The revolt of the peasants, primarily a social movement, became merged in the Slavonic Nationalist movement of which for some years there had been in the Balkans an active propaganda, largely Russian in origin. In some high quarters in Russia, Pan-Slavism was looked upon with disfavor as savoring of the Revolution; but it had a very strong hold not only on popular sympathy but also on aggressively minded patriots for whom Slavonic union under Russian leadership was a parallel and a counterpart to Teutonic union under Prussian leadership. The Tsar, honestly unaggressive, disliked the movement; Gortschakoff, without being an enthusiast for its ideals, saw in it something which might be turned to account; and he, rather than Alexander, was the real ruler. Hence Pan-Slavism, without being countenanced officially, was actually allowed free play. On the other hand, the Orthodox Slavs at least inclined to Russia as their natural protector, while Austria, with Catholic South Slavs under her own sway, regarded the Catholics in the Balkans as falling in her own, not the Russian, sphere; little though her Slav subjects had profited by their loyalty to the Empire in the time of upheaval. Thus there were cross currents in the Nationalist aspirations of the Slavonic area and in the aims of its would-be protectors.

Through the Consuls of the Powers in Bosnia the insurgents appealed to Europe. Their demands were moderate and reasonable enough—religious freedom, equality before the law in practice as well as in theory, definite instead of arbitrary taxation. If these could not be otherwise secured for them, then the formation of Bosnia and Herzegovina into an autonomous tributary principality. Failing this also, a grant of land in some foreign State whither they would emigrate rather than continue to live under the present intolerable conditions. But at the back of the demands was the conviction that their concession by the Porte, unless the Powers took actual responsibility for their execution, would be of no more effect than all the other specious promises of reform which had never begun to materialize. As a matter of course the Porte did promptly publish new promises; equally as a matter of course, the insurgents ignored them and went on their insurgent way. This was convenient enough for the Porte, which could point with complacent self-laudation to the admirable generosity of its own proposals and to the absolute necessity of enforcing submission upon the obstinate rebels who remained defiantly in arms.

Unfortunately, however, for the Sultan his personal extravagance, coupled with the corruption which honeycombed the entire administration, had made such wreck of the Turkish finances that he had driven at this inopportune moment to a partial repudiation of the public debt; whereby other interests were affected which foreign governments could not afford to ignore, apart from the widespread sympathy among their peoples—especially in Russia—for the victims of Turkish misrule.

It was at least imperative that whatever action any of the three Empires might take should be taken in concert. As a result of the diplomatic consultations, the Hungarian minister, Count Andrassy, issued a Note to be submitted to the Powers for presentation to the Porte. Neither by force nor by mere promises of reform, said the Note, did it appear that the Turks could or would maintain order; their troops were defeated and their promises were received with incredulity. The source of the evil, now threatening a general conflagration which it might not be easy to restrict even to the Balkans, was in the misgovernment and the system which fostered it. The Powers then must urge the Porte to give effect to its promises and actually to institute the most pressing reforms—recognition of the Christian religion, abolition of tax-farming, application of the taxes to local objects, establishment of a free peasant-proprietary in place of feudal serfdom (which had ceased throughout the Austrian Empire during the upheaval, while the Tsar had more recently emancipated the Russian serfs), judges holding office by a secure tenure; to give the reforms reality, local elective councils which had already been promised; and finally, the appointment of a mixed committee of Moslems and Christians in equal numbers to supervise and enforce the effective carrying out of the whole scheme. The Note added that unless the Sultan formally pledged himself to these reforms, the Powers could not, as hitherto, use their influence to restrain the insurgents. On its general acceptance by the French and British Governments, it was duly presented to the Porte (January 1876).

The Porte promptly accepted the Note, excepting only the stipulation as to the application of the taxes, and proceeded, as usual to do nothing, with the obvious excuse that nothing could be done while Herzegovina was still in a state of armed rebellion. The insurgents, perfectly aware that the Turk would continue to do nothing without direct coercion, went on fighting. The revolt was extending in Bosnia. Montenegro and Serbia were both manifestly preparing for armed intervention, and the latter gave the command of its armies to Tchernaieff, a Russian general with a high reputation. Bulgaria was astir. The Moslem population of Turkey, already fiercely resenting the interference of the Christian Powers in the affairs of the Moslem Empire, was now fanatically convinced that there was a great Christian plot against Islam afoot; already in Albania Moslems and Christians were waging on each other a savage war of reprisals; and early in May the French and German Consuls at Salonica—not yet included in the kingdom of Greece—were murdered by the Mussulmans.

Thereupon the three Emperors issued the Berlin Memorandum (13th May). It proposed to enforce upon both sides, by the combined action of the European fleets, a two months' armistice, which would enable Turkey to inaugurate the reforms. If she did not use her opportunity, farther action would then be taken. France and Italy accepted the Memorandum, but it was rejected in England by the Disraeli Government, which had been in office since 1874; and Disraeli emphasized the refusal by sending a British squadron to Besika Bay, as in 1853. The chance of agreed action by the Powers was practically at an end. Suspicion of and hostility to the extension of

INTERNATIONAL RELATIONS

Russian influence in the Balkans and over Constantinople had been again the keynote of British policy in the Near East since the fall of the Gladstone Ministry. Only a few weeks before the issuing of the Andrassy Note, Disraeli by a theatrical but particularly effective stroke had purchased the Khedive's preponderant shares in the recently constructed Suez Canal, and had thereby secured to the British Government practical control of the new short-cut to India which French, not British, genius and energy had created; and the *coup* was at least suggestive of a more "spirited" and less acquiescent foreign policy than had been followed since the most aggressive days of Palmerston. British, not Russian, influence and interests were in Disraeli's view to dominate the Eastern question, with that time-honored corollary of the integrity of the Turkish Empire to be maintained at any price which was an insuperable barrier to any effective coercion of the Porte. In May 1876 there was, moreover, this special excuse for the British action in breaking away from the Concert, that the Imperial Governments had not taken the British into their confidence until their own scheme was already formulated.

The Berlin Memorandum was still-born. Before the month was out Bulgaria had become the theater of sanguinary insurrection repressed by unrestrained massacre. On 29th May the feeble-minded Sultan Abdul Aziz was deposed, and his place was taken by his nephew Murad, the nominee of the fanatical Moslems—and he in turn, it may be noted, failing to rise to due heights of fanaticism, gave place three months later to his very able but most sinister brother, Abdul Hamid. In the course of June the tale of the Bulgarian atrocities, unspeakable in their horror even when the largest possible allowance has been made for sentimental and interested exaggeration, was published to the world. On 2nd July Serbia and Montenegro declared war on Turkey.

The desire of every Russian Government to gain free access to the Mediterranean through the Dardanelles was in itself undeniably legitimate; just as it was impossible for Great Britain to contemplate with equanimity the aggregation in the Black Sea of a powerful fleet with a secure entry to the Eastern Mediterranean, where it could dispute the British ascendency. Moreover, the Power which had this maritime ambition was also the one Power which could threaten British dominion in Asia by land. But this Russian aim could be achieved only through the collapse of the Power which held the gateway between the Mediterranean and Black Sea, and only by bolstering up that Power could England prevent Russia from achieving her ambition. Nothing short of the complete confidence of each in the whole hearted and straightforward goodwill of the other could remove this obstacle to a genuine agreement between Russia and Great Britain on the question of the Near East. Such a frank understanding was a solution which Nicholas—in all honesty, probably though the British imputed to him a deep-laid and unscrupulous hypocrisy—had vainly sought in the past to attain through an agreed partition of the "sick man's" heritage. In 1876, as in 1853, the British Government was determined to uphold the Turkish Dominion, and there was no Power in Europe equally resolved on its destruction. Russia could not, even if she would, play openly for the possession or the direct control of Constantinople.

But behind the Russian Government was the Russian people passionately sympathizing with fellow-Slavs and co-religionists subjected to the rule of Oriental Mussulmans. That oppression the Russians were resolved to end—however that object might be mixed up with the territorial ambitions of some. The Tsar wished to end it without challenging Europe, and by the action of united Europe; but if united Europe failed to act, it was more than doubtful whether he would be able to resist the popular pressure for intervention at any price, backed as it would be by the avowed or unavowed expansionists. It was of supreme importance that in such an event he should not find himself faced with the direct antagonism of Austria; and early in July Tsar and Emperor arrived at a personal understanding at Reichstadt that if Russia were driven to take Bulgaria under her protection by force of arms, a similar rôle should be conceded to Austria in Bosnia, though both monarchs were anxious to avoid an armed intervention which might kindle a general conflagration. For Bismarck the primary desideratus was such an agreement between the two as would save him from the inconvenient necessity of supporting one against the other.

The essential question remained: how far would Disraeli be able to go in resisting the application of coercion to Turkey? The country was torn between two deep-rooted sentiments rather than opinions—distrust of Russia and sympathy for the victims of Turkish misrule. Gladstone, roused to emerge from his retirement by the Bulgarian atrocities, was the incarnation of the latter; Disraeli, who this summer became Earl of Beaconsfield, of the former, which predominated certainly in Parliament, and perhaps—but much more doubtfully—in the country. But the politicians in the Government were farther divided between those who were willing and those who were unwilling to face war in defense of Turkey, the Foreign Secretary, Lord Derby, son of Disraeli's former chief, being among the latter. The immeate need, however, was to devise a common policy of action or inaction on which the Powers could at least for the time agree.

Farther, as the summer passed into autumn, the Turkish arms proved increasingly successful in the Balkan War. Serbs and Montenegrins were not in harmony; in spite of their Russian commander and some thousands of Russian volunteers, the former met with a series of defeats, and appealed for British mediation. The Porte offered only terms impossible of acceptance, and on 25th September the British submitted a proposal which would restore to Serbia and Montenegro the same status of independence as before their declaration of war, and would confer autonomy on Bosnia and Bulgaria. The Porte rejected the terms, and the British Government fell back on a demand for a month's armistice, and reference of the whole question to a conference of the Powers which was then to meet at Constantinople.

Since refusal would explicitly have been followed by withdrawal of the British ambassador, Abdul Hamid promptly offered a five months' armistice. Serbia rejected it, as it would merely have given the Turks time to organize conquest; but a Russian ultimatum reduced it to two months, which was accepted, as also was the conference.

The representatives of the Powers, pledged to the integrity of the Turkish Empire and to abstention from any schemes of individual aggrandizement, assembled at Constantinople seven weeks later (23rd December). But the Sultan checkmated the conference by producing a brand-new scheme of the most comprehensive reforms on the most approved models, including parliamentary institutions for the whole empire—designed by the Liberal Minister Midhat Pasha, whom he had selected precisely for this purpose. But no one was to interfere with Abdul Hamid in the congenial task of transforming the paper Constitution into a working system.

The Russian envoy withdrew in disgust. The rest of the diplomatists agreed on a proposal for autonomy in Bosnia, Herzegovina, and Bulgaria under control of an international Commission. The Sultan declined any sort of international control, and the conference broke up.

Every one knew that if the Powers failed to persuade Turkey by concerted action, the Tsar would perforce take the matter in hand himself. Though his efforts to obtain positive support from Bismarck were unsuccessful, the previous agreement at Reichstadt now took the form of a definite though secret treaty with Austria, which secured the neutrality of that Power (upon conditions which have never been definitely made known) in the event of a Russo-Turkish war. Russian armies were already upon the Pruth. Nevertheless Russia made one more effort to avert war, resulting in the London Protocol of 31st March (1877), which received the British assent as well as that of the other Powers. The Powers would allow the Porte time to give effect to the new Constitution; if the results were unsatisfactory they would then proceed to such action as the circumstances demanded. Meanwhile, partly as a result of British mediation, Serbia made peace with the Porte on terms of the restoration of the *status quo ante bellum*.

Abdul Hamid, after going through the farce of laying the protocol before the new "Parliament," rejected it, with the stock—unanswerable—reply. Turkey was a sovereign State, recognized definitely by the treaty of 1856. No sovereign State can permit any foreign Power or Powers to exercise control over its internal administration, nor could Turkey recognize any such right in a Concert of the Powers.

On 16th April Russia concluded with Rumania a Convention sanctioning the free passage of Russian troops through the principality; on 24th April she declared war, and her troops crossed the Pruth, and the Rumanian Convention became an Alliance.

III.—*The Russo-Turkish War, 1877-1878*

Abdul Hamid may have reckoned on armed intervention in his defense by Great Britain—a not unnatural interpretation of the language of the British Prime Minister, who believed that the war would have been avoided in 1853 if England had then adopted an uncompromising attitude. Russia, however, was unconvinced, and if Beaconsfield was personally in favor of a still more emphatic opposition to Russian action he failed to carry the cabinet with him. Great Britain, like Austria, demanded from Russia promises subject to which she would remain neutral. The third course, a frank co-operation with Russia, would have prevented the war, because Turkey would have submitted; but frank co-operation was incompatible with the suspicious hostility which, rightly or wrongly, had possessed nearly every British Government for more than half a century.

Abdul Hamid, then, was disappointed. French intervention was out of the question; Germany would not move unless Austria needed her support; Austria and Great Britain were both temporarily satisfied with a watchful neutrality. Turkey was without allies, and across the Danube Rumania was in practical alliance with Russia.

Above Belgrade the Save, and below it the Danube, which is there joined by the Save, formed the northern boundary of Turkey, separating it from Austria as far as the "Iron Gate," a hundred miles east of Belgrade, and from Rumania from the Iron Gate to the Black Sea. The Danube, flowing from west to east, takes a northward turn at Silistria, some seventy miles from the sea, turning east again at Braila and Galatz. The area between the sea and the Danube below Silistria is the marshy province of Dobrudja, at that time Turkish territory—a bad country for military movements. The business of the Turks on the declaration of war was to prevent the Russian passage of the Danube and entry into the Bulgarian plain, and to this end their troops were distributed—neglecting the Dobrudja itself—the main body in the quadrilateral of Silistria, Rustchuk, Shumla, and Varna on the east, about Widin on the west under Osman Pasha, who had been serving in the Serbian war, and at Sistova and Nicopol in the center. The Turkish fleet not only commanded the Black Sea, but patrolled the Danube itself. Large forces, however, were also engaded in Bosnia and the Montenegrin War. The Russians, if they established themselves on the Danube plain, would then be confronted by the Balkan range before they could reach the basin of the Maritza and Adrianople, from which they could threaten the Turkish capital.

A couple of months passed after the declaration of war before the Russians had succeeded by a series of daring exploits in sealing up the Turkish flotilla on the river at Nicopol, Rustchuk, and Braila, and blocking the entrance by the river mouth at Sulma. On 22nd June a Russian force effected a crossing into the Dobrudja, and succeeded in concentrating upon itself the attentions of the main Turkish army in the quadrilateral. The result was that in the early morning of the 27th the real main attack of the Russians carried the passage at Sistova, from which the Turks were driven. The plan of the campaign was that a masking force should contain the great Turkish army—already distracted by the Dobrudja diversion—on the Russian left; another acting on the Isker, to the west of Nicopol, was to contain the Widin forces on the Russian right; while the main body would seize the Balkan passes and pour down on the Maritza and Adrianople. Possibly the object of the old Turkish commander, Abdul Kerim, was precisely to lure the Russians into making this attempt, and then when the Russian center was entangled in the mountains or hurrying recklessly forward, to close in from east and west on the containing forces, crush them, severing the Russian communications, and then shut the trap on the main body. That is a quite intelligible explanation of the inaction which permitted the Russian advance; but at the same time it created such alarm at Constantinople that Abdul Kerim was superseded, and no attempt was made to carry out his plan—if it had ever existed.

The Russian advance-guard under the brilliant cavalry general Gourko, swooped on the Bulgarian capital, Tirnova, where it was hailed with acclamation by the populace, turned the eastern flank of the main Balkan pass, the Shipka, by a route almost unguarded because it was not unreasonably supposed to be impassable—the Hankoi —and then attempted to storm the Shipka itself. The attack was repulsed; but the defenders, who had no water supply, evacuated the position (19th July), and it was held by the Russians for the remainder of the war. A renegade German, Mehemet Ali, received the command in place of Abdul Kerim; Suleiman Pasha was summoned hastily by sea from Montenegro to head the troops in Rumelia and stay Gourko's advance; and in the meanwhile, as the Russian troops streamed over the Danube at Sistova, a column of them was dispatched to seize Nicopol and carry on the operations according to program on the Isker. Nicopol fell on 16th July, and Russian hopes of an immediate and glorious termination to the conflict ran high.

They were grievously disappointed. Abdul Kerim, not yet degraded had ordered Osman, with his comparatively large force at Widin, to relieve Nicopol. Finding himself too late for this, Osman seized a commanding position at Plevna (19th July), on the flank of any southward advance of the Russians. A Russian column, unaware of this stroke, appeared at Plevna next day with a like abject in view, attempted to carry it in the face of Osman's superior numbers, and was completely repulsed with heavy losses. For ten days Osman was entrenching and fortifying. On 31st July the attempt was renewed, still with insufficient forces; it was again repulsed, still more disastrously; and meanwhile Suleiman was driving in Gourko's advanced troops upon the Shipka, cutting to pieces at Eski Zagra a "Bulgarian legion" which had joined the army of liberation. Lovtcha, between Pleva and the Shipka, was occupied by Turkish troops from Sophia, though it was brilliantly captured by Skobeleff some weeks later. On the Russian left, Mehemet Ali thrust back upon the lines at Biela, covering Sistova, the containing force which was commanded by the Tsarevitch.

August passed into September without more marked successes on either side, while Russian reinforcements were accumulating, and Suleiman was wasting time and lives in sanguinary but vain assaults upon the now impregnable Russian position in the Shipka, instead of masking it while conveying active aid either to Mehemet Ali on the northeast or to Osman on the northwest. In September the Russian chief, the Tsar's brother, the Grand Duke Nicholas, struck what was intended to be the decisive blow, launching against Plevna forces which more than doubled those which defended it. But the blow recoiled disastrously upon the heads of the Russians. By furious and prolonged fighting, the Rumanian divisions and a Russian brigade captured the Grivitza redoubt on the northeast of the lines, from which they were not again ejected. Skobeleff, the most brilliant of Russian soldiers, stormed an outwork (Kavanlik) on the south, where he held on unsupported and under a heavy cross-fire, but only to be ejected next day by a series of six successive desperate assaults. And along the whole intervening front the Russian attack was shattered (11th September). Plevna remained defiantly invincible.

Nor was the news from the theater of war in Asia reassuring. The campaign in the Caucasus and Anatolia had opened with Russian successes, and the Turks had been driven back, but under the leadership of Mukhtar Pasha they were now flinging the invaders over the frontier again. In the two months since the capture of the Shipka the whole position had been reversed.

But the Turks made no use of their advantage. Osman could not trust the new levies which reached him from Sophia enough to take a bold offensive on his own account. Vigorous co-operation between Suleiman and Mehemet Ali might have placed the whole of the Russian forces in a very critical position; jealousy and intrigue prevented any such action; Mehemet Ali was ousted from his position, and the supreme command was entrusted to Suleiman, who was both incompetent and corrupt. The Russians gave up the vain attempt to storm Plevna, and instead entrusted its investment to Todleben, the hero of Sebastopol, by whose enveloping lines all Osman's communications were gradually closed, till starvation seemed likely to succeed where the bayonet had failed. At last, on 9th December, Osman made a desperate effort to cut his way out. Failing in the attempt, in which he was himself somewhat severely wounded, he had no choice but to surrender unconditionally on the following day with his whole force. And meanwhile the tide had turned in Armenia too. On 14th October Mukhtar Pasha suffered a heavy defeat at Alaja Dagh, and was forced to retreat to Erzerum, and a month later Kars was taken by storm.

Whether or not the Russians had done rightly in allowing Plevna to hold up their whole advance, its fall was decisive. Serbia again declared war. Gourko swooped suddenly on Sophia, captured it (January 4, 1878), marched by the great Roman road down the Maritza valley to Philippopolis—half-way to Adrianople—meeting on the way and utterly routing Suleiman with his main force, which was scattered to the winds (17th January), and advanced to Adrianople. While Radetzky held his grip on the Shipka, two columns under the Tsarevitch and Skobeleff carried out an enveloping movement through the snow-clad mountain passes on east and west, and the troops which had been vainly battering at Radetzky found themselves assailed on three sides, and were forced to surrender (9th January). On 20th January the Russian advance guard was in Adrianople. There, eleven days later, peace preliminaries were signed between Russia and Turkey.

IV.—Peace with Honor, 1877-1881

The surprise passage of the Danube, the capture of the Shipka Pass, Osman's first victory at Plevna, the third great repulse at Plevna, and its final fall had been the first dramatic moments of the war. The last was the signal for other Powers to bestir themselves, since it practically insured the speedy and overwhelming triumph of Russia, and an immediate necessity for the utmost vigilance lest she should use her victory in a manner detrimental to the interests of Great Britain and Austria. For it could hardly be doubted that, apart from external intervention, Turkey would have to submit to any terms Russia might choose to dictate. And although it was common knowledge that the Tsar personally had no disposition to challenge either or both of those Powers, it was by no means certain that he would be able to resist the pressure of a triumphant military party led by the generals, with Grand Duke Nicholas and the Tsarevitch at their head.

Lord Derby took instant occasion to remind the Russian Ambassador that British neutrality had been secured by the promise that Russia would make no attempt to occupy Constantinople or to obtain control of the Dardanelles; and on 16th January the British Ambassador at St. Petersburg warned the Government there that no changes could be made in the terms of the treaties of 1856 and 1871 without consent of all the signatories. In response to an appeal from the Porte for British mediation, a Note was addressed to the Tsar, to which the reply was considered so unsatisfactory that the British Mediterranean Squadron was ordered to enter the Dardanelles (23rd January); though next day Besika Bay was substituted as its destination, and Derby withdrew the resignation which he had at first tendered. On 28th January Parliament was invited to vote £6,000,000 for armaments, followed upon the publication of the demands submitted by Russia to the Porte, which included a very ambiguous clause concerning Russian rights and interests in the Dardanelles. The clause, however, was withdrawn from the peace preliminaries signed on 31st January. On the other hand, the line to which the Russians were permitted to advance was so close to Constantinople that the British Fleet again threatened to enter the Sea of Marmora "to protect British subjects," Russia replying that if they entered the Bosphorus Russian troops would enter Constantinople "to protect the Christian population." At that point the altercation was suspended. Neither party was willing to force a war; though each had advanced to the very verge, neither actually crossed the line.

Austria indeed was only less nervous than England, and when on 5th February Andrassy proposed a conference of the Powers, Russia could hardly decline—with Austrian troops concentrating on the Carpathian frontier on the flank of her communications with Turkey, with Rumania growing restive, and with Rumelian Moslems seething round the Russian and Bulgarian forces in Rumelia. Nevertheless, while she acceded to the doctrine that the Powers were entitled to maintain the existing treaties, she sought to strengthen her own position by translating the Convention of Adrianople into the Treaty of San Stefano (3rd March); taking the line that while the Powers might modify the clauses which admittedly touched the treaties it lay with her to accept or reject their views on points which she did not herself recognize as affecting them. Britain found herself alone on contending that the whole treaty in all its details should be subjected to the decisions of the Congress to be held at Berlin, which took the place of the originally proposed conference to be held at Vienna. This difference between the Russian and British Governments was so acute that at the end of March the Reserves were called out, Lord Salisbury took the place of the pacific Lord Derby at the Foreign Office, and some weeks later the Royal Prerogative was called in to bring Indian troops to Malta without authorization from a Parliament, whose consent to so bellicose a measure would have been doubtful.

In fact the Treaty of San Stefano intensified the alarm already aroused at Westminster and Vienna by the Adrianople Convention. Russia claimed the cession of the part of Bessarabia incorporated in Rumania, which was to have the Dobrudja by way of compensation. The complete independence of Rumania, Serbia, and Montenegro was to be recognized, with some accession of territory to the two latter. Bulgaria was to become an autonomous principality, under Russian supervision and in Russian occupation for two years, which could only mean that it would remain thereafter a Russian dependency; and the Bulgaria of the treaty covered the larger half of what was left of European Turkey. Father, Russia, in lieu of the cash indemnity claimed by her, was to receive territory in Asia—Batum, Kars, Ardahan, and Bayazid; fairly solid acquisitions for a Power which had formally repudiated any desire for territorial aggrandizement. But the grand crux in the whole proposed settlement was the question of Bulgaria, which, broadly speaking, embraced all Rumelia, Macedonia, and part of Thrace, including some coastline on the Ægean Sea.

Now it was not likely that the Powers would interest themselves greatly in the diverse claims of the various Balkan peoples, beyond making more or less provision for States independent of Turkish control. This was emphatically demonstrated in the case of Rumania, which, having rendered quite invaluable service to Russia, was rewarded by having to accept the Dobrudja instead of Bessarabia which Russia wanted. Rumania was of no consequence to the Powers, and could get from them nothing beyond mildly benevolent expressions of sympathy. So, too, it was apparently of minor importance that the new Bulgaria would not only be a very much bigger State than any of the others, but would absorb territories and populations in which one—or more—of them considered that it had a much better title. What did matter to Great Britain was that the new State, bigger than the rest of Turkey in Europe, and itself in effect a dependency of Russia, could dominate Constantinople; while for Austria its inclusion of Macedonia interposed a barrier blocking her aspirations for commercial expansion to Salonica. Also the Russian expansion in Armenia was ominous from a British point of view, though more as affecting Persia than Constantinople; while the Austrian engagements with Russia had stipulated for Austrian control in Bosnia as a counterpoise to Russian domination elsewhere.

Russia sought unsuccessfully to win over Austria, probably by offering her the control of Bosnia. The very probable combination against Russia of the Dual Monarchy and Great Britain was in itself a serious risk to take, but the deciding factor may well have been the painful realization that her restraining influence upon an Austria hostile to Prussia during the Franco-German War had not won for her the support of Germany in the present crisis. Her attitude grew more conciliatory; and at the end of May a basis of understanding was reached with Lord Salisbury. The new Bulgaria was to be cut in three, the northern division forming the new principality; eastern Rumelia south of the Balkan range was to be separate from it, but largely autonomous; Macedonia and the Ægean coast would remain under Turkish rule; Great Britain would assent with extreme reluctance to the cession of Bessarabia, and of Batum, Kars, and Ardaham, but Bayazid was to be given up. England would urge upon the Powers generally consideration of Greek claims on Thessaly and Epirus—which that State would herself have endeavored to assert by force of arms in February if she had not been restrained by the unanimous prohibition of the Powers.

Austria had already demanded a diminution of Bulgaria and her occupation of Bosnia and Herzegovina. Before the Congress met at Berlin in June, Great Britain had farther concluded a secret compact with Turkey by which—in the event of Russia retaining the Armenian districts—she would guarantee the rest of Turkey's possessions in Asia, subject to the carrying out of reforms with British co-operation; and incidentally, Britain was to occupy and administer the Island of Cyprus, paying over its surplus revenue to the Turkish Government.

On these lines the Congress reconstructed the Treaty of San Stefano at Berlin, under the Presidency of Bismarck, who played the part of moderator and pacificator, the "honest broker" whose sole object was to persuade every one to accept equitable adjustments of contradictory claims. The lesser Bulgaria, erected into an autonomous principality, was farther shorn of some territory on the Serbian marches which were transferred to Serbia, now recognized as completely independent. The borders of Montenegro were also somewhat enlarged. But the Sanjak of Novi Bazar, dividing Serbia from Montenegro, which the San Stefano treaty would have shared between them, remained Turkish, with a right of entry for Austrian troops. East Rumelia became more or less autonomous, but under a governor appointed by the Porte, and with Turkish garrisons in the frontier passes of the Balkan range. The claims of Greece on Macedonia were found unconvincing; in Epirus and Thessaly they were left to adjustment by negotiation between Greece and the Porte. Bosnia and Herzegovina were handed over for an indefinite but theoretically terminable period to the administration of Austria. In Asia, Russia retained Kars and Batum on condition of the latter remaining unfortified. Beaconsfield's counter-stroke, the private treaty with the Porte, was outside the scope of the deliberations of the Congress, providing no excuse for hostile action however angrily it might be resented; it infringed no compacts or treaties.

Russia had saved but a fragment of what the Treaty of San Stefano would have given her, Austria was established in Bosnia, and Great Britain had in Cyprus a new Mediterranean outpost; Beaconsfield had scored a somewhat intoxicating diplomatic triumph. British influence was supreme at Constantinople, and the Turkey England had rescued still stood as a bulwark of the British Empire, while a considerable Christian population had been delivered from Turkish rule.

But the Eastern question was no nearer to a settlement. There was no single State in the whole Balkan Peninsula which was not bitterly disappointed; each one was left still thirsting for more territory which it looked upon as its own by right of nationality or as essential to its own progress; each still found itself in a state of dependence upon some foreign Power whose irksome control it could not afford to defy openly; and each was violently jealous of its neighbors, above all of Bulgaria, whose claims had only sprung into prominence in 1876. As to Bulgaria itself, it was shut off from its expected access to the Ægean Sea, and the most genuinely Bulgarian district, East Rumelia, was severed from it. Finally, the settlement practically created a new problem of Macedonia, with a population which was an inextricable mixture of Greek, Slav, Bulgar, and Mussulman, while geographically it had that access to the Mediterranean which was intensely coveted not only by both Serbia and Bulgaria but also by Austria.

Rumania had lost instead of gaining by the aid she had rendered to Russia, and it was chiefly against Russia that her resentment was directed—a temper quite agreeable to Austria, to Bismarck, and to Great Britain, which had been at no pains to heal the ill-feeling. Serbia and Montenegro, however sorely disappointed, had both gained something. Greece got nothing at the time, though three years later when Gladstone, champion of small nationalities and "peoples struggling to be free," was again at the head of the British Government, British pressure procured the cession to her, by the Porte, of a part of Epirus and the major portion of Thessaly.

A prince was provided for Bulgaria in the person of Alexander of Battenberg, elected under its new Constitution at Russia's suggestion in April 1879. While the Constitution was being shaped by an assembly of Bulgarian notables, the direction of affairs was virtually in Russian hands, and Russia—very mistakenly as the event proved—hoped to find a tool in her nominee. The Constitution, academically admirable and excellently adapted to a population trained in self-government, was very ill-fitted to one newly emancipated and wholly without experience not only of self-government but of decent administration of any kind. The prince was to appoint his ministers or Executive Council, but they were to be responsible to the National Assembly or Sobranje elected on the basis of universal suffrage and equal electorates—inevitably, under such conditions, productive of a chaos of factions. Jealousy of the Russian control was already seething when the prince was installed; he was regarded as a Russian agent, and only a fraction of the Sobranje could be found to support his ministry. The Sobranje was dissolved, but a new election in 1880 was attended by no better results, and after an experiment with a radical ministry, a *coup d'état* in 1881 placed the whole control in the hands of the prince. Six months earlier, the Tsar-Liberator had been murdered by Nihilists in St. Petersburg.

Finally, the Berlin Congress set the seal upon the mutual hostility of Russia and Great Britain, making reconciliation and concord between them impossible for years to come; but also it has made the rift within the lute of the *Dreikaiserbund*. Bismarck had been forced to side with Austria against Russia, and Russia did not forgive him.

V.—*The Aftermath of the Berlin Congress,* 1881-1889

The essential aim of Bismarck's foreign policy was to secure the closest possible co-operation with Austria, coupled with a friendly attitude towards and on the part of Russia lest she should be driven towards a French alliance; while the isolation of France was to be completed by creating or preserving friction between her and England on one side, Italy on the other. The great stumbling-block in the way of the first part of this program was the Balkan Peninsula, where Russian and Austrian interests clashed. The whole scheme was shaken to its foundations by the Turkish war and the Berlin Treaty, when the Chancellor was forced to support the Austrian pretensions against the Russian claims. Still he strove to soothe and salve the wounded susceptibilities of the Tsardom, though only with superficial success; but in other respects his projects prospered.

In the first place the check to Russia in the Balkans encouraged her to seek elsewhere compensation at the hands of the Powers which had been most active in thwarting her; so that her energies were rather concentrated upon her Asiatic ambitions and her rivalry with the British in the Middle East. Such entanglements between those two could bring to Bismarck nothing but satisfaction. There was no open dissolution of the Dreikaiserbund, but a new secret agreement in 1879 strengthened the bond between the Dual Monarchy and the German Empire—an additional insurance against possible accidents.

In January of the same year, MacMahon's resignation of the French

Presidency placed the recently born Republic on a basis somewhat more stable, though its equilibrium was still uncertain. Both conditions were agreeable to the German Chancellor: a monarchical restoration, whether Legitimist or Bonapartist, would be more pregnant with danger of disturbance than a Republic with perpetually changing ministries. But further, he had already, at the Berlin Congress, encouraged Lord Salisbury to encourage France to turn her eyes away from the "gap in the Vosges," and to pursue aspirations in Africa which contained no menace to Germany, but were comfortably likely to procure irritation in Italy. In 1881 France, with the entire goodwill both of the British and the German governments, proclaimed her protectorate of Tunis.

The desired result ensued. Italy had ambitions of an expansion by way of Tunis and Tripoli corresponding to the Algerian expansion of France. Now France had stepped in before her. The ill-will aroused made her willing and eager to accept overtures from Bismarck, even to the extent of reconciliation with her old enemy Austria; and in the next year, in spite of Irredentist sentiment, she joined in the Triple Alliance with the Central Powers, on what was understood to be a strictly defensive basis aiming at the preservation of peace in Europe, though the terms of the compact were not published. This reversal of Italian policy was made with the less difficulty owing to the death of the liberator-king, Victor Emmanuel, the accession of his son Humbert, the almost simultaneous death of Garibaldi, the hero of the Irredentists. Nor was the combination unwelcome to the British; for events in Egypt in 1882 set up an anti-British sentiment in France which at intervals during the next twenty years threatened to issue in an open rupture.

The little rift between Germany and Russia seemed in danger of widening when Alexander II. was murdered by Nihilists in 1882; for his son and successor, Alexander III., was of the Pan-Slavist and anti-German school. It proved, however, that he had no inclination to stir up European complications, having indeed troubles enough to absorb him in his own country, and there was a formal renewal of the Dreikaiserbund in 1884. Bismarck succeeded in preserving at least the appearance of concord and at the same time maintaining the Triple Alliance, which was renewed in 1887.

But Bismarck's power, assured as long as the old Emperor lived, might not outlast his death, since he had never enjoyed the confidence of the liberal Crown Prince and his English wife. He, however, was already a dying man, and survived only a few weeks after the passing away of William I. in his ninety-first year at the beginning of 1888. When, some three months later, Frederick III. followed his father to the grave, the destinies of Europe passed in to the hands of a new controller, as yet an unknown quantity—William II. For the moment the old pilot remained at his post. He had learned to brook no control save that of the old Emperor, whom he had always been able to win over to his own point of view. The new Emperor was young, versatile, of an unbounded self-confidence, with no desire for the guidance of experience, no doubt as to the infallibility of his own judgment, which was not precisely in harmony with that of the man who had made the German Empire. Within two years of his accession the Chancellor found the position intolerable, and the resignation which had been forced upon him was accepted without hesitation. Thenceforth the Kaiser went his own way, untrammeled by the prestige of a minister whom all Europe—whether it hated, feared, or merely respected him—acknowledged as its master-statesman.

Meanwhile, if the Balkans were not threatening to bring about an immediate European conflagration, it was manifest that the Berlin Congress had not established a permanent and peaceful settlement in that region, which was destined to be a storm-center.

In Bosnia, Austria found the task of establishing her "temporary" authority by no means easy, the resistance arising chiefly among the fanatically Mohammedan section of the population. The insurrections, however, which followed upon the first entry of Austrian troops were firmly repressed, and Austria may at least claim the credit of having, after the initial troubles, given to the occupied territory a more efficient and equitable government than it had ever known. The curious mixed Austro-Turkish occupation of the sanjak of Novibazar, severing Serbia from Montenegro was doubtless intended primarily to hold the door open for an ultimate Austrian advance to Salonika; but it kept in a state of constant irritation the two Slav states on either side or other of them, as had been proposed in the Treaty of San Stefano. of it, and its own Slav population which craved for union with one

Montenegro, on the other hand, could not establish control over the Albian districts which had been alloted to her; not only the Mussulmans proving defiant, but also the Christians, who as Catholics were no less hostile to the "Orthodox" Montenegrins. Ultimately the Porte was induced by a threatened seizure of Smyrna to agree to the substituted cession of other districts, which included Dulcigno on the Adriatic and gave Montenegro a seaboard, though with little enough harborage. Greece found still less satisfaction in the passively benevolent suggestions of the treaty; and it was only with extreme difficulty that she extorted from the Porte, under pressure from the Powers especially from England, a new boundary which gave her Thessaly and a portion of Epirus.

It had been the obvious intention of Russia, when she framed the abortive Treaty of San Stefano, to create a Bulgaria bound to her by every obligation of gratitude and interest, and standing out unmistakably as the predominant state among the Balkan principalities.

Through Bulgaria so constituted her own effective control of the peninsula, if not immediately of Constantinople, would have been assured. In this design she had altogether overreached herself. In the first place, the Powers had at once taken alarm and insisted on restricting the new Bulgaria to less than half the proposed area, the rest of which was left partly as it had been before, partly as a new province with a separate status, Eastern Rumelia. But she had further failed in the purpose with which she had created Bulgaria: it was not to be an instrument in her hands at all.

In the far past Bulgaria had a history of her own, and despite centuries of repression the Bulgars had a latent craving to revive their ancient glories. They did not intend their country to be the tool of Russia; they were ambitious of an independent hegemony in the Balkans, possibly of themselves inheriting Constantinople. Moreover, Russia by her treatment of Rumania, both during and since her protectorate of the Trans-Danube principalities, had not won confidence in her disinterestedness, her generosity, or her character as a ruler. She had repaid Rumania's very valuble assistance in the recent war by robbing her of Bessarabia. She showed her hand in 1878 by a clumsily displayed assumption of controlling authority at Sofia; and she alienated Bulgaria as she had alienated Rumania.

The Battenberg candidate for the principality, the Russian Tsar's nephew, was young and inexperienced, honest, not without capacity ambition and courage, but he lacked the full measure of the astuteness and the nerve required to play his very difficult part with decisive success. It seemed at first that his sympathies were with the Russian party, but that he would not hold his own against an anti-Russian Sobranje. The *coup d'état* by which he acquired practically dictatorial powers in 1881 was approved by the new Tsar Alexander III., who expected his cousin to play into his hands and surrounded him with Russian generals—Kaulbars and others. But their domineering methods drove him into the arms of the anti-Russian party, which was increasing in strength under the same provocation. In 1883 Prince Alexander restored the suspended Constitution, and the Russian generals left the country. The Tsar became definitely hostile to the prince.

Meanwhile Eastern Rumelia was very ill content with its position as a Turkish province under a Turkish governor. The exclusion from Bulgaria of a district so essentially Bulgar was an intolerable absurdity, resented with unanimity both by his own inhabitants and by the Bulgarians. In 1885, when Prince Alexander had gone far towards winning the confidence which his subjects had at first withheld, Eastern Rumelia quietly carried through a bloodless revolution in the course of twenty-four hours, sent its governor over its borders, and proclaimed its own union with Bulgaria. Three days later the prince, urged thereto somewhat emphatically by the Sobranje, was in its capital, Philippopolis.

Bulgaria had torn up a whole series of clauses in the Berlin Treaty. Prince Alexander's audacity filled Tsar Alexander with wrath, for it could bring no profit to Russia. Also it created intense excitement in Greece and in Serbia, both of which were instant in demanding for themselves compensation for Bulgaria's aggrandizement.

Milan of Serbia had recently assumed the royal title; the rivalry of the House of Karageorgevich made his position somewhat precarious; there were already various causes of friction between Serbia and Bulgaria, besides a deep-rooted jealousy. Backed by popular enthusiasm, Milan declared war, anticipating a triumphal procession to Sofia. In a three day's battle at Slivnitsa (16th-18th November) the dream was shattered—Serbia lay at the feet of the victor; but Austria intervened. The war was ended a fortnight after its opening. It had effected nothing for either state beyond intensifying their mutual hostility. But Eastern Rumelia was incorporated with Bulgaria, while the Porte sought to save its own dignity by nominating Alexander to the vacant governorship of the province, which it affected to regard as still subject to itself. The jealous irritation of Greece would have carried her into an armed conflict with Turkey, in search of a compensatory cession of territory, in the following year, had she not been restrained by the appearance of a blockading European fleet on her coasts. But her wrath with both Turkey and Bulgaria smouldered, ready to blaze out on any provocation.

Bulgaria won her unification but lost her prince. A group of Russophil malcontents in the army, reckoning on effective countenance from the Tsar, planned his fall, captured Alexander in his palace by a night surprise, compelled him to sign his abdication, and carried him to the Danube and into Russia. The conspiracy had no backing in the country; the minister Stambuloff took effective control, and Alexander was back in his capital in a fortnight. But the shock had broken his spirit; the Tsar loomed too terribly behind the conspirators, and in obedience to the Tsar's disapproval of his return, expressed in answer to a telegram from himself, he abdicated again, and retired from Bulgaria (September).

Stambuloff, thoroughly anti-Russian, remained virtually dictator. It was not till July 1887 that a new occupant for the precarious throne was found in the person of Ferdinand of Saxe-Coburg, wary, crafty, patient, and ambitious; ready to ignore the disapproval of Russia and the other Powers—and to bide his time; to remain himself as yet in the background, leaving the government in the powerful and not too scrupulous hands of Stambuloff. And so for a while Europe shelved the Eastern question, and Turkey, as of yore unmoved by pressure, continued to mark time.

CHAPTER XLVIII

THE EUROPEAN STATES, 1871-1889

I.—The Latin States, 1871-1889

THE Franco-German War destroyed the Second Empire in France and created the new Empire in Germany. It was the concluding move in the policy which had sought the consolidation of the German states under Prussian supremacy, establishing in the center of Europe a military Power with which no other Power, except a Russia on the defensive as in 1812, could hope to contend with success single-handed. Austria had already been decisively beaten, though by Bismarck's politic foresight she had been spared humiliation in order that she might be converted into an ally. France had now been beaten still more decisively, and had been spared no circumstance of humiliation; not her alliance but her helplessness was what Bismarck wanted. So long as she could be kept from a close accord with Italy, nothing was to be feared from either of those Powers, provided at least that they were kept apart from Russia and that Austro-Hungary realized her own interest in maintaining the closest possible alliance, not as mistress but as partner, with a Germany from which she was definitely excluded. Bismarck gave to Germany the hegemony of Europe. But Germany, not content with hegemony, was presently to seek world-dominion. On that quest she went to wreck before fifty years were passed, and the great fabric which "blood and iron" had framed and cemented was shattered in the war of 1914-1918. While Bismarck's hand controlled Germany's destinies she was growing ever more powerful. Yet before he fell from power new conditions had arisen. France had ceased to be helpless, and the Franco-Russian understanding which was always Bismarck's bugbear was on the verge of materializing.

At the conclusion of the war France seemed, and was intended to be, prostrate: her military might crushed, her organization shattered, the whole state a welter of warring factions. But beneath the surface was an intensity of national vitality which was rapidly to effect in her a miracle of recuperation, despite a season of desperate turmoil followed by a long period of unstable government.

The first necessity was to hold within bounds that very ardor of patriotism which had inspired her to a heroic defiance of the conqueror. The surrender of Paris and the submission of the Paris Government to the armistice terms were fiercely resented by Gambetta and other members of the National Government at Bordeaux, who would fain have gone on fighting while there was still a Frenchman living. The summoning of a new Assembly in accordance with the armistice terms was decisive: the country demonstrated very clearly that it realized the hopelessness of a further struggle. It returned very few partisans of the Republican patriots who, as a provisional government, had continued to hurl defiance after Sedan but had failed to fling back the invader. Two-thirds of the members elected were Monarchists of one kind or another; but they were chosen—and they knew it—not because they were Monarchists, but because they represented the national cry for peace. But above all the elections proved that the provinces, as distinguished from Paris, looked to the veteran Thiers as the man of the hour—Thiers, who had helped to overthrow the Bourbons, championed a vigorous foreign policy in the flat days of Louis Philippe, and fostered the Napoleonic legend; Thiers, who had resisted the Third Napoleon and called for war with Prussia in 1866—but had denounced with shrewd warnings the war of 1870 and the refusal of peace terms when much might still have been saved. To all intents and purposes, the elections of 1871 invested Thiers with the authority of a dictator, and it was Thiers who settled the terms of the peace.

France is not Paris, but Paris has very frequently, in its own estimation, been France. Paris had overthrown the Bastille and the *Ancien Régime* together. In 1792 the Paris Commune had become the controller of the French Government. Paris had dethroned Charles X. and Louis Philippe. Paris had its own ideas. It was imbued with Socialism, and looked askance at the Monarchist Assembly; it was furious with the humiliation of the peace preliminaries; and it was armed, for the National Guard had been allowed by the terms to retain their arms. A Central Committee of the National Guard virtually took control in the name of the Commune, ignoring the orders of the Assembly at Bordeaux. When the latter resolved to return, not to Paris but to Versailles, the Committee summoned the soldiery generally to defy orders and stand by the Republic. On 18th March the Government troops attacked the National Guard; the attack, less than half-hearted on the part of the men, failed; the Government commanders were captured and "executed" by the insurgents.

In the terrible weeks of civil war in and about Paris which followed, the Government triumphed. It was the victory of the provinces over Paris. It is needless to go into the details of that fratricidal struggle. While negotiations were passing, Thiers was gathering fresh forces at Versailles; when hostilities were renewed, neither side gave quarter. On 21st May the Government troops forced their way into Paris; at the end of another week of desperate fighting they were masters of the capital. Prisoners held as hostages were slaughtered by the Communists, who, as they retreated from point to point, fired public buildings and private houses. The victors were no less merciless. Some 20,000 Communists were shot down; thousands more were imprisoned or deported. The Red Terror was stamped down in blood once more, and the bulk of the country looked upon Thiers as its savior.

For two years Thiers reigned supreme, first as "Chief of the Executive," and then as President of the Republic. The final Treaty of Frankfort had been signed on 18th May, three days before the final week's struggle with the Communists. The terror was suppressed. The intriguing of the three Monarchist factions—Legitimist, Orleanist, Bonapartist—at once became active. The Republicans were largely identified with dreams of *revanche,* though in Bismarck's eyes they were less dangerous than either a Legitimist or a Bonapartist restoration with the traditions of Louis XIV. or the great Emperor to emulate. There were fervent Republicans in France, but no widespread enthusiasm for a Republic. The personal predilections of Thiers were in favor of Constitutional Monarchy. But in the critical spring months he had insisted that the establishment of peace demanded the whole energies of the country, which must not be distracted by questions as to the future form of government; and when peace was secured he saw in the continuation of the provisional government—under his own direction—the one guarantee for recuperation, and in the Republican form that in which each Monarchist faction would acquiesce, in preference to the victory of one of the other factions—the admitted second best of all parties, which was better than a "best" hotly opposed, though for diverse and contradictory reasons, by a large majority.

In those two years he succeeded in carrying through three Herculean tasks—the establishment of local government on the principle of local cen-councils elected by manhood suffrage, with mayors and *préfets* who were in effect officers of the central government; the reorganization of the army on a basis of universal conscription which created no little anxiety in Germany; and the raising of domestic loans which procured the repayment of the last franc of the war indemnity and the withdrawal of the last German regiment from French soil in 1873. But before that time it had become clear that he had definitely resolved on the permanence of the Republic and the rejection of each and all of the schemes for a monarchical restoration; the Monarchists of the Assembly united for his overthrow; and the Legitimist Marshal MacMahon became President at the end of May (1873) to retain that office for six years.

Now there was one point on which the partisans of Legitimist Constitutionalism, and Bonapartism were in agreement—each sought to favor and to be supported by the Ultramontanes, the advanced Clerical party of which the Bourbons and Napoleon's Empress Eugénie (who survived till 1920) were devoted adherents. Primarily the presidency of MacMahon meant a Clericalist régime, not a restoration of the Bourbon candidate, the Comte de Chambord, the Orleanist Comte de Paris, or the "Prince Imperial," their heir to the claims of Napoleon who died in England in 1873. The second had declared his readiness to subordinate his own title to that of his Legitimist cousin; but the Comte de Chambord made himself impossible, something after the fashion of the "Old Pretender," by refusing to abate a title of his claims by Divine Right, symbolized by the Bourbon lilies as against the tricolor. The marshal was an entirely honest soldier whose Legitimist sentiments were not so strong as his conscientious determinaton to act strictly according to law; he was not to be used as a tool by a dynastic faction, nor was he the man to play the part of Monck on his own initiative. The majority of the National Assembly was Clericalist, though dynastically divided; and the result was a Clericalist government with no agreed dynastic program. But in the country the moderate abstract preference for some form of monarchism as against a republic did not carry with it Clericalist predilections, and was transformed into a definite preference for the Republic as it became inceasingly evident that every form of monarchism would also be Clericalist.

For the fundamental tenet of Ultramontanism was the papal supremacy recently affirmed by the Vatican Council's decree of Infallibility. Alliance with Ultramontanism involved support of papal pretensions elsewhere than in France; and without strengthening France against Germany it annoyed Bismarck, who was then engaged on the *Kulturkampf* in the Empire—the old battle of the State and the Church—while at the same time it drove into Germany's arms the Italian monarchy, to which the Vatican remained irreconcilably hostile.

By the beginning of 1874 the weakness of a government which agreed in the wish to restore monarchism but was hopelessly divided between its candidates made itself felt when the Legitimists turned out the Orleanist minister, the Duc de Broglie, thereby encouraging the Bonapartists, who were enabled to secure a majority in the ministry. Meanwhile, however, Thiers and the Conservative Republicans came to terms with the more democratic Republicans headed by Gambetta, while fear of Bonapartism was also drawing towards them the more moderate among the Orleanists and even the Legitimists. At mid-summer the Assembly was actually induced to pass, though by a very meager majority, a vote in favor of the definite adoption of a republican constitution. A series of elections in the autumn pointed unmistakably to the predominance of republican sentiment in the country. In the course of 1875 a succession of enactments established a republican constitution—a compromise under which the ministers were responsible to a chamber elected by universal suffrage. The elections of 1876 were decisive. MacMahon found that in spite of the considerable administrative powers still nominally retained by the President he could only work through a ministry which had the support of the Chamber of Deputies. Exercising his powers, he dissolved the Chamber and appealed to the electors at midsummer 1877, only to meet with decisive defeat. The death of Theirs left Gambetta the indisputable head of the Opposition. For a moment the President dreamed that he could hold his own and would neither submit nor resign, but before the year was out he realized that a successful *coup d'état* or civil war were the only remaining alternatives. For MacMahon neither was admissible, and he chose submission. That is, he appointed a Cabinet which was not Gambettist but was prepared for and accepted "compromises" which were complete victories for the Opposition. The President realized that he was thoroughly beaten, and in January 1879 he laid down his office, in which he was succeeded by Jules Grévy. The battle was finally lost and won, and the moderate Democratic Republic was permanently established in France.

The constitution of the Republic was itself a working compromise, much more effective than any of those logical schemes of checks and balances which had been devised by the constitution-mongers of previous revolutions. The President was at the head of the State, holding office for seven years. He was irremovable, except on the ground of treason; he might be reappointed; and he was elected not by the popular vote, but by the two chambers of the legislature sitting together. Theoretically, he was the head of the army; he chose the chief of the ministry, who formed that body very much after the British fashion—with no obligation to select them from any particular party, but with the practical need of keeping them in harmony with each other and supported by a majority in the legislature. Party government in the British sense is possible only where there are in effect two great parties, with a tolerably definite line of cleavage. In the French chambers there were not two great parties but many groups capable of a large variety of permutations and combinations, so that for many years no ministry held office for any long time, while various ministers reappeared in successive combinations. The fundamentally democratic character of the whole system issued from the actual fact that ministers practically found themselves responsible to and dependent on the support of the Chamber of Deputies, whose members were elected for a term of four years by manhood suffrage. The other chamber, the Senate, was perhaps intended to exercise the real control, certainly to counteract the more dangerous proclivities of popular electorates. Senators held office for nine years, and ultimately were chosen by official bodies in each department; but their functions proved in practice to be analogous to those of the British House of Lords. In actual fact the position of the President of the French Republic approximated more nearly to that of the constitutional monarch in England than to that of the more powerful President of the United States.

During the prolonged period of Grévy's presidency, the minister who for the longest period had the largest share of responsibility for the Government's policy was Jules Ferry, who, like the President, was a representative of the bourgeoisie. Gambetta exercised great influence, but was actually in authority only for two months, and died soon after (1882). Nevertheless it was he who enunciated the doctrine which was most markedly developed in domestic affairs—that "Clericalism is the enemy." To develop secular education and withdraw it from Clerical control was the main part of Ferry's work. For clericalism, in France at least, meant Ultramontanism, Ultramontanism meant hostility to the Republic, and Clerical control of education meant the training of a generation in reactionary ideas. Bonapartism had perished with the death of the Prince Imperial in South Africa (1879), but Bourbon legitimism was still to the young Republic almost what Jacobitism had been a hundred and fifty years before the House of Hanover in Great Britain, though the Bourbon princes were hardly less impossible (and for very similar reasons) than James II. and his son. At the same time France was recovering from that fear of the extreme revolutionary elements which the Commune troubles of 1871 had revived; and in these she followed the lead given by Great Britain a decade before, in legalizing the trade unions of workmen, hitherto prohibited.

France, however, wonderful as had been her recovery since the great catastrophe, was now entering upon a period of isolation (soon to be remedied by a *rapprochement* with Russia). Her appropriation of Tunis in 1881, followed by her abdication and the British occupation in Egypt in 1882, introduced a new note, of discord in her relations first with Italy and then with Great Britain, thereby weakening her in her relations with Germany and hampering French expansionists in the East—uneasiness over her Tonkin adventure was the immediate occasion of Ferry's fall in 1886. She had not yet emerged from an era of rapidly fluctuating ministries.

Italy had achieved the great work of liberation from every form of foreign domination, and the scarcely less difficult task of unification as a single state, though remnants of Italia Irredenta still remained on her Alpine border and on the Adriatic. But the great effort had exhausted her; the exalted mood which carried her to triumph through so many difficulties and reverses was over, the moment of heroic inspiration was past. Her record in the following years was somewhat dreary. Indefiniteness of aims and uncertainty as to methods made the first period of conservative government one of marking time; and when a theoretically progressive ministry came into office under Depretis in 1876 its elements were so heterogeneous and so mutually antagonistic that only a statesman of the first rank, endowed with clear judgment and consummate tact as well as supreme driving power, could have given them a real unity and a common policy. Such a man was not forthcoming, and government became a mere business of organizing majorities by intrigues with various factions and individuals, and concessions dictated not by national but by sectional interests, woefully unfruitful. The north, trained to a respect for law, could indeed enjoy a reasonable prosperity under a settled, if inefficient, government; but in the south the tradition and practice of centuries had identified law with arbitrary oppression and had given a greater influence among the people to illegal and anti-legal secret societies than to any legal authorities. The law ceased to be brutally oppressive, but remained virtually inoperative. Italy had not yet solved the question, what she was going to make of her emancipation and her unity; so far she had only secured the conditions precedent—or a part of them—for essential progress, though at the same time she was meditating premature schemes of extra-European expansion which could only materialize adequately when she should have set her own house in complete order. When France in 1881 virtually annexed Tunis, the prize which she had hoped to gather into her own garner, she could offer only ineffective protest; and found herself impelled in the following year to the alliance with Germany and her secular antagonist Austria, which gave her a qualified support in Europe at the expense of her most deeply rooted traditional sentiment. Later still, while Depretis was still at the head of affairs, her expansionist visions led her—with the goodwill but against the counsel of Great Britain—into the Erythrean adventure which in 1887, and again afterwards, brought her into disastrous collision with the semi-civilized state of Abyssinia.

Spain, or rather the affairs of Spain, had taken an involuntary part in the great drama of 1870, much as she had complicated international politics at intervals during the preceding half-century; but she exercised no direct influence on them, nor had the vagaries of her endless domestic imbroglios any determining effect on the progress of democratic developments elsewhere. For some time after the assassination of Prim and the accession of Amadeus of Savoy her state continued to be chaotic. Amadeus found himself in an impossible position—in no real sense a king, but merely the unwilling occupant of a precarious throne. Carlist claims were revived by another Carlos, nephew of the last pretender, the figurehead rather than leader of the extreme Clericalists and Absolutists. Amadeus, resolved to rule constitutionally or not at all, choose the latter course and resigned his crown in 1883. The proclamation of a republic only led to an outbreak of particularism, the country disintegrating itself into "cantons" which set the central government at defiance. Manifestly it was only through the army and the Cortes acting together that any sort of order could be restored. Emilio Sastelar, as dictator, and the soldier Pavia, accomplished the task with vigor and promptitude. But a republic could only mean a reversion to the old rule of military dictators, a prospect only less intolerable than Carlism; and the chiefs combined to effect a Bourbon restoration, calling to the throne Alfonso XII., the young son of the ex-Queen Isabella. The restoration was generally accepted; Carlism collapsed, deprived of the support of the Monarchists for whom it had been the sole alternative, who now rallied to Alfonso, and constitutional monarchy was again established. On his death in 1885, the situation was saved by the posthumos birth of a son to his widow, Maria Christina, to whom the regency was secured, and who discharged the functions of her office with tact, dignity, and wise judgment during the years of the minority of Alfonso XIII.

II.—*The German Empire,* 1871–1889

Unlike the establishment of the French Republic, the welding of the new German Empire was mainly the work of one man, its creator, Bismarck. When William I. was acclaimed German Emperor in the Hall of Mirrors at Versailles the work was by no means completed; and even that success had not been achieved without serious difficulties and the exercise of most skilful management. The old king would fain have held to the historic title of King of Prussia; failing that, both he and the Crown Prince would have claimed that of Emperor of Germany. But that would have been resented by the other princes as implying the overlordship of which Bismarck wanted the substance, while he knew that its form should not be displayed with any ostentation. If Baden was eager and Saxony ready for union, Bavaria and Würtemburg were jealously tenacious of state-rights, and insisted on safeguards. The Catholicism of the south was a bar to union with the Protestant north. And behind all was the age long hostility of particularism to any real subjection to a central authority.

Nevertheless the constitution provided for the Empire did not differ essentially from that of the North German Confederation. With the exception of certain privileges accorded to Bavaria and Würtemberg, the Imperial authority had in its own hands not only the control of foreign affairs, of military organization in peace as well as in war time, and of a common fiscal policy, but also of railways, ports, and telegraphs. Its machinery made formal concessions both to liberal and to particularist sentiment, but without practically detracting from the supreme power of the Emperor and his Chancellor. Ostensibly there was parliamentary government through the Crown and two chambers, the Federal Council *(Bundesrath)* and the elected Diet *(Reichstag)*. Of the sixty-two members of the Bundesrath (after admission in 1874 of the provinces taken from France), the several state governments each nominated a fixed number: Prussia seventeen, Bavaria six, Saxony and others four each, and the rest in proportion. The Reichstag was elected by manhood suffrage, the several states being represented in proportion to their population.

But this popular body had effective control neither of legislation nor of administration. In England, when the representative chamber was dissatisfied with the administration, it could bring government to a deadlock by refusing supplies until a ministry was formed to its liking; the logical result was that ministers had become responsible to the House of Commons, and ultimately to the electorate which chose that House. The guarantee of Responsible Government is the representative chamber's control of the purse-strings. If its control can be in practice overridden, as by Bismarck in Prussia in the early "sixties," it becomes no more than an advisory body whose opinions can be ignored by the executive, though it may be impolitic on its part to do so. And thus it was with the Reichstag. Moreover, in legislation the initiative lay with the Government; the Reichstag could only discuss measures submitted to it, though those measures could not become law without its assent.

The laws themselves were introduced in the Bundesrath by the ministers who were appointed by the Emperor and acted by his orders, the Chancellor, Bismarck, being the official channel of communication with him. As shaped in the Bundesrath they came before the Reichstag; and as shaped by the Reichstag they required the assent of the Emperor—which was not given, as in England, as a matter of course. The Emperor's control of the executive was limited practically only by the requirement of the Bundesrath's assent before a declaration of war. While William I. lived, he was in fact guided by Bismarck, though not always without acute differences of opinion, when the Chancellor more than once was only able to get his way by making his own resignation the only alternative. When William II. came to the throne, chancellors and ministers found the situation reversed, and dismissal their only alternative to carrying out his behests. Bismarck's direction of the Kaiser was a purely personal influence; when another Kaiser chose to dispense with his services, there was no appeal. The popular share in the government was practically limited to the Reichstag's power of rejecting legislation and its right of criticism.

Unity of military organization and unity of fiscal policy formed a strong basis for a genuine unification and an inclusive nationalism, though no effective concession was made to the spirit of democracy. Bismarck had taught the Germans to worship Power, and in realizing that "Union is strength" they learned to prize union even at the cost of other ideals. At the same time, Bismarck's concessions to Bavaria and Würtemberg cloaked the practical absorption which they feared, reconciling them—not wholly, but, as the event proved, sufficiently—to the new order without shaking the Prussian predominance which was of the essence of Bismarck's scheme. Though fourteen votes of Bavaria, Würtemberg and Saxony in the Bundesrath were sufficient to veto changes in the constitution, in everything else Prussia could in effect command, though the minor northern states which were practically at her orders, the majority which was all that she required. The Chancellor was President of the Bundesrath, and he made it his business to prevent the stirring up of such awkward constitutional questions as would alarm particularist susceptibilities until habit should have inured all the states to the supremacy of the Imperial authority.

In one direction, however, Bismarck was destined to meet with defeat. It was the last phase of the age-long contest between the secular and the spiritual authority. The supremacy of Prussia, a Protestant state, was always distasteful to the Papacy, and the loss of the temporal power had been accompanied by that increasingly aggressive assertion of the supremacy of the spiritual power and of Jesuit activity called Ultramontanism. Prussian Protestantism had already taken alarm; anxiety was especially aroused by the anti-Russian propaganda in the Catholic Polish provinces. The Vatican decree of Papal Infallibility immediately preceding the outbreak of the Franco-Prussian War acquired the aspect of a direct challenge; for the validity of the decree was disputed by not a few of the ablest of the "Old Catholics" in Germany. Their resistance was met by their suspension, as teachers, at the hands of the Catholic bishops; and their cause was not aided by the support they received from the anti-Clericals.

Bavaria was Catholic, but the Bavarian court resented papal interference, and especially the unconstitutional enforcement of the Vatican decree within Bavaria when it had not been recognized by the royal authority. Finding itself unsupported by the Bavarian chamber, it appealed to the Imperial Government; so that it was actually on the motion of a particularist and Catholic state that to the laws of the Empire was added a clause penalizing the official interference of priests in political affairs. The contest being thus inaugurated, Bismarck anticipated certain victory in the campaign upon which he now embarked in Protestant Prussia. In May 1873 the May Laws were passed, forbidding the intervention of the Church in civil affairs, imposing conditions upon the education of the clergy, subjecting their schools to state inspection, and otherwise placing them under state control. In the Prussian assembly, however, the Center or Catholic party was particularly efficient and well organized. The Old Conservatives withdrew their support from a policy which was claimed as its own by Liberalism. The Lutheran clergy feared secularism as the goal of state-controlled education. The Pope protested, while Bismarck proclaimed that "we shall not go to Canossa" like the Emperor Henry IV. in the days of Gregory VII. The struggle—the *Kulturkampf*—raged for some years; the bishops persisted in their suspension of the Old Catholics; the state refused to regonize as valid marriages performed by recalcitrant clerics and went on to require a civil ceremony in all cases. The Liberal support aided Bismarck in establishing the Empire; but when the time came for new departures of a kind which Liberals would certainly resent, a reconciliation with Clericals and Conservatives became a necessity. At a fortunate moment Pius IX. died; and if his successor, Leo XIII., was no less firmly devoted to the papalist doctrines, he knew how to give an air of decent compromise to the surrender which the Chancellor was now ready to make if it could be tolerably cloaked. Under cover of a new financial program which attracted public attention the troublesome points in the struggle with clericalism were yielded. Bismarck did not go to Canossa, inasmuch as he avoided public humiliation; but his surrender though gradual, was complete.

The Zollverein had laid the foundations of German unity by developing Free Trade within the German area and maintaining at first reduced tariffs on imports on its frontiers, though finally almost abolishing them, in place of the old policy by which every German state had carried Protection to the utmost limit on the hypothesis that it could thus render itself self-sufficing. Applied to a small state or even one comparatively large, as Prussia had been, the theory was absurd. To render the German Empire self-sufficing or something like it was another matter. Every industry which has to face foreign competition is more alive to the direct advantages it will reap from being protected than to the indirect disadvantages from which its individual members will suffer by the protection of other industries. Free Trade in Great Britain had rapidly found a practically universal acceptance outside the agricultural community, because the British producers found they had, at that time, nothing to fear from competitors. Few industries on the Continent were in that happy position. German producers were ready enough to be protected against British competitors. Independence of foreign supplies was an appealing motive. High tariffs provided a *quid pro quo* for bargaining with other highly Protectionist states. Germany was suffering from severe economic depression following upon the unnatural inflation produced by the influx of the indemnity moneys which had poured in from France with such unlooked-for rapidity; it was not difficult to attribute the existing conditions to a false economic policy in the past. Bismarck found no difficulty in carrying manufacturers and agriculturists with him in reverting to Protection (1879). As in England a rapid advance followed upon the adoption of Free Trade, similar effects followed in Germany upon the return to Protection. In either country the *post hoc, propter hoc* argument was accepted with conviction; and many years passed before a Free Trader was regarded by the majority of Germans as anything but a doctrinaire, or a Protectionist by the majority of Britons as anything but a crank.

Protection was in fact a part of that policy which might be called Imperial Socialism with which Bismarck was now resolving to combat Social Democracy, which was a steadily growing force. Individualism demands for the individual the utmost freedom of action compatible with general order and security of person and property; its opposite, Socialism, claims that it is the business of the State to direct and control individual action in the interests of the community. "Social Democracy," regarding the community as consisting of the manual workers, would place that control in the hands of the laboring proletariat, on the hypothesis that they would derive therefrom the maximum benefit, the assumption being that the section of the community which controls the government exercises its direction in its own interests. All such state regulation, however, is "socialistic," whether the government is absolutist or democratic. In Bismarck's view, the ground might be cut from under the feet of the Social Democrats if the very undemocratic German government applied regulation—and took its share in financing it—to the advantage of the working man, who would be less eager for political power if he prospered increasingly under a régime which denied it to him. Popular demand for political control had hitherto been met simply by repressive legislation, which had not succeeded in crushing the revolutionary propaganda, which continued to be attended by occasional acts of violence—two attempts on the Emperor's life were made in 1878. The repressive measures were intensified in consequence; but the new policy was inaugurated to provide a remedy of a different kind. Thus it was Germany which in the following years took the lead in establishing a system of state aided compulsory insurance against sickness, accident, and ultimately old age, to which both employers and workman were obliged to contribute. Although with a different object, the same principle—of state initiative and control, as opposed to unfretted and unaided individual energy and enterprise

III.—Russia in Europe, 1871–1889

In the early years of Alexander II. his naturally generous and sympathetic character led to his great endeavor to introduce in Russia reforms intended to be extremely, even extraordinarily, liberal. Their efficacy had been very largely wrecked, partly by the failure to apprehend the economic conditions, partly by the influence of the interests which saw themselves threatened, partly by political timidity, partly by the psychology of the Russian people. The serf was liberated from serfdom without recovering what he conceived to be his rights in the soil. The class-basis of the Zemstvo spoiled it as an instrument of genuine local self-government. Vacillation transformed timidly benevolent intentions in Poland into an iron tyranny. Relaxation of the intellectual censorship let in not the culture of the West, but only such fragments of it as were revolutionary or as could be given a revolutionary interpretation. The masses remained under a grinding poverty. And the outcome of it was the birth of Nihilism, the doctrine of despair, which countered tyranny by terrorism and deliberately sought to produce not a new law but chaos.

Nihilism gripped not the people but a small number of highly emotional and imaginative persons, of acute intellect and unbalanced judgment. Socialism with its schemes of reconstruction had its own advocates, politically more dangerous, but less prominent than the Nihilists made themselves, because the methods of the latter were more startling; and their propaganda issued mainly from presses outside Russia. The hotbed of revolutionary sentiment of all kinds was to be found among the university students, passionately sincere but pathetically lacking in guidance, and driven perpetually to increased recklessness by every application of what was meant for salutary discipline but was in fact arbitrary and merciless repression. The panic of reaction saw in every wild and futile plot which was concocted and discovered evidence of a powerful organization at work which could only be crushed by doubling and redoubling the tryanny, which only gave rise to more and wilder plots and multiplied the activities of every shade of revolutionary propaganda.

The military failures in the first phases of the Turkish war and the diplomatic defeat which followed it made matters worse, while the division between the revolutionary groups, became more marked. Trepoff, the head of the Russian police, was deliberately assassinated by a young girl, Vera Sasulitch; the revelation of police methods at her trial resulted in her acquittal. Assassinations multiplied; in April

1779 the Tsar's life was attempted; the Government replied by dividing Russia into military governorships where governors held and freely exercised arbitrary powers. The Nihilist group declared war on the Government, though it had little support—the bulk of the revolutionaries were not in favor of methods of assassination. The Tsar was not and did not wish to be blind to the existence of intolerable grievances. Early in 1880 an attempt to blow up the Winter Palace, following attempts to blow up trains in which the Tsar was traveling, emphasized the danger, but strengthened the position of the moderates who pleaded for reforms while repudiating Nihilism. The Tsar called to the head of affairs Loris Melikoff, a champion of the doctrine that the people ought to be considered by but not to control the government which was at the absolute disposal of the Tsar in person. A reorganization of the Zemstvos which would make local self-government a reality, discrimination between incendiary conspirators and the innocent population among whom they lurked concealed, and a reasonable freedom of honest suggestion, were the medicines he devised and began to apply. But the demands for some sort of elective assembly, whether purely consultative or possessing the authority of a parliament, were too insistent to be ignored, and he proposed the appointment of a mixed commission nominated by the Crown and by the Zemstvos, to examine and report on the question to the Tsar. On March 13, 1882, the Tsar provisionally approved the minister's proposal, but on the same day fell victim to a Nihilist plot. A bomb was thrown which killed some of his escort, a second bomb ended the tragic career of the Tsar-Liberator himself.

The senseless crime was the death-blow both of Nihilism itself and of reform, as well as of Alexander II. It revolted the common folk, who still held the person of the Tsar in religious reverence; it choked the growing sympathy evoked by the grievances which were at the root of the revolutionary movement; it gave to demands for reform a false color of revolutionary intent; it provided the reactionaries with an apparently unanswerable argument. In effect, it established the reaction in power for a score of years. Most of the conspirators were caught, tried, and put to death amidst universal execration, in spite of the threatening manifestos put forth by the terrorists. Popular sentiment had been carried over to the side of the autocracy. The new Tsar, Alexander III., issued ten days after the murder a proclamation which was practically the knell of reform, and the Melikoff ministry resigned. A few weeks disposed of its "Slavophil" successor, which sought the remedy for disease not in representative councils but councils of nominated experts, and desired a revival of the old body known as the Zemsky Sobor, whose business was merely to listen to expositions of government policy. Such methods failed entirely to touch even the most moderate demands that the popular voice should be heard; and the reappointment of the reactionary Dmitri Tolstoy confirmed the system of unqualified despotism. The old severities and the old repression were revived in full force, and were for the time effective, mainly because the shock of the Nihilist excesses alienated popular sympathy from the whole revolutionary propaganda.

Finland was external to the general Russian system. It had been joined to the empire early in the century under constitutional guarantees of its own. There was hardly even a Russian leaven in its population; free from the evils of rule by the Russian bureaucracy, it had not, like Poland, either invited or defied Russian domination or Russianizing influences, and so far had not become, as Poland had been ever since the partitions, a hotbed of anti-Russian feeling. In Poland throughout the reign of Alexander II.—and his son's accession brought no change—the Russianizing policy adopted on the suppression of the last rebellion was maintained; but it succeeded only in intensifying Polish hostility and the sentiment of Polish nationalism.

The Russian rural population had been freed from the incidents of serfdom but still lived under conditions of extreme hardships, extreme ignorance, and a strong sense that it had been cheated out of its rights in the soil. The fatalism and the rooted attachment of a peasant class to traditional practices, beliefs, and loyalties, formed the preservative which retained their suspicious antagonism to revolutionists. But there existed in Russia, mainly in the west and southwest, another element or section, capable of being rendered not merely revolutionary but intelligently and intensely anti-social, being already by immemorial tradition and practice largely outcast, repressed, severed from the rest of the community, while its own members were closely linked together by a common tradition and a common religion.

In every state of Christendom the Jews, when tolerated by governments and protected against the popular animosity inspired by their separation, their religion, their financial craft, and other racial characteristics, have been supporters of the rule which gave them security; their numbers have everywhere precluded them from any sort of armed resistance since the days of Vespasian; but their loyalty has been a matter not of sentiment but of expediency, a grudging return for a grudging and generally insulting protection. The country in which the Jew lives a sojourner and an alien is not his country; the emotion which in others is patriotism is in him appropriated not to any state but to his own scattered race. Deprived of the government's protection, he is ready to become its active enemy, and the enmity is none the less dangerous for being covert. It is only where his racial grievance has ceased to exist, where there is no political or social barrier between him and the Christian, that he is truly a citizen of the country of his habitation, and ceases also to be liable to outbreaks of popular aversion, begotten of fear, distrust, and fanaticism.

The Russian Jew, then, had hitherto enjoyed from the Russian government that measure of protection, scanty enough, which had served to keep him loyal; in the reign of Alexander II. there had been some relaxation of the disabilities under which he suffered. But at the time of the Tsar's murder a movement of anti-Semitism was spreading over Central Europe; it had reached Russia, producing a crop of local outrages; here was a fresh direction in which the spirit of unrest might find an outlet. From the Panslav point of view, the Jews were a sore in the body politic; they were offensive to the rigid orthodoxy of the throne. The government, instead of making genuine efforts to protect the Jews against popular outbreaks, practically gave them its sanction, and went on in 1884 to impose new disabilities, as well as reviving those which had lapsed or had been abolished. The persecution thus inaugurated and continued throughout the reign, sometimes with circumstances of repulsive savagery comparable to those practiced by the Turks, implanted in a section at least of the Russian Jews the spirit which was to bear the deadliest fruit when the long-deferred revolution came at last and the whole Russian system went down in awful ruin.

IV.—*Great Britain and Ireland, 1871–1889*

The Franchise Act of 1867 for the first time gave a direct voice in the government of the British Empire to the manual workers, though still excluding agricultural and casual labor. At the outset Labor, hitherto but little organized, gave its vote in the main for the Liberal party. That party, however, under Gladstone's leadership was no longer that which had been led by Palmerston, whom no one could accuse of anything which could be called Radicalism. Its watchwords were Peace, Retrenchment, and Reform. In its zeal for peace it was open to the charge of readiness to surrender even vital interests in the face of a truculent adversary; in its ardor for retrenchment, of neglecting expenditure necessary to national security; and the Immediate expression of its reforming tendencies did not excite popular enthusiasm. It took the first great step for providing education for the masses; curiously enough, it organized army reforms which immensely increased the efficiency of the forces; it removed the grievance of an Anglican Church Establishment in Roman Catholic Ireland, where also it at least alleviated the grievances of the peasantry; but every one of these measures alienated at the time more support for the party than it gained. It accepted for the first time the great principle of arbitration in an acute dispute with a foreign power, but with results so disadvantageous to the country that for a long time to come the new principle was discredited in the popular mind. And what it did to meet the demands of the newly enfranchised workmen was so little that when Parliament was dissolved in 1874 they turned more hopefully to the New Conservatives educated by Benjamin Disraeli.

Socialism at that time had no hold upon the British working class. Proudhon's theory that private property is robbery, and the Marxian doctrines of state control over the materials and methods of production where the State meant the manual laborers, did not appeal to the skilled artisans who then enjoyed the suffrage. What they wanted was the power of bargaining with their employers on an equal footing. Unless they could take effective action in combination, the bargaining was not on an equal footing: the individaul workman being helpless, he must bargain through his Union. Their quarrel with the middle-class Liberals lay in this, that the latter regarded the Union as imposing intolerable restrictions on the right of the individual working man to make his own terms, and as imposing those restrictions by a practical terrorism. The curious result followed that it was Disraeli's Conservative government, posing as the real friend of the working man, which gave the Unions their charter, by sanctioning picketing when a strike was in operation. An ingenious compromise was also devised at this time between protective (not protectionist) legislation for the working man and the principle of free contract—a process by which the law imposed obligations on landlord or employer, but permitted the tenant or employee to free him from the obligation by accepting a contract to that effect which he was rarely in a position to refuse.

Dissatisfaction with the conduct of affairs, especially in India and Africa, overthrew the Beaconsfield administration and returned the Liberals to power in 1880. But, as in Gladstone's first administration, Irish difficulties absorbed so much time and energy (besides the complications in Egypt and elsewhere, to be discussed later) that no great progress was made in democratic legislation until, in 1884, the Reform Act of 1867 received its logical completion in the extension of the franchise to the agricultural as well as to the urban laborer—a question over which a grave collision threatened between the hereditary and the elective chambers. Lord Beaconsfield had died soon after his fall from power, and the Conservative chief, the Marquess of Salisbury, regarded it as the special function of the Peers to protect the country against the recklessness of an uneducated democracy as represented in a Liberal House of Commons. The collision was avoided by a compromise, and the Act was passed which practically conferred the vote on all working men in regular employment; though this was still a long way from manhood suffrage, and the idea of conferring the vote upon women, on any terms, was still generally regarded with disdainful amusement rather than serious apprehension.

The democratic movement then made marked progress during these years; it had in fact been recognized as inevitable even before the death of Palmerston, and Conservatism had sought not so much to stay it as to direct it into channels where it could still be held under guidance. But at the same time Irish Nationalism had entered upon a new phase under a new leader; and finally the inclusion of Ireland in the Franchise Act of 1885, giving the vote to the Irish peasant, brought the whole problem of Irish autonomy into the sphere of practical politics and party programs, and wrecked the old party organizations for twenty years.

The policy of British governments in Ireland, since Catholic Emancipation, had always kept before itself two aims—the removal of grievances and the enforcement of law and order. The second process regularly invalidated whatever conciliatory effects the first process might otherwise have produced, and the mass of the population retained and acted upon its immemorial conviction that defiance of law and of all legally constituted authority was in itself meritorious. Popular opinion persisted in regarding the law as something imposed by an alien authority, and therefore repugnant to the idea of liberty, whether the law itself were good or bad and its administrators just or unjust. The obvious solution was to leave the Irish to govern themselves, but to this there were two vital objections. Autonomy would leave the Protestant minority at the mercy of the Catholic majority, the hitherto dominant class at the mercy of those to whom in the past they had shown little enough consideration; and autonomy would be used as a lever for a complete independence even more embarrassing to England in time of war than the independence of a hostile Scotland had been in the Middle Ages. On the face of things there was no more reason for regarding the British government in Ireland as alien than in Scotland; it was so in practice, because in dealing with Scotland it was guided by Scottish public opinion, whereas in Ireland the public opinion of the majority held aloof from it altogether.

Now after the scotching of Fenianism, Gladstone's unusually drastic efforts to remove grievances failed as completely as those of previous ministers. The recrudescence of lawlessness necessitated the renewal of coercion, and the Irish Repealers, led by Isaac Butt, continued to urge that since, conspicuously, the British Government might make laws for Ireland but could not govern her, she could be made autonomous. No one else paid heed to their arguments. But during Disraeli's rule a new form of artillery was brought to bear, inaugurated by Joseph Biggar and turned to account by Charles Stewart Parnell. Led by these two, the small group of uncompromising Home Rulers entered a course of organized obstruction which all but paralyzed the machinery of parliamentary debate. Butt had endeavored to convince Parliament; Parnell sought not to convince but to dictate to it. Parliament was to be coerced into granting Home Rule. When Gladstone returned to office in 1880, Parnell had established himself securely as the chief of a substantial following.

Throughout the "Eighty" Parliament the struggle was incessant. Liberalism was extremely anxious to drop coercion, to which all its instincts were opposed. In spite of Gladstone's Land Act, bad harvests and the consequent inability—genuine or otherwise—to pay rent produced new crops of evictions; the relaxation of coercive measures produced a new crop of outrages and the new form of terrorism within the law which came to be known as boycotting. An organization was set up called the Land League, which, without sanctioning outrage, encouraged resistance to eviction. The American Fenians of the "Clan-na-Gael" and the secret society of the "Invincibles" in Ireland carried on the war of assassination undenounced, while Parnell used the agrarian agitation as a weapon wherewith to fight the British Government. New Coercion Acts followed inevitably, but were accompanied by a new Land Bill setting up courts for the fixing of Fair Rents and establishing security of tenure and alienation. Parnell's own attitude, however, led first to his arrest and imprisonment, and then to his release on the understanding that he would exert his influence to check lawlessness, the Land League having in the meantime been suppressed. He was hardly out of prison when the new Chief Secretary for Ireland, Lord Frederick Cavendish, was murdered by Invincibles in Phœnix Park. The Irish party repudiated all association with the crime, but fought their hardest against the new Coercion Bill, which followed as a matter of course, though it was again immediately succeeded by an Act in relief of tenants whose rents were in arrear.

In June 1885 a Government defeat on a side issue placed Lord Salisbury in office. The new ministry passed a new Land Bill—the Ashborne Act—to provide tenants with the means for purchasing their holdings from willing landlords, and the relations between the Irish Secretary, Lord Carnarvon, and Parnell seemed to point to some measure for Irish self-government much in advance of anything hitherto entertained by the Liberal party. This appeared indeed to be almost a certainty when Parnell, on Gladstone's refusal to formulate a scheme, called upon all Irishmen to support Conservatives against Liberals at the approaching general election, which took place in December, upon the new franchise. Four-fifths of the Irish members were Home Rulers, and their number was precisely that of the Liberal majority over the Conservatives.

Without the support of the Irish neither a Liberal nor a Conservative government would be secure in office for a week; even with it the Conservative position would be worse than precarious. Lord Salisbury burnt his boats by announcing that further coercive measures were required. The ministry was promptly turned out, and Gladstone took office, to bring in a Home Rule Bill which alienated a fourth of the supporters. The Bill was rejected, and the Conservatives, supported by the Liberal Unionists, came into power. Thenceforth the Liberals as a party were committed to the principle of Irish autonomy, their opponents to the rejection of all demands for a separate Irish legislature; the parliamentary cleavage was between Unionist and Liberals, although for some years the seceding Liberals maintained their separate organization, declined to merge themselves in the Conservative party, or even to join it in a coalition government, and while giving a general support to Lord Salisbury succeeded in imparting a strong Liberal element to his administration.

The extension of a democratic franchise to Ireland had created a new situation in that country. Hitherto it had been possible to claim that the demand for autonomy had been mere sectional clamor; now it was manifest that while in one portion of it Home Rule was viewed with intense repugnance, at least three-fourths of it made the claim—a fact which gave a new color to the argument common to the extremists and the reactionaries in other lands that British advocacy of "liberty" elsewhere could only be regarded as hypocritical so long as the Irish demand remained unsatisfied. A nationalist and a democratic development arrived simultaneously. It is further to be remarked that a nationalist movement in another portion of the British Empire—India—found its first expression in the inauguration of the "National Congress" in 1887; and that all this was coincident with the birth of the Imperial Nationalism which seeks to draw closer the links which bind the whole British commonwealth together. The popular imagination was in some degree touched by the pageant of Empire in the Jubilee celebrations (1887) when Queen Victoria completed the fiftieth year of her reign; when also the first Colonial Conference gave form to the consciousness that a mere intimate mutual examination and discussion of matters of common interest throughout the Empire was much to be desired, though as yet there were only a few visionaries who had dreams of Imperial Federation.

CHAPTER XLIX

OUTSIDE EUROPE, 1871–1890

I.—*America and Australasia,* 1871–1889

GENERAL peace, a reasonable prosperity, and freedom from violent political agitations had long distinguished the empire of Brazil from the turbulent republics of Latin America; but at the time when the latter were settling into conditions of comparative order and stability the placidity of Brazil was becoming disturbed. The paternally benevolent rule of Pedro II. did not prevent the gradual dissemination of republican doctrines, and a section of the community, already annoyed by the abolition of the slave trade in 1850, was further irritated by the decree in 1871 that thereafter all children should be born free whatever the status of their parents, and finally by the abolition of slavery in 1887. The monarchy, if efficient and benevolent, attracted no ardor of loyalty; a military plot for the emperor's deposition in 1889 met with no opposition from Pedro himself, who had always cheerfully anticipated such a termination to his political career. Brazil became a republic, and the imperial family retired from the stage.

In Mexico the ascendency of Juarez was finally established by the overthrow of his ill-fated "Emperor" Maximilian. On his death, in 1872, Porfirio Diaz, the most distinguished of the republican generals in the struggle with Maximilian, became the leading personage in Mexican politics, and from 1877, with a short interval, held the presidency and ruled the republic for the rest of the century and for some years longer—a strong, competent, and not unjust dictator, not more scrupulous than others in the shedding of blood, but not in mere wantonness or vindictiveness.

Under the sway of Diaz Mexico found stability and something like security, though no personal rule based on military despotism gives sure promise of permanence. Mexico was the most successful of the northern equatorial republics in establishing an effective government, because her dictator was a man of exceptional capacity, who was able to maintain his grip on the reins of power over a long period; the prolonged rule of one man generally coincides with a period of comparative tranquillity, either because the country has become weary of turmoil or because the one man's character and capacity are exceptional.

A disintegrating factor over the whole area from Mexico to Bolivia was the large proportion of the Indian races to those of European blood, and of negroes—originally imported from Africa—over a large part of it. In the southern states the European element, already more dominant, was strengthened by an appreciable and growing European immigration.

In the southern region Chile, almost from the outset, had enjoyed greater stability than her neighbors under a government which was oligarchical or aristocratic rather than democratic in name and despotic in fact. The system was maintained, except for a brief period of reforming activity under President Balmaceda (1886–1891), which brought about a conflict between President and Congress, wherein the victory of the latter secured the continuance of the old aristocratic order. A war between Chile and Peru (1879–1883), in which the victory lay with Chile, was notable as giving the first illustration of the ironclad battleship in action. The war was the outcome of boundary disputes with both Peru and Bolivia, and left Chile in possession of all the disputed territory. There were boundary disputes also between Chile and Argentina, but these were settled in course of time without armed conflict, though more than once war had seemed almost inevitable.

Argentina, with Chile, is the most European of the Latin American states in character. From the middle of the nineteenth century, after the sanguinary despotism of Rosas, it was in some sort a federation of provinces in which the province of Buenos Ayres sought to secure a supremacy for itself—not without warrant, since as an independent state it would have monopolized commerce, being as necessary to the development and progress of the rest of the country as Ulster to Ireland. Although for a time this purpose seemed likely to be successful, the province was not destined to play the part of Prussia in Germany. In 1880 its hegemony was defeated by the separation of the town and district from the rest of the province. Buenos Ayres became conspicuously and irresistibly the capital of Argentina and the seat of the central government, but as a national, not a provincial, capital. Under the able rule of President Roco (1880-1886) substantial advance was made towards political consolidation; the natural resources of the country, the inducement of growing commerce, and the exceptionally large immigration from Europe were all influences favorable to order and progress, and Argentina may be said to have been launched at last on a career promising a stable prosperity, though not for some time to come free from perodical crises.

The republics of South America, though most of them enjoying paper constitutions on the most approved models, were in effect not democracies but military despotisms; democracy had crudely attempted to assert itself among peoples wholly without political training or experience in self-government. The tradition and practice of self-government had been bred in the English-speaking peoples of North America for centuries; the British Colonies, separated from the immediate control of the Mother Country with its landed aristocracy, developed naturally and necessarily into pure democracies in which military dictatorships were almost unthinkable, and such class distinctions as survived socially carried with them no political privileges or disabilities in the eye of the law. Their governments were designed to reflect the considered will of the people, though they did not necessarily or always answer immediately to the design. After 1789 in the United States, and 1849 in Canada, modifications of the constitution in this sense were matters of detail. For both, the main constitutional problem left was the satisfactory settlement of the relation between the state governments and the central government; though Canada, as a federal state within the British Empire, had her share of the corresponding problem, still at that time to be defined as that of the relation between the Mother Country and her Colonies—no longer an acute one, since the Imperial Government had no inclination towards pragmatical and self-assertive intervention; its fault was rather apathy. Both in the United States and in Canada the main question had in 1870 reached settlement, though with some adjustment still to be completed —in the former through the Civil War and the North's decisive victory, in the latter through the British North America Act.

When Lincoln was murdered, the "Republican" wing of the Union Coalition defeated President Johnson, captured the succession to the presidency for its own nominee, and retained it till 1885; carrying, in its first years, its own Reconstruction scheme, and attaching the governments of the South to its own party by the disfranchisement of the "rebels" and enfranchisement of the emancipated negroes. The intolerable reign, in the South, of the "carpet-baggers" and "scallawags" forced upon the former Confederates what may be called the counter-reconstruction, which, taking the law into its own hands, gradually restored the ascendency of the whites. The reaction which set in during General Grant's presidency failed only by a hair's-breadth to secure the presidential chair for the Democratic candidate at the 1876 election. If in the government the Republicans succeeded in maintaining the party predominance, their policy, so far as reconstruction was concerned, had already gone to pieces. Setting that question aside, it is difficult to recognize any clear basis of principle in the party divisions, while party machinery developed into an unedifying system of corruption and wire pulling, and party ambitions were apparently directed mainly to desire to share or appropriate the spoils of office. The growing sense that all this was neither good business nor sound morals was perhaps more than anything else responsible for the election of Grover Cleveland, the Democratic candidate, as

President in 1884, on a vague platform of administrative reform.

During his presidency, however, an old issue, long quiescent, came to the front with a new significance. The industrial population had greatly increased of late years, partly because the altered conditions of the South had driven it to development in manufacture, and also owing to labor immigration from the overstocked labor market of Europe. The United States revenue accumulated growing annual surpluses over annual expenditure, derived from the tariffs which were maintained not for revenue purposes—their only defense in the eyes of Free Traders—but solely for the protection of American industries. Cleveland raised the issue by advocating the removal of such taxes on imports as were not necessary to the preservation of necessary industries, and on that issue the Democratic victory of 1884 was reversed by the election of the Republican candidate, Harrison, to the presidency in 1888.

Hitherto the States had concerned themselves wholly with affairs on the American Continent or in American waters; they had been as zealous to avoid entanglements elsewhere as to prevent European intervention in America. But the time had now come when, whatever their natural reluctance might be, they could no longer hold themselves entirely aloof. They were on the fringe of the vortex of world-politics which refused to confine itself to one hemisphere, and the first question with which President Harrison had to deal opened a new chapter in the history of America's international relations.

Confederation was the first step towards Canada's development of individual nationhood. With one exception, there were no fundamental differences between the people of her several states; the most serious barrier to complete unification lay in the elements of racial and religious antagonism between the French population of Quebec and the British who were overwhelmingly predominant everywhere else. Permanent union was practically assured when all the North American Colonies with the exception of Newfoundland came into the federated Dominion. Party government on the English model kept the "Conservatives" in power for more than a quarter of a century and laid down the main lines of Canadian policy. By 1880 Canada had become definitely Protectionist—that is, she erected tariff barriers with the express purpose of securing home industries against outside competition—modified at a later date by differentiation in favor of British products. Economic advance was at first slow: the resources of a vast country with a small population had not been probed, communication was difficult, and capital lacking. Delay in the promised building of a trans-continental railway led British Columbia to threaten secession; but the financial difficulties were at last overcome, and the completion of the Canadian Pacific in 1885 gave an immense impulse to active development, and fostered unity by penetrating the geographical barriers which tended to segregation.

Canadian affairs were not seriously complicated by a "native" question. The Indian tribal population had dwindled till its numbers were small, and the Indian reserve gave it sufficient territory to satisfy its requirements. Only the French half-breeds on the Saskatchewan gave some trouble, fomented by Louis Riel the former rebel, who commanded some sympathy from the French of Quebec.

British Australasia, like Canada, was not troubled by any grave native question. It was only in New Zealand, the youngest colony, that the vigorous Maori had provided a stubborn problem for a short time; and in 1870 they were reduced to a somewhat morose acceptance of the inevitable, which passed gradually from negative acquiescence into positive loyalty. Australia, younger than Canada, was a stage behind her colonies in the development of nationhood; the several colonies were content with their autonomy; union, after the Canadian example, was a counsel which they were in no haste to adopt, though it was not over-tactfully preached to them by English Imperialists. There was, indeed, no barrier to union so strong even as the difference between French and British in South Africa; but on the other hand, there was no urgent pressure to overcome the normal reluctance of particularism to subject itself to any external authority. The movement towards federation began only when combined action became necessary to impress colonial demands on the Imperial authorities during the "eighties"; when other European nations besides the British had started upon the quest for unappropriated but exploitable portions of the earth.

The exciting cause lay in French and German claims to occupy Melanesian and Polynesian islands which Austrialia regarded as her own heritage, and as giving those Powers a position in the Pacific detrimental to her. It was only when the Imperial Government was somewhat rudely roused from its inaction by the urgency of colonial opinion that it in some degree mollified Australian sentiment by effecting a partition of New Guinea with Germany, and a little later joined with the United States in averting a German occupation of Samoa.

II.—*Asia:* (1) *The Far East, 1871-1889*

In China, during the long minority of the Emperor Tung-Chih, the regency was shared between the two Dowager Empresses Tzu An and Tzu Hsi. In 1872 Tung-Chih came of age, but within three years he died; the dowagers nominated as his successor another infant, Kwang Hsü, and resumed the regency. The death of Tzu An in 1881 left Tzu Hsi supreme, and for many years that masterful lady continued to be the real ruler of China.

The efforts of Europeans to find new methods of penetrating the Celestial Empire for commercial purposes were accompanied by the usual crop of embarrassing incidents. A British expedition from Burma into the southern province of Yunnan—sanctioned by the Tsungli Yamen, the equivalent of a Chinese Foreign Office—resulted in the murder of a British official, Augustus Margary; and the usual dilatoriness of the Chinese authorities in carrying out demands for an inquiry nearly brought about a rupture (1875), which was, however, averted by the shrewd management of Li Hung-chang, a statesman of progressive ideas and opportunist methods.

French rivalry or jealousy of the British produced its own complications in the south. The "Empire" of Annam (Cochin-China or Indo-China) was in a vague way a dependency of China. France, permanently excluded from India, was still not without traditional aspirations for an eastern dominion; while Napoleon III. still ruled, she had turned her eyes upon Indo-China and upon Tonkin, the northern province of Annam, as a possible basis for the penetration of China on one side and Siam on another. She had already occupied Saigon at the southern end of the peninsula, and the operations of French explorers in the north brought about in 1875 a treaty between the Saigon governor and the Annam Government, which made sundry concessions but failed to give effect to its promises. In 1882, when Jules Ferry was at the head of the French Government, a French expedition was sent to take the troubles in hand. A fresh treaty ceding territory to France was made with Annam, but was promptly repudiated by China as Annam's suzerain. Naval and military operations were renewed; the piratical confederacy of the Black Flags was called in against the French. A disaster to some French troops (1884), due to a quite unaccountable panic, brought about the fall of the Ferry Ministry early in 1885, but had little practical effect on the successful naval campaign which was being conducted by Admiral Courbet; and the fall of Ferry was immediately followed by the news that China had in effect yielded. The Treaty of Tientsin (June 1885) formally established the French protectorate over Tonkin and Annam. The position thus secured by the French, coupled with their obvious policy of acquiring at least a dominant influence in Siam and in Burma, provided Lord Dufferin then Viceroy of India, with the convincing if undeclared reason for the annexation of Burma in the same year—formally proclaimed on January 1, 1886.

The Tientsin agreement too was largely due to the dexterity of Li Hung-chang, whose insight was mainly responsible for the innovation, engineered by him with no small difficulty in spite of stubborn opposition, which authorized the building of a railway line from Tientsin to Peking and from Peking to Hankow on the Yang-tsze.

If the utility of railways had at last penetrated the offical Chinese mind, the attendant dangers loomed larger than ever. In peace, and still more in war, the foreigner was likely enough to reap more advantage from them than the native. Nevertheless in 1889 Li achieved his aim.

The West had not yet begun its scramble for mouthfuls of the East which came into active operation during the next decade—unless we regard the French protectorate in Tonkin as its opening manifestation. The more serious menace to China and to Japan also lay in the north, where Russia was prospecting for an ice-free port, with eyes surreptitiously fixed on Manchuria and Korea. Europe was as yet content with pressing for additions to the number of open ports conceded from time to time by the reluctant Tsungli Yamen. Japan, having just passed through her amazing revolution, with her statesmen as conscious of her immediate weakness as of her potential power, was in no haste to challenge a trial of strength with any one, though fiction was threatening with China in the Korea and with aggressive Russia at more points than one.

The Mikado's empire in the twenty years following the revolution was mainly occupied in organizing itself upon the new lines it had laid down, offering a unique instance of a state successfully reconstructing itself upon a scientific adaptation of foreign models to its own requirements rather than by a gradual adaptation of indigneous institutions to changing conditions. Only once was the new order threatened by internal revolt. Of the old clans none stood quite so high in power and prestige as the Satsuma; none had more jealously cherished its own independence, though Ito, the ablest of all the champions of progress, was a Satsuma Samurai; none now so deeply resented the social reconstruction which abolished the Samurai privileges. In counsel and in war Saigo had been first among the Satsuma Samurai; at the revolution he had taken a leading place in the new government; then, resenting changes which he had never contemplated, he retired to his own province among his own clansmen.

There, out of reach of interference, he organized them on the traditional lines. Satsuma, at the extreme south of Japan, was geographically isolated by mountain and sea. Officials sent thither by the central government were refused admission. The rest of Japan obeyed the central authority while Satsuma stood aloof. In 1876 a measure was passed which in effect forced the Samurai to seek their livelihood in any form of civil employment, while for any such employment the vast majority were wholly unfitted by training. Then Saigo arose at the head of his clansmen "to ask some questions." Overtures from the Government were rejected; Government troops took the field. The six months, struggle was decisive. The new troops showed unlooked-for fighting qualities; the clansmen were outnumbered, enveloped, and gradually overwhelmed; in the last desperate fight the remnant who refused to surrender were practically annihilated. What Culloden was to the Stewarts, the fight at Kagoshima was to the champions of the old Japanese tradition. It was the *coup de grâce* of a cause already lost, a cause making an almost irresistible appeal to romantic sentiment, but to cold reason indefensible.

The magnitude of the revolution is not easy to realize. No picture of any European, or indeed any other, state at any time corresponds to that of Japan in the middle of the nineteenth century. The bulk of the population was then divided rigidly into four classes: the Samurai—who formed the one and only military class—the farmers, the artisans, and the traders. Above these stood the Mikado, surrounded by the old noble families, a privileged but powerless group, entirely apart from the rest; below them, equally apart, the Helots of the nation, the out-caste Eta and Hinin. None but the Samurai had a voice or a hand in any department of government. The Daimyos, the great territorial magnates, each one the almost independent prince of his own country, were themselves of the Samurai class, not of the ancient nobility. To the Daimyos, the Samurai of his district—his clan—owed and paid unquestioned and devoted allegiance and obedience; they were his army, they supplied his counsellors; they were the lords of the acquiescent population, but they were the utterly loyal servants of the Daimyo. Supreme among the Daimyos was the hereditary Shogun, the acknowledged acting head of the whole state under the fictitious sovereignty of the remote Mikado. And the whole desired and believed itself to be entirely cut off from the contamination of the foreigner. The foreigner declined to be barricaded out, and threatened to break down the barriers with the strong hand. The Japanese slowly discovered that the foreigner had at his disposal a machinery undreamed of in Japan, rendering him irresistible. And the wise men of Japan resolved to learn, and to apply everything that the foreigner could teach them. It was primarily with intent to destroy this intensely unpopular movement that the fiction of the Mikado's sovereignty was transformed into a vital reality; but in the process, what in Europe would have been called "the reaction" became more progressive than the Shogunate, and sought national salvation in such a subversion and such a reconstruction, not only of institutions but of ideals also, as have never been achieved elsewhere except through seas of blood.

The gradual erection of parliamentary institutions was a comparatively simple matter, even in a country where representation was unknown, though it took twenty years to work out. The principles summed up in such a phrase as the "liberty of the subject" could without difficulty be officially endorsed, though their particular application might involve occasional problems not readily solved. But at the root of the whole matter lay the abolition of a conception of the social structure which till the hour of the revolution had never been called in question, and the adoption in its place of a new conception which had never before been presented, not only by those hitherto unprivileged by the very class, which, as a class, had everything to lose and nothing to gain by the change. Only the voluntary surrender of their privileges by the Daimyos and the Samurai made the revolution possible.

Class distinctions were not, indeed, wholly abolished. The territorial nobles were merged in the ranks of the ancient nobility while surrendering their clan-lordships. The rest of the Samurai became simply the *Shizoku,* the gentlemen, with their tradition of gentlehood but without privilege; the whole of the rest became the Commons, with no legal discrimination between classes or occupations. Service and promotion under Government were thrown open to all, without distinction. The Japanese army had consisted of the contingents of the Samurai of the several clans; it became now a national army recruited from all ranks on a basis of universal service, and though it was first called upon to display its quality in the Satsuma civil war, it proved its fighting capacity from the beginning. Even Saigo's Samurai found the once despised and submissive citizen a soldier who could hold his own.

The first confirmation of the revolution was the abdication of the Daimyo's feudal authority and the Samurai's allegiance to him; but these things meant appropriation of the revenue of the former to the State instead of to the maintenance of the Samurai. The compensation arranged for the latter left them almost beggared, nor were they fitted by their purely military training to compete successfully for a livelihood with traders and artisans. It was the disastrous condition to which they were reduced that brought Saigo of Satsuma finally into the field. Nevertheless, instead of joining the revolt, they remained invincibly loyal to the government—an application of the *noblesse oblige* spirit for which it would be difficult to find a parallel. The Commons, it must be owned, were unqualified gainers by the change; yet it is hardly less surprising to observe in them the development of the corporate national spirit, which is not readily generated in a folk newly emancipated from a state of acquiescent serfdom.

Parliamentary institutions were slow of formulation. The first National Assembly was drawn exclusively from the Samurai class; the second (1875) might be called an Assembly of Notables, local officials appointed not by election but by the central government.

But its second meeting, in 1879, under Ito's presidency, gave birth to elected assemblies for purposes of local administration, which introduced the representative principle; and next year the growing agitation was quieted by the promise of a National Parliament in ten years' time. The preparation of a thoroughly thought out constitution was entrusted to Ito, who paid a prolonged visit to Europe to study all available models. Upon his advice, the working system of administration was remodeled, somewhat on the lines of a British Cabinet, in 1885; and in 1889 the new Parliamentary Constitution—also the work of Ito—was promulgated; though, to the disappointment of the democratically disposed, it copied the German rather than the British precedents in its distribution of powers, making ministers responsible not to Parliament but to the Crown.

While reconstruction was in progress, Japan had to walk warily and with the utmost self-restraint in her dealings with foreign Powers; for as yet she herself had not achieved the status even of a minor European State. She failed to obtain any mitigation of the treatise forced upon the Shogun Government which withdrew foreign residents from Japanese jurisdiction; she was outside the European and American pale; even the goodwill of Great Britain did not as yet suffice to win her effective recognition. Nevertheless the firmness, the moderation, and the diplomatic skill displayed by her in regard to sundry complications and difficulties in her relations with other states began to compel a somewhat surprised and rather patronizing respect for her in Europe, and were significant of the seriousness of her endeavor to take her place within the charmed circle.

III.—Asia: (2) The British and Russian Empires in Asia, 1871–1889

The advance of Russia in Central Asia was gradual but continuous. In 1848 her southern boundary had run due east from the shores of the Caspian to the southern extremity of the Sea of Aral, and thence with a north-easterly trend to Lake Balkash. In the next twenty years she had pushed southward over Turkestan, along the whole of this line east of the Amu Darya to the borders of Bokhara and Khokand or Fergana, and in 1868 she had annexed Samarkand from Bokhara; while the Khan of Bokhara was placed in much the same position as Indian princes like the Nizam and Sindhia, with a Russian Resident at his court.

The last advance had been made by General Kaufmann, somewhat against the will of the Tsar. Kaufmann, left in control of the new province, presently found sufficient excuse for renewing the "Forward" policy in the aggressive activities of the young Khan of Khiva (on the west of the lower Amu Darya), and in 1873 he advanced against

Khiva, which was captured in June. Again very much after Indian precedents, the Khan was required to cede to the victor the left bank of the Amu Darya, of which the navigation thus passed completely under Russian control, though the Khiva Khanate, like Bokhara, was not actually annexed.

The next stage was the conquest of Khokand, with the usual justification—agressive activity accompanied by flagrant misgovernment on the part of its Khan. In the campaign of 1875 young Skobeleff won his first laurels. Khokand fell an easy prey to the Russians, who set up a new Khan supported by a Russian garrison. Then the Khokandis rose and cut the garrison to pieces. Thereupon Skobeleff smote the insurgents; and in March 1876 Khokand was annexed as a province of Russian Turkestan. But by this time the Balkan insurrections were in full swing; scarcely a year later Russia declared war upon Turkey, and military activities in Central Asia were necessarily held in check, while Skobeleff was more than confirming, in the Balkans, the reputation won by his achievements in Turkestan.

Lord Mayo in India, and his successor, Lord Northbrook, as well as the Gladstone government in England, regarded the Russian advance in Asia as being, like the British expansion in India, the inevitable result of contact upon a wide border between a western Power and an Oriental civilization. There was room in Asia for both Russia and Britain; the expansion of one ought not to be looked upon as a threat to the other, and a frank mutual understanding, a delimitation of what afterwards came to be known as spheres of influence, would be the best security against a dangerous collision of interests, though mistrust or bad faith on the part of either would make the security very precarious. The Tsar and Gortschakoff took, or professed to take, the same view. Consequently, in 1873, the basis of an understanding was arrived at by the two Powers, with the idea of preserving Afghanistan and the Pamirs as buffers between them. This, however, did not prevent the British advocates of the Forward policy from viewing with apprehension every step taken by Russia which brought her nearer to Afghanistan. Distrust of Russia and advocacy of the Forward policy very soon became the keynote of the Disraeli of Beaconsfield administration, which displaced that of Gladstone in 1874. Lord Northbrook gave place to Lord Lytton in 1876, in which year the differences between Great Britain and Russia in the Near East became increasingly acute, while the annexation of Khokand emphasized the general belief that Russian repudiations of any aggressive intent were pure hypocrisy. Whether or no there was real bad faith on the one side, there was certainly on the other very deep and not unreasonable mistrust, amounting to scarcely veiled hostility.

Indian mistrust of Russia always meant one thing—fear of the establishment of Russian influence in Afghanistan. Every Amir enthroned at Kabul knew that if he admitted Russian influence he would forfeit British friendship, and that even suspicion that he admitted it would have practically the same effect. But such suspicions could never be completely suppressed unless the British had full knowledge of what was going on in Afghanistan, and they could only have such knowledge through an accredited representative on the spot—a Resident. On the other hand, every Amir knew also that the presence of a Resident would be intolerable to his own subjects, in whose eyes it would be merely the preliminary to dictation, followed by annexation. Since the reinstatement of Dost Mohammed in 1842, every British Governor-General had recognized that whatever advantages the admittance of a Resident might bring, the practical effect would be to arouse Afghan hostility to the utmost, and probably to bring about a secret understanding with Russia.

While Dost Mohammed reigned at Kabul, after his restoration, there had been no cause for anxiety. Later, Lord Mayo had won the complete confidence of Sher Ali. But after Mayo's tragic death, the Russian advance on Khiva had inspired more alarm in the Amir than in the British Government, and he had made overtures in 1873 for a closer British alliance and stronger guarantees of British protection. Those overtures had been declined by a government anxious to avoid compromising obligations. His relations with the British became strained, while his dread of Russian aggression increased. It was obviously natural for him to begin contemplating the wisdom of coming to an understanding with the aggressive Power in view of the uncertainty of British protection.

There were then two alternatives: to secure the goodwill of Afghanistan by adequate guarantees of protection, or to bar the doors to Russian intrigue by the presence of a Resident. In 1877 Lord Lytton put forward the second demand; the Amir declined it. Down to this time it is fairly certain that Sher Ali had done his best to keep the Russians at arms length; but Afghanistan was now almost as suspicious of British as of Russian aggression, the more so owing to the recent British occupation of Quetta on the Baluchi frontier of Afghanistan, by arrangement with the Khen of Khelat. In April war was declared between Russia and Turkey, and for twelve months there was a brooding menace of war between Russia and Britain. Kaufmann from Turkestan used the opportunity to seek to establish Russian influence at Kabul. In 1878 Lord Lytton learned that a Russian mission had been received there, at the moment when the Berlin Congress was sitting. The Amir declared that though it had been forced upon him it had been promptly dismissed. Lord Lytton dispatched a British mission, but it was stopped on the Afghan frontier.

Taking this as an act of deliberate defiance, the British Government promptly dispatched an ultimatum, followed by an army of invasion, which entered Afghanistan in three columns. After one sharp fight at Peiwar Kotal, Sher Ali abdicated in favor of his son, Yakub Khan, who submitted perforce to the British terms in the Treaty of Gandamak (May 1879). A Resident and his staff were sent to Kabul; some six weeks after their arrival they were massacred in a rising at Kabul. The degree of the Amir's complicity was never made clear. British troops at once seized Kandahar and marched on Kabul, which they occupied. Yakub abdicated and was deported. The government pending settlement, was assumed by General Roberts, who, avoiding the old blunder, cantoned his troops outside the capital at Sherpur; but his rule scarcely extended beyond the limits of the encampment, which was repeatedly attacked and successfully defended throughout the ensuing winter. Pretenders to the vacant throne appeared—Abdurrahman, a nephew, and Ayub Khan, a son, of Sher Ali. The former had been for some time living in exile in Russian territory, where he had learned a heartfelt distrust of Russia; the latter was at Herat. In spring, the Kandahar force, leaving a garrison, marched up to Kabul, joining Roberts. The Beaconsfield government at Westminster fell, and Gladstone returned to office.

Once more there was to be a complete reversal of policy: the old principle of non-intervention in Afghanistan was to be resumed. Lytton retired, and his place was taken by Lord Ripon. Abdurrahman was recognized, and preparations were being made for an evacuation when Ayub Khan moved upon Kandahar from Herat. The garrison marched out to meet him and met with a disastrous defeat at Maiwand. Then Roberts executed the famous march to Kandahar, covering three hundred miles in a difficult and hostile country in twenty days, and finally inflicting a crushing defeat on Ayub before Kandahar.

Once more the British power had been decisively demonstrated. Yet the plain fact remained that to retain Afghanistan under British control would involve permanent military occupation, at enormous cost, of unproductive territory peopled by passionately hostile tribes. The strategic advantage—disputed by different schools in military circles—of maintaining the hold on Kandahar was accounted as more than counterbalanced by the political disadvantages of remaining in Afghanistan. A treaty was struck with the recognized Amir, Abdurrahman, who very soon proved himself thoroughly capable of enforcing his authority unaided. Adjustments of frontier were made for the purpose of establishing some sort of control, whether Afghan, or British, over the hill tribes of the marches. The Amir received subsidies, and undertook to have no independent relations with any foreign Power; the British left him to control the Afghans without interference on their own part. The Amir did not love the British, but he loved Russia still less. Her refusal to intervene to save Sher Ali from the results of her own uninvited intrusion in Afghan affairs in the welfare of Afghanistan was entirely selfish. What Abdurrahman cared for was a free hand in his own dominions and a sense of security against Russian aggression. And he had reached the shrewd conclusion that British interests were a guarantee stronger than any written pledges, that Britain would protect Afghanistan from absorption by expanding Russia. Also he was as emphatic as any of his predecessors in his determination to have no official British Resident in his dominions—a demand which was not likely to be repeated, or even to find responsible advocates, until more than willing acceptance of it should be very thoroughly assured.

Kaufmann's attempt to bring Afghanistan under Russian influence had been unauthorized; having failed, it was officially disapproved. Further activity upon that line was banned. But there was still a vast area, mainly desert, between the Caspian and the upper Amu Darya where Russian authority had not yet sought to establish itself, and to which Kaufmann's attention was attracted in the customary manner. It was occupied by marauding tribes, whose main centers were at Akkal and Merv. Their predatory energies demanded suppression. In 1879 Russian troops advanced against their fortified camp at Danjil Teppe in the Akkal region—and met with a disastrous and even humiliating repulse.

Skobeleff, however, was now free to take up the Central Asian task, which he would not have been unwilling to leave to others had it been possible for him to march either on Constantinople or on Vienna. Whatever official views might be, in Asia Skobeleff's objective was India, and if he had had a free hand the British Forward school would have been more than warranted in their most alarmist predictions. He had not a free hand, and he was cut off by death before he could thoroughly force the hand of the Russian Government. But in 1880 the immediate aim was to avenge on the Teke Turkomans the defeat at Danjil Teppe. That purpose was accomplished at the close of the year. The Tekkes, entrenched at Geok Teppe, offered a desperate resistance for three weeks, in spite of such a bombardment as they had never before experienced; but in the final storming they lost more than ten times as many men as the Russians, the Cossacks cutting them to pieces when they had been driven from their entrenchment into the open. The horde was broken up, and all resistance was abandoned. Persia, a constant sufferer from the Turkoman marauders, over whom she was supposed to enjoy a sovereignty which she was wholly incapable of even attempting to enforce, cheerfully accepted a treaty which transferred them to the Russian dominion.

There remained unsubdued the Merv area, which was definitely neither a part of Persia nor of Afghanistan, and a great range of debatable land on the south of it, the Afghan frontier being very indefinite. The Turkomans had learnt at Geok Teppe the lesson that Russia was not to be resisted. The diplomacy of intrigues of the Mohammedan soldier, Ali Khan—otherwise Colonel Alikanoff—induced the tribes in the greater part of this region to tender their voluntary submission in 1884, and the acquisition of Merv brought the Russian dominion in direct contact with the debatable land and into dangerous proximity to Herat.

The time, therefore, had arrived when a definite fixing of boundaries had become imperative. Proposals had already been put forward by the British Government for delimitation of the frontiers by a mixed commission. These proposals were now accepted both by the Russian Government and by Abdurrahman. The British and Russian commissioners met in the debatable land, but the opposing claims of Russia and Afghanistan appeared to be insoluble. Both laid claim to Pendjeh, which forty years before—when Russia was still hundreds of miles away—had been recognized by the British as in Afghanistan. Afghan troops proceeded to occupy it. The Russians responded by seizing another debated point, the Zulfikar Pass, and on March 30, 1885, Alikanoff forcibly ejected the Afghans from Penjeh.

For a moment it seemed that war was inevitable. Gladstone, the most fervently pacific of statesmen, expressed in unmistakable language the British determination to stand by the outraged Afghans. At it happened, Abdurrahman was at that moment at Rawal Pindi in the Punjab, visiting the newly arrived viceroy, Lord Dufferin, who gave him similar assurances. Had he chosen—as he would have been well warranted in doing—to make the Pendjeh affair a *casus belli*, the British would have been in honor bound to render him full military support. The Amir's shrewdness saved the situation. He did not mistrust the British—Lord Dufferin won his personal confidence as thoroughly as Lord Mayo had won that of Sher Ali—but he perceived that to make Afghanistan a battlefield for the two great Powers would be only less disastrous to the country than its subjection to one or other of them. Russia did not want war (Skobeleff had been dead two years). A formal expression of regret that Alikanoff had acted under a misunderstanding cleared the way for a renewal of amicable negotiations; some questions were referred to the arbitration of the King of Denmark, and the threatened storm blew over. The Amir was satisfied to give up Penjeh provided that he held the Zulfikar Pass; and the demarcation commission proceeded on its way. In 1887 its labors were concluded by the definitive acceptance of boundaries sufficiently satisfactory to all the parties concerned.

A feature of the crisis eminently agreeable to the British was the aid in the expected war—an offer which led to the subsequent formation of an "Imperial Service Force" among the native states for purposes of Imperial defense. The native princes had shown a genuine loyalty in the past, and it is probable that the sentiment had been further quickened by a measure much criticized and little approved in England at the time—the Imperial Titles Act, by which in 1876 the title of Empress of India—*Kaisar-i-Hind*—was added to that of Queen of Great Britain and Ireland. Little as it appealed to the average prosaic Briton, it touched the Oriental imagination, ranging Victoria with Akbar "the Great" and Shah Jehan, the most magnificent of the once mighty Mughal dynasty.

During Lytton's viceroyalty the financial strain imposed by the Forward policy, as well as the outlay on display entailed of necessity by the Queen's assumption of the Imperial title resting on appeal to the imagination of Orientals, greatly increased the difficulties of the financial administration; and on the top of these came the great famine of 1877, with the need of heavy expenditure on relief. Nevertheless, the Government was able by rigid economical reforms to face the immediate reduction of revenue by a heavy reduction of tariffs on imports, which, as in England in the forties, was followed by increased trade. While Bismarck in Germany was on the point of reverting to Protectionist principles, Free Trade doctrines were in England practically unchallenged, though in India itself the Free Trade measures, met with strong opposition in the Viceroy's Council. Opposition of another kind was encountered by the Vernacular Press Acts, imposing a severe censorship on the native papers.

Under Lord Lytton's successor the application of Liberal principles to the government of India advanced in a manner which excited unfortunate apprehensions and hostility in the European community, which held generally that the prosperity of the country depended upon a British control which required full recognition of the British as the ruling race. A measure known as the Ilbert Bill proposed to subject British residents in India to the criminal jurisdiction of native judges. The Bill was subsequently passed in a modified form which actually worked satisfactorily; but its introduction brought about an agitation which revived old antagonisms, and strengthened among the British residents hostility to any increase in the share in effective government extended to the natives. Considerable extensions were in fact made, not without apprehension on the part of the Government, but with warm approval on the part of the vocal section of the Indian population, whose full liberty of utterance was restored by the repeal of the Press Acts.

That section, a very limited one derived almost exclusively from one class, which was eager for a share in political power, established itself on a new footing when Lord Ripon had given place to Lord Dufferin, by the institution of the "National Congress," which claimed to be the "Voice of India," and was so at least in the sense that no other voice of India was audible; though its claim to represent a real national or Indian as distinguished from a merely sectional sentiment has never been admitted by the British in general or by the ruling authorities.

Under Lord Dufferin (1884–1888) the North-west Frontier and Afghan questions were, as we have seen, finally settled; and further, the British dominion was rounded off by the third Burmese War and the annexation of the country. The gross misrule of King Thebaw might perhaps have warranted but would not have brought about his overthrow, which was actually decided upon in view of his league, expected if not actually formed, with the French in Indo-China; which the British could not regard with equanimity at a time when French policy was not only developing expansionist tendencies but was permeated by suspicion and jealously of the British, springing mainly from the occupation of Egypt.

IV.—The Europeans in Africa: (1) Tunis and Egypt, 1871–1889

The course of events in North Africa during the period under review has a marked bearing upon a fundamental feature in Bismarck's policy—his desire to foster ill-feeling between France on one side and both Britain and Italy on the other. It was with entire satisfaction that he saw in Tunis and in Egypt a happy occasion for perpetuating mutual irritation between France and these two Powers, with whom it would be embarrassing to him that she should be on cordial terms.

In 1878 France had advanced a long way towards the recovery of her international status. Her attitude with regard to the Eastern Question was uncertain; that she should come into the Berlin Congress with a disposition to support Russian claims was most undesirable from the point of view of British diplomacy, and might lead to a *rapprochement* between her and Russia equally undesirable in the eyes of Bismarck. French jealousy of British designs in Egypt was already alert, and it was probably to secure acquiescence in the occupation of Cyprus that Lord Salisbury, at the Berlin Congress, hinted that France might find in Tunis compensation for the diplomatic successes of Beaconsfield. With assurance also of Bismarck's approval, France had no apprehension of trouble if she acted upon Salisbury's hint. Tunis lay on the borders of Algeria; the tribes of the interior were under little enough control, and there was the usual necessity for the European Power on the spot to extend its authority. Italy, which had its own dreams of African expansion, woke up in 1881 to the fact that by the Treaty of Bardo with the Dey France had acquired the protectorate of Tunis, with the open approval both of England and of Germany. It was too late for her to take any action, but her alienation from France was complete, and next year Victor Emmanuel and

Garibaldi were hardly in their graves when she formally entered the Triple Alliance with Germany and her old enemy Austria.

The story of the British occupation of Egypt requires a retrospective note. In 1841 Mehemet Ali had been recognized as the practically independent sovereign of Egypt, though still under the nominal suzerainty of the Porte. In his last years he had done much for the country, most of which had again been undone by his successor, Abbas. He in turn had been succeeded by Said Pasha, whose intentions were good while his abilities and energy were small. Said gave his assent to the design of the Frenchman Lesseps to cut a canal through the Isthmus of Suez connecting the Mediterranean with the Red Sea and so with the Indian Ocean. Palmerston in England opposed the whole scheme, though he was quite alive to its commercial utility, because he saw in it a perpetual source of inevitable friction between England and France and a probable menace to British naval ascendency in the eastern Mediterranean. England in consequence took very little share in the project. In 1869, ten years after its inception, the canal was completed and opened as the property of a Company in which the Khedive Ismail, Said's successor, held half the shares, while the bulk of the remaining shares were in French hands.

Ismail flung away money as though his resources were unlimited. A mere fraction of the product of his merciless taxation found its way to his exchequer, the rest was absorbed by the officials. To meet the enormous expenditure he built up a huge, ever-increasing debt, by raising successive loans at ruinous interest, and selling everything saleable. At last (1875) his only available asset was his interest in the Suez Canal, of which the cash value was as yet doubtful. Disraeli, warned of the situation, seized his opportunity and bought his shares for £4,000,000, thereby acquiring for the British Government the dominant control of the company and the canal which had hitherto been in effect French. Politically and financially it was a stroke of remarkable ingenuity and brilliancy; but it had the effect, foreseen by Palmerston, of stirring to their depths the susceptibilities of the French, who found themselves ousted from their apparently secure predominance by this bolt from the blue. Nor was its significance lost upon Russia.

The sale did not save Ismail from bankruptcy. In 1876 he suspended the payment of the interest on the vast loans he had raised in foreign countries; with the result that the "Caisse de la Dette" was formed, under the Khedive's authority, of commissioners from France, Austria, Italy, and ultimately England, with two controllers, one French and one English, to supervise Egyptian finance and protect the interests of the Khedive's creditor's. This inaugurated the period of the Dual Control.

Financial direction carries with it, of necessity, a degree of administrative intervention at least. Foreigners—British and others—were increasingly employed in the Khedive's service; Ismail found himself obliged ostensibly to give way to their reforming zeal. Then (1879) he sought to recover his former absolution in defiance of European opinion. The Turk hoped to recover his own long-lost control; but the outcome was that the Powers united in requiring the Porte to depose Ismail in favor of his son Tewfik, and in effect to reinstate the Dual Control.

Tewfik was young, amiable, and without experience. The Porte endeavored to assert its own authority and to limit that of the Khedive. The locusts who had battened upon the down-trodden population in the past, whose activities had been curtailed by the intervention of the foreigners, were equally hostile to these and to the threatened intervention of rival locusts from Turkey. There was no discipline in the mutinous army; it was easy for them to raise the cry of "Egypt for the Egyptians," to find a nominal leader and actual tool in an army colonel, Arabi Pasha, and to rouse Moslem fanaticism against the Infidels. Tewfik himself practically powerless and in danger of depotism unless he submitted to the dictation of which Arabi was not the deviser but the mouthpiece and the instrument.

Thus at the beginning of 1882 Egypt appeared to be on the verge of a catastrophic revolution to the accompaniment of a general massacre of Christians. It was the moment of Gambetta's ascendency in France, and the French and British Governments were in accord. They had not assumed any official control in Egypt; but they sent a joint note to Tewfik which practically bound them to support his authority and incidentally gave color to the outcry against "foreign intervention," which grew more clamorous and threatening. Armed intervention was a last resort for which neither Power had any inclination—in England the ultra-pacific Gladstone Ministry was in office, and France was afraid that any military entanglement would be turned to account by Bismarck—but both governments sent naval squadrons to demonstrate before Alexandria in May; and meanwhile an international Conference on the Egyptian Question was summoned to meet in June.

Before it could take shape, events had outrun diplomacy. The revolutionists ignored the naval demonstration; the mob in Alexandria rose and massacred a number of Christians; Arabi was strengthening the fortifications; Europeans everywhere were taking flight. Arabi's batteries were too much for the patience of the British admiral, and while Abdul Hamid at Constantinople was still hesitating about joining the European Conference, he took the responsibility of opening a bombardment on the forts. The French squadron would not co-operate without orders from the French Government, which was technically debarred from giving them without consulting the Chambers. It retired; so did Arabi, leaving the town to the mob, which indulged in an orgy of pillage and outrage. Order was at an end.

The British Government could not evade its moral responsibility for restoring order; Europe acquiesced somewhat doubtfully while an expedition was prepared, the Khedive remained paralyzed, and Arabi made ready for at least a show of fighting. The bombardment had taken place on 11th July. Six weeks later, the British force had disembarked at Ismailia, evading Arabi, who retired to an entrenched position at Tel-el-Kebir, where his forces were attacked and dispersed by the British on 13th Sept. A week sufficed to complete the collapse of the rebellion. Arabi and a few other ringleaders were formally condemned to death—a sentence commuted to deportation and easy confinement in Ceylon.

The British Government had acted very much against its own will, impelled by the logic of events and the pressure of public opinion. By leaving the whole business to England, France had ruled herself out of any title to partnership in the settlement which could be undertaken by no one else, least of all Egypt by herself unaided, or Turkey for equally obvious reasons. Government must be restored, and by the British. The fact could not be denied, however reluctantly it might be admitted. The Gladstone Ministry persuaded itself that a short term of civil reorganization would suffice, and that the military occupation, acknowledged as immediately necessary, would be brief. But if the re-establishment of the Khedive's authority was not merely a return to the old welter of tyranny and misrule tempered by occasional anarchy, a new system would have to be created. That could be done only by British administrators. And it could be maintained only by the presence of a competent military force, which must also be British until efficient native administrators and an efficient native force should have been trained by the Khedive's British advisers. To which end Sir Evelyn Baring (afterwards Lord Cromer) was appointed "Agent and Consul-General," and Sir Evelyn Wood the first Sirdar of the embryo Egyptian Army—pending the British withdrawal.

Egypt proper may be defined as including the Nile basin from the Mediterranean coast up to the Second Cataract and Wadi Halfa. Above this the Nile flows down from its sources in the great lakes through the eastern Sudan, a vast region populated by untamed tribes of negroes, Berbers, and Arabs. In this area Mehemet Ali has asserted a sort of sovereignty, and in Ismail's time British officers in the Khedive's service, Sir Samuel Baker and "Chinese" Gordon, had done much towards making his authority a reality, and checking, though by no means suppressing, the slave trade which was there particularly active. Garrisons were established; but at the close of Ismail's career as Khedive, Gordon threw up the task in which he had had little enough support from the government, and the Sudan fell back into the habitual anarchy from which it was reluctantly emerging.

While Tewfik was struggling helplessly with his difficulties, there appeared in the Sudan a Mahdi, a fanatic who conceived himself to be the promised successor of the Prophet of Islam, with a mission which included the overturning of the existing Mohammedan order with its Khalif at Constantinople and his political lieutenant at Cairo. The Sudanese rallied to the new prophet, whose power soon menaced not only Egyptian authority in the Sudan—which at the most amounted to very little—but Egypt itself. The Gladstone government recognized no obligation to aid the Khedive in restoring his shadowy authority in the Sudan, but it could not forbid him to make the attempt on his own account. He did so, with disastrous results. An Egyptian force, undisciplined and ill-bound, was dispatched to the Sudan under a British officer in the Khedive's service, Hicks Pasha; in the desert it was overwhelmed and annihilated (September 1883).

Still the British Government declined to undertake the reconquest which the Khedive certainly could not accomplish without its aid. The Mahdi and his Emir, Osman Digna, were now threatening the garrisons in the Sudan. The only alternative to the reconquest was the abandonment or the withdrawal of the beleaguered garrisons. Under pressure from the advisers in Egypt Gladstone agreed to effect the withdrawal, and the task was entrusted to General Gordon (January 1884).

The appointment, in the circumstances, was a tragic blunder. Gordon was one of the men who accomplish apparent miracles by the faith and matchless fortitude which seem to have no rational basis. But such men will go not any other man's way, but their own. Governments demand not a mystical but a rational basis for the doings of their agents. Gordon dictating a policy to a government prepared to carry out any demands he should make upon it might have performed unimagined marvels; fettered by one which had chosen him to carry out a policy dictated by itself, he was an unmanageable subordinate. Forced to give up his first proposal that he should be allowed to "smash the Mahdi," refused his second astonishing demand that he should be given to co-operate with him Zoebehr, his sometime antagonist as a most notorious slayer, he still went on his own way regardless of instructions and of repeated warnings that his proceedings must in no case involve the sending of a military expedition to his assistance. Confident that the necessary aid would nevertheless be forthcoming, he advanced with the scantiest escort as far as Khartum, and was there shut in by the Mahdi's hordes at the end of March.

There he remained month after month. The Home Government slowly woke up to the fact that nothing could bring him out again but the military expedition which had been consistently refused from the beginning; but it still declined to admit that there was any need for haste, and persisted in the belief—confirmed by the messages which came through from Khartum—that he could hold out indefinitely. It was not till the autumn that an expedition at last started, pushed its way up the Nile, reached Metemmeh—some hundred miles from the beleaguered town—after a couple of sharp fights in January, and arrived at Khartum on the 28th, only to find that the place had been rushed by the Mahdi and that Gordon himself had fallen while the march from Metemmeh was in progress.

Gordon's view had been that the Mahdi ought to be "smashed" at once and order established in the Sudan. The Government had held that however desirable that might be for Egypt, it was for the time neither necessary nor practicable; for the present, at any rate, the Sudan should be left to its own welter. For Gordon, if it was, as he deemed it, a duty, it was practicable to the eye of faith. For the Government, it would involve at least operations of inexpedient magnitude. A dozen years later it became both expedient and practicable, and the Madhi was smashed; but in the meanwhile the Government adhered to its program. The Sudan, with the exception of the Red Sea ports, was abandoned till its reconquest was organized by Sir Herbert Kitchener.

Egyptian reconstruction, however, proceeded apace under the administration guided by Baring, and in the face of difficulties which were complicated by the constant jealousy of France; to that country, ousted by Britain first from the control of the canal which had been created by her own enterprise, and then from the dual financial control in Egypt, the British occupation was a perpetual grievance which for years effectively served Bismarck's ends by precluding any really cordial relations between the two countries and peoples. But under British influence the old standing methods of oppression were gradually abolished. The peasant was no longer flogged; the *corvée*, the forced labor on the canals, disappeared, and the fellahin received wages, however small, for their toil. The able financial administration checked the universal corruption and applied the revenues to the public service; a strict economy transformed the annual treasury deficits into an annual surplus, which presently admitted a material relief of taxation, even while a constantly increasing expenditure on public works was being met out of income; and the works, especially in the way of irrigation, greatly increased the productiveness of the country. The fellahin enjoyed an unprecedented prosperity and immunity from oppression, and—most unexpected perhaps of all the developments—proved themselves capable of being trained into thoroughly efficient troops, amenable to discipline, and more ready to fight than to mutiny: a remarkable reversal of the earlier dictum that Egyptian soldiers could mutiny but could not fight. As early as 1887 it became possible to entrust to them the defense of so important a Sudan frontier post as Wadi Halfa.

V.—The Europeans in Africa: (2) South Africa, and the Partition, 1871–1890

In South Africa, the Sand River and Bloemfontein Conventions had set up two autonomous Dutch or Boer states, separated by the Vaal River, between the Limpopo, the Drakensberg Mountains, and the Orange River. The Orange Free State flourished under a model republican government; the South African Republic beyond the Vaal, was a small Boer population scattered over a very wide area, and with an empty exchequer, occupied a very precarious position, having on the south-east border the powerful and aggressive Zulu kingdom organized wholly on military lines. North of the Limpopo were the Matabele, who had been driven over the river by the Boers. On the west of the republics were the unwarlike Bechuana tribes and the Kalahari Desert. An expanding Transvaal would penetrate the African interior through Matabeleland and North Bechuanaland unless those territories were first occupied by an expansion South Bechuanaland from Cape Colony or the Orange Free State.

An accident prepared the way for British expansion. The British Government purchased from a Griqua chief the territory known as Griqualand West (where diamonds had been discovered), though it was claimed by the Orange Free State, which at the time did not make good its title. When it was proved later (1871) that the Dutch title had actually been sound, the Government paid the Free State a lump sum in compensation and retained the diamond fields, which still later became the gateway for an expansion that would have been blocked had they formed a part of the Free State.

Then the Transvaal Boers became involved in war with a Kaffir chief, Sekukuni; dissensions among them threatened disaster. Disaster might very well lead to a great Kaffir incursion, followed by a Kaffir flood in which the military Zulus would be the dominant element; there would ensue a welter of wholly barbaric warfare such as had never yet been experienced. British intervention was obviously necessary, since it seemed clear that the Boers, unsupported, could not hold their own against the Zulus, and would be wiped out—after which the deluge could no longer be checked, but would descend in the Orange Free State and on Natal.

The British intervention effectively curbed Sekukuni; but Shepstone, the commissioner in charge of affairs, went farther. The Transvaal, he judged, could not be left to itself, having neither money nor troops; independent settlers in the territory would welcome annexation, which would place it under the immediate protection of the

British Government. Only a few protesting voices were raised among the Boers, conscious of the Zulu menace. In 1877 the Transvaal was annexed by proclamation, and the South African Republic ceased to exist.

The situation, in fact, warranted grave anxiety. There were threatenings of a Kaffir rising in Natal, though these were nipped in the bud by the detection and deportation of the chief who was mainly responsible for them. A new High Commissioner for South Africa, Sir Bartle Frere, arriving at this juncture, found boundary disputes between the Transvaal Boers and the Zulu king, Cetewayo, which were in pressing need of settlement. But Frere found ample grounds for judging that Cetewayo did not want a settlement—that he was, in fact, preparing a war of aggression. As in India, so also in South Africa, every interest, native and European alike, imperatively demanded that Britain should claim the authority and discharge the duties of a Paramount Power responsible for the maintenance of peace and security, and incidentally for the restraint of ultra-barbarous customs. Therefore, while the boundary award conceded most of the Zulu claims, he appended to it demands for the abolition of sundry particularly sanguinary Zulu laws and customs, and the acceptance, in accordance with all precedent in India, of a British Resident. War was the obvious alternative.

Cetewayo ignored the ultimatum. On the expiry of the time-limit laid down, British troops crossed the Zulu frontier from Natal (January 10, 1879). A few days later a considerable force encamped at Isandlwana was completely surprised and annihilated by the Zulu warriors, though British honor was redeemed in the same night by the heroic and successful defense of Rorke's Drift, covering the communications with Natal. The disaster made any further move forward impossible until the arrival of reinforcements from the Cape; but about midsummer the conflict brought to its inevitable issue near Ulundi, the Zulu capital, where the Zulu army was completely shattered. Cetewayo was captured; the country was divided for a time into districts under native chiefs controlled by a British Resident. Later the king was restored, but on his death the rule of his son, Dinizulu, proved so unsatisfactory that in 1887 Zululand was annexed and placed under British administration, with the acquiescence of the Zulus. The disaster at Isandlwana required a scapegoat for the Government, and Frere paid the penalty for the blunders for which he was in no way responsible—the usual fate of British governors and soldiers who take risks with unpleasant consequences. Those who so suffer have at least the consolation of knowing that they are in good company.

Incidentally, Bonapartism in France received its *coup de grâce* a few days before Ulundi. Since Napoleon III.'s death in England in

1873, it had centered upon his young son, the "Prince Imperial," who joined the British forces in Zululand as a volunteer and was killed in an ambuscade, leaving no effectual representative of the Napoleonic tradition.

Ulundi ended the Zulu menace. An impression prevailed in some quarters in England that the Zulus were amiable though valiant aborigines—"blameless Ethiopians," who would have desired nothing but to be left in peace to tend their herds if they had not been goaded into a just irritation by the intrusion of the Boers and the unwarrantable arrogance of British Imperialism. As a matter of fact, they were a conquering tribe from the north; they had not been established a century in Zululand, where they had dispossessed or exterminated the comparatively peaceful tribes previously in occupation, precisely as their Matabele kinsmen were doing in another quarter; they were a terror to all their neighbors; and they were organized as a military community whose young men were not permitted to marry till they had "washed their spears"—not with water. Only the presence of the Europeans had held them in check. Frere's ultimatum at most precipitated an inevitable collision which, if left to Cetewayo's initiative, would have been attended by unimaginable horrors, and by the extermination of the white population, probably in the Transvaal and very possibly in Natal. With the disappearance of their military organization disappeared also the prospect of any native insurrection of more than local significance.

But there went, too, at the same time the one motive which had in some degree temporarily reconciled the Transvaal Boers to reabsorption in the British dominion. The Transvaalers were nearly all of them either stalwarts of the Great Trek of 1836, or sons of those stalwarts, imbued with the same intensity of resentment against the British supremacy, which they regarded as belonging of right to the Dutch in South Africa. Now they no longer stood in need of Imperial protection, and their resentment against the Imperial authority broke out again, the more because the annexation had been carried out without their assent. Their demand for retrocession was, in fact, receiving favorable consideration from the Gladstone government in England, newly returned to power in 1880, when they took the law into their own hands and on Dingan's Day— the anniversary of their great defeat of the Zulus forty-two years before—proclaimed the Restoration of the South African Republic—a direct act of rebellion.

Little effective resistance was expected by the small force which promptly advanced from Natal under Sir George Colley to suppress the insurgents. But in two successive engagements the regular troops were outmaneuvered and defeated by bands of farmers, at Laing's Nek and Majuba Hill (Feb. 27, 1881). Still the Home Government was not to be deterred from the decision which it had already reached, that the annexation had been a blunder, right was on the side of the rebels, and justice demanded the retrocession. Policy obviously required that the Boers should be made to understand thoroughly that they had not won a pusillanimous submission by the victory at Majuba; yet that was precisely what they were in effect encouraged to believe. Without further display of force an armistice was arranged, and a convention was entered upon which reinstated the Transvaal Republic—with complete autonomy, but with express acceptance of British suzerainty and control over all foreign relations, and also of the presence of a British Resident at the capital, Pretoria. In 1884 the revised Convention of London made no reference to suzerainty and withdrew the Resident.

However lofty the motives of the British Government may have been, to its enemies at home and to most Englishmen in South Africa retrocession coming on the top of an easy defeat in arms was an act of criminal folly; to its friends at home and to some South Africans it was an act of unprecedented and perhaps quixotic generosity; to the Transvaalers it was glorification of their own prowess and a conclusive proof of the inherent pusillanimity and inefficiency of British governments and of the British people—a conviction which was to be dissipated only by another war some years later.

Between 1880 and 1890 the African Continent was in effect partitioned between the European Powers. Hitherto, since the Dutch Colony at the Cape had been transferred to Great Britain, no other great Power except France had interested itself in the Dark Continent. Till the middle of the ninteenth century the interior was almost unknown. Spain had a foothold in West Africa at one or two points north of the equator; Portugal on a long strip of the west coast south of the Congo, and another strip of the east coast, facing Madagascar, from Mozambique to Delega Bay; French and British had held coastal stations for trade purposes, but very little more, at various points between Senegal and the mouth of the Niger. There had been no expansion inland, except the Boer Trek over the Orange River and the Vaal. The French occupation of Algeria under the Orleans monarchy had implanted in French minds the idea of a French Empire in Africa, towards which the second conspicuous step was the establishment of her protectorate over Tunis in 1881. Exploration of the nearly impenetrable interior had been left almost entirely to private enterprise, to missionary societies, and to geographical associations, and had provided little inducement to the pioneers of legitimate commerce. Not for commercial purposes, but primarily from a fervent desire to spread the gospel and to stop the slave trade, David Livingstone gave his life to the explorations which incidentally suggested unrevealed possibilities in the heart of Africa. Livingstone far more than any one else gave the impulse which drew into the field in the seventies H. M. Stanley and Joseph Thomson, and brought into the ken of Europe the regions of the great lakes, and of the Congo, the Niger, and the Benue. The upper Niger, however, was rather the field of the French, who in the same decade were unostentatiously pushing east from Senegal, and were established on its headwaters by 1881.

Leopold II., King of the Belgians, was now taking a lively interest in African exploration. Stanley, having explored the Congo, and failing to attract the British commercial community, turned to Leopold, who organized the International Association of the Congo, with Stanley as its administrator in Africa (1879). Meanwhile the French were exploring to the north of the river. Presently the Portuguese, waking up to a new situation, began to assert on their own account obsolete claims to occupation and possession in the interior. Germany, too, had suddenly realized that Africa contained the only territory not yet under European control, and meant to have nothing less than her share. The outcome was the assembly of a conference of the Powers at Berlin (November 1884).

The Niger was removed from the consideration of the conference by the manifestly established rights of the British to the control of its lower waters. Broadly speaking, the conference recognized the claim of the Internationl Association to Congoland on the south of the river, and including its outlet, of France to the territory on the north of it which became the French Congo, and of Portugal to the coastal territory from the mouth of the Congo to that of the Cunene. Freedom of legitimate trade and suppression of the slave trade were guaranteed. The work of the conference was hardly completed when Leopold assumed the personal sovereignty over the Congo territory, obtaining the assent of the Powers thereto, and naming it the Congo Free State. Thenceforth it was to all intents and purposes the private estate of the King of the Belgians.

In securing Nigeria, the lower Niger, and the Benue, British enterprise only just succeeded in anticipating the French on the west, and then, through the energy of the explorer Joseph Thomson (1885), the Germans, who had taken advantage of facilities bestowed by the British Niger Company to start a process of annexation in the Cameroons (south-east of Nigeria), whence they were pushing up to Benue. They had at the same time (1884) secured a foothold between the west of Nigeria and the British Gold Coast, where they proclaimed their protectorate of Togoland.

The German activity had begun in 1882 in German commercial circles. Bismarck was no great believer in German expansion oversea, but he saw in it possibilities which might be turned to account to the detriment of France and in bargainings with Britain. In 1883 Germany occupied Angra Pequeña on the south-west coast, and when it became clear that remonstrances on the part of the British Government—though it declined then and afterwards to surrender its own position as Walfish Bay—need not be very seriously regarded, she annexed the whole territory, which became known as German West Africa (1884). In the same year, however, she was foiled in an attempt to plant herself at St. Lucia—south of Delagoa Bay on the east coast—which, had it succeeded, would have given or was intended to give her access to the Transvaal from the east as well as the west.

In 1884 Karl Peters, coming from the island of Zanzibar (an Arab sultanate, where British influence was established) to the mainland north of Portuguese East Africa, started treaty-making with various chiefs—thus beginning the creation of German East Africa—in spite of the resentment of the Sultan of Zanzibar, who claimed the sovereignty. Farther north, again, however, the British were already establishing a claim in Uganda, and the British and Germans spheres of influence were delimited by agreement in 1886.

At the same time, the prospect of British penetration northward from the Cape was being threatened by raids from the Transvaal into Bechuanaland which compelled British intervention—the more on account of the recent German settlement at Angra Pequeña. In 1885 Bechuanaland became a British protectorate (a part of which was presently annexed to Cape Colony), severing German West Africa from the Transvaal, and providing the base whence Cecil Rhodes and his South Africa Company, pushed northwards over Rhodesia, to the shores of Lake Nyassa and Tanganyika. The delimitations reached what was meant to be their final settlement in the Anglo-German agreement of 1890, which established a permanent German barrier between the British in Uganda (British East Africa) on the north and in Rhodesia on the south. Incidentally the British protectorate of Zanzibar was recognized, in exchange for the cession of Heligoland in the North Sea—a harmless and graceful concession as it then appeared to Lord Salisbury. For the young Kaiser had not yet announced the unexpected doctrine that the future of Germany was on the sea.

To conclude this portion of our story: Abyssinia was left, the one definitely independent state in Africa. On its northern border the Italians began their unhappy venture in Eritrea; on the east of it, the "horn" of Africa was partitioned into British and Italian Somaliland. It remains only to remark that France, without intervention of any other Power, established in 1885 her protectorate over the great island of Madagascar, which nine years later issued in its complete annexation.

CHAPTER L

FEATURES OF THE NINETEENTH CENTURY

I.—*The European System*

WHEN Bismarck fell precisely three-quarters of a century had passed since the year of his birth, in which the Vienna Congress had taken upon itself the reconstruction of the European system. Of its reconstructed system little enough was left; and no man had done more to shatter it than Bismarck himself.

The two cardinal points in the Vienna program had been the reestablishment of governments on legitimate principles, and the preservation of peace through the concerted counsels and action of the Great Powers. The corollary of the first had been the continuity of particularism in Germany and Italy; of the second, the Holy Alliance between Russia, Austria, and Prussia; of both, the preservation of the Austrian Empire and the effective hegemony of Austria in a disunited Germany.

The gossamer threads by which Alexander sought to unite the monarchies had been re-inforced by the stronger bands woven by Metternich, so far as the three Powers were concerned; and though the Holy Alliance had failed to draw Britain and France into its orbit, it had for nearly forty years succeeded in avoiding or preventing any international conflagration. But it had been weakened by the fall of Metternich and the instability of Frederick William IV.; it failed to prevent the Crimean War, and ceased altogether to operate for the next sixteen years, during which the Prussian Chancellor and the French Emperor between them erased "the Treaties" of 1815. Bismarck recalled, and even gave some sort of material body to, its ghost in 1872, but his Dreikaiserbund finally dissolved into the elements at the moment of his retirement in 1890.

Gone, too, were the fragmentary Italy and the divided Germany which Metternich had cherished. Austria had been shorn of her hegemony in the latter and of her domination in the former, where the Bourbon incubus had also been exorcised and legitimism itself was dead and buried. Italy was united under a dynasty which had hitherto been saved from entire insignificance only by the fact that it bestrode the Alpine passes between Provence and Piedmont. Germany, after ousting Austria altogether, had attained unity through what was in fact—though the fact had been ingeniously veiled—absorption by Prussia; and Prussianized Germany was unmistakably the greatest military Power on the Continent, not there to be challenged single-handed by any other country whatsoever. That subversion of the Vienna conception of the Balance of Power had also been Bismarck's handiwork; it was he who had raised Prussia from third to first in the dominant trio; he had even incidentally helped Italy towards the completion of her unification. But here again, for over forty years, till first Napoleon III. and then Bismarck intervened, the Vienna settlement had held its own.

So was it with the integrity of Austria's Empire. The establishment of the Sardinian ascendency in Italy and the Prussian hegemony in Germany had thrust her back, forcing her to recognize herself as the Dual Monarchy, restricting her aspirations for development to the Balkan area, excluding her from Germany and Italy alike, compelling her even to a partial and incomplete acknowledgment that in the structure of states it was no longer safe to ignore nationality—a notion hardly less monstrous in the eyes of the old Congress than demands for popular control in affairs of state.

Bismarck overturned the Vienna settlement in the interests of Prussia. Had there been no Bismarck, Napoleon III. might have done it in the interests of France. But the German knew exactly what he wanted and how to get it, while the French Emperor was swayed by ill-defined dreams and sudden impulses. The Vienna settlement stood in the way of the aggrandizement both of Prussia (and by consequence Germany) and of France; but it was Prussia that effected its overturn to her own advantage. Bismarck was not satisfied with the Balance of Power as established under it; when he had readjusted this to his own satisfaction, the old association could not be restored, but his object was achieved. Germany, under his régime, was the arbiter of Europe. The Concert of Europe, which he had brushed aside when his own aims were at stake, was revived, for use when it would not run counter to what he, standing for Germany, was resolved upon. As, before his entry, it had kept the peace almost to the end, so after he had achieved his purpose, it kept the peace which Germany desired to maintain—till it suited her to break it.

The monarchs, at Vienna, were weary of war; apart from this, the root principle on which they acted was that the authority of a monarch must not be questioned or his acts criticized. Only the attitude of Britain, and then of France also, restrained them in some degree from enforcing that principle outside their own dominions. Their utmost concession was that a benevolent monarch might, of his grace, do his subjects the favor of listening to their counsels. But

FEATURES OF THE NINETEENTH CENTURY 149

in 1890 it was only in Russia, Austria, and Germany that that principle survived—and in two of them only in a modified form—in spite of its apparent triumph in 1849. Constitutionalism, already long secured in Great Britain, was established in all the Latin states also, as well as in Holland and Scandinavia, though in France it was in the form of a constitutional republic. Outside the three empires absolutism was dead, legitimism almost dead, and the right of the whole people at least to a voice in governmental affairs was established—theoretically even in Austria and Germany, though there they had no substance of control. And again outside the three empires the doctrine of nationalism—so subversive of authority and so detestable to Metternich—had so far triumphed that in the United Kingdom Irish autonomy had become a question of practical politics; that Bismarck had to justify his robberies from France and Denmark by claiming the stolen territories as *Germania Irredenta;* that European Turkey had become an aggregate of virtually independent states; and that, going farther afield, Colonial autonomy—an aspect of nationalism—had become an established fact throughout the British Empire. Even in the Austrian Empire Magyars and Teutons were on an equal footing.

All that was left was the doctrine of the preservation of peace through the Concert of the Powers. For nineteen years the peace had remained unbroken; but the uneasy truce of the next twenty-four years rested not on their harmony but on the dread of an Armageddon, a world war; while all Europe groaned under the crushing weight of ever-growing armaments, and each nation resentfully viewed its neighbor's progress in the grim competition as a menace to itself, driving it always farther and farther upon the same deadly course. Only Britain, confident in her navy, incredulous of such a crime against humanity as the deliberate provocation of a world-war, lagged behind the rest in her military preparation.

America, too, had definitely separated itself from the European sphere. In 1815 South America was still nominally under the sway of the monarchs of Spain and Portugal. But the Monroe doctrine, backed by Canning's policy, had very soon severed Spain from her American possessions; Brazil had parted from Portugal. Europe had not intervened. The temporary lapse of Monroeism while the United States were plunged in civil war had permitted Napoleon III. to embark on his Mexican venture, but that venture had been decisively closed when the consolidated United States found themselves free to attend to matters outside their own internal struggles. More emphatically than before, the Monroe doctrine stood as a rampart between South America and any attempts on the part of European Powers to exploit any portion of it under their own flags. Though

Germany might hunger for Brazil, she had to be satisfied with "peaceful penetration."

On the other hand, the United States still maintained for themselves as well as for the southern continent the doctrine of the political separation of the two hemispheres—recognizing neither interest nor obligation which could involve the republic in the complications and disputes of the Western world. Nevertheless, there had been in Samoa just a preliminary hint—no more—that she might find herself forced to discard her aloofness, drawn inevitably if reluctantly into the arena of world politics.

At the moment when Bismarck fell, the isolation of France was passing, as her *rapprochement* with Russia was becoming a certainty. It was precisely the situation which Bismarck had always feared, which for twenty years he had successfully averted, and to guard against which he had brought Italy into the Triple Alliance. He had striven to keep Russia in line with Germany, not because he trusted her, but because he feared her enmity. The Dreikaiserbund represented the ideal—complete concord between the three empires would give them a European preponderance so overwhelming that they could pursue their common aims without more than a superficial respect for anyone else. The fundamental difficulty in Bismarck's scheme lay in the fact that Russian and Austrian interests in the Balkans were irreconcilable. So long as the antagonisms there could be smoothed away or ignored, amity might be preserved. But periodically they became acute; if Germany were forced to take one side or the other, the Power she opposed would become hostile to her. If one must be alienated it was better that it should be Russia. For while Russian hostility might threaten Germany with a military attack, she would still have Austria beside her; whereas Austrian hostility, though not threatening a military attack, might issue in the disintegration of the German Empire itself, undoing the work of 1866 and 1870. Further, so long as Germany stood by Austria, Austria was bound to stand by Germany: whereas if Austria were alienated from Germany, to the strengthening of Russia, there was no security for the abiding friendship of the eastern Power.

The events of 1876-1878 forced upon Bismarck the choice which alienated Russia. The rupture was patched over, but the attachment of Italy to the two Central Powers in 1879 was significant of Bismarck's consciousness of danger ahead. The accession of Alexander III. brought anxious moments; they passed. The Bulgarian affair was more critical, yet the very attenuated bond was protracted in 1887 for three years—simultaneously with the renewal of the Italian alliance. How long Bismarck, with an assured tenure of power, might have succeeded in preserving it, may be a matter of doubt. But in the three years from 1887 to 1890 the prospect of a Franco-Russian *rapprochement* was becoming more marked. The fall of Bismarck clinched matters. The bond was not renewed, next year there was an ostentatious display of friendship between the republic of the West and the autocracy of the East; and though as yet no formal alliance was announced, the Entente had become an actually established fact. Something like an equilibrium, though not an overstable one, was set up.

Great Britain stood outside in an isolation which those who liked it called splendid, and those who did not called dangerous. But her attraction at this stage was towards the orbit of the Triple Alliance (which in Lord Salisbury's eyes was a guarantee of peace), not to the Entente. In fact the common prejudice against or hostility to England of Russia and France was a main motive in bringing about the Franco-Russian conjunction. At the bottom of it were the constant friction between France and England over Egypt and in Indo-China, and the much more deeply seated friction between Russia and England in the Near and the Middle East. The illwill based on distrust between Russia and England was mutual and almost ineradicable; between France and England it was not mutual and vanished when French distrust was overcome, but that was a consummation still distant. For the time being, all the probabilities were that the British Empire would stand entirely apart from any European conflict, but that if it should be drawn into such a conflict it would be on the side of the Central Powers. As between Italy and France, and as between Austria and Russia, Britain's interest and her sympathies would be with Italy and Austria, while she had as yet no reason to suspect a development of hostility to herself in Germany. Aggression on the part of the Central Powers was not to be anticipated, and aggression on the part of the Entente would, in the circumstances, be so extremely rash that the equilibrium was not likely to be gravely endangered.

Nevertheless it is improbable that Bismarck would have been satisfied with this situation; he could not regard a Franco-Russian alliance otherwise than as a menace to Germany, and his diplomacy would have been directed to separating them from each other—encouraging Russia to turn her eyes from the Balkans to Central Asia and the Far East, and France to turn hers from the Rhine to the Nile and the Niger. But Bismarck no longer controlled German diplomacy and German policy. What Germany's new master would do no one could tell, except that he would go his own way. The one thing definitely expected, from the strained relations which had subsisted between him and his English mother and Anglophil father, was that he would be hostile to Britain, an enemy of things British; yet the fall of Bismarck was immediately followed (1890) by the treaty as to Africa, which not only Germans regarded as highly advantageous to the British. Nothing specific could be inferred from his occasional histrionics concerning the German army or in magnification of his own office as German War Lord and Vicegerent of an apparently German God of Battles; it was only obvious that there would be much clanking of the German sabre—that it would be drawn from its sheath with any other object than stage-display was matter of doubt. The world was rather disposed to look upon these things as the vagaries of a young man with an exaggerated idea of his personal importance in the cosmos and a passion for posturing in the limelight. He would grow out of them. Whether behind it all he had a definite policy remained to be seen. But, immediately, there was no sign of his seeking to draw closer again to the Tsar, and some appearance of a wish to remove the impression that he was inimical to his mother's country, discernible through his erratic methods of self-expression.

On the other hand, if the Tsar's Government was manifestly turning to France as a more helpful ally, it was clear also that in Europe at least he was not likely to initiate a bellicose policy; and that neither Russia nor France, however anxious they might be to embarrass Britain and to take every available advantage of her, would willingly overstep the last bounds and entangle themselves in an armed conflict with her which Germany might turn to her own profit at their expense. Such an opportunity Germany was not likely to pass by; it was more probable that she would, on approved Bismarckian principles, endeavor covertly to create it. If either of those governments, yielding to their Chauvinists, should be drawn into a serious embroilment, they would be playing straight into Germany's hands. Thus while no one could calculate the possible effects of an explosion of exasperated patriotic sentiment, especially in France, no country was in a position to seek war deliberately. Least of all the Central Powers, since Germany's rapid industrial development pointed emphatically to peace for herself as the way to commercial prosperity.

II.—Labor and Capital

The State system of Europe and the governmental systems of the European states had undergone a revolution during the seventy-five years since Waterloo; but the old map of Europe was still recognizable. The same Great Powers were still there, though Prussia had assimilated the rest of Germany and Austria had lost her Italian possessions. The same minor kingdoms were still there though with notable exceptions, since Hanover had been absorbed by Prussia, and Naples by Sardinia, which had expanded into the kingdom of Italy. To the list of them Belgium had been added, and sundry principalities in what had been the Turkish Empire. Moreover, with the exception of France, the monarchies big and small were still monarchies in form, though in Great Britain and the Latin and Scandinavian states they had become, in greater or less degree, democracies in essence. In essence as well as in form Russia was still an autocracy; so in essence were the other two empires, though both had made formal concessions to the theory of parliamentary government. Castlereagh would have recognized the political Europe he knew, changed but not transmuted out of all knowledge.

Changes still more fundamental had taken place within the lifetime of Gladstone and Bismarck. If some one who died in Waterloo year could have been resuscitated in 1890, he would have found a world which differed more from that in which he had lived than the world he knew differed from that of Shakespeare, perhaps even of Chaucer; though at the very outset of the nineteenth century the coming economic revolution was already visibly inaugurated in Great Britain. Outside the British Isles it had not then taken tangible form. Only England and Scotland were transforming or had transformed themselves into manufacturing countries; they alone were beginning to be conscious of the miraculous possibilities of invention and the infinite complexity of the social problems for which the introduction of steam-driven machinery was to be responsible; in them alone a hungry proletariat was swarming round smoke-begrimed factories, seeking work and food for man, woman, and child, and in machinery which "took the bread out of their mouths"; only in them were to be found as yet these outward and visible signs of the problem, portentous and as yet unrealized, of capital and labor, which was to develop throughout the nineteenth century—the new variation on the old age-long problem of rich and poor. An age-long antagonism, because at the root of it lies the sense that material wealth, mainly the product of labor, is unjustly distributed, at the expense of the worker for the benefit of the employer; new, because between the employer and the worker a new relation was created.

In the old world the rich man was either the owner of the soil, who exacted from the man who worked it a share, reasonable or unreasonable, of the produce, in the form of rent; or he was the middleman, the merchant, who bought one man's produce and sold it to another at a higher price; rarely in comparison he was the capitalist who provided the materials and the tools for the manufacture of goods, paying what price he chose to the artificer. Occasionally he was the capitalist who leased to his neighbors the money which he did not want to spend himself. Class hostility in the past had been mainly directed against the landowner, because the great bulk of the population was primarily engaged on the soil. Insurrections and attempted revolutions on the motive of the poor against the rich had always been in the main risings of agricultural populations against the owners of the soil and their exactions in money, in kind, or in service; from the servile revolts in classical times to the French Revolution itself. Comparatively speaking, the grievances of the artificers against their employers had been insignificant.

Now in the nineteenth century there set in in Europe an era of rapid increase in population. Only a small proportion could be profitably engaged on tillage and pasture. Ever-growing numbers were seeking to earn their daily bread in some other employment; and for other employment they had to go to the capitalist, to the man who could provide the materials and the tools for manufacture on a large scale, or to him who was engaged in buying and selling again on a large scale—wholesaler or retailer; to the former as manual workers, to the latter as clerks or shop assistants—unless they could accumulate or borrow enough capital to start manufacturing or buying and selling on their own account. And the capitalist could make his own terms with them. He could get as much labor as he could employ for such a wage as sufficed to keep body and soul together, though he might discover by degrees that it would pay him to give more for the sake of increased efficiency. He could do so, because he could afford to wait longer than the laborer; to the latter the alternative was immediate starvation; he could not manufacture on his own account, because the tools available for him, which had served him in the old days, did not enable him to compete as a producer with the owner of the new machinery. He must have wages here and now or starve; and there were so many others in the same position that, of he refused what was offered, a few days would see the job being done by some one else in his place. The capitalist, the owner of the machinery, the provider of the materials, had become the enemy who ground down his wages and exploited his labor, in place of the landowner. Capitalists, not aristocrats, were the objects of his animosity. And associated with the manufacturing capitalists were the captalists of trade, big and small—the bourgeosie—and the money-lending capitalists, the bankers and the usurers; because they were obviously in the category of employers, wage-payers, and not obviously in the category of laborers, wage-earners.

All through the nineteenth century the mass of the populations were becoming increasingly urban proletariats, manual laborers, depending for their livelihood upon the amount of the wages which the capitalist employer thought fit to pay them; and broadly speaking the employers thought fit to pay no more than what they deemed necessary for efficient service; if they did give more they took credit for their benevolence. For more than half a century after Waterloo the laborer was virtually at the mercy of the employer, subject to some limitations imposed by humanitarian legislation—approved by employers who wished to be benevolent but were restrained by the

FEATURES OF THE NINETEENTH CENTURY 155

exigencies of uncontrolled competition. Otherwise the law, guided by unqualified doctrines of individualism, declined to fetter "freedom of contract." The action of employers in general emphasized the belief that the interests of the employer and the laborer were antagonistic. The whole position, then, was frankly intolerable to labor. Either the laborer must be able to bargain on equal terms with the employer—which as matters stood was not the case; or the law must intervene on his behalf—which it refused to do except by extending some protection to women and children. The solution therefore must be found either by combination among the workmen or by obtaining for labor the control of legislation.

The governments were too strong. All the efforts of labor to get control of legislation were routed in every quarter between 1848 and 1851. Combinations among workmen for the purpose of collective bargaining were still ineffective—partly because, for various reasons, only a comparatively small and intelligent section of the workmen, almost confined to Great Britain, made this their objective; partly because some of the combinations or trade unions were actually formed brought discredit on the whole movement by the lawlessness and tyranny of their methods; partly because the unions, even after their formation had been sanctioned, were still without any legal status. But in Great Britain the Trade Union movement held the field after the collapse of Chartism in 1848; and within the next thirty years it had gained the support of the great bulk at least of skilled workmen, it had repudiated the methods of lawlessness, and the unions had acquired the legal status and the freedom of action which made collective bargaining practically effective. In a set battle between employers and employed—a strike or a lock-out—the odds were still heavily in favor of the employers, but only at a cost which made reasonable concession without conflict preferable to a fight and a victory. And the leaders of the movement were still convinced that effective bargaining was better than legislation, more to the advantage of both parties, holding that capital and labor, employers and employed, had joint as well as, or even more than, conflicting interests. In another ten years trade unions had obtained a corresponding recognition in France.

But on the European continent the attitude had been different throughout. The antagonism of capital and labor was the fundamental conception. In England what the mass of the laborers demanded was fair pay and decent conditions for their work; if they could get that out of the employers they had no rooted objection to the employers being wealthy. Only a small proportion were seriously troubled by the idea that everything which went into the rich man's pocket was stolen from the poor man. Even the Chartists had demanded only strictly democratic reforms which should give to the numerically preponderant classes a preponderant control over legislation. That was a totally different thing from the continental Socialism which demanded a total reconstruction of the economic bases of society, starting with the hypothesis that all private wealth is robbery and only the community has rights of property; wholly subordinating the individual to the community; maintaining in effect that the community consists of the manual workers, who alone have claims upon it, and alone have the right to control collectively the materials, the means, and the methods of production and distribution. In these doctrines there was no room for collective bargaining; it was at best a mere palliative, at worst a sham remedy serving only to postpone the day when Socialism should triumph. It was only the opportunists of Socialism who regarded it as a useful stepping-stone to the real thing, the creation of the social-democratic state in which, however, the *demos,* the People, was to mean not the whole people but only the "workers."

By the time that labor combinations in Great Britain had won a secure legal position, Russia and Ireland were perhaps the only countries left in which the agrarian problem still counted for more than the industrial; and it was probably only in Great Britain that the socialistic solution of the industrial problem had not found favor with the majority of the industrial working class, though like the "middle classes," the peasantry elsewhere who had acquired proprietary rights, as in France, were as firmly convinced of the rights of property and as much opposed to an arbitrary redistribution of wealth as any capitalist manufacturer or banker. But in England the working class had simultaneously obtained a strong though not a controlling influence in the political machine, and could reasonably hope to obtain by constitutional methods such legislation as seemed to them urgent. It was mainly among the unorganized sections of labor that revolutionary doctrines found determined advocates. On the Continent generally there was little prospect of a similar emancipation of trade unions, and practically none of their exercising a direct influence on legislation. Therefore the working class could rest its hopes only on the overthrow of the existing order, and the substitution for it of the socialistic ideal.

Lest their demand should obtain to the insurrectionary pitch of insistence, Bismarck inaugurated in Germany his paternal Socialism— state intervention and state regulation of industry, not by a democratic government but in the interest of the workers; an intervention more active than that of the democratized governments in England. Between conciliation and repression he checked, but could not stay altogether, the rise of the socialistic tide. Socialism is the negation of freedom of contract. In Great Britain almost alone of European states the doctrine of freedom of contract held its ground, but with

FEATURES OF THE NINETEENTH CENTURY

the proviso that such freedom cannot be recognized as existing unless the parties to the contract are in fact as well as in theory on an equal footing.

Nevertheless the recognition of the right of combination had not eliminated the belief that the interests of labor and capital are antagonistic, and that the profits of one can be increased only at the expense of the other; it left untouched the moral argument of the laborer's positive right to a larger share in the profits, as distinguished from the expediency of granting it to him, and the opposed argument of the owner's right to manage his own business as he himself thought fit. A parallel question was being vehemently debated—the moral right of proprietors of the soil to the land of which the law recognized them as the owners; the right of the community to expropriate them with or without compensation and to make itself the universal landlord; the claim of the peasantry that neither the community nor the landlord but the actual tiller of the soil was the real owner; the comparative expediency of acting upon the several doctrines. Moreover, it was only organized labor which had achieved the power of collective bargaining, and organized labor only covered skilled employments; improvements in the position of the unskilled could only be enforced by the indefinite pressure of public opinion.

This was the position in the country where labor was at the least disadvantage in its conflict with capital, and best disposed to the view that the individual interests of both would be best served by mutual recognition of and insistence on common interests, and by mutual accommodation where the interests clashed. On that doctrine in its broadest sense, coupled with the Mazzinian teaching that we should think first not of our own rights and our neighbors' duties but of our neighbors' rights and our own duties, provides the only basis, except the domination of irresistible force, for peace upon earth. How far those principles were, and are, from being established we have seen in the Great War and its aftermath. In them is still to be found the only key to the problems with which we are faced to-day, unless the German solution was the right one. For Bolshevism as a doctrine is neither more nor less than the German doctrine, applied to social and industrial instead of to international relations.

The continental view of the industrial and agrarian questions emphasized more than in Great Britain the antagonisms between capital and labor, and at the same time introduced a strong cross-current materially affecting some aspects of nationalism. In the sixteenth century, and in a diminishing degree during the seventeenth, there had been a conflict between "Popery" and "Heresy" which cut across national divisions, setting up loyalty to Catholicism or Protestantism in rivalry to the loyalty of national patriotism. So Socialism in the nineteenth century sought to oppose the cosmopolitan solidarity of labor in the common class war against capital to the sentiment of racial patriotism; assuming that expansion, empire, and war were pursued in the interests of rival capitalist groups and to the detriment of all workers. The theory gained ground, but it was to be observed, when matters came to the practical test of the Great War, that a solid majority of Socialists in every land were as ready to fight for their respective countries against the alien aggressor as the capitalists themselves, each convinced that his own country was fighting on behalf of the whole community—or of humanity—not in the special interests of its capitalists; though probably, till the moment came, few students of the Socialist press would have prophesied with any confidence that this would be the case.

III.—*Science and Welfare*

A century of revolution had immensely altered the state systems of the Western world, which may be said to have come to birth four hundred years earlier. Exploration and exploitation had more or less completed the European expansion over non-European territories which had begun at the same epoch. The idea of democracy had established itself, and was apparently well on the way to realization. The industrial revolution had transformed the old opposition of rich and poor into the new antagonism between capital and labor; the mechanical inventions which produced and attended it had reduced huge distances to insignificance, so that a message from Calcutta to London was delivered on the same day, and a messenger could follow it in three weeks instead of six months.

It may very well be that in days to come the social historian will declare that the well-being of mankind was more advanced by the progress of medical science in the nineteenth century than by its political, mechanical, or economic developments. It would hardly be an exaggeration to say that in the nineteenth century, and especially the latter half of it, the business of healing, and still more of preventing, disease made an advance greater than in the two thousand preceding years. When it opened, leprosy, indeed, had long been rare; since the seventeenth century there had been no visitation of the bubonic plague which, as the "Black Death" and under other names, had occasionally devastated Europe in the past; epidemic cholera had not made its way to the west; but all were still to be feared. At the end of the century it had become almost inconceivable that, except under wholly abnormal conditions, any of these pestilences would ever again recur with virulence in the west. During the century typhus practically disappeared. The fell disease now known as tuberculosis is still responsible for a mortality terrible indeed, but known to be largely preventable, and not comparable to the ravages it inflicted even a hundred years ago as "decline" or "consumption." Before Jenner substituted vaccination for inoculation, a great percentage of the population died of smallpox, and a third of the rest went through life bearing the marks of a malady which a hundred years later had ceased to be a dreaded scourge. There was no known preventive or cure for the "hydrophobia" which, as "rabies," was brought under control before the last decade of the century, when the source of malaria was also traced home; and typhoid attained a pestilential severity only under campaigning conditions, where it was still responsible for more deaths than enemy shells and bullets.

The change was indeed partly due not to medical discovery but to medical insistence on fresh air and ventilation, general cleanliness, improved drainage, and the isolation of infectious diseases. The value of these had indeed always been known in a general way, but their importance was enormously emphasized by the gradual revelation that most diseases are generated by specific bacteria, many of them readily absorbed by the media of infected air, water, and milk. The detection of the microbic origins of disease led to the identification of one after another of the specific germs, which could in consequence be subjected to cultivation and experiment; from which followed the demonstration that the cultivated germ could in some cases be used by injection as a prophylactic or preventive, as vaccine forestalled smallpox, in others as a counteracting curative after the disease itself had been set up—of which rabies provided the first and diphtheria presently the most striking examples. In the twentieth century typhoid was definitely brought within the small range of diseases which could be effectively countered by inoculation.

Hardly less vital was the immense advance in surgery which, till the middle of the nineteenth century, had been precluded by the single fact that the surgeon could only operate upon the conscious patient. The discovery that the patient could safely be rendered unconscious and completely passive by being placed under chloroform was revolutionary. It made possible operations which had hitherto been unendurable and, if attempted, could only have had fatal results; it made easy and safe others which had been difficult and dangerous. It made practicable investigations conducted on the living body, which had heretofore been practically confined to corpses. It revealed surgical methods of eradicating diseases in individual cases, of which no one had hitherto dreamed. It permitted a much wider experimentation at greatly reduced risk to the voluntary or involuntary subject. And the application of anæthetics was followed by the development of antiseptic surgery, the protection of wounds from the introduction of the deadly poison germs which so often proved fatal when the actual work of the surgeon had been accomplished with entire success, by insuring the sterilization of the wound itself and of everything which could come in contact with it: a principle which was itself the outcome of the discovery of the microbic character of disease, and of the fact that what is "clean" to the eye is not necessarily sterilized—that is, free from the infinitesimal organisms which breed putrefaction and death.

In brief, sanitation, medicine, and surgery, the business of curing diseases, ascertaining their causes and stopping them at the source, and providing the conditions under which they should have the least chance of spreading, made unprecedented strides during this half-century. The industrial revolution, by herding the population in towns and factories, had threatened to ruin the physique of the industrial peoples; but the menace was countered first by the restrictions on the labor of women and children, and then by the development of control over disease. Life is preserved through infancy and childhood, maintained through maturity, and prolonged to old age, in a degree undreamed of a hundred years ago, when the conditions still did not differ profoundly from those which prevailed in the days of Hippocrates and Galen. So great was the change that some anxious observers have suggested that the progress made is itself destined to entail degeneration by preserving the inferior as well as the superior specimens of the Western races, and progressively lowering the average type, the standard preserved by the natural process of the elimination of the unfit.

That phrase brings us to the consideration of an aspect of the scientific developments of the nineteenth century which has profoundly influenced modern thought. The great astronomers, from Copernicus and Galileo to Newton, had demonstrated the insignificance of the earth as an atom in an infinite cosmos—not without shocks to the sentiment which identified the religion of Christianity with a literal acceptance of the words of the Hebrew scriptures, but infinitely enlarging and glorifying the conception of the Divine Majesty. Early in the nineteenth century it was the turn of the geologists to challenge the Babylonian and Tebraic cosmogony by demonstrating that life had existed on this planet for countless thousands of years before the creation of Man. The last entrenchments of the old belief—not, as some imagined, of Christianity itself—were stormed when the biologists proved that the differentiation of living organisms into species was the result of a process extending over ages untold, not of a single creative act, and that somewhere in an incalculably remote past Man himself shared a common ancestry with the anthropoid apes—a theory easily misrepresented as the doctrine that men are descended from monkeys.

The publication of Charles Darwin's *Origin of Species* in 1859 was in certain aspects the most epoch-making, or epoch-marking, event since Newton's *Principia*. It was the definite enunciation of the theory of the Evolution of Species by Natural Selection, the survival of the forms of life best adapted to their environment—which has preserved the ant and the rabbit beside Man, but exterminated the Plesiosaurus and the Megatherium. Man had grown up from a lower order. If the accepted doctrine—that Man was the specially created head of creation who, by his own act, had fallen from his high estate—was essential to Christianity, then either Christianity or Darwinism must be false. Darwinism was so strongly based upon facts that Christianity was forced to a fresh consideration of its fundamentals, a readjustment of the essentials of its faith and the adventitious adjuncts of its profession. It realized by degrees that the hypothesis of the Fall was adventitious, not essential; but ecclesiastical authority, clinging to its tradition, had suffered no blow so severe since the days of Luther. Nevertheless, Darwinism was but the further confirmation of the gospel of the astronomers, that the world and the universe are governed not by caprice but by law; while it still offered no solution of the ultimate paradox, the mystery of pain, which has baffled mankind since the days of Job.

Evolution, however, provided a new armory for political theorists of the most diverse types. It substituted the social organism for the social contract. It elevated heredity into the primary factor in progress. It confirmed the division of mankind into essentially superior and essentially inferior races; in another view it proved the precise contrary. The individualist claimed that to curb his freedom of action was to prevent development, the Socialist that the organism as a whole must adapt itself to the environment. The reformer argued that Man had displayed this quality which distinguished him from and gave him superiority over the rest of the creation—the capacity for adapting his environment to himself—and found therein the way of salvation. The optimist found a law of progress from worse to better, the pessimist a law of change only, under which the survival of the fittest might mean the survival of anything but the best or the most admirable: which indeed provided no guarantee against the multiplication of degenerates in a protective environment or the failure of the otherwise fittest in productiveness. In short, while the doctrine was incapable of a highly spiritual and inspiring interpretation, its common effect was to discredit all creeds deriving from authority or springing from an emotional basis, and to throw men back on scientific demonstration as the only warrant for truth—with the *non sequitur* that what cannot be scientifically demonstrated is, at least presumably, false. In other words, it tended to foster the spirit of scepticism.

The Humanitarian movement, though occasionally erring in the direction of a blind sentimentality, had in the course of the century finally obliterated slavery in all civilized communities. Checked in some of its divagations by the application of sounder economic doctrines, with salutary results, it had in other cases overridden the influence of economic theory and proved the economists to be in the wrong: the reform of the English Poor Law providing an example of the former, and the restriction of female and child labor of the latter. Public opinion at the end of the century demanded everywhere, if it did not always succeed in securing, a consideration for the helpless sections of the community, and a recognition at least of the dreariness of their surroundings, which contrasts with the self-satisfied or apathetic acquiescence of previous ages in the sufferings of the poor as a part of the incurable dispensations of Providence. The same sentiment had procured a humaner treatment of prisoners in jails and an alleviation of criminal codes, especially in that of England—which before 1830 was particularly barbarous—that did not have the effect anticipated by opponents of encouraging crime, which materially diminished in proportion to the population.

It might be said that only in one sphere, warfare, no vast changes had been brought into play in the century, except in the increased rapidity of communication and transport, the strategic mobility of troops. The magazine rifle, the field gun and the siege gun only threw a heavier weight of metal for a greater distance and with greater rapidity and precision than the old muskets and cannons which had been coming into effective use in the sixteenth and fifteenth centuries. Essentially the methods of Moltke were but variations on the methods of Napoleon and Marlborough, Turenne and Gustavus; which themselves differed from those of Hannibal in little but the substitution of the musketeer for the archer, the field gun for the javelin, and the siege gun for the battering-ram. By sea, the steamship and the beginnings of the ironclad man-o'-war had made only what was practically a tentative first appearance in the American Civil War, and then in the conflict between Chile and Peru. Tremendous changes in naval construction were indeed rapidly progressing between 1870 and 1890, but they had not yet been put in the test of actual war. The torpedo had been invented but not used; underwater craft, and aircraft were still only the ingenious fictions of imaginative writers. There had been no revolution in naval warfare since the oar-driven galley had been driven off the sea by the sailing ship.

WILL TO POWER

CHAPTER LI

PRELUDE, 1890-1908

I.—Europe: *Internal Developments*

THE two principles which we have seen at work in Europe striving for realization throughout the nineteenth century—nationalism and democracy—had by no means attained their fulfillment at its close. Broadly speaking, no doubt, the Latin nations had all but completed themselves; only fragments on the borders of France and Italy were still under alien rule. Germany had deliberately severed herself from her Austrian section, which would have been one with her under a purely nationalist division, but might as matters stood be called an annexe. Up to a certain point, but still very inadequately, the Balkans had been resolved into states on a nationalist basis. But in the Austrian Empire, nationalism had achieved only the Dual Monarchy, keeping the Slavs—north and south—in subjection to Teuton or Magyar. Each of the three empires was doing its best to eliminate Polish nationality within its own borders; Russia was encroaching upon the national rights of Finland. In different degrees, Ireland in the United Kingdom was seeking to assert her separate nationality, and Norway was demanding severance from Sweden, as Scotland two centuries back had threatened to demand severance from England. In other words, half the European states still had an internal nationalist problem big or small to deal with.

Poland lay in the grip of her three masters, helpless. The spirit of nationalism was not dead, but its power of resistance to circumstances was destroyed, and played no part in the internal affairs of the three empires. Only a European cataclysm could revive Polish nationality as a political factor. Finland was only a corner of the Tsar's dominions, and if he chose—as he did—to initiate a process of absorbing it into Russia against its will, it could offer no effective resistance; though a fresh element of disaffection towards the Russian Government was created thereby, and a fresh impetus was given to the Swedish sentiment of hostility and suspicion, which insured that in the event of a Russo-German contest Sweden would have at least a strong bias towards Germany. No other state save Sweden was affected. Nor did the world at large much trouble itself over the dissessions between Sweden and Norway which ultimately led to the separation of the crowns (1905). It was not likely that Scandinavia would ever again count appreciably in the scale when great Powers were at war with each other.

Nationalist aspirations were disappointed both in the Dual Monarchy and in the United Kingdom. In the Austrian Empire, the Germans had clung to their own race ascendency till they were driven to acknowledge the equality of the Magyars. They had only played at recognizing south Slavs as a counterpoise to Magyars. The latter, insistent on their own nationality, had been throughout no less insistent on their ascendency over the south Slavs in Hungary. In the Dual Monarchy, neither German nor Magyar abated their claim to dominate the Slavs within their borders. There were indeed statesmen—even archdukes—who would have sought to solve the problem by recognizing the third nationality and working on the line of a triple union; a method which, with goodwill, might very well have effected a genuine solidarity. But the goodwill was wanting, and so far wanting that no effective step was taken; and the resentment of the Slavs at their subordination remained a latent menace to the integrity of the Empire.

In the United Kingdom, Gladstone's action in 1886 had not only brought the question of Irish autonomy into the sphere of practical politics: it had made Home Rule the crucial problem. No one in Great Britain and few in Ireland contemplated separation as either desirable or attainable; but the few Irish separatists had behind them the large body of Irish "exiles" in America. Consequently, in the view of half Great Britain, the demand for Home Rule, a separate Irish legislature and an administration responsible to it, was merely a cloak for separatist aims. And at the same time a vigorous minority in Ireland was firmly convinced that any Irish legislature would adopt a policy of vindictiveness toward Protestants and landowners, which made them passionately resolved to resist to the utmost any form of Home Rule. In the abstract, British sentiment was entirely favorable to the theory of autonomy, nationalist autonomy, within the British as well as in every other empire; but not, in the concrete, to any autonomy which would be merely a half-way house to separation, or which would enable majorities to tyrannize over minorities. In Great Britain apart from Ireland the balance of opinion for some five-and-twenty years remained antagonistic to Irish autonomy, though the Nationalist preponderance in Ireland gave a Home Rule majority in the House of Commons elected in 1892. That House accordingly passed the second Home Rule Bill in 1893; but it was rejected by the Lords, and that rejection was confirmed by the general election of 1895. The next general election in 1900 took place in the middle of the Boer War, which was regarded as the one issue before the electorate; and in 1906 the Home Rule issue was postponed to the Tariff Reform issue which had been raised by Joseph Chamberlain in 1903. It was not till 1912 that Home Rule for Ireland could again be presented as an essential feature in a Government program. It must be remarked, however, that when once a solid body of opinion had been established in England favorable to some sort of Irish Home Rule, the ultimate conversion of a majority to that point of view was a question of time—provided that the Irish themselves did not excite opposition to it under the influence of extremist agitators and intriguers. And during these years, the growing confidence of the Nationalist leaders in the honest intentions of the Liberal party in Great Britain had a moderating effect which strengthened their cause in the sister island, though it did not modify the intensity of the opposition in Ulster.

In all the Western states a system of government had been established which, whether in the form of constitutional monarchy or republic, gave the ultimate control of policy to a democratic electorate. In the United Kingdom, however, it could not as yet be said that the will of the democracy necessarily found expression in the government. If the hereditary chamber were in disagreement with the elective chamber, which theoretically at least reflected the popular will, it could not interfere with administration or carry legislation of its own, but it could completely block all legislation of which it disapproved. So long as this continued to be the case, it could not be said that democracy was fully established, however the Lords might hesitate to offer flat opposition to measures for which the democratic mandate was impossible to dispute. The hereditary chamber was still a barrier against the democratic flood. Its supporters held that its checking action during the Liberal Government of 1892-1895 was more than justified by the result; but when the process was repeated on the return of the Liberals in 1906, it became clear that a critical struggle was approaching which would involve at least some remodeling of the second chamber and its functions—possibly in a reactionary, probably in a democratic, direction. Otherwise there were no apparent signs of a positive movement in either sense.

In Great Britain, however, it was noticeable that Socialism, hitherto combated by trade union leaders, was gaining ground among the working classes; while its progress on the Continent was still more marked, and was varied by ebullitions of what is theoretically its complete contradictory, anarchism. Socialism and anarchism both start with the hypothesis that the material fruits of labor are wrongly distributed and will not be rightly distributed till the existing social system has been destroyed. But from that point they part company. Socialism in all its forms aims at reconstruction, the substitution of a new and ordered system for that which is to perish; anarchism rejects reconstruction altogether, regarding government and imposed restraints as the essential enemies of welfare. It can hold its own for more than a moment only where the conditions of life are so intolerable that the breaking of all bonds appears to be the only remedy. In Russia alone among European states have its doctrines found a soil in which they could take root enduringly.

But this is not the case with Socialism, which, primarily economic in its aims, seeks to place the control of the production and distribution of wealth in the hands of the manual workers, and by consequence to appropriate to them political control also. But the logical consequent is the practical condition precedent. Broadly speaking, the less the political power of the laborer the stronger is his inducement to adopt the doctrines of Socialism; while the higher his intelligence, the greater is his readiness to secure the ultimate aim or part of it by co-operation with the non-Socialist. Hence there was a growing tendency in France as in England for the democratic individualist and the Socialist to find themselves acting in concert—until the later development of a new phase, when power was becoming to the Socialist not a means to an end but an end in itself.

In Germany, on the other hand, where the laborer's political power was infinitesimal, he became a Socialist almost as a matter of course with the subversion of the existing order as a primary aim. In the discipline of the German army lay the only security against the revolution; and hence the rhetorical emphasis laid by the Kaiser upon his own position as War Lord, the practical glorification of the military caste, and the ultimate insistence upon a German military domination of the world. Militarism was, in brief, the antidote of Socialism.

An urban industrial proletariat is much more alive than an agricultural population to the need for organization in production; its dissatisfaction with the existing order demands reconstructive Socialism. The lowest grade of reconstruction—Communism—is apt to present itself as a sufficient and ultimate goal to the laborer on the soil unless he rises to the conception of a personal peasant proprietary under which he shall individually own as much as he needs. In Russia, outside the bureaucracy, there was no section of the population which had not given its grievances—the Jews, whose refuge was in anarchism, but only as a step towards the most anti-social form of Socialism; the peasantry, least capable of organized action but most dangerous if they could be shepherded into any revolutionary fold; a proletariat, so uneducated as to be in the main more anarchist than Socialist; a more educated section, definitely Socialist; the most educated section, which pinned its faith to reform through constitutionalism and political liberty; a Tsar, well-intentioned, but having no key to the problem, and supremely conscious that the Government must maintain its mastery at all costs (a description which applies alike to Alexander III. and Nicholas II.). Under such conditions revolution was certain to arrive whenever the multitude of revolutionary forces should become capable of organized action or the Government should be too much weakened to repress their hydra-heads; unless, indeed, such reforms should be carried through as would tangibly ameliorate the grievances. But the years passed; the bureaucracy relaxed nothing of its grip; and when at last, after the twentieth century had opened, hope dawned with a promise of a Duma—something in the nature of a representative assembly to initiate reforms—the hope was dashed. For when the Duma was summoned its constitution gave it no power, and the Tsardom fell back, as before, upon repression instead of reform as the basic security against revolution.

II.—*The European Balance*

Until the end of the century, and for some time longer, the European Powers remained uneasily combined in the two groups indicated by the position in 1890, when the Dreikaiserbund was dissolved and the *rapprochement* between France and Russia was beginning to declare itself. The three Central Powers—Germany, Austria, and Italy—were in alliance; the Power on their eastern flank was virtually in alliance with that on their western flank, and the two groups were in practical equilibrium. Great Britain stood outside both groups in "splendid isolation"; but while there were perpetually recurring sources of friction and clashings of interests between her and each of the Entente pair, there were no apparent antagonisms between her and the *Triplice*. To Italy she had always been cordially sympathetic. In her whole history she had only once been at war with Austria, and not once with Prussia; she was imbued with the idea of her blood-kinship with the Teutonic peoples; neither Germany nor Austria had ever been of any account as maritime Powers, and both apparently acquiesced in her oceanic supremacy, so that the cession of Heligoland had been regarded as a harmless piece of conciliatory politeness. Austria in the Balkans was rather to be encouraged as a useful counterpoise to Russia; German expansion in Africa had apparently been arranged for in the treaty of 1890 in a manner sufficiently satisfactory. It seemed, in short, that nowhere were the members of the Triple Alliance in rivalry with Great Britain.

On the other hand, in the five centuries preceding Waterloo, there had once been a period of one hundred and thirty years during which France and England had only once been at war, between 1559 and 1689; otherwise there had never been continuous peace between them for more than forty years. Since Waterloo they had not fought, but there had been more than one crisis, when they had been on the verge of fighting. They had a long tradition of antagonism in the past; they had still rival interests in Northern Africa and in the Farther East. Between Russia and Great Britain there had been no hostility till the close of the eighteenth century, but since then there had been unceasing rivalry between them in the Near and Middle East which had repeatedly brought them to the verge, and once over the verge, of open war. Nothing seemed more remote than a junction between Great Britain and those Powers; while the chance of war was minimized by the consciousness of France, at least, that Germany would turn it to her own advantage. Neither France nor Russia was likely to carry hostility beyond the endeavor to hamper and worry Great Britain when opportunity should occur.

Again, even in combination, their chances of succeeding in an attack upon the Central Powers was so small that they were very unlikely to make the attempt, especially while the British were on friendlier terms with the Triple Alliance than with them. Till the Triplice should assume the aggressive and force on war, the probabilities were against any general conflagration. And as yet it appeared that each member of it had nothing to gain by war, but every inducement to preserve the peace.

Ostensibly, then, harmony prevailed in the European Concert— the harmony rather of common inaction than of united action. Turkey still rejoiced in the comfortable confidence that whatever her crimes of commission or omission might be, nobody would interfere seriously less somebody else should interfere in a contrary sense—and Abdul Hamid was quite acute enough to realize that Germany was the most useful friend he could have because she had no direct interest in either the Balkans or Asiatic Turkey. The Turk, in fact, enjoyed from those Powers which upheld the integrity of the Turkish Empire the same kind of countenance which medieval rulers extended to the Jews. He was repugnant to them; they held him in contempt as a creature outside the pale; but they could not afford to dispense with him or withhold a grudging protection. None of them made more than the most perfunctory professions of friendship or any pretense at all of confidence. Each protected him only against the others, and meant him to pay more or less heavily for the protection they gave him. But Germany, having no interests of her own at stake—had not Bismarck said that to her the Eastern Question was not worth the bones of a Pomeranian grenadier?—no desire to possess Turkish territory or to interfere with Turkish misrule, would give her protection in return for privileges which would cost Turkey nothing. The Kaiser, on the other hand, saw much to be gained from the privileges to be acquired as the easy reward of his friendship; he was, in fact, prompt enough to seize his opening. The first state visit he paid to a foreign court after his accession was to Constantinople, an unaccustomed resort for the Royalties of Christendom. It was not long before the training of Abdul Hamid's armies was entrusted to German hands. The energetic and complaisant German trader made industrious use of the opportunity presented by the sudden development of Turkish goodwill, and was very soon ousting his British and French rivals; who persisted in the belief that the Turk ought to buy what they wanted to sell to him at the highest possible price, not that they ought to discover what he wanted to buy and sell it to him at the lowest possible price. Peaceful penetration among the civilian population advanced side by side with the direction of military organization and discipline, and was joined with a benevolent abstention from irritating criticism of Turkish administration. In less than a decade German influence with the Porte predominated over that of all competitors, and William II. was complacently of all Mussulmans, the spiritual subjects of the Khalif at Constantinople, whoever their temporal rulers might be.

On one point all the Powers were in accord: none of them wished for disturbance in the Balkan peninsula. Yet unrest continued to seethe in those regions. Not one of the kingdoms and principalities there was satisfied with the territories which circumstances had allotted to it. Each wanted something that had been given to or appropriated by a neighbor, each wanted something that was still under the rule of the Turk, of which diverse states wanted identical portions.

The tendency was for Rumania and Bulgaria to gravitate towards the Central Powers. Each had its grievance against Russia, neither regarded itself as Slavonic; each had on its throne a German prince, one a Hohenzollern and the other a Coburg. The opposite tendency prevailed in Serbia and Montenegro, whose grievance was against Austria, the appropriator of Bosnia and Novibazar; each was proud of its Slavonic purity, and each had a prince of its own race. In all four there was a sentiment on the whole favorable to France and to Great Britain. Greece had no inclination towards one group more than another; perhaps she had more hopes of aid towards her aspirations from the Western Powers than from any of the empires. Whenever a partition of Macedonia should become an immediate question of practical politics, Serbia, Bulgaria, and Greece would all have something—and something different—to say about it. And of the islands under Moslem dominion, Crete at least was passionately set upon union with the Hellenic kingdom—a sentiment which was warmly reciprocated, with consequences presently to be noted.

Strong as were the influences of common interests which tended to draw France and Russia together, counter-influences had postponed the *rapprochement* and continued to delay it. They were largely of a sentimental character. For more than half a century France had discarded the legitimism which was an essential part of the creed of every Tsar; she was the mother of "the Revolution" and foster-mother of every revolutionary movement—abomination in their eyes. Tsars might wish for the friendship of France, but could be cordially disposed towards no Bonapartist or republican government. French public opinion was equally condemnatory of methods of Russian autocracy, especially as extended to Poland. Alexander III. was slow to repress his natural aversion. But practical expediency carried the day. France in her isolation needed an ally; a French alliance would guarantee Russia's security in pushing forward her Asiatic projects—she would at least be much less heavily handicapped by the fear that the Central Powers would take advantage of any embarrassments which might befall her in that quarter. Probably what really clinched matters was the financial need of Russia, and the readiness of France to lend when Germany was hanging back, in 1888-1889. Immense French loans were subscribed with enthusiasm; in 1891 the visit of a French naval squadron to Cronstadt was made the occasion of an ovation, which was even outdone two years later when a Russian squadron paid a return visit to Toulon—following on a commercial treaty, while between Russia and Germany a tariff war was waging. A mutual understanding at least for mutual support in arms against the aggression of any third party—which could only have meant Germany—was certainly established; though probably not as yet a full technical alliance.

The general situation was not affected by the death of Alexander III. and the accession of Nicholas II. in 1894. The new Tsar, like Alexander I. and II., was a dreamer and an idealist with a noble conception of his responsibilities; with all their natural amiability, but with a weaker personality than either of them; even less capable than either of handling the practical problems of statesmanship; altogether lacking the clear if narrow vision of Nicholas I. and Alexander III., the iron resolution of the former, the granite immovability of the latter; his judgment was always controlled by his entourage, and his perception of character limited; like Alexander II., he was apt to move in the direction whither his idealism led him, and then to shrink back in the fear that he had gone too far. From such a man a far-seeing policy resolutely pursued and confidently directed was not to be looked for. Russia drifted, and the drift kept her to the French alliance. That it had actually come into existence was virtually announced with some ostentation soon after the accession of Nicholas, and again more definitely in 1896.

No acute antagonism between the Powers developed during these years in Europe, though the Cretan troubles and hostilities between Greece and Turkey entailed lumbering intervention by the Concert, and the disagreement of its members led the Central Empires to withdraw from co-operation with the rest. Symptoms of Chinese disintegration brought about a scramble for concessions which fluttered the chancelleries, but did not prevent the Powers from ostensibly acting together when popular hostility, encouraged by Chinese officialdom, was directed indiscriminately against the "foreign devils" in general. The action of Russia in the Far East, if viewed with suspicion by European rivals, brought about no open rupture with them but aggravated the friction between Russia and Japan. There was a critical moment in the relations, between France and Great Britain when the British reconquest of the Egyptian Sudan and the French expansion from the French Congo brought the two Powers into collision at Fashoda in 1898, but their diplomacy was equal to the occasion, and a rupture was averted. The war between the British and the Boer republics in South Africa, which began in 1899, demonstrated the isolation of the British, and the almost universal European sympathy with the Boers threatened to make the British Empire the object of a general attack; but the manifestation of British sea-power and of the consequent immediate invulnerability of the island Power counteracted the vehemence of popular sentiment, while the vigorous support of the British flag accorded by Canada and Australasia gave proof of the solidarity of the Empire which had not been anticipated on the Continent. The Kaiser, who at an earlier stage had shown a disposition to meddle, assumed the rôle of peacemaker; and the calmer counsel of better instructed opinion prevailed.

William, in fact, had realized that the naval supremacy of Britain on one side and the military supremacy of Germany on the other would make an armed conflict between the two Powers futile. He had already, in consequence, inaugurated a naval program designed to rectify this obstacle to a German world policy, on which the first Napoleon's ambitions had gone to wreck. But so far he had hardly thereby disturbed British equanimity or appreciably excited British hostility. It was obvious that he was not yet in a position to challenge the "tyrant of the seas"; till he possessed a German fleet capable of serving at least as a counterpoise to the British fleet he must wait. He pushed forward his naval program, but as yet it had not been carried nearly far enough.

So the equilibrium continued. It was not till the twentieth century was well begun that the grouping of the Powers assumed a new complexion disturbing to German ambitions. Britain and France discovered that their interests in Africa and in the East were quite capable of a friendly adjustment by mutual goodwill, and that once they were adjusted there was no sufficient reason why the mutual goodwill should not ripen into a permanent cordiality. The reconciliation for which British sentiment had always been ready enough was effected, and agreement was reached on all outstanding points of difference. But there was more to follow. Russia's differences with Japan had issued in a fierce war—and David had got the better of Goliath. Russia was badly shaken; once more her weakness as an aggressive military Power had been demonstrated; she ceased to inspire alarm in the minds of Indian statesmen; it began to be credible that India was not to be the ultimate objective of her Asiatic expansion. Following the Franco-British precedent, Britain and Russia completed a settlement of their differences; and if mutual distrust was not wholly removed, each was readier than she had ever been before to give the other credit for honest intention. No counter-triple-alliance was made, but at least it could no longer be assumed that in the event of collision between the Alliance and the Powers of the Dual Entente, British neutrality would be more benevolently disposed to the Central Powers than to their rivals. The policy of keeping France, Russia, and Britain at arm's length from each other had broken down. It could scarcely be said, indeed, that they were standing shoulder to shoulder, but it seemed that they had at any rate come into line with each other.

Meanwhile, however, a change had been taking place in Germany which was accelerated and intensified by this development. Bismarck had no love for England, some dislike and some contempt. It pleased him to see her embarrassed and isolated; but so long as her isolation continued—and that he had found it easy enough to insure—he hardly looked upon her even as a potential enemy. Yet even before his fall she was beginning to be the enemy in German eyes. German commerce was expanding, and found its progress in the world's markets hampered by the position of British industries established before she had become a serious competitor. Germany wanted new fields for her overflowing population, colonies whither it could pass without also passing under a foreign flag; she looked abroad, and everywhere the choicest exploitable territories were in British occupation. For commerce and colonization alike, Britain's great navy and her giant mercantile marine placed Germany at an immense disadvantage: British was the ubiquitous obstacle. Nevertheless, Germany advanced everywhere. She was looking forward to the day when she should overtake and pass her rival; and she had no difficulty in persuading herself that Britain was desperately alarmed by the prospect, desperately anxious to undermine and destroy German competition.

The growing conviction was intensified when in 1903 Mr. Chamberlain inaugurated in Britain the Tariff Reform reaction against Free Trade, and German competition was proclaimed in the press and on the platform as the vampire which was sucking the life-blood of British trade. Nor was it apparently modified when Protectionist doctrines were emphatically repudiated in the electoral landslide of 1906, though a fervent desire on the part of the British people to annihilate

German trade rivalry would have insured the endorsement of Mr. Chamberlain's policy. Therefore when the exertions of diplomatists and the genial tact of Edward VII. brought about the British reconciliation, first with France and then with Russia, Germany saw in it not the desire of common sense to live in goodwill and amity instead of in an atmosphere of suspicion and distrust, but a British plot born of jealousy and spite against Germany. Hate of Britain became in Germany an invincible obsession of which the mass of the British people remained complacently incredulous—aware indeed that the sentiment was prevalent among the fire-eating *Junker* class, but firmly convinced that the mass of the German people were endowed with too much stolid common sense to be seriously infected with Junkerism.

Europe's security against war was presumed at least to rest upon the maintenance of an equilibrium which would make the issue of any armed contest so doubtful that no Power or group of Powers would court so hazardous an arbitrament save in the very last resort. But equilibrium meant that every Power must attain for itself such a standard of armed strength that no other would be willing to challenge it. The British Empire, confident in its naval supremacy, and having no territorial ambitions of rivalries in which naval supremacy would not be the decisive factor, suffered less than any of the European states from the burden of ever-increasing armament which weighed so grievously upon every one of them. It was not till the twentieth century that German naval programmes showed that Britain, too, must increase her burdens and revise her methods if she was to preserve her maritime security. All Europe, however, was overshadowed by the grim specter of a possible Armageddon, in comparison with which all past conflicts would be child's-play. Was equilibrium the sole safeguard?

It is curious to remark that the principal idealist schemes of world welfare since the close of the eighteenth century have been hatched in Russia. It was Alexander I. who desired the Holy Alliance, the brotherhood of monarchs inspired by one lofty ideal. We have seen how that conception went to wreck. It was Alexander I. who imagined a supreme court of arbitration to which all states should submit their disputes. That idea did not take concrete form, though through the latter part of the nineteenth and the first years of the twentieth centuries recourse was increasingly taken to arbitration for the settlement of debatable differences. The same strain of idealism was present in Alexander II., and reappeared in his grandson, Nicholas II., who once more appealed to the world to make concord, not fear, the guardian of the world's peace.

In 1898 Nicholas issued the rescript which was a general invitation to all states—not only the Great Powers—to join in a Peace Conference at the Hague, primarily with a view to devising means for the reduction of armaments. In that particular direction the conference of 1899 and its successor of 1907 achieved nothing. Diversities of Imperial obligations in non-European territories made it impossible to arrive at any common standard. But something was done when the first conference obtained unanimous sanction for the principle of arbitration and its practical application in the form of a permanent court of arbitration to which all states should be free to submit their differences. The beginnings were made of creating a code of international law morally binding on all states so far as they individually gave formal endorsement to its details. The second conference laid down rules for the humanizing of warfare which the signatories were pledged to observe; but the vital question remained unanswered— What would happen if any of the signatories, with or without excuse, broke faith when engaged in war? For the keeping of faith there was no sanction but that of public opinion, and public opinion counts for nothing with the brigand who deems himself stronger than his victims.

III.—*Europe: The Near East*

Whatever causes of friction, jealousy, or ill-will might exist outside of Europe and Asiatic Turkey, it was difficult to see how within that area any *casus belli* between the Powers could arise except in one quarter, unless it should be created by wilful aggression. Italy had so completely, if reluctantly, acquiesced in Austria's retention of the ethnically Italian Trentino and the historically Venetian Dalmatia, that she was joined in actual alliance with her former enemy. However passionately France might crave to recover Alsace and Lorraine from the German grip, she had no chance of achieving that aim single-handed in a duel with the military Empire, and none of gaining support in such an attempt, even from Russia. But in the Balkans and the Turkish Empire there was ever-inflammable material; and if a spark were kindled no man could tell what sort of conflagration might be the outcome. It could only be said that as yet the common interest of the Powers would require that the flames should be put out as promptly as possible.

Rumania was safe. She was completely independent; she wanted no additional territories south of the Danube; what she did want was Bessarabia, which Russia had appropriated, and Rumanian Transylvania, which for centuries had been politically united to Hungary. Bessarabia provided her with a grievance against Russia, but Transylvania did not yet constitute an equivalent grievance against Austria, and her interests virtually attached her to the Triple Alliance. If she was sore at Russia's ungenerous treatment, still to seek a quarrel with her would be folly, though in the event of a quarrel between her and the Central Powers it might be worth while for Rumania to take sides with the latter. Rumania was hardly within the inflammable area.

Bulgaria, on the other hand, was in an anomalous position. She was still a tributary of Turkey; her prince was only half-recognized by the Powers, and while he actually ruled in Eastern Rumelia his authority there was not officially acknowledged by the suzerain. But the primary interest of Bulgaria was peace, consolidation, and development. Under the iron rule of Stambuloff order was maintained and Russian influences were held at arm's length, while Ferdinand kept wary watch, committing himself to nothing and to no one. In 1894 Stambuloff resigned; looking upon himself as the necessary man, he had counted upon a refusal to accept his resignation which would have established his dictatorship more firmly than ever. But he had served his turn. Ferdinand, like William II., "dropped the pilot," who was shortly afterwards assassinated. The death of Alexander III. at the close of the year prepared the way for a reconciliation with Petersburg; the good offices of William II. served the same purpose at Vienna; Abdul Hamid preferred the goodwill of Bulgaria to its hostility, and gave Ferdinand full recognition. It only remained that when a son was born to the prince he should be baptized into the Orthodox Church and so make good the long-standing breach with Russia. By the end of the century Ferdinand's position was completely established in Europe, as it had been in the principality since the year of Stambuloff's death. Patient, wary, watchful, ambitious and unscrupulous, Ferdinand awaited opportunity, and never missed it when it offered. He made no false moves. Having achieved so much, he was well content to wait a little longer to achieve more. Bulgaria began to acquire the character of a model principality, fortunate in the astuteness of its ruler and in the aid lent to him by the tactful wisdom of his clever mother, a daughter of Louis Philippe.

Serbia was less happy. She needed, what fortune did not grant her, a leader under whom she could devote her energies to internal development and organization, before she could hope actively to pursue any wider ambitions. King Milan's ambitions were more dynastic than patriotic, more personal than dynastic, and neither his wisdom nor his morals commanded respect, though he was not without popular qualities. His personal inclinations, not shared by his people, brought him under Austrian influences. He blundered into the war with Bulgaria which was so suddenly ended by the disastrous defeat of Slivnitza, and would have issued even more disastrously but for Austria's intervention. Serbian finances, already suffering from reckless administration, were brought into a still more chaotic condition. His popularity waned, and to save it he granted in 1888 a new constitution, which included ministerial responsibility to the *Skupts-*

china—the National Assembly—and then abdicated in favor of his thirteen-year-old son, Alexander.

Something was to be hoped for from the regency ministry of Ristitch and Paschitch, but four years later (1893) Alexander brought it to a sudden end by a *coup d'état*—it had not yet freed itself from the paralyzing factions of the Skuptschina—and reverted to the earlier constitution. Austrian influences again predominated. The young king's reckless marriage to a handsome woman of more than dubious character degraded the Court, and plunged it into a welter of intrigues which culminated with the murder of both king and queen in 1903 —a tragedy as ugly and sordid as any on record. The Obrenovitch dynasty was engulfed—nothing less perhaps could have saved Serbia herself from being engulfed. The unsought crown was accepted by Prince Peter Karajeorgevitch, the representative of the rival house, whose accession was the beginning of better things, of serious efforts to reform administration and to work upon the natural lines of Serbian policy—towards the unity of the scattered Serbian peoples and the rest of their south Slav kinsfolk, and towards the thing most essential to Serbia's economic development, the acquisition of an Adriatic seaboard.

In the way of any such project stood immense difficulties, for it involved the transfer from Austria to a Greater Serbia of Bosnia, Herzegovina, and the Sandjak of Novibazar, as yet occupied by her under a very pale shadow of Turkish suzerainty, and not improbably of other Jugo-Slav provinces which had long been reluctant portions of the kingdom of Hungary. And if ever Austria should conceivably be found willing to permit the transfer, Italy would have her own historic counter-claim to *Venetia Irredenta* to put forward. Also there was the further difficulty of the triangular religious antagonism over all Jugo-Slavia between Orthodox Slavs, Catholic Slavs, and Mohammedan Slavs. For the present, at least, there was nothing to be done but to spread through all Jugo-Slavia the doctrine of Jugo-Slav unity—as vigorously as Austrian watchfulness would permit. The only appeal was to the sentiment of nationalism, fostered by the unqualified detestation of Magyar rule traditional in the Slav provinces of Hungary, and the qualified resentment in Bosnia against the Austrian Government which, if it denied liberty, had provided order and comparative prosperity. Finally, in dealing whether with Slavs beyond the Serbian border or with sovereign states, the Serbians were seriously hampered by the unhappy reputation they had acquired under the rule, or misrule, of Milan and Alexander.

And, meanwhile, Serbian, Bulgarians, and Greeks alike were severally engaged in trying to persuade the hopelessly composite population of Macedonia that it was at least predominantly Greek, or Bulgarian, or Serbian; each producing flatly contradictory statistics to

WILL TO POWER

prove their own case, convincing perhaps to themselves but to no one else.

Turn we now to the Turkish Empire. In the dozen years following the Russian War it had done nothing in Europe to call down even threats of intervention on the part of the Powers. It had accepted at the Berlin Treaty the protectorate of Austria in Bosnia and of Britain in Cyprus; since then it had submitted to the establishment of British control in Egypt, and the addition of Eastern Rumelia to Bulgaria. Abdul Hamid had, in fact, tried the experiment of standing aloof from Europe and seeking to concentrate upon a Pan-Islamic policy in Asia; meeting indeed with little success, partly, at least, because half the Mohammedan world did not recognize the Ottoman Khalifat at all and a portion of the rest was doubtful in its allegiance. Its loyalty was in some degree bound up with the Turk's temporal leadership of Islam, whereof the prestige was now preserved by little else than the fact that the Imperial city on the Bosporus was still the Turkish capital. Abdul Hamid was fain to fall back on the protection of the new friend who so carefully abstained from the rôle of moral mentor so readily assumed by those who had professed friendship in the past.

During those years he had indeed felt it necessary to walk carefully in Asia as well as in Europe, lest Britain at least, having taken upon herself specific obligations by the Cyprus Convention, should become inconveniently urgent. But in Christian Armenia there were agitating signs of a revolutionary spirit for which the Turk knows only one remedy. Whatever he might do there, Russia at least was not likely to intervene—Russia was herself very nervous about the revolutionary spirit; besides which the shameless ingratitude of Bulgaria, to say nothing of Rumania, were not encouraging to a disinterested philanthropy. Perhaps the manifest sincerity of the Kaiser's goodwill turned the scale; at any rate Armenia was becoming so revolutionary that the remedy—pure terrorism—was applied even more drastically than usual.

The massacres began in August 1894. The first reports of the slaughter gave the number of victims as 7,000 to 10,000—figures which should probably be divided by ten. The news excited such horror that the Sultan had to accept a mixed European commission of inquiry; while it was sitting the slaughter went on; before it was over, the total of victims reached, on the most "conservative" estimate, 50,000. The Powers in concert could only be moved to present a scheme of reforms, which was accepted as a matter of course—no Power was ready to take more stringent action on its own responsibility—and the agitation died down. Public interest was withdrawn from Armenia by the more immediate excitement of an insurrection in Crete and a Greco-Turkish War. With characteristic audacity the German Emperor seized the opportunity to favor Abdul Hamid with complimentary messages and presents (1896).

Crete was essentially a Greek island; a very small proportion of its population was Moslem and Turkish. It had persistently clamored for union with Greece which had been persistently refused; but the Berlin Congress had procured for it some pretense of autonomy. In 1886 Greece had attempted to snatch at Crete by force of arms, Bulgaria having just annexed Eastern Rumelia; but the Powers which gave their assent to Bulgaria's action drew the line at this new development, and Greece was forced to give way. But Crete was increasingly bent upon achieving liberation; in 1896 a fresh insurrection against Moslem domination broke out. The Sultan, under pressure, made promises; no one trusted them; in 1897 the insurrection broke out again more violently—and Greek forces were dispatched to the island in its aid.

The Powers intervened. A joint squadron occupied Canea and peremptorily stopped the fighting. They issued their orders; Crete was to have immediate autonomy but not immediate union with Greece. The Greeks were to withdraw, but no more Turkish forces were to be admitted. The Greeks refused to withdraw, and the insurgents refused to lay down their arms. Greece, in fact, had got entirely out of hand, and Greek troops were invading Thessaly. The Porte declared war on Greece (April), and in a month the Greeks had been thoroughly and ignominiously beaten by the German-trained Turkish army. Greece paid the penalty in a rectification of the Thessalian frontier at her expense, and other humiliating terms.

The settlement of Crete was undertaken by the Concert, but without the support of the Central Powers, which, as friends of the Porte, dissociated themselves from the action of the rest—Britain, France, Russia, and Italy. The admirals, who, in effect, had complete control of the situation, were allowed a free hand. The Greeks had gone, and the Turkish troops were compelled to clear out, bag and baggage. Crete at any rate was to be autonomous under the supervision of the four Powers. Prince George of Greece was appointed Governor as their joint High Commissioner, a position which he retained for eight years. A constitution was adopted for the island which was drawn up by a Cretan lawyer, who was later to be known as the greatest of Greek statesmen—Eleftherios Venizelos. An early union with Greece was generally anticipated, but it did not come. In 1904 the demands became loud, still without effect. In 1905 the islanders, led by Venizelos, proclaimed the union on their own account, but for the moment could get nothing more than the appointment of a new High Commissioner, M. Zaimis, in place of Prince George. The success of his government soon warranted the Powers in promising the early evacuation of the island by their troops.

Success attended the rôle assumed by the German Kaiser. He had made himself the trusted patron of Abdul Hamid. In 1898 he paid a state visit to Constantinople, whence he proceeded to Palestine and Syria, where he proclaimed himself as—according to circumstances—the guardian of Protestants, of Catholics, and finally of all true Moslems. And in 1902 a convention with the Turkish Government gave final sanction to the project which was intended ultimately to transform the Turkish Empire into a German colony—a German railway from Constantinople to Bagdad, with Constantinople as the half-way house to Berlin.

While the Kaiser's patronage of the Khalif was thus proving highly profitable to his own schemes for establishing Teutonic ascendency in the Near East, it did not provide Abdul Hamid with deliverance from his troubles. Crafty and elusive as he was, the Sultan could not gloze over the fact that large territories had passed out of Moslem control by the Berlin Treaty; that first Cyprus and then Egypt had become virtually British possessions; that Eastern Rumelia had gone to Bulgaria; that Crete was no longer under his sway; and these things were destructive of Moslem loyalty. A party was organizing itself—the Young Turks—nationalist in its aims, which meant to obtain control of the Government and to succeed where Abdul Hamid had failed, in making the Ottoman supremacy effective; conscious also that to effect its ends it must make use of western methods and get the rule into its own hands through constitutional forms, while making its appeal to Moslems as the patriotic party. With its headquarters at Salonika, it was able, especially after the Greek War, to capture the very important section of the army which was stationed there. But the time had not yet come for it to strike.

On the other hand, it drew strength from the perpetual chaos in Macedonia, where the various divergent elements were for many years in a state of chronic insurrection. Not that the Turk was troubled by such things, but that at last a point was reached when the Powers could no longer abstain from the intervention which was above all things intolerable to Moslem susceptibilities. Austria and Russia came to terms. The proposal of Bulgaria that Macedonia should be erected into an autonomous province met with the approval of neither, while the Powers were willing to entrust them with a joint authority as "mandatories." Under their joint auspices the disturbed area was parcelled out in 1904 among the Powers—Germany standing aside—who were to supervise a reformed administration, with little enough practical effect. Germany even joined with the rest in 1905 in imposing an international commission to direct the finances of the province, thus emphasizing the grievance of the Young Turks and Abdul Hamid's inability to resist the Christian demands. But the Macedonian puzzle remained unsolved.

IV.—Asia: The Middle East

While within Europe the perturbing international factors manifested themselves in the Balkan and Ægean area, movements no less portentious, in which all the leading European Powers were involved, were taking place in the Farther East, where it will be convenient to deal first with what may be called the middle section.

After the Pendjeh affair, when an alarming crisis in the Russo-British rivalry was successfully tided over, the course of events generally tended towards a better understanding between the two great Powers. Russia had apparently made up her mind that nothing was to be gained by keeping Afghanistan in a state of perpetual uneasiness. The Amir made it clear enough that he would resent by every means in his power any British interference within his own dominions, but also that, subject to that proviso—so long as he could trust the British Government—he would be equally impervious to Russian threats and blandishments. Hence the still unsettled frontier questions in the Pamirs were amicably settled before the accession of Nicholas II. Successive British viceroys achieved that compromise between the military forward policy of Lytton and the "masterly inactivity" of Lawrence which effectively strengthened the frontier without too dangerously exciting the Amir's susceptibilities, although there were moments of anxiety.

On the other hand, as the menace of the Russian approach towards India by way of Turkestan began to lose its terrors through the agreed and finally harmonious delimitation of frontiers, danger through a Russian absorption of Persia gave renewed grounds for British anxiety. The British had a prescriptive claim to control over the waters of the Persian Gulf, which secured the free entry of commerce; but there was no contact of British and Persian land frontiers. On the other hand, both east and west of the Caspian Sea, since 1881, Russian territory—some of which had formerly been nominally under the sovereignty of the Shah—marched with that of Persia. Commercial penetration was easy and inevitable, and under the existing conditions of Persian government pointed very definitely to political ascendency; and political ascendency would mean in effect a Russian port in the Persian Gulf challenging British control there, and very probably Russian monopolization of Persian trade—besides opening a new line of pressure towards India on the flank of Afghanistan and through Baluchistan.

Nor was this all, for at the opening of the twentieth century the German railway from Constantinople to Bagdad and Basra had its sanction from the Porte—obviously with Persia and the Persian Gulf in view. A third rival was entering the field, very energetic, very insidious, and unquestionably ambitious; a common threat to Russian and British interests. But it had one beneficial effect: it quickened the disposition of the threatened rivals to adjust their interests and compose their differences lest the third party should appropriate all the solid benefits. Both were now on the friendliest terms with France; any active inclination to aggression on Russia's part met with a heavy set-back in her war with Japan; and the outcome was a convention in 1907 which defined the sphere of influence of the two Powers, and sealed the new Entente.

There was indeed still another reason for seeking an immediate understanding. The political ferment of the West in the nineteenth century, working to the two issues of democracy and nationalism, had penetrated the profound conservatism of the Oriental mind. The Western conceptions had been grasped with an extraordinary intelligence and applied with an astonishing adaptability by Japan; elsewhere they were troubling the waters. The Turks had played at creating parliamentary institutions; Egypt had raised the cry of Egypt for the Egyptians; even China in a few years' time was to proclaim a republic. The ideas themselves and the conditions necessary to their realization were little enough understood even by the majority of those who caught at them most eagerly; but they were summed up in the desire of the educated sections, who had come in contact with Western doctrines, to attain self-government through representation and to be rid of the domination of the autocrat and still more of the foreigner. The ferment was at work in Persia; the Government was likely to find itself in difficulties, to the jeopardy of the interests of the foreigners—and the latter would inevitably find plausible if not imperative reasons for intervention. In that even it would obviously be better for both that any action taken by either Russia or Britain should have its basis in a mutual understanding, not in mutual distrust and more or less veiled antagonism.

Signs of the movement were already apparent in India, and its gradual increase complicated the work of the Government there. The European living in the West rarely realizes that approximately one-half of the peninsula is ruled by native princes on traditional principles and by traditional methods; the British Government leaves the feudatory states complete autonomy as concerns the regular administration, which is wholly native. It reserves to itself the sovereign powers in relation to military establishments, war and peace, treaty making; it requires decency and order to be preserved by the rulers; it maintains the general peace; but it derives no revenues from the feudatory territories, does not administer them, does not legislate for them. But in the other half every department of government was in British hands. An army of natives was employed in the Government service, but the higher grades of the civil service and commissions in the army were reserved to Europeans; in effect no white man was the subordinate of a native. Natives held high appointments in the judiciary, but their jurisdiction over Europeans was extremely limited. Natives were admitted to advisory councils, but they were not sent there by proper election. The people which on its native soil could claim to be in fact the most democratically governed in the world was ruling half the peoples of India as a dominant race—intensely conscious of its responsibilities, earnest in its endeavors after the welfare of its subjects, deeply convinced that its own lordship was the one condition absolutely necessary to preserve the whole great dependency from falling into complete disintegration and a wild welter of war and lawlessness; but ruling by the methods of benevolent despotism. By despotic methods alone has any Eastern people ever been governed, but they are absolutely irreconcilable with doctrines either of nationalism or of democracy; of which the first assumes the spirit if not the actual fact of racial unity, and the second the equal claims of all classes in the community to a share in the effective control of the government—doctrines as repugnant to the native princes as to the European rulers over Oriental populations.

In the British view the domination of the white race was a necessity, precisely because the spirit of national unity was wanting in a population so heterogeneous as that of India: democracy was impossible to reconcile with the caste system of Hinduism, and impracticable where the vast bulk of the people were illiterates. Each might be desirable as an ultimate goal, but was attainable only, if at all, by generations of education, and the very gradual admission of natives to participation in the higher functions of government. But on the other side was the ever-present undercurrent of resentment against foreign control which was only a shade more acute than in the old days when to the Hindu the foreigner had meant the dominant Mussulman, Turk or Afghan. The racial antagonism between the Oriental and the Western was easily identified as the spirit of national unity. Popular liberty or democracy was no less easily identified with the control of government by the class which was politically ambitious, but was not in the British view the most capable of shouldering the burden of political responsibility. But it was this class which monopolized the vernacular press, organized its own political activities, and claimed to speak with the "Voice of India" in the "National Congress" which it had brought to birth in 1887. From that time its agitation for the acquisition of political powers and its campaign against the British domination became increasingly active, fostering unrest, sometimes developing into undeniable sedition, and generally embarrassing a government always anxious to satisfy legitimate demands but bound to present an adamantine resistance whenever concession could be attributed to fear, or clemency to weakness.

In all communities there is an element antagonistic to the government, of which it is conscious as a restraining, not a protective, force, and an element which is ready to believe that the existing control is exercised with a sinister intent, not in the interest of the general community. Especially this is the case where the benevolent activities of the government take forms not understood, and therefore the more easily misrepresented and misinterpreted, by the mass of the governed. Thus in India there is always a large body ready to be excited by a seditious propaganda, as at the time of the sepoy revolt. At the same time there is a widespread consciousness of the essential necessity for a paramount control attainable only through the British *raj*, which insures a solid body of loyalty, shaken only if it is suspected that the government is not strong enough to carry out its task and make its control irresistibly effective. The moral justification for the rule of the foreigner is that it is the only alternative to anarchy; if it is not a security against anarchy, if it cannot or dare not enforce its control, its justification vanishes; and if it can only enforce its control by methods which rightly shock morality, its justification fails —that is, if it is really morality, not sentimentality, that is shocked, a distinction not always easy to draw. The British raj has justified and restored the balance of loyalty through serious crisis. But the point to be dwelt upon here is not that fluctuations in that balance were engendered by the new ideas, but that the ideas themselves now for the first time germinated in a new soil and have created a new problem in the East without historical precedent—the problem of reconciling paramountcy with the self-government, the popular right to which Eastern peoples have never before laid claim, and of which, unlike the Westerns, they have hitherto in practice had no experience whatever.

V.—*Asia: The Far East*

Japan's scientific adoption and adaptation of Western ideas gave her twenty years after the fall of the Shogunate—the constitution of 1889, an army reorganized on European models with European equipment, and something more than the nucleus of a navy. Her finances were acquiring a sound basis. She was not yet recognized as a Power, but if the prudence of her diplomacy had permitted Russia's annexation of Saghalien on the north, its shrewdness had secured to her the Loo-Chow Islands on the south. China had become uncomfortably aware of her advance and suspicious of her aggression. The relations of both China and Japan with Korea were a standing source of friction; and in the eighties China was already contemplating a war with the direct object of treating her very much as Prussia treated France in 1870-1871.

That aggressive intent was restrained by Li Hung-chang's insistence on the necessity for developing an overwhelming naval and military superiority as a preliminary. But though that particularly astute Minister was thoroughly alive to what was needed, the deadly inertia of the Chinese system and the utter incapacity of the Chinese officials for organized and active co-operation proved insuperable obstacles to getting the needful thing done. While Japan was quietly, persistently, and scientifically turning to account everything she had learned or could learn from Europe for perfecting her fighting forces by land and sea to the utmost of her power, China with her much greater resources and infinitely greater man-power continued to neglect her opportunities and to effect practically no improvements till in 1894, the crisis was reached which plunged her into war with her island neighbor.

By that year the prestige of Japan as a civilized state had risen so far that Britain took the lead in accepting the treaty revision on which so much store was set by the Japanese; the treaties having been imposed on the then sound hypothesis that Japan was in the category of semi-barbaric states which are permitted only a very limited jurisdiction over other nationals resident therein—a restriction of sovereignty applied to no European or American state, however insignificant and powerless. It may here be remarked that the lead thus given was in the course of the next five years followed by all the treaty states, so that by the end of the century Japan was no longer deprived of rights universally recognized in the West.

The immediate cause of the collision between China and Japan lay in Korea. In the remote past Japan had sought unsuccessfully to annex that kingdom, which had retained its isolation and independence, save for a shadowy claim to suzerainty occasionally asserted by China. When Japan embarked upon her new course, the Korean monarch ostentatiously repudiated all further relations with the degenerate state which opened its gates to the foreign devils and its ears to their offensive doctrines. War was avoided only through the resolute self-restraint of the Mikado's Government, till in 1875 a challenge was thrown down which could not be overlooked. Korea was promptly and ignominiously compelled by a mere display of force to accept a treaty dictated by Japan, which forced her to open her gates and to admit the residence of a Japanese envoy.

At the back of Japan's intervention in Korean affairs was her fear that the peninsula would fall an easy prey to Russia, which would certainly seize any plausible occasion to take possession of Manchuria. Japan, in short, wished to preserve Korea as a buffer, much as the British in another quarter sought to preserve Afghanistan as a buffer. But the Afghans were a turbulent and warlike folk, fiercely independent, who could be counted upon to defy and resist Russia to the utmost, so long, at least, as they were tolerably free from fear of British aggression; the Koreans were a feeble folk, incapable of offering a stubborn defiance to anybody. It soon became evident that there was no prospect of organizing Korea as a vigorous independent buffer state, and the Japanese legation at Seoul soon made itself as unpopular as the British had been at Kabul in 1840 and 1879. There were serious disturbances in 1882, and again in 1884; Chinese troops, which were present on behalf of the suzerain, took part in burning the Japanese legation. But neither the Mikado nor Li Hung-chang wished for war, and a treaty was patched up, of which the effect was that both China and Japan withdrew their troops from Korea; but the Japanese Resident found his own influence countervailed and dominated by that of the Chinese Resident.

The country was desperately misgoverned; the anarchy and insurtion reached such a pitch that appeal was made to China (1894). The arrival of Chinese troops and a corresponding body of Japanese troops (in accordance with the treaty arrangements) overawed the insurgents, but it was obvious that the anarchy would break out again on their withdrawal. Japan proposed a joint insistence upon the introduction of reforms. China refused co-operation, asserting Korea's right to manage her own affairs. Japan then acted on her own responsibility; an ultimatum requiring the adoption of reforms met with an unsatisfactory reply, and Japanese troops at once occupied the capital. Two days later actual hostilities between China and Japan began (25th July) with the sinking of one Chinese man-of-war and the capture of another.

In eight months the war was ended by an armistice, followed by the Peace Treaty Shimonoseki. In the first three months the Chinese had been cleared out of Korea across its northwestern boundary, the Yalu River, and the much smaller Japanese fleet had won the command of the sea. The Liao-Tung peninsula was the next objective; Port Arthur was captured in November. Wei-hai-wei commands the entry to the Gulf of Pechihli on the opposite side to Port Arthur; there the Chinese fleet lay in harbor. The port and the fleet were captured early in February (1895). An advance on Peking was threatened; opposing Chinese armies met with more defeats. China was beaten; the task of making terms was laid on Li Hung-chang, who negotiated the Shimoneseki Treaty.

The prestige of Japan was enormously enhanced. In eight months she had won a complete and decisive victory and given a striking demonstration of the effectiveness of her organization, the value of her soldiers, and the skill of her commanders. But her success was not at all to the liking of one at least of the Great Powers, and she was firmly forbidden to reap the fruits of her toil. That Russia would throw obstacles in her way was certain—and that France would give Russia at least moral support. Britain, on the other hand, was benevolently disposed, and was not at this time on the friendliest terms with those two Powers. The presumption was that if Germany intervened at all it would be in favor of Japan, but she had not hitherto taken a prominent part in Far Eastern questions.

The action of Germany was the surprise of the hour. She deliberately ranged herself on the side of Russia. In face of the combination Britain could certainly take no strong action on the other side. Japan could not defy the veto of the three Powers. She submitted with dignity; but she did not forget.

The treaty as negotiated ceded to her the Lia-Tung peninsula with Port Arthur and Talien-wan; and besides trading rights and the island of Formosa, gave her a heavy indemnity, with the occupation of Wei-hai-wei till this should be paid off. Immediately Russia and France with suavity, and Germany in more truculent vein, warned Japan to withdraw her claim to Liao-Tung. She did so, biding her time; but she remained in Wei-hai-wei, and the indemnities she received went to her war chest; when her time came, the use she made of them was manifested. Meanwhile she found that the ejection of China from Korea resulted in the substitution of Russian for Chinese influence in that kingdom.

The three intervening Powers were duly rewarded by China. France got concessions in Yunnan (the province bordering on Tonking) and on the Yangtse; Russia was permitted to carry the Trans-Siberian Railway (begun in 1892) across Manchuria to Vladivostock instead of along the boundary river, the Amur; Germany was given her own quarters in the city of Tientsin. The scramble for China had begun—a little prematurely. The time had not come for carving her into sections.

The aims of Germany were not obvious. She had not troubled about the Far East in Bismarck's time, when she professed to have no interests of her own even in the Balkans. William II. had different views as to the Near East, and very possibly as to the Far East also in connection with his doctrine, promulgated just at this time, that Germany's future was on the seas; or conceivably he had no more subtle purpose than to assume a friendly pose toward Russia and France in circumstances which would entail no disadvantage to Germany. But it is at least easier to believe that he was aiming at bringing about precisely what presently befell—the involvement of Russia in trouble with Japan, an issue directly led up to by the events of the years immediately following. With Germany ranged on the side of Japan Russia would have held her hand; the German policy tempted her forward, and ultimately drew her into a disastrous duel, at an immense distance from her own base, with a small but highly organized Power whose base was practically on the spot. Possibly William omitted to contemplate another outcome of Germany's action—the development of the marked goodwill already subsisting between Japan and Great Britain, then and for some years to come, made her in certain respects a usually negligible factor. Her friendship with Japan would hardly bring her into collision with Germany, but might well make France hesitate to bring her fleet into the balance on the Russian side. There is no doubt that at a later stage the Anglo-Japanese alliance was encouraged by Berlin.

However, that may be, Korea at once became a source of friction between Japan and Russia in place of China. But the next move in the scramble was made by Germany. The murder of two German missionaries in 1897 provided a pretext for seizing Kiao Chau, to the south of Wei-hai-wei, as compensation. China yielded (1898), and leased Kiao Chau to Germany for ninety-nine years. For this Russia required compensation, and got it in the shape of a shorter lease of Port Arthur and Talien-wan, with the concession of a branch line of the Manchurian Railway to Port Arthur. France and Great Britain could not be left out; Kwang Chow Wan, in the far south, was leased to the former, and Wei-hai-wei (with Japan's approval) to the latter. Russia's acquisition of Port Arthur—the concession meant her early and complete control of Manchuria and Liao-Tung—brought a Russo-Japanese war perceptibly nearer.

Justification for these proceedings was found in the discovery of the Yellow Peril, the urgent need that European and Christendom should guard itself against a conjunction of China with Japan. The scientific energy of Japan, working on the vast masses of China and rousing them from the inertia of centuries to obliterate Western culture under an irresistible Mongol deluge, was a danger far more terrific than the overwhelming of the Roman civilization by the Teutonic barbarians or the advance of the Crescent against the Cross. The Kaiser, for whatever reason, was a fervent advocate of this doctrine, which had many zealous partisans, though it hardly seemed probable that China could be quickened into sufficient vitality to make the menace immediately serious. But while Germany adopted this attitude with apparent sincerity, she could hardly be suspected of promoting a conflict between Japan and Russia in the hope and belief that Japan would emerge victoriously.

China, however, was in a state of unrest. The Emperor Quang Hsu had been impressed by the advance of Japan, and sought to take example by her; but unfortunately he had not, like the Mikado in 1869, a powerful and alert body of sympathizers. He decreed reforms rational enough in themselves but abominable to public opinion; consequently in 1898 the Dowager-Empress Tzu Hsi effected a *coup d'état,* deposed him, and in effect assumed control of a government directed to thorough-going reaction, and especially to the elimination of the foreigner. Independently of this, the ominously aggressive presence of the foreigners was probably largely responsible for an insurrection in North China, analogous to that of the Tae Pings, known as the Boxer Rebellion, to which various and divergent causes are assigned. But it was certainly associated with the popular hostility to the foreigners, and while it was ostensibly directed against the government, it was, at first secretly but later openly, fostered by Tzu Hsi as a means to the expulsion of the intruders.

In 1900 troops were dispatched, officially to suppress the insurgents, with whom their relations became immediately friendly. The Peking mob attacked the foreign legations and cut them off from communication with the outside world. In Manchuria the population rose against the Russians. The Powers took united action—including Japan, whose forces were the most readily available. All supplied contingents; the allied troops marched on Peking, where they found that the legations had not, as was commonly rumored, been exterminated, but had maintained a successful resistance.

Peking was occupied with little difficulty. The allies did not use their victory to obtain further concessions, but contented themselves with additional guarantees of security; and though the Empress, who had taken flight, was in effect reinstated, severe penalties were inflicted on the authorities who had instigated the rising. The progressive section could lift their heads again, and an era of constitutional reform was inaugurated with better prospects of success than had hitherto appeared.

Japanese prestige had again been raised by the admirable conduct of the Japanese troops throughout the affair. In 1902 her position was decisively recognized by a treaty of alliance with Great Britain. It may be remarked that the Boer War, which was brought to a conclusion at the same time, had emphasized the isolation of that Power, and also her maritime supremacy, which Germany's naval program was intended to undermine. There was still extreme tension in her relations with France. The alliance meant primarily that in the event of a conflict between Russia and Japan the intervention of a third Power on behalf of Russia would bring Britain into the field on behalf of Japan. France was not prepared to challenge the British navy, hence the alliance insured that the conflict, if it came, would be a straightforward duel—which would seem to have been precisely what Germany desired; and therefore German diplomacy helped to bring about the alliance and to prevent a sincere and friendly accommodation between Russia and Japan, by which the armed contest could have been averted. Germany did not join the alliance herself, for to have done so would have been to play into the hands of Kuropatkin and others who disapproved of the entanglements in the Far East which Germany wished to encourage, and desired to concentrate upon the dangers and difficulties of the situation in Europe.

So in Russia what was called the Far Eastern or Manchurian party predominated, calculating that either Japan would give way or in the alternative would be crushed. In 1903 Japan sought a solution in the proposal that Russia should predominate in Manchuria (which she had in fact filched from Japan), and Japan in Korea. The Russians reply required in effect that Russia should have a free hand in Manchuria for all purposes, while Japan should not have a free hand in Korea for military purposes. But Japan had no intention of giving way. The Boxer affair had given her the chance of comparing her own efficiency with that of her big adversary, and she was as confident as the English mariners had been when they defied the Spanish Colossus. She proposed exclusive control, for Russia in Manchuria, for Japan in Korea. On February 6, 1904, three weeks having passed without a reply, she withdrew her ambassador from St. Petersburg. Two days later Japan opened the fighting.

She had chosen her moment shrewdly. She could put immediately into the field forces greatly outnumbering all the Russian troops then in the East; the Russian fleet there was somewhat the larger, but for the present had a squadron ice-found at Vladivostok. Russia had, of course, infinitely larger reserve of men to draw upon, but they could arrive only by the single line of the Siberian Railway, which was only approaching completion and in which there was still a great gap about Lake Baikal. It would be months, before reinforcements could be on the spot. The primary need was that before that time Japan should establish herself in Manchuria and secure the command of the sea.

On 9th February a naval engagement crippled the main Russian fleet at Port Arthur, where thenceforth an effective, if not quite complete, blockade was maintained. Thus having control of the sea, Japan could pour her troops into Korea, where Kuroki was placed in command. The Russian chief, Kuropatkin, concentrated at Liao Yang. His business was to adopt Fabian methods, avoiding a heavy engagement till he should be sufficiently reinforced to strike decisively, but checking and delaying the Japanese advance. In May the Russian force holding the right bank of the Yalu was outmaneuvered, defeated, and driven back. Within a few days the Japanese second army was disembarked on the Liao-Tung peninsula, to cut off Port Arthur on the land side; before the end of the month that object had been achieved by heavy fighting at Nanshan. The siege of the blockaded port was left to General Nogi with the Japanese third army.

It is unnecessary to follow the events of the campaign in detail. The defense of Port Arthur was long and stubborn. In spite of desperate fighting at the end of July the Japanese made no great progress; a furious attack later, in August, was repulsed with heavy loss. In the interval the Russian fleet, sallying forth from Port Arthur, was in effect wiped out by Admiral Togo. At the end of the month the two main armies, whose numbers had now been brought up to over 150,000 on each side, met in the nine days' battle of Liao Yang. At the end of it Kuropatkin was forced to fall back to Mukden, but the attacking Japanese had suffered losses considerably heavier than those of the defense. Great reinforcement encouraged Kuropatkin to assume the offensive in October. In the ensuing fifteen days' battle of the Shaho the victory again lay with the Japanese, whose losses on this occasion—some 20,000—were nearly doubled by those of the Russians. But the defeat was in no sense a rout, and on both sides there followed a long and necessary pause for recuperation in this area.

At the end of the month another sanguinary onslaught at Port Arthur was repulsed after desperate fighting. Nogi, however, could not afford to rest. Russia had been fitting out in the Baltic a fresh fleet for the East; it had actually sailed some days earlier under Rozhdestvensky. The capture of the port before its arrival was of vital importance. Reinforcements were hurried over from Japan; on 25th November the attack was renewed and maintained for ten days, at the end of which great gains had been made, but at heavy cost, and the fall of the fortress still seemed remote. But during the next three weeks more points were captured, and on 1st January the commander, Stoessel, surrendered; though it would appear that he could still have held out for some weeks, and possibly months.

The fall of Port Arthur released Nogi with 100,000 men to take part in the Mukden campaign. By the middle of February each side had some 300,000 men on the Shaho front. The Japanese right opened the attack on February 23, 1905; Kuropatkin weakened his right to meet it and then found that flank being forced back by Nogi, and only with great difficulty prevented it from being turned and enveloped as it wheeled back while his left and center maintained a resolute resistance, though the whole line was forced to retire to the positions which it held before the middle of March till the end of the war, leaving the exhausted enemy in possession of Mukden. Neither Russians nor Japanese were in a condition to renew an offensive.

Russia, however, was still to make her last bid for the command of the seas. Rozhdestvensky had waited to train his half-trained crews. At last in May he appeared in the China seas, making for Vladivostock. On 27th May Admiral Togo brought the fleet to an engagement off the island of Tsushima—and annihilated it. Tsushima was the Japanese Trafalgar. There was nothing more to be gained: the sea supremacy was finally decided; on land Russia could not hope to recover what she had lost or Japan to gain more than she had won. Through the good offices of the United States, negotiations were opened between the belligerents which issued (August) in the Treaty of Portsmouth (in the U.S.A.). Russia was to evacuate Manchuria, and to give up half Saghalien; Japan to enter into possession of the

Liao-Tung peninsula with its ports, and to hold the domination of Korea undisturbed.

Japan had definitely taken her place among the first class fighting nations of the world, by land and sea. More decisively than ever it had been demonstrated that Russia, despite her size and her impenetrability to attack, should inspire little fear as an aggressor. Incidentally, the war had laid the bogey of Russian designs against India, and so prepared the way for an understanding with Britain as well as with France. And on the other hand it had satisfied William II. that Russia would not for many years be a menace to German ambitions.

In certain aspects the war was a link between the wars of the past and of the future. It belonged to the past, as a war of maneuver; but the final Manchurian campaign had produced an extended battle-front such as had never before been known. The use of high explosives in the battering of entrenchments was born but was yet in its infancy. By sea it was the first in which the torpedo had played an important part; even the great armored battleship, with its gun-range of many thousand yards, had never before been put to the test though it had played a part as long ago as in the war between Chile and Peru. Wireless telegraphy was employed on Togo's fleet. But the motor car had not yet come into active service on land, nor the submarine under the sea, nor the airship and airplane in the sky; and poison gas was still an almost unimagined horror—the world had not yet risen to the heights—or sunk to the depths—of superman Kultur, as applied to the art of war.

VI.—Africa

The Italian venture in East Africa continued to be in the main disastrous. The interpretation of an Abyssinian treaty as conveying sovereignty to Italy was repudiated by Abyssinia; the attempt to enforce it in arms resulted in heavy defeats; and in the issue the Erythrean colony was narrowly circumscribed. Somaliland, on the south of Abyssinia, was particularly between Italy and Great Britain, but could hardly in itself prove a profitable or attractive sphere of colonization to either. On the Mediterranean, France, which had secured Tunis, and Britain, which was established in Egypt, would offer no opposition to Italian influence in Tripoli; but this set the practical limit to Italy's African ambitions.

In North Africa, exclusive of Egypt and Morocco, France had the field clear for expansion after an agreement with the British in 1890, though it was not till eight years later that boundaries were delimited in the western Sudan, where, as yet, the Khalifa, the Mahdi's successor, was Prophet and Lord to the wild untamed tribes. In the southern ocean also the claims of France in Madagascar were not disputed by any European Power; and the resistance offered to the French Protectorate by the Hovas led to its definite annexation in 1895.

In German East and West Africa the Germans were organizing their rule after their own peculiar fashion, but with no great profit either to themselves or their subjects; while in Central Africa the Congo State was being worked with much profit to the King of the Belgians and none to the negro tribes, though for this the Belgian people had no responsibility.

After the fall of Khartum, the British had insisted on the withdrawal of Egyptian troops from the Sudan to the frontier station at Wadi Halfa, until such time as the army should be fit to undertake the reconquest of the whole region, which was still formally claimed as under Egyptian sovereignty. And it was still the theory, that the British were only in temporary occupation of Egypt till she should be so reorganized as to be able to fend for herself once more.

With infinite benefit to the fellahin, the organization proceeded year by year under British administration; but while the system established such order, justice, and prosperity as had never before been known, its effectiveness depended wholly upon its being administered by white men with an immemorial tradition of public duty and responsibility which forbade them to turn their opportunities to account for private gain. The Oriental tradition being the precise contrary—that public services existed for the enrichment of the officials, who should neglect no conceivable means to the attainment of that end—all responsible work was reserved to white men; so that it could hardly be pretended that the Egyptians were being trained to the practise of self-government, or that the day when they should be fit to exercise it was drawing appreciably nearer.

But while the civil population of Egypt was enjoying an unwonted prosperity, and numbers of the fellahin were being drilled into an efficient soldiery under Herbert Kitchener's discipline, the Sudan was in a welter of anarchy, dominated by the fanatical hordes of the Khalifa, a perpetual menace to Egypt itself. In 1896 the time had come to push the frontier forward; it was carried up to Dongola. Everything was now being organized not merely for a march against the Khalifa but for a complete reconquest. The advance began early in 1898: as the army went forward, the railway followed. By the decisive engagement of Omdurman—not without one very critical moment for the British—the "dervishes" were shattered, the Khalifa's power was wiped out, and the *de facto* sovereignty of Egypt in the Sudan was established far more effectively than it had ever been in the past.

During these years the French had been extending their control over the French Sudan, from Nigeria and from the French Congo.

From the latter a small expedition had been making its way towards the upper Nile while Kitchener was preparing and starting his campaign. Ignored in consequence by the Khalifa, it had reached Fashoda —well within the area of the Egyptian Sudan—and there hoisted the French flag. There Kitchener found it. But for his advance, the valiant little party would without question have been annihilated by the dervishes. French sentiment, intensely susceptible on all matters relating to Egypt, was violently excited by the British refusal to recognize the French as already in effective possession of Fashoda, but the wisdom of the French Government prevented the incident from having any more disastrous result than some widening of the breach between the two nations; and the frontiers were delimited by mutual agreement. The south of the Egyptian Sudan now marched with the British Protectorate of Uganda. But for the section where German East Africa intervened, British dominions, protectorates, or spheres of influence extended continuously from Cairo to the Cape.

In South Africa trouble was preparing, which came to a head soon after the Sudan settlement. The convention of 1884 had left the Transvaal republic as well as the Orange Free State in complete practical independence except in relation to external Powers, though the terms had never been laid down with adequate precision. When the Boers trekked in 1836 they were British subjects, and remained technically British subjects when they migrated across the Vaal and the Orange. The British title to the sovereignty had never been formally abrogated by the various concessions of self-government; and it was still possible for Boers and British each to claim rights of which the other might challenge the legality.

The Transvaal president, Kruger, himself one of the original trekkers, believed with conviction that the Dutch had, and the British had not, the moral right to the rule of South Africa. Now the two Boer states found themselves completely encircled, with all prospect of expansion or of access to the sea cut off by the British expansion from the Cape on the west and round the north over Matabeleland, Mashonaland, and all the territory which now became known as Rhodesia. Dutch or Boer nationalism in South Africa was to be cribbed, cabined, and confined. And then there came a new development. With the discovery of gold reefs in the Transvaal, there poured in a flood of people from outside—"Uitlanders," British, German, and what-not—to exploit the mines which offered little attraction to the Boers. The revenue would profit by their admission, and they were admitted. But if they became citizens they would soon swamp the Boers, to all intents and purposes the republic would cease to be a Boer state, and Boer nationalism would be smothered. The Uitlanders were not allowed to become citizens—to be "naturalized"; in defiance of the custom of all European states and of the freedom accorded to settlers in

Cape Colony from the Transvaal itself. Moreover, they were denied sundry elementary rights, and were subjected to obligations—such as was service—usually restricted to citizens. The oppressive conditions did not keep the Uitlanders from flocking to Johannesburg, reckoning that the president would be unable to resist the outcry for their relief.

Kruger was immovable; the outcry grew louder; Dr. Jameson with a troop of volunteers rode into the Transvaal to deliver the Uitlanders (who made no move) from their "helotry," found himself in a trap, and had to surrender (1896). Every one hostile to the British Government of the day—in Britain, in Europe, or in Africa—suspected it at least of complicity. The Kaiser sent the president a congratulatory telegram which stirred much indignation. Not only did the raid immensely strengthen the position of Kruger, who managed the situation with great skill; the European sympathy evoked confirmed his conviction that he would receive more than moral support from the Powers if he set Great Britain at defiance. For three years he was secretly arming for a struggle while the situation grew more acute. In spite of "suzerainty" he made treaties, and stiffened the pressure on the Uitlanders. The British High Commissioner, Sir Alfred Milner, came to the conclusion: first, that Britain was bound to insist at all costs on a decent measure of enfranchisement; secondly, that if it were refused—an improbable event if the president understood that the British were in earnest—the resistance would not be prolonged. In any case, the British ascendency in South Africa was at stake.

But Kruger was counting on victory, wholly misjudging the meaning of the events of 1881. The Orange State and many of the Cape Colony Dutch would be with him; France was hot against Britain over the Fashoda affair; the Kaiser had sent that notorious telegram. The British had no friends, they were poor fighters, and they had no backbone. He rejected the British proposals, and in October (1899) the Boer commandoes invaded Natal.

Boers and British each entered on the struggle under a total misconception of the enemy's fighting capacity. The Free State joined with the Transvaal. At the end of the first three months all the fighting honors were with the Boers; the British had met with a series of disasters. But this awakened the Government and the nation to the fact that the business on hand was serious. An increasing stream of reinforcements was poured into the Cape; the operations were intrusted to Lord Roberts and Lord Kitchener. There was further disaster in February (1900) before the new plans were in working order. Before the month was over the tide had turned; in March Bloemfontein and in June Pretoria, the capitals of the two Boer states, were occupied; in September it appeared to Lord Roberts that the war was "practically over," and he left Lord Kitchener to give it the finishing touches.

Nevertheless the Boer resistance was maintained for another eighteen months. The farmers were past masters of guerrilla warfare, and kept up the fighting by means of small, scattered, and exceedingly mobile bands of mounted men who played an interminable game of hide-and-seek and stubbornly refused all terms short of complete sovereign independence. But the time came when they could no longer break through Kitchener's encircling lines; continued defiance had been gradually reduced to pure futility, and the leaders at last accepted the most generous terms ever offered by victors to the vanquished, in the Treaty of Vereeniging (1902); terms which included the promise of the grant of self-government at the earliest practicable date, and a heavy expenditure by the conquerors on reinstatement, instead of an indemnity from the conquered.

The Boers had never received the aid anticipated from any European Power, primarily, no doubt, because it was apparent that no intervention would have the smallest effect till the British navy was paralyzed, while there was no sort of prospect that any naval combination would stand a chance of effecting that object. On the other hand, whatever doubts there may have been as to the loyalty of other British colonies to the British Empire, these were completely dispelled by the enthusiasm with which they rallied to the flag. The British principle, established in the nineteenth century, though not yet formulated, of free dominions in a united empire, was fully vindicated; much to the surprise of foreign observers who had assumed that all in succession would seize the opportunity to free themselves from the British yoke.

The principle was carried to the extreme limit by the Government which was borne into power by the Free Trade landslide in 1906. The defeated Boer states, administered in the interval as crown colonies, were granted full responsible government, with a daring confidence that they would act upon the concessions in the spirit in which it was made, and recognize themselves as integral members of a British Commonwealth, a free union of nationalities under a common flag with common ideals. That confidence was justified by the event. Only in a comparatively small section did the bitterness of nationalist particularism survive: and Boer loyalty found its most trusted supporters in the most distinguished of the former leaders of intransigent Boer nationalism.

From beginning to end the war lasted for something less than two and a half years. It cost, all told, less than 25,000 British lives, of which only one-fifth were lost on the battlefield. The Boer losses were much smaller. It suggested no conception of what a European war would mean—whereof some foretaste was to be given in the coming Russo-Japanese War, of which the story has already been told. The Boer victories were won by rifle-marksmanship; the military lesson appeared to be that of the superiority of extended formation over mass-attack and of mobility over weight; of "digging in" and of the unexpected ineffectiveness of high explosives. It was no foreshadowing of a war in which the combatants were literally to be multiplied by far more than a hundred fold, and high explosives were to be developed in a fashion as yet not dreamed of.

The conception of a French Empire in Africa in combination with the Napoleonic Egyptian tradition had been primary sources of the constant friction between France and Great Britain; but a way to reconciliation was at last found in Morocco, where, apart from commercial interests, the uncontrolled tribes were a constant trouble to the neighboring French possessions. A clear understanding was reached between the governments in 1903 recognizing the British position in Egypt and the predominant interest of France in Morocco (already acknowledged by Italy in consideration of a similar recognition by France of her own relations with Tripoli); and this new Entente was confirmed by an agreement to refer disputed question to the arbitration of the recently created Hague Tribunal, and was followed by a frank and definitive settlement of numerous minor but irritating points of difference. There was no secrecy about it; the terms of the compact (which was not an alliance) were communicated to Germany, were received by her with apparent approval, and were warmly endorsed by Russia, now at war with Japan.

Nevertheless the *rapprochement* was not to Germany's liking; nor was the adoption by France in Morocco of that system of peaceful penetration which Germany had invented and regarded as her own exclusive prerogative. In 1905 the Kaiser made a move which was intended to break up the Entente. He intervened as champion of the independence of the Sultan of Morocco, but produced no dissension between the two Western Powers. They assented, however, to escape the *impasse* (at the cost of the French Minister's retirement) by holding the Conference of Algeciras (1906), which Germany was able to claim as a defeat for France; but at the conference her sole supporter was Austria. Practically, if not formally, the French claims were confirmed, and again further ratified by an agreement with Spain. The Algeciras Conference marks the moment when the Triple Entente became a real counterpoise to the Triple Alliance; when it became clear beyond a possibility of doubt that the rapidly developing German naval program was directed against the British maritime supremacy; and when Italy, still in the Triple Alliance, showed clearly that she declined to regard hostility to Britain, or even to France, as implied in that compact.

VII.—America and Australasia

The problems of the Old World—the northern half of the eastern hemisphere—and those of the New, which comprises its southern half and the entire western hemisphere—still present marked contrasts. The New World is outside the European and Asiatic state systems; its populations are spread over an expanse of territory very much larger in proportion to their numbers; they have no aristocratic tradition, and are natural democracies, subject to those departures therefrom which are known on the one side as plutocracy, and on the other as popular or, more properly, military despotisms. The era of the second, long dominant in South America, tends to pass away; the first has raised its head in the United States in the efforts of "Big Business" to control government; neither has threatened the democratic states comprised within the British Commonwealth. And in none have industrial difficulties presented themselves in the same light as in countries where, until abnormal conditions were created by the Great War, the supply of hired labor has habitually been in excess of the demand for it. The party divisions of their domestic politics and those of the Old World states are mutually almost unintelligible. Developments of socialism, anarchism, clericanism, in one European country, affect all the rest, but do not touch America and Australasia; Europe is unconscious whether Republicans or Democrats preponderate in the United States, whether Labor is dominant in Australasia, Liberals or Conservatives in Canada.

Nevertheless the world is growing closer together, its remoter portions less distant, less isolated. In particular, the rapid development of manufacture in the United States was expanding their commerce, bringing them into much more frequent contact with other continents; they were being sucked into the whirl of conflicting interests among other states. Hitherto, save when Commander Perry forced the gates of Japan, threatened collisions had always been concerned with the American continents—boundaries and fishing rights and the like in North America, barriers to European intervention in South America. It was with no intention of breaking away from the tradition that the States found themselves, under Harrison's presidency, involved with Germans and British in the affairs of Samoa, the first indication that their isolation was weakening.

Cleveland's second presidency, which followed that of Harrison, provided another occasion for the United States to assert that paramount interest in the affairs of the southern continent expressed in the somewhat elastic theory known as the Monroe doctrine. A boundary dispute arose between Great Britain and Venezuela; the former claiming certain territory as being within British Guiana. President Cleveland claimed (1895) that the dispute about American territory between an American and a European state must be referred for settlement to the United States. Lord Salisbury declined to admit the claim. The president, with the country solidly behind him, appointed a commission to investigate the title, with something more than an implication that the States would enforce its decision. War seemed almost inevitable. But Salisbury, with a confidence in the British case which was justified by the event, made an arbitration treaty with Venezuela, and offered every facility for the commission's investigations. There was no retraction of the doctrine laid down; from the British point of view it was a concession, not of right but of grace, by which nothing was surrendered; but it was a practical recognition that the American sentiment on the subject was justifiable; and it so thoroughly satisfied both parties that it inaugurated an era of friendly feeling which could hardly have been anticipated.

This goodwill was soon to have further expression in circumstances which brought the United States into collision with another European state, and issued in their first actual appropriation of territory outside the American continent (as distinguished from the condominium with Germany and Britain than being exercised in Samoa). The island of Cuba belonged to Spain. Earlier insurrections there had excited American interest, and perhaps in some quarters the idea of acquisition, but the American people were entirely averse from any such ambitions. There had been no intervention, and the trouble had been temporarily closed. In the interval, American trade interests in the island had materially increased. In 1895 there was renewed insurrection; Spanish efforts to suppress it were conspicuously unsuccessful; in the state of irregular and anarchical civil war, Cuba was on the way to complete ruin. The Spanish governor aimed at starving the population into submission; production was almost at a standstill. Business interests, political sympathy, humanitarian sentiment, all urged intervention; Cleveland's last message to Congress in 1896 implied that it might be necessary. But a change in Spanish policy in 1897 decided the new president, M'Kinley, that it was not warranted in the existing circumstances. He did not remain of that opinion for long. The concession of a degree of autonomy failed to conciliate the insurgents. The anarchy seemed likely to continue.

The right of intervention by a foreign Power in the domestic concerns of a sovereign state is difficult to assert, and is generally held to be warranted only when it can at least be plausibly maintained that those concerns materially affect the intervening Power or Powers. Practically, it might be said that conditions which in one hemisphere would justify intervention by the European Concert would in the other justify intervention by the United States, as occupying therein a corresponding position. The Spanish position in Cuba might be represented as analogous to that of Turkey in the Balkans or of

Bomba in Sicily, though it was not open to the same charges of hideous barbarity. Apart from claims to an authority equivalent to that of the Concert, the case for intervention lay only in the existence of American financial interests jeopardized by an anarchy which the States consequently had a right to terminate by force if other means failed: but usage authorizes the application of that right only as against states which had not—as all those in America have— the full status conferred by European civilization.

The whole question as it stood in January 1898 might have been summarized in the form—did Cuban affairs so far transcend the domestic sphere as to warrant intervention going beyond mere protest? M'Kinley assumed that the moment they did not. Next moment a different answer had to be given. The *Maine,* lying in harbor at Havana, was blown up. With popular feeling already at high tension in both countries, it was naturally the universal belief in America that the thing was not an accident; that view was implied in the findings of an American court of inquiry, whereas a Spanish court arrived at the contrary conclusion. The Spanish reply to American proposals for measures to be taken in Cuba was regarded as unsatisfactory—in fact, the whole situation was inevitably colored by the sulphurous light of the *Maine* explosion, which had taken place on 15th February. On 22nd April, for the first time since 1814, the United States were at war with the European state. Then the enemy had been Great Britain; now there was no sort of doubt that British sympathies were entirely on the American side. The fact was a guarantee, if guarantee was needed, that no one else in Europe would take action on behalf of Spain.

When war was declared, its avowed aim was to secure to Cuba the independence without which there was no hope of her recovering from her unhappy plight. After three months, the Americans were only finishing up a victory already decisively achieved. The last military operation was the capture of Manilla on 13th August, the day after the signing of the peace protocol. The war had incidentally brought a change, and a very important one, into the program: it had delivered the Philippine Islands and Porto Rico into the hands of the United States, and they resolved not to release their hold.

Unlike the European nations, the United States were not groaning under the burden of bloated armaments; but if their military organization was inadequate to the immediate conduct of a great war, they had an efficient navy; while neither the army nor the navy of the second-class state to which they were opposed was within measurable distance of efficiency. At the beginning of operations Admiral Dewey's squadron crossed the Pacific and crushed the Spaniards' Philippine squadron (1st May) at the cost of seven casualties. Manilla was blockaded, was invested by an expeditionary force, and capitulated on 13th August. As there was a Filipino insurrection in progress, the insurgents co-operated with the invaders. The Spanish West India squadron was blockaded at Santiago in Cuba at the end of May, and on venturing out a couple of months later was annihilated on 3rd July. Meanwhile there had been fighting involving some hundreds of casualties in the advance on the land side upon Santiago, which capitulated on 17th July. An expedition to Porto Rico which followed—while peace negotiations were in progress—had almost completed the conquest of that island when hostilities were closed by the signing of the peace protocol (12th August)—news of which did not reach the Philippines till after the capture of Manilla.

In the final peace treaty the Philippines and Porto Rico were ceded—not without demur—to the United States, which then found themselves involved in a prolonged contest with the Filipino insurgents, who had no desire merely for a change of masters, whereas the Americans felt that the responsibilities of the "white man's burden" had been laid upon them and could not be dropped. The annexation of Cuba had never been in contemplation; the island was temporarily occupied till it could stand by itself as an independent republic, and as such it obtained full recognition in 1902.

A fight with Spain over a Spanish-American question was rather the expression of an aspect of the Monroe doctrine than an involvement in the affairs of the Old World, but the annexation of the Philippines was a distinct entry into the arena of Old-World complications. Evidence that those complications could not be evaded by America was forthcoming when the Boxer rising forced all the Powers with commercial or territorial interests in China to make common cause; incidentally it helped to confirm the growing good will between the United States and Great Britain. Commercial interests again—and with a similar result—imposed on them participation in the Algeciras Conference. However reluctant they might be to admit the fact, it was becoming year by year more certain, as the nineteenth century advanced, that the partition of the world politically as well as geographically into two hemispheres could not be permanently maintained; though Monroeism in the West was affirmed with particular emphasis and entire success when the British and German governments endeavored to coerce Venezuela on behalf of her British and German creditors (1903). But it carried with it recognition of the principle that the extension of protection involved a corresponding acceptance of responsibility for the conduct of the protected—a principal which soon afterwards compelled the absorption of San Domingo.

Canada and Australasia, untroubled by foreign complications of their own, pursued the comparatively even tenor of their way with little disturbances save such as arose from financial difficulties.

Democracy was taking its most advanced forms in the lands of the southern ocean, untrammelled by the aristocratic or ecclesiastical traditions of Europe or the plutocratic developments of the United States—plutocratic only because of the extent to which money and business interests ran the political machine. In each of the Australasian Colonies (as they were still called) Labor parties rose, generally in alliance with Liberals or Radicals, and not generally obsessed by abstract theories. New Zealand led the way in admitting women to the suffrage. The notable political facts of the period were two: the growing sense of "Imperial" solidarity exemplified during the Boer War and after it, and the corresponding movement towards specific union in the Australasian group. The centripetal tendency was not strong enough to draw New Zealand in with the rest: as Newfoundland stood apart from the Dominion of Canada, New Zealand continued to stand apart from Australia. But in 1901 the Australian group formed themselves into a Federation, differing from Canada in that it was the Federal Government which held specified powers only delegated to it by the several states; whereas in British North America the several states had the specified powers, as delegated by the Central Government. Some years were to pass before South Africa was able to follow suit. But the federalizing system pointed clearly towards one Imperial goal—a union of free federations, each having its sense of an individual as well as a common nationality, in the brotherhood of one British Commonwealth.

CHAPTER LII

CRISIS, 1908-1914

I.—*Maneuvering, 1908-1912*

AT the spring of 1908 the equilibrium appeared to be established. In each of the two great groups the Triple Alliance and the Triple Entente, there was one Power which was most unlikely to associate itself with any directly aggressive action on the part of its colleagues directed against the other group: almost certainly, any two aggressors would find themselves faced by a triple and possibly a quadruple resistance. That, at least on the surface, was the lesson of the Algeciras affair and the Anglo-Russian settlements. But it was possible to doubt whether the equilibrium would last. Britain was under no formal obligation to give armed support to France and Russia in any event, her tradition of non-intervention was strong, and circumstances might make it possible to detach her from the Entente. The military strength of the Central Empires was more formidable than that of France and Russia weakened by the Japanese War; it might be still further increased. And meanwhile, if the Teutonic ascendency in the Near East could be developed, equilibrium might give place to a Teutonic world-ascendency, growing into domination.

The first troubling of the waters was not engineered in Germany or Austria-Hungary; for the moment, indeed, it looked like a set-back to their aspirations. The troubles in Macedonia gave the Young Turks their opportunity, and in July 1908 the "Committee of Union and Progress" at Salonika issued a demand for Midhat's Constitution, which the army there obviously intended to enforce. Without hesitation Abdul Hamid yielded to the demand, with the apparent intention of complete submission. Western Europe hailed with joyful surprise the prospect of a Turkey spontaneously setting about its own reformation upon the most approved lines of Western liberalism, and the international supervisors of Macedonia were withdrawn.

The regeneration of the Ottoman upon Western lines would have produced a wholly new situation in the Near East. The miraculous change of the leopard's spots did not take place; but the revolution was an apparent fact which led up to startling events. Within three months, on 5th October, Ferdinand of Bulgaria proclaimed complete

CRISIS

independence and assumed the ancient title of Tsar of the Bulgarians. Two days afterwards, Austria announced the transformation of her thirty years' "temporary" protectorate in Bosnia into definite annexation. Crete, which had just been evacuated by the international troops, seized the opportunity again to proclaim its union with Greece.

It was easy for the Powers to snub the Cretan disregard of their arrangements, and the Greek desire for the incorporation; a naval demonstration was an unanswerable argument. Ferdinand had taken care to insure the assent of Austria and Russia to his own move. But Abdul Hamid was not yet done with. The independence of Bulgaria and the annexation of Bosnia were a rebuff for the Young Turks; the Sultan early in 1909 was able to turn them out of office and appoint Ministers of his own choosing. He had miscalculated his strength, however; in April the young Turkish forces completed the revolution, deposed and deported Abdul, and set up in his place his younger brother Mohammed V., who was a helpless puppet in their hands. And having secured themselves in power, they proceeded to associate themselves as closely with German influences as Abdul Hamid himself. It was certain that the position of Bulgaria was strengthened, probable that the government of Turkey would be more effectively organized, while Greece and Crete had apparently gained nothing—though they were, in fact, presently to gain much, because King George of Greece discovered in the Cretan leader, Venizelos, a Minister who could render incomparable service to the Greek nation. But all these things might be called merely appendices to the Austrian annexation of Bosnia.

No one had believed that the ultimate evacuation of Bosnia by Austria—or of Egypt by Britain—was anything more than a pious aspiration. But, in either case, annexation without authority from the Concert was a defiance of treaty obligations and international law. Here was a direct breach of the understanding upon which Austria and Russia had recently been acting in the Balkans, a direct blow to Russian interests there, and almost a death-blow for Serbia, who saw her shadowy hopes of some day attaining an Adriatic seaboard wiped out; for hitherto she had been able to dream of an ultimate union with Bosnia. Technically, too, the annexation was a robbery from Bosnia's official suzerain, the Porte.

It is clear that the move was a test action, a deliberate challenge to Russia at least: if Russia submitted, her prestige in the Balkans would sink to the lowest ebb and Slavism would be broken. Serbia, with no maritime outlet, would be economically doomed, and would soon lie practically at the mercy of Austria. Conceivably, if Russia, with the Western Powers behind her, had shown a resolute front, the Dual Monarchy might have found a way to withdraw—had it been standing alone. But behind it gleamed the "shining armor" of the German Kaiser. Russia, crippled by the Japanese War, knew her own weakness; a message from the Kaiser to the Tsar convinced Russia that discretion was the better part of valor, and she withdrew her opposition. The Central Empires won an unqualified victory. Nevertheless, what Austria would have called the disease of Slavism grew in intensity within her dominions—because the victory was the victory also of the German-Magyar ascendency.

Let it be noted here that hitherto there had been in Austria-Hungary a group of which the Archduke Franz-Ferdinand, the heir-presumptive, was accounted the head, which opposed to the ascendency policy the policy of Trialism—recognition of the Slavs as a third nationality on an equal footing with German and Magyar. This might have paved the way for the voluntary inclusion of Serbia and Montenegro, forming in Central Europe a triple federation infinitely stronger than an empire dominated by two nationalities which between them numbered less than the third subordinate nationality. That solution, intolerable to the arrogance of German and Magyar alike, was now more remote than ever, since the ascendency was riveted still more securely upon the necks of the south Slavs. The joint-ascendency party was in possession; like all ascendencies, it was nervously and bitterly hostile to any diminution of its domination; it was too strong to give the Trialists a chance. But if the policy attributed to Franz-Ferdinand could have been carried through, it might have reconstructed a tri-national central Power strong enough to be independent of Germany, with results which afford ample fields for speculation.

As matters stood, however, Trialism on the one hand was cleared off the board, and on the other it had been demonstrated that the Central Powers, acting together, were not likely to meet with any very determined resistance—though they might miscalculate the limits of acquiescence. Russia, in particular, had been placed in a somewhat ignominious position, which had the double effect of increasing her latent hostility to the Central Powers and, at the same time, her fear of them; from the latter it appeared that the Kaiser's personal influence over the Tsar was developing ominously. The Teutonic triumph was rather emphasized than weakened by the Austrian retirement from Novibazar—an act of grace which mollified Turkey, Serbia, and the rather restive third partner in the Triple Alliance, Italy, at no real cost to Austria.

For two years after the victory there were no international incidents. The confidence of the Central Powers in their own growing strength was increasing. The German naval program advanced in a manner which could not but be regarded as threatening in England; but the alarmist and the ultra-pacific sections of the press there combined to convince Germany that the maritime Power was thoroughly effete and practically negligible as a fighting force—in spite of the sinister and Machiavellian diplomacy inaugurated by Edward VII. and maintained by Sir Edward Grey, which aimed at the political isolation and economic destruction of the people whose destiny it was to lead the world. The illusion was fostered by the partisan passions displayed in a prolonged constitutional crisis concerned with the legitimate powers and functions of the hereditary Chamber. France, too, had been passing through a series of domestic crises by no means conducive to the strengthening of her military position; Russia was apparently resigned to her recent humiliation. The position was promising enough to bring on another move in the game in 1911.

Algeciras had been on the whole a check more than redeemed by the events of 1908-1909. Morocco was again made the field of experiment. The Algeciras Conference had recognized that France's interests were paramount in Morocco, and that she should have a free hand there subject to her safeguarding the interests of other Powers; an arrangement ratified by private agreements with Spain and with Germany herself in 1909—the latter probably due, at least in part, to the good offices of Britain. But the Morocco Sultanate could not control its subjects; insurrection threatened its overthrow, and in the spring of 1911 French troops marched to protect the capital. Germany believed, or professed to believe, that this was a prelude to the partitioning of Morocco between France and Spain; and on 1st July the German corvette *Panther* anchored at Agadir. Ordinary international courtesy demands at least diplomatic protest as a preliminary to flourishing the mailed fist; but Germany, whatever her reason, was obviously bent on assuming a provocatively bellicose attitude, as she had indeed, done in 1905. The presumption is irresistible that she hoped either to frighten France into prompt and ignominious submission or, as a preferable alternative, for a war in which the experiences of 1870 would be repeated.

The actual effect was certainly not that which Berlin had anticipated. A protest from the British Foreign Office was ignored. It was followed by a particularly emphatic warning from Mr. Lloyd George—at that time commonly regarded as the shining light of what is now known as pacificism—which was received with a storm of wrath in the German press. But apparently it turned the scale with the German Government, which within a week assumed a pacific tone. Presumably it had suddenly made up its mind that it was not at the moment prepared to challenge France and Britain together, fearing an immediate financial crisis which it had not hitherto anticipated. Though the German Junkers raged, the Kaiser posed as a fervent lover of peace who would be perfectly satisfied with compensation in the French Congo for the commercial losses in Morocco which might result from conceding to France a free hand in that country. So the storm blew over. The French protectorate in Morocco was recognized, while

Germany acquired a substantial slice of the Congo territory. The compact was signed in November.

German public opinion, however, made it perfectly clear that it preferred the Kaiser in his more truculent attitude; and popularity was the breath of his nostrils. The French and British publics learned first that there was no binding alliance between France and Britain, and secondly that Britain had a certain sense of honor—a truth which did not so readily penetrate the moral intelligence of Berlin, where the sentiment was unfamiliar.

Before the Moroccan Franco-German agreement was signed another event had taken place which was by no means in accordance with German programs. Italy declared war upon Turkey in September. Tripoli was the cause of the trouble. For twenty years Italy had been looking to Tripoli as her own North African compensation for the French acquisition of Tunis. No one had disputed her paramount interest in that quarter; but the fact remained that German "peaceful penetration" was, unostentatiously but persistently, superseding Italian influence. Unless the latter were definitely and unmistakably established at once it would very soon be superseded altogether. Recent events had emphasized the critical character of the situation for Italy: the Young Turks, whose constitutional theories were at best only a means to their Ottoman policy, were making things difficult in Tripoli for the Italians; and the Agadir business looked like another aspect of the Kaiser's pose as the protector of Islam. Italy was more than suspicious that the good will of her big allies was superficial; and their regard for her interests secondary—but they would have no case for objecting to her self-assertion in Tripoli, and their attention was absorbed in Agadir. So Italy issued an ultimatum to Turkey demanding the recognition of her protectorate in Tripoli under Turkish suzerainty. Two days later, not having received a favorable reply, she declared war without consulting her allies.

The war dragged on for a twelvemonth. The Italians had little difficulty in securing the Tripolitan coast town; to establish their authority in the interior was another matter—as the French with their Algerian experience could have told them. The "free sons of the desert," Arab or Berber, have no craving for law and order, and their mobility enables them to avoid the pitched battles in which decisive victories can be won. No one else was drawn into the contest. Apart from Tripoli, only naval operations could be conducted against the Turks, and these were vetoed in the Adriatic by Austria, whose reconciliation with her old enemy had by no means diminished her objections to any Italian occupation of Balkan territory. Italy seized islands in the Ægean, which only excited antagonism in Greece, who looked forward to ultimate possession of the archipelago. Though the Turks won no victories, the business was more expensive and exhausting to Italy than to them, and in October 1912 Italy was content to make peace by the Treaty of Lausanne, which virtually ceded Tripoli to her, while leaving her sufficiently plausible excuse for retaining her hold temporarily on the captured Ægean islands—viewed with chagrin by Greece, indifference by Turkey, and careless acquiescence by the world at large.

But the war had the indirect effect of kindling a conflagration in the Balkans, which declared itself simultaneously with the signing of the Peace of Lausanne.

II.—*The Balkan Check,* 1912-1913

The rule of the Young Turks in Macedonia and Albania had wrought an apparent miracle. It had created the Balkan League. The nationalism of Serbia, of Bulgaria, and of Greece called for the appropriation to each of a large section of Macedonia, distinguishable as at least predominantly Serbian, Bulgarian, or Greek; but in large sections also the predominant nationality was not distinguishable, and on these each of the three fixed hungry eyes for economic as well as for racial reasons. There were also acute points of difference between the three races, all of which tended to make agreement upon a scheme of partition extremely difficult. Serbia, moreover, had a natural leaning towards Russia, Bulgaria gravitated towards Austria, while Greece had no natural bias in either direction. But the sympathies of all three were with their compatriots in Macedonia under the oppression of the Young Turk as of Abdul Hamid.

Albania was on a different footing from Macedonia. Its population was little akin to that of any of the three states; it was an area never conquered, which had always suffered not so much from oppression as from the impossibility of subjecting it to any rule whatever, good or bad, except that of some rare dominating personalty. But being in effect a hotbed of tribal anarchy and tribal feuds, for which the antagonism of Christian and Moslem was an enduring excuse, it was in every one's interest that order should be established there, while the Albanian coast-line was an object of desire, to Serbia especially as an economic need—cut off as she was from the sea— but also to Greece and to Montenegro.

There were then serious difficulties in the way of union; but obviously if the three states could successfully compromise their differences and form a compact league for the furtherance of their mutual interests, their chances would be infinitely better than if they remained divided by mutual antagonisms, suspicions, and jealousies. Of all the difficulties, however, the most serious, though not the most patent, was the secret hostility which any league would arouse in Berlin, Vienna, and Buda Pesth; for it would stand as a solid barrier to eastward penetration, and would give a tremendous impulse to the crippled forces tending to the union with Serbia of the south Slav subjects of the Dual Monarchy.

In 1911-1912 the immediate difficulties were overcome. The active initiative would seem to have come from Bulgaria, the consummation to have been due mainly to the statesmanship of Venizelos. The negotiations were successfully veiled from the diplomatists who were not concerned with them. In March 1912 a treaty was signed between Bulgaria and Serbia; failing the erection of an autonomous Macedonia, they agreed upon the Macedonian territory to be reserved to each, and referred the partition of the remainder to the Tsar's arbitration. In April there was an agreement with Montenegro. In May a treaty was signed by Bulgaria and Greece for mutual support and common action, though without reference to a specific partition of Macedonia. And meanwhile the efforts of the Young Turks to Ottomanize Albania roused that province to something like a united revolt. Turkish troops mutinied and joined the insurgents; at Constantinople the Young Turks were ejected from office and their places taken by "Old Turks." The successful insurgents of Albania broke into Macedonia, and were beginning to demand the transfer of portions of it to themselves. The time had arrived for decisive action.

In September the League appealed to the Powers with a demand for an autonomous Macedonia. The Powers gave judicious advice, which neither the League nor the Porte intended to accept; the Turkish army was in course of reorganization by German officers which, had it been completed, would have rendered the troops formidable, while the reputation of Serbia was very low. Instead of bringing strong pressure to bear on the Turks, the Powers presented a joint Note to the states of the League, warning them not to fight. The reply was a declaration of war on Turkey by Montenegro (8th October), on Turkey by Greece, and on Bulgaria and Serbia by Turkey (18th October).

The states of the League had been assigned their respective spheres: to Greece the sea, to Serbia and Montenegro northwestern Macedonia, to Bulgaria the direct attack on Constantinople. At the end of a month the Turks had been routed everywhere. Their old military organization had been thrown overboard and the new was only in course of construction. The Bulgarians had won the big victories of Kirk Kilesse and Lüle Bargas, and were fronting the Tchataldja lines before Constantinople and investing Adrianople. The Serbs had cleared the Turks out of Novibazar, smashed them in the battle of Kumanovo, and occupied Uskub, the historic capital of the ancient Serbia. They had entered Albania and dispatched a force to aid the Bulgars at Adrianople. Then they swept down through western Macedonia, driving the Turks before them at Prilep and Monastir.

Then they struck for the Albanian port of Durazzo, which they occupied on 30th November. The Greek fleet was mistress of the Ægean; a Greek squadron was helping the Montenegrins, who had sat down before Scutari, which they were determined to capture; another was threatening Avlona. The Greek army advanced on Salonika, meeting with practically no resistance, and occupied it on 6th November, just before a Bulgar column reached the same objective. On 3rd December the triumphant allies accepted an armistice, which, however, did not apply to Greece. Scutari, Janina, and Adrianople had not fallen, but those three towns, with Constantinople, were all that still remained to the Turks in Europe. And all the three fell during the spring of 1913, after the renewal of the suspended hostilities.

The astounding successes of the League during October and November produced possibly a threatening hint from Russia in regard to the Bulgar advance, certainly a warning from Austria that the members of the League would not be allowed to retain any portion of the Adriatic coast-line which they might conquer. The armistice was followed by simultaneous conferences in London between the belligerents and between the Great Powers. Agreement seemed almost to have been achieved, when the Young Turks suddenly effected another revolution in Constantinople by a *coup de main*. Having done so, they flatly rejected the proposed peace terms, and hostilities were renewed in February. In March the Greeks stormed Janina, and Adrianople fell to the joint attack of Bulgars and Serbs; in April the Montenegrins, defiant of pressure from the Powers, starved Scutari into surrender. There was a fresh armistice; the negotiations in England were reopened, and the Treaty of London was signed on 30th May.

The League had started upon the war, from which it had emerged so brilliantly, with an understanding between its members, fairly clear up to a certain point but dubious beyond it, as to their shares of the prospective spoils. Their victory was much more complete than they had ever anticipated, but the spoils to be disposed of in consequence brought in new disruptive elements. Serbia and Montenegro had wanted, and had conquered, Old Serbia and the north Albanian ports. Serbia had also conquered a great cantle of Macedonia, which had not been, so to speak, within her recognized sphere. Bulgaria's military achievement had been perhaps the most remarkable, but it was not won in Macedonia; while it was Greece that had captured the Macedonian ports which were the official object of Bulgar desires. Serbia had no claims in Albania based on nationalism, and on the basis of nationalism the Powers declared for an autonomous principality of Albania (which proved to be beyond the power of man to create). Serbia, still cut off from the Adriatic, demanded access to the Ægean

Sea, a portion of Macedonia originally assigned to Bulgaria. The Powers turned the Bulgars out of Adrianople, the Serbs out of Durazzo, the Montenegrins out of Scutari, the Greeks out of Janina. The wisdom of Venizelos enabled Serbia and Greece to come to terms, roughly on the *uti possidetis* principle; an exasperating one for Bulgaria, for she had not been overrunning territory but fighting her allies' battles on soil which reverted to Turkey. Her best chance—and it was not a bad one—was to press the appeal to the Tsar's arbitration.

Instead she adopted a fatal course. On 29th-30th June, Bulgar troops in Macedonia suddenly attacked their Serbian allies. The prolonged struggle which ensued—the battle of the Bregalnica—resulted in a decisive victory for the Serbs. The Greeks came to the aid of the latter; Rumania, which had been making demands for "compensation" in the Dobrudja area, invaded Bulgaria from the north. Bulgaria, with a very strong case for sympathy in the first instance, destroyed it by the treacherous stroke by which she had intended to establish it; and she paid the penalty. If the sudden blow at Bregalnica had succeeded it might have won her all. Being completely defeated, it lost her all, and at the end of six weeks she had to submit to the Treaty of Bucharest (August), which gave to both Serbia and Greece more than either of them would have insisted on or even have claimed before the Second Balkan War, gave a slice of Bulgarian territory to Rumania, and enabled Turkey to demand and enforce the restitution of Thrace, which had been taken from her by the Treaty of London. Bulgaria had brought these things on herself; she had no right to complain, but it was inevitable that she should resent—both because she had been in the wrong and because she had originally had right on her side. If Venizelos could have had his way, Greece would have yielded her Kavala, an act of grace which would have gone far towards effecting a reconcilation. But in Greece the spirit of aggression had been excited by the unexpected successes which had wiped out the failures of the last war with Turkey, and the influence of Venizelos was waning. Neither Greece nor Serbia, against which the unprovoked attack had been directed, would make concessions to the defeated foe, and once more the old atmosphere of brooding suspicion and jealousy enveloped the Balkans. The Greco-Serbian alliance remained, but the Balkan League was dead.

III.—*Climax*, 1913-1914

The formation of the Balkan League had been a serious menace to the program of German domination of the Near East; emphasized by the triumph of their arms, but then weakened by the split between them. The defeat of Bulgaria in the Second Balkan War was in almost equal degree a defeat of the Central Powers, as her victory would undoubtedly have been a victory for them; since she was the only one of the states, Rumania included, which had an unquestionable bias towards them and away from Russia. Her hegemony in the Balkans would have been at any rate the next best thing to an Ottoman victory in the first war. As matters stood, Serbia and Montenegro in apparent conjunction with Greece completely blocked the way to the Ægean, of which Austria had been bent on possessing herself. Moreover, Serbia had won a new prestige extremely detrimental to the proper subordination of the south Slav populations in the Dual Monarchy.

But there were compensations. If Serbia was strengthened, the League was a thing of the past, and the Young Turks, even more than before, looked to Germany for moral support and military organization. In Greece Venizelos might fall; King Constantine and his consort were more than susceptible to influences emanating from Potsdam. Ferdinand of Bulgaria would certainly act with a single eye to his own interests, which would not be identified with those of Serbia. There had been no quarrel with Rumania, which was almost a fourth partner in the Triple Alliance; and King Carol was a Hohenzollern. The conditions were not so favorable as before the wars, but the main change for the worse lay in the increased strength of Serbia, which, now joined to Montenegro and in possession of half Macedonia, blocked the way to Salonika. And Serbia, headed off from the Adriatic and still without a seaboard, could be subjected to merciless economic pressure.

How far these results had been brought about by German manipulation it is hard to guess. The immediate cause was, more than anything else, the determination of the Powers to make an autonomous principality of Albania. It mattered nothing that Albania contemptuously ejected the German princeling awarded to her, and returned to her normal condition of tribal anarchy. The decision of the Powers served Austria's purpose; it had finally shut off Serbia from the sea on that side, and had doubled her desire for access to the Ægean and the assertion of her claim to Monastir. That claim produced friction with Greece, and still more acutely with Bulgaria, and was probably more than any other one thing the cause of the rupture in the League which it was the primary interest of the Central Powers to bring about. The Albanian plan may have been born simply from Western enthusiasm for the nationalist idea, benevolently encouraged—with quite another end in view—by Teutonic diplomacy. But the end which it actually served was disruption in the Balkans. Did the Germans foresee it and work for it accordingly, or did they merely leave matters to take their course? Bulgaria's spring at Serbia had all the characteristics of German method. Its success would have solved the Serbian difficulty for Germany. Was it generated by German suggestion? The only evidence that it was so is in its a *priori* probability. There are no ostensible proofs of latent German handiwork in these matters—though the avowed hostility of Austria, shared by Italy, to all Serbian aspirations for an Adriatic seaboard, was open and avowed.

Twelve months after the signing of the Treaty of Bucharest, five great Powers and two minor states were in the grip of the world war; whereof the immediate cause was the deliberate attack of Austria upon Serbia. Would it have come if there had been no Serbia standing in the way of the German Near East program? Or was the Serbian affair in the category of the Ems telegram, a manufactured occasion for forcing the greater conflict?

Austria-Hungary wanted for herself two things—the complete riveting of the Austria-Magyar yoke upon the south Slavs, and access to the Ægean. For the achievement of either object the suppression of the Serbian obstacle was necessary. The Germany of Bismarck had been interested in the Balkans only because ascendency there was a bone of contention between Austria and Russia, and it suited her to foster Austrian rather than Russian interests when they clashed. But William II. had conceived a world policy which gave her an immediate interest of her own in the Balkans; in that policy Austria-Hungary was to be in actual fact the henchman of Berlin, the German world-power. The key for the realization of the German ambition lay in the Balkans. When *Mittel-Europa* dominated the Balkans completely, with the Porte as its dependent ally, the Turkish Empire in Asia would fall into its maw. When the undeveloped resources of that region were in possession of a Power which knew how to turn them to account, that Power would hold a position of enormous advantage. The Empire stretching from the North Sea and the Baltic to the Persian Gulf could shoulder off Russia on one side. On the other side, as in the past the British maritime expansion had turned the flank of the Moslem barrier between Europe and the Far East by a sea route, so now the new empire would turn the British flank by a land route; William II. would be the successful heir of Bonaparte, who had failed to carry the grand conception to material effect. The first step in carrying out the world policy was to carry out the specific Austro-Magyar policy.

If, then, that conception should materialize, *Mittel-Europa* would dominate the world. In possession of the Dardanelles, the Ægean, and one side of the Adriatic, its huge resources would soon give it supremacy by sea as well as by land. A world war might be necessary to the materialization; but there was the chance that the first essential, the suppression of Serbia, might be achieved without a war if the other Powers failed to come to her aid; there was the second chance, that it might be attained at the cost of war with only Russia and France, Britain standing aside. At the end of that war the rest of the world would find itself faced with a *fait accompli,* and, if it did not bow the knee, could be decisively dealt with in detail and at leisure. The third chance, that Britain might come in with Russia and France, was in German eyes improbable, though it could not be ignored; but even then as Germany reckoned, if there were a world war she would emerge from it triumphantly, since she was ready for it and the rest of the world was not—and the initiative would be her own.

But there must be no repetition of Agadir; no doubt that the Central Powers were in absolute readiness for any possible conflict, and in a position to open it, if it was to be opened, by knock-out blows—the game which Bulgaria had just failed in attempting. In 1905 the Kaiser had not been ready to risk a world war, and hoped to facilitate his program by paralyzing France, leaving no more serious obstacle in his way than a Russia disabled by the Japanese War: when Britain appeared at the side of France, he retired. In 1908 the Bosnian move had been made without inconvenient results, and the weakness of Russia stood confessed; the success of that year was sufficient for the time. By 1911 a repetition of the 1905 experiment seemed worth trial, but again the moment proved unexpectedly unfavorable for a world war. Then came the Balkan wars with their rehabilitation of Serbia. She must be crushed, whether or no the crushing involved a world war. The chances were that it would involve war with France and Russia and, not so probably, with Britain. It was on that hypothesis that the next move must be worked out.

In the summer of 1913 Austria was already impatient. Before the Bucharest Treaty was signed she was urging an attack on Serbia by the Triple Alliance, whose compact had been renewed. Italy did not sympathize with Jugo-Slav ambitions, which clashed with her own; but these clashed also with Austria's. She declined the Austrian suggestion. Since the Triple Alliance might prove a broken reed, plans must be modified accordingly. Germany imposed on her colleague an hour of patience. Great Britain was promisingly embroiled in a raging Irish controversy; it would be well to have her safely off the board while Russia and France were being disposed of. At the worst, her army was ridiculously small; and as for her navy, that which the Kaiser had created was thirsting, and all but ready, to try conclusions with it.

So while the Home Rule battle grew fiercer till there was actual talk of civil war in the British Isles, Germany and Austria prepared to strike hard, and without warning, at their own chosen moment. German agents were fostering disaffection in India, in South

Africa among the Boer intransigents, and among the extreme separatists in Ireland. By midsummer of 1914 the French army organization was still defective, owing largely to the attitude of the Socialists, who everywhere resisted compulsory service. Russia, on the other hand, was on the way to recovery. But the opening of the Kiel Canal meant much to the German navy.

The hour, then, had come. On 28th June the Archduke Franz-Ferdinand, nephew and heir to the old Emperor Francis Joseph, was assassinated in Serajevo, the Bosnian capital, by Serbs who were Austrian subjects. The anti-Austrian propaganda was rife among the Slavs of Bosnia. On the other hand, the Archduke's Slavonic sympathies were notorious; his wife—the marriage was morganatic—was of a Slav family; there was no love lost between him and the party of Teuto-Magyar ascendency, who looked forward to his accession with misgivings. Was he murdered as the Emperor's representative or as the champion of the Slavs?

Austria chose to hold the Serbian Government responsible for the crime through its scarcely veiled encouragement of the Slav propaganda in Austrian territory—the lamb downstream muddied the water for the wolf above it. She issued to her intended victim an ultimatum (23rd July), acceptance of which would be not merely humiliating but would in effect be the utter surrender of Serbian sovereignty into the hands of Austria. Serbia, helpless, yielded nearly every point, but found that no shred of resistance was to be tolerated. Austria, at once accuser and judge, would have nothing to do with the Hague Tribunal as Serbia proposed. Russia if she failed to intervene now would be wiped out of the Balkan peninsula for ever; if she intervened and war ensued, France could not escape the obligation of supporting her, and Germany would take her stand beside Austria, on the hypothesis that the adverse Powers were the aggressors.

Russia might avert war—and incidentally abdicate her position as a Great Power—by simply leaving Serbia to her fate. A conjunction of the Powers, including Germany, might avert war by insisting that the whole question should be submitted to a European conference, as urged by Sir Edward Grey. But Germany could not see her way—Austria, in Germany's view and her own, was within her rights in claiming that no one had a title to interfere between her and Serbia. Germany might have averted war by acceding to Grey's proposal, but she rejected it with expressions of regret. Britain made offers of mediation, but these Austria declined.

On 28th July Austria declared war on Serbia. On 29th July Germany made proposals to Britain for British neutrality in the event of war—in terms which implied that she expected war and intended to attack France through neutral Belgium. Even then the rejection of the terms failed to convince the Germans that there were obligations of international morality which Britain would observe at all costs. By 30th July the chances of peace—though it was professedly desired most earnestly by the Kaiser—were very dim. On 31st July Austria and Russia both ordered a complete mobilization—as a defensive measure. Throught the obscurity of those fateful days it appears that Austria even then imagined that Russia would be persuaded to retreat. She was not given the chance. On the same day Germany sent a hectoring ultimatum both to her and to France; next day, no reply having been received from St. Petersburg, she declared war on Russia. France had no choice but to come to the aid of her ally; but she pledged herself not to violate Belgian neutrality; Germany's replies to British inquiries were less explicit. On 2nd August German troops entered Luxembourg; next day Germany declared war on France and her troops entered Belgium. That night Britain sent an ultimatum to Germany, and on 4th August declared war.

CHAPTER LIII

CATASTROPHE, 1914-1918

I.—The Shock, 1914

THE political situation which gave birth to the Great War may be briefly summarized. The heir to the Austrian throne was murdered by Austrian subjects in the capital of an Austrian province. Austria chose to attribute the crime to the machinations of the Government of a small independent state, Serbia, and claimed her own right to exact as penalty what was in effect the subjection of Serbia to Austria, flatly rejecting in any shape or form all those doctrines of arbitration or mediation on which the hope of the world's peace for the future were wholly dependent. If the rest of the Powers gave way, Austria would at once in effect be supreme in the Balkan peninsula.

Unless supported by Germany, Austria would certainly have to withdraw her claim; Germany made it clear by her acts that Austria had her support. Russia had a supreme interest of her own in the Balkans; she could only give way at the cost of surrendering her interests altogether, and of deserting Serbia, which had a right to look to her for defence. Without Russia, the Western Powers could not intervene in arms. But if in the circumstances Russia gave her unqualified support to Serbia, France was bound by treaty obligations to stand by Russia, and Britain was perhaps bound by obligations of honor to stand by both. That "perhaps" was wiped out by the German violation of Belgium. It would not have been obvious to the British democracy the British interests demanded armed support of Serbia, or of Russia in a quarrel with Austria over Serbia; but that democracy realized on the instant that not their interests but a vital principle which must be defended at all costs was involved when Belgium was invaded.

Austria probably, and possibly Germany, believed that Russia would give way without fighting. Both those Powers were perfectly confident that if Russia fought they could render such an account of her and of France as would make them both permanently incapable of offering effective opposition to the dictates of the Central Empires. Germany believed to the last that Britain would not fight at all, but that in the alternative her army was a negligible quantity and her naval superiority doubtful. Her intervention would be inconvenient, but would not at the worst save France and Russia from being brought to their knees in three months or less.

As a matter of fact, principle apart, vital British interests were at stake. Had Britain, like Italy, declared for neutrality, and Austria achieved her aim in Serbia, Germany would have been established as ruler of Europe from the North Sea east to the Bosphorus and of western Asia to the Persian Gulf; in possession of the Adriatic, the Ægean, and the Black Seas—the last guarded by the Dardanelles—she would have been able to develop fleets destined to destroy the British naval ascendency. This, however, it would have been hard to induce the British people to realize. But they were becoming conscious that a decisive victory of the Central Empires over France and Russia would be followed by a life-and-death struggle between those empires and the British Empire, fighting single-handed instead of in alliance with two great Powers. That consciousness would have given the support of the majority of the British people, but by no means of the whole of it, to participation in the war. But it needed the Belgian touch administered by the Germans, the touch which carried the whole war on to a different plane, the touch which made it a war not for ascendency, but for Right against Might, to unite the whole nation in the common fervor of a sublime cause, a veritable Crusade, for which men were ready to sacrifice not their own lives merely but lives which they would have given their own twenty times over to save.

So the German calculation was vitiated from the outset. The whole of the available British forces, naval and military, were mobilized at the moment of the declaration of war; the fleet had actually taken station; save the cruisers which were still at large, no German ship could pass out of the North Sea from the very beginning. The British expeditionary force was absolutely ready—a record without precedent—and had taken its place in the French fighting line in a fortnight—lamentably small, but splendidly efficient. The Territorials, organized for home service, were raised to a stage of fighting efficiency in a quarter of the time which had been reckoned as the possible minimum. At the call, voluntary recruits poured in in unimagined numbers; Canada, Australia, New Zealand rallied to it; India sent her contingents instead of rising against the British *raj*. Intransigents in South Africa gave brief trouble, but were suppressed by the very men who, fifteen years before, had been fighting their hardest for Boer independence.

But the might of Germany was concentrated against France. Paris was the heart of France; pierce it, and the collapse of France must ensue. There is no heart to Russia; Napoleon had thrust to Moscow, and thereby destroyed not Russia but himself. With France off the board, the Central Empires would have little to fear from the Eastern Power; but Russia could not be struck swiftly off the board, and therefore France must be smitten before Russia was in a position to strike hard. The Franco-Belgian frontier, respected by Bismarck, was not prepared for defence; the short way to Paris was through Belgium. Belgian neutrality must be overridden on the plea that France meant to ignore it—with or without Belgian collusion. (Bismarck would have taken good care to construct a better case, to satisfy uneasy consciences at home and abroad.)

The plan missed success by a hairbreadth. A month after the declaration of war the German right was at the gates of the French capital. It had overrun south Belgium; its artillery had played havoc with fortresses which till then would have laughed defiance to any attack. By sheer weight it had flung back French and British through the northern gap, rolling them down till it seemed that the doom of Paris was sealed.

And then, instead of entering Paris, it began to retire sullenly. In fact, in the last moments a French concentration on Paris had been secretly effected which would have made the cracking of the nut a much more dangerous business than it seemed. But the saving thrust was delivered elsewhere (battle of the Marne, 5th September) at the critical moment, entailing retirement along the whole line. The rush had just not been strong enough. The British army had made its work appreciably harder and slower; the Russians effected an invaluable diversion by a daring onslaught in the East—though they knew their own preparation to be inadequate. They paid the penalty in the Tannenberg battle, but it may be that they saved Paris and snatched from the Kaiser's lip the cup which was never again to be raised so close to it; moreover, almost at the same moment their southern armies inflicted a heavy defeat on the Austrians in Gallicia. Nor may we overlook the fact that the heroic resistance of Belgium had first held back the torrent, and then, when the barrier had burst, continued to detain masses of German troops, both during the advance and the subsequent retreat from Paris.

The Marne battle was followed by a prolonged struggle on the Aisne. The general outcome was that by the end of September the French were holding their line from its south-eastern extremity (covered by neutral Switzerland, which was not to be violated like Belgium) at Belfort to Verdun (roughly south to north), from Verdun past Rheims to Compiègne (east to west), and from Compiègne past Arras to Ypres in Belgium, and so to the coast (south to north); the left wing being occupied by British and Belgians, while the extreme flank was covered by the opening of the dikes, and the coast road was under the fire of the British monitor flotilla.

For three and a half years that line remained stationary, only with fluctuations on the various sectors, hardly measurable on small-scale maps.

For it was at this time that the war assumed a wholly unprecedented character: it ceased on the West front to be a war of manœuvre, and became an enormous siege. No turning movement was possible when each of the armies lay with one flank covered by the North Sea and the other by Switzerland. All that either could do was to endeavor by surprise concentrations to drive a gap in the enemy lines, creating a flank which could be turned, or else to heave the enemy line back, here a little and there a little; both armies living in trenches which presently developed into a network of underground burrows, facing each other at a distance of a few score yards. Months passed, however, before the permanence of these conditions was realized, or the fact that prolonged defence was almost, and victory quite, impossible without at least an equality if not a predominance in the supply of high-explosive ammunition. From being the first to grasp this the Germans gained an immense advantage. During October this general situation on the Western front became thoroughly established: first by the German completion of the conquest of Belgium, including Ostend and the whole country east of the line running south from Ostend, and secondly by the failure of the concentrated German attack (the supposed objective of which was the road to Calais) upon the thin British line covering Ypres.

The war in the East was of a different character, and remained throughout a war of maneuver. There, Austria and Germany had to deal with Russia, Serbia, and Montenegro, the rest of the Balkan states, including the Porte, having declared neutrality. Austria had a bigger task than she could manage unaided. Her main effort was directed against Russia; but her invasion was flung back, and a counter-invasion drove her out of a great part of Galicia as far as Przemysl, while the Serbians were giving her hard work in Bosnia. Northward, the Russian boundary marched with Prussia, and here the struggle swung perpetually backwards and forwards. The Russians burst into East Prussia and were flung out again. Their line rolled back before the Prussian drive, which always just failed to pierce it at any point, while the invaders were drawn farther and farther from their own strategic railways and their supplies began to fall short. Then the Russian line stiffened, renewed the offensive, and drove the Germans back on their railway base. There new and rapid concentrations could be effected: a fresh German offensive was launched, the Russian line fell back as before till the time came for stiffening. But there was a line in Prussia where the halt could always be enforced; in Russia there was no such line, and the pendulum swung back only when Hindenburg was too far from his base to maintain the thrust. The Russian advance could always be held, the German advance could not. But the Russian campaigns imposed upon Germany the retention in the East of masses of men whose transfer to the West would have given her there an overwhelming predominance.

Meanwhile, German commerce had been swept off the seas, while that of the Allies was plying freely, interrupted by little save the exploits of a couple of enterprising German cruisers, and the presence in the Pacific of a cruiser squadron. In the North Sea another squadron had been enticed into the fight of the Heligoland Bight, but had escaped complete destruction by flight to the shelter of the island. On the other hand, the German Pacific squadron at the end of October broke up a smaller British squadron which had discovered it and dared to give battle. A few weeks later, however, it was trapped and annihilated in the Falkland Islands battle. With the capture of the *Emden* and the *Karlsruhe* the Germans disappeared from the surface of the sea, save when raiders occasionally sallied forth, to race home again before they could be intercepted after shelling some open port—described as a "fortress" on the strength of the ornamental existence there of an obsolete gun or two.

Early in November the war area was widened by the expected entry of Turkey; which gave to Russia a fresh field of operations in the Caucasian region, and to Britain on the Egyptian border (Egypt being the Turco-German objective) and on the Euphrates, where the offensive was taken for defensive purposes. It was imperative to strangle the obviously intended attempt to call Islam to arms in alliance with its German champion. Thus there was an additional and inevitable strain imposed on the British in relation both to India and to Egypt; while, even after the suppression of Maritz and De Wet by Botha and Smuts, the corresponding native problem in South Africa compelled the Union of South Africa to devote its main energies to the ejection of German influences first in the west and then in the east.

II.—*Thrust and Parry*, 1915–1917

The entry of Turkey warranted the formal repudiation of Turkish suzerainty in Egypt and the proclamation of the British Protectorate, with the assent of France and Russia; but it was of immense value to Germany, since it tempted Britain into another ill-fated venture which, if successful, would have brought almost immediate assurance of victory to the Allies. Neutral Turkey and the neutral Balkan states on one side, and the German control of the entry to the Baltic on the other, severed military communications between Russia and the Western Powers. Mastery of the Dardanelles and the capture of Constantinople would establish connection, and would bring the whole of the Balkans to the side of the Allies. Early in 1915 the British fleet attempted the task of forcing the Dardanelles, only to prove that the few experts who had deemed the feat possible were wrong. The thing could not be done by ships alone. Late in April a military force was, with great difficulty, landed on the Gallipoli peninsula, notable among them being the contingents arriving from the antipodes, the "Anzacs." No war records contain more valiant feats of arms than were accomplished by those wonderful troops, but the defence, prepared under German direction, was impregnable. In August a surprise flank attack was developed from Suvla Bay; the heights commanding the Dardanelles forts were actually reached, but could not be held, as the supports were unable to come up owing to the failure of the water supply. So vanished the last chance, though it was not till the close of the year that the British made up their minds to the evacuation of Gallipoli—which was carried out with a skill and success that command the highest praise. History records no more glorious failure—even at Thermopylæ—than the great Gallipoli adventure. It is not improbable that but for the failure of water at Suvla Bay it would have recorded no more striking triumph.

Meanwhile the lesson of the Heligoland Bight had been repeated in the North Sea (January), where a German squadron, venturing forth, only escaped annihilation by flight to the nine-fields, where pursuit could only have brought destruction to the pursuer. Manifestly, "the Day" when the German fleet was to demolish the British navy was still far off. So in February the first phase of the submarine campaign, directed without discrimination against all ships making for British ports, was inaugurated; the civilized world shuddered, and Germany struck a medal, when the Atlantic liner *Lusitania* was sent to the bottom in May with a freight of women and children passengers, many of them Americans. Another horror had been revealed a fortnight earlier, when, in the course of the perpetual ding-dong fighting all along the Western front, the British line about Ypres was pierced by the use of poison gas, explicity renounced as illegitimate by all the signatories of the Hague Conference. The gap created, however, was made good mainly by the valor of the Canadian contingent. In these fierce attacks and counter-attacks the Allies, on the whole, gained ground; though the main lesson of a fiery British thrust at Neuve Chapelle (March) had been that no marked success could be achieved without an enormous increase in the supply of high explosives, of which the Germans had an overwhelming preponderance.

In the same spring the Germans developed their great onslaught upon the Russian line, driving it back and back but never succeeding in snapping it; back till it covered Warsaw; till Warsaw was evacuated (August), and then Vilna and Brest-Litovsk; finally till the north was severed from the south by the impenetrable Pripet Marshes—and there the rush was stayed. As concerned the Russians, the Central Empires had shot their bolt. For in the south, too, the Austrians, reinforced by the generalship of Mackensen, had recovered Przemysl, which had fallen early in the year, and all but cleared Galicia of the Russians.

Yet in the midst of the Russian retreat a new ally had joined the Entente Powers. Italy came in at the end of May. Austria had refused her price—immediate possession of *Italia Irredenta;* popular sentiment and all the lessons of history were on the side of the Entente; she came in, and at once attacked her old enemy in the Trentino and on the Isonzo, where Austria stood on the defensive before Trieste. On the other hand, as the year advanced, the Balkan situation became critical. Bulgaria mobilized: was it against Serbia? Greece, under the guidance of Venizelos—who, but for the king, would have joined the Allies long before—mobilized in answer; and Allied forces, at the Minister's invitation, landed at Salonika. Constantine, however, dismissed Venizelos, declined to carry out the treaty obligation to support Serbia when Bulgaria dropped the mask (September) and attacked her on the flank, and thoroughly convinced the Allies that he was determined to do all in his power to injure their cause. For a long time to come the Salonika force was virtually only a sentinel on guard over Greece, constantly on the alert against a stab in the back from its *protégé*.

Then Serbia underwent her martyrdom. Austrians on the north, Bulgars on the east, flung themselves upon her, while the French from Salonika could only attempt an insignificant diversion in the south. From the Germans in Belgium the Austrians had learnt— if they needed the lesson—how to treat a foe whom they could overwhelm; the Bulgars wanted—and took—merciless vengeance for their defeat in the last Balkan war. The Serbs fought heroically; those who were not fighting fled with what speed they could from the terror which they might not escape. Serbia was crushed, broken, almost wiped out—but not quite; and little Montenegro remained no less indomitable; while half Greece chafed to join in the fight for freedom and the other half chafed on the curb imposed by the Allies.

So ended 1915: with some progress in the West, and little but disaster in the East, though the Turks were being hammered by the Russians in the Caucasus, and threatened by the British on the Tigris—where, however, the advanced force, after a dash almost to Bagdad, had been obliged to fall back to Kut-el-Amara, there to maintain a stubborn defence while awaiting expected relief. Austrian forces were pinned to the Italian front by the pressure in the Trentino and on the Isonzo. In January 1916 the Russians from the Caucasus were driving down upon Erzerum, which they captured; on their European front no immediate move was impending on either side.

But the time had come for Germany to seek a decision, and in February a tremendous attack was launched against Verdun. The outer French lines were driven in, but at the end of the first week the attack was held up, and there ensued in that region a period of the most intense continuous fighting yet witnessed on the Western front. The weeks passed; still the Germans crept nearer, but still they could neither pierce through nor hurl back the stubborn defence. For four months the pressure and the slaughter hardly relaxed. At the close of June another assault brought them yet a little nearer; and then on another sector of the line another great battle opened—the battle of the Somme.

Meanwhile another decision had been attempted, a blow which was meant to clear Italy off the board. In May the Austrians thrust forward in the Trentino. If they could break through there they would come down on the Lombard plain, crush the Isonzo armies from the rear, and master North Italy with ease. Again the effort fell short of its aim. The Italians were driven to the edge of the mountain positions, but there the line held, the counter-attack was delivered, and during June the Austrians were thrust back out of all the ground they had gained. In the Balkans no new movement was apparent. On the Tigris, floods held up the relieving forces, and Kut was starved into surrender after a heroic defence; but its fall did not affect the general military situation.

The Central Powers had made two great thrusts. The fight for Verdun had become only a struggle for the honors of victory; its material fruits were out of reach for the Germans. The Trentino adventure had ended in definite failure. At the end of May the German navy had sought to justify its existence by coming out of its ports, when it was engaged by Admiral Beatty, who sought to draw it into the grip of the main fleet, with which it was actually forced into contact; but the skill of the German admiral, aided by atmospheric conditions, enabled him to escape complete disaster in the mine-fields, into which Jellicoe was not to be tempted. Each side inflicted heavy losses on the other. The German fleet was not annihilated at the Jutland battle, but knew that it had escaped annihilation only by breaking off the engagement. Thenceforth it remained in its ports, relying wholly upon submarine warfare against unarmed and unguarded shipping.

While the Austrians were falling back in the Trentino, the southern Russian armies opened an offensive in the Bukovina and Galicia; and on 1st July the Allies on the Western front began the step-by-step push on the left center known as the battle of the Somme, which went on continuously for three months, carrying the north-and-south line very appreciably forward without forcing a gap at any point. The battle marked the appearance of a new and ungainly but exceedingly effective instrument of war, known as the "tank," which was at once a moving fort and an irresistible battering-ram, in its appearance highly suggestive of some antediluvian monster. The continued Russian successes, the progress of the Allies in the West, now the indubitable failure of the Verdun effort, and the capture of Goritzia by the Italians, brought Rumania at last into the fray, and she opened her campaign at the end of August by a thrust not at Bulgaria but into Transylvania—apparently, at the outset, with triumphant success. The enemy had, however, only drawn back from a weakly held front, and soon took Rumania in the rear by an attack on the Dobrudja; but for the moment it looked as if the Rumanian intervention might prove decisive in the Balkans. A blockade of the Greek ports brought King Constantine to reason, and an advance into Macedonia from the Salonika front was opened.

In the last quarter of the year the push was continued, not with the persistency of the first three months but in the form of blows, generally successful, with some local advance as their object; ground was gained here and there, and the Germans were pushed out of all that they had won in front of Verdun. The Italians made progress, slow, difficult, and dangerous, before Trieste. Russia achieved no decision in Gallicia, and Rumania, after her first successes, was fighting for bare life practically unaided. The submarine campaign was growing in intensity. In the first months of 1917 it reached such a pitch that the President of the United States at last felt that he would have the nation solidly behind him should he call upon it to desert its traditional attitude of neutrality in European affairs; not Europe but the world was involved. On 6th April war was declared upon Germany, and the States gave their energies wholeheartedly to preparations for playing their part in Armageddon.

In March the Western push was renewed with fresh vigor; but it did not reach St. Quentin, which was commonly supposed to be the British objective. Southward, the French fought their way on to the Craonne plateau. As the months passed, Bapaume was taken, the Vimy ridge was captured, the Messinese ridge was mined and carried, though the French in the south strove in vain to master the famous Chemin des Dames. In Mesopotamia the Kut disaster was retrieved by the capture of Bagdad; the Turks had been swept back from the Sinaitic peninsula, and a British campaign for the capture of Palestine was in preparation. Italian successes made the fall of Trieste itself appear imminent; the Rumanians were still fighting, though they were in sore straits. The King of Greece abdicated, and Venizelos was again in power. Except in one quarter

—despite the submarine menace to the British food supplies—all the omens were favorable to the Allies at the end of the war's third year.

But Russia had wrought havoc with herself, and was heading for hideous disaster. Sinister influences were known to be at work with the Tsardom; Russian Liberalism suspected it of secret treason to the Allied cause, and in March organized a constitutional revolution. It appeared to have been carried out with astonishing moderation and success. The Tsar abdicated; a National Government was formed, eager to carry the war to a triumphant issue. After the first shock, it seemed that the cause would gain, not lose. But with the fall of the Tsardom the foundations of government were sapped. The reins were snatched by enthusiastic but unpractical idealists. For a time the Russian armies went forward victoriously. But the worst form of revolutionary poison was being disseminated in its ranks. Extremists—then known as Maximalists and later as Bolsheviks—overturned the idealist Kerensky and seized the control, which they understood how to exercise. They wanted not victory but terror; and the first indications of their coming success were mutiny in the army and military disaster in July. Though for some months under the régime of Lenin and Trotzky, after Kerensky's fall, a pretence of fighting was maintained, Russia thenceforth ceased to count as an effective unit in the Alliance. Her share in the Great War was wrecked by the Civil War of the Revolution.

Still the Allies in the West continued their pressure; on the left the Passchendaele ridge and in the center the Chemin des Dames were carried. In Mesopotamia the British were making good; by the end of the year Allenby had struck the blow which made them masters of southern Palestine and Jerusalem. But in the Balkans there was no progress after the recapture of Monastir, and Rumania was at her last gasp. Graver still was the collapse—outcome of the revolutionary propaganda—of a section of the Italian army on the Isonzo front. At the moment when the fall of Trieste was in sight, it broke at Caporetto before a sudden Austrian offensive, escaping annihilation only by a rapid retirement covered by heavy rear-guard actions; till at last it was able to hold the Austrians in check on the Piave, still covering the way to Venice, though for a long time to come the position there remained critical. At the end of November a brilliant British thrust almost reached Cambrai, but the Germans were able to bring up heavy reinforcements, and most of the ground which had been won was lost again.

III.—Habet, 1918

The new year, 1918, had hardly begun when the Russian collapse was sealed by the Treaty of Brest-Litovsk, and emphasized soon after by the surrender of Rumania. In the West both sides were preparing for a decisive struggle. The German high command knew that it must stake everything on a tremendous throw, shattering the Allies before the American armies were ready to reinforce the fighting line. On the other side it was believed that the Allies, if they did not themselves strike first, could hold the line against any shock. But on the one hand the Germans were now drawing great reinforcements from the Russian front, and on the other there was a critical moment while the line was being reorganized—the British taking over a section which had been in charge of the French.

Ludendorff, the German chief, seized his chance, and on 21st March the grand German offensive was opened against the British. The intention was to smash through the British right, take the British armies in flank, and roll them up. Once again the terrific blow was within a hairbreadth of attaining success. The weak spot was found; the line was actually broken and hurled back reeling and staggering, in a hurricane fortnight, over the recent battlefields, over the battlefield of the Somme, over all that had been won, from Arras southwards, in three stormy years; back till the Germans were only a dozen miles from Amiens. But still the French line, strained ever westwards, kept touch; the flank was never fully uncovered, and north of Arras the British positions still held, in spite of a concentrated attack on the Arras hinge. By the end of the fortnight the rush had nearly spent itself, the French were reinforcing the British, and the break-through had failed.

On 9th April the onslaught was renewed at another point, the Messinese ridge. Givenchy held, but for nearly three weeks the once more or less straight line northwards was being pressed back into a deepening arc—on the way to Calais. Once more the farthest limit of the thrust was reached before the third week ended. And meanwhile by a tremendous effort the whole of the British losses in men and material had been made good, and the supreme command over the whole Western front had been placed in the hands of Marshal Foch.

Moreover, while the crisis was at its height, a British flotilla executed an amazingly daring attack upon the submarine base at Zeebrugge, with the object—successfully accomplished—of blocking the waterways. A similar end was less completely achieved at Ostend, and both the ports were practically put out of action.

During May there was a lull; the final blow was yet to be delivered. At the end of the month the Germans crashed on the French line east and west of Rheims. They swept it back from the Chemin des Dames, from the Craonne plateau, to the old line covering Rheims; and west of Rheims the deep Marne salient was thrust out towards Paris. But once more the rush had reached its limit within three weeks and had not broken through, and at one point the troops which had stayed it were Americans.

Again the Germans paused to prepare the last desperate stroke; and while they paused the Austrians smote on the Piave—but the blow was turned, and answered by a counter-blow. In ten days the force which had thrust over the river had fallen back across it in defeat, though the Italians were not strong enough to follow up the victory. A fortnight later, on 15th July every ounce of weight that the Germans could throw into the attack was hurled against the French front along the fifty miles whose center was at Rheims. From the outset the onslaught was held up over the eastern half; but for three days the Marne pocket stretched and strained. . . .

Foch's hour had come. Without bombardment, on 18th July, the French divisions sprang forward on the western side of the salient. Within forty-eight hours the Germans were concentrating their energies on a desperate effort to extract themselves from the Marne pocket without complete disaster. The final offensive had been completely broken in a week's fighting. The last chance of the decisive break-through had gone. Yet for another fortnight it looked as if the parrying of the blow was all that had been effected. The Germans were reducing their great wedge to a shallow arc—nothing more—probably crouching to spring again.

They did not spring again. The initiative had passed, for good and all, to the Allies, and the Americans were pouring in behind the lines, to play the part of Blücher at Waterloo. The British were in strength quite unprecedented. The moment had come for the grand Allied offensive which in little more than three months laid the Titan prostrate.

On 8th August the first blow was struck; from that time, wherever a blow was struck the pressure at that point was maintained relentlessly, the next blow falling on another sector, the next either at yet another, or in connection with the previous one, right or left of it, but not at the same point—probably where reinforcements had been rushed away to save the situation elsewhere. Every German rush had been followed by a pause of three weeks or a month. There were no such pauses now.

Rawlinson opened in front of Amiens; in the course of a fortnight the forces on his right in succession—Debeney, Humbert, Mangin—had extended the front of attack. Then on Rawlinson's left Byng thrust forward in the third week; the advancing front reached as far north as the Scarpe; in the fourth, the Canadians, coming in on the left of it, broke through the "impregnable" Quéant-Drocourt switch line; and farther north the Germans were sullenly withdrawing—not being driven in—on the salient they had pushed towards Calais in April. By the end of the fifth week, the Germans held less of the ground they had won in the spring and summer offensives than the new ground, hitherto unpenetrated, now held by the Allies. At the beginning of the sixth week, far away on the right, the Americans drove the Germans out of the St. Mihiel salient (13th September), south of Verdun, which they had held since the first weeks of the war.

During the fortnight's pause which followed in the West the East came into the limelight. The forces in Macedonia fell upon the Bulgars who had long been sulking. The chief honors fell to the gallant remnant of the Serbians, who, with the French beside them, while the British held the left wing pinned, broke through the enemy's center, completely severing the Bulgar army. The blow was decisive; at the end of the month the Bulgarian republic—King Ferdinand had fled the country—submitted to the terms dictated by the Allies in the field. In Palestine for nearly nine months Allenby had been preparing the smashing blow delivered on the 19th, the literal "battle of Armageddon" or Megiddo, which annihilated the Turkish army in the Holy Land, and then swept on to the conquest of Syria and the capture of Damascus.

On 26th September the advance in the West was renewed, day by day and week by week hammering the Germans back towards the Rhine along the whole length of the line. Of all that they had won since 1914, the last fragment on which they relaxed their hold was the Chemin des Dames. The advance continued over ground where for four years there had been no fighting at all. In the Balkans the Austrians were driven out. Allenby captured Aleppo; and in Mesopotamia the Turks met with a crowning disaster. At the end of October the Allies launched a decisive attack on the Italian front, and on the 3rd November the vanquished Austrians accepted an armistice, following the examples set by Turkey four days before. Germany, left alone and fighting for life, attempted to open negotiations through Persident Wilson, as if at the end of a drawn battle. The Allies answered by driving forward. On 5th November the Americans were in Sedan. Two days earlier the German fleet had mutinied instead of answering the call to come out and die gloriously. The Kaiser fled to neutral soil in Holland. On 11th November the Canadians were in Mons, and before noon on the same day a new German Republican Government had signed the armistice dictated to them by Marshal Foch and Admiral Wemyss. The last shot in the Great War had been fired. The Titan had been cast down.

PART TWO

THE ROMANCE OF MONEY IN PAST AGES

By RUSSELL M. KNERR

THE ROMANCE OF MONEY

THE ROMANCE OF MONEY IN PAST AGES

CHAPTER I

WHEN EVERY MAN WAS HIS OWN "MINT"

Suppose that someone who didn't know—say a man from Mars—should ask you what "money" was? You might have a hard time explaining it. You might say that it was something that was made of metal with such-and-such a thing stamped on the sides of it—a buffalo or the head of a Liberty girl.

"Then", the Man from Mars might say, "Your watch fob, since it's metal and happens to have a buffalo on it, is money?"

"No", you would probably say impatiently, "that's just a piece of jewelry. No one would take *that* for a fare in the subway!"

There you would have hit on the real nature of money. It's *something that you know everybody is going to take as payment for what you want*.

Now a pawn-broker—the best of us have made trips to his office—*might* take the fob—and give you a nickel for it! That's his business *to loan you money on security*. The pawn-broker is in a very old business. There were money-lenders when the Pyramids were building very likely, in old Egypt; and we shall later come back to this trade.

But suppose that the pawn-shop man knew that you were "hard up", perhaps that you were what is not very kindly called a "tramp." He'd know that you would very likely never come back for the fob. Then, so far as you were concerned, he'd be bargaining for your fob. (A pretty good bargain it would be for him!) Now this is what men have been doing ever since they first emerged from the jungles many ages ago—"swapping" one thing for another.

Long before money was invented men were seeing things they wanted that other fellows had. If they wanted those things more than some of the things they themselves happened to have, they'd say, "Let's swap!"

HOW MEN FIRST SETTLED DOWN TO WORK

Understand, there was then no such thing as "money". Here is an instance of how these early men exchanged what they had for what they wanted. Before written European history began the people that are now the Danes and Germans raised cattle in large droves. With some of these tribes *that was their only business.* Hundreds of years before they had lived as hunters, killing the animals that they needed to eat. *But, after a while of this hunting animals got scarce.*

Then, one day somebody—he may have been either a very early man of Europe or of Asia, or even someone living in the valley of the Nile river in upper Africa—got the idea that it would be pleasanter to "settle down"—at least for part of the year.

"Why shouldn't we train these wild oxen to settle down, too?" he cried, when the "great idea" struck him.

That was the way the savage hunting tribes took to cattle raising. Instead of going out to shoot one animal at a time as they needed it, *they began to collect them in droves.* Then they could kill them off as they needed them, and could be always sure that there would be more young cattle growing up to fill this gap.

There were several stages in the growth of these early ancestors of the modern Europeans and Asiatics: first, the wild Hunting stage: then the Cattle-raising, or wandering stage—when the tribes took their herds with them when they "moved", (often they lived in tents) and finally the Farming stage—when they settled down for good, staked off their patch of ground and began to plant "crops". For pasture land also was soon exhausted, unless you "raised your own".

Some tribes stuck to their wandering ways and others went down into the valleys and began to farm. To-day the modern "farmer" is a descendant of the men of both stages, so far as his occupation goes. Though he has the best stables and machines to plant and reap his crops, he belongs—in his work—to both the latter classes. And his cattle-growing and food-raising feed the world, so that it will never be able to altogether get beyond the farming stage, until some inventor finds how to make artificial bread and beefsteaks!

But the early planting men were more or less savage still. They had learned to make very skillful tools; they worked flint and wood and later certain metals—first of all bronze—into useful weapons, household goods and ornaments. *They had no money at first;* because they were for a time able to supply everything they needed themselves. But when they wanted to get some new herds from the

EVERY MAN HIS OWN "MINT"

men of the mountains—who came down in the winter to spend the time in the sheltered valleys—they gave them in exchange some of the rough cloth they had learned to make from flax or wool, or perhaps fine flint spear- or arrow-heads. A well-polished flint would bring sometimes as many as five head of cattle!

THE BEGINNING OF BUYING AND SELLING

When did "swapping" become buying and selling?

The answer is: When groups of men first began to pay with *one kind of thing,* or with a limited number of things, which they knew from experience others were going to accept in exchange. So long as they exchanged anything they had for anything that struck their fancy, it was simple "swapping". But when one thing—or several—whether it was skins, live animals, shells, grains, beads or arrow-heads and tools—*was found that other men wanted all the time,* and that the first bargainer had enough and to spare of—it became a man's "money".

He began to *reckon the values of other things in terms of it.* It was usually the thing he happened to raise or produce. Thus, the hunter "thought in terms of" skins, the farmers in those of grain or roughly woven cloth, the artisan in tools, weapons and ornaments. And he made little price-lists in his mind, which ran somewhat as follows: "So many of my goods are worth so many of the other fellow's!"

How did he measure its value? First of all by the time and effort it took to raise or produce it—just as men still do to-day.

The "money" of the cattle-raising tribes was the "head" of cattle. Cattle-money existed for many hundreds—perhaps thousands of years. It was a favorite form of payment* with the forefathers of the men which now form the European nations. In early Greece—some 2,000 years before the Christian era—there was a primitive people living quite different from the later Greeks who produced such splendid buildings, statues and plays long ago, and about whom you will read in other books of this series. At some time before the year 1200 B.C. some strong tribes from the North came down and overran the land, conquering the people who lived there first. The newcomers were of the strong Central European stock which began to settle down and be "cattle fanciers" years before. They made a new race, and in the later period of which the old Greek poet Homer wrote—he had heard of the customs of these early men only by "hearsay" and from old

---

* The word "fee", meaning the price of something, is pretty generally believed to be the changed form of a word which in the old European tongue meant "cattle". It was the same word from which came the modern German "Vieh", meaning "cattle".

stories—they carried on much of the "buying" in terms of so many oxen. In Homer's books we have pictures of "sales" where animals are used to pay for clothing, ornaments and armor.

WHEN FISH WERE USED AS MONEY

Men who lived near the ocean or inland waters often fished, instead of hunting. *And fish became their "money"*. To this day among the people who live in the Far North—in Iceland and other cold, sea-bound countries—fish are very popular as units of money. Explorers have told about a "price-list", or table of exchange values, that is used in Iceland. It runs as follows:

> 10 horseshoes equal 20 dried fish
> 1 tub butter equals 120 dried fish
> 1 hogshead wine equals 100 dried fish

There you have a "currency" system in operation!

The farming tribes of early Europe in the same way used measures of wheat, rye or corn to pay for what they wanted. In Eastern Europe some people to this day use quarts or gallons of olive oil to pay their bills with. Among the Mongolian Tartars, it is said, tea leaves in brick form are used as "coin". Among the people of Lapland there is a word for money which also means "a skin". Coming down to later times, we have the early colonists in America: any boy who is studying the important branch of school history will tell us that in Virginia tobacco was used in this way. Why, at this very day in many country neighborhoods the farmers take eggs to the store to get sugar in return!

But man outgrew this stage of his money development. He began to use things that were of no direct use *to represent* the value of the cattle, the skins, the food or the weapons that he needed. *Then money in its true sense came into use*. How did this happen? We do not know, because there are no written books to tell us, but by *putting together* hints which we can get from old-time coins, from the customs of savage people to-day (who are only repeating what their forefathers did many thousands of years before) we can make a pretty good "guess". It is more than "guesswork", too, for *it is the only way that it could have happened*.

For instance, there is an old Greek piece of money on which the figure of a cow is stamped or punched: there is an old Chinese piece of money that has a *shirt* on it. What can this mean except that it *was used in exchange instead of the cow or the shirt itself?* Why did the early people make these new, artificial bits of metal or some other substance to use in place of the things they had first given in exchange?

First, probably because it was inconvenient to carry a cow about with one! Instead of that, they invented "cow-hide money". When a man got a cow in exchange he was given, *not the animal itself—* that may have been kept in the pasture or pen until he wanted it— *but a small square piece cut out of its hide.* He could show that when he wanted to claim his animals. It is the same principle that is used to-day when you buy a ticket for the train or the theater. It *"stood for" or represented the value of the cow itself.* But, so far as we know, it could not, like our money, be exchanged for *anything.* It was simply a handy "pocket edition" of a cow.

But man needed a unit of money that was better than this. *He began to widen his activities in trading as his tribe grew stronger and roamed over bigger distances.* Then he found himself in a very troublesome situation, for he ran into people who *"didn't want the particular thing* he had been using as "money".

"We will gladly sell you some of our fine things, but we really can't use any of the things you have to-day!" they said.

This was quite a blow to the early man, and he realized, very likely, that the world was a bigger place than he had thought, back in his own mountains! He was angry but it had the good result of setting him to think of *some one thing that would be wanted by everybody.*

THE WAY METAL MONEY CAME TO BE USED

The things that everybody seemed to want—he and his brother-tribesmen found out through the bitter experience of refusal and "keeping their eyes open", so to speak—*were the precious metals—* bronze, gold and silver. They were compact—that is, they took up little space: they could be melted into many shapes: they were "rare" —rather hard to get—and finally, they were valuable in themselves because of their beauty or usefulness.

At first gold and other metals were not melted into a particular shape. They were used "in the rough" and were reckoned by weight. A famous race of traders—the Phœnicians, related to the forefathers of those greatest of merchants, the Jews—went sailing down the Mediterranean Sea with their little trading boats filled with goods that they had picked up in the countries they visited. It was a brave undertaking to venture out on the great waters so far as these men did in their small boats about 700 B.C.

The way traders went about their buying and selling is told by an old Greek who wrote stories about the lands he had visited in his travels around the little part of Europe and northern Africa that was then known. His name was Herodotus—pronounced in the easiest way, with the accent on "rod"—and he was the same who brought back the stories about the early Egyptians and how they had built their pyramids.* This is what he has to say about the beginnings of *Commerce* in that early day, when the races of southern Europe were still more or less savage. He is speaking of the Carthaginians, who lived in northern Africa, a daring people:

"There is in Libya (Africa) a place near the Pillars of Hercules"—this was the fancy name that the old-time peoples had for Gibraltar—"a place . . . where there are men with whom the Carthaginians trade. There they unload their cargo, ranging it along the shore, return to their boats and make a great fire. The natives, at sight of the smoke come down to the sea; and, as price of the merchandise, they lay down gold and then retire to a distance. The Carthaginians come up and look at the gold, and if it seems to them to be worth as much as the goods, they take it and go away. *But if it is not enough, they return to their ship and remain there*". You see, they didn't quite like to get close to one another!

"The natives come up and add to the gold, until the others are satisfied. Never on either side do they commit injustice"—we see in this (if we can believe the old writer) that fine business honesty was then in style! He goes on: "One does not touch the gold until it is equal to the goods. The others do not touch the cargo until the gold has been removed."

Well, that was probably the way that tribes who *could not speak each other's language* carried on their "business" in those early days. As yet there was no real coined money—at least among these men who like the Libyans were children of Nature. But we see that they had things that served the same purpose—*it is impossible for men in even a half-civilized state to get along without something to pay their bills with!*

* See "The Romance of Architecture" in the present series, Chapter I.

CHAPTER II

THE GOLD OF EGYPT AND THE LANDS OF THE EAST

THE first stamp that was placed on metal *to show that it was of good quality*—somewhat as Sterling is marked on silver to-day—brought the real dawn of coinage. The early traders had exchanged their goods for raw gold or other metals. *The first attempt to fix the value of pieces of metal used as money was by weighing them. Scales were used in drawing ancient bargains.* In Egypt they set aside a standard weight of metal called the "lamb". It was in the shape of this animal, and was probably the amount of silver or gold needed to buy one in the old days. You will remember that in the Bible the story of Job, the patient and just man, tells how he was visited by several friends when he was suffering from his famous case of boils, and among the gifts they brought him was a "lamb". When the custom came in of stamping the weight on bars of metal that had been tested, it was a great step forward. With the cheaper metals like iron and bronze, quality was not of such great importance. But in the case of gold or silver, the degree of fineness had a good deal to do with the value. So later this was also certified, under the government stamp.

It is pretty well agreed that the bar of metal came before the coin as we know it. So spikes of iron are still used to-day for money by some African tribes. And in our shipments of gold from one nation to another to-day "ingots", as they are called, are used by preference, because they do not have so many surfaces to wear off by contact as coins. The old historian Pliny says that up until 550 B.C. the Romans had no coined money, but used stamped bars of copper.* *The original names of coins were weight names.* Thus, the Roman "pondo" or pound was originally twelve ounces of good copper. (So also the English "pound sterling" is the same weight of silver.)

THE WONDERFUL COINS OF THE CHINESE

Some experts think that the Chinese had the first real money. They

---

* Copper was also used for some of the first Hebrew money. In Rome this metal was the only one used until 269 B.C., when silver was introduced. The "denarius", the chief Roman silver coin, was worth about the same as the "drachma", the Greek silver money unit—of the value of a franc at par, or about twenty cents.

were one of the earliest nations to have a fully developed civilization, for some of their old books—handed down from generation to generation through thousands of years—show this plainly. There are some stories that the Chinese themselves tell about the beginnings of their money. But these may be partly "fairy tales"! One of these says that money was first made in the year 2687 B.C. by the Emperor Hoang-ti. What did he make it of? Well, the story doesn't say, *but there is another interesting legend that tells about a prince who had coins made of "stamped earth united with strong glue" about 2000* B.C. Clay* money was among the first that man ever used.

Whether we can say for certain that the Chinese "invented" money, they certainly had coins in many wonderful shapes thousands of years ago. And a romantic lot of stories are woven about them. There were wonderful bell-shaped bronze coins that must have been copied from the tinkling gongs that hung in the temples. And there are others that imitate the outlines of cruel knives or curved swords—perhaps the same that were warm with the red blood of the wicked emperors, victims of that early day! It is said that a villain one time seized the throne of China—it was several hundred years after the day of these marvelous coinages. His name was Wang-Mang, and to prove he was a *real* king, he copied the fine knife-shaped coins of the older emperors. It was a suitable symbol of his own cruel greed—for *to get the metal for his new money he robbed the tombs of the dead of the coins that, according to custom, were buried with them* to pay their way in the other life! He was the first man, probably, to "steal pennies off dead men's eyes"!

WHEN PHARAOH WAS THE WORLD'S FIRST FINANCIER

As for the civilization of Egypt at about that time, we know that it was rich and powerful from its ruins and from the stories that we read of it in the Bible and elsewhere. It was a *moneyed* country, for the kings made their conquered subjects pay huge taxes and labor service. When the boy Moses grew up there, he saw much of the great wealth of the land, living as he did near to King Pharaoh's court. This has been set down in the most romantic way in those passages of the Old Testament that tell of the long bondage of the Jews in Egypt. There were great treasure cities, and the wonderful gold harness of the king's chariots, the jewels and precious stones of

---

* It would be fine if we could make our money of common dirt today! We know for a certainty that it was in circulation among the people of Siam, Etruria (Northern Italy), Rome and Arabia at a later day, and it is very likely that it was also used in old India, Babylon and Egypt. Later the Chinese had porcelain money, which is only another form of fine baked earth.

THE GOLD OF EGYPT

the powerful men of the country, like Potiphar, the steward of Pharaoh, who brought up Joseph in his household, were the finest that any nation then had. The treasures that have been found only a short time ago in the tomb of Tut-ankh-Amen prove this.

We know that when the Israelites got Pharaoh's permission to set out for their long tramp in the wilderness the king gave them "gold and silver"—some of it a form of stamped bars, very probably. These amounts were so large that when the Jews set up their tabernacle they melted the money and made splendid golden vessels to use in their services. Perhaps some of this gold went into the famous image of a Calf that the back-sliding people made and worshiped while Moses was up on the mountain getting his tablet with the Ten Commandments!

We have a picture of an Egyptian market place of that day carved on the wall of some old building, the ruins of which were uncovered thousands of years later. These carvings were made in the stiff style that you have probably seen in pictures—all done in straight lines and with the figures all walking sideways! But the men are carrying things that show what trades they made their living by. There are shepherds with lambs, fishermen with their fish, and farmers with grain. The shopkeepers have jewels, ornaments, tools and articles of clothing to sell. Others have oils and perfumes and liquor—yes, even "wet goods" made probably from dates and other fruit, fermented into wine. There are arguments over the finest things, which several people want to buy. Here two men are disputing over a measure of grain, and a woman—there were "bargain hunters" then as now,—perhaps a good, thrifty Egyptian housekeeper, also seems anxious to get hold of that grain!

"I'll give you a 'lamb' for the whole lot!" one man seems to be saying as he holds out his stiffly-drawn hands over it.

"No, you won't," the merchant seems to say. "I want two!"

Perhaps at last he let it go for 1 98/100, and so started the habit of selling things for $1.98!

That was the "palmy" period in Egypt, but the Assyrians were getting very strong—they were the first great military nation and they believed in "preparedness"—and it wasn't very many years before they came marching across the desert and—that was the end of a good bit of the Egyptians' gold.

The Jews escaped from the chariots and soldiers like the "sands of the seas" which Pharaoh sent after them to take them back again into slavery—and perhaps to get back some of the money he had given them! He had a "change of heart", one might say, because, you remember, he had been badly scared by the plagues and the death of all the oldest sons, and he had thought: "Better get rid of these troublesome people at any cost!" The Red Sea drowned all his men, and so he never got back with interest the "loan" he had given.

THE GOLDEN AGE OF JUDAH

When the Jews after forty years got to the ideal place where they wanted to settle down on their own "suburban building development", they founded a great nation under the leadership of Joshua. Under King David there was a great period of prosperity, a "boom" of the best kind. The nation had a great deal of fighting to do to keep the new land from the envious Philistines—you remember that David himself killed the tall Philistine champion Goliath with a sling-shot!

But David had made a very valuable treaty—it was probably never written down, but was just a matter of "good will"—with the King of Tyre, a city of the Phœnicians, the famous trading nation that we spoke of in the last chapter. Tyre was a rich and powerful city, with treasures that the ships brought in from all the seas in the then known world. The friendship of the two kings was one of the fine ones of history, and Hiram, the Phœnician, sent cedar wood for the famous Temple which was finished in the days of King Solomon. He also taught the Jews how to make ships and venture out on the sea. It was an early instance of a *trade league,* such as in the later days in Europe were developed to a great degree.

The reign of Solomon marked the highest point in *prosperity* that the Jewish nation ever reached. His country of Canaan had great stores of wealth—the description of the palace and the Temple with cedar beams tipped with gold is enough to prove this. Solomon's ships came in with gold and silver, spices and flax from all the nations of that day. His treasures were bulging with "shekels" (the name of his money has come down to us to-day as a slang term). The king's great banquets, when the musicians played the harp while thousands of the court's great man sat over their wine and beautiful dancing girls moved to the sweet strains, are vividly written in the stories of that time. And when the Queen of Sheba came to visit this land, bringing with her great camel-loads of precious things as gifts to her neighbor ruler, she was so impressed that she cried out: "You're richer even than they said you were!" She used more queenly language, but those were her sentiments! And this all grew out of the wise trade relations of old King David!

After his reign there were quarrels among the tribes of Judah; and the Assyrians, who had to march past the country to get to Egypt, fought with them. Finally the King of Babylon attacked them, and carried them away. When later some of them returned, it was a sadder and smaller Judah. This nation of the Babylonians had demanded *taxes* of the Israelites, so that you see, it was a *money* matter which, as in so many later wars, was the cause of the dispute. *In fact it was the same principle of taxation that many years later was to rouse the American colonists to revolt against England.* We can only be sorry that the brave Israelites were beaten in a struggle where they seemed to have all the right on their side.

BABYLON: RULER OF THE ANCIENT MONEY-WORLD

The name of the Babylonian king who conquered them the last time (there were several wars) was Nebuchadnezzar, whose name has come down to us in connection with the terrible temporary form of insanity which made him run wild like an animal and eat "the grass of the field". He was the founder of the Babylonian empire which came into power after the Assyrians had lost their might—after winning many victories—and had been beaten by the Egyptians and the Jews, and finally by the Babylonians themselves, who burned the proud city of Nineveh.

There is some reason to think that the Babylonians used a round, stamped coin ("stater"). Their kingdom was one of the greatest that man had ever raised: it had great storerooms for treasure and sacks of gold. *And they were the first big business people, bankers, financiers, book-keepers, in all history.* But their glory did not last long. The great palace of Belshazzar, the son of this king, was a marvel to behold, and it was there that the great feast was held on the very night when the Persians came down upon them, under the leadership of the great general Cyrus, and entered the city through a dry reservoir under the city walls. These walls were so thick a chariot could drive on them: they included 185 square miles. Not only were there palaces and houses with massive walls, but great parks and farming and cattle lands, to secure Babylon food in sieges.

That money was uppermost in much of the thought of this nation is to be seen in the pomp and pride with which it built its massive city. The proud kings used to gloat over their walls: "This I have built!" The very figure of speech in which the doom of the country is announced in the Bible is one of *buying and selling*. Belshazzar saw the handwriting on the wall: "Mene, mene, tekel upharsin!" The first part meant, as we know, "You have been *weighed in the balance* and found wanting". It was the echo of his own lust for gold and power, that now mocked his tortured mind, as the proud walls of his city fell to the shouts of the fierce Persians!

THE DAWN OF BOOKKEEPING AND CREDIT

Among these ancient peoples—though their days of power were sometimes short—the foundations of our modern money system were being laid. *Credit was being introduced*—the habit of trusting for bills that were to be paid at a certain time. *This was a step forward.* It encouraged people to go into business, for they could buy their goods on a "promise to pay", sell it at a profit and then make good. It greatly aided the "middle-men", who had existed from the very earliest times—even, perhaps, when goods were only exchanged without anything to serve as money. (*"Brokers,"* we call them to-day.) Even when the men of most tribes were wandering cattle grazers or lived in the valleys and did their rude farming, there were a few clever men who lived "by their wits", who said to the shepherds:

"See here; you have no time to go down to the people below to sell your cows and sheep. I'll take on the job of getting rid of them for grain—*providing you give me ten head of cattle for my work!*"

If the man was well-known to the shepherds, they might trust their herds to him and when he came back with the grain, loaded on the animals' backs, he got his ten cattle as his share of the bargain. Or he might have to leave with them as *security* for the loan of the cattle some raw gold or other metal. *Out of such simple dealings an elaborate business of borrowing and lending grew up.*

In the days of the great merchant peoples like the Phœnicians, the Egyptians, the Jews and the Babylonians, there were bankers. These shrewd men lent money on the security of cargoes of wheat, spices, precious stones, silks and linens and regal purple dyes that a trader might have in his warehouse, and which had been brought in by his ships. They got *interest* for their loans—how much we do not know exactly! The rate was probably pretty high in those times, for sometimes they had to pass laws to keep the too-greedy money-lenders from "skinning" others! So, you see, before there was any paper men were writing "I promise to pay" on clay tablets* in the wedge-shaped letters of the time (Babylonia).

The invention of paper (produced from the leaves of the mulberry tree) is credited to the Chinese, though the Egyptians so used the "papyrus" plant long before. It is not surprising that the Orientals should have turned their new discovery to use as money, even so early as 140 B.C. Nearly 300 years before, coins covered with leather parchment were used in Carthage. But the Chinese also later used foot-square notes made of white stag skin; and though the custom was not taken up by the western Europeans for several centuries, this "shut-in" Oriental nation in 807 A.D. issued a paper money. The

* One of these agreements from the time of Moses between Egyptian and Babylonian merchants was found and is shown in the British Museum. It is a "bill of exchange" used when three men bought things—for instance, A from B, and B from C. Instead of paying each time in gold, C paid A the amount the "bill of exchange" was made out for. Bankers "cashed" these bills.

THE GOLD OF EGYPT

reason given in old records is that there was "a scarcity of copper". *This beginning of the use of paper money is one of the most important landmarks in the history of money.** It is true that the practise later lapsed in this nation, and we do not know just how much actual *credit* was involved in this issue of paper. But the promise by a government to redeem worthless paper in actual money marks a new principle in action. *It is an official recognition of the principle of credit,* of "trusting", without which we could hardly have any of the developments of modern business.

* There was an early kind of currency called "token" money used by the Phœnicians and other races that was somewhat on the principle of paper banknotes. These were small sealed bags supposed to have certain sums of money in them and were marked on the outside with the seal of the government. The bags, as was well known, were *empty,* but they passed for the full value of the contents because the state guaranteed them. "Token" money was probably started by early man because he hadn't the amount of metal on hand to pay a debt and so gave a "token" of his promise to pay. It was the beginning of the modern "note"—a sort of early "I. O. U."

CHAPTER III

THE MONEY-BAGS OF CRŒSUS AND THE TREASURIES OF GREECE

The early history of Greece, as this people themselves told it, was wrapped up in a gorgeous tissue of romance. That is, the Greeks themselves didn't know who founded their nation, so—like the Romans—they invented a story. The lure of gold was present to the Greeks at a very early day. It is enshrined in the famous story of the "Golden Fleece", which tempted the early adventurers to sail across the then unknown limits of the Ægean Sea in search of it. Jason is the name of the bold sailor who headed this party, and though the story is partly fanciful, it is believed to be based on the voyage which some early Columbus made in search of *real* gold. The "Fleece" may probably have been gold ore, or it might have been a hidden treasure. At any rate, the story credits the expedition with success—the adventurers are known as the "Argonauts", or "sailors on the Argo", as their ship was called. Where did this early "gold fever" take them? We do not know, but there were rich mines of gold, which in all likelihood the Phœnicians visited. In Rhodesia (Africa) there are traces to-day of the mines that some of these early people worked. "Ophir" was the Jews' name for a golden land where rich treasure abounded, and it was from this source that King Solomon got some of the gold for his Temple.

Among the Greeks this longing for the bright yellow substance was very strong, though they were, on the whole, a high-minded race, not much given to the brutal and monstrous greediness of some of the Eastern nations. We have the story of the golden apples of Hesperides, which were guarded by monsters, to show that this people were only human. But we have, too, the story of the apples that *turned to ashes* in the mouth of anyone who tried to eat them, to show that they realized that shallow things might "leave a bad taste". And we got from the Greeks the famous name of Crœsus (from which comes the stock term for a "wealthy person"). There was also King Midas, who, though he had a great fortune already, made a wish that everything he touched would *turn to gold*. This was granted by one of the goddesses, but he soon found that it had its disadvantages. For all the food and drink he touched at once turned into precious metal! He was surrounded with it, but at the same time nearly starved, when the deity released him from his wish.

WHEN KINGS BEGAN TO COIN MONEY

How did the common flat, round coins come out of the metal bars? First, the old peoples seem to have found out that *round* coins were easiest to handle. The Greeks, for instance, had a country split up into separate States by the mountains that ran across it. All these governed themselves and all issued their own money. They tried coins of many shapes, including six- and eight-sided ones. But at last most of them adopted the round ones. Among the Chinese a coin shaped like a flat doughnut—with a hole in the middle—is popular. They had these at a very early time, and it is believed that *metal bars were first bent into rings,* and perhaps used both as jewelry and as money. This seems to have been the case in Egypt. And when Julius Cæsar landed in Britain in 54 B.C, the natives had a kind of iron and brass ring-money. In Europe the first stamped coins were made by the people of Lydia, a small but rich nation in Asia Minor.

The first mints grew out of the need for some central place where money could be made and guaranteed to come up to requirements. The first known mint was set up by the Greeks on the island of Aegina. Coining was usually one of the powers of kings. If private persons, instead of the government are authorized by it to make money, frauds are likely to arise. So in the earliest days of tribal life, the stamping of money, the decrees as to what its value should be, were usually decided by the ruler. We know that in ancient India there were very strict rules given in the famous Code of Laws of Manu as to punishments for goldsmiths who committed frauds—they were to be *cut to pieces with razors.* So it seems probable that in the land of the Brahmins, private jewelers made the money.

GREECE GROWS TO BE A MONEY POWER

Rulers often passed laws governing the currencies. Such a sweeping change was made in the famous Code of Solon, passed in Athens in the year 594 B.C. There had been a series of revolutions, in which the nobles who owned the soil oppressed the peasants who lived on their estates, and creditors held their debtors as slaves. Solon's chief solution, in order to help the debtor free himself from his heavy obligations, was to establish a lower unit of money, the "attic", and he also made the values of the money lower. *He gave the land to the peasants*—and he divided the people into four classes *according to incomes,* each to pay taxes and give military duty according to the amount of his wealth. This was a fine arrangement for the poor. But it must have been a blow to landowners, who were made poor "over night".

Coins have been found among the wonderful ruins discovered on the island of Crete, and these are supposed to have been made by a people who lived many centuries before the Greeks. They were in many ways 5000 years ahead of the times, for they had real *plumbing!* They were related to the people who lived in Greece before the Northern Europeans overran the land. They were very artistic and their carvings and designs for cups and other vessels were of the finest taste. It may be from them that the Greeks themselves had their best traits.

The first silver coins in Greece proper were made in Ægina, as we have found, and these were also the first engraved ones ever made. During the period of which old poet Homer writes, the people traded cattle for things that they needed—articles that only a goldsmith or armorer could make. But—*as in all races of early men*—they were largely "jacks of all trades" and did their own work.

Years later the rough and warlike people of Sparta, who "raised their boys to be soldiers" were still using iron money, so it is generally believed that this was one of the earliest forms the country had. How appropriate this rough coinage was to such a nation, who took their little sons away from their mothers at seven or younger and made them sleep on the hard rushes and do exhausting exercises for days at a time to prepare them for fighting! There is a tale of the *iron* nerve required of them. You may have heard the story about the boy who stole a fox and hid it under his blouse, but so that he wouldn't be disgraced, he shut his teeth hard and without a whimper to those who were around him let the animal eat out his stomach!

The State of Athens was, however, a very rich and luxurious one. In this State there lived the most notable men of the age, whose names have come down to us as the greatest among those of that day in literature, art, philosophy and statesmanship. Among the Greeks, who lived in little city-republics, private fortunes were a second consideration to the glory and honor of their land. An instance is the form of tax that was paid by all the citizens of Athens who were of the "better" class. This was the *duty of keeping the chorus of the great State Theater trained.* The chorus in old-time Greece was not the kind that you see in musical comedy to-day. There were no beauteous ladies in it at all, only male actors who walked in stilt-like shoes and wore big masks. Suppose that each year one of the leading men in your town had himself to take over the job of training the actors of your local stock company or *pay for it!* But that was the way the Greeks looked at things—not in the light of personal "money-grubbing" but to use the great plays of their authors—the stage was almost as sacred as the temples and was used to teach "right" ideas. This was important, because every son of a citizen had a right to speak in the assembly, which voted on every question.

THE MONEY-BAGS OF CRŒSUS

The whole makeup of this people was un-commercial.* Pericles, one of the great Greek statesmen, in his speeches used to urge the people to turn their attention to higher things than fighting and *trading*—though the famous battles of Marathon and Salamis where they beat the Persians, who came swarming by hundreds of thousands to invade their country, show that they had a good fighting arm!

PERSIA: THE LAND OF "WAR PROFITEERS"

Darius the Persian, who called himself *"the* Great King", did not succeed in planting his powerful Oriental foot on the mainland of Greece. It was a fight between ideas; the Persians were the same bloody war-lords who had laid low the proud city of Babylon. Their idea of "colonizing" was to take a land and then to "make it work for them". So long as the taxes were paid the people could do pretty much as they pleased. His system for getting in his money was very efficient. He divided the empire into provinces called *satrapies,* and put a governor, or "satrap" in charge of each. Every year the fixed amount of tax in gold and silver, grain, ivory and cattle was due to stream into the treasuries of the "Great King"—he was richer than any that had ever been known in the ancient world. It was "up to" the governors to get the money out of the people, *no matter what means they had to use.* The Persians had a reputation for being very honest, but it was an *"eye for an eye"* sort of honesty. *If they didn't pay, they lost their heads.* The amount of money that flowed into the king's treasure house each year was $16,000,000—an unheard of amount for that time. Besides, if we estimate it at the buying power of gold and silver to-day, it was *worth much more,* even as much as $120,000,000!

Darius had conquered all Asia and he was the only master of it all. The nobles and warriors of the great Persian palaces at Susa, where the king went for part of the year to live in the greatest luxury within the glazed brick walls, on which triumph scenes were baked in— did not dare to breathe when the Great King was out of good spirits! A story is told how once, in displeasure, he drew his bow and shot the little son of his cup bearer through the heart, because the latter dared

---

* It is true that they carried on a good bit of trading. (The ships of the merchants of the capital came in not at Athens, which has no sea-port, but at the nearby harbor of the Piraeus.) They were great colonizers and took over the Phœnician cities in the east of the Mediterranean, and founded Marseilles in what is now France, Alexandria (later established by Alexander the Great in Egypt), Syracuse on the island of Sicily and other towns. But what they took from these places in goods and crops, they more than made up for in the arts, sciences and ideas that they gave the whole world of that day. Everybody could learn something from the Greeks, and everybody did imitate them! Even proud and commercial Rome copied their ideas.

to repeat to him a word of gossip about the king's "drinking too much".

"We shall see!" cried Darius. "If my aim is true, they lie!"

The child fell, shot squarely through the heart.

The anguished father had to bow before the Great King and tell him that not even a god could shoot so surely. What were his feelings as, every day after that, he had to hand the golden cup of wine to the king? No doubt, he wished to poison him, and we have many cases in history of kings who met their ends in this way.

The Great King's treasure was used to keep his fine court. He lived, even while on the march, in unbelievable splendor, but still there was so much treasure left that it piled up in his storehouse year by year. Now, having sacked wealthy Babylon, *he wanted to take over the free states of Greece,* to force upon this brave, thinking people the Oriental idea of despotism, of massive palaces and dungeons, crushing taxes, *the lust for gold!* King Xerxes, the son of Darius, who led the last armies against Greece, was unbelievably childish and vain. But he built a great bridge of boats across the Dardanelles for the army to cross on, at a *tremendous cost in money* and human life. A storm destroyed it, and the silly king ordered the sea to be whipped with lashes.

The Greeks had to leave Athens and it was burned by the enemy; but they cornered the enemies' great fleet at Salamis, and while Xerxes watched from a throne he had had built on the hill above the water, all was sunk. Thus was the great *war-profiteer* kingdom of Persia broken in power, and its armies went back in defeat. The land of Persia was the land of the *daric,* as ours is sometimes called "the Land of the Dollar". Theirs was a gold coin named in honor of Darius, who first had it made when he was "crowing" over conquered Babylon. No doubt the first *darics* were made of the gold that was plundered from the land of Belshazzar. Its value now went down in the international "exchange" of that day. Persia, the Orient, had lost.

"HIGH LIFE" IN OLD ATHENS

The Golden Age of Greece followed this glorious victory—the period around 500 B.C., when art ruled Athens. It was a luxurious life, too, for the Greeks were fond of the fine things of every sort. In books of the time we learn that there were great food markets in the public streets, where things that were about to spoil—so much of everything there was among the wealthy—"were exposed for sale to retailers *at any price they would fetch*." This was an early "clearance sale" at marked down values! We know that the favorite form of social intercourse was that carried on around the banquet table. Unlike modern people, who like "music with their meals" or dancing between courses, the Greeks preferred calm conversation, while lying each on a couch around the table. Wines from every Greek colony was poured out at these meals. The cost of the banquets given by the young "men about town" was quite tremendous.

The famous *hetairae*, "female companions", as the loose women of the day were called, had often the best educations and kept splendid palaces where the most prominent men of the city spent their evenings, while their plain and virtuous wives stayed at home. The names of some of these glittering courtesans, such as the notorious Chrysis, themselves meant "golden one", and we have no doubt that they were kept at great cost. The modern "gold-digger" has not a bit of advantage over the *hetairae* of old Athens! We have the verse in the old collection of poems which says of another that "her breath smells of gold." An old poet taunts a light lady who had lost her good looks with the words, "Where now are the rich gold clasps of thy haughty ankles?" And another says of certain grasping females not too stingy with their favors: "If, my friend, you bring the coin, there is neither a porter in the way nor a dog chained before the door!" But let a poor, honest youth hang ever so many garlands— they were the "bouquets" of that day—on the fair one's door, and you may be sure that he had to stay on the threshold in the wind and rain!

The politicians of the day began to be corrupt. They could be paid to make eloquent speeches which would inflame the assembly to do almost anything in the government. Even so great a speaker as Demosthenes was said by his rivals to have received more than sixty "talents"—a talent was worth about $1,100, so he had got some $66,000—in exchange for his labors *by public decrees*. That is, the great men of that day were able to get the senate to pass for them a sort of *private bonus*. The greed for power among the lesser and baser men was strong, and they started revolutions to get control of the cities.

HOW THE FAMOUS BUILDINGS WERE PUT UP

There was a feverish activity in Athens after the end of the Persian wars—the merchant ships were going out to every great seaport city of the time, a big navy was being built and the whole city was being rebuilt in splendid and costly style. The famous buildings that are found in ruins to-day on the Acropolis, or hill above the city, were built then out of the *great surplus in the city treasuries*. This step was condemned by the other jealous cities of Greece, but Pericles replied that in the recent wars these other cities had given only money to help, "but had furnished neither horses, ships nor men". And so, since Athens had protected Greece, it had earned the sums! Anyway, the buildings crowned by the splendid Parthenon*, went up to the tune of more than 1,000 talents ($1,100,000). The money came out of the public treasuries, and it was thought a good move because it kept the mechanics and workmen of the city busy *with pay*, when they would probably have had to be supported out of the fund anyway in case of hard times!

It is not so pleasant to think of the slaves, some of whom were men taken in battle, who had to work without pay in the silver mines at Larium to help make these marble and silver-crowned palaces that are still the wonder of the world. Their average life was only two years—at the end of that time their blow-scarred and broken bodies were thrown out to rot. The system of slavery in Greece was one of its worst evils. *But there was a terrible price to pay,* because in the course of several hundred years the rich and idle class in Athens lost all their old strength, while the slaves who did all the work became more clever than they. The morals of the country went down to the lowest depravity, and we have pictures of the state of things in the comedies of Aristophanes (*accented on the syllable "toph"*). The wealthy people became "loafers", who spent their early years in vice and their later ones in sentimental regrets! Then men soon found that they need not fight, if they had enough *money with which to buy the services of soldiers*—"mercenaries", as they were called, because they were paid. The use of slaves threw the lower classes out of work and they turned soldiers.

CIVIL WARS THAT AROSE OVER MONEY AND POWER

Meanwhile more gold was flowing into the Athenian treasuries because the city had now established herself supreme among those of Greece. She increased the taxes from the other cities—more than 300—and the tax money every year amounted to 600 talents or $660,000—a much bigger sum in those days than now. But the leadership was soon disputed by the Spartans in a long and troublesome civil war, the result of which was the *weakening of the already decaying power of Greece*. No one city won, though the hard and merciless struggle lasted for twenty-seven years! The Spartans led a combination of the inland cities and Athens led those on the seacoast, and though Sparta for a time gained the upper hand, the result of the wars was that King of Persia—without raising a hand—got back all the Greek cities in Asia. He simply claimed them, and one by one, the weakened Greek States had to agree to this arrangement. But there was a strong man coming upon the scene *to give a "boost"* to trade, just as the crusaders did so many years later. This was the great general, Alexander the Great of Macedonia.

* See section on Greece in "The Romance of Architecture" in this series.

THE MONEY-BAGS OF CRŒSUS

Macedonia was a province in the north of Greece. Its people were rough shepherds and soldiers, whom the polished Athenians called "barbarians". But their king, Philip, Alexander's father, had a very commercial view of how to buy world power. He believed that anyone could be "bought". He had a great ambition to make all the other Greeks join under his leadership and finally to wipe out Persia once and for all! He used to say: "No fort can stand if you only are able to get inside it *a mule loaded with gold!*" Whether he bribed or beat them, the cities of northern Greece one by one surrendered to him. Demosthenes saw the danger to Athens and used to urge the people to get up a strong army of citizens only, *for he knew that paid soldiers do not have their heart in the battle*. Philip won over all the cities including Athens, perhaps because of his strong soldiery, perhaps because *"money talks"*. Then he put up to them his scheme of marching against Persia, and he would have led the armies himself, but he was struck down by an assassin in 336 B.C., and Alexander at the age of twenty succeeded him.

ALEXANDER AS A BOOSTER OF TRADE

Alexander "did the job" in two years, by beating the Persians three times, at the river Granicus, at Issus (where the enemy was waiting with 600,000 men), and two years later at Arbela, against a still bigger army. *The result was of the greatest importance to the money market* of Western Europe and Asia. For he let loose into trade circles gold that amounted to many millions of dollars. Where did it come from? Where else than *from the captured treasure-houses of the Persian king at Susa and Persepolis!* You see, in this elaborate net-work of wars and plundering what had been done was to hoard up a great treasure and then to send it out freely like dammed-up water! It was as if a great modern bank were to pour out its money into the streets. It would "scatter" very quickly! So it did in 330 B.C. The soldiers felt the gold they had got in the plunder "burn a hole in their pockets" and each exchanged it for what he wanted most. Some of them in these years got together quite a "pile" and came home and "lorded it" over their old friends.

But the biggest result was to stimulate trade. Sums in gold were easier to carry than in silver or copper: buying "picked-up". There was more money to borrow: the rate of interest went down. (It was usually much more than twelve per cent. in ancient times, because "market" conditions were so uncertain.) Other goods went up in price, because of brisk selling, and the increased demand for them.* Hoarding money is a bad thing for business, and the Persian king

---

* For the causes of governing "price" and value of money, see Chapter 3, Part II.

had simply kept his from "working". The Macedonian victories opened up Asia and Egypt for trading as well.

After Alexander's death his empire went to pieces, but there was a big "business boom" among these Greek cities that had been under his rule. They again founded colonies, and the whole East was Hellenic. ("Hellenes" was what the Greeks called themselves.) The greatest Greek city of the period was Alexandria in Egypt, which grew from a little colony to the size of modern Paris. For its commercial position was the "best ever"—it was near the ocean and was irrigated by canals from the Nile. It was a luxurious and wicked city, for here the courtesan Thais held her revels around rose-strewn banquet tables. The merchant ships went out to every city—Herculaneum and Pompeii, which were buried under the ashes of Vesuvius later, and Baiae, the Palm Beach of the ancient world, all founded by the Romans.

FAMOUS TRADING CITIES OF THE LATER GREECE

Rhodes was another famous Greek trading city, ruled by rich merchants and noted for its honest dealings. When it was almost destroyed by an earthquake, the other cities made haste to send a lot of gold and silver and other "relief" to the bankers of Rhodes. *They knew that if these "failed", the whole ancient money-market would be turned upside down, and they'd lose more than by sending help.* That is, the money-lenders of the city would not be able to redeem the "I. O. U's" they had given, the paper or bills of exchange, and the merchants of the other cities probably had some of these in their wallets!

We learn, too, that the people of Rhodes got into several wars on account of the early *"duties" which men had begun to charge for the privilege of bringing in goods at their ports.* One of these was with the people of Byzantium, that later was to be the capital of the East. The Byzantines were "in a huff" because the men of Rhodes wouldn't back them up in a dispute against another city, so they *declared a duty* on all ships that sailed into the Bosphorus. The Rhodians went to war about it and won. Near the harbor of Rhodes was the famous Colossus—a gigantic figure of a man which was hundreds of feet high.

Later the financial power of Rhodes—it charged duty on its own harbor—was ruined by Rome. She *took off the port tolls* in her own nearby city of Delos, so all ships put to shore there and *avoided Rhodes.* Doubtless there was smuggling and cases of "fooling" the customs inspectors in that early day, just as now, and we know that there was a great deal of piracy on the sea—so much so that the Greek ports had two *Leagues of Cities,* which were rivals, but pro-

THE MONEY-BAGS OF CRŒSUS

tected their members from robbers. (Each called the other "robbers", it is true, but they were probably a better water "police force" than none!)

Prosperity did not last long. The rich and the poor classes warred with one another. These were the twilight days of Greece. The old spirit of the race was gone. Rome did not conquer at once, but *absorbed Greece, bit by bit.** Rome had become the greatest empire in the world.

* First destroyed was Corinth in Syria which was ruled by the heirs of Ptolemy, one of Alexander's generals. (His head is stamped on an old coin.) Achaea was put under a Roman governor, and later Pompey conquered other cities in Syria and Egypt. The cruel oppression of the Roman governors—"rotters" of high birth who had the people slain in the market places and wrung their money out of them—is a terrible page in history. To make up for it, some Roman Emperors gave sums to rebuild the Greek temples—and the Hellenes were now so humble that they put up inscriptions praising their conquerors for tampering with their ancient sacred places.

CHAPTER IV

WHEN ROME WAS THE NERVE-CENTER OF THE MONEY-WORLD

ROME, the "mistress of the world," was the first great money capital *of the whole earth*. From a little village on the marshlands of the Tiber River in what is now Italy, she grew—in the space of some 500 years—to be the *richest, the biggest "land owning" city ever known*. The old stories said that Rome was founded by Romulus about 753 B.C., but this was merely an "invented" person. We know that the town got to be popular because it was near enough to a seaport—Ostia, three leagues away—to bring in goods. Groups of towns grew up around it and finally joined together, like so many "boroughs". The early days of the city, when it was ruled by seven kings, have a very "hazy" history—it may be based on fact, but nobody knows.

Tarquin, the "fifth" king, was said to have been a rich merchant who came down from the province to the north—Tuscany, the people of which were called Etruscans and were a famous trading tribe. The next king is of more importance, because *he started the first money classes in Rome*. Servius Tullius was his name, and he seems to have had a very modern theory about birth having very little to do with one's fighting ability! He organized the army in five classes on the basis of wealth—somewhat as Solon had done in Greece. The highest class in the army was of those who had property worth about $2,000. (Prices were low in those days.) They rode on horses in battle and so were called the "horsemen", or the "knights". These had next place in honor to officials of the government. The other groups were those who had property worth $1500, second class; $1000, third; $500, fourth, and $250 or less, fifth. The last class to have full armor was the fourth, and the others had to go to war *with only sticks and stones*. They called them the "disturbers" or "also rans", and their job was to go along with the regular troops and "stir up" the enemy. The death rate among the "disturbers" must have been pretty high! But this shows what an advantage a "savings account" was in old Rome.

The last king, Tarquin the Proud, as he was called, "stepped on the toes" of the high "first families" of Rome, and they turned him out of the city and appointed a governor, or "consul", to take his place. But Tarquin went to a nearby city and collected an army.

ROME, THE NERVE CENTER

He came back to seize Rome, and there is a poem about "Horatius at the Bridge", which is in most of the school readers, and which tells how one man defended the entrance to the city until the others cu' down the bridge. Tarquin didn't get in.

A WORKING MEN'S REVOLT IN OLD ROME

Struggles between the high and the low classes in Rome began at a very early time and kept up until the end of the city's great days. It was so in Greece—they helped to bring about the end of that nation and have continued throughout the world to this day. *They usually come up over the question of who is to own the land.* In Rome there were two classes* as early as the fifth century B.C. The "patricians" were the "old families", descendants of the first settlers of the Roman hills. And the "plebeians" ("people of the multitude")—though they had more money and were greater in number—were the "new rich", the sons of foreigners who had come there or of the men of other Italian cities that had been annexed by Rome. *The slaves were only machines to get so much work out of!* That was the terrible fate of enemies caught in battle. Once every five years there was a census taken, and everybody was registered by the *censors*—how much they owned!

But the "multitude" insisted on having more rights—and got them. It was the beginning of that great wave of democracy that was to sweep Europe so many hundreds of years later. One day, the "multitude" got tired of being imposed upon by the upper class, and so the men left the city with all their swords and spears in hand and camped out on one of the hills. They were going to "secede", like the Southern United States in 1861! It was a dispute rather like some of the modern strikes of laboring men, only they wanted *equal rights,* instead of more pay. This greatly scared the upper class, because without farmers and workmen to raise and make what it needed, its money would have been *worthless.* The men would have starved, for they were the "brain-workers", and in some cases just idlers, of that day. And when it was a question of milking a cow or getting in the harvest, the senators of old Rome were just about as helpless as all but one American Congressman

---

* Instead of the fashionable "400" of modern cities, Rome had only 300 "noble families"—some member of which had once been a public official. *Only they governed,* though all but slaves voted. Then there were the "knights", the richest classes, who were merchants and bankers, but were not active officials in the government. They were the men who were in "class one" in war service. After these came the "multitude", or *plebs*—the workmen and farmers—and finally the lowest class of the citizens, the "freedmen", who had once been slaves.

seem to-day! The slaves did the little jobs, the "dirty work", not the feeding of the country.

The higher class saw this very plainly and sent out a good talker to persuade the crowd to come back. He did this very neatly by telling a story about the body being helpless without the stomach, and the strikers "saw the point", and the sense of their importance put them into good humor. But they made a new law that they were to have some head men of their own, "tribunes", who had the right to protect any commoner against a charge of the law or a senate ruling by simply holding up a hand and saying "Veto!" It meant "I forbid", or "do not wish it", and that's where we got the word used in our government to-day. By the year 300 B.C., the "multitude" was having things all its own way. It had the biggest number of voters, and so they passed laws giving them the right to marry into the "old families" and get appointed to the highest offices. Candidates for election had to pass around what corresponded to modern "stogies" to them. They looked him over, and if they thought he hadn't the right ideas, he never got in. It was a sort of early Farmer-Labor Party.

ROME: PLUNDERER OF THE WHOLE EARTH

How did Rome get to be so rich? Like all other old-time peoples, the city got its wealth by either commerce or war. Those were the main business of the old-time world. The "high finance" of that day was plundering. Rome began "laying up" new territory very slowly. It took 400 years (until 266 B.C.) to get hold of the ground of her neighboring tribes in Italy to the east, south and north, and the Greek cities. After the final beating of the Samnites—the most powerful tribes who lived in the mountains above Naples, known in modern Italy as the "hang-out" of robbers—the Roman general Papirius Cursor brought back in 293 B.C. as plunder, 330,000 pounds of silver and 2,033,000 pounds of bronze (Troy weight). To be sure, he had slaughtered no end of people—practically wiping out this tribe and laying the ground so bare *that it still has the traces to-day.*

The last stand of the dying race was a very pitiful one. The priests opened the sacred book of their religion, written on pages of linen, woven out of the flax that grew there. The last battalion was ready to make the last stand, and it also was dressed in linen, while above the sacred altar a great canopy of white cloth was hung. The prayer seems to have helped very little, for the army was slaughtered to the last man, and the women and children carried away to be dragged through the streets of Rome in chains—if they lived through their brutal treatment. This was what the Romans called

ROME, THE NERVE CENTER

a "triumph", and it was chiefly a big parade for the general and his loot—one of the finest honors the city had to offer!

The "big wars" of Rome were those with the Carthaginians—the same race of Phœnicians that had gone sailing to distant shores in the early days of trading. Carthage was a great city on the North coast of Africa—about where Tunis is to-day—and it grew bigger and more powerful, thanks to the merchant ships that kept coming in from all parts of the known world. Long before the first war, the leaders of Rome used to see the danger of having a rival power facing them across the little Mediterranean "pond". They would say, "Carthage must be destroyed!" That was Rome's style of treating anything that got in her way! Meanwhile, Carthage's caravans kept bringing gold from Arabia, gems from the lands of the Euphrates, silk from China, and her ships sailed as far as Britain and its tin mines.

Before the wars with Carthage, Rome used bronze money chiefly. The old stories of the Romans said that the first king to stamp his "picture" or mark on the bronze money was Servius Tullius, the same who divided the people according to their wealth. The other tribes of Italy largely imitated the Romans. But in the Greek cities, in Naples and in Cumae, silver was used, and *when the Romans began to win battles in this area* (as early as 323 B.C.) *silver* began to flow into Rome*. When the Greek cities had been taken over, among these was Tarentium, the richest city of the Hellenes, with *treasure-houses bursting with silver and other metals*. In a short time Rome had as much silver in circulation as the countries that had been mining it for hundreds of years! She had simply "held up" the other provinces at the point of the sword and said, "Empty your pockets!"

Slowly, as the soldiers spent their booty for a "hot time in the old town", as the generals turned it into the treasury—the part, that is, that they didn't put into their own purses!—*the prices of things went up*. The soldiers bought recklessly, and *no shopkeeper was going to sell his things for the old piece of copper, when he could get as big a piece of silver for them*. Nobody wanted the old copper "pound" and it went down in value to almost nothing.

Then the army began to conquer the rich island of Sicily, which was called "the granary of the East", because of the great crops and stores it had. This entry into Sicily annoyed the Carthaginians and brought on war. Sixty-five Sicilian towns surrendered to Rome before 260 B.C. The public treasure was replaced by treasure from

---

* The first silver coin in Rome (the "denarius") was first made in 269 B.C. The gold "aureus" was not made until 207 B.C. (Lawyers charged 100 aurei). The denarius had the goddess Roma on it—she was the particular one who was supposed to have the welfare of the city in charge!

Sicily and this brought on disputes which were called the "social wars" in Rome.

But the most important result of the wars with Carthage was the enormous "war indemnity" that was demanded after. Rome had won $5,000,000, worth then six times what it is now, after the first war; $10,000,000 after the second, and all the land of the enemy except that in Africa. In the last war Carthage itself was destroyed, and Hannibal, the Phœnicians' great leader, after being once almost at Rome's gates, fled finally to the king of Bithynia, and took poison when the legion sent to capture him surrounded his place of refuge. This is the way that one of the Napoleons of the ancient world died—who almost, but not quite ruined the money power, Rome! He was a "plunger" in the old-time game of plundering, but he wasn't strong enough to hold out against a whole nation of financial geniuses.

THE GAME OF HIGH FINANCE ON THE TIBER'S SHORES

Rome now became money-mad. Its conquests had been slow at first, but "nothing succeeds like success", as the proverb says. The taste of wealth provoked a desire for more. Speculation ran a mad course in this capital of 300,000 citizens. The "knights" were the rich men of the state—that is, they corresponded to the multi-millionaires of to-day, but the "nobles" and the State officials were a wealthy class. In fact, it was a requirement that those whom the "censor" picked for senators—there were 300—had to be rich and of an old respected family.*

The bankers of Rome were at first only money-changers; then their business developed until they took deposits of money for safe-keeping, lent at high interest, sent money from place to place by "bills of exchange". The financiers of old Rome were a tremendous force in the government. They were called the Argentarii, or dealers in money. These shrewd profiteers found the new national wealth

---

* *The public officials served without pay,* so that alone would have kept out the lower classes, if there had not been other reasons. To get a public office, one had to have served in the army in ten campaigns but, as Rome was at war with only one short intermission for 500 years, this wasn't difficult! The lowest job was that of "inquirer", or "Quaestor", who looked after the state treasury, in the Temple of Saturn. There were originally two of these men, but at times the number was increased, once to forty. There were "city" quaestors and "military" ones—the former had charge of the stores of gold and silver and the public documents, and the latter supplied money to the governors and provinces. Higher offices in order were: the "aedile" who policed the city and had charge of the public grain supply: the "praetor", who acted as judge in the court; the "consul", who commanded an army and was a sort of president of the assemblies, and finally the "censor", who took the census and appointed the senators and other officials. This was the highest office.

a fine thing, for they got much of it into their own hands. *They urged on the senate the declaration of more wars.* Rome defeated the heirs of the Greek generals that had fought in Alexander's army and had divided his kingdom after his death; in this way she gained Asia and Egypt. And she put down the tribes of Gauls in Northern Italy and the valley of the Rhone, invaded Britain and even went into what is now Germany. *Finally she had all the land that borders the Mediterranean from Spain to Asia Minor,* and all this land became her "public domain". Rome was the biggest "real estate owning" city ever known. And students are pretty well agreed that *she carried on her later wars, at least, largely for the sake of money and power.* In addition to the money and lands of Carthage, Rome got the vast treasure of the rulers of Asia—Antiochus, king of Syria, gave up 140,000 pounds of silver and 1,000 pounds of gold, besides great quantities of coins, and surrendered Egypt.

Rome managed all this vast territory by appointing a sort of governor for each province. He was called a "proconsul", or "one who acted for the consul". A favorite way was to thrust into these places prominent men who were just ending their service as a public official, and they were chosen only for one year—so that most made haste to get out of the office all that was to be had in the way of money! *He had the power to put anyone to death, to collect as much money as he wanted.* (Pontius Pilate is the most famous example of Roman official.) Many of the pro-consuls were the worst kind of tyrants—*so that to be safe from a sentence of death some wealthy men paid large bribes.* The governor could lay his hand upon anything, and his assistants were not slow to follow his example. Many had the people flogged, robbed the temples and the homes. There are a few exceptions—one governor built the Jews a synagogue.

THE BLOODY TAX COLLECTORS OF OLD

But the most typical figure in the business life of Rome was the "publican". Someone had to take charge of collecting the revenues and taxes of this great world-republic, so once every five years the censors appointed contractors—wealthy men, who paid so much for the privilege of doing the State's business in a certain province. The first publicans were men of the captured countries, but after the lands in Asia were taken over, the wealthy men in the government forced a new ruling that this right was to be offered at public auction. The highest bidder got it. He had the right to collect the taxes of all sorts from the conquered country—a certain part of all crops raised, a tax in silver and a certain amount per head for inhabitants. Besides, there was money flowing in from the mines, the harbor duties and the pasture tax. The way the publicans went about getting the money became quite a joke in Rome, somewhat as our little faults in connection with the United States' "income tax" are joked about in vaudeville. "Poor people in the provinces!" the polished Roman would say, with much mirth. *"They are slowly but surely being killed off by those publicans!"*

For the poor people outside Rome, it was no such laughing matter. They could only borrow money at a high rate of interest when in need. They were bled of much more than the lawful tax, and if they didn't pay were beaten, put into jail, and sometimes even killed! A worse fate still was to be sold into slavery. *No wonder that the Jews of New Testament times used the name "publican" in the same breath as "sinner"!* There was hardly any way to "get back" at them either, for with their friends they formed such an influence in the government that even the proconsuls feared them. They sat as judges in Rome, and if one of their friends had been accused by a Roman citizen—though they seldom were—he would probably have been pardoned by a court. Meanwhile he got very rich.

The power of the money princes of Rome can be seen from some stories of the time. A Roman merchant loaned a city in Cyprus a large sum of money—for now it seemed that all the money of the world was "cornered" in Rome, and whole cities abroad were penniless. *He charged nearly fifty per cent. interest for it!* When the city couldn't pay it back, the merchant went to the Roman proconsul, demanded an army, beseiged the whole senate of the city, until some persons died of starvation. Probably, when it came to a choice between no food and paying, the city found some way, even if it had to "pawn" all its valuables.

WHEN THE KING OF NUMIDIA TRIED TO "BREAK" ROME

The rich men carried the day when Jugurtha, the king of Numidia, made war on his counsin Adherbal, who had the other half of the kingdom. When the latter took refuge in the city of Cirta, Jugurtha took it and killed all the people inside. *But among these were a lot of Roman merchants.* This raised a great "to-do" in Rome. "Declare war!" cried all the rich men. You see, they didn't know that they wouldn't be massacred next while on one of their "business trips"!

The Roman general that was sent to take him, it was believed, was bribed with some of the great treasure that the Numidian king had inherited, and soon Jugurtha had the whole country. He was the prize "buyer" of favors, the best "grafter" of his time. He was called to give an account of his acts before the Roman Senate, but here he "bought" the protection of a tribune, who could "veto" the trial. As he went, Jugurtha was reported to have said: "A city for sale, and bound to fall as soon as it finds a buyer!" The Romans went into Numidia again, and though they were beaten once, the rascal was at last dragged through Rome in chains and then left to starve to death in the dungeons under the Capitol. This place was nicknamed "the bath of ice", and the end of the money-baron king of Numidia must have been a horrible one in that cold, damp, ghastly place!

The pirates on the Mediterranean were later another menace to trade, and the rich men all said: "They must be caught!" So they gave great power to Pompey by a decree of the Senate, placing him ahead of Julius Cæsar. But the latter took things into his own hands, made his famous crossing of the River Rubicon, conquered Pompey in battle, won the job of dictator and—assassination.

Rome was now in the midst of the revolution that was to end the days of the republic in disorder. Factions fought for the government and the people were discontented because the land was being *taken from them* by the State. The luxury of Roman multi-millionaires was so great that they paid thousands of dollars for a banquet,* while the people of the country districts were cheated out of their trade of farming when all the grain that was needed began to pour in free from the captured lands. They flocked into Rome, idle, poor. The Senate got out of the "good graces" of the money class because, for once, it refused to pass a law releasing the publicans of Asia from a troublesome contract they had entered into. These were the days when three powerful men, Antony, Octavian and Lepidus, ruled. At last only Octavian was left, and he was the only ruler, the Senate being now powerless. It remained only to crown him emperor and this was soon done, as the people were demanding an end of wars and revolutions.

THE SINS OF THE MONEY-MAD EMPIRE

Rome was now in its "grand" age—the days of the distribution of corn to the poor, of free games in the amphitheater—the purple empire, wealthy, the haughtiest of the earth, but crimson with the blood of centuries of victims. The people that had been taken in war were her slaves—with their heads shaven and bruised with blows, they swarmed like dogs in the palaces of the poor. (Some rich men had several thousand slaves, so that their houses were really small villages.) These hardly-human things were thrown to the lions for the least offense.

---

* Lucullus, whose name has come down as a byword for luxurious feasting, invited Julius Cæsar to a $10,000 "home" dinner.

The emperor was the only god. Religion perished with honor. The twelve Cæsars were surrounded by men that flattered them—and won away all the important jobs in the empire. *Money flowed into her treasuries from all the nations she had robbed. Rome was now spending it for vices of the most terrible kind, for night-long banquets of wine, with showers of roses that dropped from the silk-canopied ceilings of the great new golden palaces of her emperors.* The agents of the emperor levied the taxes, and these ran like golden rivers from every corner of the Roman world into his treasure chest.

Rome had grown to be the world's largest city, as well as the grandest—she had 1,500,000 souls within her walls. The poor were idle as the rich, they slept in corners in rags, went free to the Circus—and waited till the emperor should next please to dole out his distribution of $50 or more for each man. Nero did this three times during his reign. In this terrible city the rich were no more secure, for at any time the emperor could have them put to death and take all their wealth. No doubt the great magnates of that day in their country houses, called "villas", got very little sleep in spite of their ebony beds, silken coverlets embroidered with gold, the slaves who waved fans over them and rubbed them with precious oils on coming from their marble baths. In the midst of their feasts—when whole oxen and boars were brought upon the table, while live birds fluttered from the roast when carved!—they must always have been under the shadow of the sword. Some, like the famous Maecenas, were kind patrons of poets and helped Art. But when the emperor frowned, they knew, it was time to make their wills and gash their wrist-veins! Yet like the common people of the streets, they liked to have gold thrown to them: those begged from the nobles, the nobles from Cæsar.

Rome was decaying, even while the emperors were carrying on their nightly "wild parties" by the light of human torches! Rome was now a nation of newcomers—the old families had died off; they had few sons, and the city was now made up of men from every corner of the earth, and even freed slaves.

CHRIST PREACHES THE DOCTRINES OF SOCIALISM

Meanwhile, in this strange hodge-podge of luxury and misery, the Roman Empire, Christianity had arisen. Its followers had among their teachings that the poor are blessed, "for theirs is the kingdom of heaven", and that it is easier for a "camel to go through the eye of a needle" than for a rich man to find "salvation". Side by side with the decline of Rome's power, with the increase of the civil wars that came in the third century A.D., was the steady growth of this

ROME, THE NERVE CENTER

powerful and strange belief that there was something higher than the power of money. "Render unto Cæsar the things that are Caesar's; unto God the things that are God's."

While the early "saints" shunned ease and prosperity to live in rags in a cell, Rome was finding it hard to keep her empire together. There were many new emperors; they died with strange suddenness. Sometimes there were several at once—as when the Thirty Tyrants ruled. Once when a new emperor had been assassinated, two rich men proposed to bid for the empire. One offered to pay each soldier $1,000 for it and the other a little more, and the second got it. But he didn't want to pay after he got into power and so he was killed without much delay! Finally, there were two emperors—one lived in the East (in Constantinople, built by Emperor Constantine) and the other in Rome. Power like that of the old kings of Persia surrounded the Roman Emperors of the East. The Western Goths came down from the north, and the twilight of the Empire came when they fell upon Rome and sacked it in 410 A.D.

THE DOOM OF BANKRUPT ROME

The once-proud nation of Rome had literally been bankrupted. The cause of her downfall lay at the root of her money system. The revolts of the working classes came about because the rich men in Rome plotted to ruin them. If they could not pay their taxes,— as was natural when the men were called to war and the fields lay idle—they could only borrow from the usurers at a rate so high that it could not be paid. The law provided only one solution— they could go under the condition called "nexus", or bound, and work to pay off their debts on their own farms, or they could be *sold by their creditors*. In either case they were slaves. When the grain supplies came in from Egypt and Sicily, the Italian farmers were "undersold". They had to give up their farms and became idlers. The aristocracy scorned trade, and bought more and more of the land, until it was divided into fewer and fewer great unproductive estates. The farmers who stayed as servants gradually became slaves.

There was little money coming into the Roman treasuries in the latter days—but vast sums were being spent for the luxuries; silks for the women were worth their weight in gold, and more than $400,000 annually went out of Rome to the East for splendid clothes, gems, spices and oils. To offset this loss, the emperors, beginning with Nero, began to mix cheaper metals in the coins. It was the same state of things as if the President of the United States should take out one-third of the silver in our dollars and substitute tin! At last the "denarius" was only copper coated with tin, and was officially called "no good" by the government, which was a plain admission of bankruptcy. The gold coin was also reduced to almost half its original weight.

The city of Rome ceased to be the money center of the earth, and the moving of the capital at last to Constantinople was a plain sign that this city was now the great rich metropolis of the day. In the last days a few wealthy men ruled. The end came when the money gave out which used to pour out from the capital to pay the hired soldiers which guarded the frontiers. These became fewer, the lines thinner, and the barbarians were able to break through. *Rome is the most terrible example ever known of a prosperous country that failed to "save for a rainy day".*

CHAPTER V

THE MONEY SHORTAGE OF THE GOTHIC AGE

The strong world-empire of Rome was overrun gradually by the barbarians, who first took Greece, and only spared Constantinople for a sum of money. Among the half-savage tribes of Western Europe, in the struggles between the Western Goths and their neighbors, the gold of Rome was soon scattered. The handsome coins of the Roman Emperors were not appreciated by these rude fighting men. They valued them only as so many pretty trinkets, but the gold and silver in them spelled WEALTH to them. The thing that happened with the break-up of the currency systems was a *return to "swapping."* The money began to disappear, for they melted it down into ornaments and dishes and *hoarded it. They didn't know the real way to use money. They set back the clock of world-business many hundreds of years.* These peoples were still in the cattle-raising and hunting stage, farming but little.

The barbarians were a simple lot who "got rich quick". When they first were forced down from their northern homes by the fierce Huns—who about this time came into Europe from the northeast —they had no riches. They were the original European leaders of "the simple life", and they were big, blonde fighting men who led good, hearty family lives, had no time for luxuries, and kept very "fit". It was easy to see that the weakened and dissipated Romans of the third century had "no chance", when it came to a struggle between them. But when these strong fellows from the north, with their hairy cheeks, helmets with animal horns, great muscles and armor, began to get glimpses of the Romans' golden drinking-cups, after they had captured one of the enemy generals' tents, it "gave them a new idea"!

Their simple wooden bowls and drinking-horns began to look downright shabby to them. So they made gold dishes that weighed hundreds of pounds! Some of these had to be lifted upon the table by machines. The barbarians went to extremes and showed little taste—like most folks who suddenly come into a lot of money. How did they get the gold? Well for one thing the once-proud Roman nation, that had made all the world pay taxes, had at last to *bribe the barbarians* by giving them free land or by paying in some cases many pounds of gold! Then the game of plunder yielded a great deal, especially when the Empire of the West went slowly to pieces. And the barbarians* were always fighting with one another.

They valued the gold coins of the Romans, as we have said, not for the use of them as money, but to melt them into treasure. Though it was a rough and simple life that they led, a handsome arm-ring of gold "talked louder than words". It immediately put a man into the class of Somebodies! They were great children so far as decorations went—and their pleasure in a useless piece of jewelry was just like that of a South Sea Islander who is proud of the ring in his nose.

But gold treasure had a connection with honor in the tribe. Whoever had the biggest chest of gold had a good chance to be chosen chief man of the *gau,* or county division. The connection was simple: wealth was to be had only by the best fighters. And the fighters could best take on the job of ruling, in the days when tribes were *always* fighting.

The German tribes of this time had a lot of faults—for just as they were good warriors, they were also big drinkers of mead (a sort of beer) and had a *passion for gambling.* It was said that they even gambled away their wives and children and themselves into slavery; and as they made a point of "keeping their bargains", they stuck to them in such cases.

The richest men got to be the rulers—and there were kings of these tribes, which grew up from the joining of several *gaus,* as early as 350 A.D. They got the favor of their followers by leading them to victory—and by distributing handsome gifts of gold and silver. They guarded their treasure closely, for they knew it was the secret of power. Each kept a strong box in which were the ornaments, diadems, beakers, tableware and harness of gold, minted money and bars or ingots of metal.

When an old barbarian king died, there was a struggle among his sons for possession of his treasure. One prince hurried from the battlefield as soon as he saw his parent struck down—for he wanted to get his hands on the gold before his brothers did! Terrible crimes were frequent. A king's son actually murdered his father at the advice of his bloody-minded cousin. It had been agreed that they were to divide the gold and the power. But the murderer soon got

---

* There were a large number of tribes—the Western Germans, including the Franks and the Saxons; the Eastern Germans, made up of the two branches of Goths and Vandals: the Northern Germans, (that are now the Danes and Scandinavians) and the Gauls (Celts, like the Britons related to the Irish and Welsh, but mixed by marriage with the Romans.) Out of these most nations of Western Europe have grown.

"what was coming to him," when the messengers of the cousin-prince were sent to examine the hoard.

"Thrust your arm into it and measure the depth, so that we can see how much there is!" they said.

But as the son, with the blood of his father still warm on his hands, bent down over the treasure chest,—the cousin traitorously had given the order—a messenger lifted his glittering battle-ax—and cracked open his skull! The red blood of kinsmen thus reddened much old-time gold.

This was an age of many rulers—under the king were lesser nobles. When a son came into the kingship and wanted to gain favor and make a sort of alliance with a powerful neighbor ruler, he would send messengers to say: "My father's kingdom and treasure are mine. Send to me, and I will willingly give you whatever you like of the lot!" He knew that it was simpler to do it this way than to have to give up everything after being beaten in battle!

THE RICH GIFTS OF KINGS AND NOBLES

Gifts were quite the custom—for *this was a way of buying the good graces of another*. Whenever messengers were sent from one "head man" to another, when peace was signed between two rulers of the early German tribes, presents were handed around. Not only the kings but the dukes and other men of importance, going down the line, all had their "pile." They took from the men just under them—because *the only law was might* and the weaker had to pay "tribute", or a sort of tax, to the stronger. It was hardest on the workers down at the bottom—they had to slave "overtime", and as soon as they got anything together, *it was taken away from them by the "men higher up." The lords knew that if they let anybody else get rich, he would be able to buy power and followers, and so be able to overthrow them and get to be a ruler.* So helpless were the "under dogs" that they had to be glad when their lives were not taken, too. The right of the sword was to be strong.

Kings' daughters at marriage had quite a "pile" of their own. It had been started for them when they were only a year or two old. When they were given as wife to some noble—sometimes to strengthen peace between tribes—they got a great deal more from the "free-will" gifts of neighboring chiefs and lesser nobles. (These were sometimes not so free as they were made out to be, for the givers knew that it wasn't good policy to offend a powerful king!) One chieftain's girl had some sixteen wagon-loads of silks and gold to carry with her on her wedding trip.

The early churches and monasteries each had its treasure. This was presented in the form of gifts by king and noble—gold images, vessels and even chains and jewelry. When the bishop found that his cloister was in danger from war, he sometimes thought it better to satisfy the leader of the enemy by buying his favor with a handsome piece from his treasure gold. This, together with the fear of the "holy men" which the barbarians had learned—they were afraid that these would call down the wrath of heaven—kept the church free from plundering.

King Guntram of the Franks once gave a handsome gold vessel to the church at Chalons—for the leaders with guilty consciences often used this way to make up for their misdeeds by good works. Only he could tell how he got the treasure that he made it out of, but—whether it was by murder, robbery or war—he told a very neat story to account for it!

UNTOLD RICHES THAT THE EARTH HID

One day Guntram while on a hunt—so he said, and it shows the ideas of the time—got tired and, while resting, went to sleep. His attendant kept watch—and what should he see but a small mouse, which crept out of the King's mouth! (It was in this way that the barbarians believed their souls went off on sight-seeing trips during their dreams.) The mouse tried its best to get across a little stream of water, but it found it couldn't. So finally the King's man reached out his sword and made a bridge, and the little animal went across and disappeared in a hole among the rocks, soon coming back and entering the ruler's mouth. Then Guntram dreamed, and his "soul" kept the memory of what it had seen in the cave, and he saw a great treasure lying there! So, as soon as he got awake, he ordered his men to dig—and, sure enough, there they found a vast hidden hoard of gold! (You may believe this or not, but it's a good story.) There were many beliefs as strange—that of the "divining rod" being a theory that these sticks acted like magnets to indicate gold.

Treasures play a big part in the stories of these early tribes. There is the tale about the gold of the Nibelungs—a fanciful race that lived in the earth. It was stolen one day, and so the victims laid a terrible curse on it, that brought misfortune to those that got it! Kept at the bottom of the river Rhine by the three Rhine-Daughters —a sort of imaginary fresh-water mermaid!—it was stolen by the ugly dwarf Alberich, one of the Nibelungs. He made a ring out of it, but it was taken in turn by the gods, and then by the giant Fafner, who closely guarded it in the form of a dragon. Siegfried, the hero of the early German stories, killed the monster and took it, but it brought misfortune and final death to all the mortals and to the gods who used it to ransom one of their goddesses from the

SHORTAGE OF THE GOTHIC AGE

giants. The story was the result of poetic minds working on the history of *actual bloody disputes and murders that arose over gold*. These heroes were idealized out of real fighting men that won hard wars.

The nation of Franks began to be the most powerful of Western Europe. They were united to some extent under King Chlodwig, who had taken the Christian faith and with 3,000 warriors was baptized by the Bishop of Rheims. He had sworn that he would be "converted" if he won a battle against another tribe. He won, and thus, we see, even out of bloody massacre can come a certain degree of good. But Chlodwig's religion never kept him from dispatching an enemy, and in fact it was only, according to accounts, "skin deep". When he died, his kingdom and his plunder were divided by his four sons. These four warred among themselves for the empire, one was killed in battle, the others took his land and executed his sons—one escaping by becoming a monk.

The son of another brother was Theudebert, who in 539 laid waste northern Italy and took a lot of plunder. He is important in the history of money because *he was the first Frank that ever made gold coins, bearing his own picture* instead of that of the emperor of Rome. He had a very good opinion of himself, too, for it is believed that he aimed to capture Constantinople and thus get control of the Empire of the East. On the coins was stamped the words "Our Master, Theudebert the Victor". But he did not live to see his empire expand to take in what was once all Rome, and after him there were endless civil wars again between the different princes. As in the case of Theudebert, we see that occasionally a ruler of the barbarians would set up a coinage system. These coins were usually based on the Roman, but they were not good in exchange beyond the borders of the province.

THE SOLID MONEY SYSTEM OF CHARLES THE GREAT

A real coinage did not arise until the Frankish king, Charles the Great, founded his strong empire. In the year 800 he was crowned emperor, while kneeling in St. Peter's on Christmas Day, by Pope Leo III, whom he had restored when driven from his papacy by a revolt in Rome. Charles the Great now fell heir to the perished power of ancient Rome—he, who was only the bastard son of a Frank tribal king. His great ability in battle cemented scattered tribes, and he showed a great genius for ruling. He divided his empire into counties, over each of which he set a "count." He reduced the number of his dukedoms to three and made these rulers his servants. He sent out special commissioners, who "kept an eye" on these officials *and the clergy as well*. They also saw to the collection of the taxes, the management of schools and churches. The coin established by Charles the Great was the pound of silver, or "livre", modeled after the Roman pound. It became the standard of Western Europe. Many coins have been patterned after this famous one, including the pound sterling of England. He made the payment of "tithes" (one-tenth) of the produce of all his lands compulsory: it was used to support the church. Charles reigned for forty-seven years, and died at seventy in the year 814. Upon the ruins of Great Charles' empire the "feudal" system was set up.

What really happened was the break-up of the kingdoms into small self-governed groups. The kings who followed Charles were not strong enough to keep the whole country together and enforce the laws. They let the priests get more power and go without paying taxes; and *the counts, who had once been only officers of the king, now held the counties in their own right.* The kingdom of the Franks was divided between two brother kings (843), and these two parts formed roughly the France and Germany of to-day; it was the beginning of a thousand years of war between these countries. In France *the kings were not much more powerful than their great lords, who were kings in their own lands.* There were two main classes of the people—the nobles who owned the soil, made up of warriors and churchmen; and the peasants, who worked for them. There was no central government to speak of—*each man was a law to himself, and did as he pleased in proportion to his power and wealth.* There was nothing for the poor to do but attach themselves to some strong and rich lord, who would protect them in return for their services to him. *If that lord made war on the king, they had to obey.*

WHEN MONEY AND TRADE WERE PARALYZED BY WARS

In the wars and general disorder of the time, the inland European peoples had little time to carry on trade. *Things were at a standstill. The chief curse of the dull period known as the Middle Ages was the lack of money. Whenever a nation has got to be great and prosperous, has built splendid cities, and led a thriving and cultivated life, it has been because great quantities of money have been kept flowing in and out of its treasuries through war or trade.* The great kings of the past had kept millions of subjects working in the mines and fields so that streams of wealth ran into their strong-boxes. Then had come wars, and the riches were carried off to some other place, and a new "business boom" resulted. But in the feudal days no king was strong enough to make nobles pay taxes.

In the early Middle Ages the money of the Romans gradually disappeared, and the little that was issued from time to time by some barbarian kings was only a "drop in the bucket." Besides, no mines were worked to any great extent during this time in Europe. The result was that *money almost disappeared,* what little there was being hoarded for its value as metal. In an age when there were hundreds of little feudal kingdoms in each country, France alone once had some 200 private mints where nobles made money, but it was impossible for anyone to issue a coinage that would be of much account. *So they went back to the old-time system of exchange. The prices of things went down to almost nothing,* in some cases being fixed by law.

The only thing that people had left in any quantity to give in exchange was their own work. Labor was cheap, and the rate of pay was also fixed by law, so that the people really became slaves. They were set to work to build the great castles of the lords— modeled after the Roman camps, or "castra"—with their tower or "keep" at one end, their great walls with slits from which arrows or molten lead could be sent down on an enemy, and their surrounding ditch filled with water (moat) crossed by drawbridges. From these the great lords and their followers went to plunder the land of their enemies.

THE NEW POWER OF CLERGY AND POPE

The clergy of that day lived in great stone monasteries, built by the poor laborers during long years, and they also laid stone upon stone on little pay to raise the wonderful Gothic cathedrals and churches that to-day are thought marvels. The churchmen made up the most powerful group of the old society. The archbishops were really noble lords, and led their servants to war for their king when it pleased them. They began to organize, until in the eleventh century they were the *richest, the most powerful force existing.* The monastery of Cluny was the wealthiest land-holding corporation in the feudal world. Nobles sought refuge in its walls, *taking their treasures with them.*

It was in this age that the Pope became the rival of any king. This was the natural result of his position as *head of land-holding powers.* The story is told that Bruno, Bishop of Toul, when on the way to Rome to accept the office from King Henry IV of Germany, stopped at Cluny. Hildebrand, its prior, told him to dismiss his great train of attendants and go in penitent style, barefoot. This humble entrance so appealed to the imagination of the people that he was popularly acclaimed. He made Hildebrand his minister, and the latter succeeded him, calling himself Pope Gregory.

Soon arose a famous "scrap" between Henry and Gregory, who claimed that *all the lands of the world belonged to the church,* for were they not Christ's kingdom on earth? He forbade all Christians to be faithful to their oaths to the King. He later excommunicated Henry, and Henry had a council declare the Pope "deposed." The king marched upon Rome, but his followers deserted him. Henry at last became so broken in spirit that he waited three days in the snow outside the castle where the Pope held his court. Each had charges to make against the other; each claimed rule by Divine Right.

The Prince of the Church at last received him.

"Heaven's judgment is infallible!" he said. "If I am guilty of wrongdoing, may I be stricken dead as I eat this holy wafer!"

When the time came for Henry to do the same, he "balked."

Though Gregory graciously forgave the king's sins, the story got about and the king's authority was gone forever. No longer was he alone God's Anointed. So greatly had the clergy's power grown since Charles' day! Yet Gregory never realized his aim of becoming *feudal lord of the earth.* Germany was broken up into small estates in the centuries of wars between Church and kings. And not many centuries were to go by before in that same land, as well as in Italy, the earthly power of the Pope was to be lost.

This was the age of knighthood, a class that was made up of the rich, for only they could afford a life of leisure. The knight usually had a landed estate, worked by tenants, who paid a rent in labor and produce. (It was not thought "honorable" to run one's own place as a gentleman farmer.) He was usually in the service of a great lord, who gave him this land; and in return he followed the lord on his war expeditions. *At first the amount of one's wealth fixed one's rank*—somewhat as in old Rome—the highest class being the princes, dukes and counts; the next, the barons, third the knights, and last, the squires. Later all these came to be known as the "nobles", and only the sons of these could become knights, no matter how much money another man had.

But one was not born a knight; one had to serve an apprenticeship and be "dubbed." That was the beginning of the titled nobility still existing in Europe, and the honorary titles are still given by the British King with the ceremony of the old days of adventure—a tap and the words, "Arise, Sir Knight!"

It took a lot of money to go through the period of training to be knighted, and so in the old days the poorer nobles stayed squires, and attended the knights—a sort of valet duty including making beds, but then thought honorable! The romantic warriors of the day were really big bullies, corresponding to the prize-fighters of to-day, who dispatched half a sheep at one meal, made anyone eat his words who insulted them by even a look, and could cut a man and horse in half with one blow of a sword!

WHEN EUROPE'S KNIGHTS WENT TO FIGHT THE ARABS

The combination of religious enthusiasm and of plenty of spare time and a taste for fighting brought about the crusades, or "wars of the cross." *These great movements of armies from Western Europe to Palestine had important results on the money market, which had been in a very low state for several centuries.* The aim of the crusades, as every schoolboy knows, was to rescue the sacred buildings of the Holy Land from the Mohammedans; but the "holiness" of the wars did not make the rich plunder of the East any less tempting. Just as in the case of the old Greeks and the Persians, it was a struggle between East and West that now took place—the white man against the brown, symbolized by the signs of their religions; the Cross against the Crescent. *What really lay under the wars was race hatred, struggle for power, land, wealth!*

The East was much more civilized at this time, it had a better trade with other nations, had bigger cities, greater luxury, refinements, government and intelligence. *It had got down to business, carried on commerce, become rich,* and the Arabs began to come farther and farther into Western Europe. The "infidel" East was the richest part of the world for several hundreds of years; it was the last stronghold of civilization. When the rage for crusading came on the Christians, and whole villages were deserted by the poor, by men, women and children, who swarmed over Europe like a disordered mob,—those who lived to reach the land of the Arabs saw *unbelievable wealth!*

The Arab princes, or caliphs, lived amid gold and ivory, silks and gems that made the princes of Western Europe feel like simple savages. An example is found in an auction sale held by one of these Eastern rulers in the middle of the eleventh century. Here is what the bearded old codger had among his things: a chest filled with emeralds worth $7,200,000, a turban covered with precious stones, including an immense ruby and 100 pearls, a necklace of gems worth $300,000, gold dishes and others of enamel inlaid with gold, mirrors with handles of jewels or gold, 400 cases of jewels, 6,000 gold vases; animals, such as peacocks and gazelles made of gold, trimmed with pearls and rubies; a golden palm tree with jeweled fruit.

The wave of the invading Arabs overflowed into Europe as early as 600 A.D. The Mohammedans spread into Africa and conquered Spain about 900 A.D. *They would have conquered all Europe,* but the Franks beat them at the battle of Tours. Otherwise Europeans to-day would be brown men!

The Crusaders took Jerusalem in 1099—and the city that was once the great capital of King Solomon's kingdom now became a colony of Christian Europe. The city had had many changes of fortune in the meantime—had been captured by the Romans and then after the decay of their empire had fallen into the hands of the Mohammedans. *But the plundering of the "heathens", as the Christians were pleased to call them, was as nothing beside that done by their own army. On the way to Jerusalem the route was marked by the ruins of cities that had been stripped of their wealth.*

THE PRICELESS PLUNDER OF JERUSALEM

The Crusaders' army was filled with men who had run away from their debts, serfs who had escaped from a hard slavery under powerful lords, and even criminals who had broken jail—and all, up to the great nobles who rode at the head with their hawks and hounds, wanted to get rich!

They first arrived at Constantinople, the great Christian capital of the East, plundering as they came. Here the Emperor Alexius, by force and the persuasion of rich peasants, got the great leaders, Hugo, Godfrey of Boulogne and Boemund, to swear allegiance to him. He was a wise ruler, and saw that they might take the empire of the East from him. By trickery he persuaded the Mohammedans in the city of Nicaea to surrender to him instead of to the crusaders, and the latter, though angry because they had been *cheated out of their plunder,* were "hushed up" by rich gifts to lords and pilgrims alike. Next Antioch was betrayed by an Armenian sentry, and the people mercilessly killed and *all their houses robbed of great treasure.* The siege of Jerusalem lasted a week, and on July 15 the Crusaders poured into it, murdering the Mohammedans. *Everybody was looking for gold, silver, treasure!*

The lands of the East that were taken were governed on the feudal plan. Godfrey of Boulogne was appointed Guardian of the Holy Sepulcher—which was the highest ruling power—and the other chiefs of the army had each his little "staked claim", where he built his strong castle. Besides Godfrey's kingdom, there were three others—all making up a little slice of Europe in Asia. In all there were scores of little feudal holdings ruled by lords who, in many cases, coined their own money. These were patterned somewhat after the silver pound of Charles the Great, which was divided into 240 pence. The crusaders had been aided by delegations from the large Italian cities, which had revived trade—Venice, Genoa and Pisa. These had sent fleets, and in reward they were given some of the Eastern ports.

SHORTAGE OF THE GOTHIC AGE

WHEN CONSTANTINOPLE WAS SACKED OF ITS GOLD

The second and third crusades led to the fall of Constantinople before the great armies of the West under the Venetian leader Dandolo in the year 1204. *Under the pretext of sailing to retake Jerusalem*—for the Mohammedans had got it back—he arranged for the transporting of the armies by water at a cost of $9,000,000 and the Venetians promised to divide the spoils with the others. But he prevailed on them to attack Constantinople. Alexius abandoned the capital, and the massacre was terrible. The crusaders plundered the Christian church of Saint Sophia, drank the holy wine and got drunk, and played gambling games on the holy tables in the altar.

The plunder was one of the richest that has ever fallen to an army—gold and silver, gems, silks. The plunder in money amounted to 50,000 marks (more than $5,000,000) for the Venetians and about $500,000,000, or one hundred times that much, for the other crusaders. One of the old chroniclers says of the sack of Constantinople: "There was great joy and honor for the victory which God had given them, since those who had been poor were rich and happy." The adventurer Dandolo was one of the greatest "plungers" of history—and one of the names blackest in frightful treachery. He had persuaded the crusaders to turn from Palestine to attack the Empire of the East. The Pope had cursed and excommunicated him—but *he had been successful.*[*] The Pope denounced him bitterly, but he was forced to acknowledge the traitor Emperor of the East. He was even appointed a patriarch of the Eastern church, without having to bow the knee to Rome.

THE RISE OF THE RICH TRADING CITIES OF ITALY

The most important result of the crusades, in a business sense, was the re-opening of the trade routes, which had been closed to Europe by pirates on the sea and brigands on land. The crusaders now held the main land route—the spices, gems and silks of China came by way of the Persian Gulf, the Euphrates River and then by caravan to Antioch or Damascus; and they also controlled the sea route for goods brought from India down the Nile to Cairo and then to Alexandria.

And as a result of the trade resumed between the East and the

---

[*] But the great capital of the East—taken by treachery and sodden with the blood of the victims—was destined not to stay in "Christian" hands. Two centuries and a half went by, and then the Mohammedans fell upon the city and took it in 1453. With this victory by the Turks the East became closed again to Europe, and so it remained for hundreds of years. Turkey then held a brown, powerful finger on the pulse of the Mediterranean.

West, a new prosperity set in for Europe, and particularly for the Italian cities. These began to make their own money—first the silver "grosso", then in Florence the "florin" and in Venice the "ducat" (named after the dukes who made them)—both of gold.

The thirteenth century was a time of great prosperity. Venice got to be the money center of Europe: it was the beginning of the great age of trading about which Shakespeare wrote his "Merchant of Venice". The Bank of Venice was founded in 1158, and the principles of credit were re-introduced into Europe—the bill of exchange, the letter of credit and a form of paper money. We know that strict laws were established in the Italian "business" cities—Shylock, you remember, was condemned to forfeit half his estate and only barely escaped with his life because he had conspired to take more than his rightful return on the money he lent. Prices of things went up everywhere in Europe.

Even in Western Europe a wholesome respect for business came back gradually. Before this time a noble lord thought himself disgraced if he soiled his hands in any way except with the blood of an enemy. The old-time knights were taught to scorn everything but pride, "honor". How they felt about money is well illustrated by a true story that happened in France in the twelfth century. To pretend contempt for wealth Count Bertram Raimbault at a great meeting of knights at Beaucaire had the tourney ground plowed up by twelve teams of oxen and had 30,000 pieces of silver sown in the furrows! This foolhardy act gave rise to the saying "sowing one's money", which is sometimes heard to-day. But the money would have bought some of the comforts of life for the poor serfs that worked without wages under these noble lords.

Chivalry was a splendid golden *sham;* it covered with a cloak of romance the deeds of an age that was little better than savage in its ideals. The lords and ladies dressed in silks and had precious jewels, but they had only the roughest kinds of furniture and for a long time *they ate with their fingers.* When the crusaders learned some of the refinements of life from the Mohammedans, they brought back new ideas. Slowly the civilization of Europe changed. The greatest improvement was in the lot of common folk.

The crusades helped bring about the end of feudalism. The nobles began to lose their power, partly because they were often absent from home for long periods on the crusades. Their power was based on the land they owned, but in the armies that overran the East, lord and slave were much more nearly equal in the face of danger. Often the barons sold their hereditary rights and lands to get enough money to go on these trips. Many were killed—the noble lines were wiped out, and a new aristocracy grew up. The serfs were killed in large numbers on the crusades, those that stayed at home were more valuable, and at the last the demand for these workers raised them to the state of free day laborers for pay. The new flood of gold that poured into Europe made money less "tight", and soon the dependents of the lords were able to pay a money tax to their nobles, instead of having to give their own services. This turned them into independent farmers, who thus paid rent.

Best of all, *Europe was going to work*; the cities were growing; the middle class was developing its tradesmen. Each trade had a sort of secret order called a "guild"—somewhat like the labor unions of to-day. The lords used to exact taxes from the towns, and they meekly submitted until they began to have a rich merchant class. These had enough money to resist the nobles. They could store up provisions for a seige, hire paid soldiers and buy great quantities of weapons and war machines just as well as the lords could. The lords believed that the richer the city, the more tax it should pay. But when the cities began to be bold enough to fight, they won not only the freedom from taxation, but also the right to govern themselves. Often they demanded charters at the point of the sword,—and sometimes they got them. At other times they were badly beaten by the king. The free cities were called "communes" or "villes". New towns were often established by nobles, the ground given to those who applied, and, most important, markets were established. These were held at intervals through the year, the farmers bringing in their produce. The towns were often "asylums" for those convicted of debt or minor offences. Also serfs escaped to them, lived there for a year without being claimed and became free men. But the towns were not fit to rule themselves, and the kings' power grew.

THE TERRIBLE CRIMES COMMITTED BY KINGS

The fourteenth century saw the suppression of the Order of Knights Templar. This was a body of religious warriors organized in Palestine after the first crusade. Its members took oaths like the clergy; they were a sort of knight-priests. Philip IV of France coveted the wealth of the order, and he used an opportunity when he had Pope Clement in an "awkward situation", to demand of him the suppression of this order. Philip took their lands and wealth, making a flimsy excuse of turning it over to the Knights of St. John —a rival order—but really putting it safely away in his own treasury. The crusading priests had been showered with gifts. The buildings of the order at Paris—called the Temple—were really a small city in themselves, and the Templars owned land that extended to the Seine River.

The king's plot was deeply-laid. On the pretext of starting a new crusade he persuaded one of the grand masters of the order to come to Paris from Burgundy, bringing with him 150,000 gold florins and silver enough to load ten mules. Suddenly all the men of the order were arrested and put to the torture on a charge of heresy. They lay in prison several years, before their order was abolished. Fifty were burned to death slowly—turned to ashes from the feet up —because they would not confess that they were guilty of religious unbelief. At last Philip promised to restore the lands to the church if the order itself was wiped out. The Pope yielded—he had himself been placed in the Papacy by Philip—and a council was called. The knights were condemned to life imprisonment, but at the trial of one of their leaders, de Molay, the grand master, broke out in a valiant defense. The king spoke a word to his men, and as the trial ended, the two leaders were seized. Their terrible fate has been only whispered, but it is believed that they were burned to death by night on a little island in the Seine. De Molay, dying, cried out in awful accents that Clement would meet him in the other world before forty days had gone and that Philip must do so in a year! Each died before the time was up.

The struggles between clergy and kings brought the most cruel instruments into use in wreaking vengeance that man has ever conceived. The superstition of the age could be so easily played upon that anyone who had wealth could be accused of heresy and submitted to the most horrible tortures by the Inquisition. The silly notions of the age made the final test of guilt to consist in passing successfully through an "ordeal"—that is, if he could walk through fire and not be burned or stick his arm into boiling water safely, he would be innocent. The evils that came about through the abuse of the Christian beliefs by blood-thirsty princes and churchmen brought about the rebellion of the lower classes which is known as the Reformation.

The end of the middle ages came when men began to think and act for themselves. In the field of business it came with the growth of trade and the arts in the cities, in government with the new feeling of nationality and growth of strong monarchies, in education with a greater interest and curiosity in all things. The revival of the use of money in all places, the freeing of the poor that had worked without pay for the lords, the growth of industry and commerce—all elevated the City to the place of power and brought in the Renaissance. The money shortage of the Gothic Age was over, when Columbus and other daring sailors touched the shores of a New World—the source of the Wealth of the Future!

CHAPTER VI

MERCHANT PRINCES WHO REIGNED IN BAROQUE DAYS

THE beginning of the Baroque Age was the dawn of the merchant-adventurer's day. The Middle Ages did not come to an end on a particular day, at any particular hour, as so many people are tempted to believe! *It was a steady change that undermined the old order, and the cause of it was largely economic—that is, connected with trade, business, money.* For hundreds of years business had, in fact, been dead. The people had only two real occupations—fighting and (to small extent) farming. They had been stay-at-homes, with small interests; there were no nations as we have these to-day—only collections of little independent domains ruled over fighting landlords, from whom no tenant could move away on the first of May or October! The crusades opened up the eyes of everybody to the beauty and size of the world. Just as when our soldiers went to France in 1918, the fighting men came back with a new "point of view". They came back with tastes for new foods, desires for fine clothes, new colors to look at; they had seen a brilliant new world and were not satisfied with the old life,

The growth of the towns,—concerning which we have spoken in the last chapter—was the most hopeful turn in affairs. *Here money began to be piled up.* With this capitol the building of the great cathedrals was financed. In the port cities fleets were built. People were developing new and expensive tastes. The caravans brought the spices, jewels, dyes, silks of the East to the Mediterranean ports; wool and flax from England and France were woven into fine new clothing and came through the hands of the merchants of Holland. The fifteenth century opened on a new ideal of luxury. Whole new classes of traders, brokers, merchants, "middle-men" arose to keep a stream of goods moving. *Money circulated rapidly; and that is the first requirement for prosperity. Not money stored up, useless, but being spent and then regained again in exchange for other goods, makes for a business "boom".*

The trading port cities of the North organized the Hanseatic League—a great federation of seaport towns with strict rules to protect one another's interests. It made treaties that were binding on all those who wanted to trade with them—from far-away Russia to southern Italy. It was a sort of international marine law that grew up—and there was nothing more badly needed than some kind of agreement of this sort between cities and nations. The League started trading houses in all the sea cities of Western Europe. The Universities that had sprung up began to study the old laws of the Romans, and out of these was shaped a code for Europe *which had a big effect in standardizing trade*. The new inventions, including printing, spread new ideas; gunpowder made a new kind of war necessary, just as poison gas has done to-day; but most of all, the compass helped along water travel, for men could now sail out boldly on the ocean that to them was full of all sorts of hideous sea serpents, monsters, terrors of the dark. They had been taught that, if they sailed far enough, they would get to the end of the earth and fall off!

COMMERCIAL BARONS OF RENAISSANCE EUROPE

The Italian seaside cities became rich and flourished very early, as we have seen. The great cities were ruled by tyrants, who first got rich by trade and then turned this money power into *governing* might. The Medicis in Florence are the most famous example. The very conqueror of Constantinople in 1204 had been a merchant, who later had been chosen to rule as "doge" of Venice. Comfort and luxury increased on every hand, and the Italian nobles rivaled one another in building splendid palaces, filled with the most artistic marble carvings, beautiful paintings by noted masters, and furniture and articles of personal decoration of the rarest kinds. The great era of painting and architecture in Italy was directly owing to the prosperity of the cities in which these masterpieces were produced. The term "Renaissance" or "New Birth" immediately calls up a picture of all the fine things of art and literature—and it was the rich lords of the Italian cities who acted as patrons, giving money and other rewards, to the artists who turned out these splendid things. The famous Cathedral of Pisa, the Church of St. Mark's in Venice, and other grand creations were paid for out of the wealth derived from profits of trade.

But though the men of the Renaissance built palaces and were personally gay and "polished", they were likely to go to the other extreme in joy and freedom of life. They were, in fact, in some cases really monsters. They were treacherous, murderous, cruel, even while they were patrons of art! An example is seen in the bands of brigands or robbers that lived like outlaws, and *could be bought to do the vilest crimes*. They could be bought in droves by any city that wanted some "dirty work"—an invasion of a neighbor town, or the wholesale murder of a princely house—done for a neat little sum! This type of man, when he got rich from robbery or war, if he was persuasive and bold enough, got to be a ruler. The tyrants that ruled many of the city-republics of the north were such.

The main types of mind that marked the people of this day were those of impatience with restraint, and insistence on thinking and doing for oneself; interest in the things around them—the beauty of a flower, a fine figure, a good wine! *The whole trend of things was against* "standing for" the old rule of the Church, which had told men what they must think, believe, do and say on all occasions! (To be sure, they didn't practice all of it, but it was the "theory" of the Middle Ages.) Together with this new independence, daring, came a growth of intelligence, curiosity as to the world.

This was the spirit that was preparing for the Reformation, a movement to do one's own thinking in the religious field. The Church was founded on a noble creed, but it turned out in the course of centuries to be a *money aristocracy*. From the days when the monasteries began to lay up their great wealth in feudal days and the bishops got to be equal of noble lords because they owned much land, the church got richer and more luxurious. This was warned against by men in the church itself. But the revolt came in Germany, where there was little money to pay the taxes and gifts for charity that the priests asked. Italy got richer, because it was the seat of the head of the church. The break came when a monk, Tetzel, went to canvass Germany for "gifts", giving letters of the church granting its forgiveness from sins, in case of repentance. The Church sometimes sold "indulgences" or absolutions from sin, to pay for great buildings. Those for St. Peter's brought Luther's protest.

The old manuscripts that had lain buried in the musty libraries of French and German monasteries and the buildings of Constantinople were soon brought out. They began to have a new value, because the universities were bringing teachers of the old languages from the East. They were now bought and sold eagerly, by rich collectors, copied and finally printed. "First editions", or the original writings of long dead authors, were sold for just as high prices as they are to-day. The narrow ideas of the Middle Ages were now displayed by the rich feeling for the beautiful things that the old Greek and Roman writers had. No longer did people believe that their souls were in danger if they looked at fine things, heard and saw the beauties of nature and Art. They began to laugh at the theory that the Devil was trying to ensnare them through their five senses! From the Arabs many sciences were learned—such as algebra, and from studying the old works of the Greeks, men learned again how to figure things in navigation that the old-time nations had a knowledge of. Most important of all, anybody now could be "educated", because books began to appear, and be read widely, instead of—as in the old days—the priesthood being the only class that could acquire knowledge.

ADVENTURERS AND THE LURE OF GOLD

Among the subjects that now began to be eagerly studied was geography. Everybody was eager to learn about the rich lands of the East about which travelers brought back such wonderful stories. "The wealth of the Indies" became a by-word in Europe. Among the famous travelers was Marco Polo of Venice, who in the early fourteenth century came back after much wandering in the lands of Tartary and wrote a book that took the breath away! Marco had been a sort of private secretary to the Khan, or prince of the Tartars and had gone on diplomatic errands for him during the best part of twenty years. When he came back to Europe, he was thrown into prison after being captured in a war between Genoa and his native city. While he was in jail, he dictated his story to a fellow-prisoner, who wrote it out. Marco had brought back a great deal of wealth to prove his story—so much that he was called "Sir Millions".

But, in spite of the extravagant stories, which were told about the Atlantic as well as the East—of magic islands with wonderful cities of gold which disappeared under the water at intervals—a real knowledge of the earth was growing up. From actual experience in coasting along the shores, seagoing men began to make maps called "port guides", that were wonderfully near to the accurate ones of today. Men still believed that the earth was flat and that the sun went down over the edge of it, but they were ready for new discoveries. The things that set them to looking toward the West were the crushing victories of the Turks, who in 1453 took Constantinople, and captured the cities of the Italians in the East. It was the final downfall of the Roman Empire of the East—long changed to Byzantium, with a population that was a curious mixture of many nationalities. The Turks were fighters and farmers—like the early Europeans, but much more backward, so far as trade was concerned. They put the "lid" tightly over the commerce of the Mediterranean. So it stayed for hundreds of years—until the Turk began to lose his hold bit by bit, and became the "Sick Man of Europe". This was a great calamity for trade. It set back the business of Europe, and perhaps changed its whole history!

Now was the time when the lands of the Spanish peninsula—and especially the newly-created kingdom of Portugal—rose to great power. King John of the latter country set out with a great fleet of ships and men in the year 1415 on an expedition against the Moors in

Africa. The riches of the city of Ceuta were the objective of the trip, and when King John "advertised" for men to help in the expedition, the hardened adventurers of other lands came flocking. The fleet sailed in July, and with it went 80,000 men. The city soon yielded and was plundered of its riches. Under Henry, son of John, who was appointed its governor, a great plan was made to restore the trade routes to the East and increase the power of Portugal. He was nicknamed "the Navigator", for the ships that he sent out year by year to try to find a way through some river of Africa that would lead from the west coast of this continent to the East. This was a vain dream, but in the process, Portugal found and took many new lands —the Azores, Madeiras, the settlements on the Guinea coast. The big barrier was the great, bulging cape that forms the upper west coast of Africa. The tides here were treacherous and beyond it there were terrible rumors of dangers. The hand of Satan was stretched up from the sea, they believed, to grasp the ship of an unlucky sailor! Yet here was romance in plenty—riches, gold, the magic wealth of the East beckoned these daring adventurers!

A new age of conquest had begun, although the sailors didn't know it—*the days when nations were to be great and powerful, wealthy and productive, by discovering instead of war.* In 1434 one of the Portuguese sailors finally rounded the west cape of Africa and soon other ships continued down the coast and discovered what they called the "River of Gold". Whether they found real treasure here, or whether the name referred to the rich natural scenery, is not certain. *From these trips the men began to bring back African slaves.* It was the first instance of this modern form of bondage that was to curse the African for centuries. It brought cheap labor into Portugal, and this had an important effect on the wage situation. The native laborers were left idle.

In 1486 Diaz sailed to the very southern tip of Africa and even some distance up the other side. The time was now ripe for the appearance of Columbus, the Genoese adventurer, who barely ten years later, in the service of the Spanish sovereigns, *blundered* upon the Bahamas and Cuba off the mainland of America. *He* had been sailing to the West in order to get around the globe to the great, rich East—acting on his conviction that the earth was round! The joke, it must be admitted, was on Columbus. He believed that he had reached India. Spain at one stroke became the rival of Portugal, and at last the Pope was prevailed on to draw an imaginary line several hundred leagues west of the Azores, giving Spain all to the west of it including the regions, so the Pope said, as far as India! This would have been a realm, indeed—as it included—though His Holiness didn't know it—about three-quarters of the earth!

WHEN SPAIN LOOTED THE RICH LANDS OF SOUTH AMERICA

The results to European business of the discovery of America were of great importance, as it opened up great stores of gold and silver in the new lands. The results to Spain at once were rather meager. Indeed, the Portuguese—following up the voyage around Africa of Vasco da Gama—had much a richer "haul" in the East, under Albuquerque. They had extended their conquests from Malabar, taken Malacca and Ormuz, which controlled the Straits passage and the Persian Gulf. Sudden wealth was the result, and a government weakened by bad management enjoyed a brief but brilliant period of glory, with slave labor imported to do all the work. The chances for trade were very great, but Portugal neglected them.

Meanwhile Spain had found only a little gold and a few pearls in the New World. Balboa brought back stories of a land "running over with gold", which the Indians indicated was toward the south. This was the great civilization of the Aztecs in Mexico, which they themselves had taken from an earlier cultivated race, the Toltecs. The ancient Mexicans had a very high form of culture—great fortified cities, with drawbridges, some ruins of which are standing to-day. They had a money system with definite values on a unit based on the cocoa-bean. Gold dust was measured in quills of their system, and so carried and used as money.

The conquest of the Aztecs would have been impossible for the small Spanish force, but the superstitious Montezuma, emperor of the Aztecs, let the invaders under Cortez come in because he thought they looked like gods that he had seen in a dream! The Spaniards made him swear allegiance to their king, and finally seized the emperor and made him pay a ransom as price of his safety. The Aztec empire fell after three months of cruel fighting, when Cortez, after leaving the capital for a time, returned to find it in arms against him. He was aided by some of the other Mexican tribes. The city was destroyed, the allies reduced to slavery, the great temples and sacred treasure houses looted, and the treasure—all except one-fifth which was sent to the King of Spain—divided among the invaders. What great sums of money and gold were there divided we do not know!

The greatest stream of gold and silver and precious stones now came flowing into Europe in the succeeding centuries. The wealth of Mexico that had been sent to Spain had transformed that land, and, not satisfied, the nation was looking for more conquest. Pizarro now formed his plan for conquering Peru, and in 1528 he secured a commission of the king of Spain to make the attempt. He landed with a force of only two hundred men, and luckily found the capital of the Incas—which was another marvelous civilization to find in a wilderness—in the midst of a civil war. Two princes were fighting for the rule and one had imprisoned his brother. Here the tragedy of Mexico was repeated: the trusting natives were duped by the Spaniards, their leader held for ransom and the plunder of the city carried through. The royal treasures, the gold in the temples and the property of the people amounted to millions. The ruler of the Incas was executed.

Pizarro shared the empire with Almagro, another Spaniard, who was given Chile. A struggle broke out between them, and in the civil war that followed both were killed. Thus the ill-gotten treasure of the Incas empire did not remain long in the bloody hands that grasped it! The Spaniards set up a new capital—the Lima of to-day, and another great source of wealth was added to the lands of Spain. Peru had the richest silver mines of the world, and all this precious metal poured into Europe from America, stimulating trade.

But, not yet satisfied, Spain went on to conquer Colombia, which it did easily and founded the capital of Bogota. The last conquest was of the north region of Antioquia, whose masters, Robledo and Heredia, gained a greater plunder than any previous European in America, and also won for Spain the great gold mines of the Andes, among the richest in the world. *The conquest of South America put in the hands of Europeans the best sources of gold and silver in the then known world.* The crimes committed to secure them were very black, the future of the South American countries was destroyed for many centuries, the number of the massacred and those who died in slavery under the invaders' rule was enormous—but the exploit was the greatest financial *coup* of any nation since the days of Rome.

THE AGE OF PIRACY AND THE "SPANISH MAIN"

Now began a romantic age such as the world has seldom seen. It was the day when ships sailed the sea to plunder, to capture and to sack! *It was the period of piracy as a fine art.* The gold of the world was all coming over the Atlantic from the mines worked by the enslaved people of Peru and Mexico. Beneath the whips of their Spanish contractors, they piled up an enormous treasure, and the gold-fleet came ever so often from Spain to "collect". Sometimes one shipload of treasure was worth several millions of dollars! Can one blame the daring shipmen of the day for wanting to "hold up" these boats and get a fortune in one stroke? It was a lawless age, when nations themselves became rich by plunder—and it had been in just this form of international robbery that Spain had got hold of South America. Before her, the Incas and the Aztecs had themselves plundered the land from other tribes before them. It was a network of robbery.

XX

This was the day of the "buccaneers", of "pieces of eight" (a Mexican money or metal piece worth a little more than a dollar), of "dubloons", a Spanish coin. The explorers sent out by the nations could do pretty much as they pleased; if they saw a likely-looking vessel that seemed to have treasure in its hold, and they were strong enough in men and weapons, they stopped and boarded the strange boat, or fired on it with their rude cannon, until it surrendered. Private shippers or merchants found this so much easier a life than trading that they also hoisted the black flag with skull and cross-bones!

The sea route was little known, and such men suffered under some hardships. So they valued, often more than the gold, the maps and charts with marked courses that they sometimes found in taken ships. The secret routes of the Spanish treasure ships were hard to find out, as they *changed them every time they made a trip*. They went together to a certain spot, then they separated and again met in a convenient harbor when they were loaded with their rich treasure. Once an English sea captain blundered into one of these harbors, and was amazed to find himself within hailing distance of the richest collection of money in the world! He didn't stay. It wasn't "healthy!"

Once a year Spain sent a great fleet of galleons to America, which was convoyed by ships of war, and brought back the year's richest cargo of treasure. Not only was the greatest source of gold and silver placed in the hands of Europeans, but an enormous territory—as big as another Europe—was opened for exploitation. The products of this great realm began gradually to stream across the Atlantic, and trading was greatly increased. The metals helped, too, to make trade brisker. Prices went up, the use of paper money—which had been necessary because there wasn't enough silver—was to some extent discontinued. The money market of Europe had a great "boom", the capitals were hives of industry. The Atlantic became the "Spanish Main", golden highway, to the fabled country, "El Dorado", which the early Spaniards had been seeking and about which they had read in old legends.

In Spain the Council of the Indies was appointed—a board of rich and powerful men that had charge of the finances of the new colonies. It had charge of counting out the fifth of all mine treasures, which was reserved for the government; it regulated the taxes or tribute paid by the colonies, the duties on goods sold, the religious "indulgences" or purchased exemptions from sin, granted by the priests. and the doling out of the offices in the new land, which were also paid for. The grants of the privilege to hold lands in the new world were changed from being hereditary, to be only good during one's life.

But Spain rapidly grew lazy under her prosperity. Like Rome, she left off all useful business, such as manufacturing and farming.

Too much money made suddenly, "inflation", as it is called, is a bad thing for a nation. It leads to a sort of stagnation, unless the money given out is always kept equal to that coming in. Spain stopped working, spent her great wealth, and for a day lived royally. But the day was not far distant when the "slump" came. Spain dropped from power, and, like her sister State, Portugal, lost her opportunity to hold world leadership. Her ambition to invade and conquer England was smashed in 1588, with the terrible defeat of King Philip's great fleet, the Armada.

The sixteenth century saw a changed Europe. The Baroque Age was the beginning of a new world-wide outlook in business as well as politics. It was the beginning, too, of modern capitalism—of great fortunes. The Renaissance had been the birth-time of the merchant princes of the North. Even as the art of goldworking had come to a fine climax in Italy—where the great adventurer Benevenuto Cellini and others produced coins more exquisite than any known since the days of the Greeks—the northern cities had seen the growth of brand-new industries. The shipwrights made new vessels in which bold explorers set out for the New World; the mapmakers turned out new charts by which they steered—and these improved means of going to sea had put the merchants for the first time into the class of trans-Atlantic traders, instead of coasting shippers along the little Mediterranean "lake".

NEW MONEY CENTERS OF THE TRADING NORTH

Holland and Germany now came to the fore as the leading centers of commerce and trade in the world; for the victories of the Turks had closed the East to voyagers by way of the Bosphorus, and their capture of Alexandria finally made Egypt, with its rich stores, a "closed book" to Europe. The Italian cities in this way lost their "corner" on the trade routes of the Mediterranean. The Spanish and Portuguese cities, if they had been enterprising, might have captured the trade of the world. One of the greatest opportunities ever thrown away in financial history was that of the Spanish ports! They brought gold, silver and raw materials from the New World for all Europe—but they had no manufacturing or trading organization. So it was the cities of Germany, the former members of the old Hanseatic League, that grew to be great centers of manufacturing and commerce—Frankfort, Nuremberg and Augsburg. Also powerful were the cities of the Netherlands, Antwerp and Amsterdam.

These old burghers of the North were bankers *par excellence*. They held the destinies of empires in their hands; and *for the first time in modern European history kings began to depend on private rich men for the means to carry on their wars.* These rich capitalists loaned money to their sovereigns. For money-lending had got to be fashionable! In the older days it was considerably looked down upon, and the Church itself had somewhat put it under a ban. You recall that Shylock—to use him as example once more—was spit on, kicked and cursed by the Venetians. He was of the hated tribe of money-lenders; he charged a high interest for his money! But later, even in Venice, this ban was removed, and the family of Bardi in Florence loaned money to princes even of distant lands. This had an effect on the development of banking. At first banks were only *a place to deposit one's money for safekeeping*, a sort of "check-room" for valuables. Then the idea of loaning money to others out of the money deposited grew up—just as banks do to-day. At first the idea of "making" money by these transactions was thought almost dishonest! Then gradually the *idea began to come in that the use of money was worth a certain amount, and the levy of interest became quite usual.* It was now an honorable profession, for people had realized that *money can make other money in its use, that it is a great stored up force.*

THE FUGGERS: ROCKEFELLERS OF THE SIXTEENTH CENTURY

One of the most famous families of financiers in all history was that of the German clan of Fugger. The origin of the family—as in most cases where great fortunes have been piled up—was not so very high. The first of the line to get together a "pile" was a weaver who died in the early years of the fifteenth century, leaving some 3,000 gulden. Here was the humble toiler, each night counting his precious gold pieces, and dreaming of what his boys might do with the money he was to leave them! Many fathers have done the same before and since—only this one's family was not of the modern "lounge lizzard" class: Fugger's boy kept adding to what he got! He became head of the guild of weavers in Augsburg, before that city got to be so rich. *He* had three sons—and each of them kept the family pot boiling to such good ends that one of them was able to loan an Archduke several hundred thousand florins. By that time, the family was living in very splendid castles. As a result of the money the three boys lent to Emperor Maximilian, they were made noblemen. Money talks a most eloquent language, and that was true then, as now! At the period of which we are now writing—the early sixteenth century—the family business had grown until there were branches in America and most countries of Europe. They were able to lend a hand when the emperor Charles V organized a crusade against Algiers; they even held the purse for the Pope, and were the middle-men for the sale of indulgences in their country!

An anecdote is told of Charles V, in this connection. He was on a visit of state to the French court, and one of the pleasant diversions arranged for his entertainment—doubtless also proving pleasant to the monarch who did the "showing"—was a visit to the royal treasuries.

Here the royal stores of wealth were brought out to impress him.

"What do you think of our treasure?" said His Majesty of France.

"Among my subjects", said Charles quietly, "there is a *weaver* whose wealth is greater than even that of France!"

And he was perfectly right. The Fugger family, though it no longer wove—with its hands, at any rate—was busy weaving a strong net of golden strands that connected their German city with far-off Russia, with London on the Thames, and with the wilds of America. They helped the poor, they gave money to artists—some of whom immortalized them in great paintings. We have as an example the great etcher-painter Dürer's picture of old Jacob Fugger, stern and practical, in his cap and cloak. He was one of the world's greatest merchant-bankers.

Understand, the bankers of the early sixteenth century were not the kind we have to-day—the directors or stockholders of a *public* corporation with a charter from State or nation. They were the whole bank in themselves: the money was all their own; they had made it, and it was theirs to lend on whatever terms they asked. (Banking was only money-lending on a big scale.) Often they combined a goldsmith's shop with their lending; sometimes other businesses ranging from shipping to mining or storekeeping, or manufacturing. They were combined J. P. Morgans and John Wanamakers. The money that they lent was "all there", in bullion (gold and silver bars), coined money or paper. There was no such thing as stocks and bonds and other "collateral" invented.

THE BIRTH OF THE BANKS OF TO-DAY

But banking before long took on some of the public character it has to-day. In the third quarter of the sixteenth century a real public bank was set up in Venice—*that* we mentioned in the last chapter having been of the common private type. Later an important public banking institution was founded in Amsterdam. In England the Jews were great money-lenders, until the king and nobles, heavily in debt to them, expelled them! The Lombards from Italy then settled there, giving the name to "Lombard Street". Edward III didn't pay his debt to them, causing a panic. Private banks existed in the sixteenth century—Child's lately passed out of existence by fusion with another bank.* The merchant-banker of the old type kept his hold on

* Child's Bank divided the distinction of being the last private institution in England with that of Hoare and Company. The latter since the

the financial market of Europe until well into the seventeenth century, even after shares of stock began to be common and the chartered company ruled business.

Antwerp meanwhile rose to be the most powerful port city of northern Europe. The German capitalistic cities needed a good seaside place for their outlet of trade. One of its chief charms was the hospitable attitude of Antwerp. It welcomed the representatives of the Fugger interests and other merchant-bankers who started business houses there, took off the toll duties from the port and bought off the duty privileges of the other cities along the Scheldt River—and as a result most boats that came from Portuguese ports with the rich goods of India put in at Antwerp. It was a case of a free port again triumphing over those where toll was charged. It soon threw the city of Bruges "into the shade". The most eminent trading cities of the European world were now Antwerp, Amsterdam, and London. Antwerp was predominant until it was sacked in 1576 by Spain.

Until now we have not spoken often of England in this history of money. But this remarkable and sturdy nation was now coming to the fore in trade. London's position was one of the world's best for commerce, and the Thames was now beginning to look like the forest of masts that it later became in the palmy days of the sailing vessel. England had her own ambitions to find a way to the rich Indies—that was a favorite "plunging" game of the later Baroque days. *England hoped that a way could be found through the North Sea to Russia and through Asia.* And she reasoned very logically, for if Portugal could afford to go all the way round Africa to get at her source of wealth in the East, England could go a few hundred thousand miles! You see, the sailors of that day didn't know the North intimately, nor what tremendous difficulties lay in the way of such a scheme.

ENGLISH MERCHANTS WHO ROAMED THE SEVEN SEAS

But, as in the case of Portugal's first voyages, the indirect results were more important than the real end. *It was owing to English* (and to some extent also Dutch) *enterprise that the modern idea of the stock company or business in which shares are sold, and a lot of people's money put together, came to be invented. This is one of the most important developments in the history of business.* The way it came about was this: The merchants of London who were interested in finding a way to India through the North organized a Company of Merchant Adventurers. It was not yet a stock

fusion of Child's is probably the oldest bank in London of this type. Before the day of private bankers, people deposited money with goldsmiths.

company, but it did have a charter granted by the English King, which assured them the monopoly on the rights of trade. In the middle of the sixteenth century the great English explorer, Sebastian Cabot, came back from his long trip of exploration in which he had landed at Newfoundland and claimed it for his country, and was elected governor of the Merchant Adventurers. His stories of his successful voyage to the New World set everybody's ambition on edge, and it wasn't long before an Englishman, Richard Chancellor, *did* really get to Russia by way of the North. The result was great enthusiasm, and a Muscovy Company was organized to trade with Russia, which just then was expanding till she had an important finger in the pie of Asiatic trade. Another English trading group was the Levant Company, for Eastern business.

Encouraged by her successes in the East, England turned her eyes to America. In the early days of Philip of Spain's rule, when the decadent land of Portugal—with great sources of trade, and wealth—fell into Spain's hands, the sailors of England began to come into conflict with the latter country's strict monopoly of America. The English were very eager to get cargoes of slaves, and they repeatedly came into conflict with Spain because of their plundering of her ships and lands. The quarrel as to whether trade on the Atlantic was free—as England said—or closed—as Spain tried to make out—really brought on the war and defeat of the Armada.

But the history of famous English trading companies really begins with the English East India Company, organized in 1600 as a rival to the Dutch companies that had begun to sail around Africa to the East in defiance of Portugal. This was a company of merchants who organized, with a capital of some $300,000, and secured a charter from Queen Elizabeth. This company was under the supervision of the government and the privy council; it had strict rules—not to occupy ports of the Spanish and Portuguese, to send out a half-dozen ships at least each year, not to export cargoes of English money unless they returned it. Its ships reached India by way of Africa.

Its success so alarmed the Dutch that they started their own rival East India Company, with a capital of 6,000,000 florins (about $2,500,000). Its charter gave them the privilege even of *making war* in the region between the tip of Africa and the Strait of Magellan. The Dutch also extended their activities to America, organized the Dutch West India Company, on the model of their other Eastern one.

WHEN THE MAYFLOWER SET SAIL FOR AMERICA

The age of American colonization began—of the Mayflower, of the English Pilgrims and the Half Moon of Hendrik Hudson. The

English colonial companies were chartered companies of the modern kind—the Virginia, the London and Plymouth Companies were given the right besides to coin their own money. Although in Holland the joint stock company and a sort of exchange had arisen, *the London Company is the first co-operative public corporation with shares that could be purchased by anyone for a certain amount of money, with land to be distributed in proportion to each one's stock.* It had a sort of board of directors, just like a modern corporation, and a president. It differed, however, in being a sort of socialistic, or communistic, colony: that is, everybody turned in the products of work to the company storehouse, and everybody was supplied out of that. This, at least, was the *plan*; we know now that it didn't work to perfection, that after a while, especially in Virginia, the system was given up. Elsewhere the little store of tools and food and the small amount of grain raised by the colonists, together with the terrible cold of the winter and other privations, in many cases reduced their numbers to pitiful handfuls. Even so, the trials of the pioneers brought a millionfold interest in the rich resources of the developed America of to-day.

The eagerness of those Europeans who braved perils of the wilderness rather than remain in Europe shows that *the lot of the common people was not a bright one.* And indeed the greater wealth of the big merchants—together with the change in the system of making goods when the old guilds gave way before the growth of specialized trades—made their lot hard. The rise of the prices that came with the shipment of gold from South America was a trial to the workers. The growth in power of the kings, the rise of strong nations, during the last two centuries had weakened the power of the small lords. *But as the kings increased the taxes upon them to make wars, the lords made the burden of the poor so much harder. The people now had to pay big money taxes, sometimes in addition to their payment in services.* Especially in Germany this brought on rebellions of the peasants, who were slaughtered in hundreds by the nobles in revenge! They never rose again.

In England, although the people at times were taxed cruelly high and rebelled, the feudal system had not had so strong a hold. The yeomen, or small landowners, had held their grants from the king, the estates being passed down from father to son. But under Henry VIII. the bloody "queen killer", there had been a national shortage of money—it was before the treasure of the New World poured in—and *cheaper metals had been added to the coins*, just as in ancient Rome.

The increasing use of woolen cloth made sheep-raising the best-paying business of the day. So *the farmers were turned out of their lands to make room for pastures, at the order of the rich men in the government, who passed laws for this purpose, signed by the ruler.* The result of this and of the *horrible legalized robbery* when the convents and monasteries were done away with by the king, because he wanted to get their rich treasure, was to make the roads *swarm with beggars.* In rags and full of sores, thousands of these homeless ones took to the life of the beggar, and it became necessary to pass "Vagrants' Laws", one of which sentenced them to be whipped until covered with blood!

But there was a terrible revolt coming. The seventeenth century brought greater prosperity to England, but it also brought the rise of the middle-class Puritans, stern singers of psalms. The head of Charles I fell on the block in 1649, and thirty years later the victory of the middle class was absolute, and the power of the crown was placed in the hands of a committee chosen by the House of Commons.*

* The downfall of kingly houses, or the restriction of the monarch's power, is an interesting chapter in European history, but one that is of too great a scope for this brief history of money. The underlying causes in most cases are connected with money. The French Revolution, following that of England by a century, is the most famous example, partly because of its bloodiness and excesses. The people in France had been overtaxed and cruelly treated for centuries by a series of kings, who allowed their financial system for the upkeep of the country, their commerce and trade, to go to pieces, while they spent huge sums to keep up a luxurious court. The most recent instances are, of course, those of Russia—another terrible chapter of oppression and virtual slavery for the poor, and of the Central European Empires of Germany and Austria. In the latter the defeat of 1918 at the hands of the allied nations hastened the crisis, and brought a sharp realization that royal autocracy had led the countries into fatal error. Usually the hereditary nobility and kingship lose their power when the middle class gets to be rich, a monied aristocracy.

CHAPTER VII

ENGLAND, MONIED MISTRESS OF THE SEVEN SEAS

THE story of the rise of England to be a world-empire rivaling that of old Rome is one of the most romantic in the history of money. This little island in the northern Atlantic had been originally the home of a people like the modern Welsh and Irish; the Romans conquered them, and after them in sucession the Germanic Saxons and Angles, and Normans from the mainland of Europe. From this mixture of races grew the four we commonly speak of to-day—the English, Scotch, Irish and Welsh. So much for the early history of the islands. We have already spoken of the growth of the nation during Baroque Days, and of the colonies started in America.

How did this little island power become the center of a net-work of lands in many parts of the globe? Before the seventeenth century England did not even have the three other races of the British Isles in a very tight grasp. Scotland was really an enemy country, and Ireland was a wild and only partly conquered land. But slowly the union of the races was accomplished. When James I came to the English throne (he was of Scotch ancestry) a tie was provided, and under Queen Anne in 1703 the two countries were united, so far as having one crown and one parliament was concerned. Four years later Scotland was formally united with England; but Ireland, though it was brought to terms in the civil war which ended with James fleeing to France and William of Orange becoming king, was not finally incorporated until 1800.

The two last nations to set up colonies in America had been the British and the French—and their ambitions now came into conflict. *The whole of the eigthteenth century was a big battle between these two nations for land, money, power!* It began in 1689, immediately after the revolution in England which brought the anti-French William of Orange upon the British throne. France had taken possession of the St. Lawrence River Valley, the Great Lakes and the Mississippi down to the Gulf of Mexico. *This meant that France claimed the Middle West and all Canada—three-quarters of North America!*

THE MONEY STRUGGLE OF ENGLAND AND FRANCE

England would have been shut into one-quarter of North America,

ENGLAND, MISTRESS OF THE SEVEN SEAS

if she had accepted this state of things. But she wasn't of the mind to! Her commercial prosperity had been growing by leaps and bounds. The nation, which in earlier reigns had to make a new tax levy each time it needed money, now began to borrow it from the rich middle class, giving a bond as security. This was the beginning of the "national debt", which exists in larger form to-day. In 1694 the famous Bank of England was founded to supply the need of a chartered bank to represent the government. A group of rich merchants agreed to lend the nation $6,000,000 at the rate of 8½ per cent interest, and in return they were given the right to carry on a public banking business, and later to issue paper money. This great building, still the government bank of to-day, was the storehouse of treasure from which the money went forth to wage the war against France.

The trouble began when France took the part of the throneless ex-King of England, James I, and war was declared and an alliance formed between England, Holland, Spain and Germany. The first war was not a long one, and England won an important battle on the sea against a French fleet that *was coming to invade her country*. The later battles were fought mostly on the mainland of Europe. William's army had *staying power* because of the great amounts of money behind it, and in 1695 France lost one of her fortified towns— her first loss by war in half a century! Peace was signed; but France was to lose still more later.

Just at this time the nations of Europe had a jealous eye on France. The king of Spain was about to die without any heirs, and if Louis XIV got hold of the Spanish possessions, he would rule a good slice of Europe with his gay and morally rotten court! The nations' objection was on the ground of money and power, though, and not of piety! The Spanish kingdom *was* left to Louis' grandson, and the war soon began with a vengeance! England was not at first mixed up in it, but when the French captured a group of towns lying between their land and Holland—England saw her danger and entered into hostilities.

The success of her armies under the great general Marlborough, after the death of King William and the succession of Queen Anne, was the result of a great campaign in which the English fought their way through Germany and beat the enemy four successive times! Marlborough was created duke and given a life pension of $25,000 a year and had a great palace built for him by the government. Successful generalship in those days was well paid.

But England gained a great possession at the Peace of Utrecht in 1713: Gibraltar, which commanded the little strait leading from the Atlantic into the Mediterranean—where she started the strong fort in the rock made famous by a well-known life insurance company.

In America her claims to Nova Scotia, Newfoundland and the country around Hudson Bay were recognized. And she got a valuable trade agreement from Spain, France's ally—the right to hold a monopoly of the African slave trade with the Spanish colonies for thirty years and to send to Panama one ship of goods each year.

A STOCK GAMBLE THAT "FLOPPED": THE "SOUTH SEA BUBBLE"

After this victory the money power of the nation kept growing. There was a great new flurry in speculation. Merchant companies of all sorts were formed to colonize or trade with the over-sea countries. *This was a period of "wild-cat" schemes in the money world, of stock issues that were practically worthless, of lotteries—of swindles that on the surface sounded most persuasive.* People had only known the use of stocks and bonds about a hundred years, and now they began to see that these scraps of paper, that represented a share in the great pile of wealth got together for some enterprise, could be "gambled" in, made to increase in value according to the demand.

The most famous case of a stock gamble was that known as the "South Sea Bubble". This was the floating of the stock of a South Sea Company, which was founded with a charter from the government in 1711 to trade with the Spanish colonies in America (under the new permission gained in the treaty) and also to carry on commerce with Asia. It seemed to be just as practical as the other great companies that had gained great wealth by trade and had helped to build up the power of England abroad. As is the case with many such "gilt-edge" schemes, the "best people" believed in the company. The government looked upon it very favorably, and even gave permission to the directors through an act of parliament to take over the national debt *and to issue their own bonds to cover it!* People began to invest bigger and bigger sums, the capital of the company increased enormously. There was a sort of South Sea stock fever—everybody believed it was the greatest thing ever invented! They sold their property to invest in its paper. The directors promised that great dividends would be paid, and the gossips were busy on a juicy rumor that the government was arranging to take over some of the gold mines of Peru by treaty with Spain and turn them over to the company!

Then the crash came. From selling at ten times its par value, the stock fell within a week to be worth nothing. Doubt had grown rather gradually as the enthusiasm wore off; then the same gossips began to hint that something was wrong—finally all were clamoring to sell their holdings. The term "bubble" is well chosen—the panic burst in exactly the same way. *The reason? There was nothing back of the tremendous promises made. The only way that capital can be*

ENGLAND, MISTRESS OF THE SEVEN SEAS

made to produce other money and bring a return is by setting it to work, and this is apparently what the South Sea Company failed to do. A more modest start, shrewd purchase and manning of ships, and steady trade enterprise would have brought this return. The conditions were against success from the beginning. Collapse of confidence in the scheme, a selling movement, completed the ruin. It was a case of panic, like a "run" on a bank.

The public rage was terrible. People in many cases lost all they had. There was a cry that the directors should be sown up in bags and thrown into the river! One committed suicide, one died of "heart failure", another who was innocent resigned, and a number were found guilty of fraud and put into jail. Clearly, though there were many fools, a few must have been rogues. The government was appealed to, since it had approved the scheme, to help the swindled. In the crisis the people turned to Walpole, a financial genius, and elected him to predominant power in the ministry, and the King created him first lord of the treasury and chancellor of the Exchequer. *His solution was to take possession of all the estates of the directors of the company* and turn this money over to the national treasury, to have the government give up its claim against the company, and to count up all other "assets"—with the result that the stockholders got about one-third of the par value of their stock. Those who had private claims in most cases lost their money.

WAPOLE, FINANCIAL GENIUS AND FIRST PRIME MINISTER

Walpole now became the most powerful man in the government, and though he was himself honest, he allowed a great system of corruption to grow up in Parliament. He is once said to have remarked of the House of Commons: *"All the men you see here have their price!"* Bribery was common, even in money, and political offices were regularly "handed out" in return for the member's vote. But Walpole was a great leader of men, and he really was the first English "prime minister". Before that the ministers had been almost equal, but this financier became "prime" or "first". And the prime ministers after that constituted the real government, and the kings got out of the habit of attending parliament.

Of the war with Spain, fought by the English under Walpole's rule, little will be said here, as its results were of little importance to business. The cause grew up from the abuse of the English of their treaty agreement to send one ship a year to Panama, for by a trick they sent a fleet of others after it, and reloaded the ship by night as fast as the cargo was taken off! Later an English sea captain came home with a story of having his ear cut off by the Spanish, and he kept the ear in a box to show as proof. Whatever the blame for the war, the English lost most of the battles, though one of their fleets *did* plunder treasure ships and ports and came back with considerable treasure. This war was followed by another between Austria and Prussia, which drew into it other nations; and in it England had a small share in supplying money and men, and defeated two French fleets, taking some merchant vessels. But she gained nothing in the peace treaty—nor did any of the other nations seem to!

Now began the great struggle between England and France for the possession of North America and India. It had been "brewing" for a long time. The crisis came when England gave a charter to an Ohio Company to settle on the river of that name, and Duquesne, the French governor of Canada, sent a notice to the governors of New York and Pennsylvania that France would not permit this! The fighting began, a company from Virginia under George Washington was partly successful, but General Braddock, sent from England with 2,000 soldiers, was ambushed and defeated by the French and the Indians. The school histories tell of the succession of later decisive victories that placed Fort Duquesne, Ticonderoga and at the last—in the great storming of the bloody height ending in the death of both leaders, after an epic struggle between the forces of Wolfe and Montcalm—Quebec in the hands of the English. *One last victory made all Canada the prize of the victors*—the fall of Montreal in 1760. *Most land east of the Mississippi was now England's* except a slice at the mouth of the great river, ceded to Spain by France.

India had been settled in several important places by the merchants who went there in the service of the English East India Company. When that trading group was formed in Elizabeth's day the nation didn't forsee that it was to start one of her biggest colonies! The Dutch, we have seen, soon "followed suit", but their holdings never developed to great power. The French had, however, formed their own East India Company and had among their important posts in the country Pondicherry, a settlement some eighty miles below Madras, the British outpost on the lower eastern coast. The settlements were not under the British rule, except in so far as their men were subjects, and both they and the French paid a tax to the local Indian prince who was head of the district.

During the previous war with France the governor of Pondicherry, Dupleix, had won a decided victory over the English, and a French fleet had captured Madras. This was restored to England under the peace treaty, but the struggle for the peninsula of southern India was still to be decided.

ENGLAND, MISTRESS OF THE SEVEN SEAS

THE PRICELESS WEALTH OF THE INDIAN PRINCES

India was a land of great wealth, ruled over by the chief Mogul and many smaller princes. Each had his treasure—a vast hoard of untold riches! The French knew this, and the governor Dupleix had laid plans to get this wealth into his possession. He trained natives in European methods of fighting. The southern part of India, known as the Deccan, was ruled over by a prince, Nizam; but suddenly he died, and there was a rivalry between his son and two others who wanted the rule. Dupleix formed a plot to kill the rightful ruler in a rebellion in which *French Troops helped,* and having established one of the rivals, Chanda Sahib, on the throne, Dupleix had the real control of Southern India. In reward the treasure of the dead prince was spread out before him, and he was allowed to choose jewels and money—it is said, nearly $1,000,000!

Now came the real hero of India—a man who has the same glorious record in that land as Wolfe holds in England's eyes as the saviour of Canada—Robert Clive. He went to Madras as a clerk in the service of the East India Company—a spirited boy of nineteen, who wanted to get away from "office work" in London. He made a good record in the short war that had preceded, and he now was given a command when fighting broke out again. The English had made their own alliances with other Indian princes, and, the French-ruled Chanda Sahib besieged the favorite of the English, Mohammed Ali, in the fort of Trichinopoly. Clive with a few hundred men took the city of Arcot and defended it against a terrible siege. *His victory meant the loss of French power in this part of India.*

But this was not the end. France and England were soon in the midst of the Seven Years' War. The Nabob of Bengal took Calcutta, another prominent English post, imprisoned 146 of their merchants and one woman in a cell too small for all of them to breathe, where in a hot, tropical night many got crazy and the majority died. This is known in history as the "Black Hole of Calcutta". Clive was called, took Calcutta, and after a series of other battles at last crushed France's power at Plassey; and at Wandewash, Colonel Coote and his forces fought the last important fight. *In the peace of Paris, England was given virtual control of India.*

The plunder of Bengal after the battle of Plassey was great. It is said that the whole sum realized by England or by private military leaders amounted to about $4,000,000. Clive himself got very rich—and he was only thirty-four when he made his greatest exploit. *But the robbery that went on after the war was one of the greatest in history*—the sums that went into private pockets, making the fortunes of officials, were greater than Rome had found in any one conquered province. Enormous fortunes were made in India in a short time. Graft, corruption, robbery were common. Crimes were so black that the natives rose against the white men—and Clive was forced to come back from England to try to restore order.

The only solution was to take actual command of the country. Under Clive, and under the stern Warren Hastings who succeeded him, an iron hand was kept upon the land. The charges against Hastings that were made in Parliament by Burke and others—that he robbed the Nabob of Bengal of the income due him from the Company; that he also robbed the Mogul, or chief ruler; that he took a town and killed the people for a prize of two million dollars, and imprisoned some native princesses for a ransom of six millions—were doubtless partly untrue. But the beginning of the Indian Empire was a bloody one, the treachery of the natives being partly to blame.

After many woes—and the terrible mutiny of the native garrisons in the middle of the nineteenth century, when English women and children were murdered by hundreds—the land was finally placed under the sovereignty of the British crown, with a Viceroy as governing head, and local representatives. Many miles of railroads have been laid at a great cost, but bring in a yearly profit from themselves alone of some $20,000,000. The natives have been civilized in many ways, and England has grown richer into the bargain!

THE AMERICAN REVOLUTION AND ITS MONEY SIDE

The great chapter of the American Revolution is one that must be placed on the debit, not the credit, side of England's national ledger. The details of it are known by every schoolboy, but the quarrel was a money dispute on one side of it. The colonists felt that they had worked to develop the New World for England, adding to the home country's wealth and trade. They had "back pay", or at least gratitude, coming to them. Instead they were treated like a conquered province and had tax laws *levied* upon them without their consent.

Whether some of these laws were just or not is a delicate point—perhaps, if the colonies had only been consulted in the matter they would have seen the reasonableness of their helping to bear the yearly British debt. The national debt had increased $140,000,000 during the last war with France that had won Canada, the Mississippi and India, and the yearly cost of keeping the army and navy was five times as great as it had been before the war. Just as since 1917 we have had to pay an income tax to help defray the

ENGLAND, MISTRESS OF THE SEVEN SEAS

expenses of the World War, the colonies were ordered to pay a stamp tax.

Other rulings were well meant. The severest was an attempt to keep the colonists from smuggling on the sly. The Sugar Act aimed to keep the colonies from trading with the Spanish West Indies—like the older Navigation Acts forbidding foreign trade in the hope of making all *money pour into the home treasury*. (But in reality this trade had enriched the colonies and so, too, England.) The law forbidding the colonial legislatures to issue paper money as British currency aimed to keep up the value of these notes, which was in danger of falling; this rule was good for the money interests, but hard on the poor debtor classes. Other hated laws were the Mutiny Act, making the colonists give provisions to the English soldiers—a thrifty government measure to keep down expenses—and the proclamation forbidding settling west of the Alleghany, an attempt to prevent the quarrels and injustices that had brought on the French and Indian Wars.

The reply of the Americans was to boycott English goods, and this raised a great to-do among London merchants—so much so that Parliament was forced by them to repeal the Stamp Act! Next came the Tea Act, which also made the colonists pay a duty on all the glass, paper, lead and other things that came into their harbors. All the duties except that on tea were later suspended by Parliament, but the colonists refused to drink tea, going preferably without!

The trouble was magnified by the fact that the East India Company—which had had a hand in so many national affairs—was in a bad financial state and had got permission from the government to export all tea in its British warehouses without any duty except three pence for bringing it into America. The company had stood on the edge of bankruptcy, partly owing to the turmoil and disorganization, drought and famine in India during the war there and the later evils. So the directors eagerly grasped the chance to sell their cargoes of tea, and it would have been a good thing for the colonies, as the tea could have been offered cheaper than that from Holland. But the people's pride would not permit. Everybody remembers the grotesque lark known as the "Boston Tea Party", when some Americans disguised as Indians climbed on board one of the tea ships and dumped the cargo into the water!

Angry King George shut the Boston port to all ships, but the desire to re-open trade with other nations was a strong factor in bringing forth the Declaration of Independence. Trade with England was suspended by the colonies' wish, and this had caused large money losses in America. It was realized that no foreign nation would risk England's displeasure openly by trading with

America against her orders, and so, soon after the colonial ports were again opened for trade, the Declaration was made to the tolling of Liberty Bell. What followed in the seven years between July 4, 1776 and the battle of Yorktown, all know.

WHEN SOME SCIENTISTS "STUMBLED UPON" RICH AUSTRALIA

But if England lost a great domain in America, she had meanwhile gained a new realm in Australasia—a peaceful conquest that began with a trip to study the stars! In 1768 an observation of the skies was planned from a spot in the South Seas by some learned men of the Royal Society—a group of whom set out the next year in a ship commanded by James Cook. At that time Australia was unknown, but a ship had now and then sighted land in the south, and people believed that one big continent stretched up from the South Pole, covered with ice for the most part! After the scientists had made their examination of the stars, they thought of looking into the matter of the southern continent. And so, under Cook's guidance, were discovered the two islands of New Zealand and then the great continent of Australia—the latter almost equal in size to the United States. On a later voyage, while he was trying to find that famous northwest passage for trade which had lured many men to their death in the hope of rich gains from the East, Cook was killed by savages of the Sandwich Islands. Thus ended another great man, whose name in English history went down beside those of Wolfe and Clive as winners of continents.

Australia was settled first by a great colony of men from the jails and poorhouses of England who were sentenced to exile there—and they built a strong and worthy colony, which shows what a lot of good there is in the worst of men! The Continent was cleared for pasturage, and sheep-raising is still to-day one of its great industries.

Stirring days followed the discovery of gold both in New South Wales and in Melbourne—two leading provinces of the continent. Rich veins were discovered by a man who had gone to America after the report of the gold discovery there in California in 1849. There, it is said, while he sifted the sands of the strange land to find the precious gold, the idea came to him that it was like his own in Australia! He sailed back and began his "prospecting". A few months later his great find became known—and men flocked there from all the world!

Days of lawlessness, the bloody deeds of the "bushranger", have now been forgotten, and Australia has become a rich, industrious land. England has profited enormously on her trade, and has not neglected to levy shrewd seaport duties—so that Australians sometime good-naturedly complain that, though they raise wool for all the world, England makes them send it all home in order to buy it back again at a much higher rate!

THE AGE OF STEAM AND THE GREAT ROMANCE OF MACHINERY

But, long before Australian gold came flowing back to enrich England, the great *invention of the steam engine and the perfection of factory machinery had made a new industrial world*. Before that time, thread had been spun on the familiar spinning-wheel and woven into cloth on a hand loom. That is, workers had done it by hand, each in his own home usually. But first the number of threads that could be spun at one time was increased, until Samuel Crompton invented the "mule" (1779), which could spin 200 at a time by means of a system of rollers run by water power. This invention should have been worth an enormous sum to the inventor, but, like most men of this class, he let the earnings of his great improvement go to the manufacturers, who became very rich from "promoting" it. He got from them a price of only a few hundred dollars, but in his old age the government voted him a gift of $25,000 in recognition of his services to the country.

The next important invention was a power loom to replace the century-old system of hand weaving; this was perfected by Edmund Cartwright, an English minister of the gospel. Then in America the cotton "gin" to separate the fiber from the seed by machinery multiplied by *two hundred times* the amount of this that could be sent across the Atlantic to go into the jaws of the new machinery and be turned out into cloth!

The steam engine was so much improved by James Watt (about 1785) that it could be made to turn wheels by means of shafts, instead of being only a feeble contraption to hoist and pump. The beginnings of the steam boat were the contribution of America. A great and romantic tragedy is that of the life of John Fitch, a poor carpenter, who *before any man in the world,* built a ferry boat with paddles and made his own steam engine to run it, at Philadelphia. But no one would pay any attention to him. He begged rich men in vain to give him money to "put across" his invention. At last in despair he shot himself in a saloon in Kentucky. Here was the real hero of the greatest invention of the age—one that has since made countless great fortunes and changed the whole trading system of the world—being shut out from his reward! The real prize went to Robert Fulton, who managed to "sell" his steamboat, after another, Oliver Evans, had been unsuccessful in trying to interest others in his invention of the same type.

The steam locomotive grew up slowly from little attempts to

use the steam engine to pull cars on a cable, somewhat as elevators are run to-day. A plan was suggested in America by John Stevens to build a traveling engine or locomotive, but the capitalists would hear no more of this than they had of Fitch's steam boat. We may be allowed to smile to-day, when we think of the great fortunes that these men might have made on an exclusive patent right to this invention! Perhaps it has been better for human progress, though, that the invention has been free for all nations. The honor of making the first small locomotive to haul coal in a mine belongs to the Englishman, George Stephenson (1814.) But to America's credit are the invention of the McCormick reaper, either for use in operations, the telephone, the phonograph and the electric "trolley," or tram car—the last three coming of course, later than the period of English history that we are now describing—the England of the Napoleonic wars.

CRIMES AGAINST THE WORKER AND THE "WEAVERS' REBELLION"

The growth of the factories brought both good and evil in the money welfare of the nation. The capitalists who invested in the new machinery made enormous profits. One man could now do with the aid of the power loom what *two hundred* did by hand! The employers had to pay only one-two hundredth as much for labor, in addition to the running expenses of their new plants. The greatest tragedy was that of the hand weavers, who were compelled to try to turn out as much cloth as a machine! The prices for it went down with the new plenty. This was good for people in general, but terribly cruel for the poor hand workman. He had lived on his little garden plot in his cottage which he rented out of his earnings. But now he could hardly make ends meet. Many "stuck it out" during their whole lifetime of want, but there were fierce uprisings, when the maddened weavers tried to smash the machines that had made them slaves.

This was the beginning of the mechanical age, when man slaved all day in feeding the new monsters of steel. He turned one lever all day, instead of working intelligently, with brain and heart. He started at sunrise, and stopped only when it got dark. The worker now owned nothing, he was at the entire mercy of the capitalist. The terrible results in living conditions, when the people were forced to leave their little garden-plots and come in to the cities to live in tenements in filth and misery, can well be imagined! Imprisonment for debt was common: people were sent to prison or "sponging" house.

Side by side with this were the bad results of the factory slavery of women and children. Before 1800 it had got to be the custom

ENGLAND, MISTRESS OF THE SEVEN SEAS

for the town authorities to give up the children of people who died in the poorhouses to apprentice them to employers. Sometimes bad-minded parents did the same, really selling their children *by written agreement!* In other cases, want made them send the children to work at the pitiful age of eight or ten. The evil of the apprentice system was not to last long, but meanwhile the sight of the stooped, thin little children coming from the factory gates with grimy faces so moved people that a famous woman poet, Mrs. Browning, wrote her celebrated lines about the "Cry of the Children". All these black evils came from the greed for money in the employers. Nothing was done for a number of years; then the idea of rights for the working man grew up. Strict laws were passed limiting the hours of work, and the age at which children could be put to labor in factories.

Another great evil of the time was the taking of the lands by rich men to make them into big estates, putting off the folk who had lived there. This was called "inclosing" land, or "commons", and the Parliament was so much controlled by the rich that it passed a number of laws making the noble and rich the great landlords of the kingdom. This was really a great *step backward*—almost to the condition of feudal days. The landlords divided their estates into farms, which they rented to tenants to cultivate. It was the beginning of the age of the English "country gentleman", with his hunting dogs, red coat, mug of ale and long clay pipe. He built his splendid country house, lived in ease and went forth to represent his county in Parliament. He had his own little chapel on his estate, the clergyman of which he paid directly—a "living", as it was called quite rightly. These days came to their climax just before the World War, when the workingmen's groups began to ask for the return of the land of England to the people, and a few measures were taken by the Parish Councils to have parts of estates sold and divided into small farms. The rise of the new monied class—war "profiteers"—the heavy tax now laid upon incomes from land not personally farmed by the owners, and the poverty of some of the old noble families are slowly bringing about a new split-up of the land. Many years will be required, for it.

NAPOLEON'S SHORT DAY OF GLORY AS KING OF THE EARTH

The final stage of England's struggle with France was that of the Napoleonic Wars, which ended with Waterloo in 1815. Five years before, the armies of France under the marvelous Bonaparte had extended their empire so that it seemed almost as if it might soon include the whole continent of Europe! France held its own great territory, Belgium, half of Switzerland, a strip down half of the western coast in Italy, including Rome and Florence, and what is now Holland and a part of northern Germany. Napoleon had the rest of Italy and some of Germany under his "protection", and he had forced the Continent to be "allies." But the rebellion of Russia against Napoleon's rule caused him to invade that country and to enter Moscow. Finding steady resistance, he began the famous "retreat from Moscow", losing a large part of his army by cold and starvation. He met a crushing defeat at the hands of an allied army at the Battle of Leipzig. The terms offered Napoleon were generous: he could have kept his crown and had the boundaries of France fixed at the Rhine. But he refused and the allies took Paris; the French chose a Bourbon to reign as Louis XVIII—and Napoleon left for Elba, the island in the Mediterranean, granted as his own private "country place"!

England had contributed a lot of money for the war; she had opposed Napoleon from the start, and as her share the Congress of Vienna gave her Malta, the Ionian Islands, Cape Colony, Ceylon and some other small lands. The escape of Napoleon and his short new "day" of power was ended forever at Waterloo and with his exile to St. Helena, this greatest of military "plungers" forever dropped out of Europe's "money market." France had to pay a war indemnity of $140,000,000—not very much in modern days, considering all the trouble Napoleon had given.

THE GOLD AND DIAMONDS OF AFRICA: BRITON'S PRIZE

Two of the lands given to England by the Congress of Vienna had a great deal to do with her later history: these were Cape Colony and Malta. Cape Colony gave her a foothold in South Africa. This settlement was on the tip of that cape around which the Portuguese sailed centuries before to get to the East. The Dutch had settled it. Holland was lined up, along with England against the French in the Napoleonic wars, but at a critical moment she was forced to surrender, and so became an enemy of England. A fleet was sent to South Africa, and Cape Town Castle surrendered.

The colonization of the Dark Continent was carried on partly under such heroes as the missionary and explorer, Livingstone, and partly by such rich adventurers as Cecil Rhodes, who pushed boundaries northward. The races of Europeans—the English and the Dutch (who called themselves Boers, or "farmers") were often in conflict over their differences of thought, and at last the latter emigrated northward and founded the Orange Free State and the Transvaal. The richest gains to Europe were the result of the finding of the great diamond fields at Kimberley, which became the

ENGLAND, MISTRESS OF THE SEVEN SEAS

property of England. Gold was discovered in the Transvaal in 1886, and men flocked there from Europe.

The Boer War in the closing year of the last century was a rather distressing incident. The Boers declared hostilities, and for a time won steadily, but increased armies were sent from England and the other colonies and after the Boer surrender in 1902, the two colonies were annexed, though they remained self-governing. Thus another source of wealth—gold and gems—came to England. The British loaned the Boers money free to restock their farms.

The island of Malta in the Mediterranean, together with Gibraltar, commands a very important position on that sea. The idea of keeping open the ocean path to India was now uppermost in English minds. In order to keep control of the opening to the Red Sea, the nation later occupied the port of Aden and the island of Perim. France had dug the Suez Canal, and England looked at this bit of water with eyes that could not help but be a bit envious!

Now, just at this time the Khedive of Egypt had spent money so lavishly that in a few years he had raised the national debt from $3,000,000 to $98,000,000—and Egypt was bankrupt! The Khedive held about half of the stock of the canal, and he offered it for sale. Before France knew what was happening, Disraeli, the wily British prime minister, had bought the stock—and so England had the largest share in the famous waterway!

BANKRUPT EGYPT AND ENGLAND'S GUARDING OF THE NILE

Meanwhile a sort of bankruptcy court of the principal powers was appointed to supervise the accounts of Egypt; and it was agreed that the lavish spending had to stop and—what was more—the debt would have to be slowly paid off by taxation. Europe felt that Egypt couldn't keep its own books, and—as much of the money was owing to them—it would have to be done for her!

The supervision was finally given to England and France alone, and all went satisfactorily until the Egyptians started a rebellion against all foreigners. The Sultan of Turkey refused to put down the uprising, and after some Europeans were killed, England, deserted by France, stepped in and with a fleet captured the harbor of Alexandria. The country was not made a dependent of England. It was, until the opening of the World War, a self-governing province of Turkey, but England's influence over the foreign relations of Egypt and—since 1914—her protectorate over the nation has made her almost a mother-country.

The rich valley of the Nile has been the scene of the building of a great new irrigation system. The Delta Barrage, or dam to store up water for the dry season, was built (and later reconstructed) at the cost of $100,000,000—raised by the Egyptians under British management—and this great dam is said to increase the output of cotton each year by $4,000,000,000. Through other dams many hundred thousand acres of land have been drained for use. The improvements in lessening the taxation, and doing away with "graft" in the government, the exchange of a money tax for the drafted labor on public works—a slavery that had been going on ever since the Pharaohs built their pyramids to the tune of whips—were the great work of England.

The conquest of the savage tribes of the Soudan desert—the victory of Kitchener at Khartoum after the death of the heroic band headed by Gordon—were other vivid pages in the story of England's careful watching of the Nile valley. This immensely fertile country—where the earliest great civilization of the world sprang up ages ago—would be one of the world's greatest prizes if England should finally declare it a part of her empire. Now her interest seems mainly in keeping open the East, to guard her waterway to India and indirectly to Australia. Meanwhile she has built the great Cape-to-Cairo Railway—connecting Egypt and South Africa.

The climax of England's power as an empire is thought by some to have been reached in the closing years of the last century. When the aged Queen Victoria held her famous "diamond jubilee" in 1897, the glory of her world-empire could hardly have been surpassed. Financially England led the world: she was the "seat of exchanges" —that is, other kinds of money were reckoned in terms of the pound sterling. Lombard Street, London's money center, was the great "brain" of the financial world, from which nerves went out to every land. The great expansion of her money system came after her conquest of India,* and in later years the gold of Australia and Africa, the diamonds of Kimberley, added great sums annually.

THE RISE OF THE ROTHSCHILDS, SUPREME MONEY BARONS

The age of the banker had dawned in earnest, taking the place of the merchant's. An example is the great family of Rothschild—the name of which is famous the world over. The founder of the family was a Jew of Frankfort, Mayer Amschel, who served for a time under a banker in Hanover, and then came back to his native city to open an old coin and curio business. He lived in a house known as the "Red Shield", and from it the family later took its name. How did he make his money? Not, like old Fugger, by

* As compared to about $3,000,000 sent by the East India Company to England in 1760 (later declining to about $500,000 in 1770-80, when India was in disorder and the company's affairs in a bad way)—in the years of the Napoleonic wars the company sent about $15,000,000 annually.

weaving, producing—*he* gained it by juggling money itself,—and that is the trait of the new age of banking! The old coin business was soon given up for banking proper, and at last Amschel became attached to the court of the Landgrave of Hesse. He later was able to loan the government of Denmark 4,000,000 thaler. He had five sons, and of these Nathan was the most powerful, as he moved to England, married a wealthy heiress and was soon the master of the financial world. The family business had branch houses in many capitals, like that of the Fuggers, and each of the sons had charge of one of these in London, Paris, Vienna, Naples and Frankfort. No wonder there were chances of cornering the market!

Rothschild came to London at a time when there was a sudden need of money—and he was an expert at lending at his own advantage. There had been a great increase in England's money supply before this time, as has just been noted; and to pay for its war expenses the nation took out big loans—and in general the private merchant borrowed also at a reckless rate, because money was "cheap". But there was a sudden change, when it became scarce— partly owing to the revolutions in South America against Spain in 1809, when the rich mines stopped being worked—and prices fell fifteen per cent in the following year. There was a general panic made worse by the collapse of an immense loan of about $70,000,000 taken out by two leading houses, Baring's and Goldschmidt's. Baring died suddenly, there seemed some doubt as to whether there was sufficient security to cover the great sum, and the head of the other house committed suicide. These were the days when many merchants were ruined because their goods suddenly went down in value. All who have read Thackeray's "Vanity Fair" will remember the pathetic case of Mr. Sedley, who was stripped of all he had and then spent his days pretending to be "looking for business" in the coffee houses.

Many evils came in with the glittering but cruel rule of the money barons. The banking class was opposed to the Bank of England's habit of issuing liberal paper money, which it had been doing every once in a while, whenever there was a shortage of metals, or prices got a little high. The century from 1800 to 1900 was the age of gold—power, of capitalists. *They wanted to keep the value of money stationary, so that they could be sure of a good interest for it. The growth of the monied class with the age of steam—the triumph of the capitalist—was now shown in adoption of gold as the standard of value, in the terms of which everything had to be reckoned, instead of in silver, as before.* This stand has been taken later by most of the great nations, and the good or evil results have been the cause of much argument. Gold is probably more dependable in its value than any other kind of metal, but that does not mean that it is not dear or cheap according to the demand for it; besides, it is rare, and there have been times of great hardship for the merchant class in England as the result of it. At times when laws were passed keeping down the amount of paper money that could be issued to relieve the lack, prices have fallen as much as two-thirds! The later plenty of gold from the colonies which streamed into London to be sold at auction every Monday—rich treasure from South Africa, Australia, and from America—has made the situation better.

WHEN PARLIAMENT PASSED BILLS TO AID THE POOR

The misery of the poor was helped by a long series of reforms*— the vote was given (1832) to all men who paid $50 a year rent (!), and later the privilege of the vote was given to all men and women; the import duty on grain from the rest of the world was taken off (so that it could be bought cheaper.) *Finally in 1911 the most effective laws ever passed by a nation to help the poor at the expense of the profiteer* provided for an income tax, especially high on income over $25,000; a high inheritance tax— fifteen per cent on amounts over $5,000,000; a high tax on land that only paid rent instead of being worked by the landlord, and a tax of one-fifth on profits from sale of land. The age of the capitalist had not given way to that of the producer. The opposition of the House of Lords to this bill brought a new provision that this branch of Parliament *could never veto a money bill passed by the Commons!* The means used to compel it to sign its own liberty away was a threat that several hundred new lords would be created to outvote them if it had to be! With the recent election of a labor government for the first time in England—almost in the world—the working people were rulers!

Here the story of England's rise to a world nation really ends. The World War was a brief, terrible chapter in her recent course of rule. The growth of a great Empire in Germany within a hundred years, the rule of iron of Prussia under the fierce Chancellor Bismarck, the conceit which drove this government to its attempt at world-conquest in 1914, calling a conference of money barons at Potsdam before "backing" Austria—these were only incidents in a general drama of plotting, jealousy and greed that seemed to be acted over Europe before 1914. The war guilt is not Germany's alone, but she surely had dreams of annexing all France—while in the flush of her first victories—and, more and more, the struggle narrowed

---

* The Old-Age Pensions Act voted $1.25 a week to every person who had a yearly income of less than $800. Finally all workers who got less than this amount yearly were made to take out an insurance against sickness, which included free treatment and pension. Workers in some trades were also insured against being out of work.

ENGLAND, MISTRESS OF THE SEVEN SEAS

down to a contest between her and England. It was the war to a death of two great empires—one a world power, the other with strong ambitions to be one! The famous Hymn of Hate, "Smite England", is an expression of this feeling. The great struggle came very near to ending differently—with a Germany with boundaries pushed out to the English Channel, preparing for that step over the narrow water that would make her master of Britain.

THE STUPENDOUS PRICE OF THE WORLD WAR

The cost of that struggle of the world has never been properly counted up, but it is known that at least 9,000,000 persons died and the money loss was more than $200,000,000,000. *The money that had been stored up for years in Europe went for this bloody carnival of frightfulness.* No wonder the nations are poor to-day! They not only burned up their wealth as on a bonfire, but the war wrecked the whole machinery for producing and marketing goods. The war debts of the different countries are bewildering to think of: England's national debt increased in those four years to such a sum that she must raise five billion dollars a year in taxes to pay off interest and other expenses. So that her war debt must at least amount to more than fifty billion dollars! To America alone she pays an interest and refund of some $138,000,000 every year.

As a souvenir of her work in the war, England—who rarely leaves a conflict without a prize—has gained a "protectorate" over Palestine and Irak, former Turkish lands; gained German colonies in Africa and in the Pacific (the latter as a "mandatory", or sort of guardian, for the League of Nations.) Thus she controls in the East the rich valley of the Euphrates and Mesopotamia, where the first Asiatic civilization grew up in the dawn of time. In addition her foot has certainly been planted in Persia, the Shah having really turned over his country to the rich nation of the West. The rule of these new lands may be as wise as that which England has extended over her own dominions, and she is more than ever a world empire.

There have been pessimists who predicted that some day the whole great realm would fall apart, bit by bit, but now it does not seem to be in any danger of this. Most of the colonies are eager to stay in the Empire: the one exception was Ireland, and with the grant of permission to call herself a Free State and have her own legislature, she now seems fairly well satisfied. She will probably gain much by self-rule.

THE UNITED STATES BECOMES MONEY LEADER OF THE WORLD

The World War saw the rise of America to be the world's leading money power. The United States had, in fact, held this position for some time. But the great struggle in Europe, the help that we were able to give in men, supplies of all sorts and money loans—our turning of the tide of battle—demonstrated this fact to the world as nothing else could have! *Those who criticized the government for joining in the war* (and there were always a number of these) *can see the best proof of justness and duty of that act in the new respect which the United States has gained.* If she had not taken her place in that struggle, she would have remained a separated, "small-time" power. There is no denying the fact that the greatest sacrifices were made by the people of little incomes, that the rich in many cases got richer on the death-struggles of the bleeding and dying. *But the supremacy of America was shown to the world.* Even Germany, who taunted us and killed our citizens with her submarines in 1916, saying "the money-grabbing people will not lift a finger", learned that our rich grain-fields, our wealth, were *our strength and not our weakness. Our riches are based on the only true source of power*—production, growing, making, inventing! *The dollar is now the world's standard of exchange*: that is the real mark of financial and world power. In history the money capital has always been the "seat of exchanges", that is, other money was reckoned in terms of its coin. That power has passed from Rome to Constantinople, from Venice to Amsterdam, from London to New York!

THE
ROMANCE OF MONEY TO-DAY

The Romance of Money To-day: America

CHAPTER I

THE ROMANCE OF MAKING AND GROWING (PRODUCTION)

THE sky-line of New York! What a thrill those great towers give to one! If you take a walk down steep and narrow lower Broadway, between the walls of skyscrapers rising five hundred feet into the air on either side, shutting out the light,—they dazzle you with their great bulk and thousands of windows. They stand for piled-up wealth, for millions of acres of rich land, for mines that hide gold, silver, coal and copper, for spouting oil wells, many thousands of sailing and steam ships that dot the rivers and oceans, for great lines of railroads that span the continents, for ten million other houses and buildings that hold a hundred million souls! This is Capital, frozen—so it seems—into great ice-palaces of commerce. The stones that make these highest houses of the world were paid for out of little amounts of money placed together until they made a princely sum. The world's highest building, the Woolworth, stands among them—and everybody knows that "it was built with dimes". *That is the most wonderful thing about the romance of business: it is a great machine made of millions of little spokes, each one standing for the mite of money or service that one person has given!* In the old days each man had to do his own work—he walked or went on horses when he wanted to travel. To-day men do things by co-operation: they put their money together, for instance, and build a railroad!

To get back to the beginnings of all wealth, we must consider Work. All money comes from either property or work. The whole thing goes back to the question of *man's wants*. They have to be supplied—food, shelter, comforts, and the social life. Things are either grown or made. At first each man himself grew and made all the things he needed. Then men began more and more to *share these duties*. For they found that *in that way some could get to do things better and quicker from practise*. They got to be "specialists".

And *they found, too, that it was cheaper and easier to do different kinds of work in big lots at once.* So some of them did one kind of work and some another, and they exchanged one kind of service for another. *This was the beginning of exchange,* of "swapping", as we have pointed out in the first part of this book. It was also the way that "trades", the butcher, the baker and the candlestick maker, came to grow up!

All trades that really "produce", or are good for something, must either *make, move* or *store up* value. In the jobs we are now talking about, the first only is done. The farmer grows his grain, the tailor makes clothes, the watchmaker sets mainsprings. (We shall later talk about the job of the man who ships potatoes, suits or watches to market, and that of the other man who keeps the things for sale in his store until they are wanted.) At any rate, all of us can see what a great and wonderful system has grown up to *make* things in the United States and the rest of the world! From the man who adds a bolt to several hundred of those small automobiles known as "tin lizzies" every day, to the one who wraps loaves of bread in waxed paper with the aid of a machine—all are doing their "bit" to add to the wealth turned out in the country. We see that the labor of all these hands, if it was all used to swell one big fund, would make so big a pile of gold every day that it would almost equal in height one of Broadway's big buildings!

BUILDING RICH AMERICA: THE WORK OF THE PIONEERS

It was WORK that made the greatness of the United States. The work of the pioneers that cut down the forests, cleared the ground of rocks and stumps for farming, built their rough log houses and dug wells, is the source of our greatness to-day. *Our wealth has grown from the ring of the pioneers' axes,* their braving of the dangers of death from the arrows of the Indians. The first businesses of the American settlers were farming, hunting, fishing and lumbering. Then, too, there were the hundred-and-one trades that added to the comforts of life—the carpenter, the blacksmith, the tanner of leather. Many chores were done in the family, just as in some country districts people still kill their own animals and salt the meat. At that time they spun thread and wove "homespun".

Prices of things were low in those days, but at some of the trades people made good wages. The great business of lumbering—cutting down the trees and making them into building wood—was very popular. In fact, the cutting down of the forests went on at such a fast rate that to-day people have become alarmed about the prospect of having any left before long! Laws in some cases were passed, and the government for some time has had a Forestry De-

MAKING AND GROWING

partment, to keep the trees from getting as scarce as the Indians. But to the early Americans, trees were a great source of wealth. Saw mills were set up—somewhat slowly at first—and in the years just before the Revolution the yearly shipments of lumber brought in nearly $800,000. The trees also yielded tar, rosin, turpentine and other things that were used in England's shipping—the value of these things sent out amounted to about $200,000. "Lumber kings" exist in plenty to-day as a result of this "forest-slaughter".

Some of the biggest fortunes in America to-day were started in the fur-trading and fishing businesses. "Whaling" was one of the good old trades—more than 4,000 sailors at one time being engaged in it, and the number of ships being at one time more than 300. This was a romantic way to spend one's life! The cry "There she blows!" was the signal for the hardy men to put out their boats from the ship and to try to plunge the harpoon into the great fish's side. The danger was great and many brave men lost their lives, but the rewards were great, too. This and the other fishing trades were mostly carried on in New England, and the old skippers got very rich on their trips to the Newfoundland fisheries. Fur-trading and trapping were still more romantic, and this centered in the Hudson River valley and that of the Great Lakes. Furs brought high prices and were easy to ship. This trade brought in some $650,000 a year in early America. Our seal and other fisheries in Alaska bring in millions to-day.

Farming was the biggest business of that day, and rightly, too,—for all had to eat! The little garden patch of the settler surely wasn't likely to put him into the capitalist class. But soon the South learned that big profits could be made in tobacco. Europe had just learned to smoke within a hundred years, but already she had learned to "walk a mile" for her "makings"! This was a business that needed a large farm to be profitable and a lot of hired help or slaves, and so it soon got to interest the richest men.

The Indians had quite a few good ideas about farming—they taught the colonists to plant a dead fish with their crops as fertilizer. But this was often neglected because there was so much land that (so they thought at that time) it would never be used up! Of all the things raised tobacco, however, was easily the leader, and the value of that exported to Europe each year has been reckoned at $4,000,000! In Virginia these big plantations grew to be often 5,000 acres. This was the beginning of a ruling class of landowners that got to be stronger, as their estates were often given as a "patent" and could be handed down to the oldest son.

The later introduction of cotton (after the Revolution) had a great "boost" in the invention of the cotton "gin". It was this big new business that made slavery such a valuable thing in the

South—after it had been given up nearly everywhere else—and threatened to split the nation on the rock of Civil War. The money it earned each year was about $21,000,000, and without slave labor the output could not have been kept up, or else high labor rates would have had to be paid. So that a *money matter* really brought about the Civil War. We know of the lost fortunes that were the result of the doing away of slavery in the South. A whole wealthy class had most of its riches swept away. The three million slaves of the South themselves were "worth" $2,000,000,000.

The land in many parts of the South had been handed down from father to son for many generations, and had been first made as a gift in the early days of the colonies. In the Middle West the land had been claimed by several of the States, especially that lying between the Alleghenies and the Mississippi, after the Revolution. This was settled by turning it in to the government, which then for a time sold it to help pay the public debt and later gave it cheap to settlers in the West. The sum asked for these now priceless lands was $2 an acre, payable on the installment plan! The land went in 160-acre lots, and the low price encouraged people to buy still more. *That was the source of the great Western farms in many cases that are now owned by America's "wheat kings"*. Sometimes the early settling was a hard "pull", but the interest on that investment of sweat was high. Besides, after the Civil War western lands were *given* to "homesteaders".

OUR FACTORIES—THE MILLS THAT GRIND MONEY

The growth of factories came later. Up to the middle of the nineteenth century rough cloth was still woven on hand-looms at home.* It was cheaper at first to bring it in from Europe than to make it in our own factories. The rules of England before the Revolution forbade America to trade with other nations. She wanted all the money to come to her, as we have seen in the chapter before this. That was one of the things that provoked the Revolution. After that war England kept up her policy of restricted trade—that is, she laid tariff and other duties that kept America from trading on equal terms with her.

The War of 1812, like the Revolution, sprang up over England's attempts to intereferc with our trade. To defend our rights on the seas against the stopping and seizure of ships the later war was

---

* The first cotton factory in the country was started at Beverly, Mass., in 1787. It was run by real "horsepower". Samuel Slater has been called the "father of American manufactures". He set up a cotton plant with power machinery at Pawtucket, R. I., a few years later. Cotton cloth-making was then the biggest business of the factory world in America.

carried on. During the period of the struggle the United States were pretty much shut off from the world by the "Embargo" Act and England's hostility. *So that we had to fall back on our own manufactures.* We got to be self-dependent, and since that time—though England right after that war flooded the country with her goods (which hadn't had a market for so long)—American manufacturing has grown by leaps and bounds. The growth in the twenty years before 1900 was amazing, and since then it has got much greater in volume.* Not only has each business increased fifty times in volume, but many new trades have sprung up.

The beginning of the use of hard coal helped along our manufacturing enormously. Before that iron foundries were few, and charcoal was used. About 1840 the new way of making iron came in, and this—with the great need of rails for the miles and miles of railroads being laid in the West—gave a great "boost" to the business. Within thirty years the output of "pig" iron increased six times! The "palmy" days of the iron furnace in turn made whole towns spring up around them, and to-day many of these furnaces—now unused because a better way has come in—are still standing. New York and Pennsylvania were the biggest centers of early iron-making. Later soft coal got to be the most popular fuel for this business.

After the Civil War the process for making Bessemer steel was introduced. *This is now one of America's greatest businesses.* In twenty years before 1880 the steel and iron business grew until it turned out nearly $300,000,000 worth of product each year, and since then it has increased about five times.

To keep up this industry an enormous amount of mining is necessary, and *all the minerals mined each year in the United States amount to a billion and a half dollars!* (The time is not far distant when two billions may be produced in this way.) Of course, there is a danger that the supply may be used up in time, but that day doesn't seem to be here yet. Meanwhile, the glare of our great steel plants, of fiery ovens and rolling mills, dyes the sky!

The metal is used again for machinery—and in the making of big machines of many sorts the United States leads the world. It invented, for instance, some of those great farm implements—combined threshers, binders and reapers, as well as improved machines for planting and cultivating. Later it led in developing the gasoline engine and the motor vehicle. These made the great wheat farms of the west possible. Go with me in imagination and, leaving the glowing mills where the red-hot bars are forged and the black

* From yearly manufactures of all kinds worth two hundred millions in 1810, our annual output in less than a hundred years had grown to thirteen billion dollars—more than sixty-five times the first amount.

depths of the mines, come out into the bracing air of the northern central plains! For miles—as far as the eye can see—there stretches a level sea of grain. It gets ripe at the same time, and fast work is needed to get it in. Then the call for men goes out. This is romance, indeed! Like a great army of tanks the reapers move in a line; mowing and binding, the great machines move. Sometimes fifty of them go clattering slowly along at a time. This is the future bread of the nation. So the work goes on each year over some 500,000,000 acres of cultivated farm land.*

AMERICA'S GRAIN—THE BREAD OF ALL THE WORLD

The bread of America turned out to be that of the world as well during the World War, for the nations at war had no time to raise foods with so many men in the armies. In spite of a poor harvest in 1917 we sent 141,000,000 bushels of wheat to Europe, saved by the method of going without half of our regular lot.

There is a tragedy behind the growth of America, for in spite of the great output of our Western farms, our people are turning from the business of *growing* things. More and more manufacturing is taking the place of farming and cattle-raising—the latter—one of the great businesses of America. (The great packing houses of Chicago are the result of a live-stock industry that began in the romantic days of the frontier and still keeps the lariat-throwing "cowboys" busy on the Western ranch.) Yet it cannot be denied that from the plains more and more boys are going to the cities. They prefer a "white collar" job as a clerk on a high stool or a place as mechanic in one of those factories where each adds a bolt or screw.

The big hand of factory industry draws in the young as in a powerful net. They prefer to live in the big towns, where there is the stir of life, a smarter way of doing, saying and wearing! Often their living conditions aren't nearly so good; they are less independent, more nearly slaves—and finally *they have taken a step downward in becoming workers for wages* after being enterprise directors, managers of their own, reaping their own profits. This, of course, applies only to those who own or run their own farming and cattle businesses. For the nation at large, it is a bad sign that any farm worker quits.

---

* Our corn crop is about 3,000,000,000 bushels a year, as compared to some 788,000,000 bushels of wheat—and our rice crop is about one-third as big as the latter. Oats come next to corn in amount—about 1,300,000,000 bushels a year—but the value of the crop is considerably under that of wheat.

MAKING AND GROWING

MAKING FOODS THAT FEEDS THE MILLIONS

In America the manufacturing plant has been developed to a higher point than anywhere else in the world. The machine-making of everything imaginable—from tooth-paste to automobiles—has been reduced to a science. The multitude of products to eat alone mounts into the thousands. Our packing and preserving industry—which turns out everything from ready-cooked soups, ready-baked biscuit, stewed and sweetened fruits, baked beans, spiced pickles and relishes, the typically American "chewing gum", and hundreds of kinds of wrapper candies, sauces and dressings, breakfast cereals, and other things with which we are all familiar—is unequaled in the world to-day.

America literally lives out of cans and cartons. Not only are the things that can be kept a long time carefully wrapped and prepared, but everything that is sent to market one day and used the next is so treated. Milk, bread, butter, used to be shipped to the storekeeper in bulk; now it is carefully sealed and sent in a dust-proof wrapper. *Vast sums of money are spent every day in the United States to prepare our foods for the small consumer.* The process is a cleaner and more convenient one, but it is expensive, and the public gets a good deal less for its money by buying in the small box or bottle.

The triumphs of American manufacturing lie in its *large-scale production* and its *standardization.* Everything here is labeled with a trade name; and though this is not true only of America, the effort is to invent new and distinctive features in things ranging from cigarettes to clothes and then to convert the public to them.

Cheapness is often one result of the great quantities of product turned out. America has led the world, for example, in the making of great quantities of automobiles. It placed the motor-car within reach of the workman and the middle-class family. Owing to the genius for large-scale production of Henry Ford, the Detroit automobile manufacturer—surely one of the world's most enterprising industrialists—the little standardized car is turned out in endless streams. The factories are marvels of method, where the automobile takes shape under a succession of hundreds of hands as easily as a snowball gathers layers when it is kept rolling. This is romance; to make chariots better than those old-time kings rode in, to sell for the price of a good suit of clothes in the days when knights were bold!

Just as in England, the rise of the factories has brought both good and evil in American life. Big business in the United States has since 1840 developed in the direction of huge corporations. *America is the land of the "trust"*—a fact that has called forth a lot of jokes about our slogan "In God We Trust." These big combinations of "interests", all of which control the same business in some way or other, were formed for several reasons. *They keep down competition in selling finished goods or buying raw material,* and also in the shipping of goods.

THE HEARTLESS AGE OF THE "TRUSTS"

The trend of all sorts of businesses, including storekeeping, seems to be running in the direction of the "chain" or combination. We see tobacco, grocery, bakery, shoe, clothing and other "chain" stores. The advantages of buying in great lots, in selling in big quantities and controlling the amount put on sale and the price received, are plain. The huge amounts of money that can be invested in one business are another advantage. In fact, *the great capital needed to launch some of our modern businesses has shut out the private business man.*

The trust has a great power in monopolizing the market and shutting out the small competitor. For this reason there was great opposition to the oil, steel and other mergers of corporations under one set of directors, and the Sherman Anti-Trust Law and other measures were passed to forbid their formation.

Since then the trust has really gone on under the name of corporation, whole re-organizations having been made in the directorships and stockholders. They do an important work in standardizing business, and they are more efficient in their production than a lot of small producers. That they very often "profiteer", from both the man who buys their goods and the raiser or maker of the raw product, cannot be denied.

The position of the working people is another very big problem. It was harder, in general, in the days just after the Revolution than ever afterward in America, but in those early days workers were not at the mercy of the big employers. Those who were not farmers were small mechanics or laborers. Women hardly did any work except that in the household. A working man got from fifty to ninety cents a day! Often there was no regular pay day. If he got in debt, he could be thrown into jail. There was no way of making his employer pay him by "attaching" whatever he had made.

HOW TRADE UNIONS HAD THEIR START

The carpenter, the bricklayer, of that day had no Union to call out everybody on strike in case they were ill-treated. These were organized very slowly, and at first they were a sort of sick-benefit organization, somewhat like a lodge. In the South labor never "had

MAKING AND GROWING

a chance", so long as slavery was in style. After the Civil War there was an opening of new fields for the worker—the development of the West (where free land was offered to the settler) and the South, where the cotton crop had to be prepared for the market by *somebody!* This was the time when the factories began to grow in number, immigrants began to come from abroad, and women and children began to take a share in public employment. This was, too, the time when the trade union began to grow up.* A general national federation of workers was formed in the Knights of Labor (1869), which had a socialistic trend in advance of its time.

The passage of laws to help in the labor problems began with the States. Massachussetts passed an eight-hour law for children working in factories (1866). Later she limited the hours per week to sixty. That was a pretty modern point of view to have at this time, when matters had hardly been improved much in England with regard to labor!

The ranks of capital and labor had not really been drawn up for a big struggle as yet, and occasional strikes that were organized in cities were not serious. The earliest nation-wide "tie-up" came with the railroad strikes in 1877, the result of reduction in the pay of the employees. The strikers armed and fought with pickets and troops sent to break up the disorders. A lot of property of the railroad companies and other persons was destroyed.

Since that early time, numberless new branches of unions have been formed. Founded in 1881, the American Federation of Labor has come to be a great and well-regulated body, under a responsible head. Its aims are to avoid industrial disorders, to get results by talking the matter over with employers. Up to the beginning of the twentieth century there were more than a thousand cases of arguments, "lock-outs" and "walk-outs" every year in the United States.

One of the most serious strikes was that in the coal mines of Pennsylvania during the administration of President Roosevelt. The miners were organized under a strong leader, and seemed to have the greater amount of right on their side in the argument. They had left their work and for some time the stream of coal had stopped, while the owners of the mines were "trying to arrange a conference." The time dragged on and the approach of the autumn set the nation to worrying about a possible shortage. Word come from the White House that the difficulties were to be patched up as soon as possible. Suddenly Mr. Roosevelt is said to have lost his patience.

---

* Though there were a number of locals in the different cities, the first nation-wide union organization was that of the printers (1850). Some twenty-five national unions had been formed at the beginning of the Civil War. During and after this war many were organized.

He called a conference of the mine-owners and labor leaders and gave an ultimatum in his typical forceful way. He was unable to walk on account of an injury to his foot, but from his chair and bandages he bellowed: "Either those mines will be opened up inside of ten days' time, or I'll send the militia up there to do it!" And the mines were opened at once! Recent important strikes include the threatened one of the trainmen in 1922, which, however, was patched up in time by a wage agreement.

The laws passed in recent years include some important ones to provide for the worker's health. Many States have acts requiring factories to be inspected by officials. They report on the sanitary conditions. The loss of life by accidents is steadily being reduced by equipping all machines that are dangerous with safety devices. Of course, all danger can not be done away with, and there are still frightful disasters. But the *employer has come to realize that the worker's health is worth money to him.* Most stores, factores and other business places have elaborate "first aid" departments for the sick or injured. And many now have recreation rooms, restaurants and auditoriums for their employees.

"BETTER PAY!"—THE CRY OF THE WORKER

In two main directions the people who work have been demanding their rights. These are in *shorter working hours* and *better pay*. In 1830 there were fifteen hours in the working day. Women and children had to be at work at four thirty o'clock in the morning, and in the factories *the children were hurried in their work by overseers who went about with a rawhide whip, swishing it and sometimes even bringing it down on the shoulders of the shrinking little boys and girls.* And it was said that about forty per cent. of all workers were children at that day. The working day didn't end until eight o'clock at night in the summer time. It used to be the rule to go to work *without breakfast* and toil until seven or later— more than two hours—on an empty stomach. Then they were given about twenty-five minutes to eat their cold lunch. Again at noon another "lay-off" of the same length of time was given. Sometimes the employers kept the clocks turned a little slow to make the day longer, or so the workers complained!

The working hours for women and children have been cut down in many of the States; and in the case of children the age at which they may stop school to go to work has been fixed (usually at fourteen years) by the education laws of different States. The South is behind other parts of the country in this respect, and in the cotton factories of the South children are at work who are much younger. The working hours of the different trades has been fixed usually by agreements rather than by law. The ideal is the "eight-hour" day, but this has not been given in all trades. Some State laws provide that the employer is liable to damages for injury to employees, *if they were not careless.* Here the whole matter sometimes hinges, and it is hard for a poor man to prove that he wasn't against the arguments of the lawyers that a rich manufacturer can hire!

The rate of pay has gone up in most trades.* The rise was slow until after the Civil War. Then inside of twenty years earnings went up to almost half again as much. The rise in prices of things was very little compared with this. But, since then *the costs of living have gone up enormously.* It is not too much to say that at certain times they have doubled, or almost trebled. This was especially true of the World War period. The barest living expenses, the price of food and shelter, have in the last ten years reached a higher point than ever before in American history. The lack of new buildings during the war period had something to do with this, especially in the big cities. In New York the situation was so bad that a law was passed limiting the amount of rent increase that landlords could charge and keeping them from turning out tenants except on well-grounded complaints. Since then building has increased in New York (owing to an act making all such new buildings free of taxes for ten years) and to some extent the housing problem there is not so bad, though rents in the heart of the city are higher than anywhere else to-day. Prices of food are four or five times what they were in our grandfathers day, however. When we look at an old grocery bill of those days the low prices seem now quite a joke —eggs at ten or twelve cents a dozen, for example, instead of the thirty-five to seventy that we now pay. All this must be reckoned in the account when it is claimed that the pay of the worker has gone up. So it has, but *what's in the pay envelope doesn't go so far as it used to!*

WHAT SOCIALISM IS ALL ABOUT

The disputes between the worker and the employer all boil down to this: the first supplies the work and the other the raw material and (often) the tools, and each claims that he ought to get the greater part of the price that the finished goods bring. We said at the beginning of this chapter that all money comes from either property or work. *Both are necessary for the carrying on of business.* The man who supplied the money and material was always a little ahead of the worker—because he had something substantial to base his claim on, and he had charge of selling the finished goods!

---

* The average American family's income was $1,470 in 1910, $2,600 in 1919.

The workers, on the other hand, believe that their work is the source of wealth. "Even the capitalist's money", they say, "in the beginning came from the work of *somebody!*"

The feeling that the worker wasn't getting his share gave rise to the teachings of Socialism about the middle of the last century. The first teachers began by planning ideal colonies that really never turned out successful. They wanted to have all men divided into little groups that would own their own capital, manage their businesses and do the work, too. Robert Owen, an English manufacturer, founded several such co-operative colonies, including one at New Harmony, Ind. At Brook Farm, a group of "high-brows", New England writers and others, settled on the land in 1841 and planned to live simply and divide the things they raised into equal parts. But the hard work of handling a pitch-fork and shovel didn't appeal to the soft-handed thinkers, and so the little colony broke up!

Socialism really had its start in the teaching of Karl Marx, a German student, who by his writings did much to put it on a real, scientific basis. He gave up the idea that people could have "ideal" towns and settlements, where hard work and poverty never came, and everybody got a good slice of bacon for his general good feeling for the group! He taught that *machinery to produce things should belong to the nation instead of to private owners.* By this he hoped that the big profits now made by the employer class would be divided up between the workers. At the time this seemed like a very high-handed idea, but before fifty years had gone by from his death many of these ideas were being practised. For instance, the government of the United States took over the railroads during the World War (to keep down running expenses, it was said, and for greater efficiency) and when after some time they were returned to the private owners (1920), a Transportation Act limited the amount of profit they could make to six per cent. on the value of the railroads. *The day may not be far distant when laws like these will fix the amount of profits for all industries.* The movement is now on foot to cut down the earnings of capital (to go into private pockets, that is) and to add to the wage of the worker, and finally to cut down prices for the public. The big tax on incomes now enforced is a movement in this direction.

The best part of the new ideas about labor is the new *respect* for work that we see everywhere. From feudal days the idea of work seemed to have something "lowering" about it. To-day that has been changed. There is a new feeling that *every man's job is important,* from the ditch digger to the president of the company. We have only to look at the state of things in aristocratic England, where the prime minister and members of his cabinet are serving on a Labor Party ticket. In Scotland a working man was not long ago elected to the highest post in the realm. *This is a plain sign of the way the wind in blowing!*

The things that the worker is holding out for will all in time be gained. What does he want? In spite of the harsh things that are sometimes said about the labor unions,—shutting out of the non-member under the "closed shop" system and other complaints—they are working for just a few reasonable objects. The worker wants industry to be a co-operation of producer and financier for the object of serving the public, instead of making it a "grabbing" game and an exploitation of the many for a few. He wants a good wage for each worker, on which he can support his family and give them some of the good things of life and bring up his children to be a credit to the race.

There is to be a more even division of work—long hours are to be cut down, and all the unemployed shall have their share, even if the government has to start special jobs in useful building operations to keep them busy. The worker wants to be not only a spoke in the wheel, without intelligence and self-control, but a manager and part-owner in businesses. Finally, he wants to turn out as good product and as much of it as he can under pleasant working conditions. It is for the best interests of the country at large that he get these things, for it is the worker who keeps the great wheels turning that make our great nation's power and wealth.

CHAPTER II

THE ROMANCE OF RAIL AND RUDDER (TRANSPORTATION)

WHEN the colonists were beginning their great work of building the America of to-day, with its millions of acres, thousands of factories, all producing *wealth*—there was no way to get from the Atlantic to the Pacific. Everything west of the Allegheny Mountains was wilderness. If you wanted to get to Philadelphia from New York, you had to take a stage-coach, a sort of bus drawn by horses— and it took three days, instead of some two hours, as now! What is more, the roads were bad; there was no such thing as a State road of to-day.

The first improvement came when companies were organized to build "pikes", and these were made by a sort of stock company, everybody investing money who was able and cared to. Of course, to get out the money invested in them, toll had to be charged. (There are still toll gates on many roads and bridges that have been built in later times, but these are usually made by the State and the toll stops when the debt is paid off.) The West was not developed much until after the Civil War, and in the early days when people wanted to go there to settle they had to make the trip in a "covered wagon", or prairie "schooner", over a sort of trail or foot-path. It cost enormous sums to send goods anywhere, even in the East. The government in 1838 opened a pike from Washington, D. C. to Illinois, costing four millions.

After the roads began to be a little improved, the problem of shipping was partly solved by the digging of canals. *For it did no good to be making things that were worth huge amounts of money, if they could not be transported.* The canal for a time helped things along a great deal. To be sure, it was a slow way of shipping. In our modern days of speed the old canal boats—drawn by their mules along the narrow ditches, the animals plodding on with the tow rope at one side,—seem hardly to *crawl*! But in those days it seemed like a new and wonderful way of whisking from one place to another. Water travel is always a little easier than that on land, and even passengers traveled by canal boat.

The biggest of all waterways dug in America at that time was the Erie Canal. This was a big undertaking, for it required digging a ditch all the way across upper New York State, some 250 miles. From the Hudson River just above Albany the route along the Mohawk River, "hitting" Schenectady, Utah, Syracuse, Rochester, Buffalo and other towns and ending in the eastern end of Lake Erie. Of course, this also connected New York with the other Great Lakes. *It had an enormous effect on the growth of the Middle West and even on that of New York City.* The completion of the canal (it took eight years) was celebrated by the pouring of a bottle of water from the Great Lakes into New York Bay, and the opinion of the day was that East had met West. The Erie Canal was a great financial success, for though it was expensive to dig, it soon paid itself from freight tolls. Besides, the time and cost of shipping goods at once went down.

The State of Ohio later built another canal, linking up Lake Erie with the Ohio River. This canal made a still better road inland to the Middle West, and farming there took on a new "spurt", as the grains could be shipped down to New York or to other markets where they would fetch a good price. In many other States—especially in Pennsylvania—networks of canals were dug; and these are still used to-day as a cheap way to carry coal and other kinds of freight.

FROM "COVERED WAGON" TO TWENTIETH CENTURY LIMITED

The great work of developing the country came with the railroads. This invention, we have seen, helped to change England's national life within a few years. But England is a little island, and *in America the railroads had the job of binding together a land of more than three million square miles.* America, the great trackless continent, inside of a century became America, the thriving, cultivated land of homes and countless industries! *And it was all owing to the railroads.* A nation of more than a hundred million souls from every country on the globe has become welded into one people with one spirit! No wonder the great railroad pioneers are called "empire builders"! This is the romance of the rails—that they whisk a plodding, weak human being over two thousand miles of space in the same time that it takes him to walk a hundred.

America, the rich, the as yet unconquered, was waiting for the brain that would invent a machine to bind her two seacoasts together with a steel chain. If suddenly to-day the great railroad system of our country were to go to pieces utterly, *absolute paralysis would result!* The whole business of the country depends on the railroads. We know how serious was the threat of a general strike of the trainmen a few years ago. It would have meant starvation for great numbers of the people in a few days.

Our whole life is dependent on getting food supplies from the farms to the big cities. Wealth, money, rich treasure flies on the wings of the wind with every train that roars past us as we stand like a pigmy by the tracks and feel the hot breath of the steel monster! The magic carpets, the Seven-League Boots, dreamed of in old stories are not to be compared to the marvels of the steam railroad—and, for that matter, the newer electric system that is slowly gaining ground.

At first the idea of laying rails for cars to run on came to people, before the idea of steam was suggested. The first rails were wooden, with a strip of metal nailed on top to make them "wear". Later, of course, came the all-steel rail which improved matters. Meanwhile, one man experimented with the idea of having *sails* on cars and letting the wind run them. The only draw-back to this was that the car was likely to "reverse" and be blown back again the way it came! It was also a slow and untrustworthy way of travel, though it actually "worked". Then the idea of horsepower was tried. We all remember the old "horse-cars", used on the street railways even into the early twentieth century.

On train lines a fearful and wonderful "engine" was invented, where the horse was put in a sort of enclosure on board and made to tread a mill that operated the car! The people of that day sat on the platform around the sides, and this slow car was called the "Flying Dutchman"! When the Baltimore and Ohio was opened in 1830—ground had been broken two years earlier by Charles Carroll, the last living signer of the Declaration of Independence—the short run of thirteen miles to Ellicott's Mills was made in an hour and a quarter by such a horse-tread car.

After about two years steam was introduced on this pioneer line. John Stevens, as we have said in the chapter on the growth of England, made a steam locomotive—a sort of stationary boiler mounted on a platform and machinery connecting with a cogged system that drove the enormous hoop-like wheels. There were many short lines used for business purposes, in the mines and in other industries.

From all these little beginnings, the railroad grew to have a real business value. The chief use was to carry goods from points on waterways to others where they could be floated down to seaside ports. The cost of building and of running the railroads was still very high. Capitalists were rather slow in taking up the idea, and even passengers made their trips partly by canal boat and partly by the "steam cars". ("Car" would probably be more correct, for at first one big coach could carry all that wanted to ride.) The New York Central Railroad, in the Grand Central Station in New York, still keeps on view the string of little toy-like cars and the little engine that made early trips over that line.

WRESTING THE WILDERNESS FROM NATURE

As the cost of the building of great cross-country lines was enormous, the government through an act of Congress gave aid to several companies. Lands in the West were given to the Union Pacific Railroad so that it might build its line from Omaha westward to Utah, and the Central Pacific was also given several million acres of land to construct a road from Sacramento, Cal., into Utah. Money was also loaned by the government, because *it saw plainly the importance of linking the West with the East.* The whole growth of the country depended on this. When finally, in 1869, the two roads were joined with a golden spike, there was a great excitement over the whole country. *It was the beginning of a new era of development.*

The job of laying the roads through the wilderness was not so easy as it sounds in the statement. *It was a great struggle of man against Nature,* a romance of human determination and muscle in the face of almost superhuman difficulties! The empire builders had to wrest the country from a thousand natural guardians—the desert, great mountains, bodies of water, that had to be bridged and tunneled. Engineering marvels were common. The money cost of the great undertaking was vast. *The railroads were the work of all the people*—they put their money together, bought stocks of the new companies and helped in every way. They influenced the State and National legislatures to help with other measures. Above all, the enterprise of a few great railroad builders like Hill was responsible for the conquest of the continent. The greatest spurt in railroad building came after the Civil War. Between 1860 and 1880 the amount of mileage was increased from about 30,000 to some 90,000,* and the age of speculation in railroad management set in.

The first stage of the industry had now been ended—a great and fine work of heroic men who dared many dangers to lay the new paths of progress. But, just as the money men had been slow to take up the invention when it was new and risks were involved, so *now they pounced on it in the hope of getting rich by monopolizing.* This is a chapter in American money history that is not so fine as the one before it. After the coast-to-coast line was finished in 1869, there was a great railroad "boom". The West in particular

---

*At the beginning of the twentieth century it had grown to some 200,000 miles.

was soon honeycombed with railroads. Inside of ten years the amounts of tracks laid were doubled.

Everybody was mad to invest money in the new form of speculation. And unscrupulous promoters took advantage of this "investment fever" without delay. New roads sprang up everywhere—many of them were never built, but the people were persuaded to buy their paper on the strength of great promises. It was a repetition of the "South Sea Bubble" on a smaller scale in many cases. The money needed for the work of extension, consolidation, of the great roads was so enormous that, for the first time, the people as a whole were invited to become joint owners. The great managers, financial barons, at the head, to be sure, often got the greatest profit. And there were even cases where the stock issued was enormously greater than the road and equipment were worth. This is called "watering" stock, and it caused much woe.

THE AGE OF RAILROAD "GRAFT"

Several big lines now had "through" connection from the East to Chicago, and each naturally wanted to get as much of the business as possible. They tried to "underbid" each other on freight rates. Then they combined in what were known as "pools", an arrangement to divide the whole earnings in the regions that they covered among them, in proportion to the mileage of each road or the service rendered.

For the sake of some cities that had less desirable situations in trade the roads fixed cheaper freight rates, which they called "differential". This was a pretty fair way of giving cities a share in business that they couldn't have got otherwise; but *in the case of private businesses there soon grew up a system of "special rates" that was very unfair to others.* It was the big, rich corporations that could influence the roads to give them reductions—and so the small business was under a still greater disadvantage. It often happened, as it was bound to, that *the men who owned controlling shares in the railroads also had steel mills, meat packing houses and mines.* So a little "family agreement" fixed up things so that the regular rate was seemingly paid, but afterward a refund of part of the sum was made—a "rebate", as it was called. This, of course, soon "leaked out", and a great protest went up from the small shippers. Scandal raised an ugly head, and the newspapers began to print "scareheads."

Another evil was the increased use of free permits to ride, "passes", which were given to politicians, newspaper men and in short everybody with influence or "pull"—whether willingly by the railroads or because the powers insisted on them, is hard to say. *Large sums of money were being taken out of the pockets of the small stockholders* in this way and being transferred to a few influential men. It was a sort of "painless extraction."

The complaints about the high rates for small shippers and cheap ones for big were first heard from the West, where the farmers of the great grain regions demanded action to settle the question. Several of the States appointed commissions in the "seventies", and these were given power to set the limit of rates. They sometimes passed very strict local laws, and these were soon repealed on the complaint of the roads.

The mistake was soon made of trying to cure the evil by hampering the usefulness of the roads, which was just about as sensible as cutting off a leg to cure rheumatism! The idea had now grown up that the railroads were the "melon" of Big Business, instead of being part of the machinery of the country, without which it couldn't get along. But the railroad interests, to make up for such meddlesome interference—in cases, that is, where it was not wisely applied—influenced the legislatures of other States to prevent the forming of commissions. These local bodies, in any case, were not fitted to deal with the transportation problem, which is an interstate, or nation-wide, one.

The romantic history of the railroads now led to Congress and the courts. The first countrywide step which had any real effect at control of rates and other grievances was the creation of the Interstate Commerce in 1887. This was formed of five men by the provisions of the Interstate Commerce Act, which did away with "rebates", pooling, and rates which differed with distance or other considerations.*
The commission was to act as a jury to hear complaints on any breaking of the law.

Since the roads were forbidden to form "pools", they now went in for the same thing under a different name—"rate agreements"! They punished members of these little "agreeing" groups if they violated the rules for rates laid down by the others. These were later condemned as violating the Sherman Anti-Trust Law. Since then the control has been gradually passing into the hands of a few little groups of money kings, who are able to buy up small roads or to lease them for operation. A still more effective way is to "corner" their stock when that is possible, using the same method that Disraeli did a century before to get possession of the Suez Canal. The expense of

---

* Other laws passed in recent years were the Hepburn Act (1906), which forbids granting of free passes, carrying of a railroad's own products, and gives the Commission power to limit a freight rate of a railroad if a shipper complains: the Valuation Act (1913) which provides for an appraisal of the actual value of American railroads, in order to fix legal rate as a proper return on that investment. The decision has not been reached yet. The value is estimated at $19,000,000,000.

running railroads operates to place them in the hands of the richest men—or those with widespread interests.

THE GOVERNMENT AS RAILROAD "WATCHDOG"

The results of all these State and national laws has been to cut down the earnings of the roads. This was a good thing in so far as it also reduced the freight and passenger rates, but at the same time *the cost of running the roads was mounting steadily.* This led to some of the smaller ones going into the hands of receivers. It also has cut down the returns on the money invested by stockholders, and they have been led to sell their shares. When this selling became noticeable at times, of course, *the whole value of the stock took a sharp decline.* The most serious result was that the roads had to "retrench" in their expenses, and so cut down on all improvements, new cars and roadbeds, number of men, and the like. The "service" suffered a great deal, as was natural.

Suddenly the nation entered the World War. As we have noted in the chapter before this, the government took over the railroads as a war-time measure. It had the national Treasury behind it, a country of tax-payers to support it. The governing board was made up of experts, but they naturally were not so familiar with problems of actual management as the owners. The latter were guaranteed their profits. The big end was to rush war supplies to central shipping depots, to carry men for embarkation for the "front"—and expense didn't count! It was time that mattered! Under such conditions, the war record of the government was fair as railroad operator, even though the deficit was about a billion and a half dollars.

It was not until nearly two years after the signing of the Armistice that Congress was ready to return the roads to their owners. And meanwhile, it had been trying to make up a law which would satisfy everybody that had a complaint against the way they had been run by Capital. The farmers, the manufacturers, the railroad stockholders, the employees, the labor leaders, and all the members of Congress —each had his pet theory as to how they should be run! The outcome of endless discussion was the framing of the Transportation Act of 1920, which literally "lays down the law" in almost every department of operation. Many of the rules are good ones: *by this Act for the first time in America the railroads have become strictly public works run for the convenience of the people, with the owners as holders of a privilege from the government.*

The most important ruling is the one which limits the profits to be made to six per cent (later reduced to 5¾%*). *Any profit above*

---

* This is undoubtedly a little low, as the owner of a house is under some State laws allowed to realize 8% on his investment. It is said by

5¾% must be paid back to the government. On the other hand, the government guaranteed the roads against operating loss during the first six months after their return to private ownership.

Whether the investor will withdraw his money from this form of security, to put it in something that may bring larger returns, is one of the serious problems to be decided in the next few years. This would be a tragedy for the development of an industry so closely linked up with the welfare of the country.

The real future of the railroads may lie in government ownership. (The "Plump Plan", suggesting that they be owned by the trainmen, is impractical.) Now they are strictly under its control; it supervises the issuing of stock, to prevent "watering"; it maintains a Railroad Labor Board, to give advice in case of disputes between trainmen and owners. Meanwhile the roads have done marvels in improving their "service" on lowered budgets and smaller forces. A great need is for more railroad building to keep up with the population.

In a sense the railroads belong to the people of America: the stockholders number some 2,000,000 persons, but investors in thousands of other forms—holders of bank accounts, insurance policies, railroad bonds—indirectly pay their money into the funds that keep these great miles of rails singing! The cost of the golden chain that holds the country together is some six billions of dollars yearly—more than that of the government itself!

THE MAGIC OF THE ELECTRIC TRAIN

The invention of the electric train and street-car has also within twenty years changed America. The problem of caring for the great streams of people who must travel to "business" and return twice a day in the great cities could never have been solved without it. In New York, when street traffic got to be too congested in the 'seventies, the elevated tracks were put up, and at first steam locomotives drew cars on this scaffolding above the streets. The first appearance of these created amazement in our grandfathers' day! The smoke and cinders from the engines got into everybody's eyes, to be sure, but it was Progress! The surface cars were still pulled by horses. The adaptation of electricity to the driving of cars was largely owing to that inventive genius, Thomas A. Edison. Electricity itself was hardly of practical importance before 1890. To-day we wonder how anyone ever got along without it, so much do we depend on it for our means of travel, lighting and telephone and telegraph communica-

railway authorities that in the first few years after the passage of the law, the returns only averaged 4%. Any profit above 5¾% must be paid back to the government.

tion. The surface electric cars of our great cities have been superseded by the underground "subway" train, which at a speed of nearly fifty miles an hour on express lines hurls passengers through the dark tunnels under the earth. Our engineering genius has led us to drill tubes through the solid rock under rivers, and—surely this is a miracle that would have bewildered Moses of the Red Sea!—our commuters travel under water, dry-shod, from Long Island inside of five minutes.

In the small cities and between towns the "trolley" lines have proved the great means of travel. The farming districts have been linked to the town, and business has profited. The costs of erecting power plants and trolley lines is, of course, enormous. Here another form of investment for the small money-holder has been opened, and the returns on stocks of this sort are in cases higher than those of the steam railroads under the new ruling.

The fares in most small cities have risen higher within the last ten years than they have in large cities like New York, where the companies hold a franchise agreement in some cases not to raise the fare. The last arrangement is a good one in making cheap fares, but the companies are often hampered in their expenditures. In order to "make ends meet", we are told, they are unable to supply more cars, and the resulting congestion in "rush" hours is fearful.

A crying need in American metropolises is for more civic appropriations to build subway lines. New York is up to date the most fully developed in this respect, but its peculiar crowding of millions within the space of a few square miles makes its traffic problem much the greatest of any spot on earth. Chicago needs a bigger subway system, its rambling elevated lines being somewhat unsatisfactory for speedy and direct service. Boston has laid a subway of some length, and the prospect is that within the next fifty years all American cities with a population of 750,000 will have to adopt them. Thus the millions of American capitalists have built our teeming cities.

The great increase of automobiles in the streets of American cities —in certain neighborhoods to the complete exclusion of the horse—is a sign of our national wealth. This means of travel has had a greater "boom" in America than anywhere else in the world. It is only in the United States that every farmer is able to drive into the nearest city in his own motor-car. This is the final great means for *transportation* in our vast country. The number of machines turned out annually by our factories mounts into four millions; and though many are sent to other countries, the great supply sold here each year, if they were placed end to end, would doubtless cover a great highway stretching from the East to the Middle West. *America is the land of gasoline*: the amounts spent each year for this commodity have made the fortunes of our great oil companies. The automobile has made the nation *one,* even as the locomotive.

AMERICA'S EARLY TRADE ON THE SEA

We have not spoken of the water travel of America, but that has had a steady and great—if more gradual growth than that of the land. Ship-building was one of the great businesses of the early colonial period in America. At the time of the Revolution we built one-third of the merchant ships going back and forth to England.

When that country passed her ill-advised laws forbidding us to trade with the French West Indies, it was a hard blow at the old sea-captains of that day. They had been getting rich on the rum, sugar and molasses they had been bringing from there to sell at home. The result was that they went in for "bootlegging", or smuggling, of these things. One writer estimates that nine-tenths of the colonial merchants were smugglers. The list included such notable names as John Hancock, and one-quarter of the signers of the Declaration!

The first seaport to capture the lead in our trade was Boston. After the Revolution, Philadelphia had the biggest amount of shipping. All this time New York was a "dark horse". Most trade before the day of the railroads was carried on by ocean. The big growth in our sea-trade took place between the years 1793 and 1807, when the English and the French were in the midst of the wars for the rule of America and India. *A neutral country was needed to carry the goods from the colonies of one to the other.* That was America's opportunity, and in the fourteen years our foreign trade increased five times! Not only that, but the number of our ships was multiplied by six. *This is the biggest instance of growth within a decade that the history of modern trade has seen.*

Later this trade had a setback, when the English declared the French ports blockaded, and the latter nation retorted by saying that the British Isles were, too! The result was that a number of our ships, that dared the blockades, were captured, including some $50,000,000 worth of goods, at different times. To prevent this rash daring on the part of our sea captains, Congress passed the Embargo Act, forbidding our ships to go to foreign ports. *The result was a complete paralysis of our foreign trade.* It bankrupted a lot of our merchants, threw thousands of sailors out of work.

Relief didn't come until after the War of 1812. We have already seen how, after that struggle, American manufacturers took a sudden leap. Trade did not revive so quickly, partly because the country was turning all its attention to internal growth. Foreign ports had high import duties on things brought in. But now began brisk internal trade among our States. The steamboat had been introduced on the Mississippi, and the days of the "side-wheeler" that plied down the broad river to Memphis, with a background of stately mansions, wharves with bales of cotton and singing slaves, had come in.

Coasting trade along our shores was forbidden to any ships except our own by Congress in 1817, and later treaties were signed providing for free trade for foreign nations that gave us the same privileges. But many new ships had been built by England, and she was jealous of her trade with her West Indian colonies. She wanted it exclusively for herself! It was not until 1830 that she let us trade with them, and we in turn took off some port duties for her vessels coming into our harbors.

WHEN "CLIPPERS" PUT OUT FOR FAR CATHAY

About this time our shipping took another great "spurt". It had been almost stationary for some time, and in fact had declined to almost the amount of Revolutionary days. But now began a proud period when *American sailing vessels came to be the best and speediest then made anywhere*. New York came to be the leading port of the Atlantic seaboard, a position which it holds to this day. The war of Britain and China caused a lot of the trade that England had formerly with this Oriental nation to come to us, and we built great square-rigged and swift sailing vessels to go around the Horn and up the Pacific to China.

The day of passenger traffic had arrived. The discovery of gold in California and in Australia made people eager to go there at any price, and on the voyages up the Pacific our boats stopped at both these places. The number of ships built in our shipyards increased until they made up about one-third of the world's tonnage. These were romantic days, about which old "salts" not so many years ago loved to tell tales. The great quantities of cotton that now began to pour out of the South were carried to Europe by our sailing boats at a rapid rate. It was the great crops of this product that made New Orleans, Mobile, Baltimore and Charleston jump into prominence as great port cities.

The rise of the coast shipping took place at this time, and soon it was greater than the ocean trade. The activity in coast shipping has steadily increased ever since, while our foreign merchant shipping—since the high-water mark of the years just before the Civil War fell off, especially between 1880 and 1900. The reason for this is probably to be found in the great "boom" for railroad ventures and the other great development projects of the Middle and Far West. During that period our capital was invested elsewhere. The Great Lakes, however, have had a great shipping development, beginning with the building of the Erie Canal.

THE PANAMA CANAL—ROMANTIC TRIUMPH OF ENGINEERING

One of the world's greatest engineering projects has been America's building of the Panama Canal. The site was acquired from France after that nation had unsuccessfully attempted to dig the great waterway. The cost of the site alone was $50,000,000. This narrow strip of land connecting two continents presented one of the greatest tasks ever attempted. The cost of the excavation alone ran into hundreds of millions. The building of the great locks and dams and the plans for a degree of fortification will raise the sum well into the billions.

The greatest difficulties were the tropical conditions which bred malaria and yellow fever. The story is now well-known how American doctors waged a war against the mosquito which carried the deadly germs. But when the lives of the workmen had been protected, and the vast equipment of great steam shovels and other machinery had been installed, it was found that the landslides in the Culebra Cut and other parts of the great ditch could not be kept from overflowing the finished portions. The remedy for this was found only after much effort. The opening of the canal was celebrated by the United States in the Panama-Pacific Exposition in California in 1915.

The yearly $25,000,000 toll that the Canal brings in adds to our revenues. The importance of this waterway is that it makes possible a much shorter sea trip not only from the eastern United States to the Pacific, but also from the Orient across the Pacific to New York. Much of the world's traffic is going through the Canal. It is regularly cutting off some 8,000 miles from the journey of every ship that used to have to go to the southern extremity of South America to reach the Pacific. *It is one of the world's most important means of communication.* It will stand as a monument to Goethals, its builder. Not least is its importance in the volume of trade which the United States is carrying on with the East. *The expansion of our export business between the closing years of the nineteenth century and the first decade of the twentieth was enormous. The increase was almost one hundred times that of a decade before.*

The twentieth century has seen a revival of interest in prowess on the sea. The American navy won new laurels in the Spanish-American War, under the stirring leadership of Dewey and Schley. The building of vessels for our Navy—the new submarines, destroyers and many great "dreadnaught" battleships—went on with enthusiasm. Private capital began to be invested in merchant ships. (For some years nine-tenths of our commerce had been carried by foreign ships.) Big vessels were built for the Pacific trade with the East. Millionaire railroad magnates bought not only private steam yachts that are the most luxurious in the world, but also lines of coast and ocean sailing ships for trade. The merchant marine still lacks something of being a fulfillment of its early promise in the days of 1800 and 1860. Every once in a while a loud lament is heard in the newspapers or from the floor of Congress about the "State of Our Merchant Marine!" But a forward movement is even now on foot.

AMERICA'S SEA POWER SINCE THE WORLD WAR

The dramatic entry of America into the World War, which changed so many other things, suddenly gave our shipbuilders a chance to prove themselves. *Probably never in the world's history has there been such feverish activity in vessel building!* The great need of carrying supplies to Europe caused the government, as we all know, to appoint a Shipping Board, which had charge of turning out small wooden merchant ships at the rate of a hundred every month.

Before the work could be begun new shipyards had to be hastily built. Tens of thousands of men were housed in these wooden communities that sprang up like mushrooms! The cost of the work was enormous, and it was unfortunate that the war ended when it did, for the boats were really not used, except for a brief period—part of a year, when great squadrons convoyed by battle ships and destroyers crossed the ocean like a caravan, watchful for lurking submarines!

America for years had held out obstinately in her belief in wooden ships, after iron hulls had come in. This was a backward point of view at the time, but forty years later the value of wood in an emergency was proved. Men were transported across the Atlantic at a rate that reminded one of the romantic days when Xerxes, the Persian, crossed the Hellespont, driving his army along over wooden rafts!

The loss by Germany of her boats in American harbors, the later use of these as passenger liners, placed several huge craft in American hands. With these as a nucleus, it is probable that the United States will continue to extend her passenger shipping and rival the great British Cunard and other famous foreign lines.

The port of New York is to-day the great "open sesame" to a continent—the New World that more than ever is being sought as a haven by the starving and troubled nations of Europe. The shipping that lies daily in her harbors is a close second to, if indeed it does not equal, that of London. The sight presided over by her far-famed Statue of Liberty in the bay is a dramatic one. The great trans-Atlantic liner glides out slowly down the narrows, while countless smaller steamers ply about that make the trip down the coast or up the mighty Hudson. Freight vessels are seen nearby, and countless small tugs and ferry boats.

Above loom the skyscraper office buildings, and these are not seldom crowned by a distant, whirring airplane—another mighty vehicle of the future, which America, through the pioneer Orville Wright, did much to perfect. Here is a vision of the Doorway to an Empire of the People, the world's richest, yet simplest, land! With the recent establishment of an air mail service, and the astonishing record of the airman Maughan, who showed that it is possible to fly from the Atlantic to the Pacific in *one day,* and the flight around the world lately made by another group of our aviators, a new era of transportation has been opened. One who looks into the future can foresee a day in which *all long-distance travel will be done by specially-built speed aircraft.* When that day dawns, our present state of crawling in express trains over the earth will seem as laughable as the old-time horse-tread cars or the passenger canal boats!

CHAPTER III

THE ROMANCE OF BUYING AND SELLING (STORE AND STOCK EXCHANGE)

AMERICA *is the great market of the world!* That is the third factor in the wealth of the United States: in addition to her great natural sources of riches—mines, farms and fisheries—and her enormous factories, which turn out goods faster than those of any other land and in a *greater stream;* her railroads and electric lines, which hold the world's record for speed and efficiency—*she is able to offer better prices for anything she wants than any other nation on the face of the globe to-day.* The reason she can offer them is that her production and transportation—both of which we have just been reviewing—are in a healthy state, and not destroyed by the ravages of war, like those of most countries of Europe to-day. She gets good prices for the things she can produce, and the foreign nations need her goods.

The things she grows and raises are the source of America's power. From the great sums that she gets for these things the United States can loan money to the war-drained treasuries of Europe. And for drops of those golden streams of wealth Europe's producers send their own goods here to sell with eagerness. Finally, the United States is not so hampered by debt—though her war deficit was a large one—that her credit has been impaired. *It is because of her production, again, that she can sturdily overcome this debt. America's workers are her wealth.*

The machinery of her markets is as great as that of her growing, manufacturing and shipping. It ranges all the way from the great stock and other exchanges of the great cities like New York and Chicago, where stocks and other goods are quoted according to the rise or fall of prices; through an elaborate system of brokerages and jobbing houses, to the wholesalers, and finally to the retail dealers. These, in turn, range from the great merchant princes and owners of chain or department stores to the smallest dealer with his little shop of assorted goods, where sales rarely amount to more than a half-dollar.

The romance of buying and selling centers around values and prices. This is true whether the business is the packing and selling of meats or the exhibition of a fine oil painting or object of art in the windows of a Fifth Avenue dealer. Different businesses are organ-

BUYING AND SELLING

ized each in its own way. The "middle-man" or commission merchant has a big place in American business. Another very typical figure is the "traveling salesman", which we adopted from the English "commercial traveler", but developed in our own way, to be a model of practical business sense and audacity. The individual "buyer" for business houses is a familiar figure.

But the two institutions for which the United States are especially responsible are the *department store* and the *mail-order house*. The first was developed by such merchant geniuses as A. T. Stewart, whose fashionable store in lower Broadway, New York, was the mecca for fashion in the 'seventies; Marshall Field, the great Chicago merchant, and John Wanamaker, who probably introduced a new ideal of big, complete and comfortable equipment in his great and palace-like stores in New York and Philadelphia. Not only are all stores brought under one roof, but numerous educational features, like concert halls are included. The development of the cheap department stores in "chain" arrangements—like the pioneer ones of Woolworth—are made possible by American large-scale production and buying.

Other native developments are those of the combined drug and other merchandise stores; the arcades and underground communities of shops in our subway railroad stations and those in the great metropolitan terminals, and the "credit" or installment plan payment businesses. Developments of our selling talents are the plan to give a rebate, such as tobacco coupons, "trading stamps" and other things which can be redeemed in payment on other goods. The automatic restaurant is also typical of a country where all are "equal" and servants are scarce or costly. The selling of "insurance" has been developed until 40,000,000 Americans hold policies worth $8,000,000,000.

The mail-order house, which has several large representatives in the Middle West, is well adapted to an immense country where towns are distant from one another, as is the case in some parts of the United States. These houses issue large catalogues, with illustrations, and flood the mails. The plan of selling by mail is particularly developed in America, along with all other kinds of advertising, the electric sign, the "billboard" and others.

We must now take up briefly the question, "What makes prices?"

The normal value of a thing is the cost of its production in time, effort or money, as we said in connection with the "swapping" of early men. Yet prices vary. To understand the whole romance of buying and selling, one must realize that it is pretty much of a gamble! It seems easy enough to buy goods and sell them at a profit for the workmen have put into the making of them, the shipping of them, and the storekeeper's important business of arranging them for the convenience of the buyer. This would be the case, perhaps, if a spade were always a spade, in the business sense—if this "normal value" didn't differ from "market value"—if all goods were, that is, always worth the same amount of money. But a lot of natural and accidental circumstances enter into the price of things. There are in particular two things that control this rise and fall of value—and have done so ever since the first man started out to trade his arrow heads!

THE ROMANCE OF SUPPLY AND DEMAND

The first factor is *how many people want the same thing at the same time*. This is known as the "demand". For instance, eggs might suddenly go up in price because everybody took it into their heads to eat three at breakfast instead of two. Manufacturing companies understand this principle very well, and for that reason they try to persuade us by artful advertisements that we need more of their particular goods—that, in fact, our health depends on it! Connected with this factor of demand are often natural conditions, like change of seasons. Thus, coal is in demand in winter and ice in summer. Straw and felt hats are "up" at one time of the year and "down" at another. Some of these changes can be foretold in advance; others can't. Public taste is very fickle.

The second thing to be considered is *how much of the thing there is to go round*. This is the "supply". When things are plentiful, prices go down lower than when they are scarce; just as when a lot of people want to buy something, prices go up higher than when only a few do. These are two general rules that are always operating to regulate prices. For instance, the price of eggs goes up at the time of year when the hens do not lay such big quantities. In the case of coal, when the demand is greater than the supply, the price goes up. This scarcity of coal may be caused by any one of a number of things. Either the supply may be smaller than usual because of lack of miners at work, or some other reason; or the demand may be greater, because of a colder winter than usual, or other cause.

WALL STREET, THE WORLD'S MOST FAMOUS MONEY LANE

For the biggest operations in buying and selling in the United States, we must look at the work of Wall Street in New York. (La-Salle Street in Chicago is a close second.) Wall Street is the most famous financial district of the New World, as most of us are well aware. It is not really a street, but a whole neighborhood. Like a great system of electric wires, each connecting with another, lie the great banks, where surplus money—the profits of manufacturing and

BUYING AND SELLING

other business—is stored: the Clearing House, where orders to pay out money stored in any of the country's banks, or orders for the sale of stocks or bonds, are settled; the various exchanges, where selling and buying go on, where money is re-invested—the New York Stock Exchange and the New York Curb Market, where the dealing, as also in the third member of this group, the Consolidated Exchange, is in stocks and bonds—and the Cotton, Produce, Sugar and Coffee Exchanges, where the buying and selling is only in these goods. Besides all these great houses there are the thousand of brokers, or agents in these sales, the bankers, the financiers, the corporations, that control different businesses.

Buying and selling is the subject of this chapter; and so we will wait to speak of the great system of lending and borrowing that makes all business possible until the chapter that follows. It is enough to know now that the money is the golden fuel that makes the whole trade system of the world turn round. It is an endless chain, and it is hard to find the real "starting point" of the process. We shall try:

The manufacturer, the farmer, create *value* by their work. Each trades his product at the market price to the jobber or wholesale dealer. From what he gets for it he must pay the costs of making or growing it. Whatever is left is the "surplus", or "profit". This he can invest either in property, such as real estate, or deposit it in a bank on interest; or pay his living expenses, or new raw materials or tools; or buy securities, which range from acknowledgments of a loan, such as notes, bonds and mortgages, or shares of stock, which represent shares in the ownership of a business. In the same way the shipper, the jobber or wholesaler, and finally the retail dealer make their profit, and invest their surplus. The money may be invested in many ways: they may put it into other businesses by buying shares of stock, which rise and fall by the rules of supply or demand. To see these rules "working", let us go to the New York Stock Exchange.

WHERE MONEY FATES ARE SEALED—THE STOCK EXCHANGE

The work of this famous institution may seem very hard to understand for one who is not in the financial "game". But it really, at bottom, amounts only to the kind of "swapping" that the early man did! Let us go up to the balcony overlooking the floor, where visitors are admitted. (Only members are allowed on the floor; there are 1,100 of them, only from a third to one-half of whom come down on an average day.) We can look down on the famous floor. It is a great room five stories in height, lighted by enormous windows from ceiling to floor at two ends, and by myriad arc-lights sunk into its great paneled top. The floor is crowded by the members, who are usually members also of a brokerage house. They are gathered for the most part around the "stock posts"—there are twenty-five of these around the floor, which have around them leather cushioned seats much like those encircling columns in some hotel lobbies. The stock post is an upright bearing a big number, and on each are price reports of some twenty stocks, on signs with movable letters that are changed from time to time. One post is known, for instance, as the "steel post", another as the "oil post". *Here all the trading goes on, by bids conveyed by word of mouth.* One can tell what stocks are "active", that is, in which there is brisk trading, by looking at the size and excitability of the crowd around that particular post. When business is brisk, big crowds gather; there are excited bidding, shouts, surging to and fro. The floor at the end of the day is littered with torn paper memoranda. Sometimes one or two million shares are traded on a busy day.

How are sales made on the floor of the New York Stock Exchange? By the old method of barter that has been used for millions of years by mankind. We must keep in mind that shares of stock are receipts for a certain amount of money invested in a business; that they represent a part ownership in that business, however small it may be, and so are a fractional share of the capital with which it is run. *According as the business is profitable, at any particular time, the capital invested will bring returns.* This yearly return is known as the "dividends", or profit paid to stockholders in proportion to their investment. There are two kinds of stock, "common" and "preferred". The first is not guaranteed to yield any particular percentage of dividend on the investment: whatever the profits, they are divided among the stockholders. "Preferred" stock has a specified percentage of return guaranteed.

Now, the amount of dividend being paid regulates the value of the stock as an investment, and partly helps to set the price of it. Thus the stock market is like a sensitive barometer, telling how profitable businesses are. A stock is listed on the Exchange, like goods in a store, and priced according to demand. It is said to be at "par", when it sells for exactly 100% of its face value per share, in most cases $100. The prices are spoken of in terms of percentages: For instance, when steel is selling at 95½, it means that it is worth $95.50 a share. Supply and demand "work" in the case of stocks just like other things, causing their rise or fall in price. Sudden active buying will make the prices soar, sudden selling make them fall.

The sales are made by members of the exchange by the simple method of bargaining, as we have said. Each is usually the agent who handles a transaction for the real owner. *The man who has the stock to sell often lives in some distant city.* He may 'phone the order to sell to the office of the brokerage firm in New York, or that firm may have a branch office in the other city, which wires the order over its private telegraph line. This is sent by 'phone to the floor of the Stock Exchange, where each brokerage firm has its own telephone in long rows of these instruments, each attended by a clerk.

So great is the haste that these receivers are never replaced on the hook: they have long cords by which they dangle over the hook itself. Every movement counts in the romantic game of high finance! When an order comes in to buy or sell, the clerk quickly touches a switch at the side of the 'phone, and a number flashes on one of the the two big announcing-boards on the great walls of the exchange. The member on the floor sees it, and hurries back to his clerk to get the message.

HOW A SALE IS MADE ON THE NEW YORK EXCHANGE

Now he is out again in the thick of the crowd on the exchange! He goes up to the crowd around the "steel post". He has been notified by a customer in Kansas City, let us say, to sell 200 shares of steel stock. He is usually told the lowest price that the customer will sell for, and as a good broker, he must try to get as much more than that as he can. His percentage on the sale is strictly fixed by the laws of the Exchange, binding on all members, with a lowest rate to outsiders of one-eighth of one per cent, ranging to one-sixth according to the amount involved.

"What's the market for Steel?" he may ask a bystander.

"96¾ bid. Offered at 97¼."

"Sell two hundred at 97⅛", he may shout to the brokers near him.

"Sell one hundred at 97⅛," says another, lowering his price to avoid being "undersold".

"Give 97 for two hundred", replies the obstinate bidder.

"Sold two hundred at 97", says our broker. He knows that his customer is in need of the money at once, and he is afraid that his rival with the hundred shares will underbid him if he hesitates. Besides 97 was the price that the customer mentioned!

"Take it", says the buyer. The sale is now clinched by verbal agreement.

"Sold you two hundred Steel for 97", says our broker.

"Bought of you two hundred Steel for 97", says the other.

On the floor of the Exchange there are a number of men with black caps and uniforms. They are the "reporters", to whom all sales and prices must be told under a ruling of the institution. That one now jots down the sale, amount and price on a small pad. He goes up to one of the four telegraph operators who sit in little enclosures behind rails on the exchange floor.

The operator on an automatic telegraph sending instrument with a typewriter keyboard taps out the sale and price. This goes to a second relay of operators in a room in the upper part of the building, where it is transferred to the ribbon of the stock ticker and sent out over the whole country on these remarkable machines. *A few minutes after a sale is made on the New York Stock Exchange, the price is ticked off by the magic ribbon in the broker's office in distant San Francisco,* and copied on the board in chalk figures by the boy who marks quotations. By this American product of inventive skill distant coasts can be linked in the twinkling of an eye, and for the first time in the history of money the price of things can be kept uniform everywhere there is such service.

The ticker isn't the only wonderful means of communication in the Stock Exchange, for under the floor there are more than thirty miles of pneumatic tubes connecting the private telephones along the walls with the trading stations on the floor. By means of this service, orders and requests for prices can be sent out on the floor without the use of messengers. Great automatic gongs are part of the system: they start the trading day at ten in the morning and end it at three in the afternoon.

As soon as a sale is made on the Exchange, the brokers who have been parties to it, 'phone their offices the price and other particulars, and this is telegraphed to the customer, in the same or a distant city. Often the sale is made while he waits for only a very few minutes in the branch office. The completion of the sale is made through the New York Clearing House the same day, and the certificate for the stock is delivered to the purchasing brokerage firm in New York the next day. The purchaser pays for it by check or otherwise at the branch office where he has an "account", and the man who sold it receives his payment from his brokers, who deduct their commission. Regular speculators have standing accounts with their brokers, who furnish loans for "margin" investment.*

New York's Stock Exchange has had an interesting history. It is not much more than a century and a quarter old. In general it was modeled after the London 'Change, which was established in the eighteenth century. It differs in some important ways. The London system has a sort of middleman, called a "jobber", who sets the prices in transactions for the brokers, whereas our own do this for themselves. London also stresses the rule of the committee, as distinct from the members.

---

* Buying on "margin" means to borrow a large part of the money invested in stocks or bonds, and to pay interest on that sum, depositing the securities with the broker, and protecting the investment against a small decline in the value by depositing that much surplus or "margin" of one's own money, ranging from 10% to 20%, or more.

THE ROMANTIC HISTORY OF AMERICAN STOCK "BROKING"

The New York Exchange really began with a little group of about a dozen stock-dealers who used to drive their bargains under a sycamore tree in Wall Street about the year 1800. There were only a few stock issues at that day, and the bonds of the government and those of some of the new American States. At about the time of Waterloo a permanent organization was started, there being at that time twenty-eight members. To-day, as we have said, the number is 1,100, and seats on the Exchange are hard to get. New members to gain admission must be passed by the directors. Seats last were sold for $82,000 a membership. The yearly dues are $800.

The early history of the Exchange included an instance of a rival body, the Open Board of Brokers, which was founded during the Civil War, and charged the much lower rate of 1-32% as commission. The old guard declared hostility to the death, threatening to expel any member who traded with the Open Board. But it was compelled to lower its own commission rate from ¼% to ⅛%. And not long after, when the new organization moved to the present site of the Stock Exchange in Broad Street near Wall, the two boards were merged with the third under the title of New York Stock and Exchange Board.

These were the days of great issues of paper money, especially in the North, and the value soon went down. Gold began to have such importance that a premium was placed on it. At one time a special Gold Exchange was opened, and a little later when there was a great flurry in oil, a Petroleum Stock Exchange. Neither of these lasted very long.

There were several cases of great disaster as the result of "corners" on the market at about this time. Some are connected with the supply of money and credit, and so will be taken up in the following chapters. But there are famous instances of stock speculation. This was an age when the young Exchange was the battlefield for the operations of a few big financiers, for New York was then the "melon"—so was the whole country, for that matter—of a few "big men".

The names of some of these are honorable for the service they did in building up the finances of the early Union. Such a man was the famous banker Jay Cooke, who was called "the financier of the Civil War", as his banking house was the principal representative of the Federal Government, and he negotiated the great war loans, which amounted to about $2,000,000,000. His later failure was owing to his "backing" large railroad bond issues. Cornelius Vanderbilt, founder of the prominent family of that name, was another great financier, active in the management and control of railroads. But there were

XX

"JIM" FISK—BUCCANEER OF THE MONEY WORLD

Fisk's history is a very romantic one: he was a buccaneer of the money world, a "crooked one in at least some of his dealings. He started life as the son of a New England peddler. After a very few years in elementary school, he followed in the footsteps of his father. But he was a very "sharp" fellow even in his early youth, and he knew so well how to drive a clever bargain that he soon attracted the attention of a firm of Boston merchants. They took him into the firm, and in a few years he made a great deal of money for them by shrewd dealing with the government. It was said also that he smuggled cotton through the lines from the South during the Civil War, at a time when it was very scarce in the North. The big game of finance tempted him and he opened a broker's office in New York. For several years he had a hard time of it. Then he was "taken up" as a promising recruit by a noted financier, who had himself as a poor boy driven cows through what is now Madison Square—Daniel Drew. It is believed that Drew needed a sort of "tool" in his dealings at this time, for he was trying to gain control of the Erie Railroad from the interests headed by Vanderbilt, both being among the road's chief stockholders. He set up Fisk in business with a partner, and had them represent him in dealings with the Erie stockholders. Fisk was now launched on his unscrupulous career, of which more later.

There now appeared on the scene another of the great names in American financial history—that of Jay Gould. He was a marvelously shrewd young capitalist, who had slowly increased his capital gained in the lumber and tanning business before he was twenty, investing it first in a small Pennsylvania bank, and later selling out to buy the controlling interest in the Rutland and Washington Railroad. It was just after a period of financial depression in 1859, a spell of hard times, when everybody needed money. Gould was able to buy the stock of that road at ten cents on the dollar, as it was practically bankrupt. In a very short time he had built it up until, with the reviving general trend of business, the shares were selling at 120. He thus "cleared" a profit of some twelve times his original investment! He, too, came to New York, and started a brokerage. He was ambitious to get control of the Erie. He invested in a large number of its shares, and a line-up soon took place between his interests and those of another stockholder, Eldridge.

Now a compromise was arranged between the Drew-Fisk combination and the Gould-Eldridge faction so that among them they really

BUYING AND SELLING

commanded the most votes in the directorate of the road. The result was that before long the Vanderbilt interests were forced out, so far as the directors were concerned, and Fisk and Gould were installed instead. The two latter men soon had the real control, and in 1868 Gould was made president and Fisk comptroller. The road had been on the verge of bankruptcy, and Gould ever afterward claimed that he had personally saved it from this and had built it up.

The loans he negotiated, however, put it under a debt of more than $60,000,000, and it paid no dividends for the holders of common stock for more than twenty-five years. Gould's policy to gain control of roads was usually to make the value of the stock go down by some such means, and then when the small stockholders sold out, to buy it back at a much lower price.

In some such fashion he got control of the Union Pacific, and during the ten years he owned it, the stock went up from 15 to 75. He later bought up the stock of the Missouri Pacific and increased its earnings from some two and a half millions a year to more than $61,000,000, as reported. Before 1880 he controlled some 10,000 miles of road, about 10% of that in the whole country. He also consolidated the rival telegraph companies into the great Western Union Company of to-day and got control of the Manhattan Elevated Railroad in New York. No wonder his fortune grew to be one of the most princely in America, or indeed in the world! Indirectly he may be said to have done a constructive work in building up so many public utilities, or businesses. But the profit went usually into his own pocket, and indirectly many small stockholders lost their savings.

Gould's association with Fisk was less creditable. The latter was one of the most unscrupulous men that has ever been prominent in American money history. His headquarters were the center of "graft": from them golden lines went out to the officials of New York City and State, judges on the bench, legislators and public men. Bribery and "hush money" were Fisk's favorite means of getting what he wanted.

It was the age of great expansion, of new railway building, the growth of the West, the age of new vast fortunes. New York was a growing metropolis, where men still wore side-whiskers and top-hats, and women stepped out of their smart carriages to trail their funny long skirts over the pavements into the stores that centered, with the theatrical district, around Fourteenth Street. Great hotels like the Astor House and others were far down-town. Fisk himself owned an operetta theater, and the principal actress there rode in Fisk's smart "turn-out", behind Fisk's blooded horses, and for that matter lived also in a handsome brownstone mansion owned by Fisk.

THE TERRIBLE PANIC OF "BLACK FRIDAY"

The story of one of America's greatest panics is linked up with that theater. It was the famous day of crashing fortunes and ruined men known as "Black Friday", Sept. 24, 1869. The cause of the panic was a "corner" in gold, which just then was worth abnormal prices, owing to the flooding of the North with paper banknotes, which fell until worth only thirty-six cents. In 1861 the government had suspended gold payments by banks and substituted paper. People had no confidence in the power of the government, just then burdened by heavy debts and great loans, to redeem them at once, and so "Gold, *gold!*" became the cry. Fisk engineered a monopoly by buying up all the available gold on the market, and, we are sorry to record that Gould was a party to the scheme. The value of the metal went up until it was "out of sight" and could not be had for any amount. The paper money suddenly dropped until its value was practically nil! When creditors demanded settlements, there was not enough surplus on hand to honor the requests. The payments were suspended, and then the panic broke! Men with loans outstanding to buy goods or stock were ruined, as their debts were doubled, trebled and even increased five- or six-fold.

The maddened men, faced with the prospect of poverty and disgrace, stormed Fisk's offices. They would certainly have lynched him if they could have laid hands on him. But he had fled. Days later it became known that he had crept like a scared cur to the dark and dusty theater and taken refuge backstage. There an old watchman was his only companion and brought him food, until he dared to come out again. The theater still standing at Twenty-third Street and Eighth Avenue, has long since become a vaudeville house. Perhaps the stage that now echoes to the sounds of "jazz" melodies still hides somewhere the dust that Fisk's terror-stricken, muddied feet shambled over that day, as he cowered, breathless, listening for sounds of the avenging mob, his usually plump face streaked with dirt and wrinkled in terror, his expensive cravat awry!

His end was not to come for several years. Then one day the news got about that Fisk, the great gambler, the briber of senators—he who had even once had the presumption to offer President Grant a great sum for "services" (promptly turned down)—had been shot in a quarrel with one of his former henchmen. He died soon after, and that was the end of his brief day of glory. From peddler's son to captain of finance who swayed the fortunes and directed the wills of lawmakers, he came to his end in a common brawl. His name has left no legacy except that of well-merited ill-fame.

A tragic circumstance connected with the contrasted figure of Grant—the great general, the sturdy, calm-souled President—this

BUYING AND SELLING

national hero, to whom a great marble tomb has been raised on Riverside Drive, suffered also before his end through the iron hand of Wall Street, that pocketed the savings of his lifetime, risked on unwise investments. Perhaps it was the ghostly hand of "Jim" Fisk, raised from the grave, that had its vengeance then!

FAMOUS RAILROAD "STOCK SMASHES" OF THE PAST

The romance of the New York Stock Exchange meanwhile had been very closely linked up with the growth and financing of the country's railways. We have already seen that the finishing of the Pacific Railroad in 1869, caused a great enthusiasm and a big "crop" of new railroad investment schemes. The Great Lakes were being linked with the Pacific Coast, and to get money for the building of these roads great stock issues were put on the market. The dealing in bonds to cover the immense loans for the work were, of course, immeasurably greater; but that is a subject we will review in the chapter on banking.

The panic of 1873 resulted from the failure of the roads to meet the obligations on these loans and the resulting collapse of many of these investments. For two days the New York Stock Exchange was closed to keep down the flood of selling, selling—anything to get a little money to cover the outstanding loans. It would have meant the collapse of the stock market, resulting in losses to thousands of small security-holders. One of the banking houses that went down in the crash was that of Jay Cooke, who had financed many of the loans to the railroads. But every cent of the indebtedness, principal and interest, was paid in time by the Cooke firm, and the house was able to continue. With one blow, the building of roads to the Far West stopped, and the revival did not come for five years. So the stock market faithfully reflected the bad times, as it always does, usually foreshadowing slumps months ahead.

There was a great revival of business, beginning about 1879, partly owing to the great new grain crops of the West. The wave of prosperity was largely owing to the government's redeeming the outstanding paper banknotes, and substituting a metal standard, in which debts were now paid. The banknotes were, however, again issued, as part of the currency, and they have remained so ever since. A new period of activity had its effect in *enormously increased trading on the Stock Exchange.* Between 1879 and 1881 the value of a seat more than doubled, increasing from $9,000 to $20,000.

The reaction came in 1882, when there was a sudden slump in the profits brought in by the railroads and the manufactures of the country. Much capital had been invested in the new railroad lines, and when they failed to bring the expected return, there was a sharp drop in their stocks. This came to a head in the panic of May, 1884, when several New York brokerage houses and two important banks failed.

A WORLDWIDE PANIC THAT STARTED SOUTH OF THE EQUATOR

After this came a period of recovery. The lines of railroad that had gone bankrupt were bought up by larger roads, and the work of extending the lines went on rapidly. Foreign capital now began to be put into our stocks for this purpose, and large portions of the loans for the work of building the roads came from financiers in London and other European cities. Prices began to go up, with this new burst of speculation.

Suddenly this flood of gold from the other side was dramatically choked off! The reason lay in the failure of one of London's biggest banking houses, Baring Brothers, which had been founded back in the romantic days of the East India Company by a famous old explorer and adventurer. The company had been agent for an enormous loan to the new Argentine Republic, and suddenly this South American country found itself unable to pay its interest. Barings' was now in a bad situation. It had to stand good for several million pounds Sterling. It faced ruin, and all the English capitalists who were interested in the muddle as debtor or creditor began to cable to America in the greatest haste to sell their stocks and bonds to get money! The firm of Baring was later saved by a loan of $65,000,000 generously advanced by the Bank of England and another banking house. But in America the result was a panic on the New York Stock Exchange and the failure of several brokerage houses, who couldn't meet their debts when the demand for securities fell and that for money rose, carrying prices along with them! So, you see, a little disturbance of the money market in far-away Buenos Aires has power to upset the world in distant London and New York!

Business on the Stock Exchange had a hard blow, and it didn't improve until the terrible panic of 1893 had come and, like a volcanic eruption, cleared away the gases of "inflation". After that panic— one of the worst America has known—the trading on the Exchange dropped to its lowest point in fifteen years.

THE AGE OF "FAT" CORPORATIONS AND THEIR BIG "CRASH"

We can sketch only briefly the great new era that opened in American speculation with the reorganization of the railroads that has failed, the resumption of gold as a standard under McKinley, and the issuing of enormous new quantities of railroad and corporation stock. One of the causes was the great demand for our

BUYING AND SELLING

grain during a famine in Europe, and remarkable "spurt" in our export of manufactures. American goods came to have the place in importance that they have today in the world's markets. Added to this there was passed a new tariff that raised duties again enormously, making it almost ruinous for foreign goods to be sent here. This lessened the competition for our own manufacturers, at the same time that it made it possible for them to *charge higher prices*. It was the golden age of the manufacturer, and big money interests soon took advantage of this.

Now began the age of "trusts", of determined buying up by big companies of smaller rivals. The battles to get possession of the stock of rivals were staged on the Exchange, which now had a greater volume of business than ever before in its history—in fact, sales were doubled in 1905, as compared with 1900. The large companies who wanted to buy out the stock of smaller ones in most cases had to float enormous loans to do it. They risked everything they had—with what final results we shall see later. Meanwhile, they were often successful in getting all the stocks they wanted into their hands.

One of the most famous duels on the Exchange was the "corner" on Northern Pacific Railway stock, when two groups of financial interests tried to get control of that road. *The excited buying forced up the cash price on one day in May, 1901, to $1,000 a share!* This is probably the highest price ever reached by any American stock up to this time, even under the most unusual conditions. A few weeks before it had hardly been worth par. This was a "bubble" which out-"bubbled" the famous South Sea speculation. Of course, such a high price was bound to topple. More than 3,000,000 shares of the stock had been traded in, and before the day ended the price of $1,000 for cash sales dropped to $320. The corner wrecked the market in other stocks, which took a sharp fall and then went up a little again. Pacific had come down with a mighty crash. The collapse was owing partly to a suspicion that got abroad that the brokerage houses would not be able to deliver the shares when they were due, owing to the large sums involved. The brokers who had made the sales suddenly got panic-stricken, as they saw the penitentiary looming up before them, and none of them wanted particularly to wear a striped suit! The price had been created artificially, that is, altogether by forced buying, instead of being based on the profits and prosperity of the railroad. Naturally, a number of men were ruined by their losses on all stocks, or at least weathered the storm with some trouble. At one stroke almost all investments had dropped about 15% in value. That they later recovered a little hardly repaired the damage.

But this "set-back" didn't have a lasting effect on the wave of prosperity. The immense earnings of the big corporations encouraged them to form what were called "syndicates." These combinations borrowed enormous sums from the New York banks to pay for their gambling ventures in the stock of smaller companies. The climax came about 1906, when one bank was "backing" some eighty such great, swollen ventures! The money was sunk in these businesses, in several cases, in such a way that it couldn't be collected when the "slump" came. In the case of good stocks, these can usually be sold to make good the loans that they are bought with, but the "wild-cat" scheme of the syndicates left them with only their own worthless paper, when suddenly the "Street" was plunged in a new period of depression.

This was the beginning of the panic of 1907-8, when the Knickerbocker Trust Company, one of the most reliable and long-established institutions, had to close its doors. Many banks followed suit throughout the country. The Stock Exchange was deeply affected, and did not recover until after the boom set in which marked the prosperity of the country during the World War. Sales on the Exchange in 1910 were a little more than 60% of those in 1905, and there was a steady drop until Europe was plunged into war.

THE WORLD WAR TURNS THE STOCK MARKET TOPSY-TURVY

The beginning of the world upheaval was a time of grave uneasiness in the American money world. *In particular it was feared that Europe, aflame with the fires of war, would want to sell out at once all the interests her money men held in American industries. For Europe needed money now as she had never needed it*—with the need of getting ready great armies, millions of men to feed and arm, explosives and food to be supplied in quantities greater than the world has, perhaps, ever known!

On the first definite news of the beginnings of war, the Stock Exchange was closed as an emergency measure, and it remained so for more than four months, from the end of July to Dec. 7, 1914. It was the only way to prevent a selling movement, with a crash of prices and draining of money out of the United States, that would have ruined our business and our credit. It was only with a great deal of misgivings that trade was resumed before Christmas, and then an emergency rule was made that the directors of the Exchange, if it proved necessary, could fix the lowest price for any stock that went down sharply in value. Meanwhile, much selling of securities went on in private between brokers. It was a return to the old conditions when they used to meet under the sycamore trees on the curb!

But Europe had adjusted her budget to her war needs by now. Of course, for some time her trade with us stopped short. By the middle of 1915 Europe, instead of buying back our shares, was beginning to call on us for our goods and munitions in large quantities. Our export sales soon were tremendous, and shares in companies that had war contracts, such as numerous steel plants and forge shops, went up in price greatly on the Exchange.

THE WAR "BOOM" AND THE "PALMY" DAYS OF PROFITEERING

This was the period when the "war profiteers" made their staggering fortunes. It was a period of great plenty, still vivid in the mind, when the working-man believed that his golden age had come at last, so high did wages mount in the favored industries! The entry of the United States into the war, if anything, added to the great "boom", for it increased the feverish buying of all kinds of goods, from grain to shrapnel. And, though the government appointed numerous war boards to superintend the making and selling, and in some cases took over factories (as it did the railroads), the profits made were thrust into private pockets with the greatest eagerness! While the whole country slaved and saved to buy, the earnings of a small group were enormous.

The rise in prices on the Stock Exchange had begun at the moment when it was reopened for business, at least six months before trade and production—paralyzed by the sudden collapse of its usual European peace-time markets—began slowly to "pick up". But stock prices had gone up enormously in the very first winter of war. Borrowing of money to finance the big manufacturing contracts went on at a rate seldom equaled in our money world. And this was natural, for with the great profits came surpluses of money to be profitably loaned again.

After the war came the inevitable "slump". The end of fighting came suddenly, with all the factories going full tilt, and supplied with raw material in some cases to last for a year more of good, destructive war! The demand for goods from Europe and home stopped with a sort of sickening suddenness, with large supplies on hand that would not be sold for a long time—in some cases never! In the first jubilation of victory, when New York on "Armistice Day" went mad, and showers of paper rained from the skyscrapers to the shrilling of every steam whistle and bell in America, while crowds in the streets danced in joy, drunk with the good news—the matter of money was forgotten. But the warning finger of the Stock Exchange soon pointed to a sharp decline in prices.

For two or three years the business of the nation suffered grievously. The demand for general goods and the shipments on the railroads went down steadily after the armistice until they reached their low point in the early months of 1919. The Stock Exchange was then moving upward, and soon business had a slight recovery. But the Exchange, after a record year of high "inflation" of commodity or general prices, took a sharp plunge in the late spring of 1920, so severe that it amounted to a general breakdown of all prices. The recovery was very slow, and manufacturing and sales reached their lowest point in the middle of 1921—and then started to increase very rapidly, steel doubling its production in a few months! The stock market rose rapidly in 1923, foretelling a big "boom". Now (1924) despite a decline of production in the spring, stocks are rising.

The growth of stock trading in the United States has, like all other buying and selling, had a more or less steady and enormous growth. There are Exchanges in several cities—Boston, Chicago, Philadelphia, Detroit. The Stock Exchange of New York has grown vastly in its membership. The number of stocks listed is now almost 1,000, and on some days as many as 500 of these are traded in, compared with only about 150 bought on any one day twenty years ago. This Exchange is rather strict in its rules about listing shares, as the company that does so has to make application, submitting a complete statement of its financial condition and activity. The stocks listed are, therefore, pretty good ones, though not always safe from risky conditions.

THE ROMANCE OF THE CURB MARKET

But not all good issues are on the Exchange, and to provide for the great number of others, trading used to be carried on in front of the Exchange on Broad Street. This was known as the "Curb Market", and there are other outdoor selling places like it both in London and Paris, near the Exchanges in those cities.

The Curb Market was a scene to thrill and amuse in the days of its outdoor functioning. Scenes of great excitement took place in this narrow, steep street lined with brokerage and other offices. Crowds circulated on the walks, groups formed in the street, and here selling went on just as on the floor of the Exchange. The devious system of signals that passed from the windows of the offices above to the buyers in the street had to be seen to be appreciated! There was a regular deaf-and-dumb code or finger-language in each office, and these animated "talks" went on to the accompaniment of shouts, when any clerk in the window above wanted to get the attention of the broker in the street. Here were no automatic announcing-boards, but the buying went on just about as briskly without them.

The business of the outdoor market grew so much that in 1921 a large exchange building was put up near Wall Street, several blocks

BUYING AND SELLING

west of Broadway. In the three years since then (1924) the membership has grown from 750 to 1081 regular and associate members, of which 89 are said also to be members of the New York Stock Exchange. The list of its securities has grown from 888 to 1657 in the same three years, and it has begun its own ticker service to Chicago and a few other cities.

What of the darker side of the stock trader's business? In the popular mind the game of "playing the stocks" is something like the dark undertakings of the "faro" player or the patron of Monte Carlo! There is a type of "plunger" who loses one day what he makes the next. There is no denying that there is a gambling angle to the business, that the machinery of the stock market, like the revolver, lends itself to bad as well as good ends.

It is true that *the stock exchanges throughout the world act like sensitive needles to every financial, political and governmental development*—so that there is no telling just what the market will "do" next. For instance, a little difficulty about Venezuela which came up in 1895 in Grover Cleveland's term as President caused him to send a message to Congress which threatened to plunge us into international difficulties. The prospect of this threw the Exchange into confusion; prices dropped so sharply that $400,000,000 is said to have been lost.

The powers in the financial world naturally seek to avoid such great crises, and even exert a considerable influence in cases on the legislative bodies, and in the past have done so on members of the Cabinet. This state of affairs has at different times been brought to public attention. Doubtless it is an evil, in whatever degree it exists. The real amount of "graft" at any time is, however, always exaggerated by the newspapers, whose "stock in trade" is the sensation. The theories that wars are declared *solely* to protect the property of rich men are examples of these exaggerations—this in a country with such degree of popular control of the government is on the face of it absurd!

The greatest dangers in the transactions of the stock market come from a few unscrupulous men who do not at all represent the real men of Wall Street. They are the "crooked" brokers, the hangers-on, the fraudulent security dealers. The District Attorney of New York estimates that a billion dollars are lost every year through the operations of this class of men. The large debts and few assets of brokerage firms that fail are notorious. In three years 89 firms failed—not all unscrupulous ones, of course—but with total debts of more than $116,000,000, and with really nothing to cover them in most cases. *The remedy suggested is to license all brokers* or place them under the supervision of the State Superintendent of Banks. Such legislation will doubtless be passed very soon, as there is a determined movement on foot to "clean up" the stock business, and make it safe for the conservative investor, who—rather than the "margin" spectator—is its real mainstay.

SOME "SLANG" TERMS OF BROKERS AND BUSINESS MEN

Bear: one who sells stocks for the express purpose of buying them back again at a lower price. He may try to influence the market to fall by his selling. He need not have the shares himself, but may borrow them from someone else, giving money or other stocks as security. He is said to be "short" of stocks. When he buys them back at a lower price and returns them to the one he borrowed from, he is said to "cover".

Bull: one who buys stocks with the express purpose of selling them again at a profit. He may try to influence the market to rise by buying. Like the "bear", he may borrow, but usually the money to buy with. If he deposits stocks as security with the one he borrows from, the latter is said to "carry" them. The "bull" is "long" on stocks. When he sells to make his profit, he is said to "realize".

Bucketshop: pernicious gambling business, which pretends to be a brokerage, but really does not buy or sell the stocks employed to. Is able to escape detection because it usually deals on the "margin" plan, under which the customer leaves shares and "margin" as security in return for the money he borrows to invest. Bucketshop keeper collects commissions on the "sales", keeps purchase money and margin deposits, and so is able to return money when the customer wants his stocks "sold". Often operates unfairly by keeping back correct quotations from customers.

Call: a contract sold by capitalist to broker for certain commission, promising to sell to the latter a certain number of stock shares *at given price* within a certain time. Guarantees broker against loss if market rises.

Put: a contract like the preceding, only guaranteeing to *buy* at given price a certain number of stock shares within a given time. Guarantees broker against loss if market price falls.

CHAPTER IV

THE ROMANCE OF LENDING AND BORROWING (BANKING AND FOREIGN EXCHANGE)

Credit is the big "honor system" that makes all higher business possible. The great machinery for producing and marketing in the United States would be useless if there weren't some system for pouring the necessary money like some golden oil upon the wheels and bearings whenever it is required! By this we mean that *businesses would all come to a standstill, like the "perpetual motion" machines, if they had to make their own money-motive-power as they went!* In the long run, any profitable business *will* pay for itself and have some surplus to spare, but that doesn't mean that it will turn out the profits at the time that they are needed to pay expenses. Indeed, it is the rule that the profits come in a long time after the expenses come due. This is where the money-lending system must come to the rescue, and furnish funds when they are needed to make production possible. We have seen in the early chapters of this book that credit goes back to a time when early man began his "swapping", and that the Babylonians and probably the Egyptians used it.

Let us take the case of a man who owns a factory. Call him Mr. Make—a name that is surely appropriate! He has an order from a dealer in his goods—a Mr. Sell—for a new shipment of great value.

"But to make all these goods", Mr. Make will say, "I'll need to buy a lot of raw material and the cost in wages will be enormous!"

Clearly Mr. Sell is not willing to pay until the goods are delivered, or even some little time after that! In his puzzlement, Mr. Make will go to Mr. Loan, who is in the business of "selling" credit—at a fair profit. He is a banker, and his profession dates back to a time when people left their money for safekeeping with goldsmiths, who gave them a receipt corresponding to a bankbook or a check of to-day.

"I need so many dollars' worth of credit to make some goods," Mr. Make will say. "I need it until such-and-such date, when my goods will be paid for. Then I can pay you back." And he will probably show the order he has from Mr. Sell, and perhaps some figures on how much the "making" will cost. By subtracting—an operation at which most bankers are expert!—Mr. Loan can very well see how much is going to be left in profit. If he thinks that the venture is sure enough, he will put the following proposition before Mr. Make:

"You will have to give some sort of security to us. That will be placed to your credit, and you can then pay your expenses as they come up with checks, paper orders for us to turn over the amounts. The price of this credit advance from us will be such-and-such a percentage of the whole amount. This we call our 'discount', or interest. When the time is up you will pay us the amount of money credited to you, plus this discount. Now, what kind of security will you give to us?"

Here is where a lot of forms of "business paper" come in. They were invented for just such an emergency, and they are are all written acknowledgments of debt and promises to pay.

HOW THE WORLD LOANS AND BORROWS MONEY

Mr. Make hasn't the money to deposit with Mr. Loan. If he had, he could use it directly to pay his expenses. He can get a loan on goods he owns that are stored in warehouses (by depositing warehouse receipts), or on any form of property that he has: for instance, if he owns stocks or other securities he can deposit them with the banker. If he doesn't pay back the amount at the end of the time, these can be sold to make good the debt. *This is a favorite form of borrowing among brokers,* and loans of this sort are made daily through a special desk on the floor of the Stock Exchange, which reports the amounts which different banks have for the purpose and at what rate of discount. There are two kinds of loans— the "call" loan is subject to recall by either party, and must be paid the next day if notice is given before 1 P. M., and the "time" loan, which runs for a set time, thirty, sixty or ninety days.

One of the favorite forms of borrowing is by means of a "note", and this form of loan is usually for a certain set time, though there is another form which promises payment "on demand". Mr. Make— if he has a well-organized business, and can show that his debts are smaller than the amounts owing to him—may make out such a "note", or promise to pay. It is very rarely taken except of one whose credit is of the best,* unless he can get a responsible second person to indorse it. This makes the second person liable for the debt if he fails to pay. But Mr. Make may remember that he has in his

---

* Mercantile recording, or credit rating, by special firms began about 1840. Bradstreet's issued its first yearly volume in 1857, dividing firms into classes.

LENDING AND BORROWING

purse such a note given by Mr. Sell or some other customer in payment of an earlier order. He can then indorse it, and the bank will usually credit it to him, after deducting its own discount. A special business is that of the "note broker", who buys and sells this form of paper.

There is one other form of credit, the "draft", which has a romantic history dating back to the "bills of exchange" invented by the traders of Babylon and used in Venice and other cities. The original form of the "bill of exchange", you will remember, was a written order asking another to pay a certain amount of money. So to save the changing hands of money so often, when A bought a certain amount of goods from B, and B the same number from C,—A gave B such an Order, B passed it on to C, and C collected it from A, their money-lenders acting as the agents and "cashing" the bills. This system is still used very much in Europe to-day, though in America the "note" is much more popular.

To-day, when Mr. Sell wants to pay Mr. Make, he can do it by drawing such a "draft" on his credit at his bank (the draft being one of the bankers' ways to extend credit) and making it out for payment to Mr. Make; and finally, he then will, after indorsing it, deposit it. The bank then forwards it to Mr. Make, if he lives in the same city, or to a bank in his own town, and if he writes the word "accepted" on it, it becomes good for payment in whatever bank he chooses at the end of the time marked on it. Such drafts are called "acceptances", and are also sold by special brokers.

Now, suppose that you were the president of the board of directors of a large corporation that *wanted to borrow a million dollars!* It wouldn't be very wise to give notes on the personal credit of the directors, and besides that wouldn't represent all the owners of the road, who include thousands of stockholders. To supply this emergency, the issue of "bonds" was invented. A bond was originally simply an agreement before witnesses to repay a certain amount with interest. The big bond issue of to-day still keeps this "principal", or promise to pay, in the form of a certificate.*

---

*A "registered" bond is one made out in the name of a particular person. In the coupon bond, in addition to this "principal", or promise to repay the loan, there are a definite number of coupon slips, numbered in order, which must be presented at the office of the company to collect the interest at the end of every six months. This is called "clipping the coupons." Bonds of the coupon type pay their interest to whomever presents the coupons. Bonds are usually issued for the amount of $1,000, but there are smaller issued. The bond is a loan for a definite period, at the end of which time the firm that issued the bonds must redeem them upon presentation of the "principal," or main part of the bond. The security for the bond issue is usually a mortgage on property made to a trust company as trustee. A special bond is the "convertible", which can be exchanged for stock in the company.

But bonds like stocks, rise and fall in price, and like the later are traded on the floor of the Stock Exchange. A few of the best bond issues are listed on the Exchange—about 5%, according to one estimate. By far the greater part of the sale of bonds is done through the so-called "bond houses", which have a special staff of salesmen.

The value of a bond when sold is expressed in a percentage, like that of a stock share—the amount above par being the "premium!" Thus a $1,000 bond selling at 102 will cost $1,020, and in addition the amount of interest due from the day the last coupon was "clipped" until the day of the purchase must usually be paid by the buyer. The premium on a bond corresponds to the rise in the price of stock, and is the result of the value of the bond as an investment. Bonds differ in the amount of interest they bring. The "callable" bond may be redeemed by the issuing company at some time before maturing.

"Soundness" of the company issuing them has a lot to do with the demand for them, which regulates their price. When an issue of bonds is announced, the company usually gives figures on its assets, debts and yearly earnings, as well as operating expenses. *It is very important that the total issue should be covered by the value of the property given as security under Mortgage, for many investors have lost their money when this is not the case.*

These are some of the means for getting credit, and on them hinge a whole romantic story of big business that includes the borrowing of a few hundreds by the small business man and the loans of many millions by corporations, cities, States and even nations. They are the instruments on which the symphony of business is played every day in the year by countless lenders and borrowers. *Business couldn't exist in the advanced stage if it were "every man for himself".*

THE ROMANTIC STORY OF BANKING

The story of banking in the United States, properly looked at, is one of the liveliest and most romantic ones. There is something fascinating in the very visit to a great bank—the marble floor and columns, the great room with the mahogany table where the directors meet, and into which we are sometimes able to look—above all, the barred windows behind which the men finger the great piles of banknotes and metal money! Drudgery there is, too, connected with banking, as anyone who has worked in one of these institutions can tell one! But there is a charm about the idea of vaults and strongboxes where great sums of wealth are hidden.

How did banking start? We have already spoken of the private bankers of old Venice, Florence and other cities of the Middle Ages.

The government of Venice had a high-handed way of levying "loans" on its richest men, who were given credit on the books of the Bank of Venice, and later the system grew up of paying debts by having sums put over in the bank from one man's account to another's. Later (1587) a real deposit business grew up at this bank. The beginnings of the modern "check" can be traced to a sort of receipt given to depositors in the Bank of Amsterdam (seventeenth century), and these credits were later transferred from one man to another in the banks of Hamburg and Nuremberg. As yet banks of this type didn't make a business of loaning money. The Bank of Sweden about this time began this system. The real beginning of modern banking came with the founding of the famous bank of England—which was incorporated and made loans on security.

In America of colonial days there were some not very reliable "land banks", the idea of which was to lend money on mortgages on property. They didn't, as a rule, thrive, because they had no deposits, and in some case they were forbidden by the home government or by the colonies. Things were pretty unprogressive in colonial America, as the favorite means of increasing the supply of money was by issuing floods of paper banknotes under the colonies' stamp. There was a cruel shortage of any sort of money in the early days, and for this reason the settlers actually carried on much of their business by simple "swapping", using tobacco in Virginia as money, and in some other colonies adopting the shell-money or wampum of the Indians. Where there was no money, there was no need, of course, for banks.

It was not until during the Revolution that the "Bank of North America" was started in Philadelphia, under the direction of Robert Morris, the famous "financier of the Revolution". The aim of this bank was to provide funds for the war. Its capital amounted to only $400,000—and of this $250,000 was given by the government! It got charters from the Continental Congress and from the States. The need of having a treasure chest to supply the money for the brave struggle of the patriots was pressing. In this cause the Bank of North America did a noble service. The suffering of the soldiers in the terrible winter under Washington at Valley Forge, the heroic efforts of the "Minute Men" of New England—all these brought their fruit in the glorious independence that followed, but at the same time it was the cool, practical financial sense of men like Robert Morris that made our liberation possible.

HOW NEW YORK'S FIRST BANK WAS FORMED IN A COFFEE-HOUSE

The Bank of New York—the first in the metropolis—was founded in the same year that the Bank of Massachussetts was—1784.* Some

* "Savings banks"—those used chiefly to deposit money on interest—

quaint particulars of the founding of the first of these are found in old files of now-yellowed newspapers. At first the plan was to start a bank whose paid-in capital should consist "one-third of cash and two-thirds of pledges of land". (This latter feature was a survival of the old "land banks".) But another group of men seemed to favor all-cash as a basis, so they printed an advertisement in a rival paper, which read: "It appearing to be the disposition of the Gentlemen in this City to establish a Bank on liberal principles, the stock to consist of specie (money) only, they are, therefore hereby invited to meet to-morrow evening at six o'clock at the Merchants' Coffee House, where a plan will be submitted to their consideration." The meeting did take place at the coffee house, with one General McDougall in the chair, and here it was decided to call the new bank by the name mentioned above. The bank was not allowed to deal in United States or State bonds and was not allowed to loan money on real estate. Both its deposits and its payments were in actual money. It could lend on notes, but not more than three times its paid-in capital. Its real capital was $500,000 at the start. This was the forerunner of the Bank of New York and Trust Company, one of the leading banks of the city to-day.

The most important "boost" for things financial in the early United States was the founding of the First Bank of the United States under a charter from Congress in 1791. This had an important effect on the whole money background of America, and to it was directly owing the fact that the New York Stock Exchange was soon after established. But there was great opposition to it at first, though Alexander Hamilton strongly recommended such a bank in his report as Secretary of the Treasury.

"Congress can't charter a bank! It's unconstitutional!" wailed all the "standpatters." But Congress could and did, and the first government bank opened its doors, modeled somewhat after the Bank of England. It had a capital of $10,000,000, of which the government gave one-fifth, paying it in ten yearly parts, with six per cent. interest. *The rest was sold to stockholders*, who voted in proportion to the shares they held (none over thirty votes). There were twenty-five directors. The rate for discount on loans was not to be higher than six per cent., but the bank soon loaned nearly two-thirds of its capital to the government, and there was hardly any left for lending to private persons. When the government was asked to return some of this, it had to sell its stock in the bank to do so, and so the institution really was run by public funds.

The twenty-year charter ran out and Congress refused to renew

were a later invention. The "trust company" and "building and loan" association are other typically American organizations for loaning money.

it. The central member-bank was in Philadelphia, and here the great merchant, Stephen Girard, who founded the college by that name for orphan boys, bought out the holdings of the bank and started the Girard Bank. The government banking was done from 1809 to 1816 by State banks.

THE END OF THE FIRST U. S. BANK BRINGS CHAOS

The result of the passing out of the first Bank of the United States was to plunge the national money world into chaos. For one thing, it meant the paying back of the funds that a lot of European money men had put into the stock of the bank. So that it drained the ready money out of the country. This shortage came to a climax when many of the State banks had to stop paying out money in 1814. The funds of the government were deposited in these banks, and in the financial reaction it couldn't pay the interest on the public debt, or bond loans to citizens of the country. This spelled ruin for some of the bondholders, and things were generally in a bad way, when the Secratary of the Treasury proposed that a new Bank of the United States be started. It was set up in 1816 to act as agent for the government in paying and delivering the public money of the nation. It had twenty-five member banks over the country, was capitalized at $35,000,000 (one-fifth given by the government in coin or government notes at five per cent. interest.)

In the first three years the bank was very badly run, the private stockholders neglecting to pay their shares and even borrowing money on them as security when they had not been paid. It nearly went bankrupt, before it was reorganized by Cheves, who borrowed two and a half millions from Europe to set it back on its feet. It then ran on prosperously for some years, until in the administration of President Jackson it became an object of struggle between the two great political parties—one renewing the old charge that it was unconstitutional for the congress to charter a bank—and finally in the 'thirties the government funds were withdrawn and put back into the State banks.

The United States Bank because the government refused to renew its charter when it ran out (1836), then became a private institution under a Pennsylvania charter, and in the panic of 1837 it had a blow from which it never recovered. The stockholders lost everything when it finally suspended, owing to "plunging" speculation.

Beginning in 1840, the United States Treasury system was founded, and the money of the nation was kept in this central strongbox and its branches, the Sub-Treasuries, of which one stands in Wall Street. This was the era of great activity among the State banks. *They issued large quantities of paper banknotes, and also lent money in reckless amounts.*

THE MAD RAGE FOR LAND-BUYING AND THE "GOLD FEVER" OF '49

It was the big new age of interest in the West, and people began to buy acres offered by the government on "easy terms". Everybody wanted to borrow money to invest in land. "Mushroom" banks sprang up to supply this demand, and money circulated at a dizzy rate. Between 1830 and 1836 the banking business of the country took a new leap. Banks often loaned money to land buyers, who paid to the government's land "receiver", as he was called, and he again put it back in the bank, where another buyer got hold of it. The loans went up from $137,000,000 to $525,000,000 a year.

This state of things began to scare the government, so that it issued an order to the land agents not to take notes in payment for their acres, but only good solid money! This set-back had a bad result, and together with a failure of crops and heavy investments in developing the West, brought the terrible country-wide panic of 1837. The great "padding" of the currency with paper and the thriving trade of the country had made the value of real estate nearly double in one year in New York, but after the crash it fell again just as rapidly. The prosperity of the country had shot up to a great peak—and now it dropped at a sickening rate, until 1843, when the bank loans of the country were at their lowest point in more than ten years. The government had millions of acres of land thrust back on its hands that bankrupt speculators were unable to "carry".

There was a great shortage of money, too, for there was really no gold mined in the United States. *All this was changed when, in 1848, gold was discovered in a mill race in California by James Marshall.* This was at a spot about sixty miles from where Sacramento now stands. The news spread like wildfire, and then began the rush of the so-called "Forty-Niners" who took up their belongings, "bag and baggage", and settled in the new land of gold. Stirring times followed: the "boom" towns rose overnight, with their frame houses, tents and revolver-brandishing outlaws. These were the days of the "bad man", the gambler, the bandit who "held up" the stage coach at the point of a gun. But there were great fortunes made by the "prospecting" miner, with his pick, his little pan to wash the soil he gathered in the stream for the hoped-for sight of the precious yellow metal! The way of laying claim to the land—by driving in a stake and marking it with one's name—was known as "staking a claim". The great army of gold-seekers flowed into California from all parts of the world—by covered wagon over the plains, on

LENDING AND BORROWING

ships around the southern point of South America and across the Pacific from Europe and Australia. But *the results soon began to show in the great quantities of gold in circulation.* It is said that the amount mined annually was as much as the whole world had formerly produced in that time, in one year exceeding $55,000,000.

This had a great effect in bringing about the rise of prices and general improvement in business, which set in, in the 'fifties. The money in circulation had increased from $145,000,000 to $215,000,000 in a few years before 1857. The loans of the banks took a new rise. From being only about $265,000,000 in 1842, they went up to about $685,000,000 in 1857. This more than wiped out the set-back of the previous panic, but indirectly caused another in the latter year. For the loans had been largely invested in industry, and *a sudden lowering of the tariff made competition from abroad so strong that our goods were undersold and our manufacturers "failed".* Too much speculation was also to blame for the crash.

The beginning of the Civil War had an unsettling effect on the American money world, and in fact *the general paralysis of business and manufacturing made things so scarce that prices went up to unheard-of heights.* A spool of thread cost more than a dollar. At the same time the value of paper money went down—which increased the bad money conditions. Just as in feudal times, when each great lord made his own local coins, the bank-notes were issued by the State Banks—of which there were more than 1500—and many issues were nearly worthless.

THE BIRTH OF THE NATIONAL BANKS

To cure this state of things, and make one system of money for the country, Congress in February, 1863, passed the National Banking Act. This was the system that was to be used in the United States for fifty years and under which the "First" and the "Second" National Banks in all our home cities were founded.

The most important money question in the Civil War was the floating of the huge loans for the government to "carry on" with. How could they be placed quickly and safely? The government issued bonds to cover these enormous sums, but the problem was to dispose of them. *The National Bank system solved this by making all banks that held charters from the Federal government buy great quantities of them and deposit them with the government. They were then allowed to issue bank-notes to the amount of ninety per cent. of the value of the bonds.* To keep the State banks from being strong competitors, a tax of ten per cent. was put on their issuing of bank-notes. About the only good result of this system was to make the currency very "solid", dependable, for it was good while the country stood.

This was a good emergency ruling, but it was a very poor one to run the system of the country on in normal times.* For after the war the price of the government bonds went up, as the national debt was gradually paid off and the bonds matured and were redeemed. The banks could gain more by selling them at premium than by keeping them. They then had to recall their bank-notes in proportion as their holding in bonds went down (by the rules of the National Banking Act restricting them to ninety per cent of the bond holdings.) *The result was to cut down the amount of paper bank-notes in circulation, and to cause a shortage over a period of years.* It soon began to be feared that bank-notes would disappear altogether.

The issue of bank-notes was getting scarcer and scarcer by the national banks. What was to be done? The solutions suggested were many, but the first relief through actual vote of Congress was the passing of the law of March, 1900, which made conditions more favorable for the business of the national banks. The main improvements were letting them issue bank-notes to the actual "face" value of government bonds, they were to be replaced by new ones of thirty year issue.**

The panic of 1907 was in part owing to the laws governing the banks, for many of them closed their doors although they had notes and other paper on hand that could have been turned into funds if there had only been some system to arrange this. The lack of ready reserve funds was also sadly called to public attention. So that *the next year an emergency measure was passed by Congress —the Aldrich-Vreeland Law—which gave the banks power to form "National Currency Associations" and issue more bank-notes on some other kinds of securities than government bonds.*

At the same time a national "Monetary Commission" was formed

---

* The system was called a "breeder of panics", because it also demanded that banks should keep a certain amount (25 per cent of their loans usually) on hand as a reserve fund, and *stop issuing loans when that limit was reached.* Only a percentage of this had to be kept in their own vaults, and the rest could be put into other banks—so that the stores of gold were scattered in little amounts over the entire country, and a great majority centred in New York, where they could be profitably loaned. *The great peril of this was in not having large reserves at a number of cities over the country,* in case of the sudden call for payments that usually precedes a panic or money crisis.

** Other rulings cut down the amount of tax on bank-note issues one-half, and the lowest amount of capital to open these banks in small towns was also lowered from $50,000 to $25,000. As a result many new banks sprang up.

LENDING AND BORROWING

of members of Congress to look into banking conditions. They studied systems of other countries and came to a decision nearly four years later. What America needed, they believed, was a few great central banks to do the government's business, issue paper money and keep reserves of gold on hand to tide over any such terrible crash of values as that of 1907. Banks were to be grouped by districts, then the latter in a few big regions, and finally the last into a reserve group. Congress, as is not seldom its custom, delayed action on this bill, and it was finally "shelved". Yet the idea had been noised about, and it could not be dropped so easily. Bankers all over the country were demanding action.

So that before the countries of Europe were boiling over in war, the matter had come up as a political issue, when Wilson was elected in 1912.

THE FEDERAL RESERVE BANKS ARE FORMED TO END PANICS

The Democrats didn't approve the plan in their platform, but Mr. Wilson is said to have been a strong force behind the final drawing-up of the Federal Reserve Act, which included many of the points suggested by the commission. It was introduced in Congress in June, 1913, and finally passed both houses and was signed by the President on Dec. 23. *This was the biggest forward step in banking regulation ever taken in this country.* During the ten years of its existence (1924), the Federal Reserve system has proved its founders' wisdom, and the thorough study of the previous commission. Although it has small defects, it is the best working basis for our money system ever planned.

To form a picture of what the Reserve banks are doing, one must think of a great system of dams where water is stored up at different parts of a country. *All banks are connected with one another,* from the smallest to the big central ones, and all send back and forth wealth, thus keeping the tide of riches level in the whole system. *The law provided for the division of the country into between eight and twelve districts* (the latter number was decided upon). *In each of these there is to be only one Federal Reserve bank, with capital of $4,000,000. Every national bank must (State banks and trust companies may also) give toward the capital of the Reserve Bank in their districts six per cent. of their capital and surplus.* Stock may also be sold to private holders if the capital can't be raised otherwise, but no one is to hold more than $25,000 worth. (This is a wise move to prevent private interests from controlling.) Finally, if both these can't make up the capital needed, the United States government will help*

* The whole system is to be managed by a Federal Reserve Board

This is a group of banks which makes up the highest borrowing and lending system of the country. *They were founded to make loans from one another,* not to deal with the general public, in so far as deposits and loans are concerned. *They are, in fact, banks where other banks open accounts**—"wholesale" dealers, instead of "retail", to use the terms employed in like cases in the buying and selling world.

The big aims of the banks are to control the gold supply (by buying it in home or foreign markets in exchange for stocks and bonds or for foreign "bills of exchange"). They also "cash" certain limited kinds of notes, drafts and bills of exchange held and indorsed by member banks. *This is the most important part of their dealings— affording central places where the banks of the country can turn their assets in paper into gold.* This service alone has the power of strengthening the whole money system of the country, and that gold is kept on hand to supply in case of sudden demand. By this means it is hoped to avoid panics, which always arise when the banks stop payments. *The Reserve Banks also issue paper money, and in time the old National Bank bills will be replaced.* The Reserve Board in emergencies can issue a special kind of Federal Reserve notes, backed by the government.

Let us see how the system has "worked". It had a very trying beginning, owing to the outbreak of the World War in 1914, before it actually got under way.

THE WORLD WAR BURNS UP THE MONEY OF EUROPE

All the big countries of Europe at once declared what are called "moratoria"—a rather big name for a "putting off" or "delaying", which means that the governments officially announce that they will have to postpone payment of their debts when they come due—usually for a certain time. The danger of all our gold being drained away to Europe was great, as trade for a time collapsed with Europe and the foreign powers were all trying to "cash in" on any assets that they held, to pay the great costs of the war. *The situation called for quick action.* An act was passed giving the Secretary of the Treasury power to give national banks the right to issue emergency bank-

---

of seven members, including the Secretary of the Treasury and the Comptroller of the Currency, the other five being appointed by the President and the Senate to serve for ten year terms. A Federal Advisory Council, made up of one member appointed by each reserve bank, was also planned, to make any suggestions or to consult on business conditions.

* This is done in several ways: first, the member banks make their subscription of six per cent. of their own holdings; but they also deposit other money with the Federal Reserve banks, and finally, the government also makes deposits of its great surplus money in the latter.

LENDING AND BORROWING

notes equal to 125 per cent. of their capital and surplus (instead of the 100 per cent. authorized before.) The number of "National Currency Associations" grew very rapidly, as these under the Aldrich-Vreeland Act had power to issue paper money on other than government bond holdings. It is estimated that more than $300,000,000 worth of new money was thus issued in the three months following the outbreak of the war.

The whole system for financing the crops of the country had broken down with the collapse of business and exchange with Europe. The farmers and growers of the country had been accustomed to borrow large sums to pay for the marketing of their crops. This was especially the case with the cotton crop of the South, which is annually financed by the bankers of New York and other money centers. *The danger was so great that the Secretary of the Treasury called a "Cotton Conference"* at Washington in August, and it was arranged that the national banks of the country could borrow to the extent of 70 per cent. of their capital and surplus on notes secured by warehouse receipts (given by the cotton growers and other farmers). As a result the Senate passed a "Cotton Warehouse" Bill arranging a system for licensing and inspecting of all these institutions. This was to keep a supervision on these places where the security on loans was stored, and to prevent any frauds or false issue of receipts.

THE ROMANCE OF FOREIGN EXCHANGE AND WORLDWIDE FLOW OF GOLD

One other great danger arose at this time. It was connected with the system of "foreign exchange", which is the means used to settle debts and credits between merchants of different countries. "Exchange" is the sending back and forth of paper credits (drafts, bills of exchange and letters of credit or "travelers' checks". When a man in New York buys goods from Europe, he usually pays with a check or a draft on his credit at his bank. The foreign merchant then has to take this paper to his banker, who gives him the amount it is equal to in British money. The banker, that is, buys it at current rates of exchange.

There is, at bottom, a fixed rate, or par value, of one country's money in terms of the money of another nation. How is this figured out? It originally goes back to the actual value of gold or silver in the money of each land, and according to the weight and fineness, the price of one in the terms of the other is calculated.

But this is not the actual market price as it is quoted on the international market day by day. That varies with the supply and demand for the paper credits of the countries. Trade has a lot to do with this supply and demand. For instance, when Britain is buying more goods in America than we are in Britain, New York bills of exchange are in greater demand to pay these debts than London bills are. The London banker then can sell his American drafts (which some other merchant has sold him after getting them from American customers) at a higher rate. This means that our money will take a slight rise in terms of British.

The foreign merchant can either send gold shipments through his banker (if the debt is large enough) or buy drafts. When the drafts rise higher than the cost of sending gold bars, he will do the latter. *Every great ocean liner brings in its hold a rich cargo of gold and silver bars to settle debts between the bankers of different countries.* The gold of the world thus flows first in one direction, then in another, laying up stores where exports mount.

But foreign exchange is also active in payments of other debts, such as those for stocks or bonds sold or bought. The business of buying or speculation in foreign currency has given rise to dealers in this medium alone. The rise and fall of the currencies of different nations is caused by many things—among them the quantity of the gold surplus on hand, which makes for low interest rates on loans. Any great national debt or halting in trade has the power of causing the exchange value of a currency to plunge downward. Excess issue of paper money, with few assets to "back" it, of course makes the value go down both at home and abroad.

What happened at the beginning of the World War was a sharp demand for gold from the United States. We had about $150,000,000 worth of debts in Europe, and since foreign nations had suspended payments, there was no guarantee of this being made up for by sums in gold flowing back into the United States. Under the circumstances it was absolutely necessary to pay in some other way than with gold, for the scarcity here would have been so great that all prices and rates of interest would have shot up enormously.

Because the usual foreign exchange system was ruined by the outbreak of war, a "Gold Fund" Committee was appointed to meet in conference in Washington. This group of bankers proposed that a big collection of gold to equal the amounts of the debts be got together among the leading banks of the country. This amount was later reduced to $100,000,000, and a first installment was sent to the Canadian branch of the Bank of England. With this as security, we could now issue drafts or other forms of paper and send them to pay our debts in England, instead of by sending gold. A special committee took charge of issuing this paper.

THE STAGGERING LOANS OF THE WAR YEARS

Through all the complicated banking jobs that we have spoken of in the last few pages runs the *same principle* that Mr. Loan explained

LENDING AND BORROWING

to Mr. Make when he came to borrow money. It is this: *to give any kind of paper credit or promise to pay, you must first have the security to back it up with.* If you look at a dollar bill of the United States, you will find that it says: "This certifies that there has been deposited in the Treasury of the United States of America *one silver dollar payable to the bearer on demand."* A ten dollar bill changes this wording to "ten dollars in gold coin". Security backs up all the operations of foreign exchange, and the workings of the Federal Reserve Banks. And it also is the guarantee for the loans advanced by private bankers—the enormous bond issues and international loans for which America leads the world in acting as agents. Leading nations alone do not usually give an actual mortgage on their property, but issue bonds or other credits on their governments.

The World War was a breeder of loans throughout the world, and many of these funds to cover the enormous debts of the time were got from American bankers. The general total of Europe's debts to the United States, largely made during this period, has been estimated at $12,000,000,000. Some of these amounts, of course, have gone to rebuild nations after the war stopped, and their business and banking had been paralyzed. Of this huge sum, nearly $10,000,000,000 was lent to England, France, Italy and Belgium, and Russia (before the last-named nation dropped out of the war).

The funds for the war that we gave were about $22,000,000,000. At least, this latter sum was appropriated by special acts of Congress during the first few months of our participation in 1917. How was it raised? *By the issue of bonds direct to the people, instead of to a few bankers.* This was a new departure in American emergency finance. Our government really took a leaf out of the book of France, which had issued bonds for as small amounts as one franc (about 20 cents at par.) The result was that France before 1900 had become a nation of thrifty small investors, 3,000,000 shopkeepers and workmen holding government securities.

The United States issued five loans, the familiar "Liberty" Bonds, the first and second of these raising $5,000,000,000 in amounts as small as $50 before October, 1917. The other three issues made up, with these, $17,000,000,000. In addition to the bonds, "War Savings Stamps of $5 and "Thrift Stamps" of 25 cents helped to swell the sum. Everybody remembers the bands of valiant workers who sold these securities without being paid for their services. *It was a financial campaign that for success is unrivaled in money history.*

The money raised in this way was added to by the great sums brought in by the war taxes. These we shall talk about in the next chapter. But out of the loans raised by our people came the more than nine billions loaned the Allies. The interest on this sum in many cases is still to be paid. England adopted a refunding plan in

1923 to pay back $23,000,000,000 yearly and interest. Others may follow suit. The funds that went to the Russian nation will probably never be repaid. The other nations of Europe, in the terrible "slump" period after the war, when they were faced with bankruptcy, could hardly be blamed for trying to appeal to our "unselfish" spirit. We had gone into the fight, as Mr. Wilson said, without seeking "indemnities or material compensation"—pay for our sacrifices. There began to be some voices heard from abroad which suggested that the debts be canceled, that the money we had loaned was to be considered "our contribution towards the war". This was received with some alarm in America, and did much toward cooling off our wartime patriotism.

The old spirit of caution had asserted itself among the money powers of the United States, and the Congress turned down flatly the plan of the "League of Nations", so that—one of the greatest ironies the world has seen—we remained outside of the band of governments that was to secure peace to the world. *The plan we had invented was spurned by us after the foreign nations with some misgivings had entered it.*

Yet the idealistic trend of America—which had "backed" the world court established at The Hague several years before the war—asserted itself when that tribunal was reformed on a stronger basis. We have our representatives in its sittings, and several important decisions have been handed down in recent years. *It is vitally important that we remain a big and determining voice in this world court,* because war must be prevented, when that is possible, by "talking the matter over" in case of disputes. *War has always, and always will, ruin business, not only for the fighting countries, but for the whole world.*

BANKRUPT GERMANY CALLS ON AMERICA FOR AID

The mischief of ruining one country financially did not seem to occur to the Peace Congress of Versailles, when in 1919 it decided to beggar Germany in such a thorough way that she could not start an international rumpus for some time to come. Indirectly that is the very thing it did to world trade—upset it very thoroughly for some time to come. Of course, the war itself was to blame for part of the paralysis.

The terms offered Germany did not permit of a refusal—when there seemed some doubt of the "down and out" country accepting, the Allied armies made all signs of moving from their positions on the bridge-heads on the Rhine and taking "peaceful" possession of the country. This is not to suggest that weak-minded sympathy should have poured upon a nation that had laid waste a large part of the territory of two neighbor nations. The "reparations" or war indemnities fixed upon by the Versailles international gathering—$30,000,000,000, to be paid before 1934—were the largest ever levied on a nation, but it was generally thought to be just. *But in addition to this, further amounts that were left undetermined can be demanded from Germany in the future, the amounts to be decided by a commission of the conquering nations.* This was the same thing as demanding that Germany indorse a blank check at the point of a pistol, the amount to be filled in later!

If there had remained a way to pay it easily—as France did after the Franco-Prussian War in 1870—things would have been well. But rules were put into the treaty restricting the taxation that Germany could lay on her subjects. She had to give up the rich coal mining and manufacturing districts of the Saar and Ruhr valleys to France, and an International Commission was to govern the first district for the fifteen years allowed for the debt payment. The mines are being worked by money interests of France, and if at the end of the fifteen years, the inhabitants vote to return to German rule, the latter country must buy out France's interest in the mines. The revenge of the German workman was "passive resistance", or ceasing to work. This reached such a degree of effectiveness that the industry of the country was reduced to nil. France's revenge was to occupy the district with armed troops, a measure that provoked much criticism throughout the world, as it was really an aggressive act of war and contrary to the spirit of the treaty.

The amount of the total reparations was set at $132,000,000,000 in April, 1921. Meanwhile, to make up for the great lack of money, Germany was issuing paper notes at a record rate. Her printing presses turned them out by the millions. This inflation, or blowing up of her currency, for a short time brought a feverish prosperity. *But there was nothing to back up these issues with.* The fundamental rule of banking had been violated, and the natural result was that *they went down in value at a terrific rate.* The greatest fall in value came in the year 1923—a general collapse.

The plan to commandeer German industry has not been really successful. Strikes have been constant, and coal mining in the Ruhr has often stopped. The business of the country is reviving to some extent, but for a time the other nations boycotted her goods—another fatal step. Now a few kinds of goods are finding their way to America, sold for ridiculously low prices.

The real wealth of the country is concentrated in a few hands, like those of the Stinnes and Krupp interests. The workman gets very little pay, the number of unemployed is said to be steadily rising. The middle-class and "educated" classes suffer terribly, and about the only class that has a bearable life—apart from the money barons—is that of the farmers, who raise their own food. The rich have fled the country, spending so much money in foreign travel that a tax was for a time placed on this form of amusement. People of other nations who visit Germany are also subjected to high taxes on hotel bills, theater and travel expenses.

The inability of Germany to pay her reparations led the leading nations to form a Commission, headed by General Charles G. Dawes of the United States. These men went to Germany in 1923 and made a thorough study of conditions. The result was the so-called "Dawes Plan" to re-establish the country on a solid basis. The paper mark (which fell from being worth 23.8 cents to almost the vanishing point of a little more than two ten-trillionths of a cent) is to be restored to normal value. *The main solution recommended is to establish a gold bank in Berlin, with a large loan of gold from the other nations.* Several forms of security are to be given for this loan, the most important being a mortgage on all the railroads of the country. As an aid to getting the plan working, the reparations are to be postponed for a certain time.

This plan is favored by the Germans themselves, and with a call for a conference of allied government and banking interests in London in the summer of 1924, the salvation of Germany in the near future seems reasonably certain.*

THE HUGE GOLD FLOOD IN THE UNITED STATES

What has been the result of America's loaning of money to all the world? It has given her a prestige that she could not claim before. *All the nations are her debtors.* Gold is flowing into the United States in ever-increasing streams. Her exports are greater than the amount of goods that other nations send in, because her machinery for production is uninjured by the war. All this must be paid for, and it is these sums, as well as the great refunds in gold on the debts other nations owe, that are filling our treasuries to the bursting point. It is estimated that the United States (1924) has at least one-fifth of the world's gold. This is a most unique condition, but as yet there seems no way to send back sums great enough to make up for it.

The nations of Europe had been forced to turn to paper currencies during the war, but now there is a movement on foot in Germany,

---

*Two other nations have been also aided by the United States. Austria, which was cut off from all her farms and mines and factories, when the Versailles Congress parted her from Hungary, was saved by a loan of many millions and was restored to normal after a period of terrible inflation. Hungary also has issued a loan of $50,000,000, part of which was secured in the United States.

Sweden, Poland and even Russia to restore the currency to the gold basis; and the coinages of Great Britain, Holland and Switzerland are slowly returning to normal value in terms of gold. The big tendency to make loans from the United States to re-establish sound gold currencies will probably help to return some of the gold to Europe. Our investors will also put more money in foreign stocks and goods, when a more settled condition prevails over there.

FOREIGN EXCHANGE PRICES
Value of Foreign Coins in United States' Money

Nation	Coin	Par Value (in dollars)	Value July 1, 1924 (in dollars)
Britain	Sovereign	$4.865/8	$4.323/4
France	Franc	.193	.0514
Italy	Lira	.193	.04301/4
Belgium	Franc	.193	.0453
Germany	Mark (paper)	.238	.000,000,000,024
Austria	Crown	.203	.0000141/8
Czecho-Slovakia	Crown	.203	.02933/4
Denmark	Krone	.208	.1606
Finland	Finmark	.193	.0251
Greece	Drachma	.193	.018
Holland	Florin	.402	.376
Hungary	Crown	.203	.00125
Norway	Krone	.268	.1342
Poland	{ Mark	.238	.0000191/4
	{ Zloty*	.193	.193
Portugal	Escudo	$1.0805	.0274
Rumania	Leu	.193	.0042
Russia	Rouble (pre-revolutionary)	.514	.000011
Spain	Peseta	.193	.1329
Sweden	Krona	.268	.2655
Switzerland	Franc	.193	.1777
Yugoslavia	Dinar	.193	.0117
FAR EAST			
China	Tael	....	.74 (Peking)
India	Rupee	.4865/8	.3063
Philippines	Peso (silver)	.50	.4925
Java	Florin	.402	.37
Japan	Yen	.498	.4188
SOUTH AMERICA			
Argentina	Dollar (paper)	.4244	.3256
Brazil	Milreis	.3245	.1081

* Issued July 1, 1924, to replace old mark, at ratio of 1,800,000 marks to one zloty.

The most important result of the great plenty is to make the prices of things very high—as always happens when money abounds—and the *rate of loaning money in the United States unusually low.**

Whatever the future financial state of Europe, America seems now to have world leadership in money matters. The pre-eminence of her great banking houses—like those of J. P. Morgan & Company—the fame of her great capitalists—Rockefeller, Astor and others—are blazoned across the world's money scroll. Above all, *the dollar is the world's standard of value.*

---

* The great surplus in the Federal Reserve Banks led them to reduce their rediscount rate (at which they "cashed" the notes and other papers of member banks) to 3½%. Private capital is given (July, 1924) under "call" loans for even 2%. The loans made from the banks of the country by private individuals for purchase of stocks and bonds has risen to a record point, and trading on the Stock Exchange has grown brisker, raising prices. A suggestion has been made that "savings banks" also lower the interest paid to depositors, but this is not very likely to happen.

CHAPTER V

THE ROMANCE OF NATIONAL HOUSEKEEPING (U. S. TREASURY AND MINT)

Each of us is a member of some nation, which protects us in a hundred ways. We couldn't get along otherwise, and in return we must help pay for this. How does the government of the United States "keep house"? Annually it keeps its books, and enters there all the enormous expenses of keeping up its post office, its other civil service departments, its army and navy, its executive and legislative departments, and the interest on the public debt. *This is the most romantic part of the money story of any nation*—the cost of running the government itself. Just like the housewife who must manage her home, "making ends meet", the United States must every year make out a bill of what the year's expenses will, on the average, cost. It must then be sent to Congress to be passed for "appropriation" from the Treasury. *The United States government has the biggest and best-oiled machinery for this purpose of any country to-day.* While other nations are groaning under after-war debts, our Treasury in June, 1924, had a surplus of $505,000,000.

Not only the national government, but every State and city, including the smallest towns, have a way of raising money. These have to pay for their public schools, their asylums, homes for the poor, prisons, police systems, city lighting and water; building of bridges and streets and other expenses. *The branch of money activity which takes care of these things is known as "public finance"*—to mark it off from the "private" kind that we have been talking about until now. The theory is that public money is collected from those best able to pay, or according to wealth.

Here comes up the subject of *taxes*. These are really modern inventions (in the personal, periodic and evenly-distributed form we have them to-day.) In ancient Greece, as we have said, the most important men of the land kept up the theaters and games, but this was not secured by any law, rather by the weight of *public opinion*. In Rome, it was only under the Empire that heavy land and poll taxes came in, and the first was really a form of excessive rent. *The whole theory in ancient times was that the public moneys were got from those conquered in battle, not from citizens.* In times of emergency, to keep up the army, there were special money levies. According to one's wealth, one sometimes had to pay the cost of keeping several sailors in the navy of ancient Rome.

In the Middle Ages no government was strong enough to collect taxes for the whole country. The serf gave his services to his lord, and the latter protected him. Money was rare, and not until the growth of the cities did a real system of "housekeeping" in the towns begin. The feudal lords had demanded a few taxes on roads, markets and on the towns in their domains. But when the rich class of burghers, or city fathers, began to rule the free towns, they began to keep a treasury, or fund out of which to pay expenses. They began to lay "poll" taxes on each person, on the ownership of buildings and even on goods. They also borrowed money, and thus started "city debts."

TAXES—RICH INCOME OF THE MODERN STATE

National taxes came along more slowly. In England the feudal land-holding system was in style for a long time, though here the king had more power than on the Continent. He had a census taken of all property—the famous "Domesday Book"—on which taxation was based—a sort of rent in proportion to the land held, and collected by the sheriff. He had a sort of financial council, called the "Exchequer"—a name said to have been taken from the checkerboard pattern on the table-cloth over which the money passed that was paid into the treasury. Money was charged for public offices, and many fines were introduced. The poll tax, or tax per head, was especially hard on large families, and the peasants used to say that "they had their children from God, but the King charged them for it!"

But, along with the growing share of the people in British government, came their control of the tax system. The feudal service was made payable in "shield-money," and in the famous Magna Charta, or bill of rights, the barons made the king promise that they would not have to pay levies without the consent of the general council—neither "shield" nor other money except for certain special things, as when their sons were knighted. The execution of Charles I followed his stubborn attempt to lay taxes against public will, in the famous Ship Writs. In the revolution of 1688, when the power passed to a committee chosen by the House of Commons, the tax privilege in England definitely passed to the Parliament. The gradual cutting down of the power of the Lords, has since made taxes scaled to the income of the common people, and heavy on the rich.

The American States won their independence in a struggle over taxes. Under the Constitution they were allowed to lay taxes on property. They had been rather haphazard about their collections of public money in the days before colonies became States, and under British rule when bills had to be paid it was often found that the treasury, like Mother Hubbard's cupboard, was bare! The sale of lands helped to make money for the town governments, and then, too, there were cruel forms of fines and taking of property in the case of those accused of crime or—in New England—of "witchcraft". The States, then, for a time kept on in this easy, comfortable, not-caring-for-to-morrow way.

Before 1800 the States had begun to take censuses of property, slaves held and numbers of persons subject to poll tax. At first only a few kinds of property were taxed, and land, houses, horses, and other things, were valued all alike at a set rate. Finally, the laws were extended to include *all* kinds of possessions, except those that were especially exempted. The setting of definite values on each piece of property, "assessment", gradually grew up.

The great growth of the amounts collected by the States in taxes came with the increase of wealth in the country. The most interesting thing about this part of "public finance" is that the State originally collected less money than the Federal government; that soon (about 1840) they had begun to raise almost ten times as much, and that since the decline in the movement for developing the country, and especially since the Civil War, they have lowered their revenues to about one-fifth of the nation's, and the cities have grown to be big taxing powers, getting in about two-thirds as much as the government. The biggest part of real estate taxes is reaped by the cities, though some States also charge an additional percentage rate. But the States to-day get their biggest yield from taxes on "personal" property—such as stocks and some bonds—and from levies on corporations and inheritances. So it is often said that the cities have grown at the expense of the States, and even of the government.

AMERICA'S SCHOOLS SUPPORTED BY WILLING HANDS

The big public schools system of the country—better than any found in other nations—costs a huge sum to keep up. *This is by far the biggest item in the State and city budgets.** It amounts to

* The other expenses of the States and cities—to sum them up briefly *in their order of importance*—are: interest on their debts (bond issues, etc.), roads and bridges, charity (poor relief, free hospitals), salaries of employees, new State and city department buildings, police departments, courts, upkeep of old buildings, fire departments, prisons and reformatories, lighting, water, city and State officials' pay, legislature members' salaries, boards of health, parks and piers, State militia and other items. Some cities also run transit lines and ferry service.

several hundred millions each year. And with the movement for better salaries and pensions for teachers, it is every year being increased. Most cities have a "school" tax. In the West and Middle West especially, big colleges and Universities are often supported by the State. There are normal schools for training teachers free. Some cities also have colleges which they support.

The biggest and oldest Universities of the East, and of some other parts of the United States, are supported by private gifts; they have boards of rich trustees, who have an important "say" in how they are run. This is sometimes said to be an evil, as it puts a "damper" on the sort of teaching that can be done in these schools. *No theories that object to the rich men's control of things can be taught in certain of these colleges.* The teachers that dare to do this are sometimes asked to resign, and so it is a good thing for the rights of the honest working man that there are free schools where his sons can have just as good training as the pampered heirs of the rich man! Of course, not all endowed schools are so "narrow" in their point of view; but their fees for students are often so high that the poor boy, even though he "works his way," can not pay them. *The right to learn surely belongs to every man and woman.*

The romance of the national government's housekeeping centers around two big institutions—the Treasury and the Mint. (There are, in fact, several United States Mints in different cities, but they really form one big system.) The purpose of the Treasury is to store the money which comes into the national purse through taxes on imports and internal revenue, and a number of other sources. The object of the Mint is to coin our money and to keep it in good condition so far as wear and tear is concerned. There are limits to the work done by both—the Federal Reserve Banks, for instance, are now used to store public money, and the government printing offices do the actual work of making paper bank-notes, or "bills."

THE BEGINNINGS OF TAXES ON GOODS WE BUY

The romance of the golden streams of money that flow into our nation's Treasury is closely wrapped up with "indirect" taxes. By these we mean taxes laid on new things made or bought—which in the end are paid by the "consumer". (This is in contrast with "direct" taxes, or those on property which one already has, from which the States and cities draw their money.) There are a number of exciting stories connected with the beginnings of these taxes. The nation needed money soon after it had been formed. The Constitution had given the power to lay seaport duties to the central government, and *the States were especially forbidden to do so*. But the customs duties did not bring in enough money.

"We must lay taxes on things made in the country!" said Alexander Hamilton, the first Secretary of the Treasury. He put the matter before Congress, but it didn't seem greatly in favor of it. Perhaps even those early Congressmen disliked taxes! At last, however, the Act of March 3, 1791, was passed. What were the things taxed? Principally our old friends liquor (now, alas! no more!) and tobacco. The first was copied from the liquor taxes of England. But a great "to-do" was raised over the country. The West grew a lot of corn, and many of its farmers made a lot of money by distilling it into whisky. In fact, the gallon of this drink was used to pay bills, as money was scarce! This seems like a form of currency that would be worth a great deal, but we must remember that these were the days long before "prohibition" was thought of!

The result was the famous "Whisky Rebellion", when the farmers in some States—notably western Pennsylvania—told the tax collector to go about his business. *It was a sort of armed defiance of the government, and finally it got to be so widespread that the militia was called out to end it.* This was not hard, but the process cost a lot of money—$1,500,000, it is estimated, or about three-eighths of the whole yearly revenue of the government, from internal taxes *and customs, too*. The tax was, for a time, a failure, though later it grew to be a big money source. The tax on tobacco and sugar, and a "direct" tax on the States, which had to be paid in proportion to the number of citizens, were also part of the system started by Hamilton.

But in the elections of 1800 the Democratic Party won, and in the Jefferson administration the old internal taxes were taken off. *For ten years the whole money to run the country came from customs*. Then the War of 1812 brought the need for a lot of money to fight it. Then the people of that day had to bear the same costs as we moderns since 1917. The Party of the People had to do just what it had before opposed—lay a heavy tax on "spirits", tobacco, sugar, iron, paper, leather and other products, as well as levy a stamp tax and a direct tax on the States. The nation that had its birth in a protest against such money seizures now had to do the very same thing to pay a war debt as Britain had done! Two years after the war ended (Act of Dec. 17, 1817) the duties were taken off.

The main tax history of the United States is one of heavy burdens at time of war. We can sketch here only the three great periods of such levies—the Civil, Spanish-American and World Wars. For more than forty years before July 1, 1862, there had been absolute freedom from internal rules of this sort. There was not even a tax on liquor and tobacco. With the Civil War came a bigger need for money than had ever been felt in the country. The nation was split in two, was in its very death throes, and in the emergency *taxes were laid on almost everything that could be found!*

People who complained about the World War conditions should remember that our grandfathers had to pay tax percentages on a steadily greater number of articles—as well as on occupations, sales and dividends, incomes, inheritances, corporation and small firms' profits, and also a stamp tax. *And this was at a time when the production of the country was crippled, when prices went up to several hundred times the normal rate, and money was so scarce it almost disappeared!*

The most important result of the Civil War taxes was that, when they were gradually repealed, the duties on liquor and tobacco were kept—and they remained in effect permanently, but the high war whisky tax of $2 a gallon was reduced to fifty cents in 1868. In this year tobacco was first put under the adhesive stamp system, and boxes and packages are still marked in this way at present.

The Spanish-American War was a short one, but it brought in under the War Revenue Act of 1898 a new set of taxes. One of the most novel was a levy of ten cents a pound on tea—the first time this had been done since the days of the "Boston Tea Party" before the Revolution. Other new taxes were laid on business documents, trades, inheritances, flour, medicines, perfumes, wines and chewing gum. (The last form of delicacy had meanwhile been invented!) The yearly sum added to the revenues under this act was more than $148,000,000. The taxes were soon after taken off.

THE HUGE REVENUES OF THE U. S. SINCE 1917

The most far-reaching taxes ever laid were those during the World War. The two first War Revenue Bills provided for a yearly tax of $4,000,000,000—an unheard of amount before this time! *The new ideas of heavily taxing large profits, and of exempting the income of the poorer classes and their necessities of life, were put into effect for the first time in the United States—perhaps in any war taxation plan in history. This was part of the movement for a fair division of profits to the worker.* Much of the huge sum was raised on taxes on incomes—the rate of this tax ranging from two to sixty-five per cent., the latter amount on the very largest incomes, those amounting to millions of dollars.* Inheritance and "excess profits" taxes also went to swell the yearly amount. The remainder came largely from the so-called luxury taxes, laid

---

* The biggest income tax yield for one year was in 1919—$1,269,630,000.

on numberless things, ranging from expensive clothing, jewelry, candies, perfumes, to theater admissions, automobile supplies, telephone messages, tobacco, ice cream and various drinks. Taxes on occupations were also revived.

The speedy cutting down of these taxes in normal times is bound to come in a very few years!* The income tax has never been popular in the United States except in "emergencies"—at least on moderate earnings. The new laws of 1924 have cut down the rate of tax on incomes 25 per cent., and with other reductions in the "luxury" taxes that went into effect July 2 of this year it is said that the taxpayers will be saved some $35,000,000 annually. The taxes removed were those on theater tickets costing less than 50 cents, and on telephone and telegraph messages, candies, soft drinks, and certain leather goods, and the 5 per cent. levy on auto supplies was cut in half. It is estimated that in the Republican administration 1921-4 the whole tax burden was relieved $1,250,000,000 (yearly.)

To sum up, the Government gets in its largest yearly taxes at present from incomes and excess profits ($1,842,144,418 in 1924). *The next highest amount comes from tobacco.* When we open a package of cigarettes costing twenty cents, we see on the outside a stamp costing six cents. The amount brought in by this one industry in 1923 was more than $309,000,000. What about liquor? The passing of the Eighteenth Amendment, or "Prohibition" Law, cut off a yearly sum of more than $250,000,000. The liquor interests shook the threat of bankruptcy before the eyes of the government. This hasn't happened—in fact the money has hardly been missed! It must be remembered that we are not now on a normal tax schedule, and in that case the lack of this big sum would be more important. In the long run, the "consumer" had to pay this tax, and now he is probably only paying it in another form.

A great number of evils are connected with taxes as we have them to-day. There are always loopholes where the clever escape, and the burden that falls on the others is increased. One of the questionable things in force to-day is the keeping of certain kinds of bonds off the tax list.** Of course, the Government could not get so many people to buy its bonds if it also taxed them—that would be "burning the candle at both ends"! States, cities and other corporations have also issued many "free" bonds. But the result

---

* The proposal of President Coolidge (1924) to call a national conference of Federal and State officials to adjust and lower taxes will aid.

** Thus, while taxes had increased 127 per cent. in five years, the number of these tax-free investments had gone up 66 per cent. in ten years (1924).

is that rich men invest their money in these and other tax-free securities, *instead of putting it into the industry of the country*. This cuts down our yearly production and makes business slow up at times.

A new Tax Appeals Board of 28 men was created in 1924, to pass on any taxpayer's complaint of unjust taxation against the government.

TARIFF: BONE OF CONTENTION BETWEEN BIG BUSINESS AND THE PEOPLE

The customs and tariff laws of the nation make up another side of the romance of revenue. Before the Constitution was enacted, the different States had made their own laws charging duties on foreign goods brought into the country to be sold in American markets for "home" use. As some of them were low and some high, a sort of rivalry sprang up, to charge lower rates and thus attract more shipping, between the ports—a "commercial war." The confusion that resulted made the framers of the Constitution put an iron-clad rule into it that *only the Federal government could lay these duties*. A tariff act was passed in the same year, though it was not of great importance at the time, as we were doing more shipping by sea ourselves than making our own goods. Our ships carried goods of other countries then at war, and our own manufacturers were not yet big enough to need "protection". Later we made treaties promising equal port privileges in return for those in foreign ports.

Here comes up an old dispute between the people who believe in a high tariff—to keep foreign manufacturers from competing in price or "underselling" our own—and those who think trade ought to be "free". There are things to be said on both sides. Tariffs are very delicate matters because they both bring in money to the Treasury, and effects prices for goods. The most up-to-date point of view is to accept "free" trade, as the more business there is, the better for ourselves as well as the foreign countries. But few countries except Great Britain have quite got into this unselfish state of mind at present.

The manufacturers want the tariff fairly high in their particular line, and the people who buy their goods want it low, as *the more goods, the greater the supply, and the lower the price*. The government can't do without its revenues from this source, but it also knows that if the tariff is too high, foreign trade will stay away—and the customs income will suffer. The result is that the United States have wavered from one point of view to another. The tariff laws have been changed a great number of times, and at any one stage of our history have usually been a very mixed list of rates on different things, with special clauses passed through the Congress for the benefit of the butcher, baker and candlestickmaker! This wouldn't matter so much if such changes didn't have a far-reaching effect on business, and in some cases even spell ruin if they caused prices suddenly to plunge or go up.

The American ports were closed during the War of 1812, and when they were opened a general tariff bill was passed on April 27, 1816. This marked the real beginning of our customs laws protecting our own factories. *The big object of the act was to help the new cotton and woolen cloth-making trade.* Later additions were made to protect the new iron foundries from foreign competition.

At this time the country was pretty much agreed on these tariffs. But soon struggles began to break out between different parts of the nation—for each had its "pet" industry that it wanted to shield, and each was just as bitterly opposed to paying higher prices for things made in some *other* part of the United States, just because *that* neighborhood wanted to keep out foreign competition! The South gradually began to frown on high tariffs of any sort—partly because she had her own system of slave labor, instead of free, paid workers, and chiefly raised and shipped raw cotton, instead of making things, and so had little to fear from abroad. But the middle and Far West, with their farms and mines, and New England with her woolen factories, were so strong that *they pushed through Congress higher and higher tariff rates.*

This came to a climax with the Tariff Act of 1828, when rates were made so high that they wrung a roar of protest from the whole South, and the cry was soon taken up elsewhere. It was called a "tariff of abominations"—so hard did it press on the price-paying public! This "palmy" period of tariff for protection came to an end in 1832, when the charges were lowered. In the following year— to settle the disputes between the different sections of the country— the "compromise" plan was adopted, which arranged for a gradual reduction to 20 per cent on everything, and within ten years this had been done.

DUTIES, BEFORE AND AFTER THE CIVIL WAR

Between this time and the Civil War, the low rates were only designed to bring in revenue to the government. The one exception was in 1842, the period after the panic of 1837, when money was badly needed by the Treasury, and high duties were laid—as much as 75 per cent. on some goods—including iron and sugar. The famous Walker tariff of 1846 was the Democrat's attempt to reduce these rates, and it succeeded fairly well, though it was inconsistent—keeping coffee and tea free, and laying a heavy import duty on woolen goods. This period was marked by the beginning of the warehouses in which goods from abroad are kept by the government until the customs duties have been paid on them. In 1857 a reduction of about 5 per cent. was passed, but the panic of this year caused a repeal.

The final stage of our tariff history begins with the Civil War. Just as the taxes on liquor and tobacco were permanent relics of that fight, the high "protection" systems on customs to-day is. The need for money had made the taxes increase enormously, and *many of these "internal revenue" levies were on the manufacturer. In order to even things up for him, the tariff was raised higher and higher, so that he wouldn't be ruined by foreign goods swamping the market at a time when our own manufacturers were pretty badly disorganized.* That is, if the government taxed the factory-owner so much a ton on his product, it had to add a greater percentage on the tariff for that sort of goods. *But when the taxes were taken off, the tariff remained.* In spite of a temporary lowering of ten per cent. in 1872 (later repealed) and a revision ten years later, things stayed pretty much as they were.

A yearly Treasury surplus of $100,000,000 had existed in 1872. The next year saw another panic, and it had at once been necessary again to raise the tariff. Ten years later the surplus again existed, and a tariff commission was appointed to study the matter. "Reductions of twenty per cent.", the commission advised. In spite of this, the reduction was very small, averaging five per cent.

The next champion of reduction was President Cleveland, who in his annual message of 1887 practically pledged himself to this cause, if the Democrats should win the elections the next year. The Republicans won, and jubilantly went on to *raise* the average rates to about fifty per cent. in) the "McKinley Tariff Bill". But sentiment was against this move, and, in 1894 the "Wilson Bill" was passed bringing duties down to an average of about forty per cent.

Two years later the political seesaw brought the Republicans back into the majority, and the "Dingley Bill" of 1897 again raised duties to an average of 57 per cent. Manufacturing for some years took a new "spurt." Some new industries shot up over night, such as *the tin plate business. Because of the high protection by the tariff, this developed a great corporation inside of a little more than a year!* It was later bought by the great Steel Corporation, which was founded from many small plants in 1901. The evils that came in with this law included much higher prices, and some very unfair "discrimination" in prices between goods sold to foreign firms and those in the United States. Those abroad were given reduced rates. *The evil was that the money went into a few pockets, not into those of everybody.*

The cry for a change in rates came up increasingly, as the big businesses grew fatter and fatter! The demand was strong in the administrations of Roosevelt, but for some reason this great fighting leader and just thinker was never moved to start these reforms. The man who did accomplish it was President Taft, who in 1908 in a public message asked for a definite program of reduction. The result was the "Payne-Aldrich Bill" of the following year. Hearings were held during many months, and every business that wanted a "good rate" in the new tariff sent its tearful and entreating representatives! The result was a very slight betterment in a few cases,* but general levels stayed about the same. The real improvement came four years later.

One of the most sweeping changes in recent years was made by the "Underwood-Simmons Bill" of 1913. This law doubtless gave the business interests many a pang, for it put an enormous number of things on the free list, including cattle, wheat and flour, potatoes, pig iron and *even wool*. The Democrats, under the Wilson administration, were "doing the thing up brown." The party has come to be associated with low tariffs, partly because much of its voting power is made up of the price-paying, not the capitalist class, and it is the ruling party in the anti-tariff South. Yet the yearly yield to the government was not so much smaller than under the previous rates—$308,025,125 in 1921, as compared with the sum of $318,891,395 under the Payne-Aldrich Act in 1913.

THE WORLD WAR INCREASE AND THE "FLEXIBLE" TARIFF

This schedule stood during the enormously expensive activities of the World War. It lasted, in fact, just as long as the Democratic administration did—and no longer. There is no doubt that the after-war debt was a sufficient reason for wanting a slightly higher rate—so that these added sums could make up for the gradual lowering of the war taxes. Production abroad was smaller, and so the revenues had to be "given a boost." The Republican Congress in 1922 held a series of hearings covering a number of months, from which the "Fordney-McCumber Bill" emerged. It became a law in the autumn of that year. It moved rates upward, and took off the free list most

---

* Wool and cotton were heavily protected, but hides and petroleum were made free, and the duties were lowered on rough lumber, print paper, coal and iron ore. The rate on pig iron seems to us to-day to have been enormously high—$2.50 a ton, for in the latter tariff of 1913 it was made free, and to-day it is only .75 a ton.

of the things that the former tariff exempted. *In fact, the rates were in many cases higher than in the Payne-Aldrich schedule of 1909.**

At the same time, it must be remembered that raising of tariff rates does not necessarily make prices higher. Sometimes it does when the majority of the supply of some goods comes from a foreign country. Then high rates effect the supply from abroad to such an extent that local manufactures can't make up for it. But this is seldom the case when the local supply is able to meet the demand—a very common condition. In the long run it comes down to the matter of "demand"—hence "necessities" should generally be made free or at least low in tariff rates, and luxuries higher. Present high prices (1924) are owing to a number of things—i.e., gold "inflation."

The most important new ruling of this law was for a "flexible" tariff schedule—the first time this had ever been tried in this country. The President was given the power—in cases when, after careful investigation, he finds our rates of duty do not equalize the costs of production of articles between the United States and the principal foreign competing country—to set the rates that will make these equal. Thirty days after he announces this in a proclamation, the new rates are effective. But he can't change them more than fifty per cent.—either higher or lower—and not until after the U. S. Tariff Commission has "thoroughly investigated" prices.

The money that flows into the Treasury includes also the interest on bonds and other securities owned by the government, which includes the various debts of foreign nations, and this averages about $100,000,000 yearly. It has also loaned large sums to the railroads of the country since these were returned to private ownership—and these bring in a good-sized sum for interest.**

AMERICA'S HUGE EXPENSE ACCOUNT AND THE "PORK BARREL"

On the other side of this romantic slate of "high finance" stand the huge sums that the government spends every year. *America was*

---

* Some examples of increases under the Fordney-McCumber Act are: sugar,—.0168 a pound, 1909; .0125, 1913; .022; linen cloth,—30%, 1909; 30–35%, 1913; 35–55%; silk cloth,—45%, 1909 and 1913; 55%; wheat,—25 cents a bushel, 1909; free, 1913; 30 cents a bushel. Cotton thread was raised from 15%, 1913, to 20–35%. Tobacco rates were raised greatly. Wool is an important exception, for though it was free in 1913 rates, it had been 33–36 cents a pound in 1909, and in 1922 was set at a flat rate of 31 cents a pound. Pig iron (already mentioned) $2.50 a ton, 1909; made free in 1913, and was placed at 75 cents a ton—a notable exception. The rate on liquors was greatly raised—perhaps, to discourage "bootlegging"(?).

** The sums paid in interest and refund of principal average some $55,000,000 yearly, against new loans of about $13,000,000 in 1923-4.

for years a spendthrift nation. No amounts seemed too large, no end to the rich treasure which flowed in every year seemed in sight. It was only at times of war, when expenses increased hugely, or at times of a country-wide panic, that the nation was brought face to face with a serious shortage of funds. She spent lavishly the rest of the time—and *the system for spending was not of the best.* In fact, the United States gave out each day in 1915 as much as in the entire year of 1790! This huge increase came largely in recent years—the expenses going up nearly 400 per cent. in the thirty years before 1908. When the amounts went up to a billion dollars a year, the country began to grow uneasy. But just before the World War the year's appropriations reached $1,098,000,000 —this in a "normal" year!

The reasons given for these big expenses were the growths of the government's business—it had to take care of all the new territory being developed, especially in the Far West, and care for the great new millions of its population. The salaries of the government officials also went up steadily, to keep pace with the new rises in prices and standards of living. *But the biggest cause was the lack of a central group to take charge of the yearly outlay.* The founders of the Republic had made a Constitution fitted for a small country, and in the matter of expenses it provided only for the simple state of things in colonial days.

The only rule made with regard to this matter in the Constitution was that no money should be drawn from the Treasury except as the result of appropriations made by law, and that Congress should have the power to "pay the debts and provide for the defense and general welfare of the United States". The President was also given power to make recommendations as to the spending program. But all estimates were submitted to Congress through the Secretary of the Treasury, "and in no other manner," and he was to prepare these and include them in the book of estimates submitted to Congress. *The result was that the whole matter rested with Congress—it acted on the President's advice and the Secretary's "estimates,"—as these were revised by the President and then sent by special messenger—entirely as it was minded to.* The revenue bills had to originate in the House, and since the great growth of the country's business had made it impossible to debate everything on the floor, these matters were generally given to committees. *The evil came in here—that none of the members of Congress was without some "interest" in the appropriations.* There were 531 Congressmen, each representing his "district", and each locality wanted more and more money to use for its own purposes! A harbor dredged, a new court house built—and he could be sure of a warm welcome at home!

It has been said that no bill which is passed through Congress— subject, of course to Presidential veto, except by two-thirds vote— *does not in the end amount to so much money gained or spent. Government has a tremendous power*—it can decide the fate of orphan boys and penniless widows, by giving or withholding sums for charity institutions, or by cutting down the pensions of old soldiers can bring them to poverty and early death! It can decide whether the children of the nation in some cases are to be ignorant and criminal or fine and well-educated—by appropriations for public schools. Or it can make the working people the slaves or the equals of the business interests, or can make thousands the victims of frightful accidents on the railroads and other public service institutions by failing to pass laws for prevention, inspection and the like! *In all these humane matters money plays a big part, and it would be "false economy", to say the least, to "save" money in causes that cry out for it.*

THE CRY FOR NATIONAL SAVING AND THE BIRTH OF THE BUDGET

The big cry for "economy" that went up increasingly over the country before 1921 was not for a mere *cutting down* of the amounts spent. It was for that operation which every good housewife knows —"getting the most for one's money". It was notorious that there were "leaks" of the public money in Congress. The so-called "pork barrel" bills—those aimed at getting a fat appropriation for a particular district were passed oftener than they should have been. Often these were not deliberately planned to misuse the money of the people, but the *necessity* of some of these outlays was very slight. Court houses were built in little towns that certainly didn't need them, and then to make them "good for something", bills were sometimes passed providing for a new court session every once in a while! Or a river was widened at a huge expense where the amount of commerce didn't warrant it. Finally, one of the biggest wastes was in the running of the civil service and other government departments—the staffs were much larger than were needed. On the other hand, appropriations were sometimes delayed or withheld when needed.

The World War for a time made economy impossible—it was during this struggle that the United States learned to think lightly of billions. But before we went into the fight, there was a definite movement springing up in this country for a national "budget" system. We had our annual "estimates" for the coming year, to be sure, prepared by the Secretary of the Treasury and revised by the President, and these were called "budgets", but what was needed was a central committee to take charge of the balancing of what we received and

NATIONAL HOUSEKEEPING 395

what we spent. In 1915 the movement had reached big proportions, the Chamber of Commerce of the United States organizing a campaign to attract public attention to the need. The days of haphazard spending were now doomed, but the entry into the war for a time put all thoughts of reform out of mind.

The Republican administration of 1921 has to its credit the introduction of the "budget" system. To understand what is meant by this term, we must go back to the history of the British government. The parliament had a big leather bag which is said to have been used for many years to hold the papers sent in to the House of Commons to explain the money resources of the country and its needs. This bag was known as the "Budget". At last it came to be used or any statement drawn up and showing the money on hand and the objects on which it was going to be spent. Before the United States adopted this plan, it was already in use by most of the nations of the world—under different names, but still at bottom the same—a system for balancing the amounts spent against the sums on hand. *The budget tells these things: how much money it needed for carrying on the government during the next year; how much money is on hand; from what sources more is expected to come in, and how much shall be used to carry on each separate function of the government.*

The big question in the United States was, who should have the job of preparing this yearly statement? This was a delicate matter in a democratic country, as the power of commanding the money of the country might have resulted in setting up one man as supreme—a dictator. The President might have been given sole powers, but the Constitution has expressly kept the money appropriation rights for Congress. The Secretary of the Treasury seemed a likely candidate, but his powers had also been laid out for him. It seemed best to create a new officer who would be altogether disinterested, and be apart from the other government machinery.

The framers of the Budget Law of June 10, 1921, had on their hands one of the most important jobs ever undertaken in this country. The way they solved the matter was to create a Bureau of the Budget, headed by a Director and his staff. This organization acts in co-operation with the President in revising the estimates sent in by hands of all the government departments. (This means revising *downward,* in the average case!) Under the Budget and Accounting Act the only lawful estimates for the year's appropriations are those that the President sends to Congress. *There was also an important change made in the methods of Congress—instead of scattering the power to pass on money bills, the authority was centralized in the Appropriations Committees of the Senate and House.*

The custom was started of calling together the whole "business organization of the government" for a "budget conference" twice a year. At these meetings the President is heard, the Director of the Budget (the first to hold this office being Gen. H. M. Lord) sometimes also speaks, and those attending include some 2,000 persons —members of the Budget Bureau staff, Cabinet officers and all heads and sub-heads of departments and independent offices of the government. The theme of these meetings is economy. The President outlines his program, setting the limits of expenditure, and calls on the government officials to aid in this campaign. The very first conference, under President Harding, set the keynote of intensive saving.*

The biggest effort now being made by the government is to pay off its public debt. All surplus that can be spared is put to this purpose. The enormous war loans of 1917-8 brought a great interest payment, and by reducing them so much is being saved. Within three years (1924) it has been cut by some $2,722,000,000 (interest saved is more than $120,000,000 a year). As it is, the whole debt is estimated at about $21,254,000,000 in 1924. When cash is not on hand, the Treasury pays with new 2¾% short-term certificates.

The passage of several new laws have laid large new costs on the national Treasury. These are the World War Adjusted Compensation Act (1924), or soldiers' bonus bill, which, it is said, will take $132,000,000 in the first year after its enactment. This is the latest pension bill to be added to the yearly expenses—the other soldier pensions of the Civil and Spanish-American Wars costing about $180,300,000 in 1914. In addition there are civil service employees' retirement funds and pensions for retired teachers of the District of Columbia. A retiring allowance for members of the diplomatic and consular services was also fixed under the Rogers Act (1924).

THE MINT, AND THE STRUGGLE BETWEEN SILVER AND GOLD STANDARDS

The United States Mint was founded by law in 1792, but our currency really began seven years before, when the Continental Congress adopted the dollar as our money unit. The name "dollar" came from "Thaler", a German coin (short for "Joachimthaler", or "coin from the Joachim valley", where the silver was mined).

---

* The Budget Bureau has done an important work in the few years that it has been in action. Immediately on its creation in 1921, it went over the estimates for the following year, which had already been made up—the result being that it cut the actual expenses by $1,742,738,189, as compared with the year before. The other reductions are estimated by the Director of the Budget as follows: 1923, $263,033,233; 1924, about $200,000,000, the latter year's total being $2,000,000,000 lower than 1921, the last year before the budget system was adopted. Total spent: 1921, $5,538,000,000; 1922, $3,795,000,000; 1923, $3,697,000,000.

At this time the States were coining paper money, much of it almost worthless. The Constitution forbade this, and also put an end to paper money by the government for more than fifty years. The coinage system adopted in 1792 was the "decimal" plan—ten cents equal a dime, ten dimes a dollar, ten dollars an eagle. The coinage was a double standard, that is, both gold and silver were recognized, the first being worth fifteen times as much as silver, according to weight. The weight of the silver dollar was fixed at 416 grains (later reduced to 412½ in 1837). The amount of fine metal in the different coins was also set by law, and changed several times. A silver "trade dollar", which was short on the amount of metal, was recognized as "legal tender", or coin which the government recognizes as good in payment, for a number of years, but was later not taken at full value. We have already sketched the period of "greenbacks", or paper money issue, following the Civil War.

The dispute between the people who voted for gold as the standard and those who stood for silver in time grew to be a burning question. In 1873 the gold dollar of 25.8 grains was declared the "standard". Five years later Congress passed the "Bland Allison Act," making the standard the old silver dollar of 412½ grains, and it was also authorized to coin between two and four millions of them every month. This was the beginning of the great flood of silver in circulation. The climax came with the "Sherman Act" of 1890, which quite overloaded the money market. It provided that the Secretary of the Treasury should buy some $50,000,000 worth of silver each year, and coin it into dollars. To pay for the metal the Treasury was to issue notes *redeemable either in silver or gold*. The evils that arose were the result of igorance—the "free silver" enthusiasts (those who wanted the government to coin the money without charge) were under the delusion that what made for "good times" was lots of money afloat. But they did not think that "bad money drives out good"—a coin worth less stays in circulation, while the more valuable is kept. There followed a great increase in the amount of money issued, thus "blowing up" prices and making people reckless in their borrowing until their debts, too, grew enormous. In this case it was a great addition of silver to the United States currency, authorized by law, and the result was to make gold go out of circulation, often to be hoarded. It was bought up by the people, as the dollar of silver was worth only 51 cents actually. Suddenly the bad effects became plain, and the great quantities of new paper notes issued to be redeemed began to make people uneasy. Suppose, they thought, that the government couldn't buy them back? Gold began to get scarce, and at the same time everybody began to want it.

The National Treasury was getting in less money than usual

because of new tariff acts that had been passed, suddenly cutting down the amount of duty on things brought into this country. And Congress had passed great appropriation bills which drained the treasury from another side. The result was that in 1893, at a time when the outstanding loans to new railroads and manufacturing industries were enormous, the value of government silver notes fell. Gold was at a premium, but paper money went down in value sharply, *so that debts were many times increased.*

To add to the disorder, came failures of four important railroads (which couldn't meet their loans and other expenses, owing to the sudden drop in the value of their stock and other assets). In one year nearly 600 banks alone failed in the United States, and the number of merchants and manufacturers that were bankrupt was appalling! Businesses closed and people were thrown out of work, and the suffering was terrible. The men who were starving rioted or organized outlaw demonstrations like the famous "Coxey's Army". The Stock Exchange was threatened with closing in July, but managed to "carry on" with the aid of foreign capital that now was shrewdly invested in the lowered stocks and other investments. This was one of the worst money disasters that has ever swept over the United States. It paralyzed business for months, and in 1894 the trading on the Exchange fell to the lowest point in fifteen years. The government saved the situation by selling enormous new issues of bonds for gold, and so stemmed the tide with this fund.

That troublesome experience put an end to the plans for making money more plentiful by coining a lot of silver. *In the Currency Act of 1900 the "standard" of our money was made, once and for all, gold.* By this we mean that the dollar is reckoned in the terms of so many grains of gold, even though it is made of silver. This year was the beginning of the creation of big gold reserves in the Treasury, and since the adoption in 1914 of the Federal Reserve Banks, this is now kept in these institutions, instead of in the Sub-Treasuries. The gold standard is now generally in use over the world, whereas for many years both gold and silver were recognized. *The history of money is that of a gradual going up of these standards: from the days when men used clay for their money, afterwards silver, and finally gold.* That the United States has more gold than any other land to-day accounts for her "prosperity".

CONCLUSION: THE SCALES THAT BALANCE THE WORLD'S PRICES

The two biggest disaster-periods in our money history were when we tried to swell the amount of money in circulation—by paper money in the 'sixties and by silver coinage in the 'nineties. Between these two eras of violent public political campaigns—of the "Greenback"

NATIONAL HOUSEKEEPING

and "Silver" parties—we had a lot of panics for the opposite reason—that money was scarce, instead of cheap. *These are the two big dangers—that the money of a country is either too scarce or too plentiful.* In the latter case, it is almost sure to go down in value.

To get a true picture of the world's money background we must think of a pair of scales. On one side are *all the goods in the world* —if one could imagine that!—and on the other *all the money.* The ideal state of things is when the two sides balance. What else is in the scales besides the goods on one side, and the money on the other? With the goods there are *price tags*—changeable every day, so that, as we have said in the chapter on buying, rates can rise or fall with the *supply* and the *demand* for them.

Those are the two chief things that regulate prices of any goods, but *there is another, and that is, how much money there is on the other side of the scales.* Just as when the money of the conquered countries flowed into Rome, and in our own day when the gold of Europe has flowed to America to settle foreign debts, *prices went up.* To balance the added money, we may say, heavier price-tags must be added on the opposite side of the scales!

There is one other thing about money: it is different from any other sort of goods in the world because it is not meant to consume— it is only meant to be used for a time and then passed on. Its value is not the same at all times. * Apart from the rise and fall of prices for goods (caused by supply and demand), *money itself rises and falls in value, of buying power.** *Money is more valuable according to the speed with which it changes hands.* It is for use as a *means,* not an *end.* So to the picture of the scales we must add the new and strange sight of money in the one pan always being *in motion*! We can think of it as a whirlpool, churning at different rates of speed. This is surely a "new one" on the men who study physics, or the science of matter and motion. *Here is a stuff that gains in "weight" in proportion as it whirls about*!

The whole science of banking is the business of keeping this stream of money flowing. *The most fatal thing that can happen is for it to stop!* This is what causes all panics. The aim of all governments is to keep their money in this fluid state: *when it freezes into the ice of a "cornering" or hoarding,* or else flows down and out the drain pipe of foreign debt-payment—the business man mops his brow and

---

* You may say that it is only "supply" and "demand" for money that makes this happen, but *it is a different kind from that for other goods.* It is "demand for the use of money for a certain time", not for using up. The supply is not just how much there is off hand to loan, but *how often the same sum can be used by different men.* A hundred dollars loaned to seven different men in succession is about as valuable as seven hundred that is only to be had by one man (for the same time as each of the seven had the $100.) Time of use is the new thing to consider.

says, "Good night!" What the real cure for wavering prices of goods and values of money is, has been agreed upon by hardly two men who have studied it!*

But by far the greater job is that of keeping the stream of money flowing evenly—and so keeping money-values level. When some genius finds a system to do this over the entire civilized earth—as in time someone may—he will have earned the thanks of a freed money world! What is needed is a series of world-wide "locks" or "dams," where the stream may be checked or added to. Those who look into the future can see a time when the financial system of the world will not be split up into little, badly communicating parts. It will be a big page in the program of the future—when the world will surely be better organized—and when that day comes, the Romance of Money will be a brighter record than it is now!

* Some say that the price of goods should be kept steady by having a "sliding-scale" of money, so that the dollar would sometimes be reduced to seventy-five cents, let us say, when goods were low. This would cause them to go up proportionately. This is probably an impossible plan, as prices of different goods vary.

THE READER'S GUIDE

INTRODUCTION

In justice to the contents of "The Outline of Knowledge" and to those who wish to derive the greatest benefit from it, use of "The Reader's Guide" which follows is recommended. It is in no wise obligatory. Readers who prefer to devote their attention to some one specific study or subject, without correlating it with others, are entirely free to do so: each of the twenty volumes of this compendium of the world's knowledge is complete in itself.

On the other hand "The Outline of Knowledge", which may be said to represent the quintessence of the more than 5,000,000 books existant, has been prepared with one great truth constantly in view: *that every American has a right to acquire the essence of a college education without being bored.*

A diversified acquaintance with all *practically* as well as *mentally* and *spiritually* useful subjects is within the reach of every owner of "The Outline of Knowledge". And the "Outline" differs from every other collection of its kind by making the acquisition of this knowledge a pleasure instead of a task.

"The Reader's Guide" maps out a tentative educational course, starting from the beginning and following a logical line of consequent development. It takes for granted that in the half or three-quarters of an hour the reader may devote to it every day for a year, that he will read from twenty to forty pages of text, more or less. Yet the course is an elastic one. This represents an average of pages arrived at, though many a reader will be sufficiently interested to read more. The individual links of a reading course cannot, of course, always be of absolutely equal length, like the units of a string of sausages. Some may be somewhat longer, others somewhat shorter, for their length is fixed by their subject, not by arbitrary pagination. If our subject ends with page 28 we do not carry on two more pages merely to make thirty. And if the reader wishes to pass at once to some particular period of the world's history, some phase of religious or philosophic thought, some movement in literature or science in which he is especially interested, he can pick up the course at any given point and read.

All references conform to the following order and refer to the individual volumes of "The Outline of Knowledge": Vol....., Chapter....., pp...... and each unit of "The Reader's Guide" represents a week of seven days. The reader should not be intimidated by the number of "Chapters" he may be called upon to peruse. These Chapters are in nearly all cases intentionally short. They avoid the prolix and carry the reader along in a vivid, gripping, colorful flow of narrative.

FIRST WEEK

MONDAY

All things have a beginning. And the beginning of everything on the earth below and in the heavens above is told in the first three chapters of "The Romance of Evolution".

Vol. I, Chapters 1, 2, 3, pp. 1—30.

TUESDAY

The story of the unfolding of the entire vegetable kingdom out of the *first life-cell* and its ultimate development into the fauna of to-day is continued and completed in three short chapters. In connection with Vol. I, Chapter 6, "Trees and the Romance of Flowering Plants", we suggest a pleasant side excursion to another volume of the "Outline". Then begins the tale of "Earth's First Living Animals", whose first two chapters bring us to a great event in Evolution's story, *the laying of the first egg to boast a shell!*

Vol. I, Chapters 4, 5, 6 and 7, pp. 31—51
Vol. I, Chapter 8, 9, 10, pp. 52—67.
Vol. XV, "Lebanon of the Flourishing Cedars", pp. 238—243.

WEDNESDAY

The thrilling, romantic details of "Life's Reptile Nightmare on Land" (and in the sea as well) are unfolded in the pages which follow, and carry us to the first step which leads life out of the reptile into the mammal class, the development of a creature with a *four-chambered heart,* the very first of mammals, without whose coming man might never have been evolved.

Vol. I, Chapters 11, 12, 13 and 14, pp. 68—91.

THURSDAY

From the origin of the four-chambered heart and the eventual birth of the first *warm-blooded* creature, synonomous with the coming of mother-love to earth, the fascinating story of the evolution of life from atom to ape is continued. And then, in the depths of Nature's jungle-laboratory, we assist in the wonderful experiments destined to produce the *Common Ancestor* of the highest type of ape and the lowest form of man.

Vol. I, Chapters 15 and 16, pp. 92—120

FRIDAY

The four chapters, covering æons of years, of the Second Part of "The Romance of Evolution", the fascinating tale of "Man and Ape" explain how one particular family of mammals was chosen as the *original stock* of human development. We are shown the *first human footprint in the sands of time,* and the four outstanding types of earliest man-apes or ape-men established by Science are called upon to tell their own life stories. Then, in another chapter, the development of men's blood- but not soul-brethren, the great apes is traced, and the stage prepared for the coming of the "True Man"

Vol. I, Chapters 17, 18, 19 and 20, pp. 123—150

SATURDAY

And now, with the coming of the "Reindeer Men", earth's first "True Men", we learn how inconceivably strange, repellant and primitive a life *we* lived in the twilight time of the race. We follow the Reindeer Men "Over the Edge of the World"; we thrill to the romantic theories Science has woven about the movements of the primal groups of earth-folk, the Azilians, the "People of the Painted Pebbles", and Neolithic or Stone Age men, and we follow with keenest interest early man's tangled race-trails, for they are *our* race-trails as well! The gradual separation of man into tribes and races differing in kind, color and appearance, the whys and wherefores of these millennial charges, and the actual development of articulate language out of grunts and cries is traced. In this connection we may well spare a few minutes to consider "The Growth of Language" (2), as described from another angle, in "The History of Literature"; and the section "Primitive Man" in "The History of the World".

Vol. I, Chapters 21, 22, 23 and 24, pp. 151—175

Vol. XI, Chapter 1, pp. 2—7

Vol. IV, Chapter 1, pp. 2—6

SUNDAY

Curiously enough, the first Sunday of our course offers a highly appropriate subject for consideration: *the beginning of religion*. No story ever told exceeds in fascination that of the growth of religion in the human soul, and with the chapter entitled "Groping for God and Finding a Snake", should be read "How Religion Came to Be", the Introduction to Vol. II of the "Outline". One supplements the other. Following "How Religion Came to Be", Chapter I of "The Story of Religion" should be read. It deals with "The Soul", the human soul, *in which, of which and through which* religion developed.

In connection with one of the most vivid subdivisions of the chapter dealing with "The Soul", that entitled "The Head Soul" (Vol. II, p. 11), the reader will enjoy the corroborative *contemporary* glimpse of the horrors of skull-worship contained in the article, "Formosa and Its Head Hunters", in the "Travel" volume of the "Outline". And in the same volume the article "With Cannibals in the South Seas" may be read in sequence to the subdivision of the chapter

on "The Soul" in "The Story of Religion" which it supplements.
   Vol. I, Chapter 25 pp. 176—183
   Vol. II, Introduction and Chapter 1, pp. 1—17
   Vol. XV, "Formosa and Its Head Hunters", pp. 358—363
   Vol. XV, "With Cannibals of the South Seas", pp. 349—357

SECOND WEEK
MONDAY

Turning once more from things divine to things mundane, from the skies to earth, a short chapter, brimful of interest, "Marriages Not Made in Heaven", deals with earth's primitive forms of mating and marrying. Following it we have a chapter on "How Art Came into the World". "Life-reels" of the Bronze Age give us the intimate feeling and contact with our ancestors who stand on the farther side of the threshold of history proper. In connection with the *mental* life of later Neolithic Man the chapters on "Fetishism" and "Animal Worship" in "The Story of Religion" as well as the first three pages of "The Romance of the Dance" may profitably be read. Here, too, we may trace the simple beginnings of something that interests every human in the world—money!

   Vol. I, Chapters 26, 27 and 28, pp. 184—199
   Vol. III, Chapter 2, pp. 18—26, and Chapter 6, pp. 52—60
   Vol. II, "The Romance of the Dance", pp. 475—478
   Vol. XX, "The Romance of Money in Past Ages", Chapter
      1, pp. 231—236

TUESDAY

The "Romance of Evolution", the story of the development of all life in general and human life in particular, from the birth of the vital spark in the Infinite to the point where man sets his foot across the threshold of actual history, ends with a glorious, colorful, thrilling yet scientifically motived story, the wonderful "Romance of the Lost Continent".

In literature the lost continent of Atlantis has supplied the germ lived under the most perfect conditions possible, the ideal republic which has been the dream of the greatest writers and philosophers. Plato developed it in his "Republic"; and Bacon in his "New Atlantis" (1624) in which he makes science the key to universal happiness. And if the reader would enjoy a visit to some glorious Atlantide cities of ideal happiness, let him turn to the pages of Sir Thomas More's "Utopia" (Vol. XVI) and to Tommaso Campanella's "Civitas Solis" (Vol. II), to discover a world where all is perfect.

   Vol. I, Chapter 29, pp. 200—213
   Vol. XVI, Sir Thomas More, "Utopia", pp. 142—238
   Vol. II, Tommaso Campanella's "City of the Sun", Chapter 23, p. 285

THE READER'S GUIDE

WEDNESDAY

Before considering man in the valley of the Nile, the cradle of history, some readers may prefer to hark back to various specific *scientific* viewpoints of special phases of humanity's development already painted in broader and more sweeping lines in "The Romance of Evolution". If so, the science of Geology offers colorful pages regarding the "Myths of the Earth's Origin"; and the science of Biology supplies four fascinating chapters which should be read in succession: "The Science of Life"; "What is Life", "The Physiological Idea in Life" and "The Origin of Life".

Vol. VI, "Geology", Chapter 1, pp. 1—10
Vol. VI, "Biology", Chapters 1, 2, 3, 4, pp. 197—234

THURSDAY

What has just been said with regard to the chapters of "Geology" and "Biology" to which the attention of the reader has been drawn, also applies to the science of "Anthropology"—which includes *the entire past of man!* This first evening, after reading an Introduction which "places" the science of Anthropology as such, we may consider the chapters which deal with "Man's Place in Nature", "Individualities in Structure" and "The Unity and Variety of Man".

Vol. VII, "Anthropology", Introduction, Chapters 1, 2, 3, pp. 323—356

FRIDAY

Our second anthropological evening will cover "The Racial Divisions of Man", "Prehistoric Archeology"—which goes into stimulating detail regarding the way in which the dead stones, implements and inscriptions of the past supply the skeleton of fact which scientists clothe in the flesh and blood of actuality—and a wonderful chapter on "The Development of Culture". In the "Travel" idea of *all* the descriptions of the ideal commonwealth, whose people volume of our series, the articles dealing with "The Singing People of the South Seas" and "The Pigmies of the Philippines" may be read as present-day literary tid-bits.

Vol. VII, "Anthropology", Chapters 4, 5, 6, pp. 357—386
Vol. XV, "Travel", "The Singing People of the South Seas", pp. 192—202 and "Pigmies of the Philippines" pp. 225—231

SATURDAY

Ancient Egypt, the Egypt of the Pyramids, is the first country to confront us on the threshold of history. It is a land whose tale is so diversified, so fascinating, so full of thrilling interest, that we will devote several consecutive evenings to it.

First, glance over the two short pages of the Introduction to "The Romance of Human Life Through the Ages". They will give you an idea of how manifold are the subjects which we have to consider in their proper correlation. Then, for your *historic background,* into which all later details fit, read the chapters which deal with Ancient Egypt in "The History of the World". You will be surprised to find how clear and interesting they are. And now let us take up the famous work of the "Father of History", Herodotus, the first great writer who combined a modern "news sense" with a fascinating style, and follow his account of how he got to the land he wished to study and describe at a time when only gods moved with the swiftness of the automobile or the aeroplane.

    Vol. I, "The Romance of Human Life Through the Ages", Introduction, pp. 219, 220

    Vol. IV, "History of the World", Chapter 2, pp. 9—16; Chapter 3, pp. 22—37; Chapter 4, pp. 43—45

    Vol. XVI, Herodotus, "Egypt", pp. 1—18

    Vol XX, "The Romance of Money in Past Ages," Chapter 2, "When Pharaoh Was the World's First Financier", pp. 238—240

SUNDAY

Nothing is more stimulating and broadening than the comparison of our own faith with the beliefs of nations dead and gone. In Vol. II, "The Story of Religion", under the head of "The Religion of Ancient Egypt", the tale is told. And the reader should supplement this twentieth-century study of a dead faith, with the account of the intelligent sceptic Herodotus, who wrote when that faith was still alive. To complete your knowledge turn also to the short section in the "Romance of Architecture", Vol. III, called "The Mystery of the Pyramids", and learn how these monuments reflected the *Egyptian's belief in the immortality of the soul!* Music, in Ancient Egypt, was closely associated with religion, and in the same volume, in "The Romance of Music", the first chapter gives us fascinating sidelights on their interrelation.

    Vol. II, Chapter 9, "The Religion of Ancient Egypt", p. 88

    Vol. XVI, Herodotus, p. 18 (35)—p. 38 (76)

    Vol. III, Chapter 1, pp. 14, 15, "The Romance of Architecture"

    Vol. III, Chapter 1, pp. 320—323, "The Romance of Music"

THIRD WEEK

MONDAY

Monday is a workday, and we shall devote it to the colorful record of actual, everyday life in ancient Egypt. Herodotus's chatty, vivid traveler's notes on the strange people whose manners and customs he observed open up a new world, a dead world which lives again in his winged words, for our incredulous appreciation. And the "Pictures of Life in Ancient Egypt", in Vol. I, "The Romance of

Human Life Through the Ages", supplement the information Herodotus gathered from the Egyptian priests with a wealth of quaint and thrilling fact which the patient labors of scientists have established on the basis of the hieroglyphics.

> Vol. XVI, Herodotus, "Egypt", p. 38 ¶77—p. 62 ¶122
> Vol. I, "The Romance of Human Life Through the Ages",
>   Chapter I, pp, 221—243

TUESDAY

In "The Romance of Architecture", Vol. III, after reading the Introduction ("What Architecture Means"), "The Land of the Pyramids" should first be read. Then, in Herodotus's rambling style, we get the impressions of a traveler who saw the Egyptian monuments 300 years before Christ was born. "The Chisellers of Ancient Egypt", in "The Romance of Sculpture" gives us a glimpse of Egyptian sculpture; and we may supplement this whole vivid study of ancient Egyptian art with some twentieth-century impressions contained in our "Travel" volume.

> Vol. III, "Romance of Architecture", Introduction, "What Architecture Means", pp. 9, 10; and Chapter 1, pp. 11—20
> Vol. XVI, Herodotus, "Egypt", p. 63 ¶124—p. 91 ¶182
> Vol. III, "The Romance of Sculpture", Preface and Chapter I, pp. 139—141
> Vol. XV, "Travel", article "Climbing the Pyramids", pp. 452—454

WEDNESDAY

There are other ancient empires whose life story is no less interesting than that of Egypt—the empires of the Mesopotamian valley, Sumeria, Chaldea, Babylon and Assyria. First taking up their historic background in (Vol. IV), "The History of the World", we pass to their human, red-blood aspects of daily existence in "The Romance of Human Life Through the Ages", Chapter 2, the "Life Romances of Babylon and Assyria". In Vol. XX, "Babylon, Ruler of the Ancient Money World", and "The Dawn of Bookkeeping and Credit" tell us how. Various selections from the individual books of "The Romance of the Arts" will round out our knowledge of this by-gone world.

> Vol. IV, Chapter 2, pp. 16—21 and Chapter 4, pp. 53—66
> Vol. I, "The Romance of Human Life Through the Ages", Chapter 2, pp. 244—253
> Vol. III, "The Romance of Architecture", Chapter 2, pp. 21—23
> Vol. III, "The Romance of Sculpture", Chapter 1, pp. 141, 142
> Vol. III, "The Romance of Music", Chapter 2, pp. 324—326
> Vol. III, "The Romance of the Dance", Assyria, pp. 479, 480

Vol. XX, "The Romance of Money in Past Ages", Chapter 2, pp. 237—243

THURSDAY

And now for an interlude before we continue the unrolling of history's great scroll. Let us spend an evening or two with nature taking Chapter V (Vol. VI), "The Mystery of the Cell", out of which the teeming millions of Egypt and Assyria as well as all else that lives and breathes, was evolved. Chapters on "Seeing the Creature Grow", "Organic Functions" and "Life Processes" will make us realize that these processes of organic growth apply to plants as well as men, and form a natural introduction to an evening of Botany.

Vol. VI, "Biology", Chapters 5, 6, 7, 8, pp. 235—278

FRIDAY

Botany is one of the most fascinating subjects in all nature study. And the first five chapters of "Botany" (Vol. VII), lead us from "Early Development" through "Plant Structures", special "Reproduction Structures" and "Classification", to an art every one should acquire: "How to Know the Flowers".

Vol. VII, "Botany", Chapters 1, 2, 3, 4, 5, pp. 1—47

SATURDAY

That the Chaldean astrologers were probably the first to make any record of the physical phenomena of science supplies us with a natural connecting link for a study of the wonderful science of physics. The first four chapters of "Physics" (Vol. VIII), beginning with "The Analysis of Matter", explain "Radio-Activity", "The Properties of Matter" and "Heat", and fix firmly in our minds the scientific fact of the correlation of ether-born heat and energy (which we have learned to know in "The Romance of Evolution") and the mighty forces of the atom.

Vol. VIII, "Physics", Chapters 1, 2, 3, 4, pp. 99—138

SUNDAY

We will gain an idea of the Assyrian religion in "The Story of Religion", Chapter 9, under the following paragraph-heads: "Babylonian and Assyrian Sun-Gods", "Ishtar and Astarte", and "A Religion of Grown-Up Children". Then, as a happy imaginative rounding-out of our Friday evening's "Botany", we may pass to "Stone, Tree, Plant and Flower Worshipers", Chapter 8, of "The Story of Religion", and devote the remainder of our time to the savagely cruel yet sanitarily civilized secular life of ancient Creta, the earliest development of Greek civilization. Our historic outline will be found in Chapter III of "The History of the World", entitled "The Ægean Isles and Coasts". The more vivid, intimate illumination of this historic outline will be found in Chapter 3 of "The Story of

Human Life Through the Ages", entitled "The Land of the Double Axes"; while in "The Romance of Architecture" the specific art development of old Mycenæ is described in "The Palaces of the Sea-Kings".

> Vol. II, "The Story of Religion", Chapter 9, pp. 93—96
> Vol. II, "The Story of Religion", Chapter 8, pp. 73—80
> Vol. IV, Chapter 3, pp. 37—42
> Vol. I, "The Romance of Life Through the Ages", Chapter 3, pp. 254—258
> Vol. III, "The Romance of Architecture", Chapter 6, pp. 39, 40

FOURTH WEEK

MONDAY

We must now leave the isles of Greece and return to Asia, the Asia which is teeming with still other races and peoples besides the Egyptians and Assyrians. Our historic background for the story of the Hebrews will be found in Vol. IV, Chapter 4, "The Semitic Area from 1200 to 538 B.C." "The Romance of Human Life Through the Ages", Vol. II, Chapter 4, gives us "Glimpses of Human Nature from Old Semitic Lands", in particular a wonderful account of the Hebrew crossing of the Red Sea from an *Egyptian* angle, and sidelights of life in ancient Tyre; as well as an insight into the character of the wild desert Arabian tribes of the time. No account of the ancient Hebrews which does not deal with their finances would seem complete. In Vol. XX these are discussed under the heading: "The Golden Age of Judah".

> Vol. IV, Chapter 4, pp. 43—57
> Vol. I, "The Romance of Life Through the Ages", Chapter 4, pp. 259—270
> Vol. XX, "The Romance of Money in Past Ages", Chapter 2, pp. 240, 241

TUESDAY

This Tuesday evening, following out the developments of the evening before we may regard, educationally speaking, as a species of Jewish holiday. To this end we recommend in "The Story of Religion", Vol. II, the chapter entitled "The Religion of the Hebrews and Judaism". Chapter 9 of the same volume gives an interesting portrait of Lillith, "The Sorceress of the Jewish Paradise"; Vol. IX contains an historical introduction to "The Psalms", Vol. XI reviews the Bible as a whole; and Vol. III contains studies of two cultural developments, "The Dances of the Jews", and "The Legends of Joseph". In connection with the religious beliefs of the Phœnicians, read in "The Story of Religion", Chapter 9, the sections "Moloch" and "Astarte, the Ishtar of Syrian Hieropolis"; and in "The Romance of Human Life Through the Ages", in Chapter 8, the thrilling "Sacrifice to Moloch".

Vol. II, "The Story of Religion", Chapter 15, pp. 144—160
Vol. II, "The Story of Religion", Chapter 9, p. 94
Vol. IX, "The Psalms", p. 311
Vol. XI, "Sacred Book of the Ancients", Chapter 3, pp. 15—18
Vol. III, "The Romance of the Dance", pp. 481, 482 and pp. 488, 489
Vol. II, "The Story of Religion", Chapter 9, pp. 94—96
Vol. I, "The Romance of Human Life Through the Ages", Chapter 8, pp. 314—317

WEDNESDAY

To-night we will set about preparing ourselves for an intimate acquaintance with two ancient nations, Persia and Greece, whose destinies are inextricably interwoven for hundreds of years. Our preparation will consist of a quiet, studious reading of a single illuminating chapter of "The History of the World".

Vol. IV, Chapter 5, pp. 69—89

THURSDAY

First we will read the vivid pages of the short chapter in Vol. I, "The Romance of Human Life Through the Ages", called "Out of the Persian Past". Then, with no falling off of interest, we will take up various art developments of the ancient Persians, their architecture (2), their sculpture (3), their music (4), their dance (5), and their money (6). In Vol. II, Chapter 2, "The Story of Religion", their faith, Zoroastrianism, is described under the head of "The Noblest of the Sun Cults"; in Vol. XI, chapter 4, the sacred books of the Persians are specifically dealt with; and in Vol. IX, "Sacred Writings", the reader should read the Preface, "The Bible of Zoroaster", p. 137, and may dip at leisure into the Zend-Avesta itself (pp. 138—198) to enjoy some of its fine moral lessons and teachings, if so inclined. As a literary dessert every reader will enjoy the thrilling tale of "The Ring of Gyges". It shows the tragedy of the soul-conflict due to diametrically opposite ideas of decency.

Vol. I, "The Romance of Human Life Through the Ages", Chapter 5, pp. 271—275
Vol. III, "Romance of Architecture", Chapter 3, "Persia's Towers of Silence and Royal Halls", pp. 24—26
Vol. III, "Romance of Sculpture", Chapter 1, "The Persian Stone-Cutters", p. 143
Vol. III, "The Romance of Music", see "The Music of the Ancient Persians", pp. 326, 327
Vol. III, "The Romance of the Dance", see "Persian", p. 481

Vol. XX, "The Romance of Money in Past Ages", Chapter 3, "Persia, the Land of War Profiteers", pp. 247—248

Vol. XI, Chapter 4, pp. 26—29

Vol. IX, p. 137

Vol I, "The Romance of Human Life Through the Ages", see "Asian Greece", pp. 288—296

FRIDAY

Two sources supply our reading matter for this evening. We have learned to know the ancient Persians; we must now make the acquaintance of their foes, the ancient Greeks. Let us prepare our historical background of appreciation by reading "The Crash of East and West", i.e., of Persia and Greece, in Chapter 6 of "The History of the World"; and as a delightful excursion into the field of biography follow it up by reading Plutarch's "Life of Themistocles", the greatest of Greek heroes of the "Crash" in question.

Vol. IV, Chapter 6, pp. 90—101

Vol. XVI, Plutarch, "Themistocles", pp. 241—265

SATURDAY

To-night instead of establishing our historical background by means of a chapter in "The History of the World", we will devote the entire evening to one of the most brilliant, vivid, illuminating biographies ever written—Plutarch's "Life of Pericles". It will give the reader the feeling of direct contrast with the "famous Age of Pericles", the greatest epoch in the history of ancient Greece. To complete, it is the most eloquent and moving speech the great politician ever made, in his own words, which have been preserved for us.

Vol. XVI, "Plutarch's Lives", Pericles, pp. 266—299

Vol. XVIII, "Famous Orations", See Pericles's "Funeral Oration on the Athenians Who First Fell in the Pelopennesian War", pp. 253—259

SUNDAY

Once more Sunday has arrived—a fitting day for a peep into the religious life of ancient Greece. First of all, let the reader turn the pages of "The Story of Religion", Vol. II, until he reaches Chapter 14, which deals with "Greek and Roman Mythology". Let him read from the beginning of the chapter to and including the section entitled, "The Religious Mysteries and the Greek Philosophies". He can then turn with understanding to Vol. XIX, and in "The Tales of Ancient Greece", make the acquaintance of some of the loveliest legends of the old Greek gods.

Vol. II, Chapter 14, pp. 130—134

Vol. XIX, "The Tales of Ancient Greece", pp. 281—307

412   THE READER'S GUIDE

FIFTH WEEK

MONDAY

The gods of Greece and the old Greek heroes belong together. And to understand the human life, politics and the arts in the Age of Pericles, we should feel at home in Greek legend and literature. In Vol. XI, in "The History of Literature", the chapter devoted to "The Classic Epics" explains Hesiod, the "Illiad" and the "Odessey" of Homer, and other leading works, as well as taking up Virgil's "Æneid", which continues Homer's tale of Troy Town. This may be supplemented by reading in Vol. XIX, Hawthorne's lovely retelling of "The Tale of the Golden Fleece". Then, too, we have what is perhaps the greatest drama of the heroic times of Greece, Æschylus's tragedy of "Agamemnon". If the reader does not care to follow it at length, let him at all events read the admirable "Introductory Remarks".

>   Vol. XI, "The History of Literature", Chapter 5, "The Classic Epics", pp. 34—42
>   Vol. XIX, "The Golden Fleece", pp. 308—333
>   Vol. XVII, Sophocles, "Agamemnon", pp. 1—53

TUESDAY

We may well assign one more evening to some other wonderful efforts of the Attic imagination, before reverting to the lower plane of the historic everyday—though the historic everyday in ancient times is very colorful. If we read Æschylus's great tragedy "Agamemnon", we are in duty bound almost, to make the acquaintance of the "Antigone" (Vol. XVII, pp. 57—95) by the second great Greek dramatist, Sophocles. And in connection with it, to understand how the Greek theater was conducted and what it was like, we should first read Vol. III, "The Romance of Architecture", Chapter VI, "The Glory That Was Greece". Incidentally, any reader who in leisure moments not included in the reading course wishes to dip into Æsop's delightful "Fables" (Vol. XIX, pp. 425—502), should first read in Vol. VI, "Zoology", Chapter I, "Zoology in Fable", pp. 391—394.

>   Vol. III, "The Romance of Architecture", Chapter 6, "The Glory That was Greece", pp. 39—47

WEDNESDAY

It is time to vary our excursions into Greek literature by visiting with live, everyday human beings, instead of the idealized creatures of the poet's fancy. Chapter 7, Vol. IV supplies the historic background for the Age of Pericles; and Chapter 6, Vol. I, "The Romance of Human Life Through the Ages", well called "Some Curious Phases of Ancient Greek Life", initiates us in strange developments of the political and sex life of the ancients. In connection with these sparkling, spicy pages we also may drink our first draught of Attic philosophy, in Vol. II, second portion of Chapter 14, from the section beginning "The Religious Mysteries and the Greek Philosophies", to "Earlier and Later Roman Beliefs". In Vol. XIII, "Philosophy", the choicest wisdom of Plato and Socrates, embodied in the latter's gratest "Dialogues", "Phædo or the Immortality of the Soul" (pp. 1—62), and the "Phædrus" (pp. 63—116) will allow the reader to delve deeper into his realm of thought.

> Vol. IV, Chapter 7, "Athens, Sparta, Thebes, Syracuse", pp. 102—113
>
> Vol. I, "Romance of Life Through the Ages", Chapter 6, pp. 276—287
>
> Vol. II, "Story of Religion", Chapter 14, pp. 133—143

THURSDAY

We now know something of the *people* of the golden age of Greece, the Age of Pericles. It is time to turn to their accomplishments in the field of *art*. First, let us meet the great Greek sculptors in "The Great Sculptors and Statues of Greece", and reading the preceding summary of the development of painting, the great "Painters of Ancient Greece." We may then turn to the dance in ancient Greece, and end with a modern development, some of the most famous operas of the contemporary repertory which are founded on Greek legendary subjects. This last will help show us how important a part Greek culture still plays in our lives to-day. And here, too, though it is not an obligatory reading, we promise the reader that once he gets into the spirit of the greatest "musical comedy" of ancient times, "The Frogs", by Aristophanes, that he will not regret reading it (Vol. XVII, Aristophanes, "The Frogs", pp. 159—209). Money—pig-iron and purest gold—in ancient Greece is considered in Vol. XX, in the chapter entitled "The Moneybags of Crœsus and the Treasuries of Greece."

> Vol. III, "The Romance of Sculpture", Chapter 2, pp. 145—151
>
> Vol. III, "The Romance of Painting", Chapter 1, pp. 206—208
>
> Vol. III, "The Romance of Music", Chapter 4, pp. 334—337, (2d par.)
>
> Vol. III, "The Romance of the Dance", p. 482, 383
>
> Vol. III, "The Romance of Opera", pp. 434, 435, 436, 441, 442, 448
>
> Vol. XX, "The Romance of Money in Past Ages", Chapter 3, pp. 244—253

FRIDAY

To-night we may dip into the intimate *romance* of history, and devote some time to the emotional side of ancient royal and republican lives, in the Orient and in Greece.

XX

Vol. II, "The Personal Romance of History", Chapter 1,
  pp. 357—360, 368, 369
Vol. II, Chapter 2, pp. 370—375
Vol. II, Chapter 3, pp. 376—380

SATURDAY

To-night we return to our historical background. We will move from the Age of Pericles to that of Philip and Alexander of Macedon. To relieve this more serious reading we may turn to some of the great English poets and enjoy the fruit their imagination has drawn from the inspiration of ancient Greek legend and mythology. There is Ben Jonson's "Hymn to Diana"; John Keat's "On First Looking into Chapman's Homer"; Tennyson's "Ulysses"; Matthew Arnold's "The Song of Callicles"; and Shakespeare's wonderful, passionate "Venus and Adonis".

Vol. IV, Chapter 7, from section 111 on, pp. 113—133
Vol. XII, pp. 189, 190, 191, 244, 245, 86—117
Vol. XI, pp. 235—448

SUNDAY

We have already studied the religion of the ancient Greeks and their systems of philosophy, yet a reading in "Biology" is appropriate enough on a Sunday, for a consideration of the wonders of science invariably suggests the thought of a Supreme Being to whose creative instinct they are due. Resuming at "The Origin of Species in Plants and Animals", we may continue through "The Kinship of All Life" to "Evidences of Organic Development", subjects treated in a more informal yet no less informative way in "The Romance of Evolution".

Vol. VI, Chapters 9, 10, 11, 12, pp. 297—334

SIXTH WEEK

MONDAY

From the lofty plane of pure science we again return to the lowlier strata of human interest. In order properly to understand the Age of Alexander we must become acquainted with the reign of his father, King Philip of Macedon, who immediately preceded him. Chapter 8 (1), of "The History of the World" gives us our historic background. The cultural side may be represented by a study of Chapter 3 of "The Romance of Sculpture", entitled "From Praxiteles to the End of the Hellenistic Age." Since the reign of the Macedonian king Philip was almost completely occupied by the famous "two-man" struggle between himself, the representative of autocracy, and Demosthenes, the most fanatic and eloquent defender of the ancient liberties of decadent Greece, we turn to Plutarch's stirring account of this life-long battle between the two greatest men of their time, one of the truly great biographies of all history.

Vol. IV, Chapter 8 ¶1 "Philip", pp. 134—137

Vol. XVI, Plutarch, "Demosthenes", pp. 300—320

Vol. III, "The Romance of Sculpture", Chapter 3, pp. 149—153

TUESDAY

To-night we enter upon one of the most wonderful periods of all history, the Age of Alexander. Chapter 8 (II, III) in "The History of the World" tells the tale of the empire of Alexander the Great and of the kingdoms his generals founded upon its ruins. Then, in "The Romance of Human Life Through the Ages", we get the stirring *human* scenes which illustrate, enliven and clarify history's pages. In "The Personal Romance of History", Chapter 3, beginning with "Alexander's First Love", and running to the end of the chapter, the *heart-story* of earth's greatest conqueror is told; while in Chapter 3 of "The Romance of Money in Past Ages", the section entitled "Alexander as a Booster of Trade" will round out what has gone before.

Vol. IV, Chapter 8, "The Macedonian Supremacy", pp. 137—150

Vol. I, Chapter 7, "Some Pictures from the Age of Alexander", pp. 297—304

Vol. II, Chapter 3, "The Personal Romance of History" pp. 380—384

Vol. XX, Chapter 3, pp. 351, 352, "Alexander as a Booster of Trade".

WEDNESDAY

This evening's allotment of reading runs full sixty pages, yet what wonderful pages they are! They throw new lights and shadows on the incredible, spectacular career of Alexander of Macedon. It is a master biography traced by a master-hand—Plutarch's. It *is* history yet it reads like romance, and in connection with, the readings of the evening will enshrine the great Macedonian forever in our memory!

Vol. XVI, Plutarch, "Alexander", pp. 358—418

THURSDAY

With special reference to the world of *thought* of the Alexandrian epoch, we may once more read, in Chapter 14 of "The Story of Religion", the sections entitled "Aristotle" and "The Inwardness of Aristotle's Philosophy". And here, too, we may make a detour into a special *scientific* field, and read the first two chapters of "Medicine" (Vol. VIII) which cover all the ancient Greeks of Alexander's day knew of the subject, as well as whatever ideas of medicine were held by the ancient peoples of the Orient whom Alexander conquered. Here, too, a portion of Chapter 2, of "Geology", may be read. It is called "The Beginnings of Map-Making", and outlines to us the world as men knew it, physically, to the end of the Macedonian supremacy.

As supplementary reading, left to the reader's initiative, the three books of Aristotle's "Ethics", contained in the volume devoted to "Philosophy" (Vol. XIII, pp. 117—168), give the lofty ethical deductions of Alexander's famous teacher.

Vol. I, "The Story of Religion", Chapter 14, pp. 137—138
Vol. VIII, "Medicine", Chapters 1, 2, pp. 313—338
Vol. VI, "Geology", Chapter 2, pp. 11—24

FRIDAY

Before leaving Greek thought and Greek civilization to begin the study of the ancient Roman world, we may well devote another evening to "Physics". In the book of "Physics", the chapters: "The Sources of Light", "The Speed of Light", "Reflection and Refraction", and "The Nature of Light", will enable us to compare the *exact* and authoritative *knowledge* of science to-day! with the vague gropings of the early great thinkers.

Vol. VIII, "Physics", Chapters 5, 6, 7, 8, pp. 139—175

SATURDAY

The time has come to move on to another world of race and thought, and take up the story of "The Rise and Expansion of Rome", from 753—133 B.C., in the five sections of this chapter of "The History of the World"—"The Story of Early Rome", "The Institutions of Early Rome", "The Growth of the Roman Power in Italy", "The Struggle with Carthage" and "Expansion and Degeneration".

Vol. IV, Chapter 9, pp. 151—181

SUNDAY

To-day we will turn to fascinating detail studies of various phases of Roman life and culture belonging to the period historically described above. First, we may read Chapter 8 of "The Romance of Human Life Through the Ages" in its entirety. Then, in Vol. XX, Chapter 4, we may turn to three sections entitled: "When Rome was the Nerve-Center of the Money-World"; "A Workingman's Revolt in Old Rome"; and "Rome, Plunderer of the Whole Earth". In "The Personal Romances of History", Chapter 4, from the beginning to and inclusive of "The Tragedy of Virtuous Lucretia" should be read.

Vol. I, "The Romance of Human Life Through the Ages",
    Chapter 8, pp. 305—323
Vol. XX, "The Romance of Money in Past Ages", Chapter 4, pp. 254—258
Vol. II, "The Personal Romance of History", Chapter 4, pp. 385, 386

SEVENTH WEEK

MONDAY

In "The History of the World' 'the chapter entitled "A Century of Revolution", which takes us from the beginning of the revolutionary era to the death of Mark Antony, demands an entire evening of the course in order to be properly assimilated and digested. It deals with the world and the age of Cicero, Pompey, Julius Cæsar and Cleopatra.

>   Vol. IV, Chapter 10, pp. 182—209

TUESDAY

To-night we may fill in last night's historic outline with a wealth of fascinating detail regarding old Roman life and *morals* in "The Romance of Human Life Through the Ages", Chapter 9. In Chapter 4, of the "Romance of Money in Ages Past", read three sections entitled: "The Game of High Finance on Tiber's Shore", "The Bloody Tax Collectors of Old" and "When the King of Numidia Tried to Break Rome". And, to end on a more sober note, three of the greatest speeches ever delivered in ancient Rome (Vol. XVIII): Marcus Porcio Cato's "Speech in support of the Oppian Law", Cicero's "First Oration Against Catiline", the democratic extremist of the day; and Cæsar's "Speech Delivered on the Treatment of the Catilinarian Conspirators", whose attempt he is thought to have encouraged.

>   Vol. I, "The Romance of Human Life Through the Ages",
>   Chapters 9, pp. 324—328
>   Vol. XX, "The Romance of Money in Past Ages", Chapter 4, pp. 358—361
>   Vol. XVIII, "Famous Orations", pp. 260—278

WEDNESDAY

This evening we again devote to one man, yet Plutarch's life study of Rome's greatest orator and politician tells us so much about Rome and Roman affairs in general as well as about Cicero in particular, that we are carried along on the flow of his narrative without a single dull moment.

As a short, natural supplement to the life of this great master of the eloquent word, the reader might turn to Ralph Waldo Emerson's beautiful essay on "Language", in Vol. XIV ("Essays") of "The Outline", pp. 291—295. In addition, if having become interested in Cicero the *man*, you wish to make the acquaintance of Cicero, the *author*, his wonderful "Lælius or an Essay on Friendship", is at your disposal for supplementary reading (Vol. XVI, pp. 92—131).

>   Vol. XVI, Plutarch, "Cicero", pp. 321—357

THURSDAY

Pompey, the true champion of Roman aristocracy as Cæsar was the pretended one of Roman democracy, also has been made the subject of one of Plutarch's glowing biographies. It naturally follows that of Cicero, and is quite an enjoyable and informative to read.

>   Vol. XVI, Plutarch, "Pompey", pp. 465—508

FRIDAY

This evening, in the natural sequence of historic event, brings us to Julius Cæsar, whose name is still a household word in every home and school throughout the United States. Cæsar's biography, too, has been written by Plutarch and completes and supplements the two great preceding biographies which we have read.

>Vol. XVI, Plutarch, "Cæsar", pp. 419—464

SATURDAY

Where, among these illustrious Romans, is the famous Mark Antony, the reader may have asked. Antony's life-story already has been outlined in last Monday's chapter of history. To tell it in its intimate detail it is inseparable from that of the lovely Cleopatra, and to this pair of famous lovers, whose lives can no more be parted in a reading course than in reality, we will devote this evening. Chapter 1, of "The Personal Romance of History", beginning with the section "Cleopatra, the Serpent of Old Nile", to the conclusion of the chapter, unfolds what is perhaps the most thrilling and fascinating romance of love and politics the ancient world affords.

>Vol. II, "The Personal Romance of History", Chapter 1, pp. 360—369

SUNDAY

It is time to turn to the religious and philosophic beliefs and theories of the ancient Romans. Here the simplest and most direct way is to consider them as a *unit,* from the early days of the Roman republic to the introduction of Christianity in the Roman empire. To do so we turn to Chapter 14, of "The Story of Religion". It is entitled "Greek and Roman Religion, Mythology and Philosophic Thought", and beginning with the section entitled: "Earlier and Later Roman Beliefs", we read through to the end of the chapter. To this may be added certain especially interesting cultural and scientific aspects of the old Roman civilization: architecture, sculpture, medicine, music and the dance. In Vol. XIII, "Philosophy", uplifting moral thoughts of the greatest of Stoic philosophers of Rome—Greek Stoic philosophers already have been considered in "The Story of Religion", Chapter 14—are offered him in "The Moral Discourses of Epictetus" (pp. 169—252).

>Vol. II, "The Story of Religion", Chapter 14, pp. 140—143
>Vol. III, "The Romance of Architecture", Chapter 7, "Roman Architecture", pp. 48—57
>Vol. III, "The Romance of Sculpture", Chapter 4, pp. 154—156
>Vol. VIII, "Medicine", Chapter 3, "The Romans", pp. 339—346
>Vol. III, "The Romance of Music", Chapter 5, "Music in Republican and Imperial Rome", pp. 338—340

THE READER'S GUIDE

Vol. III, "The Romance of the Dance", see "Dancing in Ancient Rome", p. 483

EIGHTH WEEK

MONDAY

Before resuming history's tale with the beginnings of the Roman empire, we might make an excursion to the Orient. There two great empires of the past, India and China developed apart from the rest of the world. Let us first consider India. "The History of the World" gives us an admirable historic background (Chapter 12, 1). Then, in "The Romance of Human Life Through the Ages", Vol. I, Chapter 12, "Glimpses of the Indian and Chinese Soul", should be read. Finally, in "The Story of Religion", Vol. II, "The Brahminic Religions of Ancient India" are discussed in Chapter 12.

Vol. IV, Chapter 12 ¶1. "The Far East", (1. India), pp. 248—255

Vol. I, "The Romance of Human Life Through the Ages", Chapter XII, pp. 347—358

Vol. II, "The Story of Religion", Chapter 12, "The Brahminic Religions of India", pp. 113—123

TUESDAY

To-night we may take up some of the fascinating cultural developments of the old East Indian civilization. We may turn to its architecture, music and dancing, in the various books of Vol. III, "The Romance of the Arts", and to these we might add an interesting modern glimpse of old religious superstitions which have survived the ages in "Travel", the article entitled "The Superstitious East Indian", and a present-day view of "Bombay, the Queen of Indian Cities", in the same volume. As supplementary reading to these two chapters, the authentic "Bible of Brahmanism", in Vol. IX, "Sacred Writings", pp. 1—72, is available. A delightful fable from the old Sanskrit "Hitapodesa", to which the reader may be more apt to turn, will be found in Vol. XIX, p. 502.

Vol. III, "The Romance of Architecture", Chapter 4, "Architecture's Land of License", pp. 27—29

Vol. III, "The Romance of Music", Chapter 3, "Music in India", pp. 328—333

Vol. III, "The Romance of the Dance", p. 480, "India", "The Blue God".

Vol. XV, "Travel", pp. 336—342

Vol. XV, "Travel", pp. 364—371

WEDNESDAY

A special development of ancient Hindoo religious belief and one which has spread to other lands is *Buddhism*. First of all, we must read the vivid chapter devoted to "Buddhism", in "The Story of

Religion", in which special attention has been paid the life, teachings and miracles of Gautama Buddha, the founder of this faith. This, if he wish, the reader may supplement with some of the beautiful *suttas* which make up the "Bible of Buddhism" (Vol. IX, "Sacred Writings", pp. 73—136). Obligatory, however, if we are to gain an idea of the *spread* of the Buddhist faith, is the reading of Chapter 4, of "The Story of Religion", the short concluding sections which deal with Buddhism in China and Japan. In addition there are admirable pages dealing with Hindoo religious thought, Vedic and Buddhist, in Vol. XI, "The History of Literature", and the same volume also contains a chapter devoted to the old Sanskrit hero tales, "The Epics of the Orient".

Vol. II, "The Story of Religion", Chapter 13, pp. 124—129
Vol. II, "The Story of Religion", Chapter 4, pp. 37—40
Vol. XI, "The History of Literature", Chapter 3, pp. 20—25
Vol. XI, "The History of Literature", Chapter 6, pp. 43—54

THURSDAY

Our historical background is supplied by the second section "China", of Chapter 12, of "The History of the World", and thence we may pass at once to the great Chinese religions, Confucianism and Taoism, in "The Story of Religion". *These chapters should be read in the order given below.* In "The History of Literature" certain pages are devoted to Confucianism and as non-obligatory supplemental reading we have (Vol. IX, "Sacred Writings", pp. 199—268) "The Bible of Confucius". And now for some cultural aspects: Human Life is touched on in Vol. I; architecture and music in Vol. III; and, for a lighter moment of pure enjoyment we may turn to Vol. XIV.

Vol. IV, Chapter 12, pp. 255—259
Vol. II, "The Story of Religion", Chapter 5, "Chinese Mythology and Ancient Worship (Confucianism), pp. 41—51
Vol. II, "The Story of Religion", Chapter 4, "Taoism and Chinese Buddhism", pp. 37—40
Vol. III, "The Romance of Architecture", Chapter 5, "Where Nature is Architecture's Twin", pp. 34—38
Vol. III, "The Romance of Music", Chapter 3, "Music in the Land of the Yellow Men", pp. 330—333
Vol. XIV, Lamb's Essays, "A Dissertation on Roast Pig", pp. 486—491

FRIDAY

In Chapter II of "The History of the World", "The Roman Empire", 29 B.C.—A.D. 395, the sections: 1. "The Principate", 2. "The Julian Emperors" (Augustus to Nero); 3. "The Flavians and Antoines"; 4. "The Prætorian Emperors"; 5. "The Reconstructed Empire" and 6. "The Rise of Christianity, carry us up to the period of the breaking-up of the empire, and will supply the historic background essential for the proper understanding of subsequent readings.

Vol. IV, Chapter II, ¶1, 2, 3, 4, pp. 210—247

SATURDAY

To-night we may fill in our preceding historic outline with all picturesque and colorful *human* interest which, if properly presented makes history the most interesting study in the world. First, let us read Chapter 10 of "The Romance of Human Life Through the Ages", next read in "The Personal Romance of History", Chapter 4: "Was Cæsar Romantic?" "Mysterious Tiberius", "The Man who Taxed Marriage", "Messalina", "A Ruling Passion Strong in Death", "Poppæa, the Empress who Bathed in Milk", "Octavia and Poppæ", "Nero's Love-Kick", "Material for Psychoanalysis Rather than Romance". This may be followed (Chapter 4, "The Romance of Money in Past Ages") by the sections: "The Sins of the Money-Mad Empire", "Christ Preaches the Doctrine of Socialism", and "The Doom of Bankrupt Rome".

> Vol. I, "The Romance of Human Life Through the Ages", Chapter 10, "From Augustus to Augustulus", pp. 329—339
>
> Vol. II, "The Personal Romance of History", Chapter 4, pp. 386—393
>
> Vol. XX, "The Romance of Money in Past Ages", Chapter 4, pp. 254—264

SUNDAY

This is the first *Christian* Sunday of our reading-course! The story of imperial Rome and that of Christianity are connected and interwoven, and Chapter 17 of "The Story of Religion", entitled "From Christ's Nativity to the Earthquake Martyr", will bring us to the reign of the philosopher Emperor Marcus Aurelius. In "The Romance of Human Life Through the Ages", read Chapter II, "A Quartet of Martyrs"; John Milton's "On the Morning of Christ's Nativity" (Vol. XI, Milton, pp. 463—470), and Dryden's "Song for St. Cecilia's Day" (Vol. XI, Dryden, pp. 281—283).

> Vol. II, "The Story of Religion", Chapter 17, pp. 184—192
>
> Vol. I, "The Romance of Human Life Through the Ages", Chapter 11, pp. 340—346

NINTH WEEK

MONDAY

In "The Story of Religion", Chapter 18, "Gnosticism", and Chapter 19, "From Heliogabalus to Julian the Apostate", cover the period of our historic outline chapter (last Friday), and show developments full of engrossing interest. As supplementary reading to Chapter

18, the reader will find in Vol. XIII, ("Philosophy", pp. 253—305) the sublime "Meditations of Marcus Aurelius".

    Vol. II, "The Story of Religion", Chapter 18, pp. 193—198

    Vol. II, "The Story of Religion", Chapter 19, pp. 199—216

TUESDAY

We now stand, historically, on the threshold of the Middle Ages, and, can afford to turn from man to beast, thinking as we do that in this period of history beast may set men a good example. We already have read the chapter entitled "Zoology in Fable" in the proper connection. This evening three chapters on: "Development and Distribution" in the bestiary, and on "The Lower Invertebrates" and "The Higher Invertebrates" prepare the way for socialistic and communistic studies of insect nature.

    Vol. VI, "Zoology", Chapters 2, 3, 4, pp. 395—430

WEDNESDAY

One of the most fascinating phases of nature-study in the zoological branch is that of "Insect Social Communities". The reader will remember some of the weird and ghastly marriage and other details of insect social existence from "The Romance of Evolution", and Chapter V of "Zoology" gives further vivid information regarding insect family and community life. In the chapter "The Vertebrates", (1) "Fish", and in the chapter "The Vertebrates", (2) "Amphibia and Reptiles" are discussed in detail.

    Vol. VI, "Zoology", Chapters 5, 6, 7, pp. 431—464

THURSDAY

Thursday evening completes our direct study of "Zoology", by taking up the habits, nature and character of "The Vertebrates", (3) the "Birds", and "The Vertebrates", (4) the "Mammals", and completes the fascinating detailed description of the animal life of the world.

    Vol. VI, "Zoology", Chapters 8, 9, pp. 465—508

FRIDAY

Our session of vacation study in nature, though we have finished with "Zoology", calls for a logical conclusion of two evenings devoted to "Biology". Having concluded the tale of animal *life,* we quite naturally pass to the scientific theories which determine its development and, in particular the scientific explanation in detail of the *Darwinian theory* of "Natural Selection". This chapter of "Biology", together with its supplementary chapters, "Sexual Selection" and "Factors Other Than Selection", should be read in sequence.

    Vol. VI, "Biology", Chapters 12, 13, 14, pp. 313—350

SATURDAY

For Saturday, to conclude our week of nature, we have reserved what are, perhaps, the two most thrilling of biological chapters. One is the chapter on "Heredity", of tremendous interest because of its importance in individual human life, and its bearing on the theory of evolution. The other is the chapter on "Adaptation", which deals with the adaptation of organisms to their environment, the way and manner in which they adjust themselves to their surroundings and living conditions.

Vol. VI, Chapters 15, 16, pp. 353—383

SUNDAY

Turning once more from nature to man, we may resume the story of the decline of the Roman empire and the beginnings of the Middle Ages—in view of the day—by reading in "The Romance of Architecture", "The Catacombs" and "The Early Christian Churches"; in the "Romance of Music", Chapter 6, "The Early Music of Christianity", from "The Catacombs to Charlemange". Chapter 14, sections 1, 2, of "The History of the World" outlines "The Teutonic Conquest" and the empire's dissolution. Supplemental matter will be found in Chapter 13, of "The Romance of Human Life Through the Ages". Here, too, may be read a wonderfully interesting special chapter (Vol. IV) "Some Aspects of the Ancient World", as we pass to the Middle Ages and say farewell to the world of antiquity.

Vol. III, "The Romance of Architecture", Chapter 8, pp. 58, 59

Vol. III, "The Romance of Music", Chapter 6, pp. 341—344

Vol. IV, Chapter 14, 1, 2, pp. 273—284

Vol. I, "The Romance of Human Life Through the Ages", Chapter 13, pp. 359—372

Vol. IV, Chapter 13, pp. 260—272

TENTH WEEK

MONDAY

For a number of varied aspects of those Dark Ages when the barbarian tribes gradually developed into king-ruled nations on the ruins of the Roman empire, and the Christian Church continued to wax in power, we turn this evening to various volumes of the "Outline". First, section 3, of Chapter 14, "The History of the World", deals with "The East, the Goths and the Franks". Then, in "The Romance of Money in Past Ages", Chapter 5, we may read from "The Money Shortage of the Gothic Age" to and inclusive of "When Money and Trade Were Paralyzed by Wars". Various pages in Chapter 21, "The Western Church", in "The Story of Religion", from the beginning of the chapter to and inclusive of the section "From Pride of Power to Shameful Decay", are well in order; and "The Northern Epics", Vol. XI, Chapter 7 tell the stirring legends of the great barbarian nations of the north. Here, as cultural supplementary reading the student may turn to "The Story of Religion", Chapter 9, pp. 87, and read the section beginning "Norse Mythology's Artistic Gift to the World", and ending with "What Edda and Nibelungen Ring Reflect."

Vol. IV, Chapter 14, 3, pp. 284—290

Vol. XX, "The Romance of Money in Past Ages", Chapter 5, pp. 265—271

Vol. II, "The Story of Religion", Chapter 21, pp. 232—235

Vol. XI, Chapter 7, "The Northern Epics", pp. 55—69

TUESDAY

To-night we will vary our study of decadent civilization with an excursion into the realms of primitive barbarism. We will study the African in one of his most interesting developments—that of snake-worship. As Chapter 7, "Snake and Serpent Worship", in "The Story of Religion" will show, snake worship was and is not confined to the African. Yet the specific developments of this hideous belief are so thrilling in their detail, especially as regards the Dahomeian snake-cult and Voodism, that they preempt the attention. To complete this evening's study in black, we may turn to some modern aspects of life in the Orient, culled from the volume of "Travel".

Vol. II, "The Story of Religion", Chapter 7, "Snake and Serpent Worship", pp. 61—72

Vol. XV, "Snake Fakirs and Serpent Worship", pp. 62—68 (this article in particular, may serve as a supplement to Chapter 7, Vol. II); "Patrolling the African Game Country", pp. 83—91; and "Life Among the Kikuyu", pp. 315—328

WEDNESDAY

We return from our African excursion to pass from Rome to Byzantium. Preceding sections of our historical outline already have described the founding of Byzantium or Constantinople by the Emperor Constantine the Great. We take up the story with section 4, Chapter 14, of "The History of the World", entitled "The Era of Justinian"; and then read section V, "After Justinian". In Chapter 16 (1) we have "The Iconoclasts" and (6) "Italy and the East". Besides these chapters, Chapter 8, "Byzantine Architecture", pp. 60—62 in "The Romance of Architecture"; and certain pages in "The Romance of Painting" should be scanned. In "The Romance of Sculpture" the Byzantine chisselers, and the "Byzantine and Arabian Schools" of therapeutics are considered in Vol. VIII.

Vol. IV, Chapter 14 (3,4), pp. 291—303

Vol. IV, Chapter 16 (1), pp. 323—328, (6) 346—352.

Vol. III, "The Romance of Architecture", Chapter 8, pp. 60—62

Vol. III, "The Romance of Painting", Chapter 1, pp. 209, 210

Vol. III, "The Romance of Sculpture", Chapter 4, p. 156

Vol. VIII, "Medicine", Chapter 4, pp. 347—357

THURSDAY

We have gained an idea of the history and the arts of the Byzantines. Now we will turn to life itself in ancient Byzantium. In Chapter 14 of "The Romance of Human Life Through the Ages", we have two illuminating historical tales. Chapter 6 ("Empresses of Byzantium"), "The Personal Romance of History", gives glimpses, terrible, startling, yet authentic, of what the lives of these imperial ladies were like. A vision of a great day in the history of the Greek empire is in Chapter 5 of "The Romance of Money in Past Ages", captioned "When Constantinople Was Sacked of Its Gold!"

Vol. I, "The Romance of Human Life Through the Ages", Chapter 14, "Human Documents of Byzantium", pp. 373—383

Vol. II, "The Personal Romance of History", Chapter 6, "Empresses of Byzantium", pp. 402—413

Vol. XX, "The Romance of Money in Past Ages", Chapter 5, p. 275

FRIDAY

Before turning to the startling rise of Mohammed and Islam, let us give another glance at the earlier Middle Ages outside the Byzantine world. To this end we may read in succession, in "The History of the World", Chapter 14 (6), "The Teutonic Conquest of England"; Chapter 15 (3), "The West", 630—720; and Chapter 16 (2), "The Deeds of Charles the Great", (3) "The Empire of Charlemagne", and (4) "The Disruption of the Carolingian Empire", supplemented by Chapter 5 of "The Personal Romance of History", "Some Romances of Medieval Days".

Vol. IV, Chapter 14, (6), pp. 303—306

Vol. IV, Chapter 15, (3), pp. 315—322

Vol. IV, Chapter 16, (2, 3, 4), pp. 329—337, and pp. 337—339

Vol. II, "The Personal Romance of History", Chapter 5, pp. 394—401

SATURDAY

Byzantium, the Greek empire of Constantinople, came to an end in the fifteenth century when it was conquered by the Turks. Before we pass on to a concluding chapter which shall deal with its religion—the Greek Catholic faith—let us turn to Vol. XV of "The Outline". In "The New Melting Pot on the Bosporus" we see Constantinople as the most impoverished and expensive city of

Europe, the hopeless haven of Russian imperialist refugees, where the Turkish flapper doffs her veil as she gains woman's rights. In "Constantinople, the Edge of the Orient", we have a colorful description of the actual city, and in "How Constantinople Spends Its Sabbath", we may follow the manner of worship to-day of Moslem, Jew and Christian, in mosque, synagogue and church of what was once old Byzantium.

    Vol. XV, "The New Melting Pot on the Bosporus", pp. 1—9

    Vol. XV, "Constantinople, the Edge of the Orient", pp. 372—377

    Vol. XV, "How Constantinople Spends its Sabbath", pp. 77—82

SUNDAY

To-day's religious reading comprises two of the most interesting chapters of "The Story of Religion". First, in Chapter 20, "The Greek Catholic Church", in order to preserve the continuity of the narrative, the story of Greek Catholicism is told from the beginning to the present day. Then we may turn to Chapter 21 of the same volume, "The Western Church from the Fisherman Bishop to the Papacy's Height of Power". In this last chapter the reader should begin with the section "A Family of Female Pope-Makers" and read to the one entitled "The *Unum Sanctum* Bull"

    Vol. II, "The Story of Religion", Chapter 20, pp. 217—231

    Vol. II, "The Story of Religion", Chapter 21, pp. 235—242

THE ELEVENTH WEEK

MONDAY

In "The History of the World", Chapter 15, (1, 2,) Chapter 16, (1, 6), and Chapter 17 (4), "The East, 920—1072", we continue the tale of Islam from the time of Mohammed to the time of the Turkish ascendancy (1072).

We are now prepared to consider from the vantage ground of historical appreciation and in all their interesting detail the various phases of Mohammedan life and customs.

    Vol. IV, Chapter 15, (1), pp. 307—315
    Vol. IV, Chapter 16, (1), pp. 323—328
    Vol. IV, Chapter 16, (6), pp. 346—352
    Vol. IV, Chapter 17, (4), pp. 371—375

TUESDAY

Most interesting will the reader find Chapter 15 of "The Romance of Human Life Through the Ages". It is entitled "Echoes of the Romance of Islam", and following upon an historical "Introduction" and a brief study of "The Spirit of Islam", we have four fascinating tales in which leading phases of that spirit are illustrated. To supplement these the reader may turn to Chapter 7 of "The Personal Romance of History", entitled "Romances of the Mohammedan Orient".

> Vol. I, "The Romance of Human Life Through the Ages", Chapter 15, pp. 384—400
>
> Vol. II, "The Personal Romance of History", Chapter 7, pp. 414—423

WEDNESDAY

Let us now turn to the *culture* of the Saracens. In "The Romance of Architecture", Chapter 10, "Mohammed and the Mosque", gives the most true, illuminating account of the ideas and ideals of Islamic architecture, perhaps, ever written. This chapter should be followed by the Section of Chapter 4, in the same volume, dealing with Mohammedan architecture of India. In "The Romance of Painting", see "Mohammedan Painting", Chapter 1; and in "The Romance of Music", Chapter 7, "Music and Mohammed"; while in "The Romance of the Dance" the reader may turn to "The Dances of the Mohammedan East" and "Scheherazade".

> Vol. III, "Romance of Architecture", Chapter 10, pp. 74—84
>
> Vol. III, "Romance of Architecture", Chapter 4, pp. 29—33
>
> Vol. III, "Romance of Painting", Chapter I, pp. 210, 211
>
> Vol. III, "Romance of Music", Chapter 7, pp. 345—347
>
> Vol. III, "Romance of the Dance", pp. 489—490

THURSDAY

Special attention has been devoted in the "Outline" to Mohammedan *literature*. First of all, for non-obligatory literary reading we have the selections from "The Koran" (Vol. IX, "Sacred Writings", pp. 354—508). Every pious Mohammedan regards the Koran as the master production of Arabic literature, and its introduction, "The Bible of Islam", should be read in any event. Lighter literature is represented by a delightful choice of tales from the immortal "Arabian Nights"—they do much to make the spirit of oriental life clear to the occidental—and in "The History of Literature", in Chapter 6, "The Epics of the Orient", offers us the glowing legends of the heroic days of Persia by the Mohammedan poet Firdausi.

> Vol. XIX, Arabian Nights Tales: "Ali Baba and the Forty Thieves", pp. 33—38; "Aladdin and the Wonderful Lamp", pp. 60—67
>
> Vol. XIX, "The Arabian Nights", pp. 378—424
>
> Vol. XI, "The History of Literature", see Chapter 6, "The Epics of the Orient", pp. 43, 54.

FRIDAY

Friday is the Mohammedan Sabbath—what would be more in

keeping with the day than a reading of Chapter 16 of "The Story of Religion"? It is entitled "Mohammedanism (The Religion of Islam)", and covers the whole subject of Mohammedan religious and philosophic thought.

> Vol. II, "The Story of Religion", Chapter 16, "Mohammedanism", pp. 161—183

SATURDAY

As a relief from our more serious Mohammedan studies we may conclude what is practically a Mohammedan week by some "Travel" glimpses, brilliantly written, of interesting nooks and corners of the Mohammedan world of to-day: "Cairo, Old and New"; "In Cairo's Teeming Thoroughfares"; "Beirut, the City of Saturn"; "Ibrahim of Algiers"; and "Putting in at Algiers".

> Vol. XV, "Travel", pp. 279—285
> Vol. XV, "Travel", pp. 27—32
> Vol. XV, "Travel", pp. 252—256.
> Vol. XV, "Travel", pp. 426—430 and pp. 445—448

SUNDAY

We must now return from our visit to the Orient of to-day to the Western World of the Middle Ages. We would suggest for this purpose—though certain sections of Chapter 17 already have been read in special connections—that the reader give his attention to "The History of the World", Chapter 17, "From Henry the Fowler to Hildebrand", and to Chapter 18, "From the Accession of Gregory IX to the Accession of Innocent III", which will bring him to the thirteenth century of our era. Read in connection with them Chapter 21, Vol. II, from "A Pen Picture of Pope Innocent III" on to the end.

> Vol. IV, Chapters 17, 18, pp. 353—405
> Vol. II, Chapter 21, pp. 243—246

TWELFTH WEEK

MONDAY

These pages of secular and religious history will have given the reader an excellent insight into the struggle between the popes and the emperors in the Middle Ages, the struggle between the lords temporal and the lords spiritual of mankind. Of thrilling interest are the "Glimpses of the Medieval Peep-Show" afforded by Chapter 16 "The Romance of Human Life Through the Ages". To these we may add two love romances of real life, those of "Abélard and Héloise" and "St. Elizabeth of Hungary", in Chapter 8 of "The Personal Romance of History". To conclude, see in the "Romance of Music", Chapter 8, "Cloister and Hearth in Music".

> Vol. I, "The Romance of Human Life Through the Ages", Chapter 16, pp. 401—415

Vol. II, "The Personal Romance of History", Chapter 8, pp. 424—426

Vol. III, "The Romance of Music", Chapter 8, pp. 348—353

TUESDAY

A highly dramatic century in the world's history is the thirteenth, and one rich in ill luck for a number of famous personages. If we devote this evening to the perusal of Chapter 19 of "The History of the World", entitled "The Era of Innocent the III", we will find that we are ready to enjoy the following evening's reading in the light of the knowledge we have gained.

Vol. IV, Chapter 19, pp. 406—433

WEDNESDAY

Of the two readings suggested for to-night, one deals with religion and the other with money. After the reader has enjoyed Chapter 5 of "The Romance of Money in Past Ages", beginning with: "The New Power of Clergy and Pope", and reading to the end of the chapter; he may read Chapter 22 of "The Story of Religion", from the beginning to and inclusive of the gripping section entitled "The False and Mythical Legend of Pope Joan".

Vol. XX, "The Romance of Money in Past Ages", Chapter 5, pp. 271—278

Vol. II, "The Story of Religion", Chapter 22, pp. 247—255

THURSDAY

We must not forget the *art* of the Gothic Age. Chapter 9 of "The Romance of Architecture" deals with the "Gothic Style", and gives us marvelous descriptions of the greatest of Gothic cathedrals. In the "Romance of Sculpture", the Gothic Age is considered in Chapter 4; and in Chapter 3 of "The Romance of Painting" we meet the "Great Painters and Great Paintings of the Gothic Age". Finally, in "The Romance of the Dance", we have, in section 4, "Dancers and Dancing in the Middle Ages".

Vol. III, "Romance of Architecture", Chapter 9, pp. 66—73.

Vol. III, "Romance of Sculpture", Chapter 4, pp. 157—161.

Vol. III, "Romance of Painting", Chapter 2, pp. 212—220.

Vol. III, "Romance of the Dance", (4), pp. 484—486.

FRIDAY

The Fourteenth Century, 1307—1380, the century in which the Roman popes lived in exile in the French city of Avignon, is an interesting one, and the reader will enjoy the clear, comprehensive view presented of it in Chapter 20 of "The History of the World".

Vol. IV, Chapter 20, "The Fourteenth Century", pp. 434—462.

SATURDAY

For to-night's quota of reading we may turn again to Chapter 22 of "The Story of Religion", entitled "Along the Way to the Reformation" and resuming it where we left off, begin with the section headed "The Inquisition" and conclude with the miracle-tale of "Christ in Flanders". The English poet Geoffrey Chaucer (1340—1400) we have just reviewed. As supplementary period reading we may call attention to the selection from his famous "Canterbury Tales" (Vol. XI, Book I "English Poetry", pp. 125—158). In Vol. II, "The Lovers of Toledo", "The Pope's Mule" and "Christ in Flanders", show three aspects of religion: religious bigotry, religious humor and religious reverence, contrasted in three gripping tales from master pens.

> Vol. II, "The Story of Religion", Chapter 22, pp. 255—274

SUNDAY

Few literary works supply a finer subject for Sunday reading than the famous English dramatist Christopher Marlowe's "The Tragical History of Dr. Faustus." In English it is the next greatest work to Goethe's "Faust".

> Vol. XVII, "The Drama", Christopher Marlowe, "Dr. Faustus", pp. 213—249

THIRTEENTH WEEK

MONDAY

Before we take up the chapter entitled "The Passing of the Middle Ages" in "The History of the World", we must deal with three special Medieval developments: (1) *Literary*; (2) *Scientific* and (3) *Racial*. We will begin with (1). The "Faust" tragedy we have just read is absolutely Medieval in character and spirit. We will follow it this evening with one of the old traditional poems of the Middle Ages, "The Gest of Robyn Hode"—we might mention that because of its length we have not made it an obligatory reading number. Read, in "The History of Literature", Chapter 8, "The Epics of Chivalry", and Tennyson's "Morte d' Arthur" and his "Sir Galahad" in Vol. XII.

> Vol. XI, "Traditional Ballads", "A Gest of Robyn Hode", pp. 158—209
>
> Vol. XI, "History of Literature", Chapter 8, "The Epics of Chivalry", pp. 70—81
>
> Vol. XII, "English Poetry", pp. 191—197, and pp. 201—203

TUESDAY

Following our evening devoted to literary aspects of the Middle Ages, we may profitably read an interesting chapter on "The Development of Culture" (Vol. VII). For the Middle Ages, though they are also known as the "Dark Ages", are the connecting link between antiquity and the modern world.

Vol VII, "Anthropology", Chapter 6, "The Development of Culture", pp. 378—386

WEDNESDAY

To-night and to-morrow night will be devoted to romantic and humorous aspects of the science of chemistry, vividly told in two chapters which should be perused in sequence. In Chapter 2, "Chemistry", we first have a summary of "The Chemical Knowledge of the Ancients". The succeeding chapter, "The Early Alchemists", tells the thrilling story of a man's century-long struggle to turn base metals into gold by means of the mythical "Philosopher's Stone", the universal solvent.

Vol. VII, "Chemistry", Chapters 2 and 3, pp. 402—422

THURSDAY

Upon the two more serious chapters of "Chemistry" which we read last night may most appropriately follow a reading of one of the wittiest comedies—for all that to modern taste the frank and outspoken humor of its age may seem a trifle coarse—which English literature has produced. It is "rare old Ben Jonson" (b. 1573) the bricklayer and soldier dramatist's masterpiece, his play entitled "The Alchemist".

Vol. XVII, "The Drama", Ben Jonson, "The Alchemist", pp. 253—354

FRIDAY

We have come to the third (3) special Medieval development to be considered. It is one racial and political, to which we will devote special attention before coming to the concluding readings which deal with this great division of world history. To-night we are concerned with the Orient during the Middle Ages and specifically with the Mongols, the teeming hordes of yellow men who overthrew the Mohammedan kingdoms of Asia and for a time threatened to overrun Europe. Nine clear, gripping pages of "The History of the World", will enable us to place in their proper historical frame these descendants of the old Turanian races. This may be followed by the wonderful "Pictures Out of the Mongol East" in "The Romance of Human Life Through the Ages".

Vol. IV, Chapter 17, "Slavs and Magyars", pp. 375—379

Vol. IV, Chapter 19, (from the second last paragraph, p. 427 to the end of section, p. 428)

Vol. IV, Chapter 22, "The Far East in the Middle Ages", pp. 496—499

Vol. I, "The Romance of Human Life Through the Ages", Chapter 17, pp. 417—430

SATURDAY

To complete our Mongol studies we must turn to-night to Chapter 3 of "The Story of Religion". It is entitled "Shamanism", and gives in detail an account of the special religious "attitude of mind" which is part of the make-up of the yellow race. Samuel Taylor Coleridge's fantastic poem "Kubla Khan", an imaginative masterpiece evoked by a Mongol theme; some brief considerations of music in Mongol lands, and an account of a modern art development of old Mongol tribal dances will appropriately end an interesting evening.

Vol. II, "The Story of Religion", Chapter 3, "Shamanism" pp. 27—36

Vol. XI, "English Poetry", pp. 391—393

Vol. III, "The Romance of Music", Chapter 3, pp. 332, 333

Vol. III, "The Romance of the Dance", see "The Dances from 'Prince Igor'", pp. 505, 506

SUNDAY

The Middle Ages are so vastly important in the history of mankind and so filled with color and interest that four evenings are by no means too much to devote to a final summary of all they meant to man, before taking leave of them. Let the reader turn to-night in "The History of the World" to Chapter 21, "The Passing of the Middle Ages" (1340—1485). It is indispensable to a proper mental grasp of the succeeding chapter, summarizing "Aspects of the Middle Ages".

Vol. IV, Chapter 21, "The Passing of the Middle Ages", pp. 463—495

FOURTEENTH WEEK

MONDAY

In this chapter, "Aspects of the Middle Ages" beginning with (2) "Economic Conditions", in Vol. IV, we continue in Volume V (3) with "Intellectual Conditions", and end with (4), a special study of "The Art of War" during this period of history.

Vol. IV, "Aspects of the Middle Ages", pp. 496—506

Vol. V, "Aspects of the Middle Ages, pp. 1—12

TUESDAY

And now, before finally dismissing the Middle Ages, let us once more look back and take a peep at them through the glowing veil of pure romance. "The Romance of Opera" (Vol. III), is a comprehensive guide to the repertory of this great art form. At the same time it is more. If we group some of the greatest operas whose scene of action and story are strictly Medieval, we get surprisingly colorful and poetic glimpses of Medieval life from the emotional side. In connection with these stories the Introduction to "The Romance of Opera" (Vol. III, p. 383) "What is Opera", may be read with profit.

Vol. III, "The Romance of Opera"

"Don Giovanni" (pp. 390, 391); "Mefistofile" (pp. 400, 401); "Faust", (pp. 414, 415); "Amore dei tre Rei" (pp. 386, 387); "Pélleas et Mélisande" (pp. 425, 426); "Tristan and Isolda" (pp. 457, 458); "Le Roi d'Ys" (p. 429); "Euryanthe" (pp. 436, 437); "Oberon" (pp. 447, 448); "Robert le Diable" (pp. 428, 429); "Grisélidis" (pp. 415, 426): "Der Freischütz" pp. 439, 440); "Tannhäuser" (pp. 455, 456); "Lohengrin" (p. 444); "Jongleur de Notre Dame" (pp. 417, 418); "Robin Hood" (p. 463); "Rienzi" (pp. 450, 451); and "William Tell" (p. 432).

WEDNESDAY

When next we take up history's tale we begin the story of the modern world with the "Age of Transition" (1485-1520). Before we do so, however, let us, for the time being, revert to the primitive! Chapter 2 of "The Story of Religion" and read from "The New Guinea Kainama" to and inclusive of "The Taboo", dealing with the Polynesian savage. Then, in "Travel" the articles "Hobnobbing with Fiji's Aristocracy", and "Australia's Mandate in the Pacific".

Vol. II, "The Story of Religion", Chapter 2, "Fetishism", pp. 20—23

Vol. XV, "Travel", pp. 15—19 and pp. 40—46

THURSDAY

Passing from the primitives of the South Seas, we will find among those who dwell around the Poles tribes that reproduce the life of the Stone Age in a species of *bone* version. Take, in Chapter 2 of "The Story of Religion", the section "The Eskimo", and read to the end of the chapter. Then turn to "On the Northeast Tip of Asia", and learn how the Mezinkas lead their physically and morally unclean lives. Thence pass to "MacMillan's Quest of Crocker Land" where girls marry at fourteen and wives are "swapped" with frequency. And "Along the Unknown Reaches of the Mackenzie and Peace Rivers", we find the Nunalmiute Eskimo eating his decayed fish in a land glamored with the lure of scenic romance.

Vol. XV, "Travel", pp. 298—303
Vol. XV, "Travel", pp. 386—390
Vol. XV, "Travel", pp. 186—191

FRIDAY

A visit to "The Country of the Dyaks", which we may profitably make to-night in continuation of our studies in the primitive, will take us to Sarawak. Then before passing from these vivid studies of present-day primitive man back to the beginning of "Modern Age in History" every reader might read the First Epistle of the great English poet Alexander Pope's (1688-1744) "Essay on Man". It deals with the Nature and State of Man with Respect to the Universe". It will suggest to the reader trains of thought he may take pleasure in developing.

Vol. XV, "Travel", "In the Country of the Dyaks", pp. 329—335

Vol. XI, "English Poetry", Alexander Pope, "Essay on Man" Epistle 1. "Of the Nature and State of Man with Respect to the Universe", pp. 289—295

SATURDAY

We have left the Middle Ages to take up the eternal march of historic event at the point where the story of the Modern world begins. Broadly speaking it may be said to run from 1485 to 1520, The first section of "The History of the World", Chapter 23, gives us a general view of "The European States" during the time mentioned. This general view we may profitably supplement with the special readings indicated in various fields illustrating its men, thoughts and events.

Vol. V, "The History of the World", Chapter 23, pp. 13—22

Vol. II, "The Story of Religion", Chapter 22, pp. 274—278

Vol. II, "The Personal Romance of History", Chapter 8, pp. 433, 434

Vol. I, "The Romance of Human Life Through the Ages", Chapters 18, pp. 431—440

SUNDAY

To-day's reading should begin with Chapter 23, section 2 of "The History of the World". It is a brief, eloquent account of "The Birth of the Reformation". With it should be read the intensely interesting portion of "The Story of Religion", Chapter 24, entitled "The Revolt of Independent Christian Thought Against the Church of Tradition", from the beginning to and inclusive of the section "Leo and Martin". We may conclude the evening by making the acquaintance of "The Great Painters of the Renaissance", in Chapter 3 of "The Romance of Painting".

Vol. V, "The History of the World", Chapter 23, "The Birth of the Reformation", pp. 22—28

Vol. II, "The Story of Religion", Chapter 24, "The Revolt of Independent Christian Thought Against the Church of Tradition", pp. 287—293

Vol. III, "The Romance of Painting", Chapter 3, "The Great Painters of the Renaissance", pp. 221—226

FIFTEENTH WEEK

MONDAY

From the religious ideas of the Age of Transition we will turn to-night to some non-religious developments of thoughts, philosophic and scientific, of the time. In Chapter 23 of "The Story of Religion", the reader should begin with the section entitled "The

Thought of the Renaissance", and read to the end of "Tommaso Campanella's 'The City of the Sun'" (already considered in another connection). This may be followed by the fascinating chapter of "Chemistry" entitled "The Later Alchemists", and a corresponding chapter in "Medicine" called "The Close of Medievalism".

> Vol. II, "The Story of Religion", Chapter 23, pp. 281—286
>
> Vol. VII, "Chemistry", Chapter 4, pp. 423—433
>
> Vol. VIII, "Medicine", Chapter 5, "The Close of Medievalism". pp. 358—368

TUESDAY

It is now time to take up some of the interesting art developments in the Renaissance Age. In "The Romance of Architecture", Chapter 11, "The Renaissance", to become acquainted with the great buildings of that age, and the *ideas* and architects that produced them. In close connection is the subject of "Sculpture in the Renaissance", Chapter 5 of "The Romance of Sculpture"; while in "The Romance of the Dance", we have (5) "Court Dances of the Renaissance and the Baroque"; and in "The Romance of Music", Chapter 9, "The Renaissance and the Baroque in Music". We may conclude with two little "human interest" pictures of Renaissance life drawn from "The Romance of Human Life Through the Ages", Chapter 18.

> Vol. III, "The Romance of Architecture", Chapter 11, pp. 85—94
>
> Vol. III, "The Romance of Sculpture", Chapter 5, pp. 162—167
>
> Vol. III, "The Romance of the Dance" (5), pp. 486, 487
>
> Vol. III, "The Romance of Music", Chapter 9, pp. 354—357
>
> Vol. I, "The Romance of Human Life Through the Ages", Chapter 18, pp. 444—449

WEDNESDAY

Two interesting Renaissance study contrasts may be united in this evening's readings, one purely *practical* the other *intellectual*. For the first we may turn to Chapter 6, of "The Romance of Money in Past Ages", and read the first two sections of the chapter, entitled respectively: "Merchant Princes Who Reigned in Baroque Days" and "Commercial Barons of Renaissance Europe". For our evening's intellectual pabulum we may then pass to three of the finest essays of Michael de Montaigne (1533-1592): "Of Profit and Honesty"; "Of the Incommoditie of Greatnesse"; and "How One Ought to Governe His Will".

> Vol. XX, "The Romance of Money in Past Ages", Chapter 6, pp. 279—282
>
> Vol. XIV, "Essays", Michael, Lord of Montaigne, "Three Essays", pp. 66—104

THURSDAY

We already have made the acquaintance of the "Humanist" thought of the Age of the Revival of Learning, the Renaissance, on Monday last. Since between Dante (d. 1321) and Pope Leo X, "who enjoyed the papacy" (d. 1521) the great wave of humanism rose and fell a few pages (Chapter 9 of "The History of Literature") which admirably summarizes Dante will begin our reading for this evening. Following this we will turn to some special culture developments of the *later* or *"High"* Renaissance, before giving three evenings to the greatest drama, with a Renaissance atmosphere, ever written. In "The Romance of Sculpture" read Chapter 6, "Michel Angelo and Benvenuto Cellini"; and in the "Romance of Painting", Chapter 4, "The Great Painters of the Italian High Renaissance", whose outstanding personalities are the romantic figures of Leonardo da Vinci and Raphael Sanzo.

> Vol. XI, "The History of Literature", Chapter 9, pp. 82—89
> Vol. III, "The Romance of Sculpture", Chapter 6, pp. 168—174
> Vol. III, "The Romance of Painting", Chapter 4, pp. 227—237

FRIDAY

An evening of poetry—poetry which lets some of the great painters of whom we read last night, tell their lives, their dreams and their aspirations in the winged words of one of the greatest of English poets, may appropriately follow on Thursday's reading. Let us turn, therefore, to Robert Browning's wonderful "Andrea del Sarto" (See "The Romance of Painting", p. 233) in Vol. XII, "English Poetry", and follow it with his "My Last Duchess", a great painter's impression of a great lady, a Duchess of Ferrara, of his day. Both poems give a deep insight into the artistic spirit and feeling of the Renaissance.

> Vol, "English Poetry", Robert Browning, pp. 218—224, and 213, 214

Through a typographical error in Volume XII the poems of Robert Browning have been listed under Charles Kingsley. The "Sands of Dee" and "Young and Old" are the only poems of Kingsley we have included. The remaining poems listed under "Kingsley" are those written by Robert Browning.

SATURDAY

Shakespeare is a poet, a dramatist of all time, raised above the narrow range of race and land, yet Shakespeare's English is "Renaissance English". He writes in the reign of the greatest monarch of the Tudor family, the "Renaissance dynasty" of England. And, he has placed the scene of action of some of his greatest dramas in the magic cities of the Italian Renaissance—Verona, Venice, Padua, Mantua, Rome. The tragedy of the "star-cross'd lovers", "Romeo and Juliet", is found in Italian tales of the fourteenth and fifteenth centuries. Shakespeare's play was written in 1591. It is a lyric tragedy at its best. His Romeo is a Renaissance lover and his Juliet (both of them representing the spirit of youth incarnate) is a Renaissance type, "evidently a portrait". As a preparation for reading this work turn to "The History of Literature", Chapter 10. There we may follow "The Development of the Drama" as a whole from the beginning to the second paragraph of p. 95. Skipping two pages we may then turn to p. 96 and, beginning with the last paragraph of the page read the three successive paragraphs devoted respectively to Marlowe, Shakespeare and Jonson. Then we have an exhaustive study of "Shakespeare's Life and Works", in Vol. XII. Now we are taking up "Romeo and Juliet", in etaoinshrdluetaoinnu may read from the beginning to the scene in "Friar Laurent's Cell".

Vol. XI, "The History of Literature", Chapter 10, p. 90, p. 95; then 96, 97

Vol. XVIII, "The Drama", Shakespeare's "Romeo and Juliet", pp. 1—26

SUNDAY

From the scene in "Friar Laurent's Cell", where he reflects that "Virtue itself turns vice being misapplied", we may this evening continue with p. 26 reading to where the poor girl, turning on her old nurse, declares "If all else fail, myself have power to die!"

Vol. XVIII, "The Drama", Shakespeare's "Romeo and Juliet", pp. 26—54

SIXTEENTH WEEK
MONDAY

Our evening begins with Act IV of the tragedy. It opens in Friar Laurent's cell, dwells for a time in the Capulet house, and then passes to Mantua, where, at the first tidings of Juliet's death coming from Verona, Romeo buys a poison before setting out for his love's tomb. There he drinks the poison "with a kiss", and Juliet awakening and finding him dead, thrusts a dagger into her heart. "Romeo and Juliet" among all Shakespeare's plays has the perfect conclusion, its hero and heroine remain "forever young and still to be enjoyed".

Vol. XVIII, "The Drama", Shakespeare's "Romeo and Juliet", pp. 55—75

TUESDAY

Following Shakespeare's "Romeo and Juliet", nothing offers a more moving and beautiful final reading in the more romantic and poetic aspects of the Renaissance than a poem by John Keats and a dramatic tale by the Hungarian novelist Jokai. Keats' "The Eve of Saint

Agnes", as a pendant to Shakespeare's tragic lovers it gives us a pair of happy ones, an elopement filled with the spirit of Renaissance romance. Following it read in Chapter 18, "The Romance of Human Life Through the Ages", the weird and terrible story of the woman who was "Too Beautiful!"

>Vol. XI, "English Poetry", John Keats, "The Eve of Saint Agnes", pp. 437—446
>
>Vol. I, "The Romance of Human Life Through the Ages", Chapter 18, "Too Beautiful!" pp. 440—444

WEDNESDAY

To-night we take up one of the most interesting practical developments of the Age of Transition, Chapter 23, "The History of the World", in section 3, "The Round World". It deals with the discovery by Vasco da Gama and Christopher Columbus respectively, of the route to the East and to the West Indies, of the "New World". As supplementary reading see in "Geology", Chapter 2, "The Beginnings of Map-Making"; and in "The Romance of Money in Past Ages", Chapter 6, "Adventures and the Lure of Gold". In "The Romance of Opera" we also have a colorful imaginative sidelight on the character of one of the great explorers.

>Vol. V, Chapter 23, "The History of the World"; "The Round World", (3) pp. 28—33
>
>Vol. VI, Chapter 2, "The Beginnings of Map-Making", pp. 17—19, second last paragraph
>
>Vol. XX, "The Romance of Money in Past Ages", Chapter 6, "Adventurers and the Lure of Gold", pp. 282, 283
>
>Vol. III, "The Romance of Opera", pp. 409, 410

THURSDAY

And now, in connection with the "New World" Columbus discovered, let us gain an idea of the two great Indian civilizations the Spaniards found and destroyed there, those of Aztec Mexico and Inca Peru. "The History of the World", Chapter 24, section 5, "The New World", tells the tale of the Spanish conquests with vivid briefness. Next, in "The Romance of Money in Past Ages", Chapter 6, "When Spain Looted the Rich Lands of South America", shows the rich tribute the conquered empires yielded. The architecture, dance and music of the Aztecs and Peruvians have not been overlooked in "The Outline"; and in "The Romance of Human Life Through the Ages" we find a tragic tale of a king of Tezcuco, one of the subject kings of the Aztec emperor Montezuma.

>Vol. V, "The History of the World", Chapter 24, (5), pp. 56—60
>
>Vol. XX, "The Romance of Money in Past Ages", Chap-

ter 6, "When Spain Looted the Rich Lands of South America", pp. 284, 285

Vol. III, "The Romance of Architecture", Chapter 14, pp. 117—122, "Aztec Mexico and Inca Peru".

Vol. III, "The Romance of the Dance" (7), "Aztec and Inca Dances", pp. 491—493

Vol. III, "The Romance of Music", Chapter 15, "The Romance of Music in America", pp. 379, 382

Vol. I, "The Romance of Human Life Through the Ages", Chapter 16, pp. 415, 416

FRIDAY

To-night we will devote to the picturesque religion of the Aztecs, which mingled the cult of bloody human sacrifice and fragrant flower-offerings and to that of the Incas of Peru. Both are described in Chapter 10 of "The Story of Religion", under the title "The Great Sun Religions of America". In Chapter 8 of the same volume we also call attention to the paragraph sections entitled: "The Children's Drinking Festival", "Sacred Flowers", and "The Lily of Mictlan".

Vol. II, "The Story of Religion", Chapter 10, pp. 97—107

Vol. II, "The Story of Religion", Chapter 8, pp. 78—80

SATURDAY

In Chapter 24, "The History of the World", Section 1, we meet two leading figures, King Francis I of France and the Emperor Charles V of Germany. With the historic background it supplies we may combine some separate biographic studies. Then, Chapter 5 of "The Romance of Painting" brings us into intimate touch with the great painter Titian, who painted Charles V, and with other painters of the time. As a special study of medical science in "The Era of Charles V", and somewhat later, we may conclude with chapter 5 of "Chemistry", dealing with "The Period of Medical Mysticism".

Vol. V, "The History of the World", Chapter 24 ¶1, pp. 34—38

Vol. II, "The Personal Romance of History", Chapter 9, p. 446 and Chapter 8, p. 434

Vol. II, "The Romance of Painting", Chapter 5, pp. 238—244

Vol. VII, "Chemistry", Chapter 5, pp. 434—445

SUNDAY

Beginning with "When Protestantism Takes Shape", Chapter 24 (2), we read on to the end of section 4 of this chapter, "France, Britain and Scandinavia". Rereading the section entitled "Leo and Martin" in Chapter 24, "The Story of Religion", in connection with our history, we may then pass to the one entitled "Luther and Lutheranism", and complete in outline our knowledge of the faith founded by Luther. In the same chapter, beginning with the section "The Anabaptists", we may follow the exciting adventures of "A Brigham Young of 1532".

>Vol. V, "The History of the World", Chapter 24, "The Era of Charles V", ¶2, 3, 4, pp. 38—56
>
>Vol. II, "The Story of Religion", Chapter 24, "The Revolt of Independent Christian Thought Against the Church of Tradition", pp. 291—298

SEVENTEENTH WEEK

MONDAY

The "Era of Charles V" is succeeded in history by "The Era of Philip II", his son. This period is one of intense interest: it is that of the Valois kings of France, of Henry VIII and Elizabeth in England, of Mary Queen of Scots, of John Calvin, of the Armada and the St. Bartholomew's Massacre. Let us read to-night its first section "Storm and Stress" (1556—1572). Our historic background established we may then enjoy a brilliant biographical sketch of King Philip II, and the pages which deal with the four "Vicious Valois" brothers. In Chapter 24, "The Story of Religion", the section "The Huguenots" tells the whys and wherefores of the St. Bartholomew night massacre; and then we may visit the "Escorial"; and finally visualize the galleons of Spain in Macaulay's great poem "The Armada".

>Vol. V, Chapter 25, "The Era of Philip II", ¶1, pp. 61—69
>
>Vol. II, "The Personal Romance of History", Chapter 9, "The Vicious Valois" to "Henry the Degenerate", pp. 446—449
>
>Vol. II, "The Personal Romance of History", Chapter 12, "King Philip of Spain", pp. 490, 491
>
>Vol. II, "The Story of Religion", Chapter 24, "The Huguenots, pp. 298, 299
>
>Vol. II, "The Romance of Architecture", Chapter 2, "The Escorial", pp. 92, 93
>
>Vol. XII, "English Poetry", Macaulay, "The Armada", pp. 279, 280

TUESDAY

We continue to-night in our chosen historic period. Sections 2 and 3 of "The Era of Philip II", dealing with "The Breaking of Spain" and "The End of the Spanish Ascendancy", tells among other things the historic tale of the great Armada which Macaulay's poem has just illustrated. A thrilling picture of love and war when men lived by the sword in the depraved days of Valois France may accompany our historic reading.

Vol. V, "The History of the World", ¶2, 3, pp. 69—82

Vol. I, "The Romance of Human Life Through the Ages", Chapter 19, pp. 450—458

WEDNESDAY

To-night's historical reading, Chapter 25 (5), "The History of the World", entitled "India", gives us an opportunity to supplement the historian's accounts of this golden Asian land with some fascinating additional material. In Chapter 11, "The Story of Religion", read "An Oriental Example of Royal Tolerance" for a glowing pen-picture of the Mongol emperor Akbar of India (1542—1605); and in Chapter 17, "The Romance of Human Life Through the Ages", to glimpse the human side of the Mongol Emperor Humayun. The industrious reader should he feel inclined, may improve the opportunity to enjoy the great English philosopher Herbert Spencer's essay on "What Knowledge is of Most Worth".

Vol. V, "The History of the World", Chapter 25 ¶5, pp. 82—84

Vol. II, Chapter 11, "The Story of Religion", p. 111

Vol. I, "The Romance of Human Life Through the Ages", Chapter 17, pp. 424—430

Vol. XIV, "Essays", Spencer, "What Knowledge Is of Most Worth", pp. 412—450

THURSDAY

The year 1558 was that in which Queen Mary of England, wife of King Philip of Spain, died. It was also the year when Fiorentino published his tale *Il Pecorone,* which develops the germ idea of Shakespeare's "Merchant of Venice", the idea of the enforced payment of a given bond. As Shakespeare's drama develops it, it may be said to give us the spirit and environment of Italy in the Age of Philip II, seen through the glasses of English genius. For tonight we may read from the beginning up to the wonderful scene in Portia's house.

Vol. XVIII, "The Drama", Shakespeare's "Merchant of Venice", pp. 188—210

FRIDAY

In Portia's great scene, with which we begin this evening's reading, she stands out against the terrible, remorseless Shylock as "a splendid beauty-breathing Titian does against a magnificent Rembrandt", to quote the poet Heine. We may follow her as she walks in gardens of statues, flowers, fountains and whispering ghostly music", until we reach the point (Act IV, Scene 1) where the Duke of Venice begs Shylock not to exact his pound of flesh.

442   THE READER'S GUIDE

Vol. XVIII, "The Drama", Shakespeare's "Merchant of
Venice", pp. 211—232

SATURDAY

This night's reading concludes the "Merchant of Venice", and ends with the famous Act V in Portia's garden and the happy close, happy for all but Shylock.

Vol. XVIII, "The Drama", Shakespeare's "Merchant of
Venice", pp. 232—250

SUNDAY

From the world of Shakespeare's imagined usurer we will return to the realities of his character's period. To-night we will consider England and Scotland, in the light of its great historic figures, already reviewed in the preceding "The Era of Charles V" and "The Era of Philip II". In Chapter 24, "The Story of Religion", the sections entitled "The Mennonites", "Calvin and Calvinism", "John Knox", "Presbyterianism" and "The Anglican Church" may be read with profit. In addition should be read "Essays" 4, 18, 19, and 20 by Francis Bacon, Queen Elizabeth's Lord High Keeper of the Seal. They are inspired by or touch upon the men and events of his time.

Vol. II, "The Personal Romance of History", Chapter 9,
pp. 439—453

Vol. II, "The Story of Religion", Chapter 24, sections
indicated.

Vol. II, "The Story of Religion", Chapter 27, "Francis
Bacon", pp. 336—337.

Vol. XIV, "Essays", Francis Bacon, pp. 6—9; 10; pp.
43—52.

EIGHTEENTH WEEK

MONDAY

This evening's reading is solidly but interestingly historical. Chapter 26 of "The History of the World", entitled "Before the Thirty Years' War", and the first four sections of Chapter 27, "The Era of the Thirty Years' War" (1648) carry us to the conclusion of this great conflict and prepare our further study of the life and personalities of the time.

Vol. V, "The History of the World", Chapters 26 and 27,
pp. 85—116

TUESDAY

The "human interest" material supplementing last evening's historic reading is colorful and vivid. In "The Romance of Money in Ages Past", Chapter 6, we may read from "The Age of Piracy and the Spanish Main" to and including "The Fuggers: Rockefellers of the Sixteenth Century". In "The Romance of Human Life Through the Ages" we have, Chapter 19, "In the Heydey of the Great God Loot" and "The Army Wife"; and, Chapter 20, "The Soldier Monk" (1597—1651). In "The Story of Religion" we may read Chapter 25, "The Counter Reformation and the Church of Tradition", from the beginning to the end of the section "The Net Results of the Religious Wars".

> Vol. XX, "The Romance of Money in Past Ages", Chapter 6, pp. 285—289
> Vol. I, "The Romance of Human Life Through the Ages", Chapter 19, pp. 458—466
> Vol. I, "The Romance of Human Life Through the Ages", Chapter 20, pp. 467—472
> Vol. II, "The Story of Religion", Chapter 25, pp. 307—310

WEDNESDAY

Continuing from the preceding evening we may read to-night Chapter 9, "The Personal Romance of History", from "La Reine Margot" to the end of the chapter. In Chapter 12 of the same volume, see "Alphonso, the Monster of Portugal"; while "Hapsburg Loves", Chapter 11, contains a pen-picture of the Emperor Rudolph II, (1552—1612). Four short chapters in "The Romance of Painting", Chapters 6, 7, 8 and 9, may profitably close the evening.

> Vol. II, "The Personal Romance of History", Chapter 9, pp. 449—453; Chapter 12, pp. 493, 494; Chapter 11, pp. 480—482
> Vol. III, "The Romance of Painting, Chapters 6, 7, 8, 9, pp. 245—258

THURSDAY

Chapter 27 (5, 6) "Europe Outside the Empire, 1603—1648" and "Overseas, 1600—1648", make up our history reading for the evening. In connection with these pages the reader may turn to "The Personal Romance of History", Chapter 10, from the beginning to "Louis the Fourteenth"; "The Romance of Architecture", Chapter 14, "The Romance of the Cliff Dwellers"; and to "The Birth of the Banks To-day" and "English Merchants Who Roamed the Seven Seas" in Chapter 5, "The Romance of Money in Past Ages". He may conclude with Oliver Cromwell's great speech at the "Opening of the Protective Parliament", in 1654.

> Vol. V, "The History of the World", Chapter 27, pp. 116—125
> Vol. II, "The Personal Romance of History", Chapter 10, pp. 454—456
> Vol. III, "The Romance of Architecture", Chapter 14, pp. 122—124

Vol. XX, "The Romance of Money in Past Ages", Chapter 6, pp. 289—291

Vol. XVIII, "Famous Orations", Oliver Cromwell, pp. 279—290

FRIDAY

Whenever Cromwell's name is mentioned another great name in another field occurs to us. It is that of his friend the poet John Milton (1608—1764). "Paradise Lost" and "Paradise Regained" are considered in "The History of Literature", Chapter 9. In Vol. XI we recommend especially: "On the morning of Christ's Nativity", "Comus", "The Passion", "To the Lord General Cromwell", and "On the Late Massacre in Piedmont".

Vol. XI, "The History of Literature", Chapter 9, pp. 86—89

Vol. XI, "English Poetry", pp. 463—470; 482—506; 480—482; 473, 474

SATURDAY

Chapter 28 of "The History of the World" is devoted to the great and splendid Age of Louis XIV. For to-night we will read from "The Mazarin Period" (1) to the "Ottoman Aggression", covering the years between 1648 and 1696.

Vol. V, "The History of the World", Chapter 28, "The Age of Louis XIV", pp. 126—148

SUNDAY

Continuing the study of the historic aspects of "The Age of Louis XIV", we will read to-night from "The Ottoman Aggression" (4) to the end of the chapter, which brings us to the year 1715.

Vol. V, "The History of the World", Chapter 28, "The Age of Louis XIV", pp. 148—177

NINETEENTH WEEK

MONDAY

In view of the scheme of development followed we suggest that this evening the reader begin at "The Edict of Nantes", in "The Story of Religion", Chapter 24, and read through to Chapter 26; then Chapter 27 to and inclusive of the section "The English Empiricists". As supplementary non-obligatory reading in this last connection the reader may turn to "Philosophy", and delve in the principles of René Descartes and "The Thoughts" of Blaise Pascal (b. 1623).

Vol. II, "The Story of Religion", Chapter 24, pp. 299—306; Chapter 25, pp. 307—319; and Chapter 27, pp. 336, 337

Vol. XIII, "Philosophy", René Descartes, "The Principles

of Philosophy", pp. 306—354; "The Thoughts of Blaise Pascal", pp. 355—388

TUESDAY

A variegated wealth of reading may now supplement what we have learned in the two evenings past. With regard to "The Age of Louis XIV", we gain colorful vistas of architecture, painting, dance, music, finance and medicine—Louis XIV, according to sober History, was largely purged to death—in the days of the "Sun King".

    Vol. III, "The Romance of Architecture", Chapter 12, pp. 95—103

    Vol. III, "The Romance of Painting", Chapter 10, pp. 259, 260

    Vol. III, "The Romance of the Dance", (8, 9) pp. 493—496

    Vol. III, "The Romance of Music", Chapter 9, pp. 354—357

    Vol. XX, "The Romance of Money in Past Ages", Chapter 6, pp. 279—293

    Vol. VIII, "Medicine", Chapter 7, pp. 386—396

WEDNESDAY

There is no more vivid love-life in history than that of Louis XIV, nor are other kings whose hearts got the better of their discreation forgotten in the "Outline". "Fallen" indeed, in the higher moral sense, are the monarchs of whom we read, hence we may with profit finish our evening by perusing "God's Love to Fallen Man", a sermon by John Wesley, a contemporary of Louis XIV.

    Vol. II, "The Personal Romance of History", Chapter 10, (from "Louis the Fourteenth" to "Louis the Fifteenth"), pp. 456—465

    Vol. I, "The Romance of Human Life Through the Ages", Chapter 20, pp. 472—480

    Vol. II, "The Personal Romance of History", Chapter 12, (from beginning to "Bonnie Prince Charlie"), pp. 486—488.

    Vol. XVIII, "Famous Orations", pp. 291—299

THURSDAY

The Age of Louis XIV is also that of Queen Anne in England, and in this connection we will turn to English literature, and enjoy some of the greatest works the time produced. Jonathan Swift (1667—1745) is a great master of plain speech in the writing of his age. Two amusing evenings will cover his "Travels into Several Remote Nations of the World, by Lemuel Gulliver" (1726). The first four chapters carry us to Gulliver's description of the land of Lilliput.

Vol. XIX, Jonathan Swift, "Gulliver's Travels", pp. 334—356.

FRIDAY

Resuming Gulliver's narrative with Chapter 5, we continue our story to its climax in the hero's return home to England from his first voyage.

Vol. XIX, Jonathan Swift, "Gulliver's Travels", pp. 356—377

SATURDAY

John Dryden (1631—1700) is a great English poet and playwright (see note, p. 451, Vol. XIV). Of the three essays by Dryden in Vol. XIV, "The Essay on Dramatic Poetry" probably is the most valuable. In addition to the "Essays", the reader may also turn to Dryden's "Ode", in Vol. XI, and since the essay as a literary form is continually being submitted to the reader, Chapter II, "The Essayists and Historians", may be read in the "History of Literature".

Vol. XIV, "Essays", John Dryden, "Three Dramatic Essays", pp. 451—479

Vol. XI, "English Poetry", John Dryden, "Ode", pp. 278—281

Vol. XI, "English Poetry", "The History of Literature", Chapter 11, pp. 104—107

SUNDAY

Alexander Pope (1688—1744) was vain and often insincere, yet he is one of the great poets of Anne's reign, and if we consider Swift we must not forget him. His "Essay on Man", Epistle One, we already know. We will turn this evening to the remainder of the poem and enjoy: 2. "Of the Nature and State of Man with Respect to Himself"; 3. "Of the Nature and State of Man with Respect to Society"; and 4. "Of the Nature and State of Man with Respect to Happiness".

Vol. XI, "English Poetry", Alexander Pope, "Essay on Man", (2, 3, 4) pp. 296—318

TWENTIETH WEEK

MONDAY

Before we revert to our historic thread a reading of some of the loveliest and most famous individual English poems from the time of Queen Elizabeth to that of Queen Anne will be of pleasure and profit to the reader. The poets chosen are: Edmund Spenser (1553—1599) Prothalamion; Michael Drayton, (1563—1631), "To the Virginia Voyage"; Francis Beaumont (1586—1616), "On the Tombs in Westminster Abbey"; William Drummond, (1585—1649), "Saint John Baptist", "For the Magdalene"; Robert Herrick (1591—1674), "The Mad Maid's Song"; Henry Vaughan (1622—1695) "Beyond the

Veil"; Abraham Cowley, (1618—1667), "Cheer Up, My Mates"; Sir William Dàvenant (1605—1668), "Dawn Song".

 Vol. XI, "English Poetry", pp. 215—219, 244, 245, 247, 248, 254, 260, 261, 272, 265

TUESDAY

Let us turn now from our literary studies to world history, reading Chapter 29, "Russia, Prussia and Turkey, from 1713—1739". In these pages the name of Peter the Great stands out. In "The Story of Religion", Chapter 10 ("Another Russian Child of God") and Chapter 11, "The Personal Romance of History", we find complementary studies of this remarkable man. Then, to complete the evening, read Thomas Carlyle's striking essay on "Biography", and obtain new viewpoints on the biographies of celebrated men which we are continually reading:

 Vol. V, "The History of the World", Chapter 29 (2), pp. 185—189

 Vol. II, "The Personal Romance of History", Chapter 11, pp. 475—485

 Vol. II, "The Story of Religion", Chapter 10, pp. 97—107.

 Vol. XIV, "Essays", Thomas Carlyle, "Biography", pp. 188—200

WEDNESDAY

In to-night's reading "The History of the World", Chapter 29, (3), "The War of the Austrian Succession", we may turn in connection with the name of Walpole, Queen Anne's great finance minister, to some brilliant pages of "The Romance of Money in Past Ages", Chapter 7, reading from "England, Monied Mistress of the Seven Seas" to and inclusive of "Walpole, Financial Genius and Prime Minister". To conclude the evening, turn to that sublime commentary on the vanity of all earthly ambition and read Thomas Gray's "Elegy in a Country Churchyard".

 Vol. V, "The History of the World", Chapter 29 (3), pp. 189—196

 Vol. XX, "The Romance of Money in Past Ages", Chapter 7, pp. 294—298

 Vol. XI, "English Poetry", pp. 318—322

THURSDAY

In Chapter 29 of our world history we now have reached section 4, "Between the Wars, 1748—1756". The reader will notice that Longfellow's wonderful poem "Evangeline" is mentioned there in connection with the brutal deportation of the French inhabitants of Acadie by the British (1775). The reader should not fail to turn to this poem when he has accomplished his historical stint and enjoy its delightful pages.

Vol. V, "The History of the World", Chapter 29, (4), pp. 196—201.

Vol. XII, "English Poetry", William Wadsworth Longfellow, "Evangeline", pp. 340—376

FRIDAY

As a preparation for several evenings of special readings section 5, Chapter 29 of our world history, "The Seven Years' War, 1756—1763", is invaluable. With it, this evening, we may combine a glance at "American Architecture", Chapter 14, "The Romance of Architecture"; and study the lives of some *Russian* ("Earlier Romaninoffs", "Catherine the Great"), *Saxon*, ("The Father of Two Hundred Odd", Chapter 9, "The Personal Romance of History") and *Spanish* ("From Philip II to Ferdinand VI, "Chapter 12, *idem*) royalties. Then for a tid-bit which combines historic truth with piquant fact read "Galafas" (A Tale of the Dunkerque Galleys) in "The Romance of Human Life through the Ages".

Vol. V, Chapter 29, (5), pp. 201—210

Vol. III, "The Romance of Architecture", Chapter 14, pp. 124—128

Vol. II, "The Personal Romance of History", Chapter 11, pp. 475—480, Chapter 12, pp. 491, 492

Vol. I, "The Romance of Human Life Through the Ages", Chapter 21, pp. 496—498

SATURDAY

We cannot neglect the opportunity offered by "The Outline" to read Lord Macaulay's famous historical study of "Frederick the Great" with reference to "The Seven Years' War" of last evening. It glows with life, it fascinates with its descriptive brilliancy and power, it makes the great king of Prussia move and live before our eyes. Our first evening's reading will carry us to Voltaire's arrival in Berlin.

Vol. XIV, "Essays", Lord Macaulay, "Frederick the Great", pp. 201—230

SUNDAY

Our second night's reading of Macaulay carries us from the beginning of the friendship between the Prussian king and the French philosopher to the end of Frederick's military career, for it is to "the end of his career as a warrior" that Macaulay carries his hero. The reader will lay down this biography with regret.

Vol. XIV, "Essays", Lord Macaulay, "Frederick the Great", pp. 230—261

TWENTY-FIRST WEEK

MONDAY

Let us close our ears to the roar of cannon on the battlefields of

Europe for a few evenings to revert to literature. In the year 1770, while Frederick the Great was settling with the Austrian Emperor Joseph II the Partition of Poland, Oliver Goldsmith (1728-1774) was writing the "Deserted Village". It really is *two* villages: in its prosperity an *English* one, an *Irish* one in its decay. Yet the junction of the two villages has made it quite the loveliest thing of its kind written in English—in spite of the fact that its political economy and its natural and moral philosophy are all wrong.

> Vol. XI, "English Poetry", Oliver Goldsmith, "The Deserted Village", pp. 334—343

Tuesday

Upon Goldsmith's great sentimental poem should follow his incomparable five-act farce "She Stoops to Conquer". It paints the manners, morals and ideas of his own time with richest drollery and when produced in Convent Garden (1773), kept pit, boxes and galleries in a constant roar of laughter.

> Vol. XVII, "The Drama", Oliver Goldsmith, "She Stoops to Conquer", pp. 441—470

Wednesday

To-night's reading concludes our delightful Goldsmith farce. We resume at p. 470, where Hastings enters.

> Vol. XVII, "The Drama", Oliver Goldsmith, "She Stoops to Conquer", pp. 470—499

Thursday

With to-night's resumption of our readings in "The History of the World", temporary interrupted for literature's sake, we enter (Chapter 30) "From the Peace of Paris to the French Revolution", upon a very interesting period, one rich in event and development in every field of human activity. Let us first read, Chapter 30, (1) "Great Britain and Birth of the United States". Together with it we should peruse the eloquent Addresses of Edmund Burke, the British statesman who was a firm friend of the colonists and their backer against Lord North and George III. They include the "Address to the British Colonists of North America", and the "Letter to Dr. Benjamin Franklin".

> Vol. V, Chapter 30, (1), "Great Britain and the Birth of the United States", pp. 211—219
> Vol. XIV, "Essays", Edmund Burke, "Addresses", pp. 105—128

Friday

Continuing our illustrative readings for the period of the winning of our independence are three great American orations which every American should know: Patrick Henry's "Give me Liberty or Give me Death!" (1775); George Washington's "First Inaugural Address" (1789); and Thomas Jefferson's, "Democracy Defined" 1801).

With them should be read, in accordance with the references which follow, the accounts of American architecture, sculpture, painting and music; and in "The Personal Romance of History", Chapter 14, from the beginning to the end of the section "An Emperor of the Creeks". Finally, read in "The Romance of Money", Chapter 7, "The American Revolution and its Money Side".

    Vol. XVIII, "Famous Orations", pp. 300—310
    Vol. III, "The Romance of Architecture", Chapter 14, "The Colonial Style", "Mount Vernon", pp. 128, 129
    Vol. III, "The Romance of Sculpture", Chapter 2, pp. 198, 199
    Vol. III, "The Romance of Music", Chapter 15, p. 380
    Vol. II, "The Personal Romance of History", Chapter 14, pp. 503—504
    Vol. III, "The Romance of Painting", Chapter 20, pp. 307—309
    Vol. XX, "The Romance of Money in Past Ages", Chapter 7, pp. 300—302

SATURDAY

There are certain poems of patriotism directly inspired by the men and events of the time of the Birth of our Nation. Even if some may be already known to the reader he may revert with pleasure to: Robert Burns' "Ballad on the American War"; William Cullen Bryant's "Song of Marion's Men"; Ralph Waldo Emerson's "Concord Hymn"; Henry Wadsworth Longfellow's "Paul Revere's Ride"; Oliver Wendell Holmes' "Old Ironsides"; and Rudyard Kipling's "The Rhyme of the Three Captains" (Paul Jones).

    Vol. XII, "English Poetry", pp. 176—178; 299, 300; 314, 315; 337—340; 393, and 476—479

SUNDAY

Owing to the specific plan of "The Story of Religion" the reader is advised, for a general resumé and a comprehensive view of the developments of religious thought of the eighteenth century to reread Chapters 24 and 25 of "The Story of Religion" in their entirety.

    Vol. II, "The Story of Religion", Chapters 24 and 25

TWENTY-SECOND WEEK

MONDAY

Turning to the philosophic thought of the eighteenth century we will find (in addition to what has been said anent the theories of Voltaire, Rousseau and other French philosophers of the "Age of Reason" in Chapter 25 of "The Story of Religion") that reading from *Pierre Bayle* on (Chapter 27, *idem*) the philosophic thought of the eighteenth century has been brilliantly epitomized in the sections which follow up to "German Philosophy from Fichte to Eucken".

THE READER'S GUIDE

Turning then to Jean Jacques Rousseau's own writings, let us read Part One of his famous "Dissertation on the Origin and Foundation of the Inequality of Mankind".

> Vol. II, "The Story of Religion", Chapter 27, pp. 336—356
> Vol. XIII, "Philosophy", Rousseau, "Dissertation of the Origin and Foundation of the Inequality of Mankind", Pt. 1, pp. 433—458

TUESDAY

In Part Two of Rousseau's famous "Dissertation" he advocates a return to the innocence and simplicity of Nature, crying: "what a sight would the perplexing and envied labors of a European minister of state present to the eyes of a Caribean!

> Vol. XIII, "Philosophy", Rousseau, Pt. 2, "Dissertation on the Origin and Foundation of the Inequality of Mankind", pp. 459—483

WEDNESDAY

Our reading in the "History of the World" for to-night is section 2, Chapter 30, "India, 1761—1786". In connection with it "The Priceless Wealth of the Indian Princess", Chapter 7, in "The Romance of Money in Past Ages", should be read. Then, as a supplementary literary tid-bit the reader may turn to "Travel" and read "The Spectacular Prince of the Garden of India", of Baroda and its Maharajah to-day.

> Vol. V, "History of the World", Chapter 30 (2), pp. 219—223
> Vol. XX, "The Romance of Money in Past Ages", Chapter 7, pp. 299—300
> Vol. XV, "Travel", pp. 142—150

THURSDAY

In "The History of the World" we take up (section 3, 4, 5, of Chapter 30) "France, 1763—1789". This is the France of King Louis XV, the wretched royal contemporary of Frederick the Great. It is the France in which the writings of philosophers like Rousseau were helping to prepare the French Revolution. It is the France of Madame de Pompadour and du Barry. Its architecture, sculpture, painting, music and dance have been remembered in "The Outline", as the following references will prove:

> Vol. V, "The History of the World", Chapter 30 (3, 4, 5) pp. 223—237
> Vol. III, "The Romance of Architecture", Chapter 12, "French Rococo", pp. 103—106
> Vol. III, "The Romance of Sculpture", Chapter 8, "The Rococo", pp. 178, 179
> Vol. III, "The Romance of Painting", Chapter 10, pp. 259, 260

Vol. III, "The Romance of Music", Chapter 11, "Romance of the Violin" (to Paganini) and Chapter 13, "Romance of the Piano" (to Franz Liszt), pp. 362—364; 370—371

Vol. III, "The Romance of the Dance", 9, "La Grande Guimard", pp. 496, 497

FRIDAY

To-night we will conclude our study of Rococo France, the France of Louis XV. Biographical studies cover Louis XV, "Bonnie Prince Charlie" and their lady loves ("Personal Romance of History"); and the brilliant thumbnail sketches in "From Rococo to Revolution" ("Romance of Human Life Through the Ages") should prove highly enjoyable. In addition the reader may dip at will into Rousseau's "the Social Contract", (Vol. XIII, "Philosophy", pp. 487—506).

Vol. II, "The Personal Romance of History", Chapter 10, "Louis the Fifteenth"; Chapter 12, *idem,* "Bonnie Prince Charlie" pp. 488

Vol. I, "The Romance of Human Life Through the Ages", Chapter 21, "From Rococo to Revolution", pp. 481—484; "The Eighteenth Century in Other Lands", p. 495

SATURDAY

The reading of Chapter 30 (6), "Europe, 1786—1792", and all of Chapter 31, "Three Centuries" (1. Dropped Threads, 2. Political Aspects, 3. Economic Aspects) prepares us for the French Revolution and the fall of the Bourbon monarchy in France.

Vol. V, "The History of the World", Chapters 30 (6), and 31, pp. 237—256

SUNDAY

Sunday does not seem a day on which to let the Revolutionary tocsin ring out with brazen clamor. Hence let us gleam a few interesting vistas of King Louis XVI and the "old regime" before it is swept away in a torrent of blood and fire. "The Personal Romance of History", Chapter 10, contains an interesting study of "Marie-Antoinette and Her Lovers". In the "Romance of Painting", Chapter 10, see "Greuze, the Painter of Artificial Innocence"; and in "The Romance of Human Life Through the Ages", Chapter 21, the touching tale "A Love Which Came Too Late". It may be followed—a piquant contrast—by the delightful study of eighteenth century "Medicine", Chapter 8, "The Contributions of the Practitioner".

Vol. II, "The Personal Romance of History", Chapter 10, pp. 468—469

Vol. III, "The Romance of Painting", Chapter 10, "Greuze", p. 262

Vol. I, "The Romance of Human Life Through the Ages", Chapter 21, pp. 498—501

Vol. VIII, "Medicine", Chapter 8, pp. 397—407

TWENTY-THIRD WEEK

MONDAY

To-night we enter upon the most momentous event in Modern History, the French Revolution. In "The History of the World", section 1, Chapter 32, we will read "The Fall of the Monarchy, 1789-1792", which carries us down to the proclamation of the Republic. The glowing eloquence of a "voice from the tomb" survives to our day in Danton's great speech "To Dare, to Dare Again; Always to Dare", delivered to the National Assembly (1792); and it, with an account of "The Paris Bastile", may conclude the evening's short allotment of reading.

Vol. V, "The History of the World", Chapter 32 (1), pp. 257—268

Vol. XVIII, "Famous Orations", Danton, "To Dare, To Dare Again, Always To Dare", p. 311

Vol. III, "The Romance of Architecture", Chapter 9, pp. 72, 73

TUESDAY

Before beginning with the rule of the Convention, the next period of the French Revolution, we should read a wonderful first hand account of the events of our historic period by a famous contemporary, Thomas Paine (1737-1809). After fighting for freedom in America, Paine (1791) wrote his famous "The Rights of Man" as an answer to Burke's "Reflections on the Revolution in France", which condemned the Revolution and its makers. It is full of wonderful living pictures of the happenings of the time and defends the revolutionary ideas which brought them about. We will read to-night from the beginning of "The Rights of Man" to p. 160, the line: "The French Constitution says there shall be no game laws! . . . "

Vol. XIV, "Essays", Thomas Paine, "The Rights of Man", pp. 132—160

WEDNESDAY

This evening may conclude the reading of "The Rights of Man", beginning at the point at which it was laid aside, and continuing to the end, with the declaration of these rights by the French National Assembly.

Vol. XIV. "Essays", Thomas Paine, "The Rights of Man", pp. 160—187

THURSDAY

To-night's reading will conclude the history of "The French

Revolution", in Chapter 32, with the sections (2), "The Convention and the First Coalition, 1792-1795", and (3), "The Directory, 1795-1799". As a corollary let the reader turn to Napoleon's (5) rousing addresses to his soldiers, from the "Address to the Army at the Beginning of the Italian Campaign" (1796) to that on "The Conclusion of the First Italian Campaign" (1797).

> Vol. V, "The History of the World", Chapter 32, (2, 3) pp. 268—286
>
> Vol. XVIII. "Famous Orations", Napoleon Bonaparte, "Addresses", pp. 312—314

FRIDAY

Two other French revolutionary vistas may be enjoyed this evening, before passing to the next chapter in "The History of the World". The reader may glance at the colorful picture of "The Festival of the Goddess of Reason" in "The Story of Religion". Then, in "The Romance of Human Life Through the Ages", he may turn to one of the weirdest and most compellingly terrible tales ever told, "Royal Hearts".

> Vol. II, "The Story of Religion", Chapter 25, "The Festival of the Goddess of Reason", pp. 315, 316
>
> Vol. I, "The Romance of Human Life Through the Ages", Chapter 21, "Royal Hearts", pp. 484—495

SATURDAY

Our period of world history, speaking collectively, is one of revolution, reaction and reform. Chapter 33, "Napoleon, 1799-1815", takes us from the Consulate to the pinnacle of Napoleon's imperial glory and power. With these pages read Napoleon's "Address to the Troops After the War of the Third Coalition".

> Vol. V, "The History of the World", Chapter 33, pp. 287—313
>
> Vol. XVIII "Famous Orations", Napoleon Bonaparte, "Addresses", (1805), p. 315

SUNDAY

In the pulsing pages of Chapter 27, "The Story of Religion", we learn of the lives and theories of the great German philosophers of the Napoleonic Age (reading from "Immanuel Kant" to the end of "Schopenhauer, the Philosopher of Pessimism"). As optional reading, showing the eighteenth century background of philosophic thought from an English angle, the interesting "Treatise of Human Nature" by David Hume (1711-1776), Rousseau's friend and admirer, may here be recommended ("Philosophy", David Hume, "Treatise on Human Nature", Vol. XIII, pp. 389—432).

> Vol. II, "The Story of Religion", Chapter 27, pp. 344—348

THE READER'S GUIDE

TWENTY-FOURTH WEEK

MONDAY

From the philosophic thought of the Napoleonic era, as exemplified by thinkers from Kant to Schopenhauer, we may now pass to the fields of art, to architecture, sculpture, painting, music and the dance, and find much enjoyable material bearing on the Napoleonic Age.

Vol. III, "The Romance of Architecture", Chapter 12, "The Empire", pp. 106—108

Vol. III, "The Romance of Sculpture", Chapter 8, pp. 178—183

Vol. III, "The Romance of Painting", Chapter 13, "The French Classic Painters", pp. 269—273

Vol. III, "The Romance of Music", Chapter 11, "Paganini", pp. 364—367

Vol. III, "The Romance of the Dance" (9). "Some Great Dancers of the Eighteenth and Nineteenth Centuries", pp. 495—499

TUESDAY

Nine gripping pages, Chapter 34, "The History of the World", describe Napoleon's "Downfall: 1812-1815". They may be followed by the "Address to the Troops on Beginning of the Russian Campaign" (1812), and the "Farewell to the Old Guard", April 20, 1814. Napoleon's amatory and heart life is detailed in "The Bonapartes as Lovers" (Vol. II, Chapter 13), reading to end of section "Jerome".

Vol. V, "The History of the World", Chapter 34, 314—323

Vol. XVIII, "Famous Orations", Napoleon Bonaparte, "Addresses", pp. 316

Vol. II, "The Personal Romance of History", Chapter 13, "The Bonapartes as Lovers", pp. 495—498

WEDNESDAY

With Chapter 35, section 1, "Overseas, 1786-1815", we take up "Ireland: and the British Expansion". With it we may read in "The Romance of Money", Chapter 7, the forceful and exciting sections from "When Some Scientists Stumbled Upon Rich Australia", to the end of "Napoleon's Short Day of Glory as King of the Earth", dealing with English economic conditions during the Napoleonic era. In conclusion, the "Travel" article, "Alexandria and the Nile Delta" gives interesting facts in connection with Napoleon's Egyptian campaign and Nelson's victory at Aboukir.

Vol. V, "The History of the World", Chapter 35 (1), pp. 324—334

Vol. XX, "The Romance of Money in Past Ages", Chapter 7, pp. 302—306

Vol. XV, "Travel", pp. 343—348

THURSDAY

In "The History of the World" our subject to-night is "America, 1789-1815", section 2 of Chapter 35. As supplementary reading we suggest Washington Irving's masterly telling of the American folk-legend of "Rip Van Winkle", who went to sleep a subject of His Majesty King George III of England, and woke up a free citizen of the United States.

    Vol. V, "The History of the World", Chapter 35 (2), pp. 334—342

    Vol. XIX, Washington Irving, "Rip Van Winkle", pp. 205—218

FRIDAY

In Chapter 36 of "The History of the World", "Europe and the Near East: 1815-1832", we have "The Vienna Settlement" (1) and "Europe in the Era of Congresses; 1815—1822" (2). The "Vienna Settlement" (1) first engages our attention. Most of the kings and princes of Europe had attended the Congress of Vienna in the year (1814), when the terms of the Vienna Settlement were laid down, and had sent their delegates to other Congresses. Let us get an idea of some of these European royalties of the Napoleonic Age to-night. To do so *England* ("Three Georges" and "The Lovely Mrs. Fitsherbert"); *Spain* ("Pathetic Ferdinand and Others"; *Russia* ("From the First Paul to the First Nicolas"); *Austria* (from Leopold I to Francis Joseph I); and *France* ("Louis XVIII and the Countess de Cayla") may be read in "The Personal Romance of History".

    Vol. V, "The History of the World", Chapter 36 (1, 2), pp. 343—359

    Vol. II, "The Personal Romance of History", Chapter 12, pp. 489, 490, 492, 493; Chapter 11, pp. 476, 477, 475, 478; Chapter 10, pp. 473, 474

SATURDAY

To-night we continue the history readings of yesterday and gain an insight into affairs in "Eastern Europe, 1820-1832" and "Western Europe" (Chapter 36, 3, 4) during the same period. In these sections the outstanding date of American importance is that of President Monroe's famous message to Congress (Dec. 2, 1823) saying intervention by any European nation in South American affairs would be considered an "unfriendly act" by the United States. This is our celebrated "Monroe Doctrine".

    Vol. V, "The History of the World", Chapter 36 (3, 4), pp. 359—382

SUNDAY

Chapter 37 of "The History of the World", still covering the general subject of "Europe and the Near East", carries us from the year 1832 to the year 1848. It is a chapter crowded with many events yet their multiplicity is not detailed in a confusing manner, but in a logical progression which links one development with the next in order, and gives the reader a clear picture.

> Vol. V, "The History of the World", Chapter 37, pp. 383—400

TWENTY-FIFTH WEEK

MONDAY

To-night, turning first to "The Romance of Money in Ages Past", Chapter 7, we may read economic facts picturesquely put in connection with our general historic period, beginning with "The Gold and Diamonds of Africa," and closing with "The Rise of the Rothschilds". Architecture, painting and music will supply other interesting cultural pages.

> Vol. XX, "The Romance of Money in Past Ages", Chapter 7, pp. 305—310
>
> Vol. III, "The Romance of Sculpture", Chapter 8, "Canova", pp. 181—183
>
> Vol. III, "The Romance of Painting", Chapter 11, (Turner especially) pp. 263—266; and Chapter 12, "Goya", pp. 267, 268
>
> Vol. III, "The Romance of Music", "Franz Liszt", Chapter 13, pp. 371, 374

TUESDAY

Strange to say, in a musical creation of this period we may find a convenient point of departure for an agreeable literary interruption of our more serious historical studies. In 1847, ten years after Queen Victoria has ascended the English throne, the great Italian composer Guiseppe Verdi produced in Milan his opera "Macbeth". It is one of the many musical reactions of the age to Shakespeare's genius, and its mention may serve to introduce a great drama to our attention. So, leaving for the quarrels and intrigues of European diplomats, we will follow the eloquent pages of "Macbeth" from the beginning of the drama to the point where Macduff cried: "Shake off this downy sleep, death's counterfeit!"

> Vol. XVIII, Shakespeare, "Macbeth", pp. 76—95

WEDNESDAY

Continuing this evening from the point at which he left off, the reader may follow the tragic drama to the passage where the witches tell Macbeth he cannot be vanquished until "Great Birnam wood to high Dunsiane hill shall come against him!"

> Vol. XVIII, Shakespeare, "Macbeth", pp. 96—114

THURSDAY

From the scene of the witches' prophecy the reader may now move with the tale to its conclusion with Macbeth's announcement of his coming coronation as King of Scotland.

    Vol. XVIII, Shakespeare, "Macbeth", pp. 115—135

FRIDAY

Chapter 38 of "The History of the World" is devoted to "The World Outside Europe, 1814—1848", and section 1 deals in interesting fashion with "South and Central America". As a supplement we may turn to "Travel" vistas of two countries, respectively South America (Uruguay, Argentina and Brazil) and Central America (Panama) for a more intimate knowledge of the manners and customs of their inhabitants.

    Vol. V, "The History of the World", Chapter 38, pp. 401—407

    Vol. XV, "Travel", see "The South American Cowpuncher", pp. 171—177

    Vol. XV, "Travel", see "The Little People of n Blas", pp. 69—73

SATURDAY

Chapter 38 (2) of "The History of the World" deals with "The United States", and in connection with it we should turn to supplementary reading for the period purely American in interest. "The Romance of Money To-Day". Vol. XX, Chapter 1, tells the thrilling tale of the pioneer work in making America wealthy: read from "The Romance of Making and Growing" through "Building Rich America". As a cultural supplement follow this, in "The Romance of Music", with Chapter 15, "The Romance of Music in America" as a whole; as well as Chapter 12, "The Romance of the Wind Instruments", and Chapter 14, "The Romance of the Orchestra".

    Vol. V, "The History of the World", Chapter 38, (2), pp. 407—414

    Vol. XX, "The Romance of Money To-Day", Chapter 1, pp. 315—318

    Vol. III, "The Romance of Music", Chapters 12, 14, 15, pp. 368, 369, 375—382

SUNDAY

Here we may profitably assign an evening to a patriotic reading of two great American orations. They are: "Dictators in American Politics", Henry Clay's oration denouncing Andrew Jackson (1834); and Daniel Webster's "Bunker Hill Oration" (1825). Every American should know them. As a reward for accomplishing a patriotic duty which should be a pleasure, the reader may then turn to "The Personal Romance of History", and read Chapter 14, beginning with "The American Vice-President Who Planned to Give His Daughter an Imperial Crown", to the end.

    Vol. XVIII, "Famous Orations", Henry Clay and Daniel Webster, pp. 360—367, 368—383

Vol. II, "The Personal Romance of History", Chapter 14, pp. 504—508

TWENTY-SIXTH WEEK

MONDAY

The third section of Chapter 38 of "The History of the World" covers British "Colonial Expansion: 1815-1848", Canadian and African "Travel" vistas which may appropriately be considered in this connection are: "Canada's Great Eastern Game Preserve", "In the Heart of the Canadian Rockies", and "A Visit to the Falls of the Zambesi", which Livingston called "the most wonderful sight I visited in Africa".

Vol. V, "The History of the World", Chapter 38, (3), pp. 414—422

Vol. XV, "Travel", pp. 110—117; 503; 391—393

TUESDAY

Interesting is the course of development of the white man's control of the East described in "Asia" (History of the World, Chapter 38 (4), during this period. It is the epoch when China ceded the great port of Hong-Kong (1847) to Great Britain; and Commodore Perry (1853) opened Japan to American trade. With this evening's history reading, therefore, we may combine two "Travel" articles on the Chinese: "Peking, the Fantastic", and "The Peculiar Heathen Chinee".

Vol. V, "The History of the World", Chapter 38 (4), pp. 422—430

Vol. XV, "Travel", pp. 214—218; 118—125

WEDNESDAY

To-night's reading, in line with what has gone immediately before, will be specifically Japanese. We have three delightful articles: "Welcoming the New Year in Japan"; "The City of Ten Thousand Temples"; and "Macao, the Monte Carlo of the Orient".

Vol. XV, "Travel", pp. 20—26; 162—170; 304—308

THURSDAY

Our reading of this evening will consist of Chapter 39 of "The History of the World" devoted to "Aspects of the Period" we have been considering, aspects "Political" (1), "Economic and Social" (2). It supplies enough food for thought to suffice for an evening's work.

Vol. V, "The History of the World", Chapter 39 (1, 2), pp. 431—446

FRIDAY

In connection with the political ideas discussed in Chapter 39, (1), of "The History of the World", the reader may turn to-night to "The Romance of Money To-Day", Chapter 2, "The Romance of

Rail and Rudder", and read "From Covered Wagon to Twentieth Century Limited", to "The Age of Railroad Graft". Next comes "America's Early Trade on the Sea" and "When Clippers Put Out for Far Cathay". In Vol. II, Chapter 27, "Modern Philosophical Thought", then read from the close of the Schopenhauer article to "Herbert Spencer", for a *resumé* of earlier nineteenth century philosophic and economic thought. As supplemental non-obligatory reading, the English philosopher and political economist John Stuart Mills' "Essay on Liberty" (Vol. XIV, "Essays", pp. 350—361) may be recommended.

    Vol. XX, "The Romance of Money To-Day", Chapter 2, pp. 328—332; 337, 338

    Vol. II, "The Story of Religion", Chapter 27, pp. 348—350

SATURDAY

We resume the course of historic event with Chapter 40 of "The History of the World", a period of "Nationalism and Democracy", in which Europe is everywhere agitated by the turmoil of revolutionary uprisings, in Italy, Germany, Austria, France and the West, ending with the final triumph of the forces of Reaction.

    Vol. V, "The History of the World", Chapter 40, pp. 447—477

SUNDAY

A most interesting period now is discussed in "The History of the World", Chapter 41, that of the famous "Second French Empire", the empire of Napoleon III. Sections 1 and 2 carry us down to the end of the Crimean War (1856) and we have some interesting supplementary reading to accompany them.

    Vol. V, "The History of the World", Chapter 41, pp. 478—494

    Vol. III, "The Romance of Sculpture", see "Jean Baptiste Carpeaux", pp. 180, 181

    Vol. III, "The Romance of Painting", Chapters 14, 15, pp. 274—279

    Vol. XII, "English Poetry", Tennyson, "The Charge of the Light Brigade", pp. 204, 205

TWENTY-SEVENTH WEEK

MONDAY

Chapter 42 of "The History of the World" recounts the interesting story of Italy's throwing off the Austrian yoke, her struggle for independence and the resulting "Unification of Italy", with the help of Napoleon III. It takes us to the year 1817. With it we may read "The Personal Romance of History", Chapter 13, "The Emperor Napoleon III". In "Famous Orations" we also may read the great French poet and novelist Victor Hugo's address "On the Centennial of Voltaire's Death", May 30, 1878. Its connection with his enemy Napoleon III lies in the accusing words which bid philosophers "face to face with monarchs thinking of war, to proclaim the blessedness of peace."

>   Vol. V, Chapter 42, "The History of the World", pp. 495—506
>
>   Vol. II, "The Personal Romance of History", Chapter 13, pp. 499—502
>
>   Vol. XVIII, "Famous Orations", Victor Hugo, "Address on the Centennial of Voltaire's Death", pp. 317, 318

TUESDAY

In Chapter 43 of "The History of the World", we may take up "The Consolidation of Germany", and at the same time read the gripping history of the Franco-Prussian War of 1870-1871, whose legacy of hatred played its part in the initiation of the World War.

>   Vol. XX, "The History of the World", Chapter 43, pp. 1—23

WEDNESDAY

This evening's reading will include vivid selections bearing more or less directly on events and personalities just considered in Chapter 11 of "The Personal Romance of History", the late Emperor Francis Joseph of Austria (1830—1916) his unhappy and beautiful Empress Elizabeth; and "King I, the Lover, of Bavaria and the Outrageous Lola Montez"; In "The Romance of Architecture" we have a brilliant pen-picture of his mad son, King Louis II of Bavaria in "A Madman's Vision of Beauty in Stone". Two "Travel" articles: "From the Latin Quarter to Saint-Cloud" and "Corfu, the Colorful Isle", touch respectively on the favorite palace retreats of Napoleon III and the Empress Elizabeth. As a poetic contrast to these pictures of royal lives we should read James Russell Lowell's lofty "Ode Recited at the Harvard Commencement" (Vol. XII, pp. 402, 413).

>   Vol. II, "The Personal Romance of History", Chapter 11, pp. 480—485
>
>   Vol. III, "The Romance of Architecture", pp. 115, 116
>
>   Vol. XV, "Travel", pp. 494—499; 33—39

THURSDAY

In connection with the preceding chapter and illustrating its political developments, we may turn to-night to leading political ideas and ideals expressed in eloquent speeches by the greatest of German statesmen, Bismark. They are the address "Against Liberalism: A Prussian Royalist Confession of Faith" (June 1, 1847) and the famous "Plea for an Imperial Armament".

>   Vol. XVIII, "Famous Orations", Bismark, pp. 409—422

FRIDAY

As Bismark's two great speeches illustrate German political ideals and aspirations of the middle and end of the nineteenth century, so Gladstone's great address "On Domestic and Foreign Affairs" (Nov. 27, 1879) also supplements Chapter 43 of "The History of the World" with an eloquent statement of the aims and ambitions of Victorian England at home and abroad. It is an address well worth reading.

    Vol. XVIII, "Famous Orations", Gladstone, pp. 336—359

SATURDAY

Our last reading in "Medicine" carried us well toward the end of the eighteenth century. To-night we may read three clear, concluding chapters, from "Nineteenth Century Theories" through the "Modern Treatment of Disease" and the concluding "Modern Physiology", which carry the story of the healing art down to the present day.

    Vol. VIII, "Medicine", Chapters 9, 10, 11, pp. 408—436

SUNDAY

Last Monday and Tuesday evenings of this week dealt with the history of the unification of the German empire (1871), the proclamation of the King of Prussia as emperor of the land which is now a republic, and with biographical studies of some of the personalities of the period. To-night, in Chapter 44 or "The History of the World", we turn to "Asia, 1848—1871" and (inclusive of a vivid account of the great "Indian Mutiny" or "Sepoy Rebellion") may follow the development of European influence in the Orient—India, China and Japan.

    Vol. XX, "The History of the World", Chapter 44, pp. 24—43

TWENTY-EIGHTH WEEK

MONDAY

A final evening of cultural reading in connection with the three evenings immediately preceding may include selections dealing with architecture, sculpture and painting. As obligatory reading, Cardinal Newman's (1801—1890) essay on "Theology as a Branch of Knowledge (Vol. XIV, pp. 262—281) is recommended.

    Vol. III, "The Romance of Architecture", Chapter 9, "The Cathedral of Cologne", pp. 69, 70

    Vol. III, "The Romance of Sculpture", Chapter 9, "Modern Sculpture in Germany and Austria", pp. 185, 186

    Vol. III, "The Romance of Painting", Chapter 18, "Arnold Boeklin", pp. 298, 299

    Vol. XIV, "Theology as a Branch of Knowledge", pp. 262—281

TUESDAY

Chapter 45 of "The History of the World", which we may read tonight, is of especial interest to the American reader, since it deals clearly and exhaustively with the subject of "American Nationalism, 1848—1871". We get a clear, convincing non-partisan statement of the causes which precipitated the Civil War in section 2 of this chapter, "The Breach"; and in section 3 is shown the favorable partisan attitude of Great Britain with regard to the Southern States; and we have a graphic, consequent narrative of the great struggle, its battles and sieges, from the firing of the opening gun at Fort Sumter to the final surrender of Lee at Appamatox Court House.

Vol. XX, "The History of the World", Chapter 45, pp. 44—62

WEDNESDAY

As supplementary reading to follow this chapter we may enjoy tonight in connection with 1, "South America and Mexico" in "Travel", some interesting "Glimpses of the Rubber Country" (Brazil). Section 2, "The United States: the Breach", dealt with the stirring agitated years preceding the Civil War. Bearing directly upon them are John Caldwell Calhoun's great "Speech on the Slavery Question" (1850); and John Greenleaf Whittier's noble poem "Massachusetts to Virginia"; while Robert Burns' "The Slave's Lament", is the plaint of the Senegalese negro sold into Virginia slavery.

Vol. XV, "Travel", "Glimpses of the Rubber Country", pp. 203—213

Vol. XVIII, "Famous Orations", Calhoun, "Speech on the Slavery Question", pp. 384—400

Vol. XII, "English Poetry", Whittier, Burns, pp. 379—381; 142

THURSDAY

To-night, in direct connection with section 3 of Chapter 45, "The History of the World": "The United States: The War for the Union, 1861—1865" we turn to "Famous Orations" for two other great American speeches. First, let us read Chauncey M. Depew's "Speech at the Dinner (Delmonico's) to Celebrate the Anniversary of the Birth of General Grant" (April 27, 1888); and follow it with three addresses by the immortal Abraham Lincoln: the Springfield "Farewell Address" (February 11, 1861); the "First Inaugural Address" (March 4, 1861); and the glorious "Speech at Gettysburg" (November 19, 1863), popularly known as "The Gettysburg Address". Here, too, may be read the late President Wilson's "Address Delivered at Gettysburg, Pa., July 4th, 1913" with its eloquent close: "Come, let us be comrades and soldiers yet to serve our fellow men in quiet counsel, where the blare of trumpets is neither heard nor heeded, and where the things are done which make blessed the nations of the world in peace and righteousness and love!"

Vol. XVIII, "Famous Orations", Chauncey M. Depew, pp. 442—447; Abraham Lincoln, pp. 401—408; Woodrow Wilson, pp. 464—466

FRIDAY

A separate evening of Civil War poetry may appropriately conclude our literary and historical supplemental reading in connection with the Civil War: Whittier's "Barbara Frietchie", James Russell Lowell's "The Present Crisis", William Cullen Bryant's "The Death of Lincoln" and Walt Whitman's "Beat, Beat Drums!", "Vigil Strange I Kept on the Field One Night", "Ethiopia Saluting the Colors", "The Wound-Dresser", and "O Captain, My Captain!"

Vol. XII, "English Poetry", Lowell, pp. 397—400; Whittier, pp. 391—393; Bryant, 302; Walt Whitman, pp. 419—424

SATURDAY

To-night, in connection with section 4, Chapter 45, "The History of the World", "The United States: Reconstruction, 1865—1871", we may read two orations which have passed into history, and with which as with those whose acquaintance we have already made and whose acquaintance we shall make in the future, every American should familiarize himself. Henry Ward Beecher's (1813—1887), "Oration at the Raising of the 'Old Flag' at Fort Sumter" (April 14, 1865) celebrates with passionate joy and eloquence the restoration of peace to a once more united commonwealth. With it we may appropriately bracket General Grant's "Second Inaugural Address" (March 4, 1873).

Vol. XX, "The History of the World", Chapter 46 ¶1, pp. 58—62

Vol. XVIII, "Famous Orations", Henry Ward Beecher, pp. 320—335; General Grant, pp. 461—463

SUNDAY

From America we once more turn to Europe. In Chapter 46, "The History of the World", entitled "Great Britain and Greater Britain, 1848—1871", section 1 deals with "The British Isles". Contemporary "Travel" articles will aid in bringing the reader into touch with the geographical, human and social atmosphere of nineteenth century Great Britain. To "The Memorable Tower of London"; and "Along Thames Waters"; may be added poetic glimpses of the English countryside in: Wadsworth's "The Reverie of Poor Susan", "Daffodils", "To the Daisy", and Swinburne's evocative picture of "A Forsaken Garden".

Vol. XX, "The History of the World", Chapter 46 ¶1, pp. 63—67

Vol. XV, "Travel", pp. 232—237; 440—444
Vol. XI, "English Poetry", Wadsworth, 391, 382, 383, 384
Vol. XII, "English Poetry", Swinburne, pp. 293—295

TWENTY-NINTH WEEK

MONDAY

We may conclude our "Travel" glimpses of interesting corners of the British Isles with two Scotch vistas: "A Reminiscence of Edinburgh", and "The Fowlers of Kilda". "Springtime Rambles in Ireland" make us acquainted with the country and its people may conclude these entertaining and instructive *apercus* of Great Britain.

Vol. XV, "Travel", pp. 420—425; pp. 394—396; pp. 486—489

TUESDAY

The second section of Chapter 45 of "The History of the World" is devoted to "Greater Britain", under the head of "Colonial Self-Government". We learn much anent Australia, New Zealand and Africa and have wonderfully colorful "Travel" articles to lend a more intimate background to our historic progress of event. "An Adventure into the Never-Never Country" may be followed by "The real November Summerland". We cannot conclude the evening more appropriately than by reading Robert Ingersoll's wonderful "Oration on Humboldt". Humboldt (1769—1859), the great German naturalist and traveler, by his scientific researches and the publication of his epoch-making work "Kosmos" (1845—47), did much to direct the eyes of the political world to the possibilities of that colonial expansion in Asia, Africa and Australia, of which we have been reading in the history of the nineteenth century. Ingersoll's wonderful oration is at once a thrilling biography, an account of his labors and discoveries and a brief to show that "He was to science what Shakespeare was to the drama".

Vol. XX, "The History of the World", Chapter 46, ¶2, pp. 67—74

Vol. XV, "Travel", pp. 92; 455—458

Vol. XVIII, "Famous Orations", Ingersoll, pp. 451—459

WEDNESDAY

And now, with the study of Humboldt which we just have read as a point of departure, we may take up the subject of "Geology", one to which we must devote a sequence of evenings, since a clear understanding of it will best be obtained by this method of consideration. The first two chapters of "Geology" already have been read in other connotations. We may with profit, however, reread Chapter 2, "The Beginnings of Map-Making" (Vol. VI, pp. 11—25), "Geology in the Dark Ages" which carries us down to the French pioneer naturalist Buffon (1707—1788). In Chapter 4, "Laying the Rocks Bare", we become acquainted with the revelations of Humboldt's age, and see the exact knowledge of the present day gradually assuming its primary shape.

Vol. VI, Chapters 2, 3, 4, pp. 11—43

THURSDAY

Our geologic reading for to-night comprises two chapters; Chapter 5, "The Developments of Modern Geologic Knowledge" taking in the great advances science made during the nineteenth century. In Chapter 6, we find described with a wealth of interesting detail "The Composition of the Earth".

Vol. VI, "Geology", Chapters 5, 6, pp. 44—64

FRIDAY

Our two chapters of "Geology" this evening deal, respectively, with "Strata Movements and Earthquakes" (Chapter 7) and "Volcanoes and Geysers" (Chapter 8).

Vol. VI, "Geology", Chapters 7, 8, pp. 65—85

SATURDAY

To-night in "Geology" our reading covers Chapter 9, "Erosions and Landslides", and Chapter 10, "Reconstructive Processes".

Vol. VI, "Geology", Chapters 9, 10, pp. 86—104

SUNDAY

Chapters 11 and 12 of "Geology", respectively, take you first on a trip to the "Interior of the Globe", then to one of "Your Own Neighborhood".

Vol. VI, "Geology", Chapters 11, 12, pp. 105—129

THIRTIETH WEEK

MONDAY

Reading the "Life of the Past", Chapter 13 of "Geology", we learn the whole wonderful tale of how by the patient, century-long labors of the scientist the story of life on our planet has been revealed by the mute yet eloquent testimony of the rocks and fossil remains—the word "fossil" means "dug up"—which prove its existence.

Vol. VI, Chapter 13, pp. 130—157

TUESDAY

The title of our geologic chapter to-night has a romantic sound, "The Story of Crystals". And, aside from the scientific analyses which make it clear, we have actual romance in the beautiful passages quoted in this chapter from Ruskin's "Ethics of the Dust".

Vol. VI, "Geology", Chapter 14, pp. 158—168

WEDNESDAY

To-night's Chapter 15, "Descriptive Mineralogy", develops the idea that man is what he is to-day not alone because of the *cell-life* of his ancestors, but also because of the *mineral* characteristics of the substances out of which those ancestors originally were formed.

Vol. VI, "Geology", Chapter 15, pp. 169—181

THURSDAY

Chapter 16 of "Geology", our stint for to-night, is entitled "Mining and Metallurgy". Several brilliant pages are devoted to a colorful review of the *story of mining* from the earliest times, and we learn how the nations of the ancient world harried mother earth for the gold, silver, copper, tin and other metals they coveted. With this chapter our readings in "Geology" come to an end and we are ready to resume the course of our historical narrative at the point where it was temporarily suspended.

Vol. VI, "Geology", Chapter 16, pp. 182—194

FRIDAY

Chapter 47 of "The History of the World" deals with "International Relations and the Eastern Question, 1871-1889", section 1 specifically with "The European Powers, 1871-1875"; section 2, "The Balkan Ferment, 1875-1877"; section 3, "The Russo-Turkish War, 1877-1878"; and section 5, "Peace with Honor", shows matters in the Balkans in such shape that a plentiful crop of new causes for dispute would remain for future adjustment. "The Aftermath of the Berlin Congress, 1881—1889" is notable for its account of the dismissal of the great German statesman Bismarck from his post as Chancellor of the Empire by the man who now lives on the memories of vanished glories, then the young and ambitious Emperor William II.

Vol. XX, "The History of the World", Chapter 47, pp. 75—98

SATURDAY

"The European States, 1871-1889" is the title of Chapter 48 of "The History of the World", whose reading we begin to-night. In its first section, "The Latin States", we study the overthrow of the terrible Paris "Commune" of 1872; the presidencies of Thiers, the French statesman who wrote a famous "History of the Consulate and Empire" of Napoleon Bonaparte; and of the gallant soldier president Marshal MacMahon; and of Jules Grevy, and it also sheds light on the political situation in Italy and Spain. In "The Romance of Painting", Chapter 17, "French Painters from Meissonier to Matisse"; in "The Romance of Sculpture", Chapter 10, "Modern Sculpture in France"; and in "The Romance of Architecture", Chapter 13, "Modern Architecture: 'Introduction' and (1) 'France'", may be read with profit.

Vol. XX, "The History of the World", 48 ¶1, pp. 99—106

Vol. III, "The Romance of Architecture", Chapter 13, pp. 109—113

Vol. III, "The Romance of Sculpture", Chapter 10, pp. 191—197

Vol. III, "The Romance of Painting", Chapter 7, pp. 287—293

SUNDAY

Section 2 of Chapter 48 of "The History of the World" is given over to "The German Empire, 1871-1889". We learn in it how the German Empire was constituted—a union of monarchial countries instead of free and independent states. We come to know the attitudes of these different countries toward each other, and the part religion played in their prejudices and policies and in their attitude toward the central government. Following our historic and political reading we may peruse a few cultural pages in "The Romance of Architecture" and "The Romance of Painting" of specific German interest. Finally, as a vivid contrast, one which at the same time develops trains of thought all our historic reading suggests anent those hidden and irrevocable laws which govern the affairs of men and nations despite all their political and militaristic activity, we may turn with real pleasure to Emerson's wonderful essay on "Fate".

Vol. XX, Chapter 48 ¶2, pp. 107—111

Vol. III, "The Romance of Architecture", Chapter 13, "Germany", pp. 114, 115

Vol. III, "The Romance of Painting", Chapter 18, "German Painting from Cornelius to the Present Day", pp. 294—299

Vol. XIV, "Essays", Emerson, "Fate", pp. 314—334

THIRTY-FIRST WEEK

MONDAY

We will bring our reading of Chapter 48 to a close this evening with section 3, "Russia in Europe, 1871—1889", and section 4, "Great Britain and Ireland, 1871-1889". With regard to section 4 of the chapter, we learn to understand the "Home Rule" principles for which Parnell contended in the Emerald Isle and which the end of the World War has seen established in practice as well as in theory.

Vol. XX, "The History o fthe World", Chapter 48, ¶3, 4, pp. 111—118

TUESDAY

It is high time for us to return to "our own United States". We will do so in Chapter 49 of "The History of the World", "Outside Europe, 1871-1889". In connection with the first section: "America and Australasia, 1871—1889", which in the United States carries us down to President Harrison's election, we find that we have some highly interesting supplementary reading matter of distinctively

American interest. In the "Romance of Money To-Day", we may resume the wonderful narrative of the great *epic of achievement* which to all practical intents made the United States economically independent of Europe and self-supporting, the great story of American progress whose *modern* beginning was made after the end of the Civil War. Beginning with Chapter 2 ("The Romance of Rail and Rudder"), we will read in that chapter: "The Age of Railroad 'Graft'". Then, in Chapter 3, passing to "The Romance of Buying and Selling", we read from the beginning of the chapter through to "The Age of Fat Corporations and Their Big 'Crash'".

Vol. XX, "The History of the World", Chapter 49 ¶1, pp. 119—123

Vol. XX, "The Romance of Money To-Day", Chapter 2, pp. 332—334; Chapter 3, pp. 342—354

WEDNESDAY

To-night we turn to Chapter 4 of "The Romance of Money To-Day". It is devoted to "The Romance of Lending and Borrowing (Banking and Foreign Exchange)". "It continues the story we began last night. Then we pass to "The Romantic Story of Banking", and read the "Mad Rage for Land-Buying and the Gold Fever of 1849", concluding with the account of "The Birth of the National Banks" in 1863.

Vol. XX, "The Romance of Money To-Day", Chapter 4, pp. 361—371

THURSDAY

We will resume and conclude our narrative of American economic and financial development to-night, for the time being, by reading in Chapter 5 of "The Romance of Money To-Day", the title-section; "The Romance of National Housekeeping (U. S. Treasury and Mint)"; "Taxes—Rich Income of the Modern State"; and "America's School System". We may add to this stint of economic reading two other selections, the first an oration *on* James G. Blaine (1830-1890), the other an oration *by* him. "Blaine, the Plumed Knight", Robert G. Ingersoll's "Nominating Speech in the Republican National Convention at Cincinnati, June 15, 1876", always will be remembered because of its introduction of the descriptive phrase "the plumed knight", famous in its hour and day. James G. Blaine's own "Oration on Garfield" (1831-1881) delivered in the hall of the House of Representatives on February 27, 1882, is a far more important historic document. It is not alone an eloquent tribute to the great President who had fallen by an assassin's hand, like Abraham Lincoln, but also a wonderful and detailed biographical study of his life and works.

Vol. XX, "The Romance of Money To-Day", Chapter 5, pp. 381—388

Vol. XVIII, "Famous Orations", Ingersoll, pp. 448—450; James G. Blaine, pp. 500—506

FRIDAY

We will read this evening, Chauncey M. Depew's "Oration at the Unveiling of the Bartholdi Statue". But the sculptor Bartholdi's (See "Romance of Sculpture", p. 191) "Liberty Enlightening the World" is chiefly important as a *symbol* that expresses all America won in her struggle for Independence, a struggle in which France aided her. What makes the Depew oration especially valuable is an account of all that the gift of the great statue from the French to the American people implies.

Vol. XVIII, "Famous Orations", Chauncey M. Depew, "Oration at the Unveiling of the Bartholdi Statue", pp. 431—441

SATURDAY

The nineteenth and twentieth centuries are those crowded with the major portion of the scientific and cultural advance civilization has made from its beginnings. Hence, the sciences of "Mathematics" and "Electricity" which we still have to consider, will each be presented in a series of readings. Our last night's selection was the beautiful "Bartholdi Statue" oration of Chauncey M. Depew and—still harping on the American string—we will to-night pass from the historic to the purely human, and read "Five Famous American Story-Poems of Sentiment". The first of these poems is by an English, *not* an American poet, William Wordsworth (1770-1850). Yet not only is "Ruth" one of the loveliest of this great nature-poet's efforts, it also has a purely American setting. Following "Ruth", the reader may turn to John Greenleaf Whittier's (1807-1892) "Maud Muller". "Maud Muller" takes us back to the green, rustic charm of the poet's New England farm and village life, in the old *ante-bellum* days in the North, when life in the countryside was simple and primitive. James Russell Lowell's (1819-1891), "The Courtin'" is a happy counterpart to "Maud Muller". Henry Wadsworth Longfellow (1807-1882) himself a descendant of "Priscilla, the Puritan Maiden" whom he sang in his "Courtship of Miles Standish", contributes two of his finest minor poems. Both "The Village Blacksmith" and "The Bridge", as is so often the case with his verse, show *aspects of nature influencing human feeling*.

Vol. XI, "English Poetry", pp. 373—380

Vol. XII, "English Poetry", pp. 385—388; 400—402; 327—329; 330—332

SUNDAY

Our Saturday reading has been devoted to heart-stories in poetic form. To-night we may appropriately turn to "Five Poems of Religious Sentiment" (1). Isaac Watts' (1674-1748) "The Dying Adrian to His Soul", is a half-questioning valedictory to the human soul, poised for its last flight, dreading, yet hoping "it knows not what". Henry Vaughn's "Beyond the Veil", calls upon "Dear, beauteous Death, the jewel of the just", to "disperse the mists which blot and fill" this earthly perspective. In Richard Rowland's "Our Blessed Lady's Lullaby", we have one of the loveliest older English poems inspired by the Holy birth; while Tennyson's (1809-1892) "Crossing the Bar" is perhaps the loveliest poetic epitome of man's desire for the perfect passage from this life to the next. Robert Browning's "Rabbi Ben Ezra" shows his noble and distinctive doctrine of life and conduct, and may be summed up as the exposition of the thought that a man's value should not be measured by the work he had done on earth, but by the characters which he had molded.

Vol. XI, "English Poetry", pp. 284; 260, 209—213
Vol. XII, "English Poetry", p. 205; pp. 230—235

THIRTY-SECOND WEEK

MONDAY

Between poetry and mathematics there does not yawn so great a gap as appearances might indicate, for mathematics is the poetry of numbers. Poetry itself—save in modern free verse—moves in an ordered cadence whose accents and stresses recur with mathematical regularity. One of the great charms of poetry, in fact, is this mathematical rhythm, which flows and ebbs in measured and numbered syllables. Chapter 1 of "Mathematics", which we take up to-night, deals with "Number".

Vol. VIII, "Mathematics", Chapter 1, pp. 447—467

TUESDAY

To continue "Mathematics" the following chapter, "Calculation", should be read to-night. Mathematics is an exact science, naturally, and some poetic readers may feel inclined to dodge it, fearing it may be dry. Yet this chapter is an interesting one, and its interest lies in the fact that it explains the different *ways* in which calculation may be carried on.

Vol. VIII, "Mathematics", Chapter 2, pp. 468—482.

WEDNESDAY

Our survey of "Mathematics" concludes with Chapter 3, "Analytical Geometry". The reader will be pleasantly surprised, after a more serious consideration of what "Geometry" is, to find that the "analytical or algebraic investigations" of geometry very often result in values which involve the *imaginary element*. In other words this austere mathematical science has what the higher moral law would consider disreputable relatives. These relatives are all the *games of chance*. Once this discovery has been made, there is not a dull moment in the chapter.

Vol. VIII, "Mathematics", Chapter 3, pp. 483—498.

THURSDAY

It is no more than fair to allow the student who has faithfully perused the three preceding chapters a chance to relax, to turn to poetry, in a second group of "Five Famous Story-Poems of Human Feeling and Sentiment". Anthony Munday's (1553-1633) "Beauty bathing by a spring, where fairest shades did her hide", is a graceful little bit of imaginary verse, light and happy. Next we have the lovely Scotch ballad "Helen of Kirconnell", by an anonymous poet, which is as sad as its predecessor is cheerful. Gay's (1685—1732) contribution to our evening's reading is a delightful eighteenth century sailor's romance, "Black-Eyed Susan".

Like "Black-Eyed Susan", Henry Carey's (d. 1743) "Sally in Our Alley" is a simple eighteenth-century lass whose father makes cabbage-nets". Carey, sauntering along Cheapside, happened to walk behind a shoemaker's apprentice-boy who was taking out his girl, his master's daughter, heard their artless talk and out of it grew his little story poem, in which the hopeful lad tells his dream of love fulfilled. Two fine sea poems by William Cowper (1731-1800) belong to this same general period. "The Castaway" is still in tense, dramatic language an exploitation of the fate of the unfortunate sailor who is washed overboard at sea in a night of storm. "The Loss of the Royal George" was one of the tragedies of the old English navy.

Vol. XI, "English Poetry", p. 226; 252, 253; 286, 287; 287—289; 344—348

FRIDAY

No one who wishes to be generally well-informed and able to bear his part in conversation when it turns to the subject of the heavens and its stars, can afford to neglect obtaining a good outline idea of "Astronomy". In the chapters which follow "Astronomy" is handled in a clear, popular manner and in a definite historical and descriptive way. It makes no demands save on the intelligence, attention and interest the reader will not find it difficult to supply, in view of the direct and simple method in which the author has treated his subject. In view of this fact only the volume chapter and page references are given. Our first night's reading in "Astronomy" includes the short Introduction to the science as a whole, and Chapter 1, "The Growth of Astronomical Ideas".

Vol. VII, "Astronomy", Introduction and Chapter 1, pp. 77—89

SATURDAY

To-night we pass from our introductory chapter to an account of "The Evolution of Astronomical Methods of Observation".

Vol. VII, "Astronomy", Chapter 2, pp. 90—100

SUNDAY

We might devote this evening to a consideration of "A Little Group of Star Poems". If we took away sun, moon and stars from the poet many a page in the great volume of the world's poetry would be dark indeed. In the selections which follow some of the loveliest human thought in connection with the planetary inhabitants of the heavens has been assembled. William Shakespeare's striking sonnet, No. 14, is an example of how skillfully and eloquently the astronomical comparison may be used in poetry to voice a lover's ardent thoughts. Ben Jonson's "Hymn to Diana" is a direct invocation to the crescent-crowned moon goddess of the ancient Greeks. In Robert Browning's "One Word More", Cantos XV, XVI and XVII, the moon serves to show that the meanest of God's creatures has two sides or faces, and that man's two "soul-sides" reflect the blank face with which he confronts the world, and that face full of life and meaning he turns on the woman he loves. In Shelley's "To the Moon" and "The Cloud", we have gloriously beautiful pictures of the same planet.

Vol. XII, "English Poetry", p. 33; 228—229
Vol. XI, "English Poetry", p. 235; 455; 460—462

THIRTY-THIRD WEEK

MONDAY

With Chapter 3 of "Astronomy", entitled "The Physics of the Heavenly Bodies", we would suggest that the reader review Chapter 5 of "Physics" (Vol. VIII, pp. 139—144).

Vol. VII, "Astronomy", Chapter 3, pp. 101—108

TUESDAY

This evening we turn to "The Evolution of Astronomical Instruments and Methods: Celestial Photography", and "The Law of Gravitation" (Chapters 4 and 5) in the story of "Astronomy".

Vol. VII, "Astronomy", Chapters 4, 5, pp. 109—122

WEDNESDAY

To-night, in three brief but highly interesting chapters, we deal with the Solar System as a whole. Chapter 6, explains the "Planetary Distances"; Chapter 7, "The Motions of the Planets"; and Chapter 8, "Modern Investigation" in connection with the Solar System and its results.

Vol. VII, "Astronomy", Chapters 6, 7, 8, pp. 123—142

THURSDAY

Our reading lesson to-night is not an overly long one, yet it is important. Chapter 9 of "Astronomy", is devoted to "The Sun: Eclipses, Sun-Spots and Auroræ, and the Photosphere". The interesting and often fanciful conclusions earlier students of the nature and motion of the sun arrived at are given in vivid detail, and then the subject of eclipses is considered.

Vol. VII, "Astronomy", Chapter 9, pp. 143—153

FRIDAY

To-night's reading, Chapter 10, continues the subject of "The Sun", with a consideration of "The Reversing Layer: The Chromosphere and Corona: Radiation Pressure and Solar Energy".

Vol. VII, "Astronomy", Chapter 10, pp. 154—165

SATURDAY

For a succession of evenings our readings will now be devoted to the various planets. Chapter 11, "Mercury" and Chapter 12, "Venus", introduce two of the best-known. Mercury is the smallest of the major planets and the one nearest the sun. The chapter takes up the sum of human knowledge regarding the planet, from earliest times to the present day, and presents it in a sequential and interesting way.

Chapter 12 is devoted to Venus, the morning and evening star, the "Shepherd's Star", the Greek "Kallistos", "the beautiful star", and all the essential facts concerning her are given in it.

Vol. VII, "Astronomy", Chapter 11, 12, pp. 166—181

SUNDAY

While astronomically we are still "on earth", so to speak, we may appropriately pause this Sunday for a reading of some shorter serious poems dealing with earthly life, the life we lead on this earthly planet. Our selections are by poets of the Elizabethan Age. First comes "His Pilgrimage", by Sir Walter Raleigh (1552-1618). The great old colonizer of Virginia and discoverer of tobacco deals with the pilgrimage of the soul away from the earthly sphere. Ben Jonson, in "A Farewell to the World", speaks quite bitterly of poor old earth and those upon it; but Thomas Campion in "Integer Vitæ" (Of the upright life) gives us a fine idea of what constitutes a straightforward earthly existence and an honest man, summing them up in a fine concluding stanza. Robert Greene, in "Content", tries to make us realize that "The quiet mind is richer than a crown"; and William Drummond in his poem "Life", goes to the skies we have been studying for a comparison to explain that it is "like a bubble blown up in the air".

Francis Bacon (1561-1626) too, like William Drummond, thinks the "world's a bubble", and paints but a very gloomy picture of men and conditions. His is a poem which would do credit to Schopenhauer, the apostle of pessimism (See "The Story of Religion").

Vol. XI, "English Poetry", pp. 227. 228; 233; 231; 232; 229; 247; 262, 263

THIRTY-FOURTH WEEK

MONDAY

Of the two chapters we read to-night, Chapter 13 introduces us to the planet with which, whether astronomers or merely ordinary mortals, we are the best acquainted, "The Earth". Then Chapter 14, "The Moon", will show that planet dear to lovers' hearts under its more purely scientific aspects.

Vol. VII, "Astronomy", Chapters 13, 14, pp. 182—204

TUESDAY

Mars is the next star to swim into the astronomical ken of our evening readings. Chapter 15, "Mars", considers Mars from a scientific standpoint, of course, and one of the most interesting questions it raises is whether or not Mars is inhabited. It might here be said that the idea that Mars is inhabited rests on the belief that the "canals" described in our chapter are artificial and that they are the work of thinking creatures of some sort. More and more, scientific evidence tends to prove that these canals *are* artificial. Not long since, when Mars on his celestial rounds drew as near the earth as he is likely to come, men tried to establish some communication with its supposed inhabitants by means of radio. But no answer came from the planet. Hence the problem remains unsolved.

Vol. VII, "Astronomy", Chapter 15, pp. 205—214

WEDNESDAY

To-night we pass from this planet whose ruddy and incendiary light typifies the evil of militarism to the planet "Jupiter" (Chapter 16) and to "Saturn" (Chapter 17). In Chapter 17, the many interesting scientific mysteries of the planet Saturn are discussed, and this star's famous "rings" are described in detail.

Vol. VII, "Astronomy", Chapters 16, 17 pp. 215—226

THURSDAY

We come to-night to "Uranus and Neptune" (Chapter 18) and "The Little Planets" (Chapter 19). All the interesting scientific information concerning Uranus, the triumph of telescopic discovery and Neptune, whose discovery redounds to the glory of mathematical astronomy, are detailed in this chapter. Since Uranus was discovered only a short time before the outbreak of the French Revolution, the ancient astrologers did not know he existed; but modern astrologers have given him a place in their system.

Vol. VII, "Astronomy", Chapters 18, 19, pp. 227—237

FRIDAY

"Comets, Meteors and Meteorites", Chapter 20 of "Astronomy", is among one of the most interesting we could read, for comets and meteors for hundreds of years were associated in the mind of man with the belief that they foretold the coming of evil, pestilence and war, the death of rulers, the destruction of nations or the end of the world. Halley's Biela's, and Donati's comets are introduced to us, together with other falling stars without number, and the reader will find that the chapter holds his attention from beginning to end.

Vol VII, "Astronomy", Chapter 20, pp. 238—254

SATURDAY

"The stars, the Constellations and Methods of Noting the Stars" are the astronomical heads considered in Chapter 21, this evening's reading.

Vol. VII, "Astronomy", Chapter 21, pp. 255—259

SUNDAY

Two short chapters, 22 and 23, will engage our attention this evening. The first is a simple, practical guide to "How to Know the Stars", and is a directly practical way of making their acquaintance in the skies at first hand, without the aid of an elaborate telescopic apparatus and relying on the naked eye. Our second chapter deals with "The Motions and Brightness of the Stars".

Vol. VII, "Astronomy", Chapters 22, 23 pp. 260—270

THIRTY-FIFTH WEEK

MONDAY

Even among the star-families there are twins, and Chapter 24, our reading stint for to-night, is devoted to "Variable and Twin Stars".

Since our scientific chapter is short, we may add to it three "Life" poems which will complete the little cycle begun a week ago yesterday. The first is Robert Burns' "Remorse". Ralph Waldo Emerson's (1803—1882) "Good-bye", is the farewell of a city-dweller to the world of brick and stone. Longfellow's immortal "Psalm of Life" expresses a noble philosophy of living, and its verses are beautiful variations on the theme: "Life is real and Life is earnest!"

Vol. VII, "Astronomy", Chapter 24, pp. 271—279

Vol. XII, "English Poetry", p. 175; p. 313; pp. 326, 327

TUESDAY

To-night's reading quota, Chapter 25 "Nebulæ and Star Clusters", covers the whole subject of these radiant gases and star islands diffused in space with such ample and interesting detail of description that we will add no supplementary matter here.

Vol. VII, "Astronomy", Chapter 25, pp. 280—290

WEDNESDAY

What already has been said in connection with the preceding chapter applies as well to Chapter 26, "The Making of the Worlds", which may be regarded as the scientific amplification of the account already given in the initial chapters of "The Romance of Evolution".

Vol. VII, "Astronomy", Chapter 26, pp. 291—300

THE READER'S GUIDE 477

THURSDAY

Chapter 27, "Newton and Einstein", is one of the most important which our course presents, for in clear, untechnical language it gives an account of Einstein's revolutionary discoveries in physics, which have attracted such attention during the past few years, and explains so that the layman may understand it his so-called "law of relativity".

Vol. VII, "Astronomy", Chapter 27, pp. 301—308

FRIDAY

Chapter 28, the concluding chapter of "Astronomy" also deals in greater scientific detail with subjects already considered in "The Romance of Evolution". These subjects are: "Atoms, Molecules and Electrons". The reader might do well to read in Vol. I, "The Romance of Evolution", Chapter 1, "Out of the Nowhere", pp. 3, 4 and 5 (paragraph one), in connection with this last chapter of "Astronomy".

Vol. VII, "Astronomy", Chapter 28, pp. 309—319

SATURDAY

If the reader will turn back in the "Guide" to the Thirty-First Week, Tuesday, he will find the last reading in "The History of the World", Chapter 49, section 1. It dealt principally with America (1871-1889). To-night—after our scientific digressions in "Mathematics" and "Astronomy" we return to history with sections 2, "Asia (1): "The Far East, 1871-1889", and section 3, "Asia (2) The British and Russian Empires in Asia, 1871-1889" of the same chapter.

Vol. XX, "The History of the World", Chapter 49 ¶2, 3, pp. 123—135

SUNDAY

To-night, in the two succeeding sections of Chapter 49 of "The History of the World", we have the completion of the story of European exploitation and development of the economic resources of backward races in the two sections devoted to "The Europeans in Africa". Section 4 ¶1, "Tunis and Egypt, 1871-1889"; and section 5 ¶2 "South Africa and the Partition, 1817-1889". As a relief from the interesting but sordid and green-inspired tale of European exploitation in Asia and Africa, let us add to our reading for to-night the first five short sections of the "Nature" essay by Ralph Waldo Emerson, probably the greatest essayist the United States ever produced. If we read 1. "Nature", 2. "Commodity", 3. "Beauty", 4. "Language" (though it already may have been read in another connection) and 5. "Discipline", they will raise us to a loftier, nobler plane of thought, whence we may look down with contempt on the covetousness of imperialistic national ambitions.

XX

Vol. XX, "The History of the World", Chapter 49 ¶4, 5,
   pp. 135—146
Vol. XIV, "Essays", Emerson, pp. 282—300

THIRTY-SIXTH WEEK
MONDAY

In Chapter 50 of "The History of the World" we have a broadly-drawn and colorfully written view of the characteristic "Features of the Nineteenth Century" to which we are about to bid adieu. Section 1 is devoted to "The European System", and after we have read it we may appropriately turn to three poems directly inspired by the historic personality or ideal: Robert Burns' "Written by Somebody on the Window of an Inn at Stirling, On Seeing the Royal Palace in Ruin"; Robert Browning's "The Lost Leader"; and Rudyard Kipling's "Recessional", a splendidly voiced, virile hymn and *credo* of British imperialism.

Vol. XX, "The History of the World", Chapter 50 ¶1,
   pp. 147—152
Vol. XII, "English Poetry", p. 153; pp. 208, 209; pp. 438, 439

TUESDAY

Section 2 of Chapter 50 treats of "Labor and Capital" in Europe during the nineteenth century, and does so in a highly fair and direct way. In connection with this chapter we may read the idealistic poem by William Morris "The Day is Coming".

Vol. XX, "The History of the World", Chapter 50, ¶2,
   pp. 152—158
Vol. XII, "English Poetry", pp. 289—292

WEDNESDAY

To-night we conclude our review of the nineteenth century in "The History of the World" with section 3, Chapter 50, "Science and Welfare". As a cultural supplement the reader might add, in "The History of Literature", Chapters 11 and 12, devoted to "Essayists and Historians", and "The Novel and the Short Story", and in "The Romance of Painting", Chapter 16, "British Painters".

Vol. XX, "The History of the World", Chapter 50 ¶3,
   pp. 158—162
Vol. XI, "The History of Literature", Chapter 11, 12, pp. 104—121
Vol. III, "The Romance of Painting", Chapter 16, pp. 280—286

THURSDAY

One evening may well be devoted to some aspects of an art we already have considered in various connections throughout our course —the art of music. First, let us read that inspired rhapsody known as "The Chant at the Corner-Stone" by Thomas De Witt Talmage

(1832-1902), the Presbyterian clergyman, author and orator. To it we may add a group of beautiful musical poems: Shelley's noble "Music, when soft voices die"; William Collins' "Ode to Music"; Thomas Moore's stirring Irish bardic chant, "The Harp that once through Tara's halls"; Tennyson's lovely "Blow, Bugle, Blow" and that musical epitome of eighteenth century Venice, by Robert Browning, "A Toccata of Galuppi".

Vol. XVIII, "Famous Orations", De Witt Talmage, pp. 423—430

Vol. XI, "English Poetry", pp. 329, 462

Vol. XII, "English Poetry", pp. 282, 283; 188; 216, 217

FRIDAY

Poetry is so intimately connected with music that this seems a logical evening to devote to a group of four of the loftier and nobler poems of feeling the nineteenth century produced: Lord Byron's "The Prisoner of Chillon" (1816); John Keats' (1795-1821) "La Bella Dame Sans Merci" (The Lady Without Mercy); Dante Gabriel Rossetti's (See Vol. III, pp. 282, 283) "The Blessed Damozel", and Robert Browning's (1812-1889) "Evelyn Hope" is a tender farewell to a sixteen-year old girl, who died "before it was her time to love".

Vol. XII, "English Poetry", pp. 127—135; 250—254; 214, 215

Vol. XI, "English Poetry", pp. 446—448

SATURDAY

Before finally dismissing the nineteenth century culturally, we may with profit read a group of poems expressing with clever, virile insight, albeit from the point of view of the confirmed militarist imperialist of the Victorian age, the soldier and sailor (navy and merchant marine) soul of "imperial Britain" and various human phases of Anglo-Indian officialdom. In Rudyard Kipling's (b. 1865) colorful "Barrack Room Ballads", full of vigorous soldier slang and in "The Five Nations" breathes the spirit of an epoch which came to a definite end with the World War. These poems have immortalized it as definitely as Camoens "Luisade" has ambered the time of Portugal's East Indian conquests, or Beranger's Napoleonic verses the heroic days of the first empire. Hence to-night the reader may turn to: 1. Soldier Ballads (India): "Ford o' Kabul River", "Route Marchin'", "Gunga Din", "Mandalay", "The Sons of the Widow" (an excellent imperialistic ballad), "The Ballad of Boh Da Thone", "Tommy", "Danny Deever" ("Mandalay", "Danny Deever" and "The Recessional" have been set many times as songs), "Soldier, Soldier", "Troopin'" and "Screw-Guns"; also (Soudan) "Fuzzy-Wuzzy", and (Ireland) "Belts". 2. Navy and Merchant Marine: "The Ballad of the Clampherdown" and "The Ballad of the Bolivar" are true poems of ocean and engine-room, as the "Ballad of Fisher's Boarding-House" is of the wharfside boozing and crimping-den. 3. Anglo-Indian social life is revealed in: "Delilah", "What Happened", "Code of Morals", "To the Unknown Goddess", "The Lovers' Litany", "A Ballad of Burial", "The Mare's Nest", "Possibilities", "Christmas in India", "As the Bell Clinks" and "Griffin's Debt".

  Vol. XII, "English Poetry", pp. 439—506

SUNDAY

Our Sunday's reading will be a full chapter of "The Story of Religion", which may appropriately be perused at this point, where we stand on the border line between the nineteenth century past and the twentieth century present. It is Chapter 26 of Vol. II, "Religion in the Nineteenth and Twentieth Centuries", and will give an oversight of the many developments in religious thought during the period mentioned.

  Vol. II, "The Story of Religion", Chapter 26, pp. 320—335

THIRTY-SEVENTH WEEK

MONDAY

Our reading in "The History of the World" for to-night ushers in the beginning years of the twentieth century. It bears the general head: "Will to Power", and Chapter 51 itself is entitled "Prelude: 1890-1908". Section 1 of this chapter deals with "Europe: Internal Development". In connection with this section we may complete the reading of Emerson's "Nature" essay, begun last week, by perusing: 6. "Idealism", 7. "Spirit" and 8. "Prospects".

  Vol. XX, "The History of the World", Chapter 51, ¶1, pp. 163-167

  Vol. XIV, "Essays", Emerson, pp. 300—313

TUESDAY

The nineteenth and twentieth century social struggles between capital and labor, plutocratic class government and democratic individualism are paralleled by the struggle in the individual human being between lower and higher ideas of practical conduct and living. We already have read some satiric poems of a political nature. At this point we may enjoy some whose application is more personal. In both cases the satiric poet may be regarded *as a pioneer of progress!* Robert Burns was born in 1759, but much of his satiric verse is as applicable to our life to-day as it was to that of the eighteenth century. Read "What Can a Young Lassie Do Wi' an Auld Man"—it applies as well to the marriages of elderly millionaires with young girls which form part of the chronicles of the daily press, as to Scotch Jennie and her "auld man" of a century and a quarter ago. Nor has "The Henpecked Husband" changed. And "How Cruel Are the Parents", excoriates the mothers who as to-day "riches only prize", and who sacrifice their hapless daughters to "the wealthy booby". Kipling's famous "The Vampire", "My Rival" and his "General Summary" speak for themselves as satiric poems.

 Vol. XII, "English Poetry", Burns, pp. 145, 149, 135, 136, 436, 437

WEDNESDAY

Section 2 of Chapter 51 is devoted to a subject still as dangerous and as full of possibilities of evil for the future if not to-day as it was in the last decade of the nineteenth and the first decade of the twentieth century: "The European Balance". It gives us an excellent idea of the delicate nature of that hair-trigger adjustment of equilibrium, its weights, the huge standing continental armies and the great British super-fleet at sea, an adjustment which the murder of one man eventually was to upset.

 Vol. XX, "The History of the World", Chapter 51, pp. 167—174

THURSDAY

To-night, with the great mechanical and practical advances made by humanity during the nineteenth and twentieth centuries in mind, and not forgetting that these material advances, as we have seen, rested on the foundations of the big guns of all nations, ever ready to be discharged, we will turn to Emerson's essay on "Culture". It defines all that "culture" really is and means, and opens a glorious vista of the time "when the evil forms we know can no more be organized". As supplementary optional reading which deals with various *practical* phases of culture in daily life, the "Essays on Culture" (Vol. X, pp. 328—355) are recommended.

 Vol. XIV, "Essays", Emerson, "Culture", pp. 334—349

FRIDAY

Resuming our reading in "The History of the World" at the point at which we left off on Wednesday, we review in section 3 of Chapter 51, "Europe: The Near East". We follow the trend of political development in the Balkans; the spread of the doctrine of Jugo-Slav unity; the internal problems of Austria; Turkish, Armenian (1894) and Greek complication; the German emperor's identification with Turkish interests and the projection of the Berlin-Bagdad railroad plan. It is not "dry" reading. Yet for those who may fancy it dry a group of "Poems for Such as Disapprove of the Eighteenth Amendment" follows. It includes Thomas Dekker's "Cold's the Wind"; Thomas Jordan's "Let Us Drink and Be Merry"; Abraham Cowley's "Drinking"; and Robert Burns' "Scotch Drink" and "John Barleycorn". There is also Charles Lamb's essay, "Confessions of a Drunkard" (Vol. XIV, pp. 502—508).

 Vol. XX, "The History of the World", Chapter 51 ¶3, pp. 174—180

Vol. XI, "English Poetry", pp. 251, 271, 272
Vol. XII, "English Poetry", pp. 164—168; 178—180
Vol. XIV, "Essays", Lamb, pp. 502—508

SATURDAY

Section 4 of Chapter 51, "Asia: The Middle East", traces the development of a national spirit in oriental lands European nations had long exploited: Egypt, Persia, India. It presents the imperialistic European arguments which hold that while domination is preferable for the "brown brother"; and is especially interesting in view of present-day conditions, for oriental countries having taken the late President Wilson's "self-determination for small nations" principle seriously to heart, are applying it practically to throw off the yoke of England and Spain in lands formerly controlled by them. As a poetic tid-bit to accompany what we read of Anglo-Indian affairs, Rudyard Kipling's specifically *"East* Indian" poems may be read: "The Ballad of East and West", "The Last Suttee", "The Ballad of the King's Mercy", "The Lament of the Border Cattle Thief". They will repay the reader for the time spent on them.

Vol. XX, "The History of the World", Chapter 51 ¶4, pp. 180—183
Vol. XII, "English Poetry", Kipling, pp. 433—436; 451—457; 474, 475

SUNDAY

An evening devoted to a group of "Poems of Religious Sentiment" will take us for the time being to regions far removed from the struggles of worldly greed and ambition. George Sewell's "The Dying Man in His Garden", Robert Louis Stevenson's "The Celestial Surgeon", Emerson's "Brahma", and John Greenleaf Whittier's "The Eternal Goodness" express religious ideals as these poets see them.

Vol. XI, "English Poetry", pp. 329—330
Vol. XII, "English Poetry", pp. 296, 297; 313, 314; 377—379

THIRTY-EIGHTH WEEK

MONDAY

To-night, with section 5 of Chapter 51, "Asia: The Far East", we resume the detailed narrative of "The History of the World". It deals with the struggles of Japan, first with China, then with Russia, in which the Nipponese empire won a two-fold victory and established her position as the dominating power of the Far East. It is especially interesting because the Russo-Japanese War is a link between the wars of the past and the World War and wireless *telegraphy* made its first appearance on the world war stage. In connection with *wireless telegraphy,* the time seems opportune to suspend our historic reading for the moment to review the whole subject of

"Electricity", and all those developments which have made it an indispensable necessity of twentieth-century civilization.

Vol. XX, Chapter 51, ¶5, "The History of the World", pp. 183—191

TUESDAY

Let the reader bear in mind, when beginning Chapter 1, of "Electricity", which deals with "The Nature of Electricity", that this is not a practical manual. It is the story of electricity, simply and interestingly told, so that—as was the case with "Physics", "Chemistry", "Medicine", "Astronomy" and other sciences—he who reads will have the intelligent grasp of the subject which the educated man is supposed to have. Chapter 1 carries us from Thales 600 B.C.), to the modern definition of what electricity is. Chapter 2, "Electrostatics: Atmospheric Electricity", brings us to the most recent application of condensers.

Vol. VIII, "Electricity", Chapters 1, 2, pp. 191—211

WEDNESDAY

Chapter 3, "Fundamental Discoveries" clearly explains all those basic discoveries in electricity upon which the superstructure of modern achievement rests and hence is of great importance. Chapter 4, "Electro-Magneto Machinery", immediately following, shows how these discoveries were practically applied.

Vol. VIII, "Electricity", Chapters 3, 4, pp. 212—233

THURSDAY

Chapter 5, "The Development of Power Transmission", describes how electric power is subjugated, confined and "projected" or transmitted in the amount or voltage which may be required to serve all practical purposes. In Chapter 6 we have "The History of Electric Lighting", from 1800 to the present time.

Vol. VIII, "Electricity", Chapters 5, 6, pp. 234—256

FRIDAY

Chapter 8, which deals with our familiar household friend, "The Telephone", is one the reader will enjoy, even though it does not explain why he does not always get his calls. It is preceded by Chapter 7, "The Development of Electro-Chemistry", which is carried to the solution of the problem of the storage-battery by Edison and others.

Vol. VIII, "Electricity", Chapters 7, 8, pp. 257—276

SATURDAY

Our chapters for this evening are: "Electric Railways", Chapter 9, and "The Electro-Magnetic Telegraph", Chapter 10; and their contents supply the mental meal for to-night. Each gives an admirable oversight of its special field, and calls for no further elaboration in this place.

Vol. VIII, "Electricity", Chapters 9, 10, pp. 277—297

SUNDAY

"Wireless Telegraphy and Telephony", Chapter 11, the closing chapter of this well-planned *resumé* of the entire subject of "Electricity", is an appropriate one for its day. For Sunday, which offers so many educational and cultural opportunities to the "radio fan", usually finds his "set" busy carrying religious and educational addresses and music direct from their place of delivery to his listening ears.

Vol. VIII, "Electricity", Chapter 11, pp. 298—309

THIRTY-NINTH WEEK

MONDAY

Section 6, Chapter 51, of "The History of the World", "Africa", covers the period of German colonial expansion in East and West Africa, and that of the horrible cruelties of the Belgian administration of the Central African Congo State, Lord Kitchener's conquest of the Soudan and the Boer War, the consolidation of the French Moroccan empire and the near-upset of the European balance of power at the Algerciras Conference (1906). Our section read, we may do what most of the diplomats who helped avert war at the Conference did when their delicate labors were at an end—take a travel vacation. We may enjoy "Winter Days in Switzerland" or "In the Shadows of the Matterhorn", make a "Trip to Iceland" or "Venice", or go to "San Marino, the World's Smallest Republic", seeing all these places by taking up our volume of "Travel".

Vol. XX, "The History of the World", Chapter 51 ¶6, pp. 191—197

Vol. XV, "Travel", pp. 257—262; 291—297; 415—419; 397—400; 263—270

TUESDAY

In Chapter 51, Section 7, "America and Australasia", "America", naturally, of all the sections of this chapter is most important to the American reader. It covers an interesting period of our national history, beginning with Cleveland's second presidency, and going beyond the close of the Spanish-American War (1898) to our firm stand on the Monroe Doctrine when England and Germany tried to coerce Venezuela on behalf of her creditor nations in 1903. With the short paragraphs devoted to Canada and Australasia in Chapter 51, section 6, read the highly entertaining "Travel" article entitled "The Land of the Model Husband", dealing with the Australasian Marshall Islands.

Vol XX, "The History of the World", Chapter 51, ¶7, pp. 197—201

Vol. XV, "Travel", pp. 55—61

WEDNESDAY

The Spanish-American War resulted in the delivery of the Philippines as well as China from the Spanish yoke; the building of the Panama Canal falls within the same period. So this evening we may enjoy some colorful "Travels" vistas of our distant island possessions in: "Our Tiniest Dependency" (the fairy island lying midway between the Philippines and Hawaii) and in "Religious Fanatics of the Philippines". And for an original glimpse of the Canal, we may read "Panama from the Ship's Deck". The articles are distinctively American in spirit and interest.

Vol. XV, "Travel", pp. 9—14; 74—76; and 244—251

THURSDAY

In a preceding reading we have considered "Religion in the Nineteenth and Twentieth Centuries". We may turn to-night to Chapter 27, of "The Story of Religion", "Modern Philosophic Thought from the Age of the Reformation to the Present Day". A portion of this chapter already has been read in various connections, and the reader therefore (unless he prefers to review the entire chapter) should begin at the section "Immanuel Kant, the Philosopher of Protestantism" and continue to the end of the chapter.

Vol. II, "The Story of Religion", Chapter 27, pp. 344—354

FRIDAY

In connection with our last reading in American history we will come to-night to "The Romance of Money To-Day" and gather up, as deserving especial attention here, threads which were dropped some time ago. The reader will find grouped various sections which cover the general economic and financial history of the United States during the closing decades of the nineteenth century and up to the period of the World War, (though in some instances the nature of the subject discussed interferes with an exact chronological schedule). In connection with the section "The Mint and the Struggle Between the Gold and Silver Standards", William J. Bryan's celebrated address "The Cross of Gold" (Democratic National Convention, Chicago, 1896) may be read.

Vol. XX, "The Romance of Money To-Day", Chapter 2, pp. 335, 336; Chapter 3, pp. 354—356; Chapter 5, pp. 388, 389

Vol. XVIII, "Famous Orations", Bryan, pp. 483—489

SATURDAY

In the "History of the World" we find no change in political morals or methods. The Crisis of 1914 is gradually drawing nearer, and section 1 of the chapter, aptly entitled "Manœuvering, 1908-1912", shows us the results of the tortuous secret diplomacy of the European cabinets in the constant roiling of European political waters, and the war Italy initiates with Turkey in order to exploit the trade possibilities of Tripoli, a war which indirectly was to fan the slumbering embers of Balkan hatred into fresh flames. As a supplementary Italian "Travel" picture the reader might turn to "A Year in Capri" in the "Travel" volume.

Vol. XX, "The History of the World", Chapter 52 (1) pp. 202—207

Vol. XV, "Travel", pp. 490—493

SUNDAY

As a change from war and bloodshed we will turn this evening to one of the most famous "Christ" sermons ever preached. It is Dwight L. Moody's (1837-1899) "What Think Ye of Christ?" which reflects the noble soul of this Massachusetts evangelist, whose theology laid all stress on the Gospel and none on sectarian opinions. It may be accompanied by a short "nature-sermon" by Mark Twain (1835-1910) a great American whose ethical standards were always high. Our selection is his "New England Weather", an address delivered before the New England Society on December 22, 1876. It is a lovely bit of nature-painting.

Vol. XVIII, "Famous Orations", pp. 490—499

FORTIETH WEEK

MONDAY

Chapter 52, section 2, is devoted to an account of "The Balkan Check, 1912-1913", and the war between the Balkan League (Servia, Bulgaria and Greece) and Turkey. In connection with Albania, mentioned in this section, the reader may turn to the article "Interviewing the Albanian Housewife", in the "Travel" volume.

Vol. XX, "The History of the World", Chapter 52 (2), pp. 207—210

Vol. XV, "Travel", pp. 47—54

TUESDAY

Chapter 52, section 3 of "The History of the World" is entitled "Climax, 1913-1914", and gives a clear narrative of the whole sequence of complicated events which led more or less directly up to the World War. The point of view, of course, is an Anglo-Saxon one and with this premise in mind is a very fair statement of the course of events, though we are still too near those events in point of time and prejudice for their dispassionate examination. In connection with the narrative course of our history we take this opportunity of calling to the reader's attention H. G. Well's statement that *"All* the great states of Europe before 1914 were in a condition of aggressive nationalism and drifting toward war!"

Vol XX, "The History of the World", Chapter 52, (3), pp. 210—215

WEDNESDAY

To-night, in "The History of the World", Chapter 53, section 1, we have "The Shock, 1914", the actual outbreak of the World War which was to arrest the whole course of civilization, cost millions of

American and European lives, and end with a peace treaty whose practical inadequacy has been more apparent with every year which has gone since its passing. The general chapter head "Catastrophe, 1914-1918" is admirably chosen. This chapter carries the story of the war up to the time of the entry of Turkey into the conflict on the side of the Central Powers (1915). An interesting wartime glimpse of Paris is given in our "Travel" volume, in the article "Paris Under the Long Range Gun", and may be read in connection with the evening's history section.

Vol. XX, "The History of the World", Chapter 53 (1), pp. 216—220
Vol. XV, "Travel", pp. 151—157

THURSDAY

Chapter 53, sections 2 and 3, "Thrust and Parry, 1915-1917", tell the story of the World War from the entry of Turkey on the side of the Central Powers to that of the United States on the Allied side (April 6, 1917) and thence to the signing of the Armistice. As our point of departure for this evening's reading we may take an oration by the late Theodore Roosevelt (1858-1919), that great American's address on "The Right of the People to Rule", Delivered at Carnegie Hall, New York City, on March 20, 1912, it puts forth fundamental American doctrines and is a declaration of the principle of American government which will endure.

Vol. XX, "The History of the World", Chapter 53 (2, 3), pp. 220—228.
Vol. XVIII, "Famous Orations", Roosevelt, pp. 467—482.

FRIDAY

Our "History of the World" ends with the conclusion of the great struggle which it has so vividly described.

Of interest to us, as a contemporary summing up of the present economic and social situation of the United States and of the internal problems which to-day confront it, are certain sections of "The Romance of Money To-Day". They deal especially with the effects the World War has had on life in our own country, and will form the matter for to-night's reading. The reader may turn, in the following order, to the sections in question:

Vol. XX, "The Romance of Money To-Day", (pt. 1) Chapter 7, "The United States Becomes Money Leader of the World"; The sections: "When Parliament Passed Bills to Aid the Poor"; "The Stupendous Price of the World War. Pt. 2, Chapter 1, "America's Grain" and "Making Food That Feeds the Millions" to and inclusive of the final section of the chapter, "What Socialism is About". In Chapter 2, read: "The Government as Railroad Watchdog" and "America's

Sea Power Since the World War". In Chapter 3, read: "The World War Turns the Stock Market Topsy-Turvy" to end of chapter.

SATURDAY

This evening may conclude our readings in "The Romance of Money" with Chapter 4, from the section "The World War Burns up the Money of Europe", to the end of the chapter, which explains the reasons *why* the dollar is the world's standard of value to-day. Then turning to Chapter 5, the reader may begin at "The Huge Revenues of the United States Since 1917", and continue to the end of the chapter.

> Vol. XX, "The Romance of Money To-Day", Chapter 4, from section "The World War Burns Up the Money of Europe" to end of chapter; Chapter 5, begin "The Huge Revenues of the United States Since 1917" to end of chapter.

SUNDAY

Passing from the very interesting study of the economic and financial changes brought about in the United States by the World War, we may well devote an evening to three great poems the conflict inspired. They represent a few among the many poetic reactions to the struggle. In them the reader who himself may have been among those who wore his country's uniform, may find thoughts vaguely familiar to his own mind, and to which genius has given perfected expression.

THE CALL TO ARMS IN OUR STREET

(M. W. Letts)

> There's a woman sobs her heart out,
> With her head against the door,
> For the man that's called to leave her,
> God have pity on the poor!
> > But it's beat, drums, beat,
> > While the lads march down the street,
> > And it's blow, trumpets, blow,
> > Keep your tears until they go!
>
> There's a crowd of little children
> That march along and shout,
> For it's fine to play at soldiers
> Now their fathers are called out.
> > So it's beat, drums, beat;
> > But who'll find them food to eat?
> > And it's blow, trumpets, blow,
> > Oh, it's little children know!
>
> There's a mother who stands watching
> For the last look of her son,
> A worn poor widow woman,
> And he her only one.
> > But it's beat, drums, beat,

Though God knows when we shall meet;
And it's blow, trumpets, blow,
We must smile, and cheer them so!
There's a young girl who stands laughing,
For she thinks a war is grand
And it's fine to see the lads pass,
And it's fine to hear the band.
So it's beat, drums, beat,
To the fall of many feet;
And it's blow, trumpets, blow,
God go with you where you go.

This poem gives a purely human reaction to "the call to arms". It applies to the men and women of every age and every war. It does not deal with ideals or theories, reasonings or arguments. It is a simple, eloquent document of human feeling.

A CAROL FROM FLANDERS, 1914
(Frederick Nevin)

In Flanders on the Christmas morn
The trenches formen lay,
The German and the Briton born—
And it was Christmas Day.

The red sun rose on fields accurst,
The gray fog fled away;
But neither cared to fire the first,
For it was Christmas Day.

They called from each to each across
The hideous disarray
(For terrible had been their loss):
"Oh, this is Christmas Day!"

Their rifles all they set aside,
One impulse to obey;
'Twas just the men on either side,
Just men—and Christmas Day.

They dug the graves for all their dead
And over them did pray;
And Englishman and German said:
"How strange a Christmas Day!"

Between the trenches then they met,
Shook hands and e'en did play
At games on which their hearts are set
On happy Christmas Day.

Not all the Emperors and Kings,
Financiers, and they
Who rule us could prevent these things—
For it was Christmas Day.

Oh ye who read this truthful rime
From Flanders kneel and say:
*God speed the time when every day
Shall be as Christmas Day!*

The breath of "peace and good will" on earth hallowing a Christmas Day in the trenches.

"WHEN THERE IS PEACE"
(Austin Dobson)

"When there is Peace, this land no more
Will be the land we knew of yore."
  Thus do the facile seers foretell
   The truth that none can buy or sell,
And e'en the wisest must ignore.

When we have bled at every pore,
Shall we still strive for gear and store?
  Will it be Heaven, will it be Hell,
   When there is peace?

This let us pray for—this implore—
That, all base dreams thrust out at door,
  We may in nobler aims excel,
  And, like men waking from a spell,
Grow stronger, worthier, than before,
   When there is peace!

Austin Dobson, in this poem originally published in "The Spectator", embodied the aspiration which if practically realized would end war forever.

FORTY-FIRST WEEK
MONDAY

We had dropped "Botany" for the time being at a natural stopping-point, Chapter 5, "How to Know the Flowers". "Mathematics", "Medicine", "Astronomy", "Electricity", all more important in the general scheme of things, took precedence. Now, however, we may resume our "Botany" readings with Chapter 6, "Organogeny and Adaptation". It takes up the analysis of the plant cell and the interesting details of how plants adapt themselves to their conditions of life. With this more serious botanical reading William Wadsworth's "The Solitary Reaper" and his "The Reverie of Poor Susan" might be enjoyed.

    Vol. VII, "Botany", Chapter 6, pp. 48—56
    Vol. XI, "English Poetry", Wadsworth, pp. 391

TUESDAY

Chapter 7 of "Botany" deals with "The Physiology of Plants", beginning with the demonstration that the offspring of plants, like those of all other living organisms, inherit the characteristics of the parent stock. It may be followed by a perusal of Thomas Dekker's jolly "Country Glee"; Thomas Moore's "The Last Rose of Summer", and Thomas Edward Brown's "My Garden".

    Vol. VII, "Botany", Chapter 7, pp. 57—63
    Vol. XI, "English Poetry", pp. 250, 251
    Vol. XII, "English Poetry", p. 282; p. 250

WEDNESDAY

Chapter 8 of "Botany" deals with "Growth and Variation", and brings our readings in "Botany" to a close. As a poetic nature supplement read Robert Burns' "On a Bank of Flowers" and "The Fall of the Leaf", and William Cullen Bryant's "Robert of Lincoln".

Vol. VII, "Botany", Chapter 8, pp. 64—73
Vol. XII, "English Poetry", pp. 147, 148; 150; 297, 298

THURSDAY

Developing more fully the "nature poem" idea which accompanied our "Botany" readings we will follow the latter by two evenings devoted to selected poems of nature. The group selected for the evening's reading is: William Cowper's "The Poplar Field"; William Wadsworth's "Written in Early Spring"; Robert Burns' "A Rosebud by My Early Walk"; Charles Dickens' "The Ivy Green"; Thomas Campbell's "Ode to Winter"; Tennyson's "Break, Break, Break", and Robert Louis Stevenson's "In the Highlands".

Vol. XI, "English Poetry", pp. 346; 384, 385
Vol. XII, "English Poetry", pp. 152, 153; 249; 285—287; 296

FRIDAY

Four longer nature poems are recommended to the reader for tonight. They are Shelley's "To a Skylark" and "The Cloud"; Ralph Waldo Emerson's "Wood Notes" ¶1, 2, and Sidney Lanier's "The Marshes of Glynn".

Vol. XI, "English Poetry", pp. 456—458; 460—463
Vol. XII, "English Poetry", pp. 315—325; 413—416

SATURDAY

From now on the readings which conclude our Course will be literary in character, with occasional "Travel" and other relaxations to break their continuity. From our last readings in poetry we turn tonight to prose, yet without "breaking" with Nature—for the scene of action of Shakespeare's "A Midsummer-Night's Dream" is laid "at Athens and in a *Wood* not far from it". In reality its scenes are laid in a fairyland of Shakespeare's fancy, and it probably was first performed at some courtly wedding attended by Queen Elizabeth. Let us read to-night from the beginning to the end of p. 153, where Helen discovers Lysander.

XVIII, Shakespeare, "A Midsummer-Night's Dream", pp. 136—154

SUNDAY

To-night's reading in "A Midsummer-Night's Dream" begins with Lysander's promise "to run through fire" for Helen's sake and, including the woodland scenes of Act III, takes us to the end of p. 170, where Puck squeezing his poppy-juice on Lysander's eyelids, bids him fall asleep, promising that when he wakes he shall find his love.

Vol. XVIII, Shakespeare, "A Midsummer-Night's Dream",
pp. 154—170

FORTY-SECOND WEEK

MONDAY

This evening concludes our reading of Shakespeare's lyric comedy. It includes the famous woodland scene between Bottom and Titania and Oberon, Queen and King of the Fairies, and its inimitable dialogue carries us to the happy ending, after which we have the mock-tragic postlude of the death of Pyramus and Thisbe which, Philostrate declares, brought "merry tears" to his eyes when he saw it rehearsed.

Vol. XVIII, Shakespeare, "A Midsummer-Night's Dream",
pp. 171—185

TUESDAY

Upon Shakespeare's great play, which we have just read, his "Sonnets" may appropriately follow. Aside from their literary beauty the "Sonnets" have a human heart-interest, for the most valid criticism holds that they are autobiographical, that they form *an actual record* of part of Shakespeare's life during the years in which they were written! The "Sonnets" fall naturally into two series. The longer series (I—CXXVI) addressed to a man, covers a long period of time and a wide range of emotions. The man addressed is younger than Shakespeare and of higher rank. The first group of these "Sonnets" (I—XVII) is the one suggested for tonight's reading In them Shakespeare begs his friend to marry and beget children. His friend is now "on the top of happy hours". He must haste before the rose of beauty dies, to secure himself against devouring time in the persons of his descendants.

Vol. XII, "English Poetry", Shakespeare's "Sonnets",
(I—XVII) pp. 28—35

WEDNESDAY

In to-night's group of "Sonnets" (XVIII—XXV), Shakespeare presents himself as the poet whose gift is devoted to celebrating his patron (he is thought to have been some young gentleman of rank, a member of a family like the Sidneys or the Walsinghams), as well as of the friend who betrays his absorbing affection.

Vol. XII, "English Poetry", Shakespeare's "Sonnets",
(XVIII—XXV), pp. 35—38

THURSDAY

The ensuing group of "Sonnets" shows that the two friends have been separated. But the thought of friendship cheers the daily routine of travel and the sorrows of an existence which, as the poet says, is "in disgrace with fortune and men's eyes", and filled with melancholy brooding on the past.

Vol. XII, "English Poetry", Shakespeare's "Sonnets", (XXVI—XXXII), pp. 38—40

FRIDAY

We now come to a difference between the two friends. They are estranged. Alas, the poet's friend has committed a sensual fault which is at the same time a sin against friendship! He has been wooed by a woman whom the poet himself loved. The poet resents this treachery, but finally forgives his friend and bids him take all his loves since all are included in the love he himself has freely given him.

Vol. XII, "English Poetry", Shakespeare's "Sonnets", (XXXIII—XLII), pp. 40—44

SATURDAY

Again the poet goes on a journey, his mind filled with thoughts of his friend, thoughts which Shakespeare claims (LIII—LV) will be immortalized in the sonnets that embody them, a claim which time has justified.

Vol. XII, "English Poetry", Shakespeare's "Sonnets", (XLIII—LV), pp. 44—49

SUNDAY

Once again there is a parting between the two friends, and in his poems Shakespeare waits as patiently as may be for his Pythias to return; and (LVI—LXI) once more declares that his verse will bestow on his friend the gift of immortality.

Vol. XII, "English Poetry", Shakespeare's "Sonnets", (LVI—LXI) pp. 49—51

FORTY-THIRD WEEK

MONDAY

And now, in succession, the poet declares himself weary of the world but that his friend redeems it (LXVI—LXVIII); he records the rumors of some scandal affecting his friend (LXIX—LXX); and he falls into sombre musings on death (LXXI—LXXIV). Yet his friend (LXXV—LXXVII) still is his, and his own affection for him still is his argument.

Vol. XII, "English Poetry", Shakespeare's "Sonnets", (LXVI—LXXVII), pp. 53—57

TUESDAY

We now have a new departure. Shakespeare is rendered unhappy by the appearance of a rival poet, one who asserts that spirits have taught him "to write above a mortal pitch" and who, "with the proud sail of his great verse", already has won the favor of Shakespeare's patron and friend.

Vol. XII, "English Poetry", Shakespeare's "Sonnets", (LXXVIII—LXXXVI), pp. 57—60

WEDNESDAY

A new estrangement follows (LXXXVII—XC). Now the poor poet, disillusioned by the spiteful tricks fortune has played him, not alone is ready to acquiesce in the loss of friendship, but to blame himself for it. And when his friend returns to him their relations are still clouded by the poet's doubt that the former is faithful (XCI—XCIII); and "by public rumors of his patron's wantonness" (XCIV—XCVI), and for a third time the friends are parted, in summer and spring (XCVII—XCIX).

Vol. XII, "English Poetry", Shakespeare's "Sonnets", (LXXXVII—XCIX), pp. 61—65

THURSDAY

We now have an apparent interval, after which a friendship already three years old is renewed (C—CIV) with even greater and more eloquent praises (CV—CVIII); while instead of accusations the poet offers apologies (CIX—CXII) for his own offenses against friendship, and for some blot upon his name seemingly due to the conditions of his profession.

Vol. XII, "English Poetry", Shakespeare's "Sonnets", (C—CXII), pp. 65—70

FRIDAY

Once more the poet is absent (CXIII), and once more he renews his assurances that his friendship and affection are imperishable (CXIV—CXVI), and dwells upon his own unworthiness (CXVII—CXXI), for which the only excuse he has to offer is that his friend once was unkind. If his friend has suffered as he has—we quote Shakespeare's own words—he has "passed a hell of time".

Vol. XII, "English Poetry", Shakespeare's "Sonnets", (CXIII—CXXI), pp. 70—74

SATURDAY

This first series of the "Sonnets" ends with a group of four poems (CXXII—CXXV) in which time and love are contrasted and weighed and one (CXXVI) poem—not in sonnet form—which is a species of "farewell", in which Shakespeare takes leave of his friend with the warning that in the end Nature's audit must be answered. This concludes the first series of those Shakespearian Sonnets which reflect a great spiritual experience with such unexampled power and sincerity. sincerity.

Vol. XII, "English Poetry", Shakespeare's "Sonnets", (CXXII—CXXVI), pp. 74, 75

SUNDAY

Before passing on to the second section of Shakespeare's "Sonnets", addressed to a *woman,* the reader may indulge in a group of "Travel" vistas. Two are Asian and two West Indian. "Palmyra, the Queen of the Desert" and "Darjeeling" are filled with visions of scenic beauty. In "Jamaica, the Garden Island of Our Tropic Seas" we have the entertaining account of a New York business man's midwinter vacation trip to an "island of promise and fulfilment"; while "Bermuda, the Winter Haven of Lovers of the Sea", tells of ocean bathing and sailing in the Gulf Stream.

Vol. XV, "Travel", pp. 219—224; 401—407; 462—465; 482—485

FORTY-FOURTH WEEK

MONDAY

This shorter series of Shakespeare's "Sonnets" (CXXVII—CLIII) is a passionately uttered account of the great poet's relations with a mistress, a dark woman, black-haired and with great, mournful eyes. The earlier poems which we will read to-night (CXXVII—CXXXIII) are full of playful conceits. Shakespeare envies the "jacks" (keys of the virginals) "that nimble leap to kiss the tender inward" of her hand. He playfully defends her dark beauty against the fashionable blonde ideal standardized by Queen Elizabeth. These are the happier, more cheerful sonnets of the series. In them the poet thinks of love alone.

Vol. XII, "English Poetry", Shakespeare's "Sonnets", (CXXVII—CXXXIII), pp. 76—78

TUESDAY

But in the succeeding group (CXXXIV—CXL), Shakespeare turns serious. "Mortgaged" to his mistress' will, his verses show that he knows his soul goes in slavery to his body. Why, he asks, has "her eyes' falsehood forged hooks Whereto the judgment of his heart is tied?"

Vol. XII, "English Poetry", Shakespeare's "Sonnets", (CXXXIV—CXL), pp. 78—81

WEDNESDAY

He continues in the bitterness of lustful passion (CXLI) to prove that his mistress is a wanton. She has broken her bed-vow for Shakespeare's sake ("Robbed others' beds' revenues of their rents"), and Shakespeare himself is forsworn in his love for her, "as black as hell, as dark as night!" (CLVII).

Vol. XII, "English Poetry", Shakespeare's "Sonnets", (CXLI—CXLVII), pp. 81—83

THURSDAY

A last group (CXLVIII—XCVI) beginning "O me, what eyes hath Love put in my head, which have no correspondence with true sight!" concludes this sonnet-sequence of a heart unable to cast off passion's tyranny. The last two "Sonnets" (XCVII, CLIV) have nothing to do with Shakespeare's passion-romance in verse.

Vol. XII, "English Poetry", Shakespeare's "Sonnets", (CXLVIII—CLIV), pp. 83—86

FRIDAY

Before following the sonnet-sequences of the great Elizabethan poet with Elizabeth Barrett Browning's "Sonnets from the Portuguese", which Robert Browning, the poet-husband of this poet-wife called "the finest sonnets written in any language since Shakespeare", we will break the continuity of our serious reading with another journey abroad. To-night the reader may enjoy some glimpses of Russia in: "From Rostov to the Murman Coast", "At Omsk and Tomsk", and "Christmas in Russia and Her Provinces".

Vol. XV, "Travel", pp. 98—109; 271—278; 384—485

SATURDAY

Browning's statement that his wife's "Sonnets from the Portuguese"—original poems, not translations—were "the finest written in any language since Shakespeare" cannot be taken too seriously, since it ignores the wonderful sonnets of William Wadsworth. The "Sonnets from the Portuguese" have not the impassioned peace which such great poetry as Wadsworth's holds, and yet their beauty "is beyond praise". Curiously enough, as in the case of Shakespeare, these "Sonnets" also tell their author's heart-story. They are no figments of the poetic imagination, but narrate the tale of Browning's courtship of his wife in their verses. Let us take the Sonnets from I to X to-night, and follow the story they reveal. First (I) a mystic hand seizes upon the writer. At her question whether it be the hand of death "the silver answer" rings: "Not Death but Love!" Elizabeth Barrett (1806-1861) learned to love Browning in his poems before she met him in the flesh. Once they did meet he became her frequent visitor. But though he kept her room filled with flowers she (III, IV, V) "poor, wandering singer", could hardly believe her good fortune. She bids him go (VI) though since she "heard the footsteps of his soul" (VII) all her world is changed. She was not strong: What can she give him? (VIII) Should she "breathe her poison on his Venice-glass?" (IX); and yet, when men and women love, "an equal light leaps in the flame from cedar-plank or weed!" (X).

Vol XI, "English Poetry", Elizabeth Browning, "Sonnets", (I—X), pp. 419—423

SUNDAY

We continue our heart-story. Browning was six years younger than the woman he admired so passionately. With her "Cheeks as pale as these you see, and trembling knees that fail" (XI), he first thought some hopeless physical injury confined her to her sofa. But she feels that his love has snatched up her soul, "faint and weak" (XII), to put it beside his own on a golden throne. And though she contemplates renunciation (XIII, XIV, XVI) and stresses her feeling of his greatness as a poet (XVII), she assures him (XVIII) that on her lips he will find "pure . . . the kiss my mother left there when she died!" In the beautiful Sonnet XIX she barters curl for curl with her lover and then (XX), looks back upon the dead world "a year ago" before "life's great cup of wonder" had been raised to her lips.

>Vol. XI, "English Poetry", Elizabeth Browning, "Sonnets" (XI—XX), pp. 423—426

FORTY-FIFTH WEEK

MONDAY

Her physical illness forgotten Elizabeth rises to the heights of eloquent expression of her love (XXI, XXII, XXIII, XXIV). It has cured her heavy heart (XXV), her lover's coming has brought her soul "satisfaction of all wants" (XXVI), the "saving kiss" (XXVII). "God's future thundered on my past" (XXVIII) she cries, he is the great tree (XXIX) which shades her life, and in XXX we find expressed the troubled raptures of the wedding-hour.

>Vol. XI, "English Poetry", Elizabeth Browning, "Sonnets" (XXI—XXX), pp. 426—430

TUESDAY

"Ah, keep near and close" (XXXI), Elizabeth sighs after the secret wedding (London, Sept. 12, 1846), which united her to Browning against a tyrannical father's wish. Yet she feels (XXXII) like "an outworn viol a good singer would be wont to spoil his tune with". Then follow five beautiful sonnets (XXXIII, XXXIV, XXXV, XXXVI, XXXVII) which sing her fondness and, reverting to "that first kiss" (XXXVIII), she bids her lover see her soul as it truly is (XXXIX) and closes on a note of passionate reliance on him who (XL) can wait "through sorrow and sickness to bring their souls to touch".

>Vol XI, "English Poetry", Elizabeth Browning, "Sonnets" (XXXI—XL), pp. 430—434

WEDNESDAY

The four sonnets which conclude the sequence seem to reflect the improvement in Elizabeth Browning's health and spirits after her marriage during the summer of 1846. "Instruct me how to thank thee!" she cries (XLI). "How do I love thee?" she asks and answers her question with supreme eloquence (XLII). She begs her lover to mold her closer to his heart's desire (XLIII) and in a final sonnet leaves the pages of "life's first half" to "write me new my future's epigraph" (XLIV), one all joy and happiness. Not until the wedded lovers were in Pisa, Italy, in 1847, did Robert Browning see those sonnets in which his wife had poured out her soul to him in secret, with no idea of ever publishing them. And—"professional jealousy" was the last thing his noble spirit could have felt—it was to please him that she gave them to the world.

    Vol XI, "English Poetry", Elizabeth Browning, "Sonnets" (XLI—XLIV), pp. 434, 435

THURSDAY

In pursuance of our policy of alternating verse and prose in our literary readings, let us turn from poesy to humor; from love to laughter, from sonnet to essay, from Elizabeth Browning to Charles Lamb. Two of Lamb's (1775-1834) happy, light-hearted "Essays of Elia" we already have read in other connotations: "A Dissertation Upon Roast Pig", and the "Confessions of a Drunkard". These we read to-night, like those we already have read, mingle exquisite humor, cordial pleasantry and heart-touching pathos. In "Witches and Other Night-Fears", "Poor Relations" and "The Genteel Style of Writing", we find Lamb at his best. And to these "Essays", the reader may add that poem all tenderness and grace, Lamb's "The Old Familiar Faces".

    Vol. XIV, "Essays", Charles Lamb, pp. 480—485; 492—501

    Vol. XI, "English Poetry", Charles Lamb, p. 417

FRIDAY

To-night we will turn to a group of "Poems of Youth and Age", in which the poets give us an insight into the human values of the two great life stages, each of which has its own peculiar joys and sorrows, powers and possibilities. Charles Kingsley's "Young and Old"; Longfellow's "My Lost Youth"; Byron's "Youth and Age"; and Coleridge gives us comfort: "Life is but thought; so think I will That Youth and I are housemates still"; and we may close with Oliver Wendell Holmes' humorous and middle-aged "Contentment"; and Kipling's famous bachelor revery, in which the worshiper of "the great god Nick o'Teen" turns love aside because "a woman is only a woman, but a good cigar is a smoke!"

    Vol. XII, "English Poetry", pp. 206, 207; 333—335; 121, 122

    Vol. XI, "English Poetry", pp. 393, 394

    Vol. XII, "English Poetry", pp. 395—397; 500—502

SATURDAY

From our poetic considerations of youth and age we may fitly pass to an eighteenth-century work, "brilliantly written, full of keen wit and admirable portrait-painting", the Earl of Chesterfield's

(1694-1773) famous "Letters to His Son". They are especially intimate and personal because they were never meant to be printed. Two evenings have been assigned for their reading.

Vol. X, "The Book of Culture", Chesterfield's Letters, pp. 470—488 (Truth)

SUNDAY

Beginning with the section "Truth" (p. 488) of Lord Chesterfield's "Letters", the reader may now finish this work so full of interest and dry humor, though it also reveals the soul of a worldling, and reflects the morality of his age and time.

Vol. X, "The Book of Culture", Chesterfield's Letters, pp. 488—506

FORTY-SIXTH WEEK

MONDAY

To-night we will hark back from the practical prose education of city youth to the heart-poetry of childhood, childhood mainly in rustic surroundings in Wadsworth's "We are Seven"; Robert Burns' "On the Birth of a Posthumous Child"; Tennyson's lullaby, "Sweet and Low", Longfellow's "The Children's Hour", Charles Kingsley's "The Sands of Dee", and Whittier's happy idyl of American boyhood, "The Barefoot Boy".

Vol. XI, "English Poetry", pp. 380—382
Vol. XII, "English Poetry", pp. 146; 187, 188; 335—337; 206; 388—391

TUESDAY

To-night we will begin the English novelist Charles Dickens' (1812-1870) "A Christmas Carol", that inspired bit of writing which Thackeray called "a national benefit". It is a tale so clear and spontaneous that it calls for no elaborate commentary. It divides naturally into its five "Staves" and to-night we may read Stave 1, "Marley's Ghost".

Vol. XIX, "Fables and Fairytales", Charles Dickens, "A Christmas Carol", pp. 219—233

WEDNESDAY

Our reading this evening continues "A Christmas Carol" with Stave 2, "The First of the Three Spirits", ending with Scrooge's falling asleep preparatory to making the acquaintance of the second of the three.

Vol. XIX, "Fables and Fairytales", Charles Dickens, "A Christmas Carol", pp. 233—246

THURSDAY

To-night's reading continues our story with Stave 3, "The Second of the Three Spirits", and ends with the apparition of the last of these phantoms.

Vol. XIX, "Fables and Fairytales", Charles Dickens, "A Christmas Carol", pp. 246—263

FRIDAY

Stave 4, which we read to-night carries our tale to the point where the covetous old sinner, as he seizes the phantom's spectral hand in an agony of fear, promises to honor Christmas in his heart.

Vol. XIX, "Fables and Fairytales", Charles Dickens, "A Christmas Carol, pp. 264—275

SATURDAY

Stave 5, "The End of It", brings the beautiful tale to its happy conclusion, with the permanent change of heart of the former skinflint and miser, who has become "as good a friend, as good a master, as good a man as the good old city knew". With this concluding section the interesting "Travel" article "Christmas 'Round the World" may appropriately be read.

Vol. XIX, "Fables and Fairytales", Charles Dickens, "A Christmas Carol", pp. 275—280
Vol. XV, "Travel", pp. 459—461

SUNDAY

For this evening's reading we may turn to a group of poems which deal with Death, but which, instead of investing the grisly reaper with an aura of horror and despair, sing of his advent and his accomplishment in accents of resignation or wreathe his scythe with the bright flowers of hopeful fancy. They are Thomas Nashe's "In Time of Pestilence", John Donne's "Death" and "Valedictory Forbidding Mourning", Alexander Smith's "Barbara", Christina Georgina Rossetti's (1830-1894) "Song", Rudyard Kipling's "A Ballad of Burial", and Walt Whitman's eloquent "When Lilacs Last in the Dooryard Bloomed", and "The Last Invocation".

Vol. XI, "English Poetry", pp. 213, 214; 236—238
Vol. XII "English Poetry", pp. 247, 248; 277; 490, 491; 424—432

FORTY-SEVENTH WEEK

MONDAY

Our reading for this evening is a group of "Classical Fables of Ancient Greece", mainly culled from the rich Æsopian store. Æsop (circa 620—560 B.C.) left posterity a literary legacy in his "Fables" which should atone for any earthly misdeeds he may have committed.

Vol. XIX, "Fables and Fairytales", pp. 443; 441, 442; 447; 454, 455; 460, 461; 476; 486; 491, 492; 494, 495

TUESDAY

Our reading for to-night will comprise three fairytales which have special interest because they may be identified with actual historic personages. When we read "Bluebeard", we may remember that without Gilles de Retz (1404-1440), a depraved Breton nobleman who murdered innocent children in his gloomy medieval castle with unholy rites, neither the fairytale nor Crockett's novel "The Black Douglass", the Frenchman Huysman's "La Bas", and various operas, including Dukas' "Ariane et Barbe-Bleue" (See "The Romance of Opera", Vol. III, p. 411) ever would have been written.

Vol. XIX, "Fables and Fairytales", pp. 29—33; 91—100; 191—193

WEDNESDAY

Beginning with this evening the reader may take up the Francis Bacon's "Essays", except Nos. 4, 18, 19, 20, already considered elsewhere. Bacon's "Essays" are moral readings of the familiar, practical kind, whose pithy sayings have become household words, and whose quaint, rich, original style and weighty thoughts make them a contribution to English literature with which every well-informed person should be acquainted.

Vol. XIV, "Essays", Francis Bacon, pp. 1—6; 11—23

THURSDAY

We continue to-night with the reading of the following Bacon "Essays" on: "Love", "Great Place", "Boldness", "Goodness and Goodness of Nature", "Nobility", "Sedition and Troubles" and "Atheism".

Vol. XIV, "Essays", Francis Bacon, pp. 23—41

FRIDAY

This evening we may conclude our reading of Bacon's "Essays" with those on: "Superstition", "Wisdom for a Man's Self", "Dinovation", "Dispatch", "Seeming Wise", "Friendship" and "Expense".

Vol. XIV, "Essays", Francis Bacon, pp. 41—42; 53—65

SATURDAY

Once more we revert from prose to poetry in two groups of "Fantastic Poems". Our first reading may begin with John Keats' "The Realm of Fancy", move to Coleridge's oriental vision "Kubla Khan"; Tennyson's wonderful "The Lotus-Eaters", Sidney Lanier's "How Love Looked for Hell"; Lord Byron's "Darkness"; and Matthew Arnold's beautiful sea-fantasy, "The Forsaken Merman".

Vol. XI, "English Poetry", pp. 435—437; 391—393
Vol. XII, "English Poetry", pp. 197—201; 416—419; 124—126; 240—244

SUNDAY

Our second and equally beautiful group of poems of pure fantasy includes: Richard Corbett's "Farewell, Rewards and Fairies", Shelley's "A Dream of the Unknown" and "To the Night"; William Morris' "Prologue to 'The Earthly Paradise'"; and the finest flowers of the genius of that tragic figure among American poets, Edgar Allan Poe.

Vol. XI, "English Poetry", pp. 243, 244; 451, 452; 459, 460

Vol. XII, "English Poetry", pp. 288, 289; 302—312

FORTY-EIGHTH WEEK

MONDAY

From the vague fairylands of the poet's fantasy we will return to solid earth this evening with a "Travel" excursion to two little known and highly interesting countries. "The Land of the Sumoi" takes us to Finland which, in all probability, few of our readers have visited; while "To the Midnight Sun", and "To Norway for a Vacation" rounds out our trip on the printed page with first-hand views of Scandinavian life, folk and surroundings.

Vol. XV, "Travel", pp. 126—134; 436—439; 470—474

TUESDAY

It is true that a hundred phases of the tender passion are revealed in the immortal sonnets of Shakespeare and Elizabeth Browning; yet these by no means complete the tale. We will allot, therefore, two evenings to amatory poems which have been chosen from among many others.

Vol. XI, "English Poetry", pp. 232; 248—250; 228, 229; 267; 223; 224; 230, 231; 259; 387, 388; 365

WEDNESDAY

To-night we may read the second group of our amatory poetic anthology. It includes: Robert Burns' "The Golden Hair of Anna"; and his delightful "The Lass That Made the Bed to Me"; Byron's "When We Two Were Parted". "All for Love" and "Maid of Athens"; Robert Browning's "Never the Time and the Place"; Matthew Arnold's "To Marguerite"; James Thomson's "Gifts"; Christina Georgina Rossetti's "In the Round Tower of Jhansi"; Thomas Campbell's "The Soldier's Dream"; John Boyle O'Reilly's "A White Rose"; and Algeron Swinburne's "A Match".

Vol. XII, "English Poetry", pp. 146, 147; 136, 137; 122, 123, 124; 235; 245, 246; 250; 278; 284, 285; 292, 293

THURSDAY

At this point we may read two great dramas. In them the genius of two great playwrights, one the Greek Euripides, the other the Englishman Dryden, has enshrined the memory of the two women who in all history have been mankind's ideal of the woman beloved, Helen and Cleopatra.

Vol. XVII, "The Drama", Euripides, "Helen", pp. 99—111

FRIDAY

The drama moves on to-night to the end of p. 121, where Helen flings her arms with transport around the neck of her husband, Menelaus, whom she once more has found.

Vol. XVII, "The Drama", Euripides, "Helen", pp. 112—121

SATURDAY

From the point where Menelaus—he accepts Helen's story of a shadow double—rejoices to find his wife again, we continue our tale to Menelaus' plea for life to Thenoe, the Egyptian queen, on whose shores husband and wife now are stranded.

Vol. XVII, "The Drama", Euripides, "Helen", pp. 122—132

SUNDAY

To-night's reading carries on the tale (including the wonderful choral ode which calls on the nightingale with the words: "On thee who build'st thy tuneful nest protected by the leafy groves I call, O nightingale! . . . ") to Menelaus' promise to clear Helen's name of the unjust infamy which weighs it down in her native Greece.

Vol. XVII, "The Drama", Euripides, "Helen", pp. 132—142

FORTY-NINTH WEEK

MONDAY

From the stately Ode to "the celestial mother" (p. 144) we read to the end of the great drama to-night. It concludes with an apostrophe of a Helen "with a lofty soul endued, such as in female bosom seldom dwells".

Vol. XVII, "The Drama", Euripides, "Helen", pp. 142—154

TUESDAY

Beside Helen's there is only one other female name which enjoys the same reputation for romantic charm and supreme personal beauty —that of Egyptian Cleopatra. Dryden's lines in his "All for Love" may not be as austerely beautiful as those of Euripides but they are more impassioned; and he is nearer to us in point of time and human feeling than the old Greek dramatist.

Vol. XVII, "The Drama", Dryden, "All for Love", pp. 355—367

WEDNESDAY

To-night we read from the clever "Restoration" Prologue to Antony's lament, after the battle of Actium, that Cleopatra at length has wearied of his "careless days and his luxurious nights".

Vol. XVII, "The Drama", Dryden, "All for Love", pp. 368—381

THURSDAY

Our reading allotment for to-night contains many wonderful passages, such as Cleopatra's—"I have loved with such transcendant passion that I soared, at first, quite out of reason's view", and brings

us to Antony's "I am a Roman!" spoken to his friend Ventidius.
   Vol. XVII, "The Drama", Dryden, "All for Love, pp. 380—388

FRIDAY

From that meeting of Antony and Cleopatra in which she accuses the gods of "having seen her joys with envious eyes", our story takes its course to Antony's acceptance of the fate which has made him, "whose morning chambers were filled with sceptered slaves", empty of all save a heart "that swells in scorn of fate!"
   Vol. XVII, "The Drama", Dryden, "All for Love", pp. 388—397

SATURDAY

Continuing our reading from last night, we find Antony recalling Cleopatra as first she came out of Egypt, "her galley down the Cydnus rowed", smiling the smile which "a darting glory seemed to blaze abroad." We end with the dialogue in which Cleopatra, not very convincingly, exclaims that "Nature meant me for a wife; a silly, harmless household dove!"
   Vol. XVII, "The Drama", Dryden, "All for Love", pp. 398—409

SUNDAY

The dialogue continues—we mark Ventidius' happy exclamation: "Women! Dear, damned inconstant sex!"—and shows us his faithful, long-suffering Roman wife, Octavia, leaving Antony—"Poor cozened man!" never to return; for she despairs of having him whole and "scorns to take him half". Antony accuses Cleopatra, after her departure, of being false to him.
   Vol. XVII, "The Drama", Dryden, "All for Love", pp. 410—420

FIFTIETH WEEK

MONDAY

We read on, beginning with Antony's exclamation "When half the globe was mine I gave it you in dowry with my heart! . . ." and the development of his accusation is succeeded by Cleopatra's unavailing defence and her attempt to stab herself in her despair.
   Vol. XVII, "The Drama", Dryden, "All for Love", pp. 420—431

TUESDAY

The stirring, emotional love tragedy draws to its close. Her lover is told that Cleopatra has killed herself. "Now she's dead let Cæsar take the world!" Antony cries, and falls on his sword. But Cleopatra lives. She enters and the dying man, rising on his couch, hails her as "the first kind ghost" that meets him dead. Yet now Cleopatra has no reason for living. After a tender farewell from

THE READER'S GUIDE

Antony she bares her arm to the asp. "O turn me to him and lay me on his breast . . . now part us for thou canst!"

    Vol. XVII, "The Drama", Dryden, "All for Love", pp. 432—437

WEDNESDAY

As the introduction to "The Book of Good Manners" (Vol. X of The Outline) declares: "well-bred behavior is a fundamental of civilized life." A survey of the whole subject of "Good Manners", therefore, may serve to review essentials of behavior whose observance should be second nature.

    Vol. X, "The Book of Good Manners", Chapters 1, 2, 3, Pt. 2, pp. 33—52

THURSDAY

This evening's reading comprises Chapters 4, 5 and 6, "Dancing", "The Young Man in Society", and "The Young Woman in Society", in our social mentor.

    Vol. X, "The Book of Good Manners", Chapters 4, 5, 6, Pt. 2, pp. 53—73

FRIDAY

Following the preceding chapters we may read this evening Chapter 7, "Correspondence"; Chapter 8, "Riding, Driving and Outdoor Sports"; Chapter 9, "Courtship"; and Chapter 10, "The Engagement", in Part Two.

    Vol. X, "The Book of Good Manners", Chapters 7, 8, 9, 10, Pt. 2, pp. 74—94

SATURDAY

To-night Chapters 1 and 2 of "The Wedding", Part Three, may be covered. They are entitled respectively "All That Goes Before" and "Types of Weddings".

    Vol. X, "The Book of Good Manners", Chapters 1, 2, Pt. 3, pp. 98—116

SUNDAY

Chapter 3 of this section is devoted to "The Wedding Itself"; while Chapter 4 covers "From the End of the Wedding to the start of the Honeymoon".

    Vol. X, "The Book of Good Manners", Chapters 3, 4, Pt. 3, pp. 117—131

FIFTY-FIRST WEEK

MONDAY

"Good Manners in General" is the title of Part Four of the volume which is, perhaps, its most important section. Chapters 1 and 2 deal respectively with "The Niceties of Social Intercourse in Public" and "The Proprieties of Speech and Conversation".

    Vol. X, "The Book of Good Manners", Chapters 1, 2, Pt. 4, pp. 135—168

TUESDAY

"Calls, Cards and Visits" and "The Demands of the Special Occasion", Chapters 3 and 4, Part Four, will suffice for this evening's reading.

> Vol. X, "The Book of Good Manners", Chapters 3, 4, Pt. 4, pp. 169—197

WEDNESDAY

The short special chapter on "Motor Etiquette" (Chapter V) might be read as a separate entirety, since it is a brief section complete in itself.

> Vol. X, "The Book of Good Manners", Chapter 5, Pt. 4, pp. 198—207

THURSDAY

"The Courtesies of Club Life", Chapter 6, and "Correct Manners in the Hotel", Chapter 7, are the two chapters which supply the allotment for this evening's reading.

> Vol. X, "The Book of Good Manners, Chapters 6, 7, Pt. 4, pp. 208—228

FRIDAY

Reserving Chapter 8, "The Amenities of Travel" for consideration elsewhere, we take up in Part Five, "The Matron and the Social Round", Chapters 1, 2, 3 and 4. They are entitled: "After the Honeymoon", "The Home Background", "Service (The Home-Keeper and Hostess)", "Service (Servants and their Duties)."

> Vol. X, "The Book of Good Manners", Chapters 1, 2, 3, 4, Pt. 5, pp. 239—262

SATURDAY

Three special studies in Vol. X each may claim an evening before we take up the next chapters of Part Five. All are intimately associated with "The Home Background", Chapter 2, of last night's reading. "Color Harmony and Design in Dress" covers the subject of "color harmony" in general (pp. 397—409) but the feminine reader will find the practical advice as to the dress colors and designs best suited to blonde and brunette hair and complexion, a stout or slender figure, in the second section of the book (pp. 410—430).

> Vol. X, "The Book of Good Manners", pp. 397—430

SUNDAY

Physical beauty, under circumstances, may attain almost a moral level. "Physical Beauty" and the duty of its care and preservation may well engage feminine attention, and even some masculine readers may find food for thought in "First Aid to the Fat", etc., (pp. 363—367).

> Vol. X, "The Book of Good Manners", pp. 359—393

FIFTY-SECOND WEEK

MONDAY

Sex is a basic life-fact. The reader may or may not learn anything new by perusing the special study of "Sex" included in Vol. X. A necessary complement to an "Outline of Knowledge", it covers its subject in a direct, straightforward way.

> Vol. X, "The Book of Good Manners", pp. 433—469

TUESDAY

We return from our excursions into "Color Harmony", "Physical Beauty" and "Sex", to the next "Good Manners" sections, "The Formal Dinner" and "Other Formal Meals", Chapters 5 and 6 of Part Five, whose detail is comprehensively covered in the pages alloted them.

> Vol. X, "The Book of Good Manners", Chapters 5, 6, Pt. 5, pp. 263—279

WEDNESDAY

The four short chapters 7, 8, 9 and 10 of Part Five which remain —"Formal and Informal Teas", "Other Informal Meals", "Cards", "The Formal Ball"—may easily be covered in a brief reading-session as a group.

> Vol. X, "The Book of Good Manners", Chapters 7, 8, 9, 10, Pt. 5, pp. 280—295

THURSDAY

Part Six, "Funerals and Funeral Observance", brings our subject to its natural close. Death has its decencies and grief its code of good form and they are fully covered in the pages of Chapters 1, 2, 3 and 4: "Before the Funeral", "The Church Funeral", "The House Funeral" and "After the Funeral".

> Vol. X, "The Book of Good Manners", Chapters 1, 2, 3, 4, Pt. 6, pp. 299—323

FRIDAY

The fact that "the paths of glory" to quote Gray's famous "Elegy" (and all other paths as well) "lead but to the grave", does not make it necessary to have the grave yawn at the end of our reading course. In order to avoid this contingency we may return to Chapter 8, Part Four of "The Book of Good Manners", entitled "The Amenities of Travel". The subject is one whose practical usefulness is apparent. With it, as a no less practical supplement, may be read the article "Coming Through the Customs House" in our "Travel" volume. To these may be added a group of short "Far North" excursions: "The Arctic Pie"; "Farthest North and the Problem of the Pole"; and "A Trip Down the Yukon River".

> Vol. X, "The Book of Good Manners", Chapter 8, Pt. 4, pp. 229—235
>
> Vol. XV, "Travel", pp. 449—451; 158—161; 431—435; 478—481

SATURDAY

We will bid farewell to the reading course which has led us

through "The Outline of Knowledge" from the beginning of all things to the present hour in two enjoyable "Travel" excursions. In the first we fly more swiftly than the Zeppelin can bear us to Paris boulevards, where the Parisians sit gaily over their *bocs* under striped awnings, and become initiated into "The Spirit of the French Cafés". And then, the poetic and practical mingling, we may learn of "The Joys and Sorrows of Automobiling in France"; ending up with a glimpse of tulip-land as we fare "Through Holland in a Canal Boat".
Vol. XV, "Travel", pp. 309—315; 408—415; 500—503
Vol. XIX, "Fables and Fairytales", pp. 115—119

SUNDAY

It was Keats who said: "Pleasure never was at home!" The statement may be too radical, yet which reader will object to ending his weeks of reading with a flight "From Marseilles to Genoa, Along the Riviera"—that playground of moneyed Americans—and (despite the day) concluding with a visit to "Monte Carlo". Not cultural? Indeed it is, for readers who might shrink from peeping into the famous Casino, where pallid *croupiers* rake in the gold of desperate gamblers, can visit the magnificent oceanographic museum of the Prince of Monaco instead. And there in the beautiful gardens of the great gaming establishment (its walks are not always covered with the bodies of those ruined victims who have shot themselves in despair), the reader may meditate on one thing or another suggested by what he has read through the seemingly endless (?) weeks that have passed.
Vol. XV, "Travel", pp. 378—384; 475—478

IN CONCLUSION

Each individual volume of "The Outline of Knowledge" covers its specific subject or subjects from bottom to top, *perpendicularly*. The "Reader's Guide" connects these manifold subjects in a *vertical* sequence. The reader may prefer to read "The Romance of the Arts" or "The History of the World" as separate works, and he is quite free to do so if he choose. It has been a labor of love on the part of the Editor of "The Outline" to make the "Readers' Guide" as interesting, valuable and helpful as its nature would permit, so that those who use it will not find it a mere cut and dried scheme of readings, reduced to titles and page-numbers, but a vivid, running commentary on whatever subject is to be considered.

It is his hope that the reader may find as much pleasure and benefit in using it as he himself derived from planning it with the reader's best cultural interests in mind.

James A. Richards